BIRDS of EASTERN CANADA

BIRDS of EASTERN CANADA

EDITOR
DAVID M. BIRD, Ph.D.
Emeritus Professor of Wildlife Biology
McGill University

DK

DORLING KINDERSLEY

FIRST EDITION

Senior Art Editors
Caroline Hill, Ina Stradins

Senior Editors
Angeles Gavira Guerrero, Ankush Saikia

Canadian Editor
Barbara Campbell

Project Editor
Nathan Joyce

Project Designer
Mahua Sharma

Designers
Sonia Barbate, Helen McTeer

Editors
Jamie Ambrose, Lori Baird, Tamlyn Calitz, Marcus Hardy, Patrick Newman, Siobhan O'Connor, Garima Sharma, David Summers, Miezan van Zyl, Rebecca Warren

Design Assistant
Becky Tennant

Editorial Assistants
Elizabeth Munsey, Jaime Tenreiro

Creative Technical Support
John Goldsmid

DTP Manager
Sunil Sharma

Senior DTP Designers
Pushpak Tyagi, Tarun Sharma

DTP Designers
Manish Chandra Upreti, Rajdeep Singh, Anurag Tiwari, Satish Chandra Gaur

Production Editor
Maria Elia

Production Controller
Rita Sinha

Jacket Designer
Mark Cavanagh

Illustrators
John Cox, Andrew Mackay

Picture Editor
Neil Fletcher

Picture Researchers
Laura Barwick, Will Jones

Managing Art Editor
Phil Ormerod

Managing Editors
Glenda Fernandes, Sarah Larter

Publishing Manager
Liz Wheeler

Art Director
Bryn Walls

Publishers
Jonathan Metcalf, Aparna Sharma

THIS EDITION

Project Art Editor
Rupanki Arora Kaushik

Project Editor
Priyanjali Narain

Editor
Aashirwad Jain

Managing Art Editor
Sudakshina Basu

Senior Managing Editor
Rohan Sinha

DTP Designer
Bimlesh Tiwary

Senior DTP Designer
Harish Aggarwal

Production Editor
Vishal Bhatia

Preproduction Manager
Balwant Singh

Senior Production Controller
Meskerem Berhane

Jacket Designer
Gayatri Menon

Senior Jackets Coordinator
Priyanka Sharma Saddi

Jacket Design Development Manager
Sophia MTT

Design Head (DK Delhi)
Malavika Talukder

Editorial Head (DK Delhi)
Glenda R Fernandes

Managing Art Editor
Michael Duffy

Managing Editor
Angeles Gavira Guerrero

Art Director
Karen Self

Design Director
Phil Ormerod

Associate Publishing Director
Liz Wheeler

Publishing Director
Jonathan Metcalf

This Canadian Edition, 2023
First Canadian Edition, 2013
Published in the United States and Canada by DK Publishing
1745 Broadway, 20th Floor, New York, NY 10019

24 25 26 27 10 9 8 7 6 5 4 3 2
002—331866—Apr/2023

Includes content previously published in *AMNH Birds of North America* and *Birds of Canada*.

Published in Great Britain by Dorling Kindersley Limited

A catalog record for this book is available from the Library of Congress.
ISBN 978-0-74407-071-2

Printed in China

For the curious
www.dk.com

MIX
Paper | Supporting responsible forestry
FSC
www.fsc.org
FSC™ C018179

This book was made with Forest Stewardship Council™ certified paper - one small step in DK's commitment to a sustainable future.
For more information go to www.dk.com/our-green-pledge

CONTRIBUTORS

David M. Bird
Nicholas L. Block
Peter Capainolo
Matthew Cormons
Malcolm Coulter
Joseph DiCostanzo
Shawneen Finnegan
Neil Fletcher
Ted Floyd
Jeff Groth
Paul Hess
Brian Hiller
Rob Hume
Thomas Brodie Johnson
Kevin T. Karlson
Stephen Kress
William Moskoff
Bill Pranty
Michael L. P. Retter
Noah Strycker
Paul Sweet
Rodger Titman
Elissa Wolfson

Map Editor Paul Lehman

Project Coordinator
Joseph DiCostanzo

CONTENTS

DK Bird sounds app

The songs and calls of more than 180 species of birds in this book are featured on the new DK AMNH Bird Sounds app. Bird calls are usually short and simple, and are used to pass on information, such as an alarm call that warns of a predator or a contact call that helps birds stay in touch with each other. Songs are longer and made up of a complex set of notes, and are used by males to defend a territory or attract a mate. A bird may have several sounds in its repertoire, but each type is usually constant and unique to a species. As bird sounds carry a long way, you will often hear a bird before you can see it, and this app will help you to identify it.

To download the app, go to:
www.dk.com/bird-sounds-na

The birds featured on the app have this symbol next to their common name in this book.

PREFACE

SUMMER SINGER
Male Indigo Buntings sing from the highest available perch all summer long.

Publishing an all-inclusive, up-to-date reference book on the bird species that are found in any delineated geographical entity, such as a country like Canada, is a constantly evolving chore. With never-ending new data on morphology and behavior coupled with rapidly changing molecular technology and innovative Citizen Science programs like eBird, taxonomists are incessantly making alterations to the official list of the birds of the world. But that's not the whole story. Changing weather patterns are causing more and more bird species to shift their breeding and wintering ranges further north, and extreme weather events like hurricanes and tropical storms are blowing more and more birds across entire continents and oceans, leading to newly established populations in regions where they did not exist before. So, if birders and ornithologists want to have the latest and correct information at their fingertips, that means putting new editions of reference books and field guides on their library shelves every few years or so. And that is exactly what we have done with these 3rd editions of *Birds of Eastern Canada* and *Birds of Western Canada.*

These two handy regional guides offer, for almost all Canadian bird species, profiles with detailed information, including beautiful photographs and precise distribution maps; readable accounts of notable characteristics; data on identification, behavior, habitat, voice, nest construction, breeding season, and food; diagrams of flight patterns; statistics of size, wingspan, weight, clutch size, number of broods per year, and lifespan; and geographical information about breeding, wintering, and migration. While the use of scientific jargon has been minimized, a glossary identifies concepts that benefit from an explanation. The user-friendly format should permit readers to enjoy either studying one species account at a time or browsing to make cross comparisons.

As before, the Eastern and Western ranges are split along the 100th Meridian, or around Winnipeg, an invisible barrier located in a transitional zone between habitats that represents Eastern versus Western landscape types or biomes. While almost all of the bird species residing in Canada are included, a handful of birds that spend most of their time in a Canadian range far out to sea, for example, were left out of these volumes.

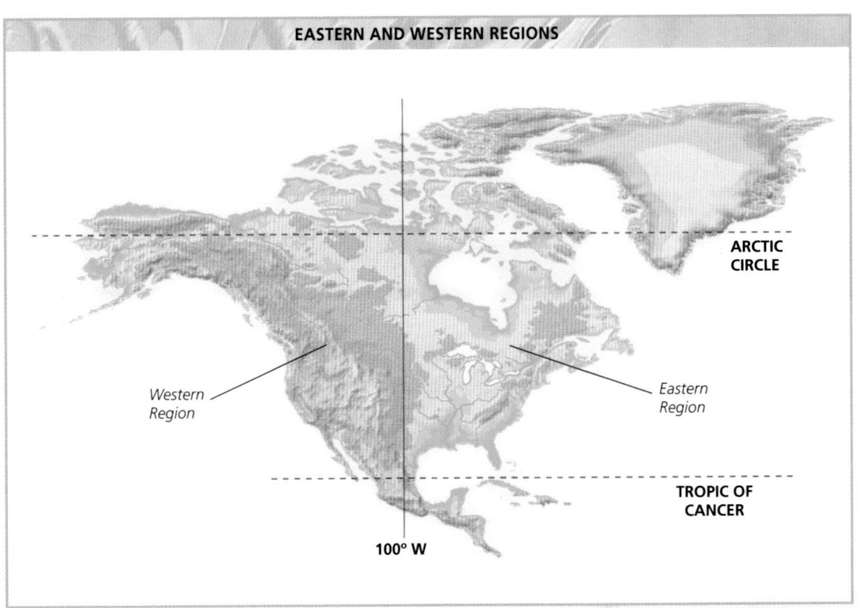
EASTERN AND WESTERN REGIONS
ARCTIC CIRCLE
Western Region
Eastern Region
TROPIC OF CANCER
100° W

During my tenure as a professor of ornithology for over 35 years, I have come to realize the real value of a concise reference work that can be conveniently carried around. I hope that these books will be useful to all persons interested in birds, whether young or older, enthusiastic birder or novice. If you are going birding, don't leave home without it!

David M. Bird
Emeritus Professor of Wildlife Biology
McGill University

TRAVELING BIRD
The Bohemian Waxwing is named for its nomadic lifestyle in the winter, as it travels around looking for fruit to eat.

HOW THIS BOOK WORKS

THIS GUIDE COVERS JUST over 350 eastern Canadian bird species. The species are organized into two sections: the first profiles common Canadian species found in the east, with each given full-page treatment; the second covers rarer birds in quarter-page entries.

∇ INTRODUCTION

The species are organized conventionally by order, family, and genus. Related birds appear together, preceded by a group introduction. The book follows the most up-to-date avian classification system, based on the latest scientific research.

Families Charadriidae, Scolopacidae, Stercorariidae, Alcidae, Laridae
SHOREBIRDS, GULLS, AUKS, AND RELATIVES
SHOREBIRDS
TERNS
GULLS
AUKS
DISTANCE TRAVELER
96

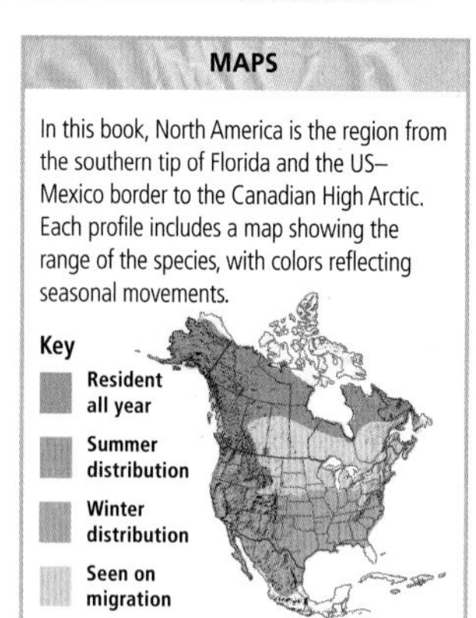

MAPS

In this book, North America is the region from the southern tip of Florida and the US–Mexico border to the Canadian High Arctic. Each profile includes a map showing the range of the species, with colors reflecting seasonal movements.

Key

- **Resident all year**
- **Summer distribution**
- **Winter distribution**
- **Seen on migration**

GROUP NAME
The common name of the group the species belongs to is at the top of each page.

COMMON NAME

IN FLIGHT
Illustrations show the bird in flight, from above and/or below—differences of season, age, or sex are not always visible.

PHOTOGRAPHS
These illustrate the species in different views and plumage variations. Significant differences relating to age, sex, and season (breeding/nonbreeding) are shown and the images labeled accordingly; if there is no variation, the images have no label. Unless stated otherwise, the bird shown is an adult.

FLIGHT PATTERNS
This feature illustrates and briefly describes the way the species flies. See panel opposite.

SIMILAR SPECIES
Similar-looking species are identified and key differences pointed out.

LENGTH, WINGSPAN, AND WEIGHT
Length is tip of tail to tip of bill; measurements are averages or ranges.

SOCIAL
The social unit the species is usually found in.

LIFESPAN
The average or maximum life expectancy.

STATUS
The conservation status of the species; the symbol (p) means the data available can only suggest a provisional status. The term "Localized" suggests that the species may be widespread but restricted to smaller areas of suitable habitat and climatic conditions.

COLOR BAND
The information bands at the top and bottom of each entry are color-coded for each family.

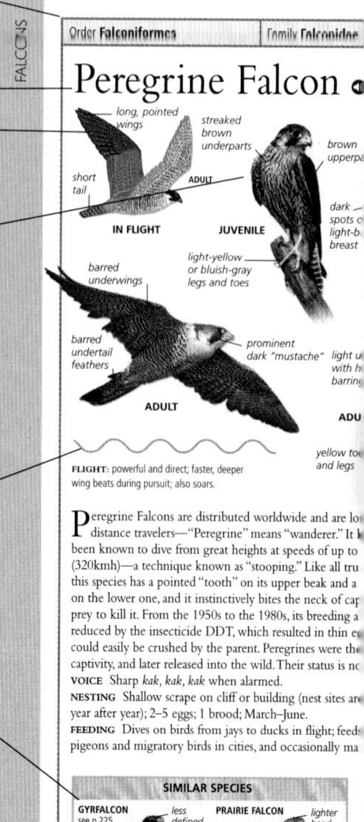

FALCONS
Order Falconiformes
Family Falconidae
Peregrine Falcon
long, pointed wings
streaked brown underparts
short tail
ADULT
IN FLIGHT
JUVENILE
light-yellow or bluish-gray legs and toes
barred underwings
barred undertail feathers
prominent dark "mustache"
ADULT
FLIGHT: powerful and direct; faster, deeper wing beats during pursuit; also soars.
Peregrine Falcons are distributed worldwide and are lo distance travelers—"Peregrine" means "wanderer." It been known to dive from great heights at speeds of up to (320kmh)—a technique known as "stooping." Like all tru this species has a pointed "tooth" on its upper beak and a on the lower one, and it instinctively bites the neck of ca prey to kill it. From the 1950s to the 1980s, its breeding a reduced by the insecticide DDT, which resulted in thin e could easily be crushed by the parent. Peregrines were th captivity, and later released into the wild. Their status is n
VOICE Sharp kak, kak, kak when alarmed.
NESTING Shallow scrape on cliff or building (nest sites ar year after year); 2–5 eggs; 1 brood; March–June.
FEEDING Dives on birds from jays to ducks in flight; feed pigeons and migratory birds in cities, and occasionally ma
Length 16in (41cm)
Social Solitary/Pairs
Lifespan Up to 20 ye
226 DATE: TIME:

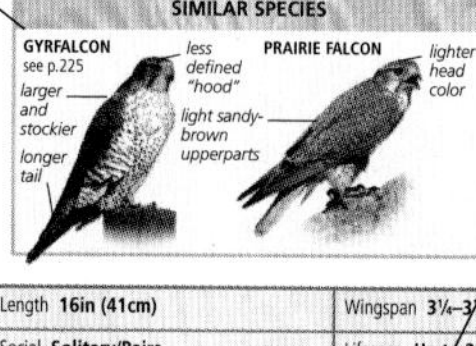

SIMILAR SPECIES
GYRFALCON see p.225
larger and stockier
longer tail
less defined "hood"
PRAIRIE FALCON
lighter head color
light sandy-brown upperparts

SYMBOLS

♂ Male	Spring
♀ Female	Summer
Juvenile	Autumn
Immature	Winter

MAPS
See panel, left. The occurrence caption describes the bird's preferred habitats and range within the North American region.

▽ COMMON SPECIES

The main section of the book features the 332 most commonly seen bird species in the eastern Canada region. Each entry is clear and detailed, following the same easy-to-access structure.

Species Falco peregrinus
yellow eye-ring
"hood"
dark "mustachial" stripe
bluish-gray upperparts

CLASSIFICATION
The top band of each entry provides the scientific order, family, and species names (see glossary, pp. 389–392 for full definitions of these terms).

DESCRIPTION
Conveys the main features and essential character of the species.

VOICE
A description of the species' calls and songs, given phonetically where possible.

NESTING
The type of nest and its usual location; the number of eggs in a clutch; the number of broods in a year; the breeding season.

FEEDING
How, where, and what the species feeds on.

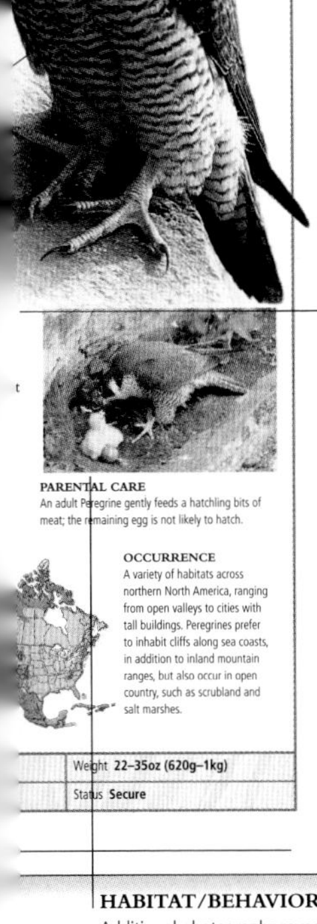

PARENTAL CARE
An adult Peregrine gently feeds a hatchling bits of meat; the remaining egg is not likely to hatch.
OCCURRENCE
A variety of habitats across northern North America, ranging from open valleys to cities with tall buildings. Peregrines prefer to inhabit cliffs along sea coasts, in addition to inland mountain ranges, but also occur in open country, such as scrubland and salt marshes.
Weight 22–35oz (620g–1kg)
Status Secure

HABITAT/BEHAVIOR
Additional photographs reveal the species in its typical habitat or show the bird exhibiting typical behavior.

Garganey
White-winged Dove
Chuck-will's-widow
Purple Gallinule
383

△ RARE SPECIES

Twenty-four less common birds are presented on pp. 383–388. Arranged in the same group order used in the main section, these entries consist of one clear photograph of the species accompanied by a description of the bird.

FLIGHT PATTERNS

Simple line diagrams are used to illustrate eight basic flight patterns.

wing beats

Woodpecker-like: bursts of wing beats between deeply undulating glides.

Finch-like: light, bouncy action with flurries of wing beats between deep, undulating glides.

Grouse-like: bursts of wing beats between short, straight glides.

Hawk-like: straight, with several quick, deep beats between short, flat glides.

Gull-like: continually flapping, with slow, steady wing beats.

Duck-like: continually flapping, with fast wing beats.

Kite-like: deep, slow wing beats between soaring glides.

Swallow-like: swooping, with bursts of wing beats between glides.

EVOLUTION

ORNITHOLOGISTS AGREE THAT BIRDS evolved from dinosaurs about 150 million years ago, but there is still debate about the dinosaur group from which they descended. Around 10,000 species of birds exist today, living in many different kinds of habitats across the world, from desert to Arctic tundra.

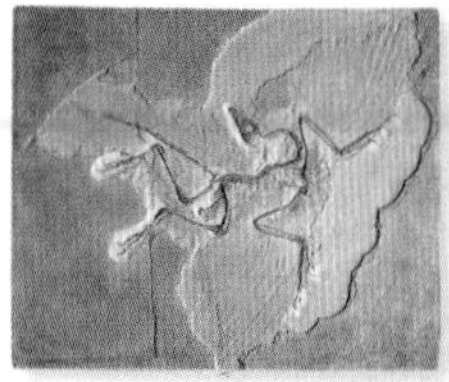

MISSING LINK?
Archaeopteryx, shown here as a 145-million-year-old fossil, had dinosaur-like teeth, but birdlike feathers.

SPECIATION

What are species and how do they evolve? Species are biological entities. When two species of a genus overlap they rarely interbreed and produce hybrids. The North American Flicker has an eastern (yellow-shafted) and a western (red-shafted) form; after the discovery that these two forms interbreed in the Great Plains, the flickers are now considered one species. In other cases, a previously single species, such as the Northern Oriole, has been divided into the Baltimore Oriole and the Bullock's Oriole. Such examples illustrate how species evolve, first by geographic separation, followed in time by overlap. This process can take millions of years.

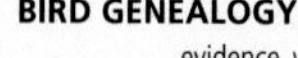

BIRD GENEALOGY

The diagram below is called a phylogeny. It shows how selected groups of birds are related to each other. The timescale at the top of the diagram is derived from both fossil and DNA evidence, which allows ornithologists to estimate when different lineages of birds diverged. The names of groups shown in bold are those residing permanently in Canada.

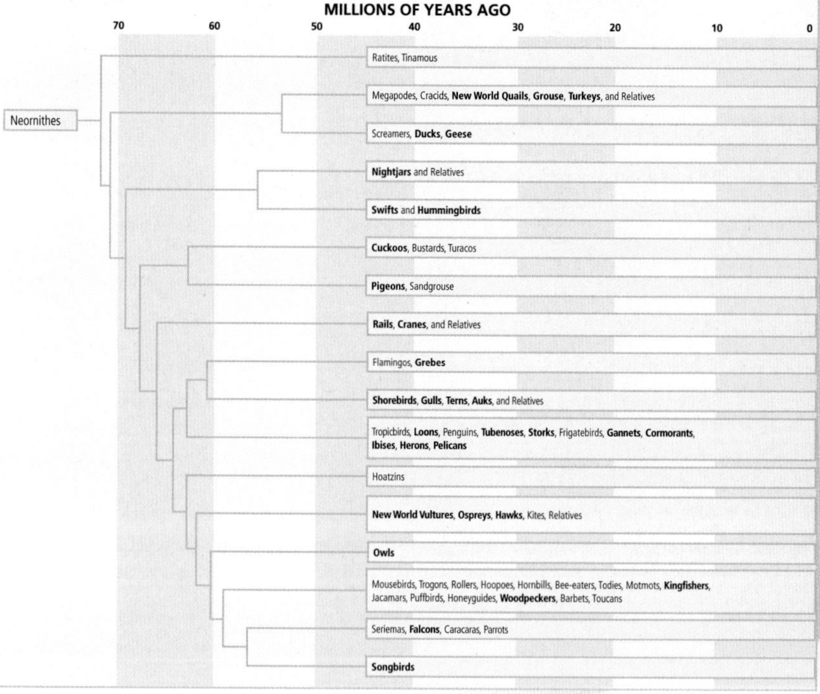

MILLIONS OF YEARS AGO

70 60 50 40 30 20 10 0

Neornithes

- Ratites, Tinamous
- Megapodes, Cracids, **New World Quails**, **Grouse**, **Turkeys**, and Relatives
- Screamers, **Ducks**, **Geese**
- **Nightjars** and Relatives
- **Swifts** and **Hummingbirds**
- **Cuckoos**, Bustards, Turacos
- **Pigeons**, Sandgrouse
- **Rails**, **Cranes**, and Relatives
- Flamingos, **Grebes**
- **Shorebirds**, **Gulls**, **Terns**, **Auks**, and Relatives
- Tropicbirds, **Loons**, Penguins, **Tubenoses**, **Storks**, Frigatebirds, **Gannets**, **Cormorants**, **Ibises**, **Herons**, **Pelicans**
- Hoatzins
- **New World Vultures**, **Ospreys**, **Hawks**, Kites, Relatives
- **Owls**
- Mousebirds, Trogons, Rollers, Hoopoes, Hornbills, Bee-eaters, Todies, Motmots, **Kingfishers**, Jacamars, Puffbirds, Honeyguides, **Woodpeckers**, Barbets, Toucans
- Seriemas, **Falcons**, Caracaras, Parrots
- **Songbirds**

CAPE
LONGCLAW
WESTERN
MEADOWLARK
Class
Aves (Birds)
Order
Passeriformes (songbirds)
Family
Parulidae (Wood Warblers)
Genus
Setophaga
Species
Setophaga castanea
Setophaga palmarum
Setophaga tigrina
Subspecies
S. p. palmarum

BLENDING IN
This magnificent species is diurnal, unlike most other owls, which are nocturnal. The Snowy Owl breeds in the Arctic tundra and if the ground is covered with snow, it blends in perfectly.

CONVERGENCE

The evolutionary process during which birds of two distantly related groups develop similarities is called convergence. Carrion-eating birds of prey are one example. Old World vultures belong to the hawk family (Accipitridae), while New World vultures are more closely related to storks. However, both groups are characterized by hooked bills, bare heads, and weak toes.

PARALLEL EVOLUTION
The African longclaws (family Motacillidae) and North American meadowlarks (family Icteridae) show convergence in plumage color and pattern.

EXTINCTION

During the last 150 years, North America has lost the Passenger Pigeon, the Great Auk, the Carolina Parakeet, the Labrador Duck, the Eskimo Curlew, and the Ivory-billed Woodpecker. Humans hunted them out of existence and/or destroyed their habitat. Some species that seemed doomed have had a reprieve. Thanks to captive breeding and release programs, birdwatchers can still see Whooping Cranes and California Condors in the wild today.

OVERHUNTING
The Passenger Pigeon was eradicated partly as a result of relentless hunting.

CLASSIFYING BIRDS

All past and present animal life is named and categorized into groups. Classifications reflect the genealogical relationships among groups, based on traits, such as color, bones, or DNA. Birds make up the class "Aves," which includes "orders." Each "order" is made up of one or more "families." "Genus" is a subdivision of "family," which contains one or more "species." A "species" is a unique group of similar organisms that interbreed and produce fertile offspring. Some species have distinct populations, which are known as "subspecies."

ANATOMY AND FLIGHT

IN SPITE OF THEIR EXTERNAL DIVERSITY, birds are remarkably similar internally. To allow flight, birds require a skeleton that is both rigid and light. Rigidity is achieved by the fusion of some bones, especially the lower vertebrae, while lightness is maintained by having hollow limb bones. These are connected to air sacs, which, in turn, are connected to the bird's lungs.

"hand"
"forearm"
neck vertebrae
bill
fused tail vertebrae
furcula
keeled sternum

SKELETON
Avian skeletal features include the furcula (wishbone), the keeled sternum (breastbone), and the fused tail vertebrae.

secondaries
tail feathers
uppertail coverts
rump
tertials
primaries

FLIGHT ADAPTATIONS

For birds to be able to fly, they need light and rigid bones, a lightweight skull, and hollow wing and leg bones. In addition, pouch-like air sacs are connected to hollow bones, which reduce a bird's weight. The air sacs also function as a cooling system, which birds need because they have a high metabolic rate. The breast muscles, which are crucial for flight, are attached to the keeled sternum (breastbone).

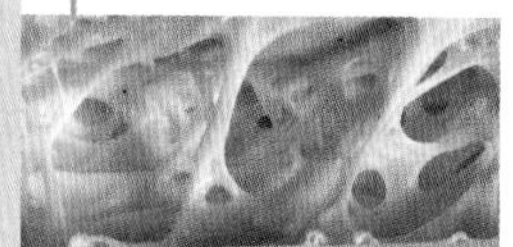

BIRD BONE STRUCTURE
Most bird bones, except those of penguins and other flightless birds, are hollow, which reduces their weight. A honeycomb of internal struts makes the bones remarkably strong.

LEGS, FEET, AND TOES

When you look at a bird's leg, you do not see their thigh, which is inside the body cavity, but just the leg from the knee down. When we talk about a bird's feet, we really mean its toes. The shin is a fused tibia and fibula. This fused bone plus the heel are collectively known as the "tarsometatarsus."

enables grip on ground

WALKING
Ground-foraging birds usually have a long hind claw.

enables strong grip on branches

CLIMBING
Most climbers have two toes forward and two backward.

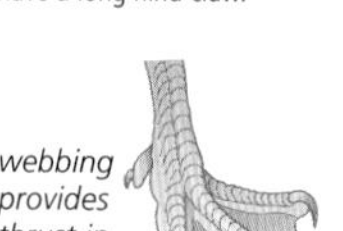
webbing provides thrust in water

SWIMMING
Water-loving birds have webbing between their toes.

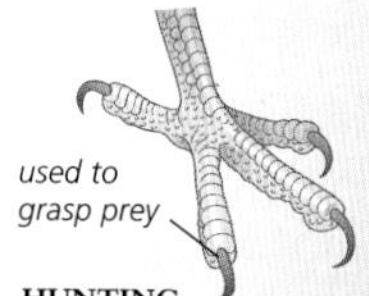
used to grasp prey

HUNTING
Birds of prey have very sharp claws or talons.

axillaries
breast
bill
undertail coverts
belly
toes

UNDERPARTS
Underwing coverts have a regular pattern of overlapping rows. Short feathers cover the head, breast, belly, and flanks. In most birds, the toes are unfeathered.

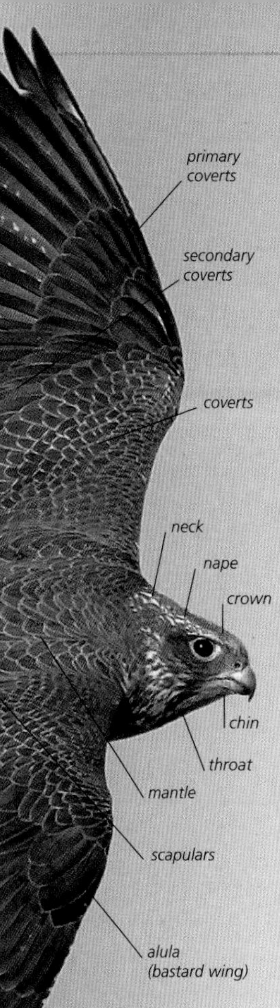
primary coverts
secondary coverts
coverts
neck
nape
crown
chin
throat
mantle
scapulars
alula (bastard wing)

FEATHERS

All birds, by definition, have feathers. These remarkable structures, which are modified scales, serve two main functions: insulation and flight. Special muscles allow birds to raise their feathers or to flatten them against the body. In cold weather, fluffed-out feathers keep an insulating layer of air between the skin and the outside. This insulating capacity is why humans often find wearing loose-fitting "down" jackets so effective against the cold. The first feathers that chicks have after hatching are down feathers. The rigidity of the flight feathers helps to create a supporting surface that birds use to generate thrust and lift.

TYPES OF FEATHERS

Birds have three main kinds of feathers: down, contour, and flight feathers. The rigid axis seen in feathers is called the "rachis."

DOWN FEATHER **CONTOUR FEATHER** **FLIGHT FEATHER**

UPPERPARTS

The wing feathers from the "hand" of the bird are the primaries and those on the "forearm" are the secondaries. Each set has its accompanying row of coverts—contour feathers that overlap the flight feathers. The tertials are adjacent to the secondaries.

WING FUNCTIONS

Flapping, soaring, gliding, and hovering are among the ways birds can use their wings. They also exhibit colors or patterns as part of territorial and courtship displays. Some waterbirds, such as herons, attract fish by creating shade with their open wings. An important aspect of wings is their relationship to a bird's weight. The ratio of a bird's wing area to weight is called wing loading, but this may also be affected by wing shape. An eagle has a large wing area to weight ratio, which means it has lower wing loading, whereas a swallow has a small wing area to weight ratio, and therefore high wing loading. This means that the slow, soaring eagle is capable of much more energy-efficient flight than the fast, agile swallow.

LONG AND BROAD

The broad, long, rectangular wings of an eagle allow it to soar. The outstretched alulae (bastard wings) give it extra lift.

POINTED

Broad at their base and tapering toward a point, and bent at the wrist, a swallow's wings enable fast flight and sharp turns.

SHORT AND ROUND

Short, broad, and rounded wings enable warblers to move between perches and to migrate long distances.

WING AERODYNAMICS

The supporting surface of a bird's wing enables it to take off and stay aloft. Propulsion and lift are linked in birds—they use their wings for both—unlike in airplanes in which these two functions are separate. Large and heavy birds, like swans, flap their wings energetically to create propulsion, and need a long, watery runway before they can fly off. The Golden Eagle can take off from a cliff with little or no wing flapping, but the Black and Turkey Vultures hop up from carrion, then flap vigorously, and finally use the air flowing across their wings to soar. This diagram shows how airflow affects lift.

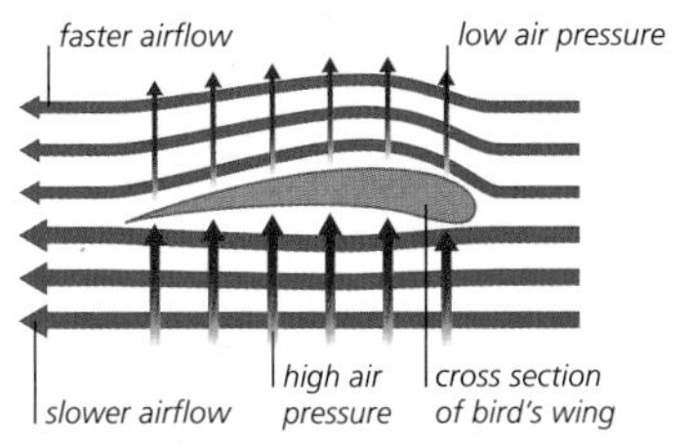
faster airflow
low air pressure
high air pressure
cross section of bird's wing
slower airflow

MIGRATION

UNTIL RECENTLY, THE MECHANICS, or the "how" of migration was poorly understood. Today, however, ornithologists know that birds use a variety of cues including visual and magnetic, whether they migrate by day or by night. Birds do not leave northern breeding areas because of the winter cold, but because day length gets shorter and food scarcer.

NIGHT MIGRANTS
During migration, ornithologists can point a telescope on the moon and count the birds that cross its surface.

REFUELING
Red Knots make a stop on their long journey to eat horseshoe crab eggs.

INSTINCTIVE MOVE

Even though many birds use visual cues and landmarks during their migration, for example birds of prey flying along the Appalachians, "instinctive" behavior must control much of how and where they move. Instinct is a loose term that is hard to define, but ornithologists generally understand it as a genetically programmed activity. They assume that natural selection has molded a behavior as complex as migration by acting on birds' DNA; this hypothesis is reasonable but hard to prove. Nevertheless, it would seem to be the only explanation why many juvenile shorebirds leave their breeding grounds after their parents and yet still find their way to their final destination.

NAVIGATION

One of the most puzzling aspects of migration is understanding how birds make their way from their breeding grounds to their destination. Ornithologists have devised experiments to determine how the different components of a navigation system work. For example, if visual landmarks are hidden by fog, a faint sun can give birds a directional clue; if heavy clouds hide the sun, then the birds' magnetic compass may be used to ascertain their direction. Night migrants use star constellations.

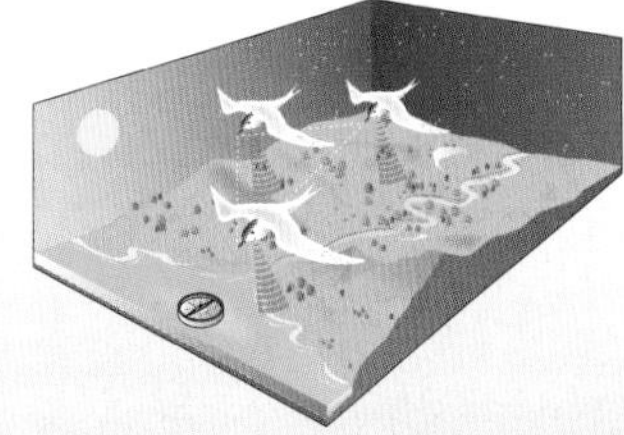

FINDING THE WAY
Birds coordinate information their brains receive from the sun, moon, stars, landmarks, and magnetite, or iron oxide, and use it as a compass.

OVERLAND FLIERS
Sandhill Cranes migrate over hills and mountains from their northern breeding grounds to the marshes of the Platte River and as far south as Texas and Mexico.

GLOBETROTTERS

Some bird species in Canada are year-round residents, although a few individuals of these species move away from where they hatched at some time in the year. However, a large number of Canadian species are migratory. A few species breed in Labrador, but winter in the Gulf of the Caribbean. Others breed in the Canadian Arctic Archipelago, fly over land and the Pacific Ocean, and spend the winter at sea off the coast of Peru. Many songbirds fly from Canada's boreal forests to Mexico and northern South America. The most amazing globetrotters, such as the Red Knot, fly all the way to Tierra del Fuego, making only a few stops along the way after their short breeding season in the Arctic tundra. The return journeys of some of these travelers are not over the same route—instead, their entire trip is elliptical in shape.

EPIC JOURNEY
The Arctic Tern is an amazing long-distance migrant, breeding in northern regions and wintering in the pack ice of Antarctica after flying a round-trip distance of about 25,000 miles (40,000km).

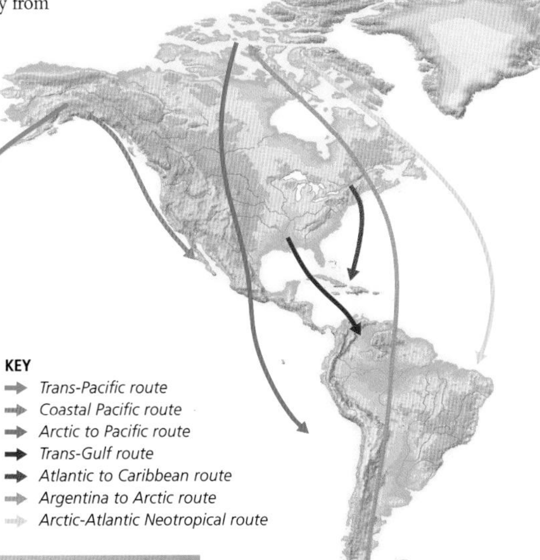

KEY
- *Trans-Pacific route*
- *Coastal Pacific route*
- *Arctic to Pacific route*
- *Trans-Gulf route*
- *Atlantic to Caribbean route*
- *Argentina to Arctic route*
- *Arctic-Atlantic Neotropical route*

MIGRATION ROUTES
The map above shows the range of migration routes that some North American species take to and from their breeding grounds.

NEOTROPICAL MIGRANT
Many wood warblers, such as this Blackpoll Warbler, breed in boreal forests before migrating to their wintering grounds in the Caribbean, or Central or South America.

V-FORMATION
Geese and other large waterbirds fly in a V-formation to allow following birds to gain lift from those in front, thereby saving energy. The lead bird is regularly replaced.

PARTIAL MIGRANT

The American Robin is a good example of a partial migrant, a species in which the birds of some populations are resident whereas others migrate out of their breeding range. Most Canadian populations of the American Robin fly south, US populations are largely resident, and quite a few from either population spend the winter in the Southwest, Florida, or Mexico.

KEY
- *Breeding distribution*
- *Resident all year*
- *Nonbreeding distribution*

COURTSHIP AND MATING

WHETHER MONOGAMOUS OR NOT, males and females need to mate for their species to perpetuate itself. With most species, the male plays the dominant role of advertising a territory to potential mates using vocal or visual displays. Females then select a male and if the two respond positively to each other, a period of courtship follows, ending in mating. The next step is nest-building, egg-laying, and rearing the young.

DISPLAYS

Mutual attraction between the sexes starts with some sort of display, usually performed by the male. These displays can take a number of forms, from flashing dazzling breeding plumage, conducting elaborate dancing rituals, and performing complex songs to offering food or nesting material, or actually building a nest. Some birds, such as grebes, have fascinatingly intricate ceremonies, in which both male and female simultaneously perform the same movements.

WELCOME HOME
Northern Gannets greet their mates throughout the breeding season by rubbing bills together and opening their wings.

DANCING CRANES
During courtship, Sandhill Cranes perform spectacular dances, the two birds of a pair leaping into the air with wings opened and legs splayed.

COURTSHIP FEEDING

In some species, males offer food to their mate to maintain the pair bond. The male Common Tern routinely brings small fish to a mate in a nesting colony, spreading his wings and tail until she accepts the fish.

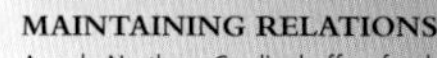
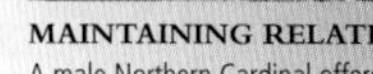

MAINTAINING RELATIONS
A male Northern Cardinal offers food to the female, which is a way of reinforcing their pair bond.

BREEDING

After mating, a nest is made, often by the female, where she lays from one to a dozen eggs. Not all birds make nests. Nightjars, for example, lay their eggs directly on the ground. In many species, incubation doesn't start until the female has laid all the eggs. Incubation, more often done by the female, varies from 12 days to about 45 days. Songbirds ranging from the temperate zone to the Arctic show a range in clutch size, with more eggs produced in the North than in the South. The breeding process can fail at any stage, for example a predator can eat the eggs or the chicks. Some birds will nest again, but others give up breeding for the season.

MATING

Mating is usually brief and typically takes place on a perch or on the ground, but a few species like swifts and swallows can mate in the air. This male Black Tern balances himself by opening his wings.

POLYGAMY

This Winter Wren collects nesting material for one of the several nests he will build.

MONOGAMOUS BONDS

Some birds, such as Snow Geese, mostly remain paired for life after establishing a bond.

SINGLE FATHER

A male Red-necked Phalarope incubates eggs in the Arctic tundra. Phalaropes are well known for their reversal of breeding roles. The female, who is the larger and more colorful of the two sexes, aggressively competes for males, and after mating with several of them, plays no role in nest-building, incubating, or caring for chicks, but tends to her territory instead. Although the chicks can feed by themselves immediately after hatching, they remain with a male before growing feathers and living on their own.

NESTS AND EGGS

MOST BIRD SPECIES BUILD THEIR OWN NEST, which is a necessary container for their eggs. Exceptions include cowbirds, which lay their eggs in other species' nests. Nest-building is often done by the female alone, but in some species the male may help or even build it himself. Eggs are incubated either by females alone, or by males or females, depending on the species. Eggshells are thick enough to sustain the weight of incubating parents, yet thin enough for a chick to break its way out. Eggs, consisting of 60 percent water, contain a fatty yolk as well as sugars and proteins for nourishment of the embryo.

NEST TYPES

In addition to the four types shown below, nests range from a simple scrape in the ground with a few added pebbles to an elaborate woven basket-like structure. Plant matter forms basic nest material. This includes twigs, grass stems, bark, lichens, mosses, plant down, and rootlets. Some birds add mud to their nest for strength. Others incorporate animal hair or feathers to improve its softness and insulation. Female eider ducks pluck down feathers from their belly. Some birds include bits of plastic or threads in their nests. Many birds make their nest or lay their eggs deep inside the empty burrows of other animals.

UNTIDY NEST
Huge stick nests, built on top of dead trees, are the hallmark of Ospreys. They also use a wide variety of artificial structures, including nesting platforms built for them by humans.

EGG CUP
A clutch of blue robin eggs in a cup lined with grass stems. Robins build their nests either in shrubs or trees, and sometimes on artificial structures like porch lights.

NATURAL CAVITY
This Northern Saw-whet Owl is nesting at the bottom of a tree cavity that was probably excavated by a woodpecker.

NEST BOX
Cavity-nesting bluebirds have been affected by habitat loss. They compete with other birds for nest sites, which may include human-made structures.

COMPLEX WEAVE
New World orioles weave intricate nests from dried grass stems and other plant material. They hang them from the tip of branches, often high up in trees.

EGG SHAPES

There are six basic egg shapes among birds, as illustrated to the right. The most common egg shapes are longitudinal and elliptical. Murres lay pear-shaped eggs. Formerly believed to prevent eggs from rolling off ledges, recent studies suggest that the pointed shape facilitates more efficient incubation. Spherical eggs with irregular red blotches are characteristic of birds of prey. Pigeons and doves lay white oval eggs, usually two per clutch. The eggs of many songbirds, including sparrows and buntings, are conical and have a variety of dark markings on a pale background.

NEAT ARRANGEMENT
Many shorebirds, such as plovers and sandpipers, lay four conical eggs with the narrow ends pointed in toward each other.

COLOR AND SHAPE
Birds' eggs vary widely in terms of shape, colors, and markings. The American Robin's egg on the left is a beautiful blue.

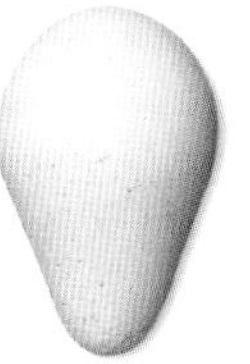

PEAR-SHAPED

LONGITUDINAL

ELLIPTICAL

OVAL

CONICAL

SPHERICAL

HATCHING CONDITION

After a period of incubation, which varies from species to species, chicks pierce the eggshell, some of them using an egg tooth, a special bill feature that falls off after hatching. After a long and exhausting struggle, the chick eventually tumbles out of the shell fragments. The transition from the watery medium inside the egg to the air outside is a tremendous physiological switch. Once free of their shell, the hatchlings recover from the exertion and either beg food from their parents or feed on their own.

FOOD DELIVERY
Tern chicks, although able to move around, cannot catch the fish they need to survive and must rely on their parents to provide food until they can fly.

PARENTAL CARE
Birds of prey, such as these Snowy Owl owlets, need their parents to care for them longer than some other bird species. They do not leave the nest until their feathers are sufficiently developed for their first flight.

FAST FEEDER
Coots, gallinules, and rails hatch with a complete covering of down, and they can feed themselves immediately after birth.

BROOD PARASITISM

Neither cowbirds in the New World nor cuckoos in the Old World make a nest. Choosing from over 200 potential species, female cowbirds deposit up to 40 eggs in the nests of several species. If the foster parents accept the foreign egg, they feed the chick of the parasite until it fledges. In the picture below, a tiny wood warbler feeds its adopted chick, a huge cowbird hatchling that has overgrown the nest.

IDENTIFICATION

SOME SPECIES ARE EASY TO IDENTIFY, but in many cases, species identification is tricky. In Canada, a notoriously difficult group to identify is the wood warblers, especially in the fall, when most species have similar greenish and/or yellowish plumage. Gulls and shorebirds are also challenging.

bright-
blue
wings
white
belly
chestnut
flanks

BLUEBIRD VARIATIONS
Species of the genus *Sialia*, such as the all-blue Mountain Bluebird (above) and the Eastern Bluebird (left), are easy to identify.

GEOGRAPHIC RANGE

Each bird species in Canada lives in a particular area that is called its geographic range. Some species have a restricted range. For example, the Whooping Crane breeds only in Wood Buffalo National Park in Alberta and the Northwest Territories. Other species, such as the Red-tailed Hawk, range from coast to coast and from northern Canada to Mexico. Species with a broad range usually breed in varied types of vegetation, while species with narrow ranges often have a specialized habitat. For example, Northern Gannets prefer steep, rocky shores.

SIZE AND WEIGHT

From hummingbird to Tundra Swan and from extra-light to heavy, such is the range of sizes and weights found among the bird species of Canada. Size can be measured in several ways, for example, the length of a bird from bill-tip to tail-tip, its wingspan, or even its weight. Size can also be estimated for a given bird in relationship with another that is familiar. For example, the less familiar Bicknell's Thrush can be compared with the well-known American Robin.

SIZE MATTERS
Smaller shorebirds, with shorter legs and bills, forage in shallow water, but larger ones have longer legs and bills and can feed in deeper water.

SEMIPALMATED PLOVER

LESSER YELLOWLEGS

HUDSONIAN GODWIT

WHIMBREL

GENERAL SHAPE

Just as birds come in all sizes, their body shapes also vary, but size and shape are not necessarily correlated. In the dense reed beds in which it lives, the streaked American Bittern's long and thin body blends in with reeds. The round-bodied Sedge Wren hops in shrubby vegetation or near the ground where slimness is not an advantage. In dense forest canopy, the slender and long-tailed Yellow-billed Cuckoo can maneuver easily. Mourning Doves inhabit rather open habitats and their plumpness is irrelevant when it comes to their living space.

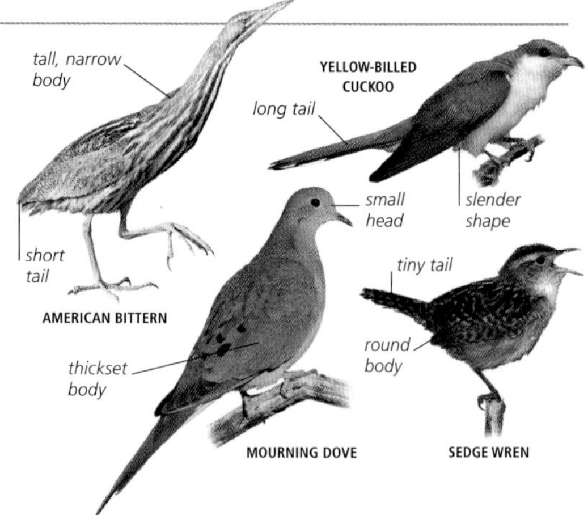
tall, narrow
body
short
tail
long tail
small
head
slender
shape
tiny tail
round
body
thickset
body

AMERICAN BITTERN

YELLOW-BILLED CUCKOO

MOURNING DOVE

SEDGE WREN

BILL SHAPE

These images show a range of bill shapes and sizes relative to the bird's head size. In general, bill form, including length or thickness, corresponds to the kinds of food a birds consumes. With its pointed bill, the Black-capped Chickadee picks tiny insects from crevices in tree barks. At another extreme, dowitchers probe mud with their long thin bills, feeling for worms. The Willet swishes its long, recurved bill back and forth in water in search of aquatic insects.

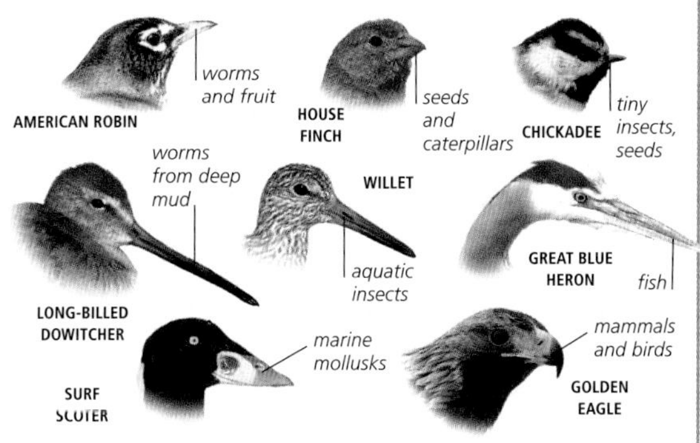
AMERICAN ROBIN
worms and fruit
HOUSE FINCH
seeds and caterpillars
CHICKADEE
tiny insects, seeds
LONG-BILLED DOWITCHER
worms from deep mud
WILLET
aquatic insects
GREAT BLUE HERON
fish
SURF SCOTER
marine mollusks
GOLDEN EAGLE
mammals and birds

WING SHAPE

Birds' wing shapes are correlated with their flight style. The long, round-tipped wings of the Red-tailed Hawk are perfect for soaring, while the tiny wings of hummingbirds are exactly what is needed to hover in front of flowers and then to back away after a meal of nectar. When flushed, partridges flutter with their round wings briefly and drop down.

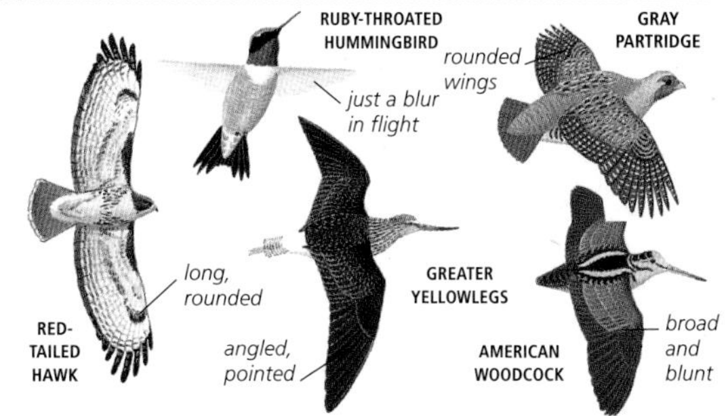
RUBY-THROATED HUMMINGBIRD
just a blur in flight
GRAY PARTRIDGE
rounded wings
RED-TAILED HAWK
long, rounded
GREATER YELLOWLEGS
angled, pointed
AMERICAN WOODCOCK
broad and blunt

TAIL SHAPE

It is not clear why some songbirds, like the American Goldfinch, have a notched tail while other similar-sized birds do not. Tail shapes vary as much as wing shapes, but are not so easily linked to a function. Irrespective of shape, tails are needed for balance. In some birds, tail shape, color, and pattern are used in courtship displays or in defensive displays when threatened.

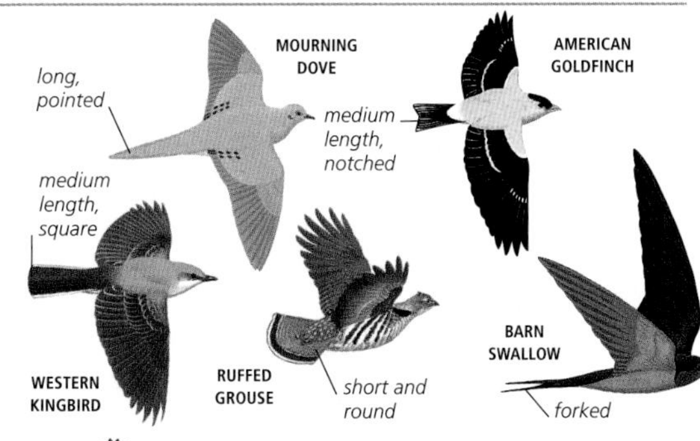
MOURNING DOVE
long, pointed
AMERICAN GOLDFINCH
medium length, notched
medium length, square
WESTERN KINGBIRD
RUFFED GROUSE
short and round
BARN SWALLOW
forked

COLORS AND MARKINGS

Melanin and carotenoid pigments largely determine color. Gray and brown birds have melanin (under hormonal influence), yellow and red ones have carotenoid (derived from food). House Finches are reddish because they eat a carotenoid-rich diet. Diversity in color and markings also results from scattering of white light by feathers (producing blue colors) and optical interference (iridescence) due to the structural properties of some feathers.

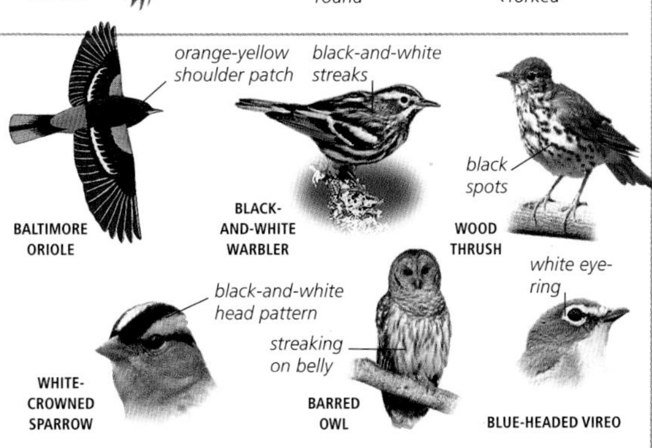
orange-yellow shoulder patch
BALTIMORE ORIOLE
black-and-white streaks
BLACK-AND-WHITE WARBLER
black spots
WOOD THRUSH
black-and-white head pattern
WHITE-CROWNED SPARROW
streaking on belly
BARRED OWL
white eye-ring
BLUE-HEADED VIREO

SPECIES GUIDE

DUCKS, GEESE, AND SWANS

RECENT GENETIC studies indicate that waterfowl are most closely related to members of the order Galliformes. Most species of waterfowl molt all their flight feathers at once after breeding, making them flightless for several weeks until they grow new ones.

GEESE

Ornithologists group most geese and swans together into the subfamily Anserinae. Geese are generally intermediate between swans and ducks in body size and neck length. They are more terrestrial than either swans or ducks, often seen grazing on dry land. Like swans, geese often pair for life. They are also highly social, and most species are migratory, flying south for the winter in large flocks.

SWANS

Swans are essentially large, long-necked geese. Their heavier weight makes them ungainly on land, and they tend to be more aquatic than their smaller relatives. On water, however, they are extremely graceful. When feeding, a swan stretches its long neck to reach water plants at the bottom, submerging up to half its body as it does so. The Trumpeter Swan is North America's largest native waterfowl, growing up to 5ft (1.5m) long and weighing up to 25lb (12kg).

DUCKS

Classified into several subfamilies, ducks are more varied than swans or geese, with many more species. They are loosely grouped by their feeding habits. Dabblers, or puddle ducks, such as the Mallard, teals, and wigeons, eat plants and invertebrates. They feed by upending on the surface of shallow water. By contrast, diving ducks, a group that includes scaups, scoters, eiders, mergansers, and the Ruddy Duck, dive deep underwater for their food.

INSTANT TAKEOFF
Puddle ducks like the Mallard can shoot out of the water and into the air.

GAGGLING GEESE
Gregarious Snow Geese form large, noisy flocks during migration and on winter feeding grounds.

Order **Anseriformes**	Family **Anatidae**	Species ***Anser caerulescens***

Snow Goose

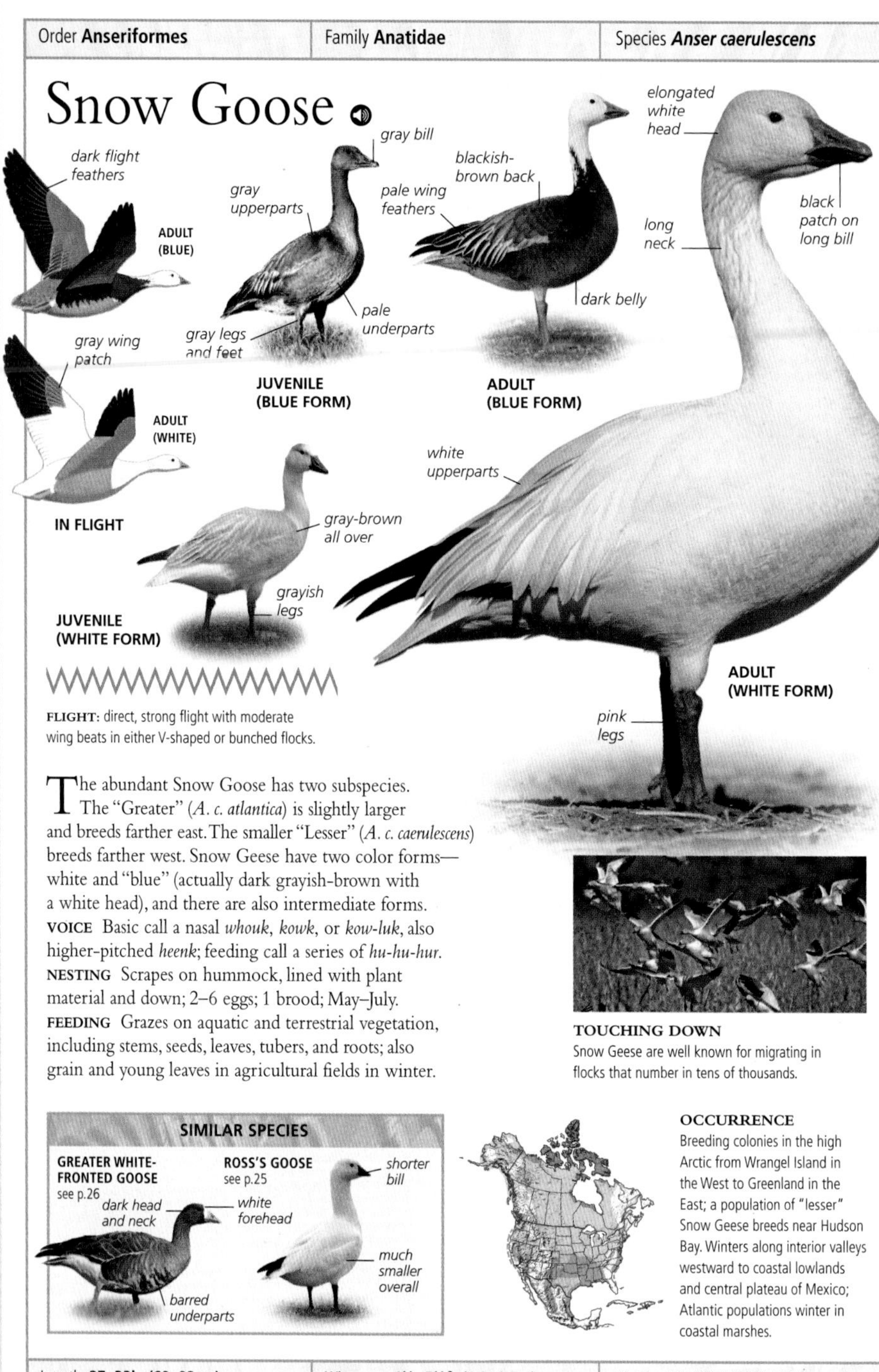
dark flight feathers
ADULT (BLUE)
gray wing patch
ADULT (WHITE)
IN FLIGHT
gray bill
gray upperparts
gray legs and feet
pale underparts
JUVENILE (BLUE FORM)
blackish-brown back
pale wing feathers
dark belly
ADULT (BLUE FORM)
elongated white head
black patch on long bill
long neck
white upperparts
gray-brown all over
grayish legs
JUVENILE (WHITE FORM)
ADULT (WHITE FORM)
pink legs

FLIGHT: direct, strong flight with moderate wing beats in either V-shaped or bunched flocks.

The abundant Snow Goose has two subspecies. The "Greater" (*A. c. atlantica*) is slightly larger and breeds farther east. The smaller "Lesser" (*A. c. caerulescens*) breeds farther west. Snow Geese have two color forms—white and "blue" (actually dark grayish-brown with a white head), and there are also intermediate forms.

VOICE Basic call a nasal *whouk*, *kowk*, or *kow-luk*, also higher-pitched *heenk*; feeding call a series of *hu-hu-hur*.

NESTING Scrapes on hummock, lined with plant material and down; 2–6 eggs; 1 brood; May–July.

FEEDING Grazes on aquatic and terrestrial vegetation, including stems, seeds, leaves, tubers, and roots; also grain and young leaves in agricultural fields in winter.

TOUCHING DOWN
Snow Geese are well known for migrating in flocks that number in tens of thousands.

SIMILAR SPECIES

GREATER WHITE-FRONTED GOOSE see p.26
dark head and neck
barred underparts

ROSS'S GOOSE see p.25
shorter bill
white forehead
much smaller overall

OCCURRENCE
Breeding colonies in the high Arctic from Wrangel Island in the West to Greenland in the East; a population of "lesser" Snow Geese breeds near Hudson Bay. Winters along interior valleys westward to coastal lowlands and central plateau of Mexico; Atlantic populations winter in coastal marshes.

Length **27–33in (69–83cm)**	Wingspan **4¼–5½ft (1.3–1.7m)**	Weight **3¾–6½lb (1.7–3kg)**
Social **Flocks**	Lifespan **Up to 27 years**	Status **Secure**

DATE: ______ TIME: ______ LOCATION: ______

Order **Anseriformes**	Family **Anatidae**	Species ***Anser rossii***

Ross's Goose

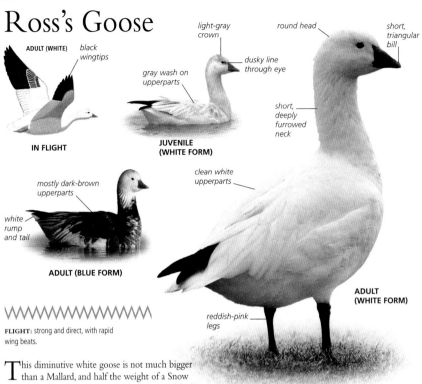

ADULT (WHITE) *black wingtips*

IN FLIGHT

light-gray crown
dusky line through eye
gray wash on upperparts

JUVENILE (WHITE FORM)

round head
short, triangular bill
short, deeply furrowed neck
clean white upperparts
reddish-pink legs

ADULT (WHITE FORM)

mostly dark-brown upperparts
white rump and tail

ADULT (BLUE FORM)

FLIGHT: strong and direct, with rapid wing beats.

This diminutive white goose is not much bigger than a Mallard, and half the weight of a Snow Goose; like its larger relative, it also has a rare "blue" form. About 95 percent of Ross's Geese once nested at a single sanctuary in Arctic Canada, and breeding pairs have spread eastwards along the Hudson Bay and to several island locations. Hunting reduced the population to just 6,000 in the early 1950s, but since then the numbers have increased to around 2 million individuals.

VOICE Call a *keek keek keeek*, higher-pitched than Snow Goose; also a harsh, low *kork* or *kowk*; quiet when feeding.

NESTING Plant materials placed on ground, usually in colonies with Lesser Snow Geese; 3–5 eggs; 1 brood; June–August.

FEEDING Grazes on grasses, sedges, and small grains.

TRAVELING IN FAMILIES
Family groups migrate thousands of miles together, usually from northern Canada to central California.

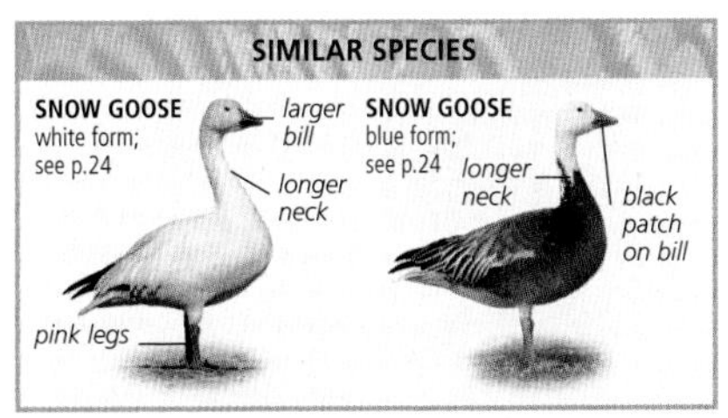
SIMILAR SPECIES
SNOW GOOSE
white form;
see p.24
larger bill
longer neck
pink legs
SNOW GOOSE
blue form;
see p.24
longer neck
black patch on bill

OCCURRENCE
Breeding grounds are amidst tundra in a number of scattered, high Arctic locations. Main wintering areas in California. On the wintering grounds, it feeds in agricultural fields, and also grasslands. Roosts overnight in several types of wetlands.

Length **22½–25in (57–64cm)**	Wingspan **3¼ft (1.1m)**	Weight **1¾–4½lb (0.85–2kg)**
Social **Flocks**	Lifespan **Up to 21 years**	Status **Localized**

DATE: ______________ TIME: ______________ LOCATION: ______________

Order **Anseriformes**	Family **Anatidae**	Species ***Anser albifrons***

Greater White-fronted Goose

ADULT
gray wing feathers
white rump band
IN FLIGHT
white tip to tail
white flank streak
brownish-gray head
pink bill with white base
darker chocolate-brown upperparts
larger body
longer legs, bill, and neck
A. a gambeli (TULE)
bright-orange legs
MALE
A. a. frontalis (TUNDRA)
brown underparts with black bands
dull yellowish-orange bill
no belly barring
JUVENILE

The Greater White-fronted Goose is the most widespread goose in the Northern Hemisphere. It is easily distinguished by its black-barred belly and the patch of white at the base of its bill. There are five subspecies, two of which are most commonly seen in North America. The "Tundra" (*A. a. frontalis*) makes up the largest population, breeding across northwestern Canada and western Alaska. The "Tule" (*A. a. gambeli*), while the largest in stature, occurs in the fewest numbers, and is restricted in range to northwest Canada.

VOICE Laugh-like *klow-yo* or *klew-yo-yo*; very musical in a flock.
NESTING Bowl-shaped nest made of plant material, lined with down, constructed near water; 3–7 eggs; 1 brood; May–August.
FEEDING Eats sedges, grasses, berries, and plants on both land and water in summer; feeds on grasses, seeds, and grains in winter.

FLIGHT: strong, direct flight; flies alone, in multiple lines, or in a V-formation.

FLIGHT FORMATIONS
This heavy-bodied, powerful flier can often be seen in tightly packed flocks.

SIMILAR SPECIES

CANADA GOOSE
see p.29
black head, neck, and bill
white chin strap

HEAVY GRAZER
Grass is the major component of this goose's diet.

OCCURRENCE
Different habitats are utilized, both for breeding and wintering. Nesting areas include tundra ponds and lakes, dry rocky fields, and grassy slopes in Alaska and northern Canada. In winter, coastal marshes, inland wetlands, agricultural fields, and refuges are used along the Pacific Coast, the southern US, and Mexico.

Length **25–32in (64–81cm)**	Wingspan **4¹/₄–5¹/₄ft (1.3–1.6m)**	Weight **4–6¹/₂lb (1.8–3kg)**
Social **Flocks**	Lifespan **Up to 22 years**	Status **Secure**

DATE: ____________ TIME: ____________ LOCATION: ____________

Order **Anseriformes**	Family **Anatidae**	Species ***Branta bernicla***

Brant

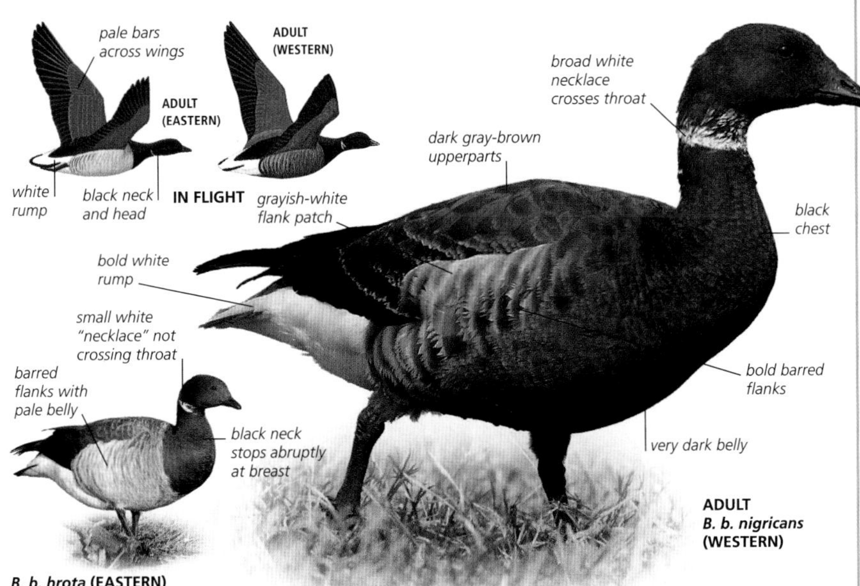
pale bars across wings
ADULT (EASTERN)
ADULT (WESTERN)
white rump
black neck and head
IN FLIGHT
grayish-white flank patch
dark gray-brown upperparts
broad white necklace crosses throat
black chest
bold white rump
small white "necklace" not crossing throat
barred flanks with pale belly
black neck stops abruptly at breast
bold barred flanks
very dark belly
ADULT
B. b. nigricans (WESTERN)
B. b. hrota (EASTERN)

A small-billed, dark, stocky sea goose, the Brant winters on both the East and West Coasts of North America. There are two subspecies named in North America—the pale-bellied "Atlantic" Brant (*B. b. hrota*), found in the east, and the darker "Black" Brant (*B. b. nigricans*), found in the west; an intermediate gray-bellied form, not yet named, breeds in the Canadian archipelago and winters in Boundary Bay, British Columbia. Unlike other North American geese, the Brant feeds mainly on eelgrass in winter.

VOICE Nasal *cruk*, harsh-sounding in tone; rolling series of *cut cut cut cronk*, with an upward inflection at the end.

NESTING Scrape lined with grass, plant matter, and down on islands or gravel spits; 3–5 eggs; 1 brood; May–July.

FEEDING Eats grass and sedges when nesting; eelgrass in winter; also green algae, salt marsh plants, and mollusks.

FLIGHT: rapid and strong; low, irregular flight formations.

GRASSY MEAL

In winter, Brants forage almost exclusively on eelgrass between the high and low tide marks.

SIMILAR SPECIES

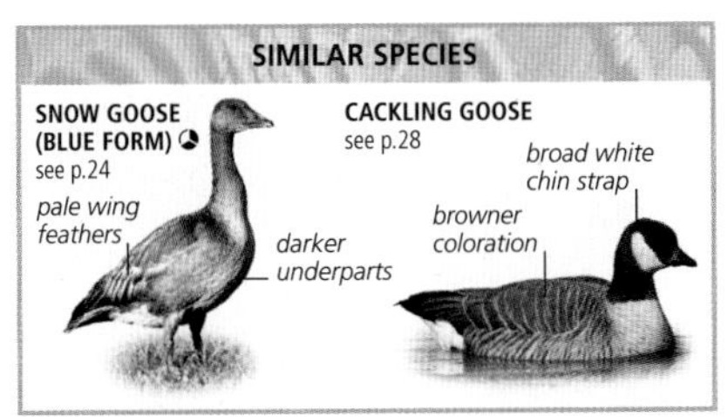
SNOW GOOSE (BLUE FORM)
see p.24
pale wing feathers
darker underparts
CACKLING GOOSE
see p.28
broad white chin strap
browner coloration

OCCURRENCE

Breeds in colonies in northern Canada and Alaska, and winters along both the Pacific and Atlantic Coasts. The western breeding population of the Brant ("Black") winters from the Aleutian Islands to northern Mexico, while the pale-bellied form ("Atlantic") is restricted in range to the East Coast.

Length **22–26in (56–66cm)**	Wingspan **3½–4ft (1.1–1.2m)**	Weight **2½–4lb (1–1.8kg)**
Social **Flocks**	Lifespan **Up to 25 years**	Status **Secure**

DATE: ____________ TIME: ____________ LOCATION: ____________

Order **Anseriformes**	Family **Anatidae**	Species ***Branta hutchinsii***

Cackling Goose

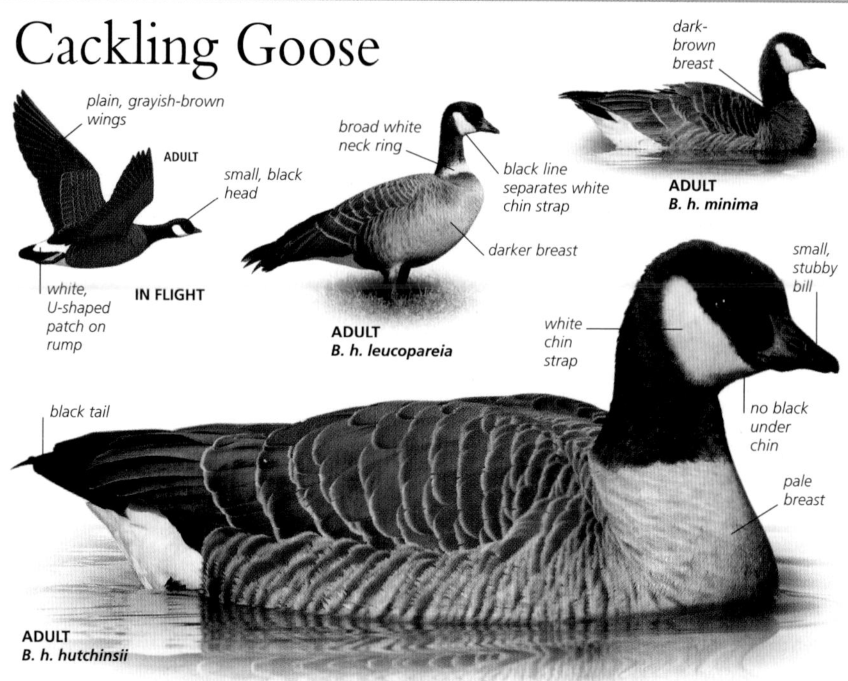
plain, grayish-brown wings
ADULT
small, black head
white, U-shaped patch on rump
IN FLIGHT
broad white neck ring
black line separates white chin strap
darker breast
ADULT
B. h. leucopareia
dark-brown breast
ADULT
B. h. minima
small, stubby bill
white chin strap
no black under chin
pale breast
black tail
ADULT
B. h. hutchinsii

The Cackling Goose has recently been split from the Canada Goose; it can be distinguished from the latter by its short, stubby bill, steep forehead, and short neck. There are four subspecies of Cackling Goose, which vary in breast color—ranging from dark on *B. h. minima* and fairly dark on *B. h. leucopareia* to pale on *B. h. hutchinsii*. The Cackling Goose is much smaller than all subspecies of Canada Goose, except the "Lesser" Canada Goose, which has a longer neck and a less sloped forehead.

VOICE Male call a honk or bark; females have higher pitched *hrink;* also high-pitched yelps.

NESTING Scrape lined with available plant matter and down; 2–8 eggs; 1 brood; May–August.

FEEDING Consumes plants in summer; in winter, grazes on grass in livestock and dairy pastures; also in agricultural fields.

FLIGHT: strong with rapid wing beats; flies in bunched V-formations.

LITTLE GEESE
Cackling Geese are tiny when seen together with the larger Canada Goose.

SIMILAR SPECIES

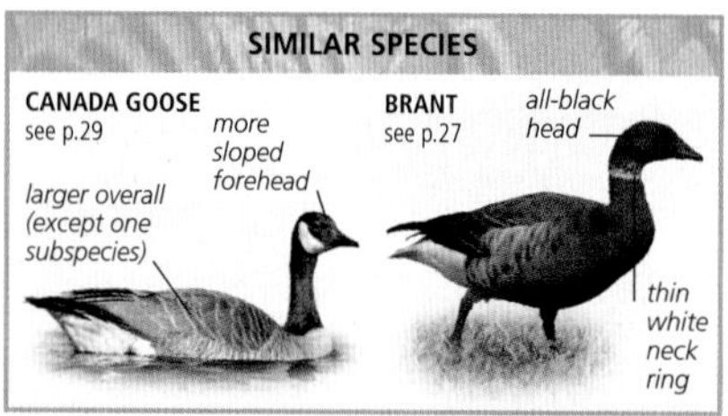
CANADA GOOSE
see p.29
more sloped forehead
larger overall (except one subspecies)

BRANT
see p.27
all-black head
thin white neck ring

OCCURRENCE
At the northernmost fringe of the Canada Goose's range, in the tundra, it breeds on rocky tundra slopes from the Aleutians East to Baffin Island and Hudson Bay. Winters from British Columbia to California, also central US, Texas, and New Mexico in pastures and agricultural fields.

Length **21½–30in (55–75cm)**	Wingspan **4¼–5ft (1.3–1.5m)**	Weight **2–6½lb (0.9–3kg)**
Social **Flocks**	Lifespan **Unknown**	Status **Secure**

DATE: ____________ TIME: ____________ LOCATION: ____________

Order **Anseriformes**	Family **Anatidae**	Species ***Branta canadensis***

Canada Goose

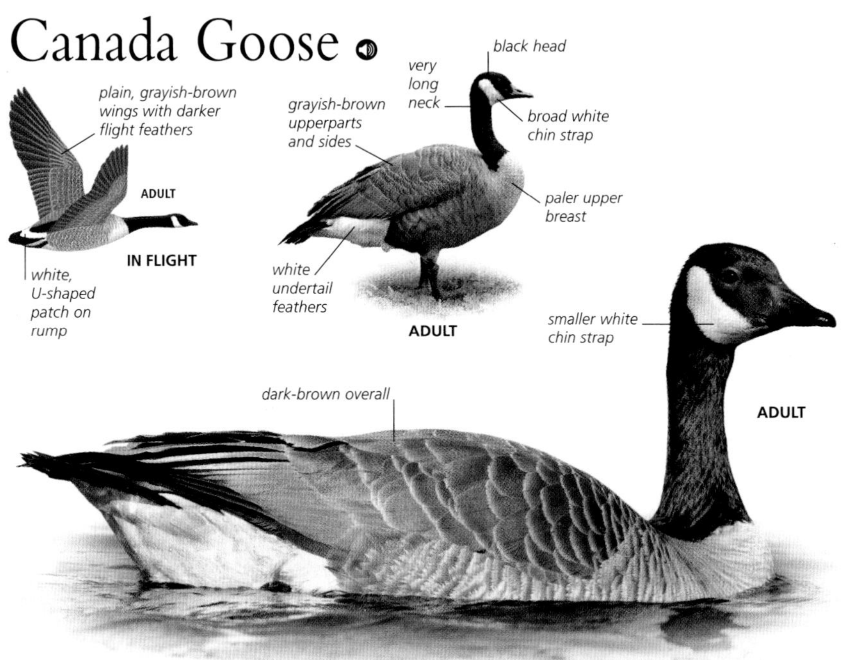
plain, grayish-brown wings with darker flight feathers
ADULT
IN FLIGHT
white, U-shaped patch on rump
grayish-brown upperparts and sides
very long neck
black head
broad white chin strap
paler upper breast
white undertail feathers
ADULT
smaller white chin strap
dark-brown overall
ADULT

The Canada Goose is the most common, widespread, and familiar goose in North America. Given its colossal range, it is not surprising that the Canada Goose has much geographic variation, and 12 subspecies have been recognized. With the exception of the Cackling Goose, from which it has recently been separated, it is difficult to confuse it—with its distinctive white chin strap, black head and neck, and grayish-brown body—with any other species of goose. It is a monogamous species, and once pairs are formed, most stay together for life.

VOICE Males mostly honk or bark; females have high pitched *hrink*.

NESTING Scrape lined with available plant matter and down, near water; 2–12 eggs; 1–2 broods; May–August.

FEEDING Grazes on grasses, sedges, leaves, seeds, agricultural crops, and berries; also insects.

FLIGHT: strong and direct with fairly slow, deep wing beats; often flies in V-formation.

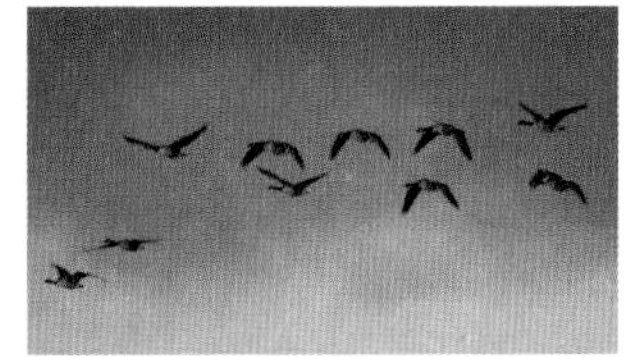

TRICK OF THE LIGHT
A low sun can play tricks—these birds are actually pale grayish underneath.

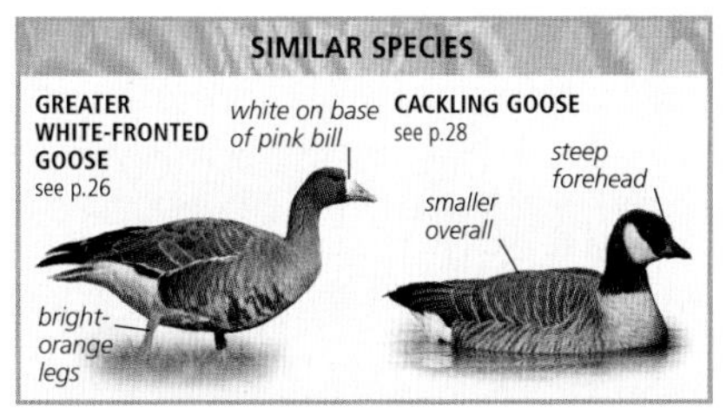
SIMILAR SPECIES
GREATER WHITE-FRONTED GOOSE
see p.26
white on base of pink bill
bright-orange legs
CACKLING GOOSE
see p.28
steep forehead
smaller overall

OCCURRENCE
Variety of inland breeding habitats near water, including grassy urban areas, marshes, prairie, parkland, coastal temperate forest, northern coniferous forest, and the Arctic tundra. Winters in agricultural fields, mudflats, saltwater marshes, lakes, and rivers.

Length **2¼–3½ft (0.7–1.1m)**	Wingspan **4¼–5½ft (1.3–1.7m)**	Weight **6½–9¾lb (3–4.4kg)**
Social **Flocks**	Lifespan **Up to 25 years**	Status **Secure**

DATE: ____________ TIME: ____________ LOCATION: ____________________

Order **Anseriformes**	Family **Anatidae**	Species ***Cygnus olor***

Mute Swan

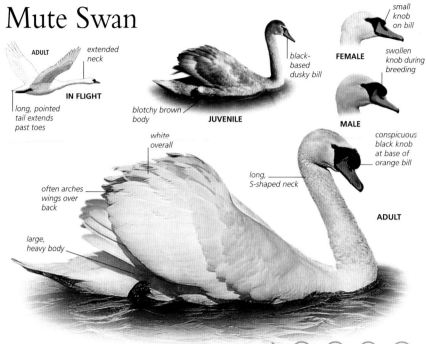

ADULT
extended neck
IN FLIGHT
long, pointed tail extends past toes

black-based dusky bill
blotchy brown body
JUVENILE

small knob on bill
FEMALE
swollen knob during breeding
MALE

white overall
conspicuous black knob at base of orange bill
long, S-shaped neck
often arches wings over back
ADULT
large, heavy body

One of the heaviest birds in North America, the Mute Swan was introduced from Europe due to its graceful appearance on water, if not on land, and easy domestication. However, this is an extremely territorial and aggressive bird. When threatened, it points its bill downward, arches its wings, hisses, and then attacks. Displacement of native waterfowl species and overgrazing by this species have led to efforts to reduce its numbers in North America.

VOICE Not mute; hisses, grunts, snorts, and snores; during courtship, trumpets, although more quietly than other swans.

NESTING Platform nest of plant materials, built on ground near water; 4–8 eggs; 1–2 broods; March–October.

FEEDING Dabbles, dips, and upends, mainly for underwater plants, but occasionally for small creatures too.

FLIGHT: strong, steady wing beats; creating a distinctive whirring and throbbing sound.

FORMATION FLYING
Groups of Mute Swans will sometimes fly in a line, and at other times, as here, they will arrange themselves in a V-formation.

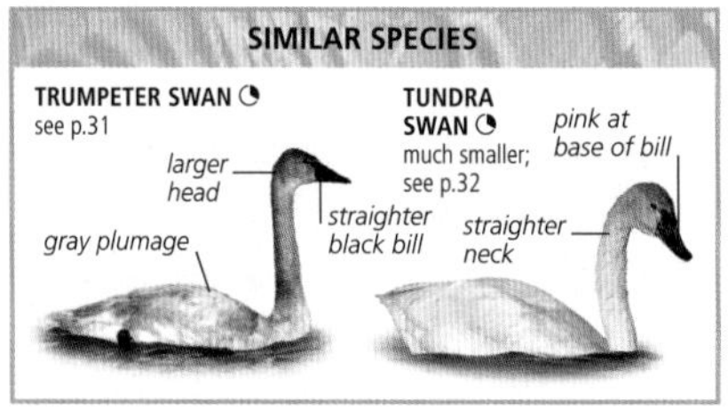
SIMILAR SPECIES
TRUMPETER SWAN
see p.31
larger head
straighter black bill
gray plumage
TUNDRA SWAN
much smaller; see p.32
pink at base of bill
straighter neck

OCCURRENCE
Bulk of population is found along the Atlantic Coast from Maine to North Carolina; smaller populations around the Great Lakes and southern British Columbia. Breeds and lives year-round on sluggish rivers, ponds, or lakes, preferring still water with emergent vegetation.

Length **4–5ft (1.2–1.5m)**	Wingspan **$6^1/_2$–$7^1/_2$ft (2–2.3m)**	Weight **12–32lb (5.5–14.5kg)**
Social **Pairs/Family groups**	Lifespan **Up to 21 years**	Status **Localized**

 DATE: ____________ TIME: ____________ LOCATION: ____________

Order **Anseriformes**	Family **Anatidae**	Species ***Cygnus buccinator***

Trumpeter Swan

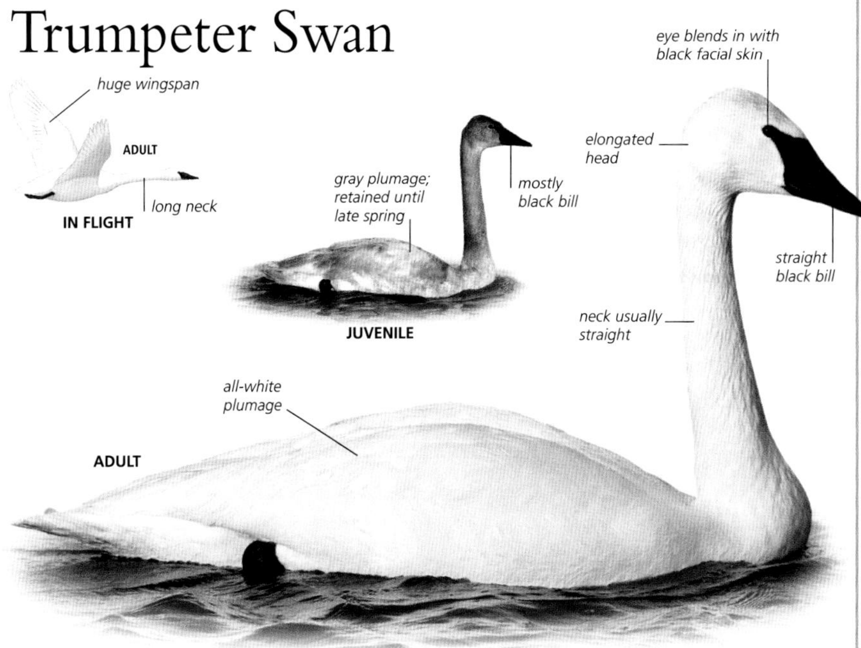
huge wingspan
ADULT
long neck
IN FLIGHT
gray plumage; retained until late spring
mostly black bill
JUVENILE
eye blends in with black facial skin
elongated head
straight black bill
neck usually straight
all-white plumage
ADULT

North America's quintessential swan and heaviest waterfowl, the Trumpeter Swan is a magnificent sight to behold. This species has made a remarkable comeback after numbers were severely reduced by hunting in the 1600–1800s; by the mid-1930s, fewer than a hundred were known to exist. Active reintroduction efforts were made in the upper Midwest and Ontario to reestablish the species to its former breeding range. The Trumpeter Swan's characteristic far-reaching call is usually the best way to identify it.

VOICE Call nasal, resonant *oh-OH* reminiscent of French horn.
NESTING Large mound made of plant matter on raised areas near or in freshwater; 3–6 eggs; 1 brood; April–September.
FEEDING Eats algae and aquatic plants, including moss, at or below the surface; feeds on grain in pastures and fields.

FLIGHT: slow, heavy, ponderous wing beats; "runs" on water's surface when taking off.

RUSTY STAINING
Trumpeter Swans often have rufous-stained heads and necks due to probing in iron-rich mud.

SIMILAR SPECIES

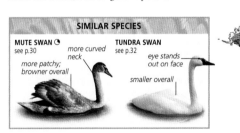

MUTE SWAN ◔ see p.30
more curved neck
more patchy; browner overall

TUNDRA SWAN see p.32
eye stands out on face
smaller overall

OCCURRENCE
Alaskan and northern Canadian breeders go south to winter; others remain year-round at local places, such as Yellowstone National Park. Found on freshwater lakes and marshes with plenty of vegetation on which to feed. Also found on estuaries in winter.

Length **4¼–5ft (1.3–1.5m)**	Wingspan **6½ft (2m)**	Weight **17–28lb (7.5–12.5kg)**
Social **Flocks**	Lifespan **Up to 24 years**	Status **Secure**

DATE: ____________ TIME: ____________ LOCATION: ______________________________

Order **Anseriformes**	Family **Anatidae**	Species ***Cygnus columbianus***

Tundra Swan

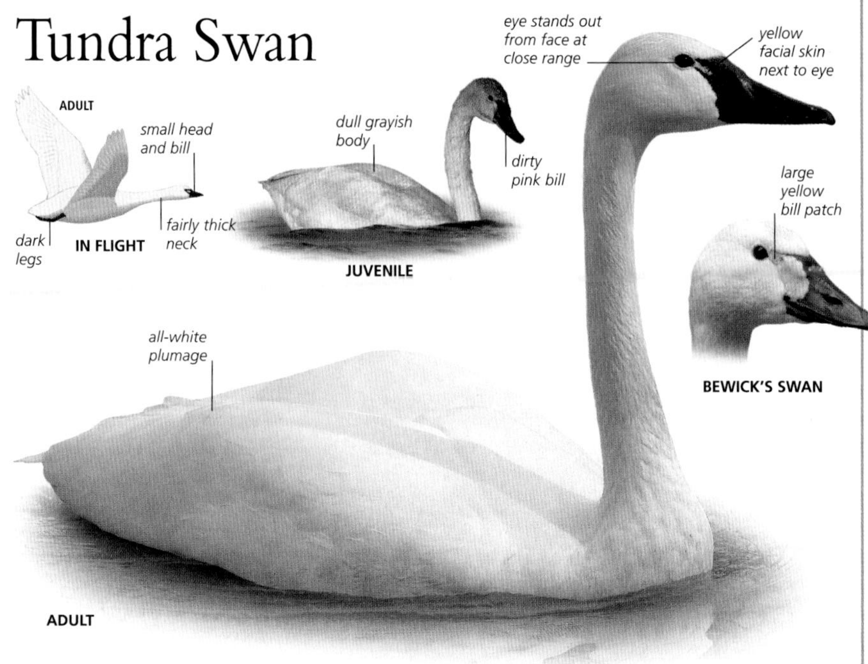
eye stands out from face at close range
yellow facial skin next to eye
ADULT
small head and bill
dull grayish body
dirty pink bill
large yellow bill patch
fairly thick neck
dark legs
IN FLIGHT
JUVENILE
all-white plumage
BEWICK'S SWAN
ADULT

Nesting in the Arctic tundra, this well-named species is North America's most widespread and smallest swan. Two populations exist, with one wintering in the West, and the other along the East Coast. The Tundra Swan can be confused with the Trumpeter Swan, but their different calls immediately distinguish the two species. When they are silent, weight and bill structure are the best way to tell them apart. In Eurasia, this species is known as Bewick's Swan and possesses a larger yellow patch at the base of its bill.

VOICE Clear, high-pitched yodeling *whoo-hooo* calls mixed with garbles, yelping, and barking sounds.

NESTING Mound-shaped nest made of plant matter near water; 3–6 eggs; 1 brood; May–September.

FEEDING Eats aquatic vegetation, insects, and mollusks; also grain.

FLIGHT: flight pattern like that of other swans but with slightly faster wing beats.

LARGE WINTER FLOCKS
Its size, white plumage, and flocking habits make the Tundra Swan a conspicuous species.

SIMILAR SPECIES

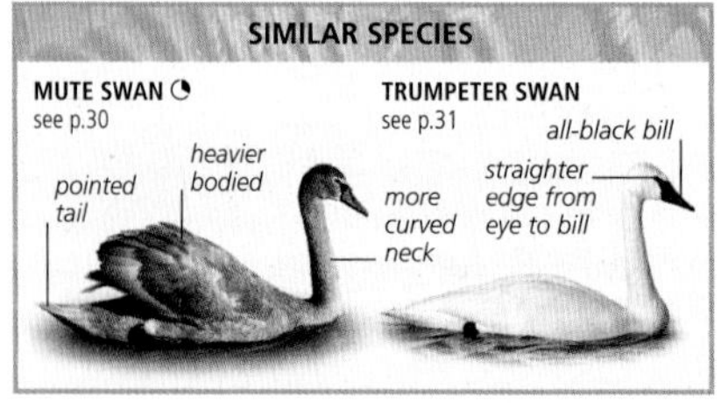
MUTE SWAN
see p.30
heavier bodied
pointed tail
TRUMPETER SWAN
see p.31
all-black bill
straighter edge from eye to bill
more curved neck

OCCURRENCE
Nests around lakes and pools in northern tundra from the Aleutians to the Yukon, and east to northwest Quebec. Winters in southern British Columbia, western US, and the mid-Atlantic states, mostly New Jersey to South Carolina. Winter habitat includes shallow coastal bays, ponds, and lakes.

Length **4–5ft (1.2–1.5m)**	Wingspan **6¼–7¼ft (1.9–2.2m)**	Weight **12–18lb (5.5–8kg)**
Social **Flocks**	Lifespan **Up to 21 years**	Status **Secure**

DATE: ____________ TIME: ____________ LOCATION: ____________

Order **Anseriformes**	Family **Anatidae**	Species ***Aix sponsa***

Wood Duck

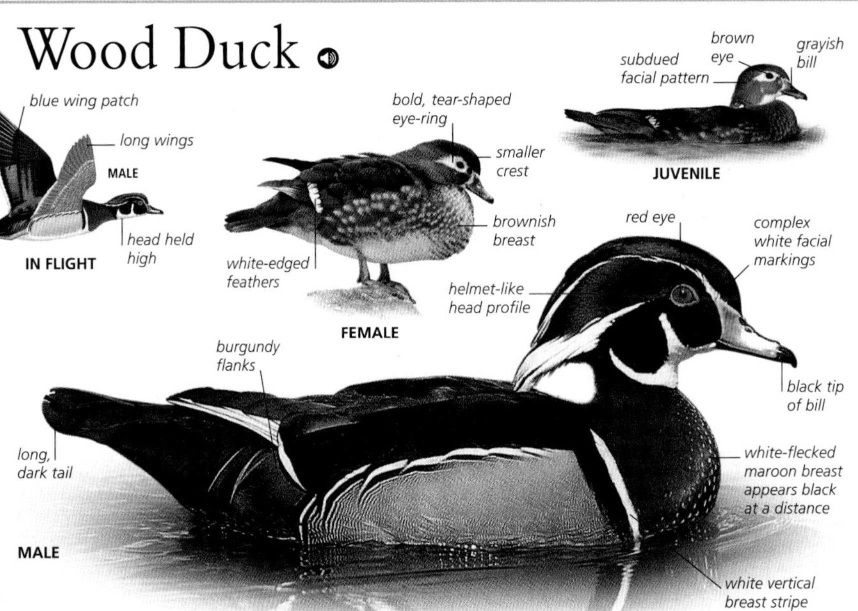
blue wing patch
long wings
MALE
head held high
IN FLIGHT
bold, tear-shaped eye-ring
smaller crest
brownish breast
white-edged feathers
FEMALE
subdued facial pattern
brown eye
grayish bill
JUVENILE
red eye
complex white facial markings
helmet-like head profile
burgundy flanks
black tip of bill
long, dark tail
white-flecked maroon breast appears black at a distance
MALE
white vertical breast stripe

The male Wood Duck is perhaps the most striking of all North American ducks. With its gaudy plumage, red eye and bill, and its long sleek crest that gives its head a helmet-shaped profile, the male is unmistakable. It is related to the Mandarin Duck of Asia. The Wood Duck is very dependent on mature swampy forestland, and is typically found in marshes, shallow lakes, ponds, and park settings that are surrounded by trees. Although it adapts to human activity, it is quite shy. When swimming, the Wood Duck can be seen jerking its head front to back. Of all waterfowl, this is the only species that regularly raises two broods each season.

VOICE Male gives a wheezy upslurred whistle *zweeet*; female's call a double-note, rising *oh-eek oh-eek*.

NESTING Nests in natural tree cavities or nest boxes in close proximity to water; 10–13 eggs; 2 broods; April–August.

FEEDING Forages for seeds, tree fruit, and small acorns; also spiders, insects, and crustaceans.

FLIGHT: rapid flight with deep wing beats; flies with head up; leaps straight off the water.

PLAIN BELLY
Wings raised, a male reveals one of the only plain areas of its plumage—its pale belly and undertail.

SIMILAR SPECIES

BUFFLEHEAD ♀
see p.55

HOODED MERGANSER ♀
narrower wings; see p.58

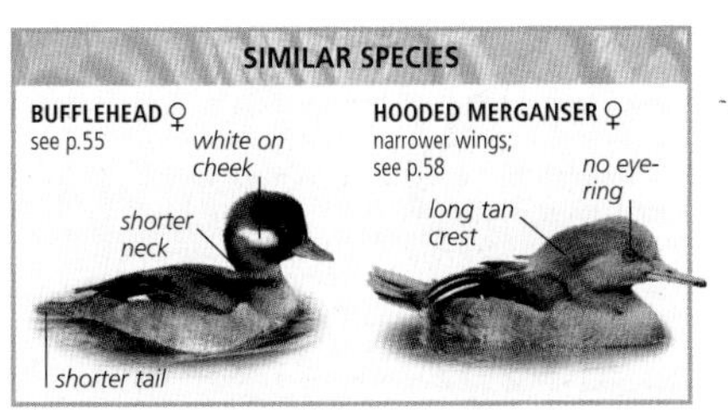
white on cheek
shorter neck
shorter tail
long tan crest
no eye-ring

OCCURRENCE
Usually found throughout the year, along rivers, streams, and creeks, in swamps, and marshy areas. Has a preference for permanent bodies of water. If good aquatic feeding areas are unavailable, the Wood Duck feeds in open areas, including agricultural fields.

Length **18½–21½in (47–54cm)**	Wingspan **26–29in (66–73cm)**	Weight **16–30oz (450–850g)**
Social **Small flocks**	Lifespan **Up to 18 years**	Status **Secure**

DATE: ____________ TIME: ____________ LOCATION: ____________

Order **Anseriformes**	Family **Anatidae**	Species ***Spatula discors***

Blue-winged Teal

powdery-blue forewing with green patch
MALE (BREEDING)
white facial crescent
white underwing stripe
IN FLIGHT
broken, contrasting white eye-ring
grayish-brown overall
pale eyebrow, dark cape, and eye-line
pale spot at base of bill
FEMALE
white facial crescent
dark, grayish head
black bill
MALE (FALL)
black spots on rich buff-brown breast and flanks
white facial crescent
long, blackish bill
rich tan flanks
warmer brown overall
MALE (BREEDING)
conspicuous white patch

This small dabbling duck is a common and widespread North American breeding species. With a bold white crescent between bill and eye on its otherwise slate-gray head and neck, the male Blue-winged Teal is quite distinctive. The Blue-winged and Cinnamon Teals, along with the Northern Shoveler, constitute the three "blue-winged" ducks; this is a conspicuous feature when the birds are flying. The Cinnamon and the Blue-winged Teals are almost identical genetically and interbreed to form hybrids. The Blue-winged Teal winters mostly south of the US and migrates north in spring.

VOICE Male a high-pitched, raspy *peew* or low-pitched *paay* during courtship; female a loud single *quack*.

NESTING Bowl-shaped depression lined with grasses, close to water's edge, in meadows; 6–14 eggs; 1 brood; April–September.

FEEDING Eats seeds of a variety of plants; feeds heavily on insect larvae, crustaceans, and snails, when breeding.

FLIGHT: fast, twisting flight; flies in compact, small groups.

OUTSTRETCHED WING
Wing stretch behavior shows the white feathers between the blue forewing and green rearwing.

SIMILAR SPECIES

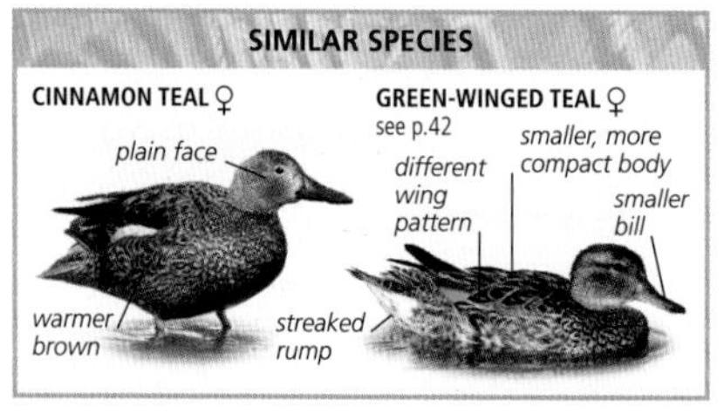
CINNAMON TEAL ♀
plain face
warmer brown
GREEN-WINGED TEAL ♀
see p.42
different wing pattern
smaller, more compact body
smaller bill
streaked rump

OCCURRENCE
Nests across North America, with highest numbers in the prairie and parkland regions of the midcontinent. Prefers shallow ponds or marshes during nesting; freshwater to brackish water and (less so) saltwater marshes during migration. In winter, prefers saline environments, including mangroves.

Length **14½–16in (37–41cm)**	Wingspan **23½–25in (60–64cm)**	Weight **11–18oz (300–500g)**
Social **Flocks**	Lifespan **Up to 17 years**	Status **Secure**

DATE: ____________ TIME: ____________ LOCATION: ____________

Order **Anseriformes**	Family **Anatidae**	Species ***Spatula clypeata***

Northern Shoveler

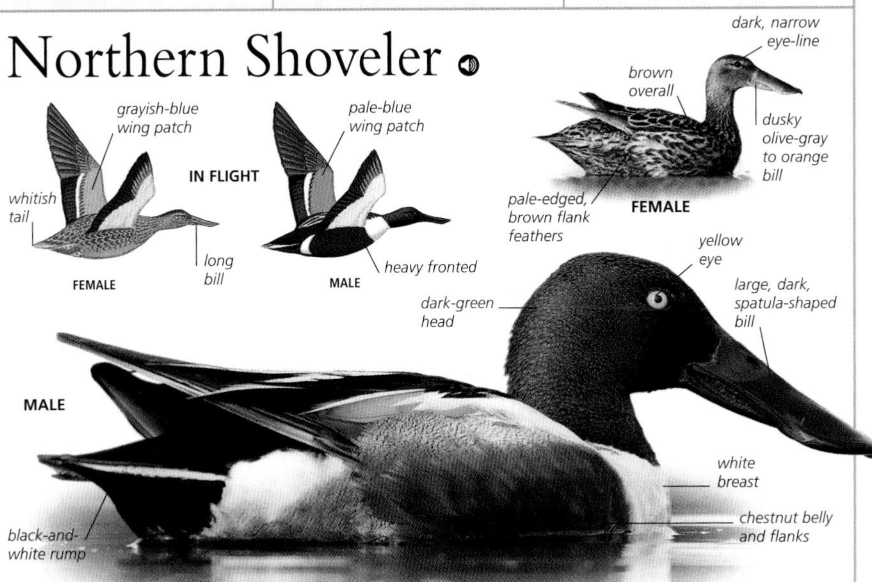

dark, narrow eye-line
brown overall
dusky olive-gray to orange bill
pale-edged, brown flank feathers
FEMALE
grayish-blue wing patch
pale-blue wing patch
IN FLIGHT
whitish tail
long bill
FEMALE
MALE
heavy fronted
yellow eye
large, dark, spatula-shaped bill
dark-green head
MALE
white breast
chestnut belly and flanks
black-and-white rump

FLIGHT: strong direct flight; male's wings make a rattling noise when taking off.

The Northern Shoveler is a common, medium-sized, dabbling duck found in North America and Eurasia. It is monogamous—pairs remain together longer than any other dabbler species. Its distinctive long bill is highly specialized; it is wider at the tip and contains thin, comb-like structures (called "lamellae") along the sides, used to filter food items from the water. Shovelers often form tight feeding groups, swimming close together as they sieve the water for prey.

VOICE Male call a nasal, muffled *thuk thuk…thuk thuk*; also a loud, nasal *paaaay*; female call a variety of quacks, singly or in a series of 4–5 descending notes.

NESTING Scrape lined with plant matter and down, in short plants, near water; 6–19 eggs; 1 brood; May–August.

FEEDING Forages for seeds; filters small crustaceans and mollusks out of the water.

UPSIDE DOWN FEEDER
This male upends to feed below the water's surface, revealing his orange legs.

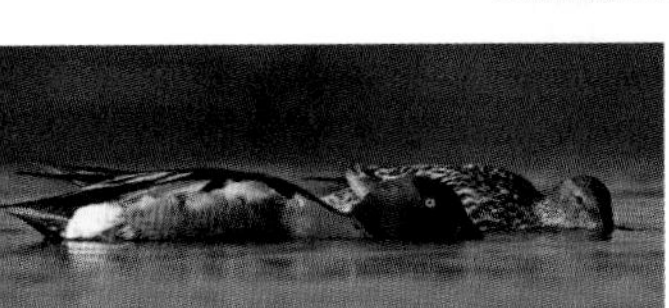

FILTER FEEDING
Their bills open, these ducks sieve small invertebrates from the water.

SIMILAR SPECIES

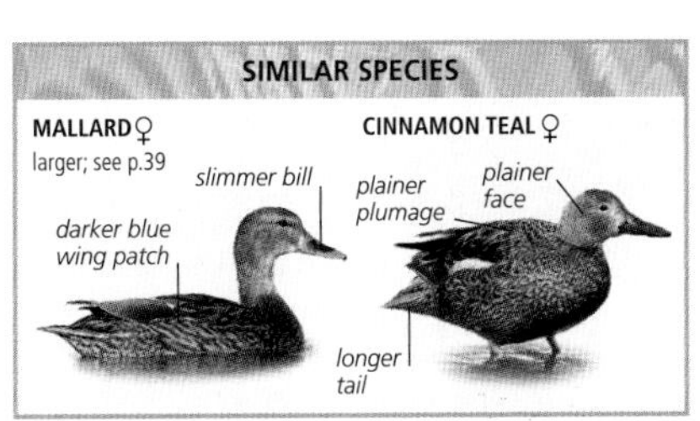

MALLARD ♀
larger; see p.39
slimmer bill
darker blue wing patch
CINNAMON TEAL ♀
plainer plumage
plainer face
longer tail

OCCURRENCE
Widespread across North America, south of the tundra. Breeds in a variety of wetlands, in edges of shallow pools with nearby tall and short grasslands. Occurs in freshwater and saltmarshes, ponds, and other shallow bodies of water in winter; does not feed on land.

Length **17½–20in (44–51cm)**	Wingspan **27–33in (69–84cm)**	Weight **14–29oz (400–825g)**
Social **Flocks**	Lifespan **Up to 18 years**	Status **Secure**

DATE: ______________ TIME: ______________ LOCATION: ______________

Order **Anseriformes**	Family **Anatidae**	Species ***Mareca strepera***

Gadwall

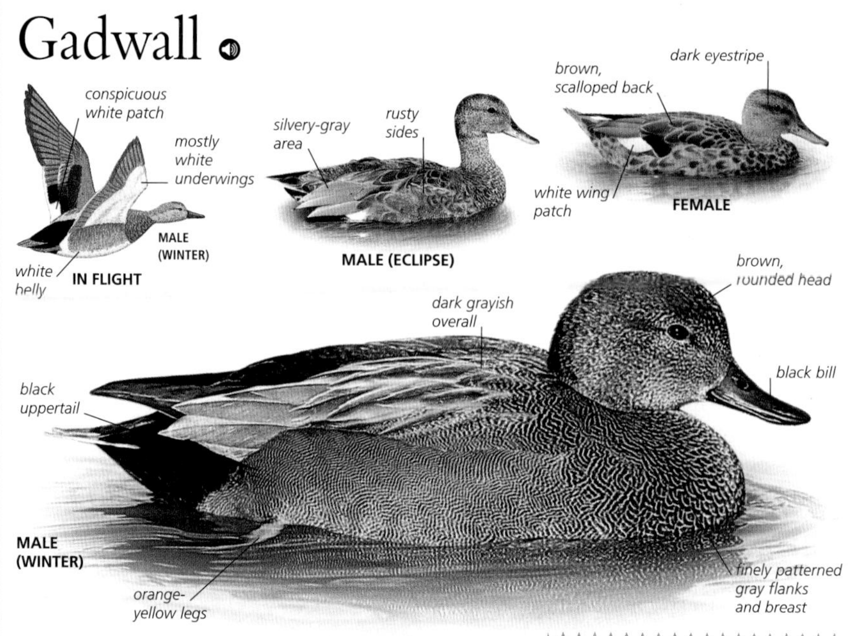

conspicuous white patch
mostly white underwings
MALE (WINTER)
white belly
IN FLIGHT
silvery-gray area
rusty sides
MALE (ECLIPSE)
brown, scalloped back
dark eyestripe
white wing patch
FEMALE
brown, rounded head
dark grayish overall
black bill
black uppertail
MALE (WINTER)
orange-yellow legs
finely patterned gray flanks and breast

Although the Gadwall's appearance is somewhat somber, many birders consider this duck one of North America's most elegant species because of the subtlety of its plumage. Despite being common and widespread, Gadwalls are often overlooked because of their retiring behavior and relatively quiet vocalizations. This dabbling duck is slightly smaller and more delicate than the Mallard, yet female Gadwalls are often mistaken for female Mallards. Gadwalls associate with other species, especially in winter.

VOICE Low, raspy *meep* or *reb* given in quick succession; female *quack* similar to that of female Mallard, but higher-pitched and more nasal; high-pitched *peep*, or *pe-peep*; both sexes give *tickety-tickety-tickety* chatter while feeding.

NESTING Bowl nest made of plant material in a scrape; 8–12 eggs; 1 brood; April–August.

FEEDING Dabbles on the surface or below for seeds, aquatic vegetation, and invertebrates, including mollusks and insects.

FLIGHT: direct flight with fast wing beats; leaps straight off the water.

BROOD ON THE MOVE
Females lead their ducklings from their nest to a brood-rearing habitat that provides cover and ample food for the ducklings to forage.

SIMILAR SPECIES

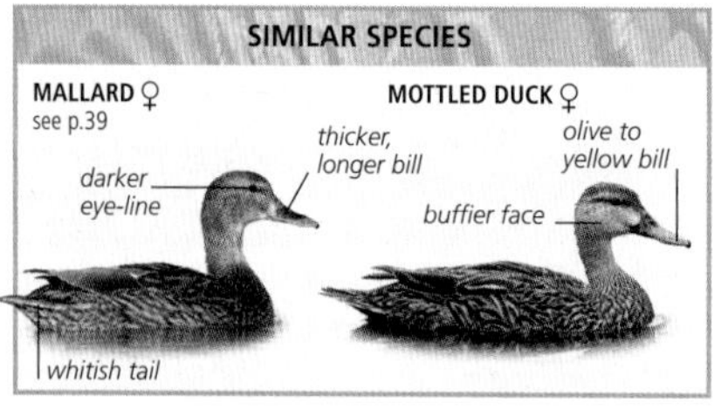

MALLARD ♀
see p.39
darker eye-line
thicker, longer bill
whitish tail
MOTTLED DUCK ♀
olive to yellow bill
buffier face

OCCURRENCE
From the western Prairie Pothole Country of Canada and the northern US, the Gadwall's range has expanded as it has adapted to artificial bodies of water, such as reservoirs and ponds. In winter, mostly found on lakes, marshes, and along rivers.

Length **18–22½in (46–57cm)**	Wingspan **33in (84cm)**	Weight **18–45oz (500–1,250g)**
Social **Winter flocks**	Lifespan **Up to 19 years**	Status **Secure**

 DATE: ______ TIME: ______ LOCATION: ______

Order **Anseriformes**	Family **Anatidae**	Species ***Mareca americana***

American Wigeon

MALE (BREEDING)
white underwing patch
gray head contrasts with pinkish-brown breast and flanks
IN FLIGHT
long, pointed tail
rufous-edged wing feathers
dark smudge around eye
gray head
narrow black line along bill
warm-brown breast and flanks
FEMALE
cream forehead and crown
green band from eye to nape
MALE (BREEDING)
black-tipped bill
black rump
pinkish-brown flanks

Often found in mixed flocks with other ducks, the American Wigeon is a common and widespread, medium-sized dabbling duck. This bird is an opportunist that loiters around other diving ducks and coots, feeding on the vegetation they dislodge. It is more social during migration and in the nonbreeding season than when breeding.

VOICE Slow and fast whistles; male's most common call a slow, high-pitched, wheezy, three-syllable *whew-whew-whew*, with middle note loudest; also, a faster *whee* whistle.

NESTING Depression lined with plant material and down, usually in tall grass away from water; 5–10 eggs; 1 brood; May–August.

FEEDING Grazes on grass, clover, algae and in agricultural fields; feeds on many seeds, insects, mollusks, and crustaceans during the breeding season.

FLIGHT: rapid, fairly deep wing beats; leaps almost vertically off the water.

COMING IN FOR A LANDING
This male's cream-colored forehead is clearly visible, as is the sharp contrast between the white belly, and the pinkish breast and flanks.

FLAPPING WINGS
This bird has a white patch on its underwing, while the Eurasian Wigeon has a gray patch.

SIMILAR SPECIES
EURASIAN WIGEON ♂
see p.38
bright-chestnut head
pinkish breast
EURASIAN WIGEON ♀
see p.38
warm-brownish head
pale throat

OCCURRENCE
As the northernmost breeder of the dabbling ducks, this species occurs from Alaska to the Maritimes. Prefers pothole and grassland habitats; found almost anywhere near water in winter. Winters south to northern South America and the Caribbean, in freshwater and coastal bay habitats.

Length **17½–23in (45–58cm)**	Wingspan **33in (84cm)**	Weight **1⅛–3lb (0.5–1.3kg)**
Social **Flocks**	Lifespan **Up to 21 years**	Status **Secure**

DATE: ____________ TIME: ____________ LOCATION: ____________________

Order **Anseriformes**	Family **Anatidae**	Species ***Mareca penelope***

Eurasian Wigeon

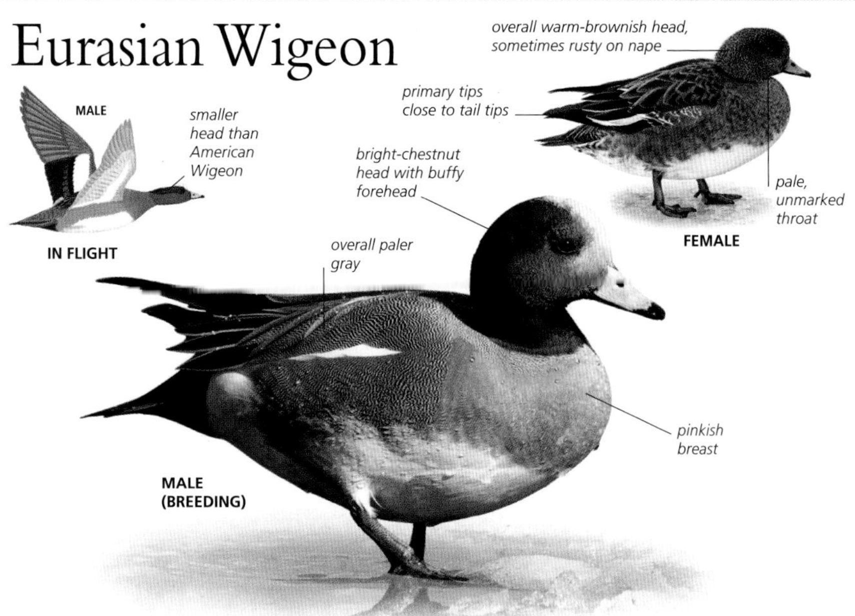
overall warm-brownish head, sometimes rusty on nape
MALE
smaller head than American Wigeon
primary tips close to tail tips
bright-chestnut head with buffy forehead
pale, unmarked throat
FEMALE
IN FLIGHT
overall paler gray
pinkish breast
MALE (BREEDING)

The adult male Eurasian Wigeon is distinctive with its bright-chestnut head and broad creamy-yellow forehead. Its bold white forewing, with a green patch bordered in black, is conspicuous in flight. Females are plain brown with a small pale bill. Eurasian Wigeons are often found among flocks of their closest relatives, the American Wigeons, and hybrids between the two species are not uncommon. In recent decades, the number of Eurasian Wigeons recorded has increased, particularly in the Pacific Northwest.

VOICE Males a two-note piping whistle, *whee-oooo* and a lower *wip-weu*; females a throaty growl.

NESTING Shallow depression lined with grass and down on the ground, usually near water; 8–9 eggs; up to 2 broods; April–August.

FEEDING Forages for leaves, stems, roots, and seeds by dabbling at surface of water or submerging the head and neck in the water; eats some insects in summer.

FLIGHT: continually flapping, with fast wing beats.

PARTY OF FOUR

A party of Eurasian Wigeon drakes show off their typical chestnut heads with buffy foreheads.

SIMILAR SPECIES

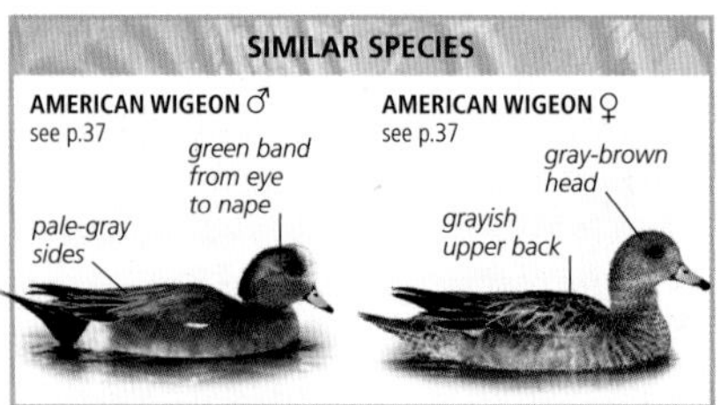
AMERICAN WIGEON ♂
see p.37
green band from eye to nape
pale-gray sides
AMERICAN WIGEON ♀
see p.37
gray-brown head
grayish upper back

OCCURRENCE

Widespread and common in Eurasia near ponds, lakes, and marshes, and open fields nearby. Breeds at northern latitudes and winters on both the Atlantic and Pacific Coasts, with small numbers found inland. Regular winter visitor to North America, especially on the West Coast, from Canada to California.

Length **16½–20½in (42–52cm)**	Wingspan **31.5in (80cm)**	Weight **17½–33½oz (500–950g)**
Social **Flocks**	Lifespan **Up to 34 years**	Status **Secure**

 DATE: ____________ TIME: ____________ LOCATION: ____________

Order **Anseriformes**	Family **Anatidae**	Species ***Anas platyrhynchos***

Mallard

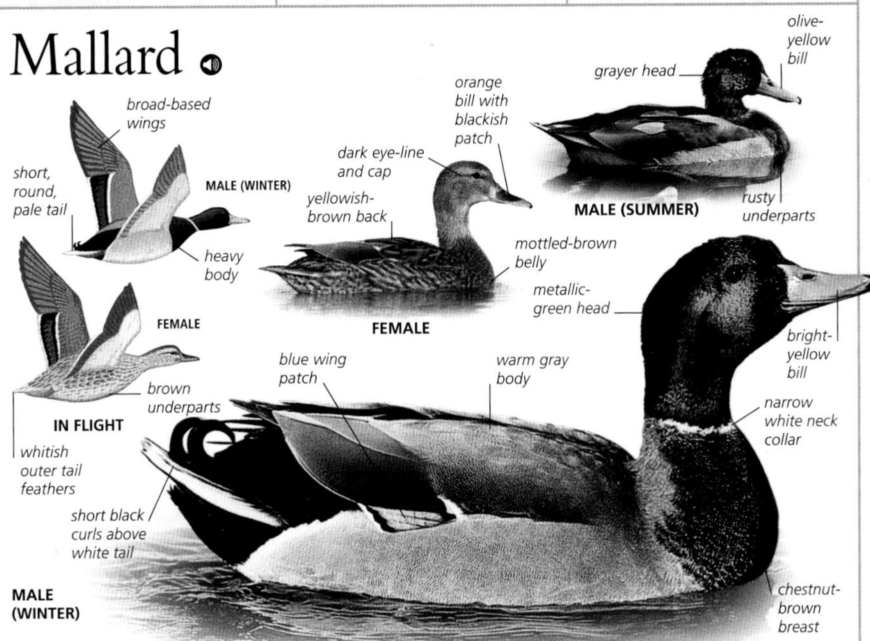
broad-based wings
short, round, pale tail
MALE (WINTER)
heavy body
FEMALE
brown underparts
IN FLIGHT
whitish outer tail feathers
dark eye-line and cap
orange bill with blackish patch
yellowish-brown back
mottled-brown belly
FEMALE
grayer head
olive-yellow bill
MALE (SUMMER)
rusty underparts
metallic-green head
bright-yellow bill
blue wing patch
warm gray body
narrow white neck collar
short black curls above white tail
MALE (WINTER)
chestnut-brown breast

The Mallard is perhaps the most familiar of all ducks, and occurs in the wild all across the Northern Hemisphere. It is the ancestor of most domestic ducks, and hybrids between the wild and domestic forms are frequently seen in city lakes and ponds, often with patches of white on the breast. Mating is generally a violent affair, but outside the breeding season the wild species is strongly migratory and gregarious, sometimes forming large flocks that may join with other species.

VOICE Male's call a quiet raspy *raab*; during courtship a high-pitched whistle; female call a *quack* or repeated in series.

NESTING Scrape lined with plant matter, usually near water, often on floating vegetation; 6–15 eggs; 1 brood; February–September.

FEEDING Feeds omnivorously on insects, crustaceans, mollusks, and earthworms when breeding; otherwise largely vegetarian; takes seeds, acorns, agricultural crops, aquatic vegetation, and bread.

FLIGHT: fast, shallow, and regular; often flies in groups.

STICKING TOGETHER
The mother leads her ducklings to water soon after they hatch. She looks after them until they can fend for themselves.

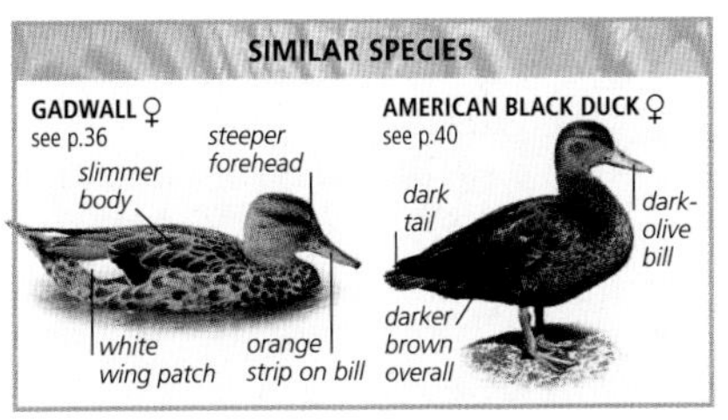
SIMILAR SPECIES
GADWALL ♀
see p.36
slimmer body
steeper forehead
white wing patch
orange strip on bill
AMERICAN BLACK DUCK ♀
see p.40
dark tail
dark-olive bill
darker brown overall

OCCURRENCE
Occurs throughout the region, choosing shallow water in natural wetlands, such as marshes, prairie potholes, ponds, and ditches; can also be found in artificial habitats, such as city parks and reservoirs, preferring more open habitats in winter.

Length **19½–26in (50–65cm)**	Wingspan **32–37in (82–95cm)**	Weight **1⅞–3lb (0.9–1.4kg)**
Social **Flocks**	Lifespan **Up to 29 years**	Status **Secure**

DATE: ________ TIME: ________ LOCATION: ________

Order **Anseriformes**	Family **Anatidae**	Species ***Anas rubripes***

American Black Duck

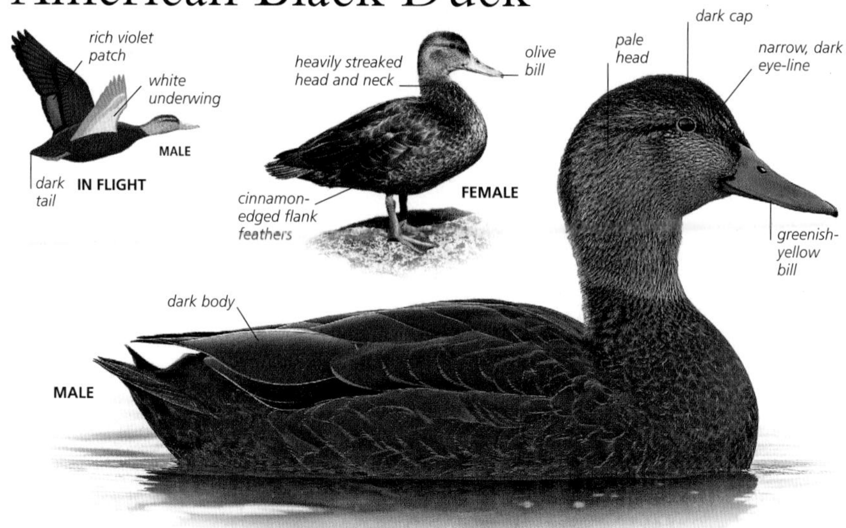
rich violet patch
white underwing
MALE
dark tail
IN FLIGHT
heavily streaked head and neck
olive bill
cinnamon-edged flank feathers
FEMALE
pale head
dark cap
narrow, dark eye-line
greenish-yellow bill
dark body
MALE

The American Black Duck, a large dabbling duck, is closely related to the Mallard. In the past, the two species were separated by different habitat preferences—the American Black Duck preferring forested locations, and the Mallard favoring more open habitats. Over the years, these habitats became less distinct as the East was deforested and trees were planted in the Midwest. As a result, there are now many hybrids between the two species. It has also been argued that the introduction of Mallards to various areas in the East has further increased interbreeding. The American Black Duck breeds throughout a wide area in the northern part of its range. When breeding, males can be seen chasing away other males to maintain their territories.

VOICE Male's call a reedy *raeb*, given once or twice; female quack sounds very similar to Mallard.

NESTING Scrape lined with plant material and down, usually on ground or close to water; 4–10 eggs; 1 brood; March–September.

FEEDING An omnivore, the American Black Duck eats plant leaves and stems, roots, seeds, grains, fruit, aquatic plants, fish, and amphibians.

FLIGHT: fast, shallow, and regular; often flies in groups.

DARK PLUMAGE
This species is the darkest of all the Mallard-type ducks that occur in North America.

SIMILAR SPECIES

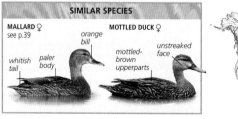

MALLARD ♀ see p.39
whitish tail; paler body; orange bill

MOTTLED DUCK ♀
mottled-brown upperparts; unstreaked face

OCCURRENCE
Nests in eastern Canada and adjacent areas of the US in a variety of habitats including northerly and mixed hardwood forest, wooded uplands, bogs, salt- and freshwater marshes, and on islands. Resident in the central part of its range, but large numbers winter in saltwater marshes.

Length **21½–23in (54–59cm)**	Wingspan **35–37in (88–95cm)**	Weight **1½–3½lb (0.7–1.6kg)**
Social **Flocks**	Lifespan **Up to 26 years**	Status **Secure**

DATE: ____________ TIME: ____________ LOCATION: ____________

Order **Anseriformes**	Family **Anatidae**	Species ***Anas acuta***

Northern Pintail

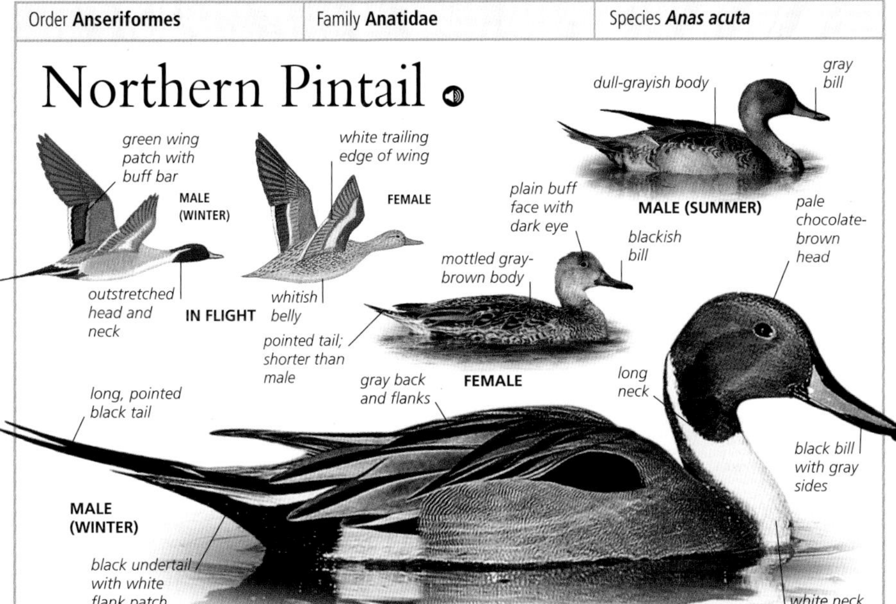

green wing patch with buff bar
MALE (WINTER)
white trailing edge of wing
FEMALE
outstretched head and neck
IN FLIGHT
whitish belly
dull-grayish body
gray bill
MALE (SUMMER)
plain buff face with dark eye
blackish bill
mottled gray-brown body
pointed tail; shorter than male
FEMALE
pale chocolate-brown head
long, pointed black tail
gray back and flanks
long neck
black bill with gray sides
MALE (WINTER)
black undertail with white flank patch
white neck and breast

An elegant, long-necked dabbler, the Northern Pintail has extremely distinctive marking and a very long tail—in fact, the longest tail to be found on any freshwater duck. One of the earliest breeders in the year, these ducks begin nesting soon after the ice thaws. Northern Pintails were once one of the most abundant prairie breeding ducks. However, in recent decades, droughts, combined with the reduction of habitat on both their wintering and breeding grounds, have resulted in a significant decline in their population.

VOICE Male call a high-pitched rolling *prrreep prrreep;* lower-pitched wheezy *wheeeee*, which gets louder then drops off; female call a quiet, harsh *quack* or *kuk* singularly or as short series; also a loud *gaak*, often repeated.

NESTING Scrape lined with plant materials and down, usually in short grass, brush, or even in the open; 3–12 eggs; 1 brood; April–August.

FEEDING Feeds on grains, rice, seeds, aquatic weeds, insect larvae, crustaceans, and snails.

FLIGHT: fast, direct flight; can be very acrobatic in the air.

FEEDING TIME
Even when tipping up to feed, these pintails can be identified by their long, black, pointed tails.

SIMILAR SPECIES

GADWALL ♀ see p.36
shorter tail; orange-sided bill; white wing patch

AMERICAN WIGEON ♀ see p.37
shorter tail; darker gray head; chestnut breast and flanks

OCCURRENCE
Widely distributed in North America; breeding in open country in shallow wetlands or meadows in mountainous forest regions. Found in tidal wetlands and saltwater habitats during migration and in winter; dry harvested and flooded agricultural fields in autumn and winter.

Length **20–30in (51–76cm)**	Wingspan **35in (89cm)**	Weight **18–44oz (500–1250g)**
Social **Flocks**	Lifespan **Up to 21 years**	Status **Declining**

DATE: ____________ TIME: ____________ LOCATION: ____________

Order **Anseriformes**	Family **Anatidae**	Species ***Anas crecca***

Green-winged Teal

MALE
green-and-black patch on hindwing
short neck
IN FLIGHT
gray flanks
dark-green ear patch
rufous head
horizontal white line on sides
lacks white vertical bar
small, narrow, black bill
A. c. crecca (EURASIAN)
black-spotted breast
darker face
steeper forehead
white vertical bar
FEMALE
finely detailed pattern
shoulder feathers with narrow, pale edges
weaker face pattern
yellowish-buff undertail feathers
MALE
JUVENILE

The Green-winged Teal, the smallest North American dabbling duck, is slightly smaller than the Blue-winged and Cinnamon Teals, and lacks their blue wing patch. Its population is increasing, apparently because it breeds in more pristine habitats, and farther north, than the prairie ducks. The species has three subspecies, *A. c. crecca* (Eurasia), *A. c. carolinensis* (North America), and *A. c. nimia* (Aleutian Islands). *Carolinensis* males have a conspicuous vertical white bar, whereas Eurasian *crecca* males do not.

VOICE Male call a high-pitched, slightly rolling *crick crick*, similar to crickets; female call a quiet *quack*.

NESTING Shallow scrape on ground lined with nearby vegetation, often placed in dense vegetation near water; 6–9 eggs; 1 brood; April–September.

FEEDING Eats seeds, aquatic insects, crustaceans, and mollusks year-round; also feeds in grain fields in winter.

FLIGHT: fast flight; often flying in twisting, tight groups reminiscent of shorebird flocks.

SINGLE PARENT
The female duck is deserted by her partner during incubation, so she must provide all parental care.

SIMILAR SPECIES

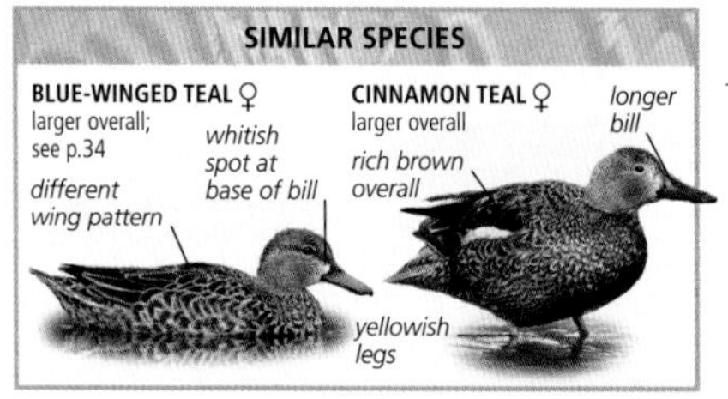
BLUE-WINGED TEAL ♀
larger overall; see p.34
whitish spot at base of bill
different wing pattern
CINNAMON TEAL ♀
larger overall
longer bill
rich brown overall
yellowish legs

OCCURRENCE
Breeds north of the tree line in Alaska and Canada—around ponds in forest and deciduous woodlands. Prefers shallow wetlands with vegetation. In winter and migration, inland marshes, sloughs, agricultural fields, and coastal marshes. Winters south of the Caribbean and in southern Mexico.

Length **12–15½in (31–39cm)**	Wingspan **20½–23in (52–59cm)**	Weight **7–16oz (200–450g)**
Social **Flocks**	Lifespan **Up to 20 years**	Status **Secure**

 DATE: ____________ TIME: ____________ LOCATION: ____________

Order **Anseriformes**	Family **Anatidae**	Species ***Aythya valisineria***

Canvasback

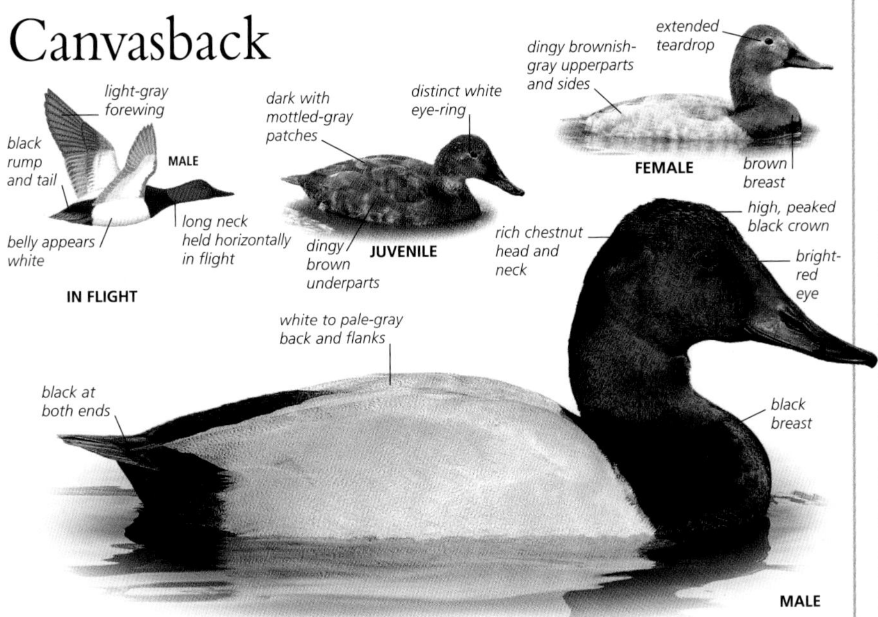
light-gray forewing
black rump and tail
MALE
belly appears white
long neck held horizontally in flight
IN FLIGHT
dark with mottled-gray patches
distinct white eye-ring
dingy brown underparts
JUVENILE
dingy brownish-gray upperparts and sides
extended teardrop
FEMALE
brown breast
rich chestnut head and neck
high, peaked black crown
bright-red eye
white to pale-gray back and flanks
black at both ends
black breast
MALE

A large, elegant, long-billed diving duck, the Canvasback is a bird of Prairie Pothole Country. Its specialized diet of aquatic plants has resulted in a smaller population than other ducks. With legs set toward the rear, it is an accomplished swimmer and diver, and is rarely seen on land. Weather conditions and brood parasitism by Redheads determine how successful the Canvasback's nesting is from year to year.

VOICE Mostly silent except during courtship when males make soft *cooing* noises; females emit a grating *krrrrr krrrrrr krrrrr*; females give loud quack when taking off; during winter, both sexes make soft wheezing series of *rrrr rrrr rrrr* sounds.

NESTING Platform over water built of woven vegetation; occasionally on shore; 8–11 eggs; 1 brood; April–September.

FEEDING Mainly eats aquatic tubers, buds, root stalks, and shoots, particularly those of wild celery; also eats snails when preferred plants are unavailable.

FLIGHT: direct strong flight; one of the fastest ducks; forms V-shaped flocks.

DEEP WATER
Canvasbacks prefer deeper-bodied waters that support the aquatic vegetation they eat.

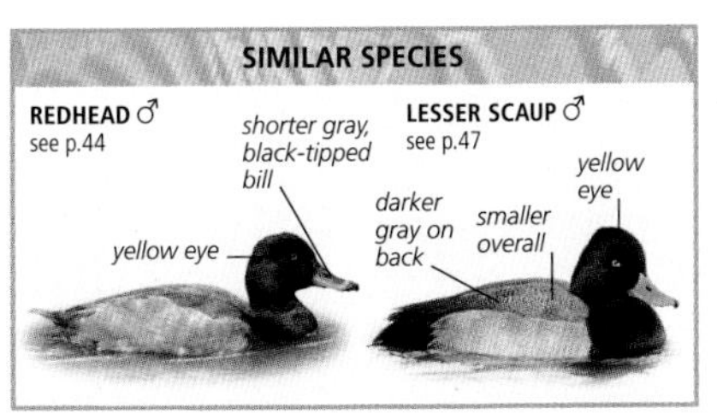
SIMILAR SPECIES
REDHEAD ♂
see p.44
shorter gray, black-tipped bill
yellow eye
LESSER SCAUP ♂
see p.47
yellow eye
darker gray on back
smaller overall

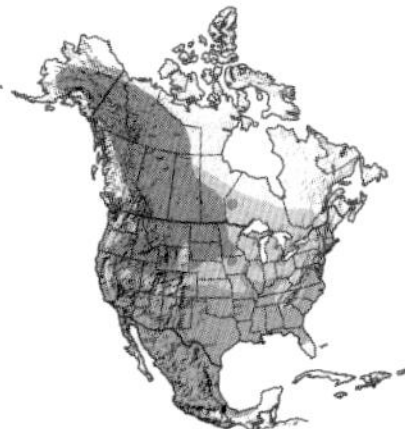

OCCURRENCE
Found in potholes, marshes, and ponds in prairie parkland, tundra; northerly forests preferred where their favorite foods grow. Winters in large numbers in large bays and lakes, and deltas, with smaller numbers scattered across North America and Mexico.

Length **19–22in (48–56cm)**	Wingspan **31–35in (79–89cm)**	Weight **1¾–3½lb (0.8–1.6kg)**
Social **Flocks**	Lifespan **Up to 22 years**	Status **Secure**

DATE: ____________ TIME: ____________ LOCATION: ____________________

Order **Anseriformes**	Family **Anatidae**	Species ***Aythya americana***

Redhead

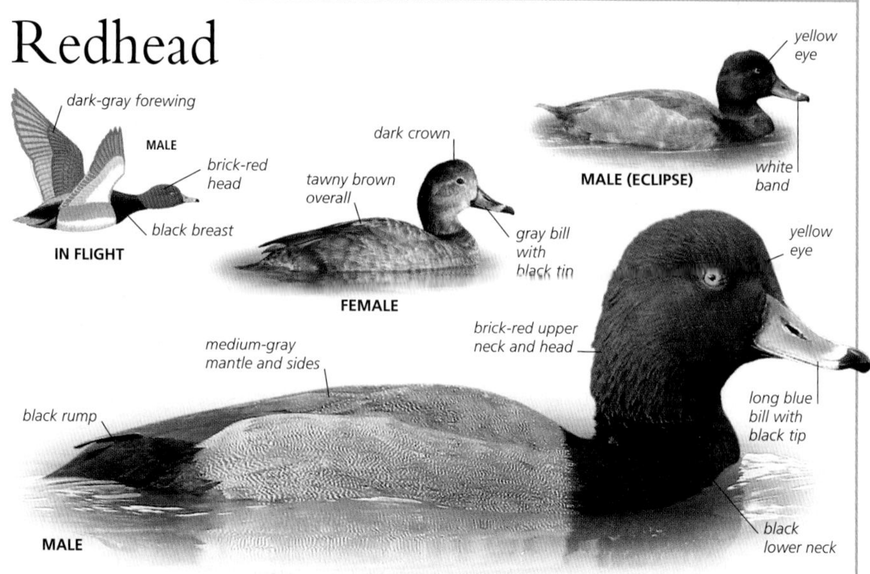
dark-gray forewing
MALE
brick-red head
black breast
IN FLIGHT
dark crown
tawny brown overall
gray bill with black tip
FEMALE
yellow eye
MALE (ECLIPSE)
white band
yellow eye
brick-red upper neck and head
medium-gray mantle and sides
black rump
long blue bill with black tip
black lower neck
MALE

The Redhead, a medium-sized diving duck belonging to the Pochard group, is native only to North America. Only when seen up close is it apparent that the male's seemingly gray upperparts and flanks are actually white, with dense, black, wavy markings. The Redhead often feeds at night and forages mostly around dusk and dawn, drifting during the day. It parasitizes other duck nests more than any other duck species, particularly those of the Canvasback and even other Redheads.

VOICE Male courtship call a wheezy rising then falling *whee ough*, also *meow*; female call a low, raspy *kurr kurr kurr*.

NESTING Weaves solid nest over water in dense vegetation, such as cattails, lined with down; 7–14 eggs; 1 brood; May–September.

FEEDING Omnivorous; feeds on aquatic plants, seeds, tubers, algae, insects, spiders, fish eggs, snails, and insect larvae; diet is variable depending on location.

FLIGHT: direct flight; runs on water prior to takeoff.

MALE DISPLAY
This male is performing a spectacular courtship display called a head throw, while remaining otherwise completely still on the water.

EASY IDENTIFICATION
The long blue bill with a whitish band and black tip is clearly visible in males.

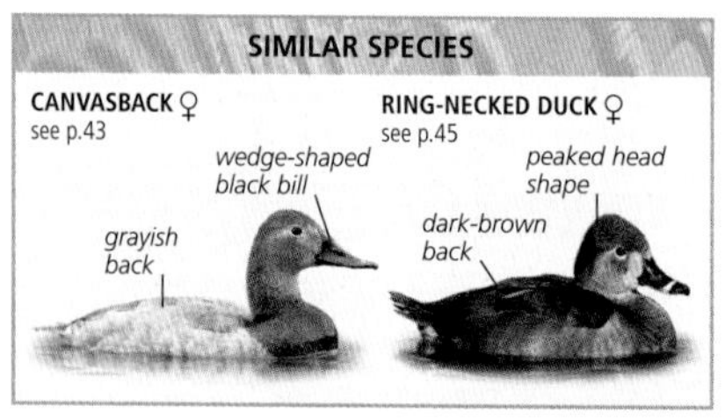
SIMILAR SPECIES
CANVASBACK ♀
see p.43
wedge-shaped black bill
grayish back
RING-NECKED DUCK ♀
see p.45
peaked head shape
dark-brown back

OCCURRENCE
Breeds in shallow wetlands across the Great Basin and Prairie Pothole Region, very densely in certain marsh habitats. The bulk of the population winters in coastal lagoons along the Atlantic Coast and the Gulf of Mexico.

Length **17–21in (43–53cm)**	Wingspan **30–31in (75–79cm)**	Weight **1⅜–3¼lbs (0.6–1.5kg)**
Social **Flocks**	Lifespan **Up to 21 years**	Status **Secure**

DATE: ____________ TIME: ____________ LOCATION: ____________

Order **Anseriformes**	Family **Anatidae**	Species ***Aythya collaris***

Ring-necked Duck

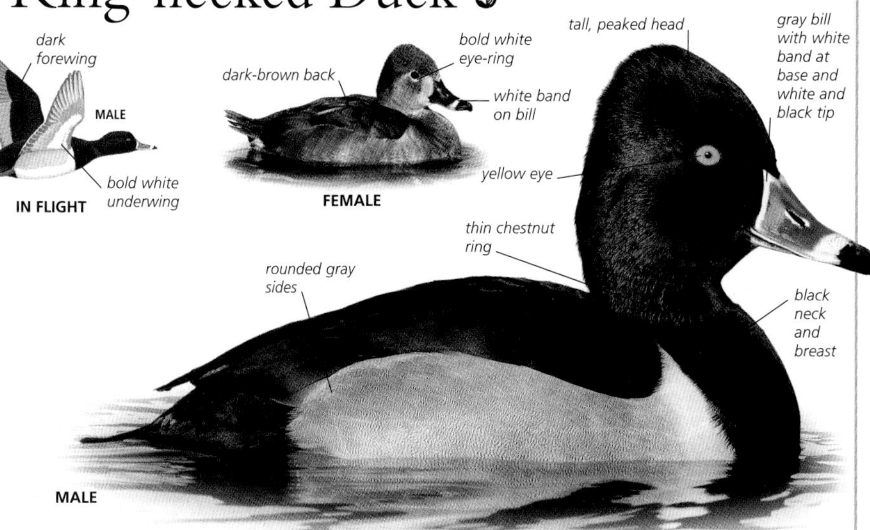
dark forewing
MALE
bold white underwing
IN FLIGHT
dark-brown back
bold white eye-ring
white band on bill
FEMALE
tall, peaked head
gray bill with white band at base and white and black tip
yellow eye
thin chestnut ring
rounded gray sides
black neck and breast
MALE

A resident of freshwater ponds and lakes, the Ring-necked Duck is a fairly common medium-sized diving duck. A more descriptive and suitable name might have been Ring-billed Duck as the bold white band on the bill tip is easy to see, whereas the thin chestnut ring around the neck can be very difficult to observe. The tall, pointed head is quite distinctive, peaking at the rear of the crown. When it sits on the water, this bird typically holds its head high.

VOICE Male normally silent; female makes low *kerp kerp* call.

NESTING Floating nest built in dense aquatic vegetation, often in marshes; 6–14 eggs; 1 brood; May–August.

FEEDING Feeds in water at all times, either by diving, tipping up, or dabbling for aquatic plant tubers and seeds; also eats aquatic invertebrates, such as clams and snails.

UNIQUE BILL
A white outline around the base of the bill and the white band on the bill are unique markings.

FLIGHT: strong flier with deep, rapid wing beats; flight somewhat erratic.

FLAPPING WINGS
Bold white wing linings are apparent when the Ring-necked Duck flaps its wings.

SIMILAR SPECIES

LESSER SCAUP ♂
see p.47
rounded head
wavy-patterned gray mantle

TUFTED DUCK ♂
crested tufts
white sides

OCCURRENCE
Breeds across Canada, south of the Arctic zone, in shallow freshwater marshes and bogs; sporadically in the western US. Winters in freshwater and brackish habitats, such as swamps, lakes, estuaries, reservoirs, and flooded fields. Migrants are found in the Midwest near stands of wild rice.

Length **15–18in (38–46cm)**	Wingspan **24–25in (62–63cm)**	Weight **1⅛–2lbs (500–900g)**
Social **Flocks**	Lifespan **Up to 20 years**	Status **Secure**

DATE: ____________ TIME: ____________ LOCATION: ______________________________

Order **Anseriformes**	Family **Anatidae**	Species ***Aythya marila***

Greater Scaup

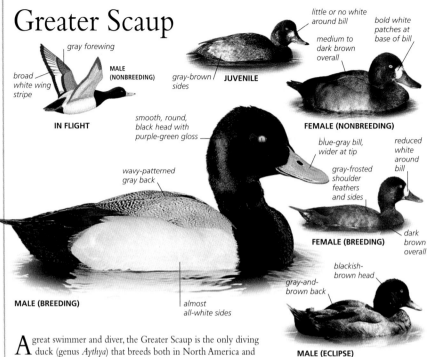

gray forewing
broad white wing stripe
MALE (NONBREEDING)
IN FLIGHT

little or no white around bill
gray-brown sides
JUVENILE

bold white patches at base of bill
medium to dark brown overall
FEMALE (NONBREEDING)

smooth, round, black head with purple-green gloss
wavy-patterned gray back
blue-gray bill, wider at tip
almost all-white sides
MALE (BREEDING)

reduced white around bill
gray-frosted shoulder feathers and sides
dark brown overall
FEMALE (BREEDING)

blackish-brown head
gray-and-brown back
MALE (ECLIPSE)

A great swimmer and diver, the Greater Scaup is the only diving duck (genus *Aythya*) that breeds both in North America and Eurasia. Due to its more restricted coastal breeding and wintering habitat preference, it is far less numerous in North America than its close relative, the Lesser Scaup. The Greater Scaup forms large, often sexually segregated, flocks outside the breeding season. If both scaup species are present together, they will also segregate within the flocks according to species. Correct identification is difficult.

VOICE During courtship, male call a soft, fast, wheezy *week week wheew*; female gives a series of growled monotone *arrrr* notes.

NESTING Simple depression lined with grasses and down, nest sites need to have dense cover of vegetation from previous year; 6–10 eggs; 1 brood; May–September.

FEEDING Dives for aquatic plants, seeds, insects, crustaceans, snails, shrimp, and bivalves.

FLIGHT: strong, fast, and agile; flocks shift and twist during prolonged flight.

FOND OF FLOCKING
Male Greater Scaups, with distinct black-and-white markings, flock together on the water.

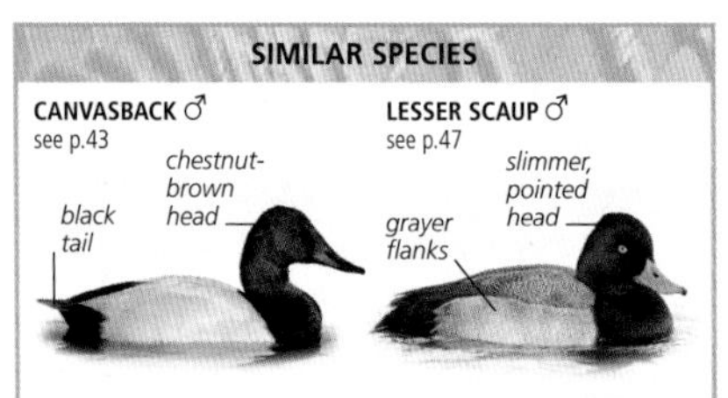
SIMILAR SPECIES
CANVASBACK ♂
see p.43
chestnut-brown head
black tail
LESSER SCAUP ♂
see p.47
slimmer, pointed head
grayer flanks

OCCURRENCE
Majority breed in western coastal Alaska on tundra wetlands; also in lower densities in northwest and eastern Canada. Almost all birds winter offshore, along the Atlantic and Pacific Coasts, or on the Great Lakes due to increased food availability. Small groups are found inland and midcontinent, on unfrozen water bodies.

Length **15–22in (38–56cm)**	Wingspan **28–31in (72–79cm)**	Weight **1¼–3lb (0.6–1.4kg)**
Social **Flocks**	Lifespan **Up to 22 years**	Status **Declining**

DATE: ____________ TIME: ____________ LOCATION: ____________

Order **Anseriformes**	Family **Anatidae**	Species ***Aythya affinis***

Lesser Scaup

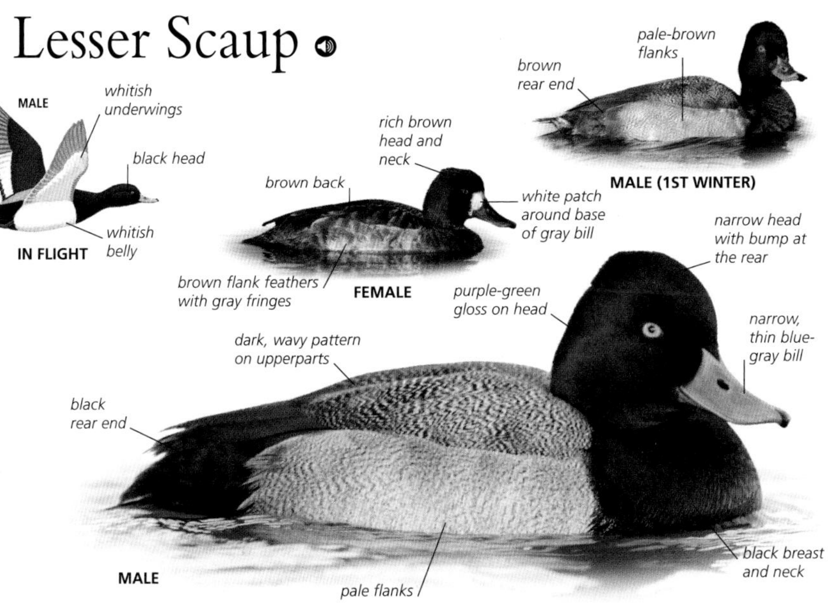
MALE
whitish underwings
black head
whitish belly
IN FLIGHT
rich brown head and neck
brown back
white patch around base of gray bill
brown flank feathers with gray fringes
FEMALE
brown rear end
pale-brown flanks
MALE (1ST WINTER)
narrow head with bump at the rear
purple-green gloss on head
narrow, thin blue-gray bill
dark, wavy pattern on upperparts
black rear end
black breast and neck
pale flanks
MALE

The Lesser Scaup, far more numerous than its somewhat larger relative (their size and weight ranges overlap), is also the most abundant diving duck in North America. The two species are very similar in appearance and are best identified by shape. Identification must be done cautiously as head shape changes with position. For example, the crown feathers are flattened just before diving in both species; thus, scaups are best identified when they are not moving.

VOICE Males mostly silent except during courtship when they make a wheezy *wheeow wheeow wheeow* sound; females give repetitive series of grating *garrrf garrrf garrrf* notes.

NESTING Nest built in tall vegetation or under shrubs, sometimes far from water, also on islands and mats of floating vegetation; 8–11 eggs; 1 brood; May–September.

FEEDING Feeds mainly on leeches, crustaceans, mollusks, aquatic insects, and aquatic plants and seeds.

FLIGHT: rapid, direct flight; can jump off water more easily than other diving ducks.

PREENING SCAUP
Ducks are meticulous preeners, and the Lesser Scaup is no exception.

SIMILAR SPECIES

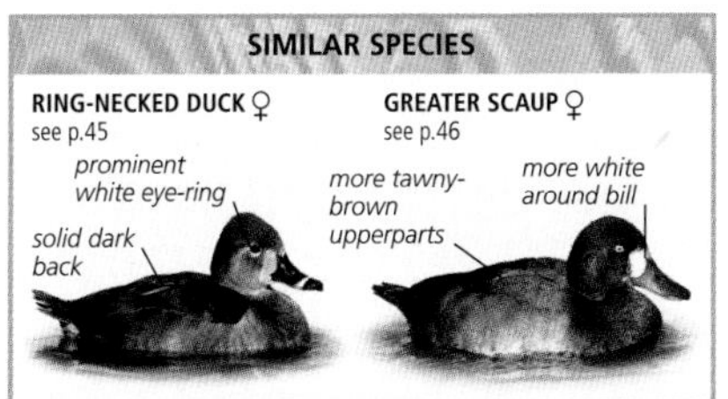
RING-NECKED DUCK ♀
see p.45
prominent white eye-ring
solid dark back
GREATER SCAUP ♀
see p.46
more tawny-brown upperparts
more white around bill

OCCURRENCE
Breeds inland from Alaska to eastern Canada in open northern forests and forest tundra, most farther north. Winters in the Caribbean, the southern US, and south to northern South America. Majority winter along coasts; others winter inland on lakes and reservoirs.

Length **15½–17½in (39–45cm)**	Wingspan **27–31in (68–78cm)**	Weight **1–2¾lb (0.45–1.2kg)**
Social **Flocks**	Lifespan **Up to 18 years**	Status **Secure**

DATE: ____________ TIME: ____________ LOCATION: ____________

Order **Anseriformes**	Family **Anatidae**	Species ***Somateria spectabilis***

King Eider

MALE (BREEDING)

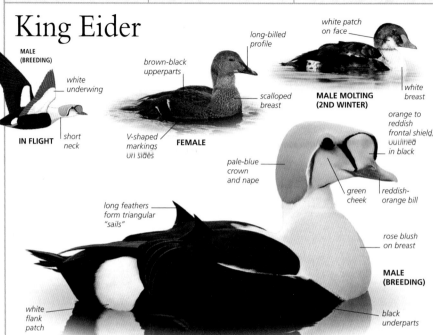

white underwing

IN FLIGHT

short neck

brown-black upperparts

long-billed profile

scalloped breast

V-shaped markings on sides

FEMALE

white patch on face

MALE MOLTING (2ND WINTER)

white breast

orange to reddish frontal shield, outlined in black

pale-blue crown and nape

green cheek

reddish-orange bill

long feathers form triangular "sails"

rose blush on breast

MALE (BREEDING)

white flank patch

black underparts

The scientific name of the King Eider, *spectabilis*, means "worth seeing," and its gaudy marking and coloring around the head and bill make it hard to mistake. Females resemble the somewhat larger and paler Common Eider. The female King Eider has a more rounded head, more compact body, and a longer bill than the male. King Eiders may dive down to 180ft (55m) when foraging.

VOICE Courting males give a repeated series of low, rolled dove-like *arrrrooooo* calls, each rising, then falling, followed by softer *cooos*; females give grunts and croaks.

NESTING Slight depression in tundra, lined with nearby vegetation and down; 4–7 eggs; 1 brood; June–September.

FEEDING Dives for mollusks; other food items include crustaceans, starfish, and when breeding, insects and plants.

FLIGHT: direct and rapid flight; migrates in long lines, abreast in a broad front, or in clusters.

GROUP FLIGHT

Migratory King Eiders move in large groups to their northern breeding habitats.

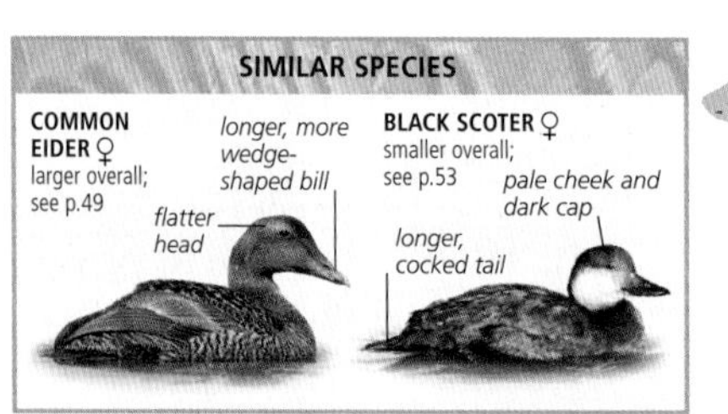
SIMILAR SPECIES
COMMON EIDER ♀
larger overall; see p.49
longer, more wedge-shaped bill
flatter head
BLACK SCOTER ♀
smaller overall; see p.53
pale cheek and dark cap
longer, cocked tail

OCCURRENCE

Nests along coasts and farther inland than Spectacled or Steller's Eiders in the high Arctic, on a variety of habitats; around low marshes, lakes, and islands; prefers well-drained areas. During winter, found mostly along the southern edge of the ice pack, in coastal waters up to 66ft (20m) deep.

Length **18½–25in (47–64cm)**	Wingspan **37in (94cm)**	Weight **2¾–4¾lb (1.2–2.1kg)**
Social **Flocks**	Lifespan **Up to 15 years**	Status **Secure**

DATE: ______________ TIME: ______________ LOCATION: ______________________________

Order **Anseriformes**	Family **Anatidae**	Species ***Somateria mollissima***

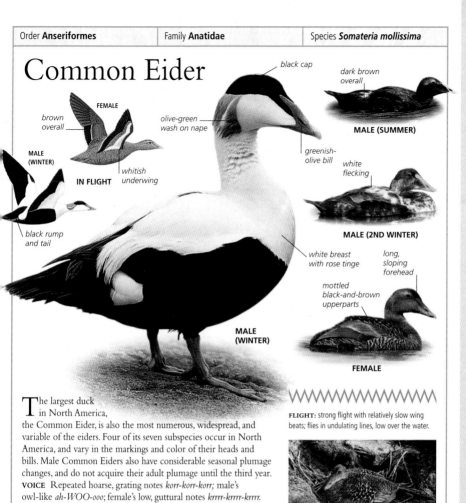

Common Eider

FEMALE
brown overall
MALE (WINTER)
IN FLIGHT
whitish underwing
black rump and tail
olive-green wash on nape
black cap
greenish-olive bill
MALE (WINTER)
dark brown overall
MALE (SUMMER)
white flecking
MALE (2ND WINTER)
white breast with rose tinge
long, sloping forehead
mottled black-and-brown upperparts
FEMALE

The largest duck in North America, the Common Eider, is also the most numerous, widespread, and variable of the eiders. Four of its seven subspecies occur in North America, and vary in the markings and color of their heads and bills. Male Common Eiders also have considerable seasonal plumage changes, and do not acquire their adult plumage until the third year.

VOICE Repeated hoarse, grating notes *korr-korr-korr;* male's owl-like *ah-WOO-ooo*; female's low, guttural notes *krrrr-krrrr-krrrr.*

NESTING Depression on ground lined with down and plant matter, often near water; 2–7 eggs; 1 brood; June–September.

FEEDING Forages in open water and areas of shallow water; dives in synchronized flocks for mollusks and crustaceans, but consumes its larger prey above the surface.

FLIGHT: strong flight with relatively slow wing beats; flies in undulating lines, low over the water.

BROODING FEMALE
Females line their nests with down plucked from their bellies, and cover the eggs with their bodies.

SIMILAR SPECIES

KING EIDER ♀ smaller overall; see p.48
flatter crown
thicker neck
shorter, more concave bill

SURF SCOTER ♀ see p.51
shorter, wedge-shaped bill
dark brown overall

OCCURRENCE
Arctic breeder on coastal islands, peninsulas, seldom along freshwater lakes and deltas near coast. One population is sedentary in the Hudson Bay and James Bay regions. Other populations winter in the Bering Sea, Hudson Bay, north British Columbia, Gulf of St. Lawrence, and along the Atlantic Coast.

Length **19½–28in (50–71cm)**	Wingspan **31–42in (80–108cm)**	Weight **2¾–5¾lb (1.2–2.6kg)**
Social **Flocks/Colonies**	Lifespan **Up to 21 years**	Status **Secure**

DATE: ____________ TIME: ____________ LOCATION: ____________

Order **Anseriformes**	Family **Anatidae**	Species ***Histrionicus histrionicus***

Harlequin Duck

MALE
dark wings above and below
short neck
pointed tail
IN FLIGHT
dark sooty-brown overall
broad face with whitish patches
scaly, pale-brown lower breast and belly
FEMALE
very round head
rust crown stripes
steep forehead
slate-blue with bright rusty sides
two white bands perpendicular to breast and neck
two white facial spots
white bands down either side of back
small, dark bill
white crescent
MALE

This small, hardy duck is a superbly skillful swimmer, diving to forage on the bottom of turbulent streams for its favorite insect prey. Despite the male's unmistakable plumage at close range, it looks very dark from a distance. With head and long tail held high, it can be found among crashing waves, alongside larger and bigger-billed Surf and White-winged Scoters, which feed in the same habitat.

VOICE Male a high-pitched squeak earning it the nickname "sea mouse"; female's call a raspy *ekekekekekek*.

NESTING Nests near water, under vegetation or base of tree; also tree cavities; 3–9 eggs; 1 brood; April–September.

FEEDING Dives for insects and their larvae, and fish roe when breeding; in winter, eats mollusks, crustaceans, crabs, snails, fish roe, and barnacles.

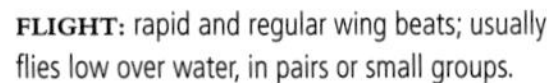

FLIGHT: rapid and regular wing beats; usually flies low over water, in pairs or small groups.

MALE GROUPS
After the breeding season, many males may gather and forage together.

PAIR IN FLIGHT
Note the crisp white markings on the slate-blue male in flight.

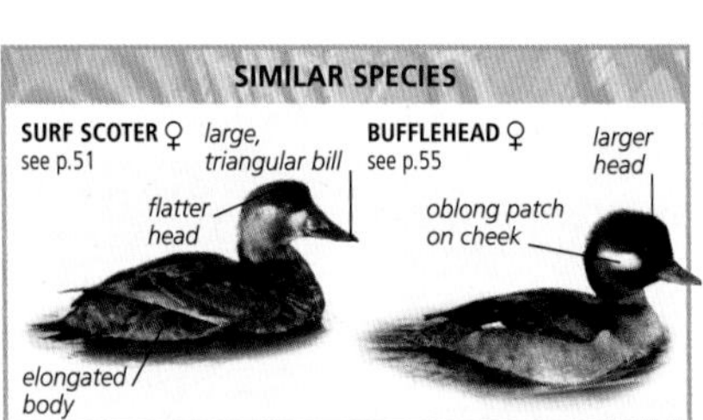
SIMILAR SPECIES
SURF SCOTER ♀
see p.51
large, triangular bill
flatter head
elongated body
BUFFLEHEAD ♀
see p.55
larger head
oblong patch on cheek

OCCURRENCE
Breeds near rushing coastal, mountain, or subalpine streams. During winter, found in small groups or mixed in with other sea ducks close to the shore, particularly along shallow rocky shorelines, jetties, rocky beaches, and headlands.

Length **13–21½in (33–54cm)**	Wingspan **22–26in (56–66cm)**	Weight **18–26oz (500–750g)**
Social **Small flocks**	Lifespan **Unknown**	Status **Special Concern**

DATE: ____________ TIME: ____________ LOCATION: ____________

Order **Anseriformes**	Family **Anatidae**	Species ***Melanitta perspicillata***

Surf Scoter

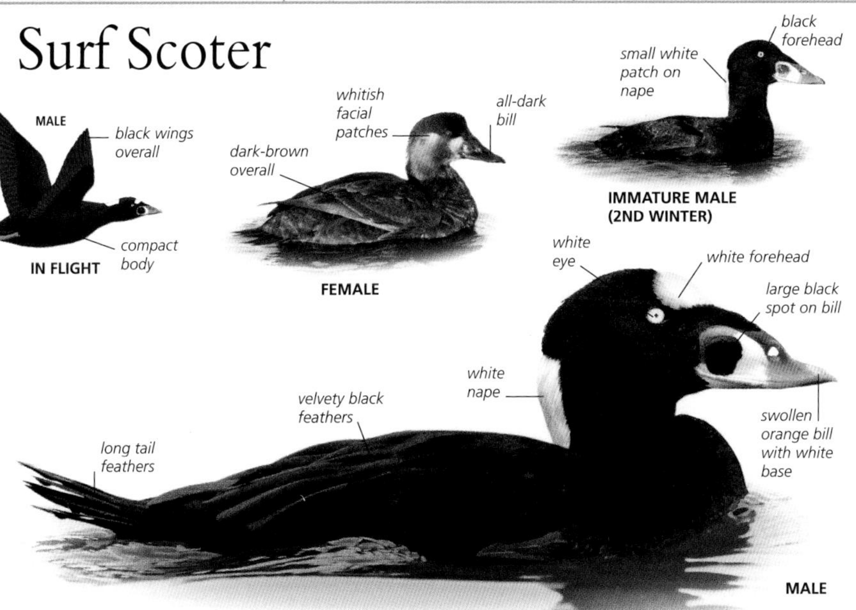
MALE
black wings overall
compact body
IN FLIGHT
whitish facial patches
all-dark bill
dark-brown overall
FEMALE
black forehead
small white patch on nape
IMMATURE MALE (2ND WINTER)
white eye
white forehead
large black spot on bill
white nape
velvety black feathers
long tail feathers
swollen orange bill with white base
MALE

Surf Scoters, one of three species of scoters living in North America, migrate up and down both coasts, often with the other species. They take their name from the way they dive for mollusks on the seafloor, in shallow coastal waters, through heavy surf. Groups often dive and resurface in unison. Black and Surf Scoters can be difficult to tell apart as both have all-black wings. The underside of the Surf Scoter's wings are uniformly black, whereas the Black Scoter's have gray flight feathers, which contrast with the black underwing feathers.

VOICE Normally silent; courting male's variety of calls includes liquid gurgled *puk-puk*, bubbled whistles, and low croaks; female call a harsh *crahh,* reminiscent of a crow.

NESTING Ground nest lined with down and vegetation on brushy tundra, often under low branches of a conifer tree; 5–10 eggs; 1 brood; May–September.

FEEDING Dives for mollusks and other aquatic invertebrates.

FLIGHT: strong wing beats; flies in bunched-up groups; male's wings hum or whistle in flight.

DISTINGUISHING FEATURES
The white forehead and bright orange bill, in addition to its red-orange legs and feet, identify male Surf Scoters.

SIMILAR SPECIES

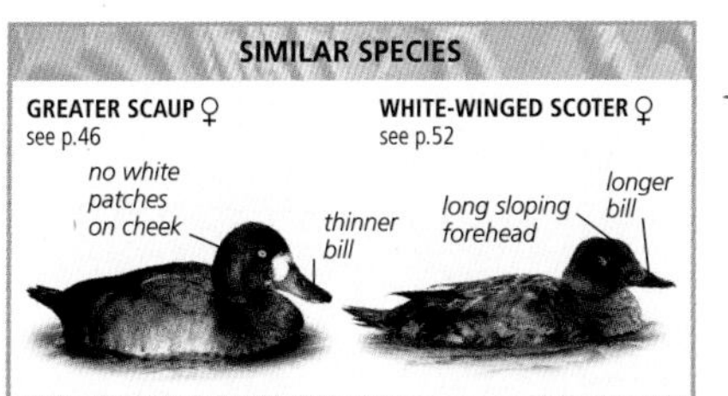
GREATER SCAUP ♀
see p.46
no white patches on cheek
thinner bill
WHITE-WINGED SCOTER ♀
see p.52
long sloping forehead
longer bill

OCCURRENCE
Nests on lake islands in forested regions of interior Alaska and northern Canada. Nonbreeders in summer and adults in winter are strictly coastal, with numbers decreasing from north to south along the Pacific Coast. In the East, most overwinter in the mid-Atlantic Coast region.

Length **19–23½in (48–60cm)**	Wingspan **30in (77cm)**	Weight **1¾–2¾lb (0.8–1.2kg)**
Social **Flocks/Pairs**	Lifespan **Up to 10 years**	Status **Declining**

DATE: ____________ TIME: ____________ LOCATION: ____________

Order **Anseriformes**	Family **Anatidae**	Species ***Melanitta deglandi***

White-winged Scoter

white wing patch

ADULT

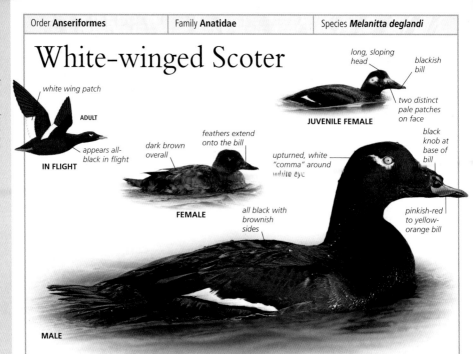

appears all-black in flight

IN FLIGHT

long, sloping head

blackish bill

two distinct pale patches on face

JUVENILE FEMALE

dark brown overall

feathers extend onto the bill

FEMALE

upturned, white "comma" around white eye

black knob at base of bill

all black with brownish sides

pinkish-red to yellow-orange bill

MALE

The White-winged Scoter is the largest of the three scoters. When visible, the white wing patch makes identification easy. Females are quite similar to juvenile male and female Surf Scoters and can be identified by head shape, extent of bill feathering, and shape of white areas on the face. When diving, this scoter leaps forward and up, arching its neck, and opens its wings when entering the water. Underwater, White-winged Scoters open their wings to propel and stabilize themselves.

VOICE Mostly silent; courting males emit a whistling note; female call a growly *karr*.

NESTING Depression lined with twigs and down in dense thickets, often far from water; 8–9 eggs; 1 brood; June–September.

FEEDING Dives for mollusks and crustaceans; sometimes eats fish and aquatic plants.

FLIGHT: direct with rapid wing beats; flies low over the water in small groups.

WHITE FLASH IN FLIGHT
Scoters often migrate or feed in mixed flocks. The white wing patches are striking in flight.

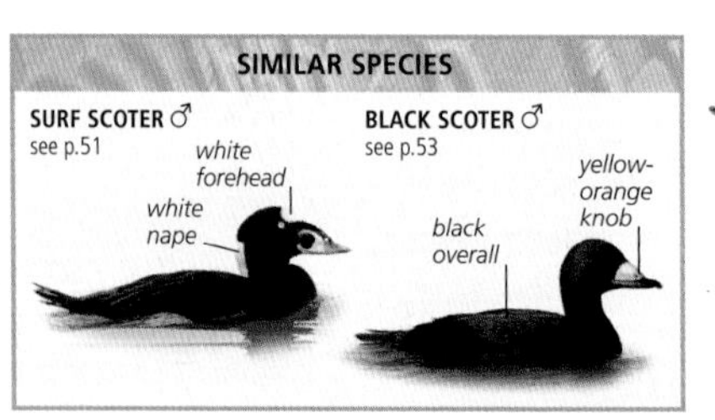
SIMILAR SPECIES
SURF SCOTER ♂
see p.51
white forehead
white nape
BLACK SCOTER ♂
see p.53
yellow-orange knob
black overall

OCCURRENCE
Majority breed in dense colonies in interior Alaska and western Canada on large freshwater or brackish lakes or ponds, sometimes on saltwater lakes. Winters along both coasts, large bays, inlets, and estuaries. Rarely winters inland, except on the Great Lakes.

Length **19–23in (48–58cm)**	Wingspan **31in (80cm)**	Weight **2¾–4¾lb (0.9–1.9kg)**
Social **Flocks/Colonies**	Lifespan **Up to 18 years**	Status **Vulnerable**

 DATE: ____________ TIME: ____________ LOCATION: ____________________

Order **Anseriformes**	Family **Anatidae**	Species ***Melanitta americana***

Black Scoter

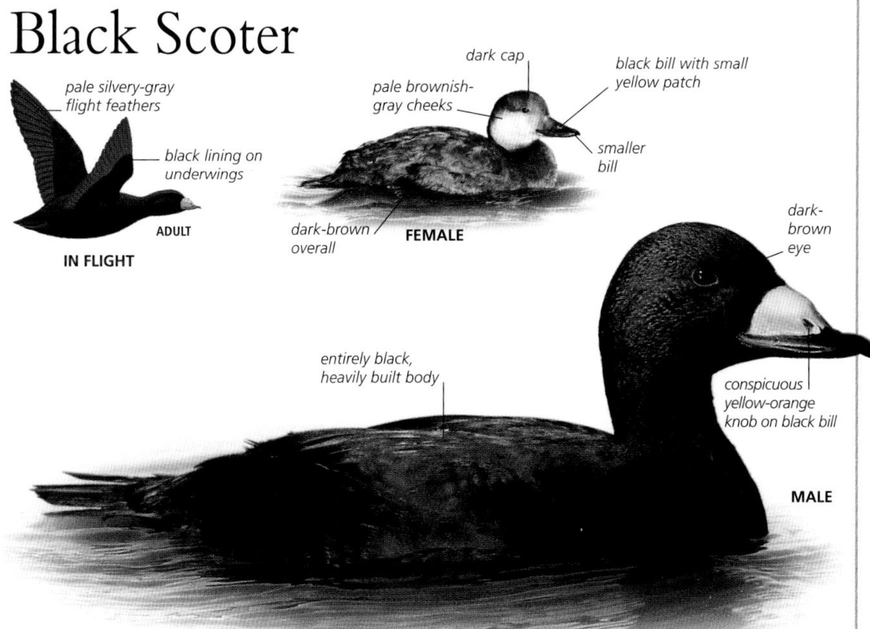
pale silvery-gray flight feathers
black lining on underwings
ADULT
IN FLIGHT
dark cap
pale brownish-gray cheeks
black bill with small yellow patch
smaller bill
dark-brown overall
FEMALE
dark-brown eye
entirely black, heavily built body
conspicuous yellow-orange knob on black bill
MALE

Black Scoters, the most vocal of the scoters, are medium-sized sea ducks that winter along both coasts of North America. Riding high on the waves, they form dense flocks, often segregated by gender. While swimming, the Black Scoter sometimes flaps its wings and while doing so drops its neck low down, unlike the other two scoters. This scoter breeds in two widely separated sub-Arctic breeding areas and is one of the least studied ducks in North America. The Black Scoter was once thought to be a subspecies of the Common Scoter, but recent studies have split the American birds from their Eurasian relatives.

VOICE Male call a high-whistled *peeew*; female a low raspy *kraaa*.

NESTING Depression lined with grass and down, often in tall grass on tundra; 5–10 eggs; 1 brood; May–September.

FEEDING Dives in saltwater for mollusks, crustaceans, and plant matter; feeds on aquatic insects and freshwater mussels.

FLIGHT: strong wing beats; male's wings make whistling sound during takeoff.

YELLOW BILL
Male Black Scoters are distinctive with their black plumage and yellow bill-knob.

SIMILAR SPECIES

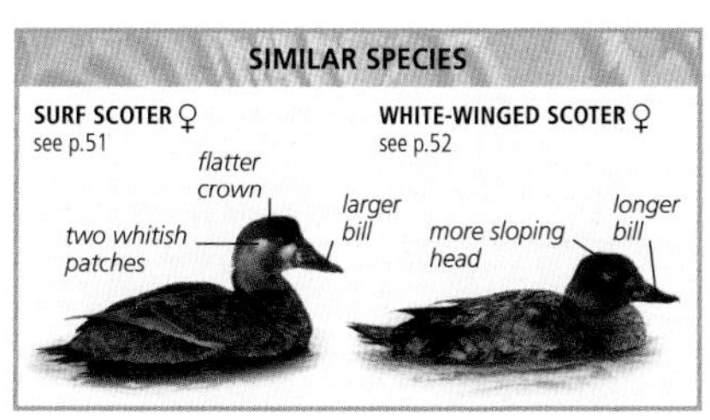
SURF SCOTER ♀
see p.51
flatter crown
two whitish patches
larger bill
WHITE-WINGED SCOTER ♀
see p.52
more sloping head
longer bill

OCCURRENCE
Breeding habitat is somewhat varied, but is generally close to fairly shallow, small lakes. Winters along both coasts. Populations wintering farther north prefer water over cobbles, gravel, or offshore ledges, whereas in southern locations, sandier habitats are chosen.

Length **17–21in (43–53cm)**	Wingspan **31–35in (79–90cm)**	Weight **1¾–2¾lb (0.8–1.2kg)**
Social **Flocks**	Lifespan **At least 8 years**	Status **Declining**

DATE: ________ TIME: ________ LOCATION: ________

Order **Anseriformes**	Family **Anatidae**	Species ***Clangula hyemalis***

Long-tailed Duck

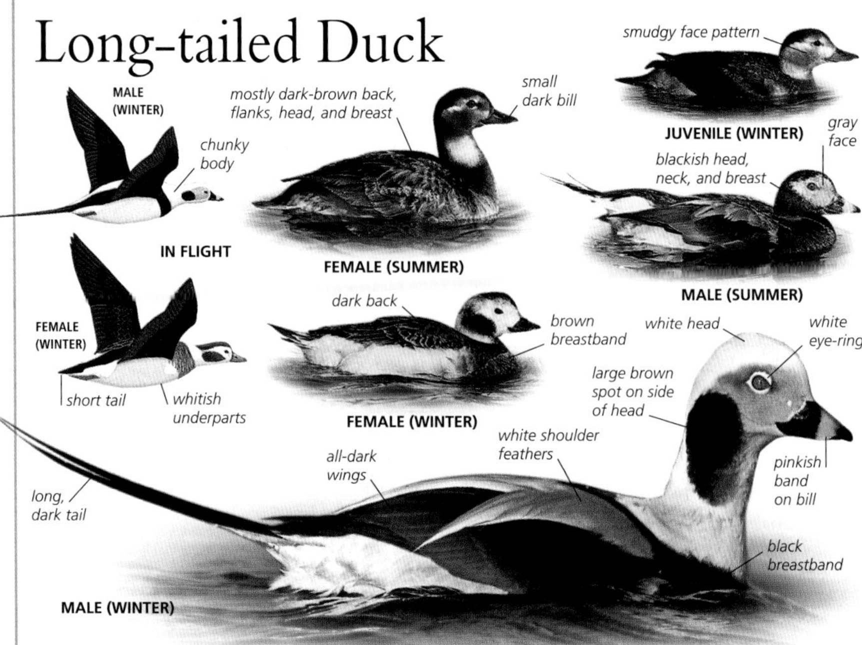

MALE (WINTER)
chunky body
IN FLIGHT
FEMALE (WINTER)
short tail
whitish underparts
mostly dark-brown back, flanks, head, and breast
small dark bill
FEMALE (SUMMER)
smudgy face pattern
JUVENILE (WINTER)
gray face
blackish head, neck, and breast
MALE (SUMMER)
dark back
brown breastband
FEMALE (WINTER)
white head
white eye-ring
large brown spot on side of head
white shoulder feathers
all-dark wings
pinkish band on bill
long, dark tail
black breastband
MALE (WINTER)

The Long-tailed Duck is a small, pudgy sea duck with a wide range of plumages depending on the season and the sex of the bird. The male has two extremely long tail feathers, which are often held up in the air like a pennant. The male's loud calls are quite musical, and, when heard from a flock, have a chorus-like quality, hence the name *Clangula*, which is Latin for "loud." This species can dive for a prolonged period of time, and can reach depths of 200ft (60m), making it one of the deepest diving ducks. Its three-part molt is more complex than that of other ducks.

VOICE Male call a *ang-ang-eeeooo* with yodelling quality; female barking *urk* or *uk* alarm call.

NESTING Shallow depression in ground lined with plant matter; 6–9 eggs; 1 brood; May–September.

FEEDING Dives to bottom of freshwater or saltwater habitats for mollusks, crustaceans, insects, fish, and roe.

FLIGHT: flies low over the water, somewhat erratically, with fast, fluttering wing beats.

UNMISTAKABLE MALE
In winter, dark wings, a white body with black breast-band, and a long tail make this male unmistakable.

SIMILAR SPECIES

BUFFLEHEAD ♀ see p.55

BLACK GUILLEMOT ❄ see p.137

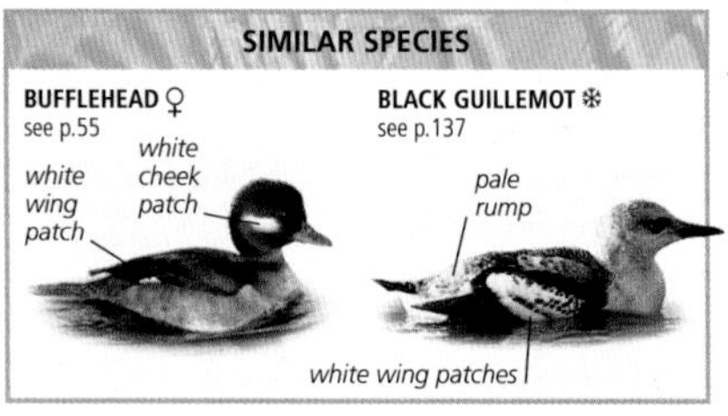

white wing patch
white cheek patch
pale rump
white wing patches

OCCURRENCE
Breeds in Arctic and sub-Arctic, nesting in small groups on islands and peninsulas on lakes, less commonly on tundra and freshwater ponds on islands. Winters mostly along rocky coasts and headlands, protected bays, or on large freshwater lakes.

Length **14–23in (35–58cm)**	Wingspan **28in (72cm)**	Weight **18–39oz (500–1,100g)**
Social **Flocks**	Lifespan **Up to 22 years**	Status **Declining**

 DATE: ________ TIME: ________ LOCATION: ________

Order **Anseriformes**	Family **Anatidae**	Species ***Bucephala albeola***

Bufflehead

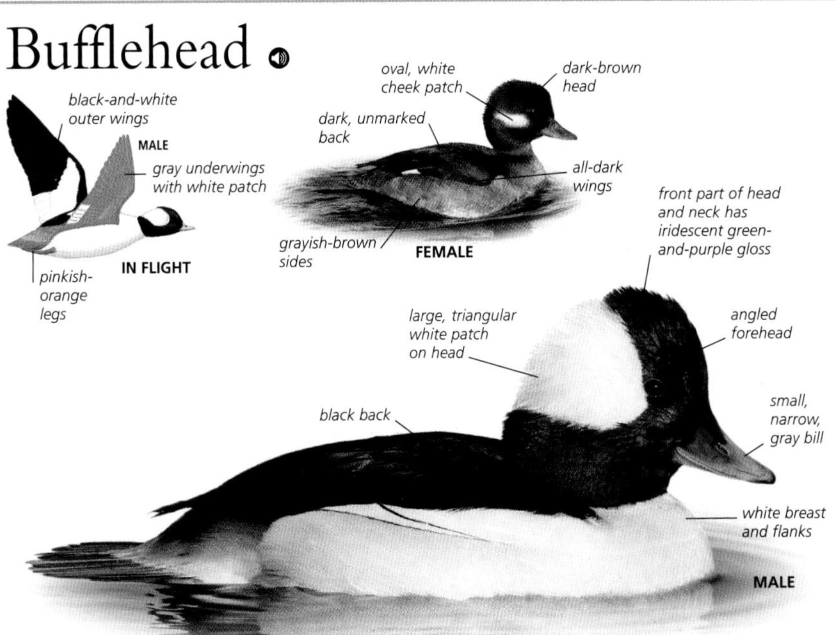
black-and-white outer wings
MALE
gray underwings with white patch
IN FLIGHT
pinkish-orange legs
oval, white cheek patch
dark-brown head
dark, unmarked back
all-dark wings
grayish-brown sides
FEMALE
front part of head and neck has iridescent green-and-purple gloss
large, triangular white patch on head
angled forehead
black back
small, narrow, gray bill
white breast and flanks
MALE

The smallest diving duck in North America, the Bufflehead is a close relative of the Common and Barrow's Goldeneyes. Males make a bold statement with their striking head pattern. In flight, males resemble the larger Common Goldeneye, yet the large white area on their head makes them easy to distinguish. The Common Goldeneye's wings create a whirring sound in flight whereas the Bufflehead's do not. The northern limit of the Bufflehead's breeding range corresponds to that of the Northern Flicker, as the ducks usually nest in abandoned flicker cavities.

VOICE Male a low growl or squeal; chattering during breeding; female mostly silent except during courtship or calling to nestlings.

NESTING Cavity-nester, no nesting material added, near water; 7–9 eggs; 1 brood; April–September.

FEEDING Dives for aquatic invertebrates: usually insects in freshwater, mollusks and crustaceans in saltwater; also eats seeds.

FLIGHT: very rapid wing beats; no flight sound, unlike Goldeneyes.

IMMEDIATE TAKEOFF
Unlike other diving ducks, the small, compact Bufflehead can take off almost vertically.

SIMILAR SPECIES

HOODED MERGANSER ♂ see p.58

RUDDY DUCK ♂ ❄ see p.61

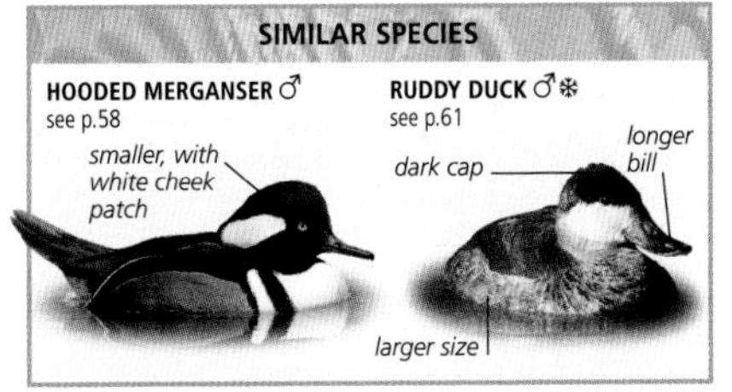
smaller, with white cheek patch
dark cap
longer bill
larger size

OCCURRENCE
Breeds in forest from Alaska to eastern Canada, in woodlands near small lakes and permanent ponds, where young are raised. Winters largely along the Pacific and Atlantic Coasts with lower densities scattered across the continent, south to northern Mexico, and in Bermuda.

Length **12½–15½in (32–39cm)**	Wingspan **21½–24in (54–61cm)**	Weight **10–18oz (275–500g)**
Social **Flocks**	Lifespan **Up to 15 years**	Status **Secure**

DATE: ____________ TIME: ____________ LOCATION: ____________

Order **Anseriformes**	Family **Anatidae**	Species ***Bucephala clangula***

Common Goldeneye

white wing patch
with two bars
FEMALE
white
collar
mostly white
inner wing
MALE
(WINTER)
dusky
underwing
IN FLIGHT
warm brown
head
bright-
yellow eye
FEMALE
white patches on
flanks and wings
MALE
(1ST WINTER)
large,
round
white spot
iridescent
green
head
extensive white
shoulder feathers
MALE
(WINTER)

Common Goldeneyes closely resemble Barrow's Goldeneyes. Found in North America and Eurasia, this is a medium-sized, compact, diving duck. It is aggressive and very competitive with members of its own species, as well as other cavity-nesting ducks. It regularly lays eggs in the nests of other species—a behavior that is almost parasitic. Before diving, the Common Goldeneye flattens its feathers in preparation for underwater foraging. The female's head shape changes according to her posture.

VOICE Courting males make a faint *peent* call; females a harsh *gack* or repeated *cuk* calls.

NESTING Cavity-nester in holes made by other birds, including Pileated Woodpeckers, in broken branches or hollow trees; also commonly uses nest boxes; 4–13 eggs; 1 brood; April–September.

FEEDING Dives during breeding season for insects; in winter, mollusks and crustaceans; sometimes eats fish and plant matter.

FLIGHT: rapid with fast wing beats; male's wings make a tinkling sound in flight.

MALE TAKING OFF

Quite a long takeoff, involving energetic running on the water, leaves a trail of spray.

SIMILAR SPECIES

BUFFLEHEAD ♀ see p.55

BARROW'S GOLDENEYE ♂ see p.57

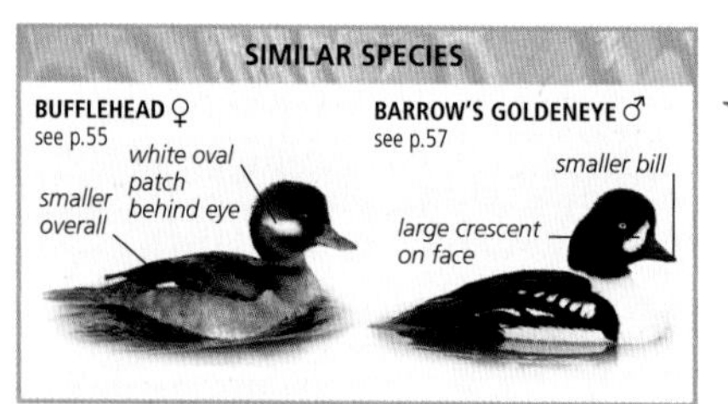
white oval
patch
behind eye
smaller
overall
smaller bill
large crescent
on face

OCCURRENCE

Breeds along wetlands, lakes, and rivers with clear water in northern forests, where large trees provide appropriate nest cavities. Winters across continent, with highest densities located from north New England to the mid-Atlantic on coastal bays and in the West from coastal southeast Alaska to British Columbia.

Length **15½–20in (40–51cm)**	Wingspan **30–33in (77–83cm)**	Weight **19–44oz (550–1,300g)**
Social **Flocks**	Lifespan **Up to 15 years**	Status **Secure**

DATE: ______________ TIME: ______________ LOCATION: ______________

Order **Anseriformes**	Family **Anatidae**	Species ***Bucephala islandica***

Barrow's Goldeneye

white wing patch
MALE
dark underwings
IN FLIGHT
narrow white wing patch
FEMALE (BREEDING)
darker brown head
steep forehead
small yellow bill
black head with purple gloss
sloping crown
grayish-brown wing feathers
white neck
MALE (1ST WINTER)
white "piano key" markings on sides
bold white facial crescent
MALE

Barrow's Goldeneye is a slightly larger, darker version of the Common Goldeneye. Although the female can be identified by its different head structure and bill color, the bill color varies seasonally and geographically. Eastern Barrow's have blacker bills with less yellow, and western populations have entirely yellow bills, which darken in summer. During the breeding season, the majority of Barrow's Goldeneyes are found in mountainous regions of northwest North America.

VOICE Males normally silent; courting males grunt *ka-KAA*; females *cuc* call, slightly higher pitched than Common Goldeneye.

NESTING Tree cavity in holes formed by Pileated Woodpeckers, often broken limbs or hollow trees; also uses nest boxes; 6–12 eggs; 1 brood; April–September.

FEEDING Dives in summer for insects, some fish, and roe; in winter, mainly mollusks and crustaceans; some plant matter.

FLIGHT: rapid flight with fast, deep wing beats; flies near water surface on short flights.

COURTING DISPLAY
A male thrusts his head back and gives a guttural call. His feet then kick back, driving him forward.

SIMILAR SPECIES

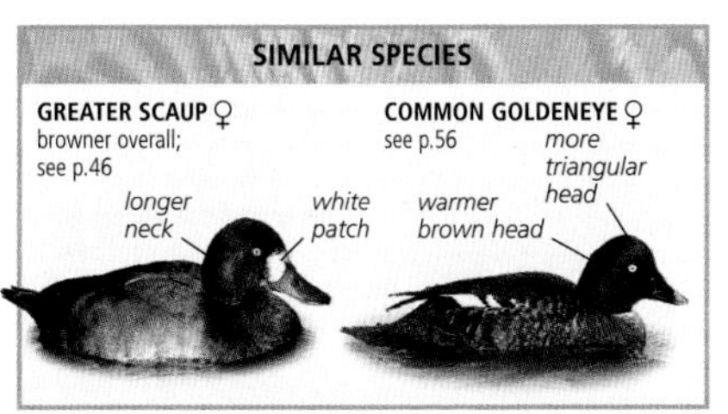
GREATER SCAUP ♀
browner overall;
see p.46
longer neck
white patch
COMMON GOLDENEYE ♀
see p.56
more triangular head
warmer brown head

OCCURRENCE
Winters along the Pacific Coast between southeast Alaska and Washington, with small populations in eastern Canada. Smaller numbers found inland from the lower Colorado River to Yellowstone National Park. Eastern population is localized in winter with the highest count in St. Lawrence estuary.

Length **17–19in (43–48cm)**	Wingspan **28–30in (71–76cm)**	Weight **17–46oz (475–1,300g)**
Social **Flocks**	Lifespan **Up to 18 years**	Status **Special Concern**

DATE: ____________ TIME: ____________ LOCATION: ____________________

Order **Anseriformes**	Family **Anatidae**	Species ***Lophodytes cucullatus***

Hooded Merganser

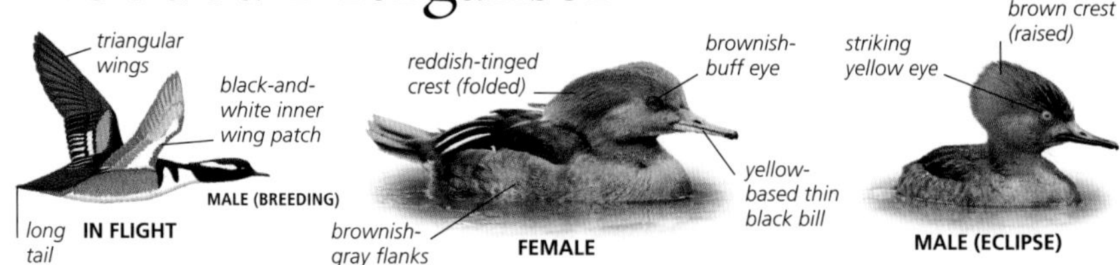
triangular wings
black-and-white inner wing patch
MALE (BREEDING)
long tail
IN FLIGHT
reddish-tinged crest (folded)
brownish-buff eye
yellow-based thin black bill
brownish-gray flanks
FEMALE
small gray-brown crest (raised)
striking yellow eye
MALE (ECLIPSE)

longish tail, often raised
crested black-and-white head (crest not raised)
yellow eye
thin, black, serrated bill
black back
white breast
MALE (BREEDING)
warm-brown flanks
bold vertical bars

This dapper, miniature fish-eater is the smallest of the three mergansers. Both male and female Hooded Mergansers have crests that they can raise or flatten. When the male raises his crest, the thin, horizontal, white stripe turns into a gorgeous white fan, surrounded by black. Although easily identified when swimming, the Hooded Merganser and the Wood Duck can be confused when seen in flight since they both are fairly small, with bushy heads and long tails.

VOICE Normally silent; during courtship, males produce a low, growly, descending *pah-hwaaaaa*, reminiscent of a frog; females give a soft *rrrep*.

NESTING Cavity-nester; nest lined with down feathers in a tree or box close to or over water; 6–15 eggs; 1 brood; February–June.

FEEDING Dives for fish, aquatic insects, and crayfish, preferably in clear and shallow fresh waters, but also in brackish waters.

FLIGHT: low, fast, and direct; shallow wing beats; quiet whirring noise produced by wings.

FANHEAD SPECTACULAR
The male's magnificent black-and-white fan of a crest is like a beacon in the late afternoon light.

SIMILAR SPECIES

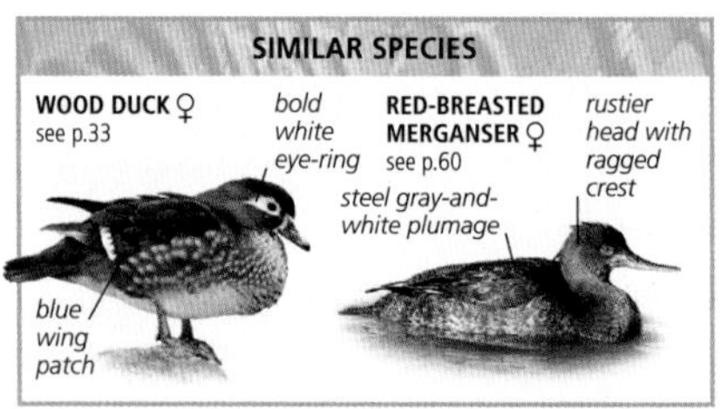
WOOD DUCK ♀
see p.33
bold white eye-ring
blue wing patch
RED-BREASTED MERGANSER ♀
see p.60
rustier head with ragged crest
steel gray-and-white plumage

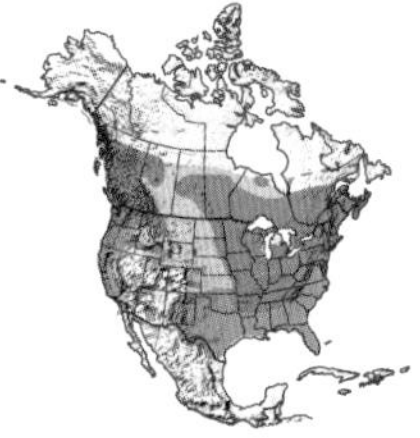

OCCURRENCE
Prefers forested small ponds, marshes, or slow-moving streams during the breeding season. During winter, occurs in shallow water in both fresh- and saltwater bays, estuaries, rivers, streams, ponds, freshwater marshes, and flooded sloughs.

Length **15½–19½in (40–49cm)**	Wingspan **23½–26in (60–66cm)**	Weight **16–31oz (450–875g)**
Social **Small flocks**	Lifespan **At least 11 years**	Status **Secure**

DATE: ____________ TIME: ____________ LOCATION: ____________

Order **Anseriformes**	Family **Anatidae**	Species ***Mergus merganser***

Common Merganser

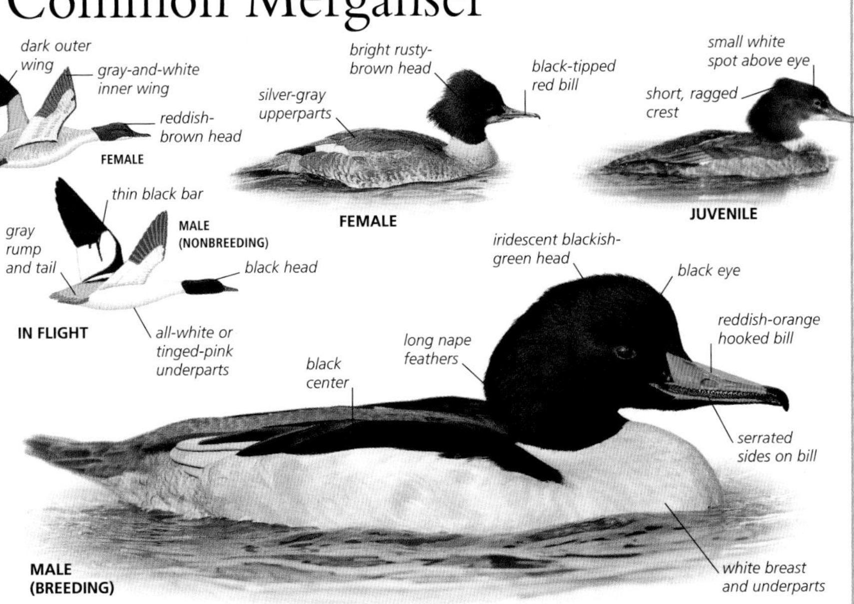
dark outer wing
gray-and-white inner wing
reddish-brown head
FEMALE
bright rusty-brown head
silver-gray upperparts
black-tipped red bill
FEMALE
small white spot above eye
short, ragged crest
JUVENILE
thin black bar
gray rump and tail
MALE (NONBREEDING)
black head
IN FLIGHT
all-white or tinged-pink underparts
iridescent blackish-green head
black eye
reddish-orange hooked bill
long nape feathers
black center
serrated sides on bill
MALE (BREEDING)
white breast and underparts

The largest of the three merganser species in North America, the Common Merganser is called a Goosander in the UK. This large fish-eater is common and widespread, particularly in the northern portion of its range. It is often found in big flocks on lakes or smaller groups along rivers. It spends most of its time on the water, using its serrated bill to catch fish underwater.

VOICE Mostly silent, except when alarmed or during courtship; females give a low-pitched harsh *karr* or *gruk*, the latter also given in series; during courtship, males emit a high-pitched, bell-like note and other twangy notes; alarm call a hoarse *grrr* or *wak*.

NESTING Cavity-nester sometimes high in trees; uses nest boxes, nests on ground; 6–17 eggs; 1 brood; April–September.

FEEDING Eats mostly fish (especially fond of trout and salmon, but also carp and catfish), aquatic invertebrates, frogs, small mammals, birds, and plants.

FLIGHT: fast with shallow wing beats; often flying low over the water.

FEEDING ON THE MOVE
This female Common Merganser is trying to swallow, headfirst, a rather large fish.

SIMILAR SPECIES

COMMON GOLDENEYE ♂ see p.56

RED-BREASTED MERGANSER ♀ see p.60

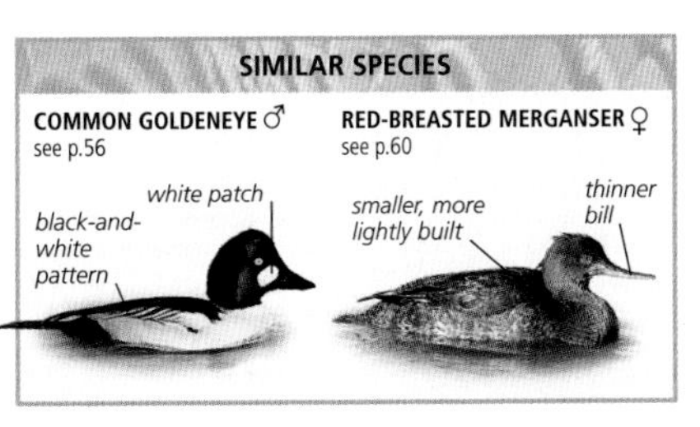
white patch
black-and-white pattern
smaller, more lightly built
thinner bill

OCCURRENCE
Breeds in the northerly forests from Alaska to Newfoundland; winters south to north central Mexico. Being very hardy, it will winter farther north than most other waterfowl as long as water remains open. Prefers fresh- to saltwater locations.

Length **21½–28in (54–71cm)**	Wingspan **34in (86cm)**	Weight **1¾–4¾lb (0.8–2.1kg)**
Social **Flocks**	Lifespan **Up to 13 years**	Status **Secure**

DATE: ____________ TIME: ____________ LOCATION: ____________________

Order **Anseriformes**	Family **Anatidae**	Species ***Mergus serrator***

Red-breasted Merganser

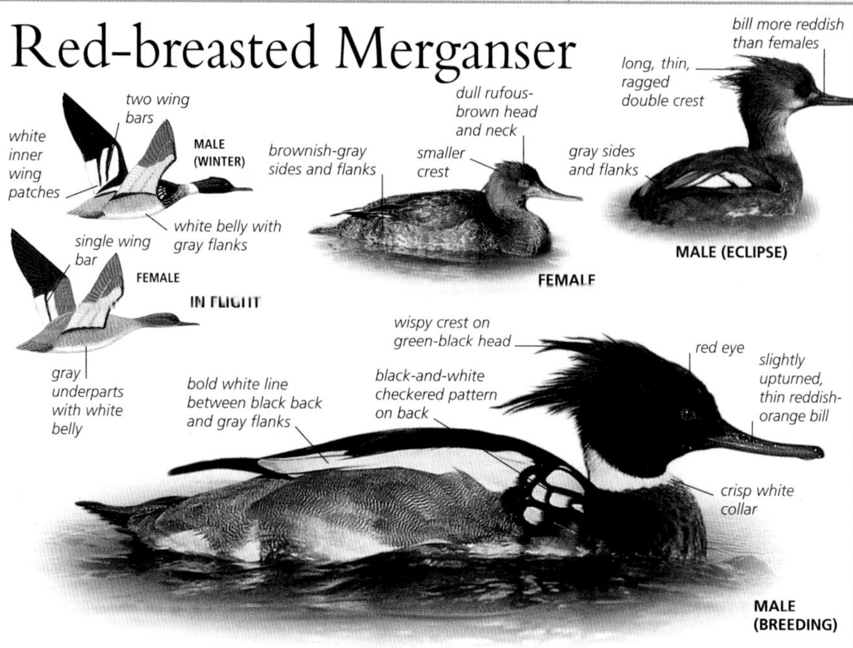

two wing bars
white inner wing patches
MALE (WINTER)
white belly with gray flanks
single wing bar
FEMALE
IN FLIGHT
gray underparts with white belly
brownish-gray sides and flanks
dull rufous-brown head and neck
smaller crest
FEMALE
bill more reddish than females
long, thin, ragged double crest
gray sides and flanks
MALE (ECLIPSE)
wispy crest on green-black head
red eye
slightly upturned, thin reddish-orange bill
bold white line between black back and gray flanks
black-and-white checkered pattern on back
crisp white collar
MALE (BREEDING)

The Red-breasted Merganser, like the other saw-billed mergansers, is an elegant fish-eating duck. Both sexes are easily recognized by their long, sparse, somewhat ragged-looking double crest. Red-breasted Mergansers are smaller than Common Mergansers, but much larger than the Hooded. The Red-breasted Merganser, unlike the other two mergansers, nests on the ground, in loose colonies, often among gulls and terns, and is protected by its neighbors.

VOICE During courtship males make a raucous *yeow-yeow* call; females emit a raspy *krrr-krrr.*

NESTING Shallow depression on ground lined with down and plant material, near water; 5–11 eggs; 1 brood; May–July.

FEEDING Dives for small fish, such as herring and minnows; also salmon eggs; at times flocks coordinate and drive fish together.

FLIGHT: fast flying duck with very rapid, regular, and shallow flapping.

KEEPING CLOSE
Red-breasted Mergansers are gregarious at all times of year, often feeding in loose flocks.

SIMILAR SPECIES

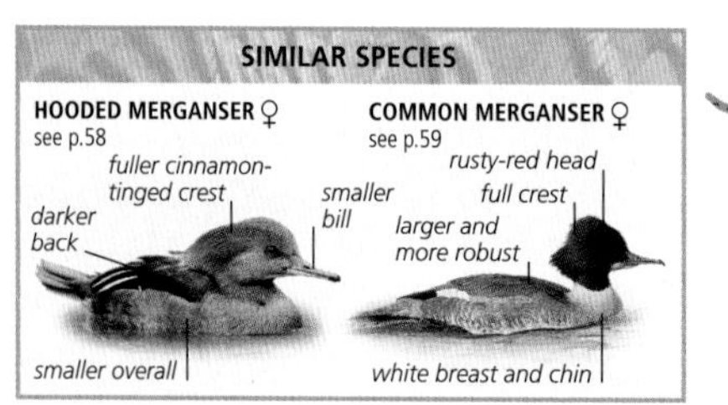

HOODED MERGANSER ♀
see p.58
fuller cinnamon-tinged crest
darker back
smaller bill
smaller overall
COMMON MERGANSER ♀
see p.59
rusty-red head
full crest
larger and more robust
white breast and chin

OCCURRENCE
Most northerly range of all the mergansers, nests across the Arctic and sub-Arctic regions, tundra and northerly forests, along coasts, inland lakes, river banks, marsh edges, and coastal islands. Winters farther south than other mergansers, mostly in protected bays, estuaries, or on the Great Lakes.

Length **20–25in (51–64cm)**	Wingspan **26–29in (66–74cm)**	Weight **1¾–2¾lb (0.8–1.3kg)**
Social **Flocks/Colonies**	Lifespan **Up to 9 years**	Status **Secure**

DATE: ____________ TIME: ____________ LOCATION: ____________

Order **Anseriformes**	Family **Anatidae**	Species ***Oxyura jamaicensis***

Ruddy Duck

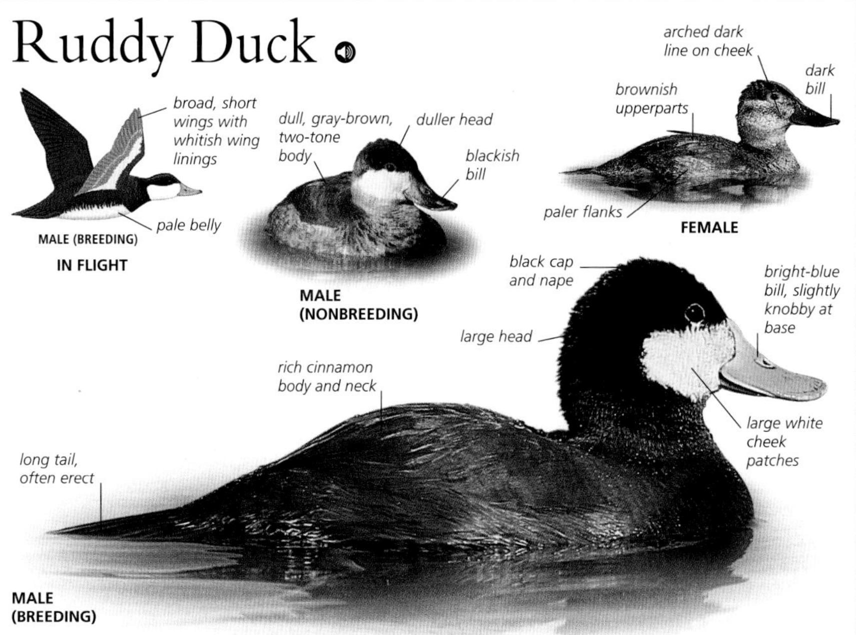
broad, short wings with whitish wing linings
pale belly
MALE (BREEDING)
IN FLIGHT
dull, gray-brown, two-tone body
duller head
blackish bill
MALE (NONBREEDING)
arched dark line on cheek
dark bill
brownish upperparts
paler flanks
FEMALE
black cap and nape
bright-blue bill, slightly knobby at base
large head
rich cinnamon body and neck
large white cheek patches
long tail, often erect
MALE (BREEDING)

Small and stiff-tailed, the Ruddy Duck is comical in both its appearance and behavior. Both sexes often hold their tail in a cocked position, especially when sleeping. During courtship displays, the male points its long tail skyward while rapidly thumping its electric-blue bill against its chest, ending the performance with an odd, bubbling sound. In another display, males make a popping sound by slapping their feet on the water's surface. Large feet, on legs set far back on its body, make the Ruddy Duck an excellent swimmer and diver; however, on land it is perhaps one of the most awkward of diving ducks. Females are known to push themselves along instead of walking.

VOICE Females give a nasal *raanh* and high-pitched *eeek*; males are vocally silent, but make popping noises with feet.

NESTING Platform, bowl-shaped nest built over water in thick emergent vegetation, rarely on land; 6–10 eggs; 1 brood; May–September.

FEEDING Dives for aquatic insects, larvae, crustaceans, and other invertebrates, particularly when breeding; during winter, also eats plants.

FLIGHT: rapid and direct, with fast wing beats; not very agile in flight, which seems labored.

HEAVY HEAD
A female "sitting" on the water streamlines her body ready to dive, making her look large-headed.

SIMILAR SPECIES

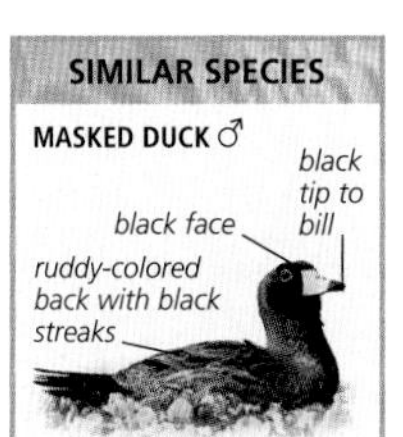
MASKED DUCK ♂
black tip to bill
black face
ruddy-colored back with black streaks

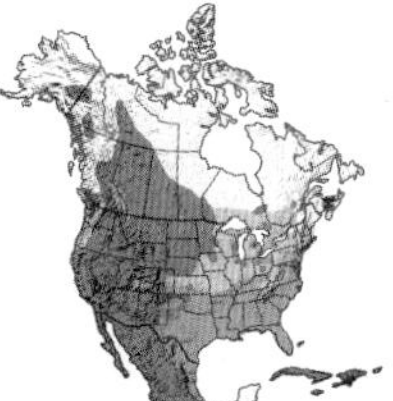

OCCURRENCE
Breeds in the Prairie Pothole Region in wetland habitats; marshes, ponds, reservoirs, and other open shallow water with emergent vegetation and open areas. Majority winter on freshwater habitats from ponds to large lakes; smaller numbers found on brackish coastal marshes, bays, and estuaries.

Length **14–17in (35–43cm)**	Wingspan **22–24in (56–62cm)**	Weight **11–30oz (300–850g)**
Social **Flocks**	Lifespan **Up to 13 years**	Status **Secure**

DATE: ____________ TIME: ____________ LOCATION: ____________

Families **Odontophoridae, Phasianidae**

QUAILS, GROUSE, TURKEYS, AND RELATIVES

THIS DIVERSE AND ADAPTABLE group of birds thrives in habitats ranging from hot desert to frozen tundra. They spend most of the time on the ground, springing loudly into the air when alarmed.

NEW WORLD QUAILS

Among the most terrestrial of all galliforms, quails are also renowned for their great sociability, often forming large family groups, or "coveys," of up to 100 birds. The five species found in western North America each live in a specific habitat or at a particular elevation, but the single species found in the East, the Northern Bobwhite, ranges over a variety of habitats.

GROUSE

The most diverse and widespread birds in the order Galliformes in North America, the 12 different species of grouse can be divided into three groups based on their preferred habitats. Forest grouse include the Ruffed Grouse in the East, the Spruce Grouse in the North, and the Sooty Grouse and Dusky Grouse in the West. Prairie grouse, including the Sharp-tailed Grouse, are found throughout the middle of the continent. All three tundra and mountaintop grouse or ptarmigans are found in the extreme North and the Rockies. Grouse often possess patterns that match their surroundings, providing camouflage from enemies both animal and human.

GRASSLAND GROUSE
The aptly named Sharp-tailed Grouse is locally common in western prairies, strutting in search of grasshoppers.

DRESSED TO THRILL
With its striking plumage, the Ring-necked Pheasant is an impressive sight when flushed out of its cover.

PHEASANTS AND PARTRIDGES

These Eurasian birds were introduced into North America in the 19th and 20th centuries to provide additional targets for recreational hunters. While some introductions failed, species such as the colorful Ring-necked Pheasant adapted well in the new environment and now thrive in established populations.

SNOW BIRD
The Rock Ptarmigan's white winter plumage camouflages it against the snow, helping to hide it from predators.

Order **Galliformes**	Family **Odontophoridae**	Species ***Colinus virginianus***

Northern Bobwhite

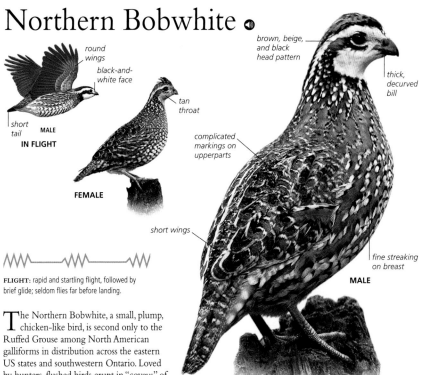

round wings
black-and-white face
short tail
MALE
IN FLIGHT

tan throat
FEMALE

brown, beige, and black head pattern
thick, decurved bill
complicated markings on upperparts
short wings
fine streaking on breast
MALE

FLIGHT: rapid and startling flight, followed by brief glide; seldom flies far before landing.

The Northern Bobwhite, a small, plump, chicken-like bird, is second only to the Ruffed Grouse among North American galliforms in distribution across the eastern US states and southwestern Ontario. Loved by hunters, flushed birds erupt in "coveys" of 10 to 20 individuals, bursting from groundcover and dispersing in many directions. Large numbers are raised in captivity and released to supplement wild populations for hunting.

VOICE Characteristic *bob-WHITE* or *bob-bob-WHITE* whistled by males in breeding season; call to reunite flock includes *hoi-lee* and *hoi* following dispersal.

NESTING Shallow depression lined with plant matter, located on ground within sight of an opening; 10–15 eggs; sometimes multiple broods per season; January–March.

FEEDING Forages for wide variety of plant matter (seeds, buds, leaves), and insects, snails, and spiders, depending on the season.

COVEY LIFE
Male, female, and juvenile Northern Bobwhites live together in tight flocks called coveys.

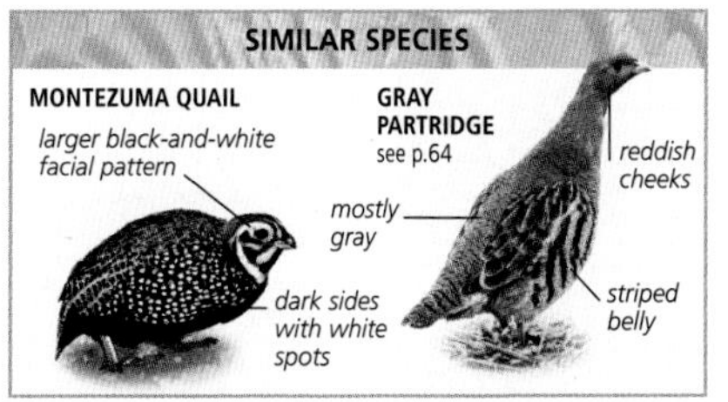
SIMILAR SPECIES
MONTEZUMA QUAIL
larger black-and-white facial pattern
dark sides with white spots
GRAY PARTRIDGE
see p.64
mostly gray
reddish cheeks
striped belly

OCCURRENCE
Widely distributed but only locally common in much of the eastern US and southwestern Ontario, and in Mexico, southward to Guatemala. Most often associated with agricultural fields, it thrives in a patchwork of mixed young forests, fields, and brushy hedges. A permanent resident.

Length **8–10in (20–25cm)**	Wingspan **11–14in (28–35cm)**	Weight **6oz (175g)**
Social **Small flocks**	Lifespan **Up to 6 years**	Status **Declining**

DATE: ____________ TIME: ____________ LOCATION: ____________

Order **Galliformes**	Family **Phasianidae**	Species ***Perdix perdix***

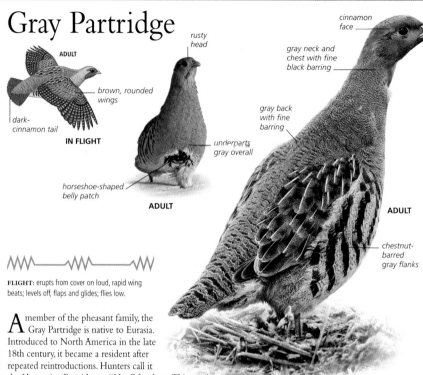

Gray Partridge

ADULT

brown, rounded wings

dark-cinnamon tail

IN FLIGHT

rusty head

underparts gray overall

horseshoe-shaped belly patch

ADULT

cinnamon face

gray neck and chest with fine black barring

gray back with fine barring

ADULT

chestnut-barred gray flanks

FLIGHT: erupts from cover on loud, rapid wing beats; levels off, flaps and glides; flies low.

A member of the pheasant family, the Gray Partridge is native to Eurasia. Introduced to North America in the late 18th century, it became a resident after repeated reintroductions. Hunters call it the Hungarian Partridge or "Hun" for short. This species has benefited from the mixture of agricultural and fallow fields, which resulted from long-term conservation programs, and its population is stable or expanding in the west. The isolated eastern populations, however, are declining due to changes in land use. This species is popular with hunters in both North America and Europe.

VOICE Short *kuk-kuk-kuk*, quickly and in a series when alarmed; *prruk-prruk* between adults and young when threatened.

NESTING Shallow depression in soil lined with vegetation, usually in hedgerows; 14–18 eggs; 1 brood; March–May.

FEEDING Eats mostly seeds and row crops such as corn and wheat; succulent green leaves in spring; insects when breeding.

NOISY TAKEOFF
When the Gray Partridge takes flight, its wings make a loud whirring sound.

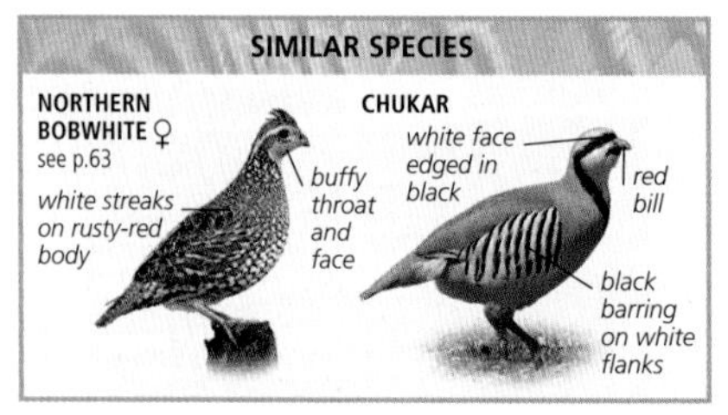
SIMILAR SPECIES
NORTHERN BOBWHITE ♀
see p.63
white streaks on rusty-red body
buffy throat and face
CHUKAR
white face edged in black
red bill
black barring on white flanks

OCCURRENCE
Primarily agricultural fields of crops including corn, wheat, and oats, as well as associated hedgerows and fallow grasslands. Most birds are nonmigratory, but there is some movement by eastern birds after breeding.

Length **11–13in (28–33cm)**	Wingspan **17–20in (43–51cm)**	Weight **12–18oz (350–500g)**
Social **Family groups**	Lifespan **Up to 4 years**	Status **Declining**

DATE: ____________ TIME: ____________ LOCATION: ____________

Order **Galliformes**	Family **Phasianidae**	Species ***Phasianus colchicus***

Ring-necked Pheasant

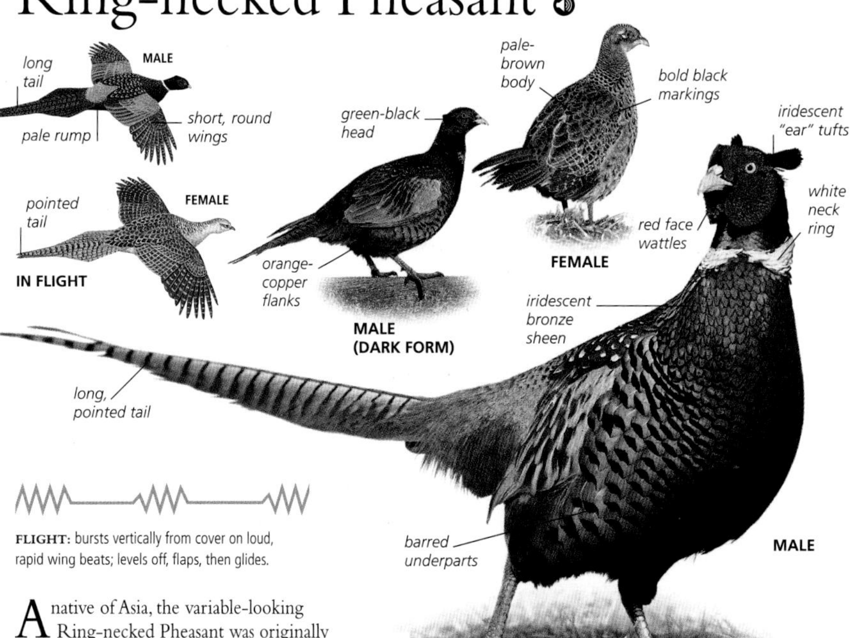
long tail
MALE
short, round wings
pale rump
pointed tail
FEMALE
IN FLIGHT
green-black head
orange-copper flanks
MALE (DARK FORM)
pale-brown body
bold black markings
FEMALE
red face wattles
iridescent "ear" tufts
white neck ring
iridescent bronze sheen
long, pointed tail
barred underparts
MALE

FLIGHT: bursts vertically from cover on loud, rapid wing beats; levels off, flaps, then glides.

A native of Asia, the variable-looking Ring-necked Pheasant was originally introduced in North America for recreational hunting purposes, and is now widely distributed across North America. Birds released after being bred in captivity are used to supplement natural reproduction for hunting purposes. In the wild, several females may lay eggs in the same nest—a phenomenon called "egg-dumping." There is a less common dark form, which can be distinguished principally because it lacks the distinctive white band around the neck.

VOICE Male emits a loud, raucous, explosive double note, *Karrk-KORK*, followed by loud wing-flapping; both sexes cackle when flushed.

NESTING Shallow bowl composed of grasses, usually on ground in tall grass or among low shrubs; 7–15 eggs; 1 brood; March–June.

FEEDING Feeds on corn and other grain, seeds, fruit, row crops, grass, leaves, and shoots; eats insects when available.

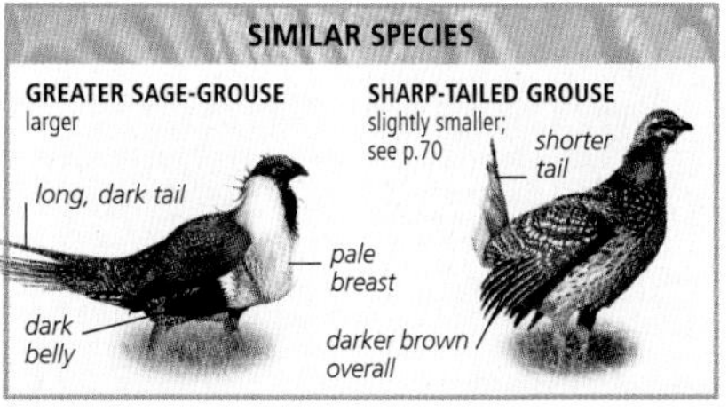
SIMILAR SPECIES
GREATER SAGE-GROUSE
larger
long, dark tail
pale breast
dark belly
SHARP-TAILED GROUSE
slightly smaller; see p.70
shorter tail
darker brown overall

FLUSHED OUT
The Ring-necked Pheasant is a powerful flier when alarmed or flushed out of its cover.

OCCURRENCE
Widespread across southern Canada and the US; prefers mixture of active agricultural crops (especially corn fields), fallow fields, and hedgerows; also cattail marshes and wooded river bottoms. The Ring-necked Pheasant is native to Asia from the Caucasus to China.

Length **19½–28in (50–70cm)**	Wingspan **30–34in (76–86cm)**	Weight **1¼–6½lb (0.5–3kg)**
Social **Solitary/Flocks**	Lifespan **Up to 4 years**	Status **Secure**

DATE: ______________ TIME: ______________ LOCATION: ______________

Order **Galliformes**	Family **Phasianidae**	Species ***Bonasa umbellus***

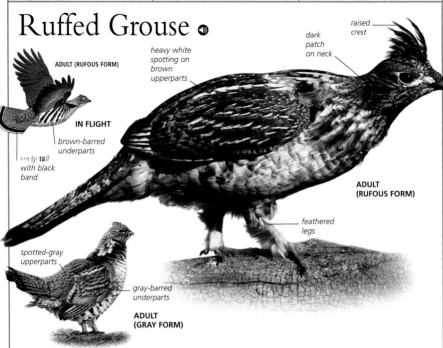

Ruffed Grouse

ADULT (RUFOUS FORM)

IN FLIGHT

brown-barred underparts

rufous tail with black band

heavy white spotting on brown upperparts

dark patch on neck

raised crest

ADULT (RUFOUS FORM)

feathered legs

spotted-gray upperparts

gray-barred underparts

ADULT (GRAY FORM)

The Ruffed Grouse is perhaps the most widespread galliform in North America. There are two color forms, rufous and gray. Both allow the birds to remain camouflaged and undetected on the forest floor, until they eventually burst into the air in an explosion of whirring wings. The male is well known for his extraordinary wing beating or "drumming" display, which he performs year-round, but most frequently in the spring.

VOICE Hissing notes, and soft *purrt, purrt, purrt* when alarmed, by both sexes; male's "drumming" display when heard from distance resembles beating fists on one's chest, *thump…thump…thump...thump… thump…thuthuthuth.*

NESTING Shallow, leaf-lined bowl set against a tree trunk, rock or fallen log in forest; 6–14 eggs; 1 brood; March–June.

FEEDING Forages on ground for leaves, buds, and fruit; occasionally insects.

FLIGHT: an explosive takeoff, usually at close range, glides for a short distance before landing.

SIMILAR SPECIES

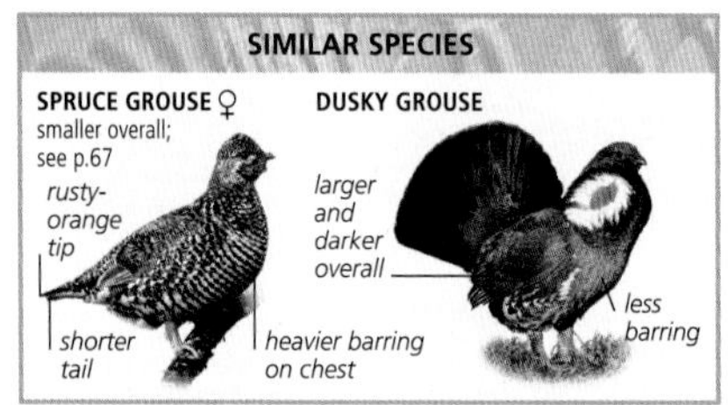
SPRUCE GROUSE ♀
smaller overall; see p.67
rusty-orange tip
shorter tail
heavier barring on chest
DUSKY GROUSE
larger and darker overall
less barring

WARM RED
The rufous form of the Ruffed Grouse is more common in hotter parts of the continent.

OCCURRENCE
Found in young, mixed habitat forests throughout northern US and Canada. Southern edge of range extends along higher elevations of the Appalachians and middle levels of the Rocky Mountains, if suitable habitat is available.

Length **17–20in (43–51cm)**	Wingspan **20–23in (51–58cm)**	Weight **20–22oz (575–625g)**
Social **Solitary/Small flocks**	Lifespan **Up to 10 years**	Status **Secure**

Order **Galliformes**	Family **Phasianidae**	Species ***Canachites canadensis***

Spruce Grouse

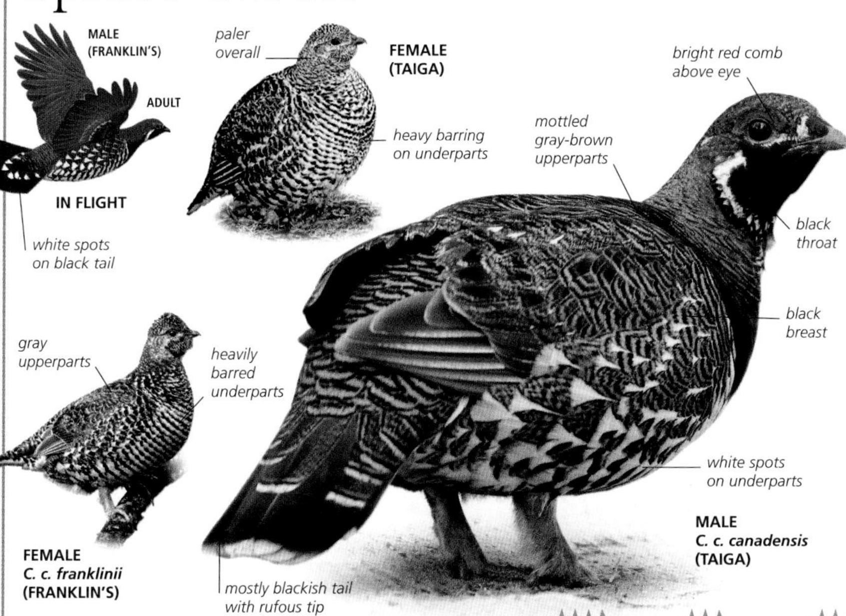
MALE (FRANKLIN'S)
ADULT
IN FLIGHT
white spots on black tail
paler overall
FEMALE (TAIGA)
heavy barring on underparts
mottled gray-brown upperparts
bright red comb above eye
black throat
black breast
gray upperparts
heavily barred underparts
white spots on underparts
MALE
C. c. canadensis
(TAIGA)
FEMALE
C. c. franklinii
(FRANKLIN'S)
mostly blackish tail with rufous tip

Perhaps because of the remoteness of their habitat and lack of human contact, Spruce Grouse are not afraid of humans. This lack of wariness when approached has earned them the name "fool hens." Their specialized diet of pine needles causes the intestinal tract to expand in order to accommodate a larger volume of food to compensate for its low nutritional value. There are two groups of Spruce Grouse, the Taiga and the Franklin's, both of which have red and gray forms.

VOICE Mostly silent; males clap their wings during courtship display; females often utter a long cackle at dawn and dusk.

NESTING Lined with moss, leaves, feathers; often at base of tree; naturally low area in forest floor; 4–6 eggs; 1 brood; May–July.

FEEDING Feeds mostly on pine but also spruce needles; will eat insects, leaves, fruit, and seeds when available.

FLIGHT: generally avoids flying; when disturbed, bursts into flight on whirring wings.

RUFOUS BAND
The male "Taiga" form displays the thin rufous band on the tip of his tail.

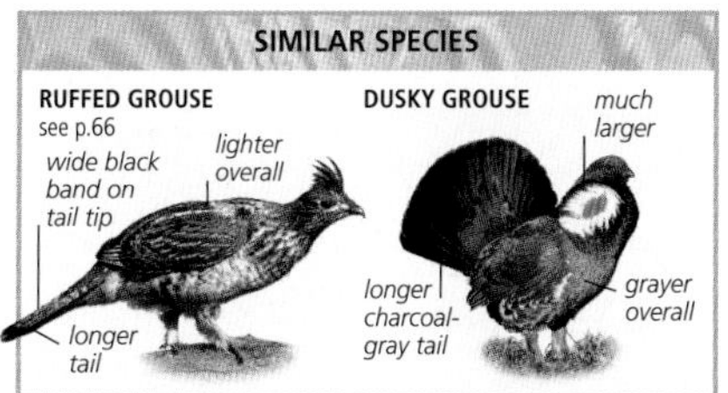
SIMILAR SPECIES
RUFFED GROUSE
see p.66
wide black band on tail tip
lighter overall
longer tail
DUSKY GROUSE
much larger
longer charcoal-gray tail
grayer overall

OCCURRENCE
Present year-round in forests dominated by conifers, including Jack pine, lodgepole pine, red spruce, black spruce, balsam fir, subalpine fir, hemlock, and cedar. Found from western Alaska to the Atlantic Coast.

Length **14–17in (36–43cm)**	Wingspan **21–23in (53–58cm)**	Weight **16oz (450g)**
Social **Solitary**	Lifespan **Up to 10 years**	Status **Secure**

DATE: ____________ TIME: ____________ LOCATION: ____________

Order **Galliformes**	Family **Phasianidae**	Species ***Lagopus lagopus***

Willow Ptarmigan

reddish-brown body
black tail
white between eye and black bill
ADULT (WINTER)
IN FLIGHT
MALE (SUMMER)
black bill
all-white body
ADULT (WINTER)
red comb
black bill
rich reddish-brown body
lacks red comb
yellow-brown body
FEMALE (SUMMER)
dark scaly bars
white belly
feathered feet
MALE (SUMMER)

FLIGHT: strong, rapid wing beats before gliding; prefers to walk.

The most common of the three ptarmigan species, the Willow Ptarmigan also undertakes the longest migration of the group. The Willow Ptarmigan is an unusual Galliform species, as male and female remain bonded throughout the chick-rearing process, in which the male is an active participant. The Red Grouse of British moors is a subspecies (*L. l. scoticus*) of the Willow Ptarmigan, but it is classified as a separate species by some.

VOICE Variety of purrs, clucks, hissing, meowing noises; *Kow-Kow-Kow* call given before flushing, possibly alerting others.

NESTING Shallow bowl scraped in soil, lined with plant matter, protected by overhead cover; 8–10 eggs; 1 brood; March–May.

FEEDING Mostly eats buds, stems, and seeds, but also flowers, insects, and leaves when available.

PERFECT BLEND-IN
Its reddish-brown upperparts camouflage this summer ptarmigan in the shrubby areas it inhabits.

SIMILAR SPECIES
WHITE-TAILED PTARMIGAN ☼
browner plumage
smaller overall
ROCK PTARMIGAN ☼
see p.69
grayer plumage
white belly

OCCURRENCE
Prefers tundra in the Arctic, sub-Arctic, and subalpine regions. Thrives in willow thickets along low moist river corridors; also in the low woodlands of the sub-Arctic tundra.

Length **14–17½in (35–44cm)**	Wingspan **22–24in (56–61cm)**	Weight **15–28oz (425–800g)**
Social **Winter flocks**	Lifespan **Up to 9 years**	Status **Secure**

Order **Galliformes**	Family **Phasianidae**	Species ***Lagopus muta***

Rock Ptarmigan

mostly gray upperparts
black tail
MALE (WINTER)
all-white wings
gray wing patch
IN FLIGHT
MALE (SUMMER)
small bill
white plumage
FEMALE (WINTER)
brown-and-black barring
white wings
mottled belly
FEMALE (SUMMER)
small, round head
red comb
small, delicate bill
"salt-and-pepper" barring on gray upperparts
black line between eye and bill
MALE (WINTER)
white belly
feathered feet
MALE (SUMMER)

FLIGHT: bursts into flight with rapid wing beats, followed by gliding and shallow flapping.

The Rock Ptarmigan is the most northerly of the three ptarmigan species found in North America. Although some birds make a short migration to more southern wintering grounds, many remain on their breeding grounds year-round. This species is well known for its distinctive seasonal variation in plumage, which helps to camouflage it against its surroundings. The Rock Ptarmigan is the official bird of Nunavut Territory.

VOICE Quiet; male call a raspy *krrrh*, also growls and clucks.

NESTING Small scrape or natural depression, lined with plant matter, often away from cover; 8–10 eggs; 1 brood; April–June.

FEEDING Feeds on buds, seeds, flowers, and leaves, especially birch and willow; eats insects in summer.

IN BETWEEN PLUMAGE
Various transitional plumage patterns can be seen on the Rock Ptarmigan in spring and fall.

SIMILAR SPECIES

WHITE-TAILED PTARMIGAN ☼
all-white tail in winter
smaller overall
lighter brown upperparts

WILLOW PTARMIGAN ☼
see p.68
larger overall

OCCURRENCE
Prefers dry, rocky tundra and shrubby ridge tops; will use edges of open meadows and dense evergreen stands along fairly high-elevation rivers and streams during winter. Occurs throughout the Northern Hemisphere in the Arctic tundra from Iceland to Kamchatka in far east Russia.

Length **12½–15½in (32–40cm)**	Wingspan **19½–23½in (50–60cm)**	Weight **16–23oz (450–650g)**
Social **Winter flocks**	Lifespan **Up to 8 years**	Status **Secure**

DATE: ____________ TIME: ____________ LOCATION: ____________

Order **Galliformes**	Family **Phasianidae**	Species ***Tympanuchus phasianellus***

Sharp-tailed Grouse

ADULT

mottled wings

IN FLIGHT

pale, wedge-shaped tail with protruding central feathers

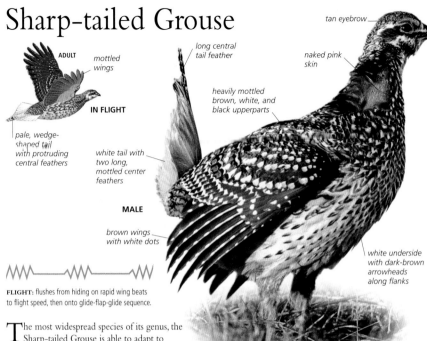

long central tail feather

tan eyebrow

naked pink skin

heavily mottled brown, white, and black upperparts

white tail with two long, mottled center feathers

MALE

brown wings with white dots

white underside with dark-brown arrowheads along flanks

FLIGHT: flushes from hiding on rapid wing beats to flight speed, then onto glide-flap-glide sequence.

The most widespread species of its genus, the Sharp-tailed Grouse is able to adapt to the greatest variety of habitats. It is not migratory, but undertakes seasonal movements between grassland summer habitats and woodland winter habitats. Elements of this grouse's spectacular courtship display have been incorporated into the culture and dance of Native American people, including foot stomping and tail feather rattling. The Sharp-tailed Grouse is the provincial bird of Saskatchewan.

VOICE Male calls a variety of unusual clucks, cooing, barks, and gobbles during courtship; females cluck with different intonations.

NESTING Shallow depression lined with plant matter close at hand as well as some feathers from the female, usually near overhead cover; 10–12 eggs; 1 brood; March–May.

FEEDING Forages primarily for seeds, leaves, buds, and fruit; also takes insects and flowers when available.

PRAIRIE DANCER
The courtship dance of the Sharp-tailed Grouse heralds the arrival of spring to the grasslands.

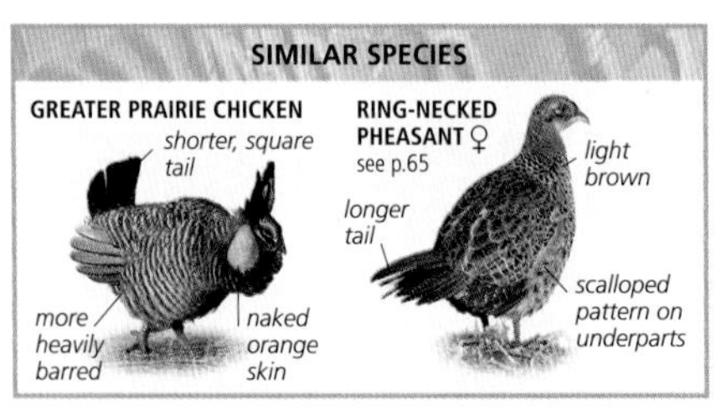
SIMILAR SPECIES
GREATER PRAIRIE CHICKEN
shorter, square tail
more heavily barred
naked orange skin
RING-NECKED PHEASANT ♀
see p.65
light brown
longer tail
scalloped pattern on underparts

OCCURRENCE
Has a northern and western distribution in North America, from Alaska (isolated population) southward across Canada to northern prairie states. Prefers a mixture of fallow and active agricultural fields combined with brushy forest edges and woodlots along river beds.

Length **15–19in (38–48cm)**	Wingspan **23–26in (58–66cm)**	Weight **26–34oz (750–950g)**
Social **Flocks**	Lifespan **Up to 7 years**	Status **Declining (p)**

DATE: ____________ TIME: ____________ LOCATION: ____________

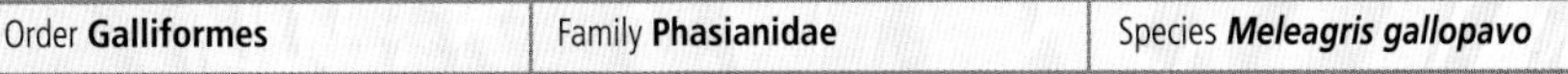
Order **Galliformes**
Family **Phasianidae**
Species ***Meleagris gallopavo***

Wild Turkey

MALE (EAST)
IN FLIGHT
rusty tail with black band
black-and-white barred wings
tail fanned in display
humped back
no feathers on head
long legs
JUVENILE
unfeathered blue-and-red head
large red wattles
hair-like "beard" on breast
dark overall
iridescent bronze-and-purplish body
FEMALE
dark body with bronze iridescence
MALE (WEST)

Once proposed by Benjamin Franklin as the national emblem of the US, the Wild Turkey—the largest galliform in North America—was eliminated from most of its original range by the early 1900s due to over-hunting and habitat destruction. Since then, habitat restoration and the subsequent reintroduction of Wild Turkeys has been very successful.

VOICE Well-known gobble, given by males especially during courtship; female makes various yelps, clucks, and purrs, based on mood and threat level.

NESTING Scrape on ground lined with grass; placed against or under protective cover; 10–15 eggs; 1 brood; March–June.

FEEDING Omnivorous, it scratches in leaf litter on forest floor for acorns and other food, mostly vegetation; also takes plants and insects from agricultural fields.

FLIGHT: after running, leaps into the air with loud, rapid wing beats, then glides.

COLLECTIVE DISPLAY
Once the population expands into new areas, numerous males will be seen displaying together.

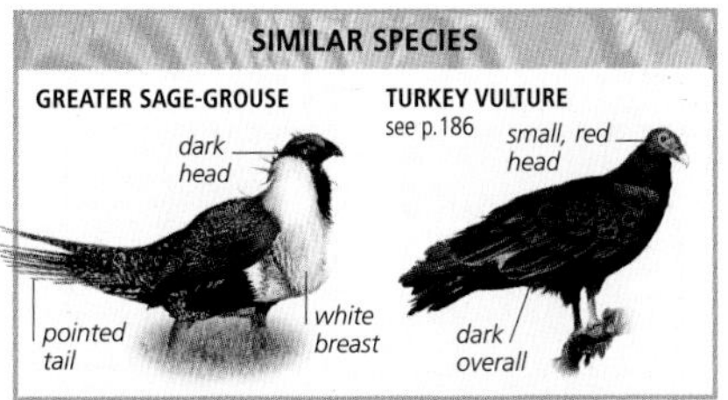
SIMILAR SPECIES
GREATER SAGE-GROUSE
dark head
pointed tail
white breast
TURKEY VULTURE
see p.186
small, red head
dark overall

OCCURRENCE
Found in mixed mature woodlands and fields with agricultural crops; also in various grasslands, close to swamps, but adaptable and increasingly common in suburban and urban habitats. Quite widespread, but patchily distributed across the US and southern Canada.

Length **2¾–4ft (0.9–1.2m)**	Wingspan **4–5ft (1.2–1.5m)**	Weight **10–24lb (4.5–11kg)**
Social **Flocks**	Lifespan **Up to 9 years**	Status **Secure**

DATE: ______________ TIME: ______________ LOCATION: ______________________________

Family **Podicipedidae**

GREBES

GREBES RESEMBLE LOONS and share many of their aquatic habits, but anatomical and molecular features show that they are actually unrelated; and they are placed in a different order: the Podicipediformes. Grebe bodies are streamlined, offering little resistance when diving and swimming. Underwater, their primary means of propulsion is the sideways motion of their lobed toes. The legs are placed far back on the body, which greatly aids the bird when swimming above or below the surface. Grebes have short tails, and their trailing legs and toes serve as rudders when they fly. The position of the legs makes it impossible, however, for grebes to stand upright for long or to easily walk on land. Thus, even when breeding, they are tied to water; and their nests are usually partially floating platforms, built on beds of water plants. Grebes' toes have broad lobes that splay when the bird thrusts forward through the water with its feet. They dive to catch fish with a short, forward-arching spring. Unusual among birds, they swallow feathers, supposedly to trap fish bones and protect their stomachs, then periodically disgorge them. Like loons, grebes can control their buoyancy by exhaling air and compressing their plumage so that they sink quietly below the surface. They are strong fliers, as well as migratory.

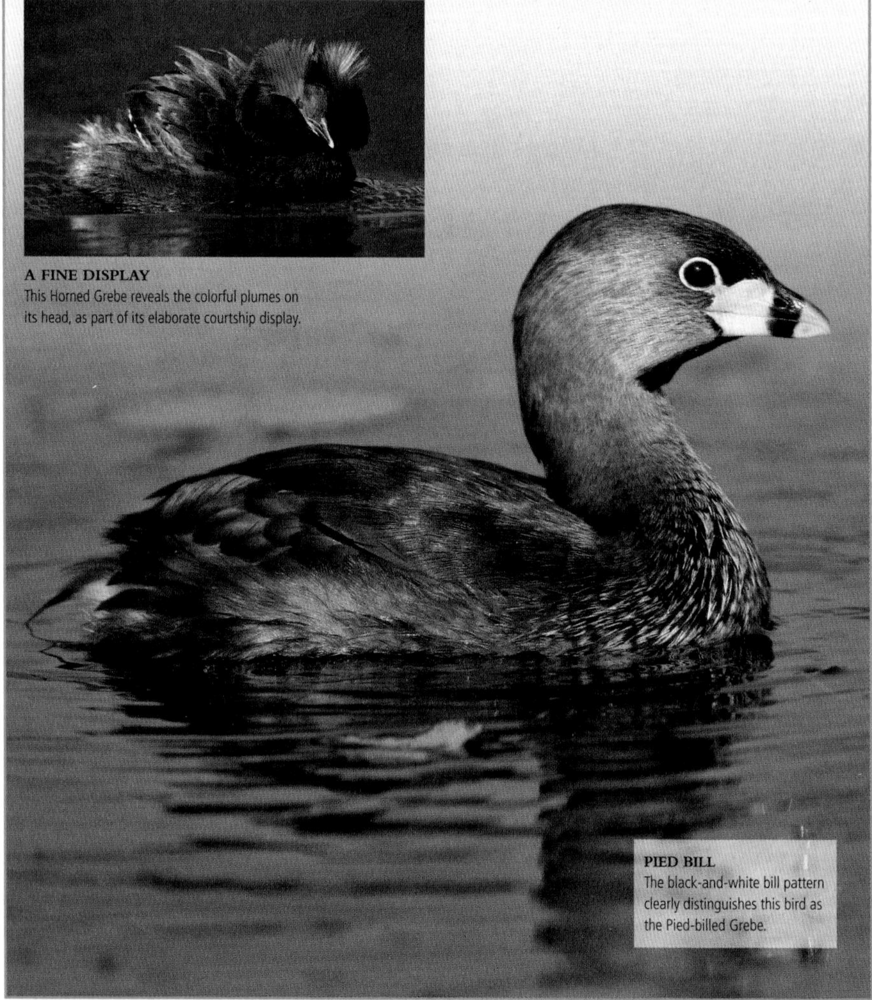

A FINE DISPLAY
This Horned Grebe reveals the colorful plumes on its head, as part of its elaborate courtship display.

PIED BILL
The black-and-white bill pattern clearly distinguishes this bird as the Pied-billed Grebe.

Order **Podicipediformes**	Family **Podicipedidae**	Species ***Podilymbus podiceps***

Pied-billed Grebe

outstretched neck
ADULT (BREEDING)
lighter flight feathers
IN FLIGHT
yellowish bill
whitish throat
ADULT (NONBREEDING)
brown eye
whitish hooked bill with a black ring
black throat patch
reddish-brown neck and breast
brownish-gray body
ADULT (BREEDING)
white undertail

The widest ranging of the North American grebes, the Pied-billed Grebe is tolerant of highly populated areas and is often seen breeding on lakes and ponds across North America. It is a powerful swimmer and can remain submerged for 16–30 seconds when it dives. In contrast to some of the elaborate displays from other grebe species, its courtship ritual is more vocal than visual, and a pair usually duet-call in the mating season. Migration, conducted at night, is delayed until its breeding area ices up and food becomes scarce. The Pied-billed Grebe is capable of sustained flights of over 2,000 miles (3,200km).

VOICE Various grunts and wails; in spring, call a cuckoo-like repeated gobble *kup-kup-Kaow-Kaow-kaow*, gradually speeding up.

NESTING Floating nest of partially decayed plants and clipped leaves, attached to emergent vegetation in marshes and quiet waters; 4–7 eggs; 2 broods; April–October.

FEEDING Dives to catch a variety of crustaceans, fish, amphibians, insects, and other invertebrates; also picks prey from emergent vegetation, or catches them mid-air.

FLIGHT: strong, direct flight with rapid wing beats, but rarely seen.

BACK OFF
When alarmed, a Pied-billed Grebe will flap its wings in a defensive display.

SIMILAR SPECIES

LEAST GREBE ☼

smaller bill
yellow eye
darker body

OCCURRENCE
Breeds on a variety of water bodies, including coastal brackish ponds, seasonal ponds, marshes, and even sewage ponds. Winters in the breeding area if food and open water are available, otherwise chooses still waters resembling its breeding habitat.

Length **12–15in (31–38cm)**	Wingspan **18–24in (46–62cm)**	Weight **13–17oz (375–475g)**
Social **Family groups**	Lifespan **At least 3 years**	Status **Vulnerable**

DATE: ____________ TIME: ____________ LOCATION: ______________________

Order **Podicipediformes**	Family **Podicipedidae**	Species ***Podiceps auritus***

Horned Grebe

flattish top of head
white cheek
black crown
white sides to neck
neck and head in line with body
red eye
ADULT (SUMMER)
ADULT (WINTER)
gold streak from eye to nape
IN FLIGHT
short, dark bill with whitish tip
ADULT (SPRING MOLT)
rufous neck
black throat
ADULT (SUMMER)

The timing of the Horned Grebe's migration depends largely on the weather—this species may not leave until its breeding grounds get iced over, nor does it arrive before the ice melts. Its breeding behavior is well documented since it is approachable on nesting grounds and has an elaborate breeding ritual. This grebe's so-called "horns" are, in fact, yellowish feather patches located behind its eyes, which it can raise at will.

VOICE At least 10 calls, but descending *aaanrrh* call most common in winter, ends in trill; muted conversational calls when birds are in groups.

NESTING Floating, soggy nest, hidden in vegetation, in small ponds and lake inlets; 3–9 eggs; 1 brood; May–July.

FEEDING Dives in open water or forages among plants, mainly for small crustaceans and insects, but also leeches, mollusks, amphibians, fish, and some vegetation.

FLIGHT: strong, rapid wing beats; runs on water to become airborne; rarely takes off from land.

HITCHING A RIDE
In common with other grebes, Horned Grebe chicks often ride on the back of a swimming parent.

SIMILAR SPECIES

RED-NECKED GREBE ❄ see p.75
brownish cap
darker eye

EARED GREBE ❄ see p.76
upturned bill
dark cheek

OCCURRENCE
Breeds in small freshwater, even slightly brackish, ponds and marshes, including artificial ponds. Prefers areas with open water and patches of sedges, cattails, and other wetland vegetation in any ecosystem. Winters on saltwater close to shore; also on large bodies of freshwater.

Length **12–15in (30–38cm)**	Wingspan **18–24in (46–62cm)**	Weight **11–20oz (300–575g)**
Social **Pairs/Loose flocks/Colonies**	Lifespan **Up to 5 years**	Status **Special Concern**

DATE: ____________ TIME: ____________ LOCATION: ____________

Order **Podicipediformes**	Family **Podicipedidae**	Species ***Podiceps grisegena***

Red-necked Grebe

head and neck in line with body
white-edged inner wing
ADULT (BREEDING)
IN FLIGHT
brownish cap
pale reddish-brown crescent near ear
ADULT (NONBREEDING)
broad stripes on cheek and ear
mostly yellowish bill
JUVENILE
broad head with crest at rear
black cap
brown eye
grayish-white cheeks and throat
chestnut-brown neck and chest
gray flanks
ADULT (BREEDING)

The Red-necked Grebe is smaller than Western and Clark's Grebes, but larger than the other North American grebes. It migrates over short to medium distances and spends the winter along both coasts, where large flocks may be seen during the day. It runs along the water's surface to become airborne, although it rarely flies. This grebe doesn't come ashore often; it stands erect, but walks awkwardly, and prefers to sink to its breast and shuffle along.

VOICE Nasal, gull-like call on breeding grounds, evolves into bray, ends with whinny; also honks, rattles, hisses, purrs, and ticks.

NESTING Compact, buoyant mound of decayed and fresh vegetation in sheltered, shallow marshes and lakes, or artificial wetlands; 4–5 eggs; 1 brood; May–July.

FEEDING An opportunistic hunter—eats fish, crustaceans, aquatic insects, worms, mollusks, salamanders, and tadpoles.

FLIGHT: fast, direct, wing beats, with head and outstretched neck mostly level with line of body.

COURTSHIP DISPLAY
This courting pair face each other, with outstretched necks and raised chests.

SIMILAR SPECIES

RED-THROATED LOON ❄ see p.159

HORNED GREBE ❄ see p.74

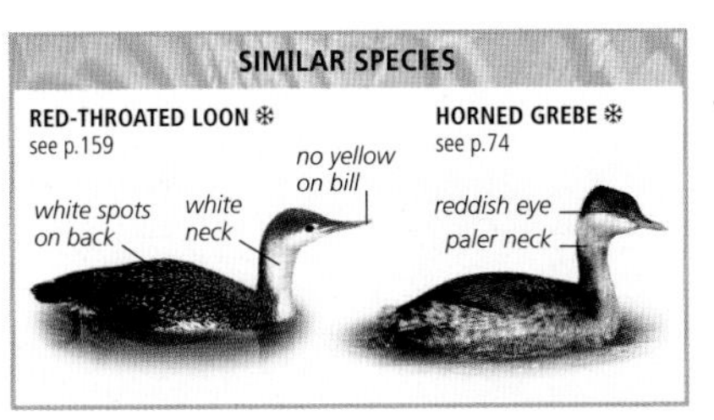
no yellow on bill
white spots on back
white neck
reddish eye
paler neck

OCCURRENCE
Breeds from northern prairies and forests, almost to the tree line in the northwest; limited to suitable interior bodies of water, such as large marshes and small lakes. Winters primarily in estuaries, inlets, bays, and offshore shallows along the Atlantic and Pacific Coasts; can also be found on the Great Lakes.

Length **16½–22in (42–56cm)**	Wingspan **24–35in (61–88cm)**	Weight **1¾–3½lb (0.8–1.6kg)**
Social **Pairs/Loose flocks**	Lifespan **Up to 6 years**	Status **Vulnerable**

DATE: ____________ TIME: ____________ LOCATION: ____________

Order **Podicipediformes**	Family **Podicipedidae**	Species ***Podiceps nigricollis***

Eared Grebe

white patch on wing
ADULT (SUMMER)
outstretched neck
IN FLIGHT
darker flanks
browner plumage
JUVENILE
dusky cheek
dusky white flanks
upturned bill
grayish neck
ADULT (WINTER)
black crest
red eye
large, wispy gold patch behind red eye
thin, upturned bill
dark back
black neck
rufous breast and sides
ADULT (SUMMER)

The most abundant grebe in North America, the Eared Grebe is quite remarkable in terms of physiology. After breeding, it undergoes a complex and drastic reorganization of body-fat stores, along with changes in muscle, heart, and digestive organ mass to prepare for fall migration. All of this increases the bird's energy reserves and body mass, but renders it flightless. It may have the longest periods of flightlessness of any flying bird—up to 10 months.

VOICE Various trills during courtship, including squeaky, rising *poo-eep*; sharp chirp when alarmed; usually silent at other times.

NESTING Sodden nest of decayed bottom plants anchored in thinly spaced reeds or submerged vegetation in shallow water of marshes, ponds, and lakes; 1 brood; 1–8 eggs; May–July.

FEEDING Forages underwater for small crustaceans and aquatic insects; also small fish and mollusks; consumes worms in winter.

FLIGHT: flies with neck outstretched, held at a low angle; rarely flies except during migration.

SALTY WATER
The Eared Grebe prefers salty water at all times except when breeding.

SIMILAR SPECIES

RED-NECKED GREBE ❄ see p.75

HORNED GREBE ❄ see p.74

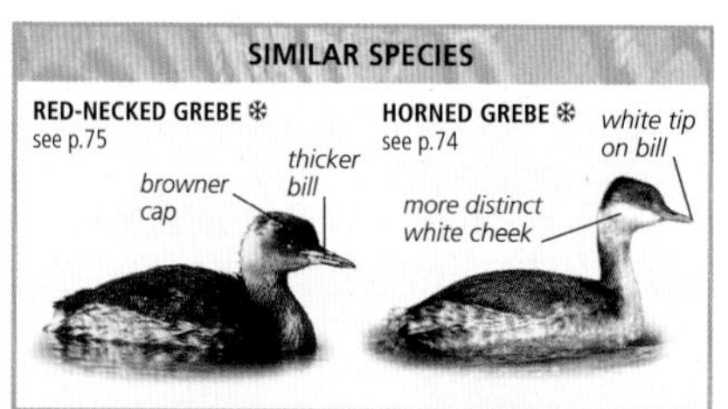
browner cap
thicker bill
more distinct white cheek
white tip on bill

OCCURRENCE
Breeds in marshes, shallow lakes, and ponds in the four western provinces. After breeding, many birds seek highly saline, slow-to-freeze waters, such as Mono Lake, where their favorite foods thrive—brine shrimp and alkali flies. Winters in coastal bays of the Pacific Coast and is a vagrant on the Atlantic Coast.

Length **12–14in (30–35cm)**	Wingspan **22½–24in (57–62cm)**	Weight **7–26oz (200–725g)**
Social **Flocks**	Lifespan **Up to 12 years**	Status **Secure**

DATE: ________ TIME: ________ LOCATION: ________

PIGEONS AND DOVES

THE LARGER SPECIES WITHIN the family Columbidae are known as pigeons, and the smaller ones as doves, although there is no actual scientific basis for the distinction. They are all fairly heavy, plump birds with relatively small heads and short necks. They also possess slender bills with their nostrils positioned in a fleshy mound at the base. Among other things, members of this family have strong wing muscles, making them powerful and agile fliers. When alarmed, they burst into flight with their wings emitting a distinctive clapping or swishing sound. Pigeons and doves produce a nutritious "crop-milk," which they secrete to feed their young. Despite human activity having severely affected members of this family in the past (the leading cause of the Passenger Pigeon's extinction in the 19th century is thought to be overhunting), the introduced Rock Pigeon has adapted and proliferated worldwide. Rock Pigeons, featuring an amazing array of plumages from all-white, reddish, and gray to all-black, can be found in habitatas ranging from downtown city centers and suburban neighborhoods to open farmlands. Among the species native to North America, only the elegant Mourning Dove is as widespread as the various species of introduced birds.

URBAN DWELLER
Rock pigeons are a common sight in cities around the world.

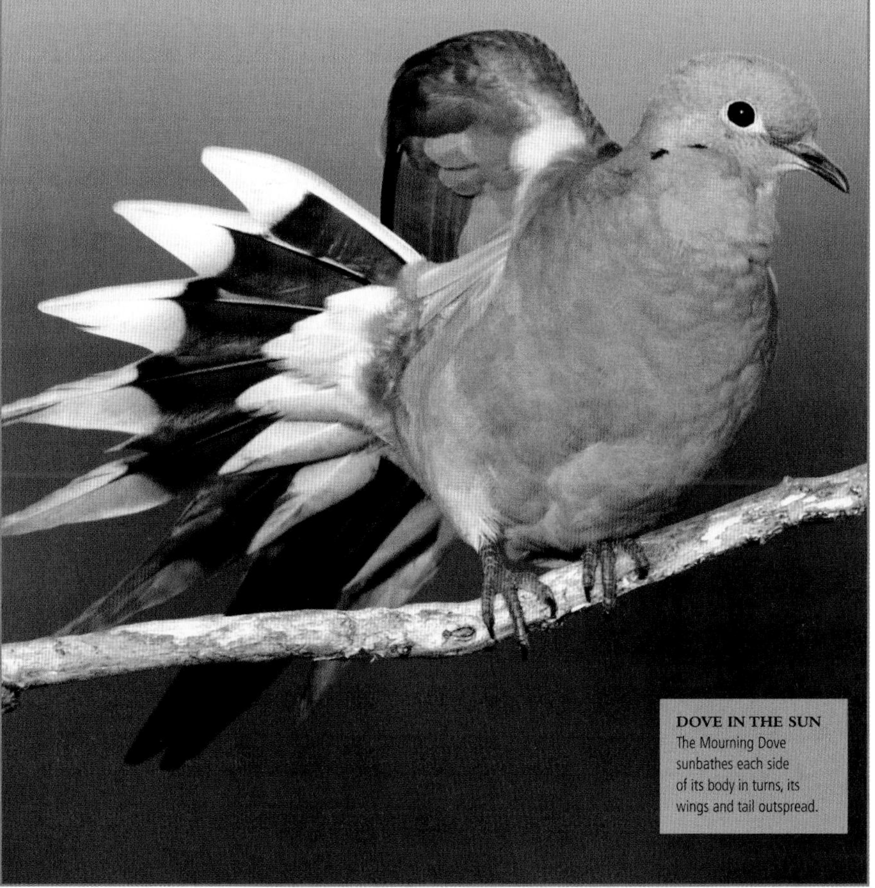

DOVE IN THE SUN
The Mourning Dove sunbathes each side of its body in turns, its wings and tail outspread.

Order **Columbiformes**	Family **Columbidae**	Species ***Columba livia***

Rock Pigeon

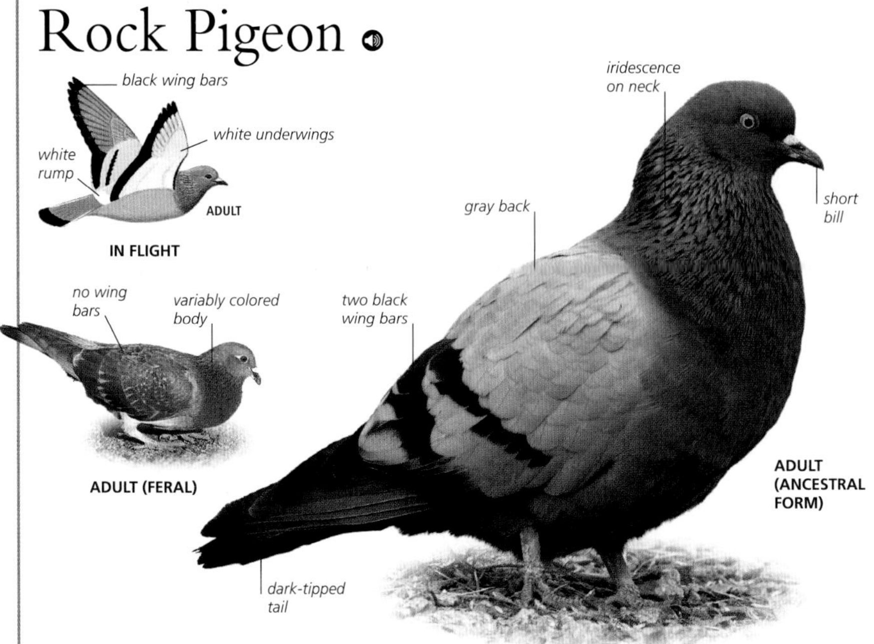
black wing bars
white underwings
white rump
ADULT
IN FLIGHT
iridescence on neck
gray back
short bill
no wing bars
variably colored body
two black wing bars
ADULT (FERAL)
ADULT (ANCESTRAL FORM)
dark-tipped tail

The Rock Pigeon was introduced to the Atlantic Coast of North America by 17th century colonists. Now feral, this species is found all over the continent, especially around farms, cities, and towns. This medium-sized pigeon comes in a wide variety of plumage colors and patterns, including bluish gray, checkered, rusty red, and nearly all-white. Its wings usually have two dark bars on them—unique among North American pigeons. The variability of the Rock Pigeon influenced Charles Darwin as he developed his theory of natural selection.

VOICE Soft, gurgling *coo, roo-c'too-coo*, for courtship and threat.

NESTING Twig nest on flat, sheltered surface, such as caves, rocky outcrops, and buildings; 2 eggs; several broods; year-round.

FEEDING Eats seeds, fruit, and rarely insects; human foods such as popcorn, bread, peanuts; various farm crops in rural areas.

FLIGHT: strong, direct; can reach speeds up to around 60mph (95kph).

CITY PIGEONS
Most Rock Pigeons in North America descend from domesticated forms and exhibit many colors.

SIMILAR SPECIES

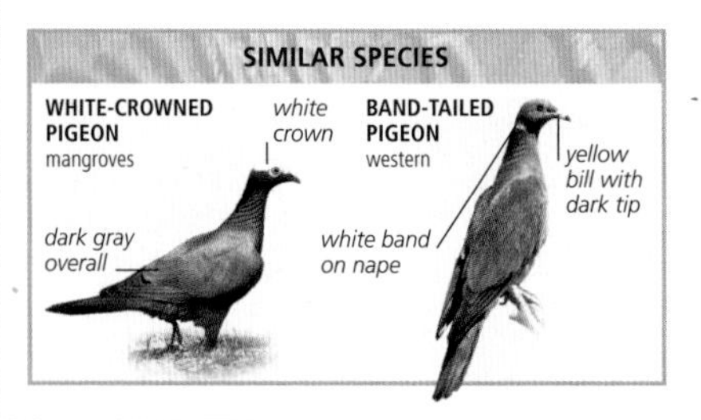
WHITE-CROWNED PIGEON
mangroves
white crown
dark gray overall
BAND-TAILED PIGEON
western
yellow bill with dark tip
white band on nape

OCCURRENCE
Across southern Canada and North America; nests in human structures of all sorts; resident. Original habitat in the Old World was (and still is) sea cliffs and inland canyons; found wild in some places, such as dry regions of North Africa, but feral in much of the world.

Length **11–14in (28–36cm)**	Wingspan **20–26in (51–67cm)**	Weight **9–14oz (250–400g)**
Social **Solitary/Flocks**	Lifespan **Up to 6 years**	Status **Secure**

DATE: ____________ TIME: ____________ LOCATION: ____________

Order **Columbiformes**	Family **Columbidae**	Species ***Zenaida macroura***

Mourning Dove

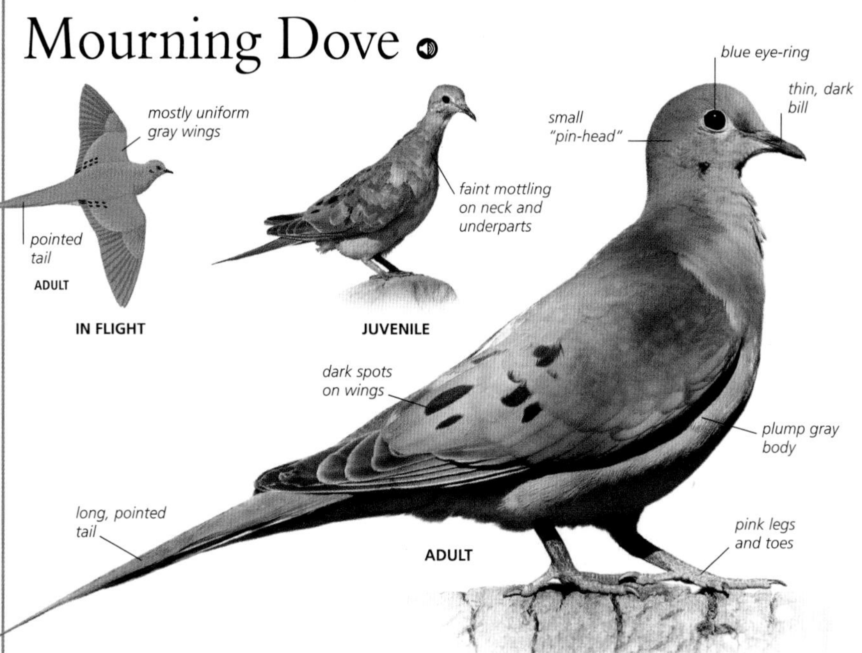
mostly uniform gray wings
pointed tail
ADULT
IN FLIGHT
faint mottling on neck and underparts
JUVENILE
small "pin-head"
blue eye-ring
thin, dark bill
dark spots on wings
plump gray body
long, pointed tail
ADULT
pink legs and toes

One of the most familiar, abundant, and widespread North American birds, the Mourning Dove is a long, plump, medium-sized dove with an undersized head. It has a gray body with a pale, rosy breast and black spots on folded wings. While coveted by hunters—as many as 70 million are shot annually—the Mourning Dove is also well known to those who live on farms and in suburbia. Found all across North America, the species is divided into two subspecies—the larger, grayish-brown *Z. m. carolinensis*, east of the Mississippi River, and the smaller, paler *Z. m. marginella* in the west.

VOICE Mellow, owl-like call: *hoO-Oo-oo, hoo-hoo-hoo.*

NESTING Flat, flimsy twig platform, mostly in trees, sometimes on the ground; 2 eggs; 2 broods; February–October.

FEEDING Forages mainly for seeds on the ground; obtains food quickly and digests it later at roost.

FLIGHT: swift, direct flight, with fairly quick wing beats; twists and turns sometimes.

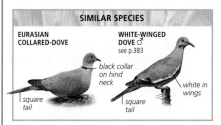

SIMILAR SPECIES

EURASIAN COLLARED-DOVE — black collar on hind neck; square tail

WHITE-WINGED DOVE ♂ see p.383 — white in wings; square tail

FAMILIAR SIGHT
The Mourning Dove is North America's most widespread member of this family.

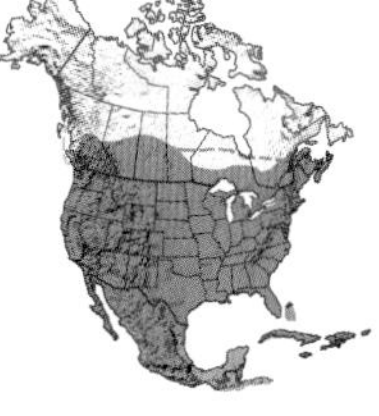

OCCURRENCE
Breeds in a wide variety of habitats but shuns extensive forests; human-altered vegetation favored for feeding, including farmland and suburbia. Winters in small to medium sheltered woodland while feeding in grain fields; winters in southern Mexico and Central America.

Length **9–13½in (23–34cm)**	Wingspan **14½–17½in (37–45cm)**	Weight **3–6oz (85–175g)**
Social **Pairs/Winter flocks**	Lifespan **Up to 19 years**	Status **Secure**

DATE: ______________ TIME: ______________ LOCATION: ______________________________

Family **Cuculidae**

CUCKOOS

THE FAMILY CUCULIDAE INCLUDES typical cuckoos, anis, and roadrunners. Cuckoos favor forested areas, anis prefer more open bush country, and roadrunners are found in dry, bushy semi-desert or desert regions. Cuckoos are mainly insectivorous, specializing in caterpillars from the ground or gleaned from foliage. Anis have a more varied diet. They are sociable, blackish, heavy-billed birds, found only in Florida and along the Gulf Coast in the US but are more widespread in Central America. Roadrunners are ground-feeders, rarely flying but able to run fast in pursuit of prey, which ranges from insects through small lizards to snakes (famously including rattlesnakes) and small rodents.

NIGHT SINGER
During the breeding season, the Black-billed Cuckoo will often call throughout the night.

Family **Caprimulgidae**

NIGHTJARS

THE NIGHTJARS ARE ACTIVE mostly around dusk and dawn, and so are not well known to many people, although their remarkable songs and calls may be more familiar. Common Nighthawks are easily seen and may even be spotted over suburban areas, but most nightjars are elusive species. Some inhabit scrub and bushy slopes and plains, while others are found in woodlands. They are medium-sized birds with pointed wings and long tails. They have tiny legs and minute bills but very wide mouths: they catch flying insects such as moths in the air, directly into the open gape. Their mouths are surrounded by bristles that help guide insects in when the birds are foraging.

SITTING PRETTY
Unusually for birds, members of the nightjar family, such as this Common Nighthawk, often perch lengthwise on branches.

Order **Cuculiformes**	Family **Cuculidae**	Species ***Coccyzus americanus***

Yellow-billed Cuckoo

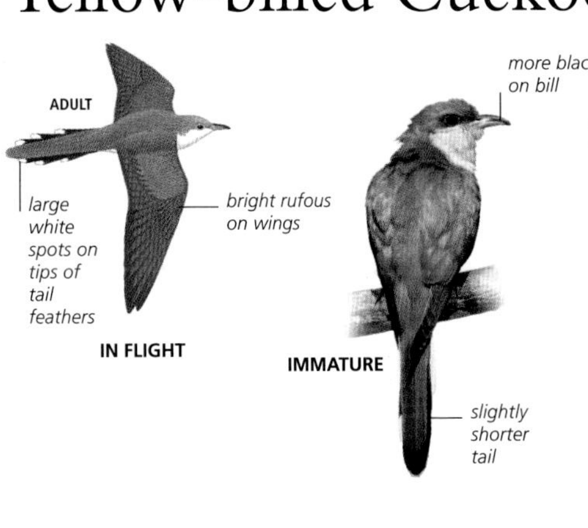
ADULT
large white spots on tips of tail feathers
bright rufous on wings
IN FLIGHT
more black on bill
IMMATURE
slightly shorter tail

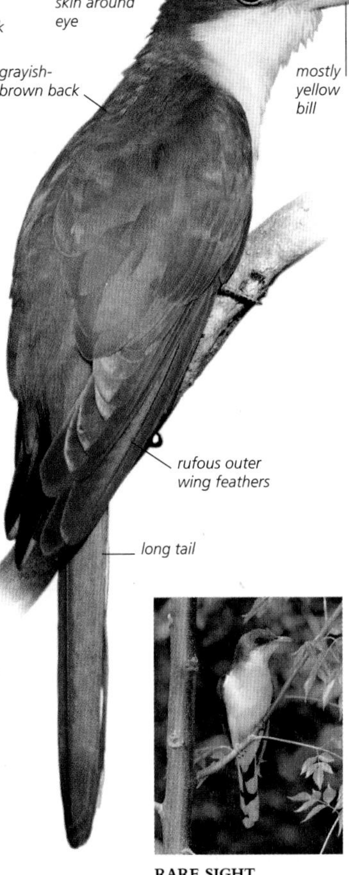
bare yellow skin around eye
grayish-brown back
mostly yellow bill
ADULT
rufous outer wing feathers
long tail

FLIGHT: flight is swift, using long strokes to maintain level pattern.

The Yellow-billed Cuckoo is a shy, slow-moving bird, with a reputation for fairly odd behaviors, including its habit of calling more often on cloudy days. This tendency has earned it the nickname "rain crow" in some areas. In addition to raising their young in their own nest, females often lay eggs in the nests of more than a dozen other species, especially during years with abundant food. The host species may be chosen on the basis of how closely the color of its eggs matches those of the cuckoo. This brood parasitism is the rule of many species of Old World cuckoos, and is the origin of the word "cuckold."

VOICE Call a series of 10–12 low notes that slow down as it progresses, *ca ca ca ca coo coo coo cowl cowl cowl.*

NESTING Flimsy oval-shaped platform of small sticks and branches, often lined with leaves and strips of plants; 2–4 eggs; 1–2 broods; May–August.

FEEDING Mostly consumes insects, such as grasshoppers, crickets, katydids, and caterpillars of several moth species; also eats seeds.

RARE SIGHT
Given the habitat they prefer and their skittish nature, a clear view of a Yellow-billed Cuckoo is rare.

SIMILAR SPECIES

BLACK-BILLED CUCKOO see p.82
all-black bill
no rufous on wings

MANGROVE CUCKOO
black mask around eyes
buffy undertail and belly

OCCURRENCE
Has a wide range in the US; extends into southeastern Canada. Found primarily in open forests with a mix of openings and thick understory cover, especially those near water. Winters in similar habitats in Central and South America.

Length **10–12in (26–30cm)**	Wingspan **17–20in (43–51cm)**	Weight **2–2¼oz (55–65g)**
Social **Small winter flocks**	Lifespan **Up to 4 years**	Status **Declining**

DATE: ______________ TIME: ______________ LOCATION: ______________

Order **Cuculiformes**	Family **Cuculidae**	Species ***Coccyzus erythropthalmus***

Black-billed Cuckoo

long tail

small white spots on tips of tail feathers

ADULT

long wings

IN FLIGHT

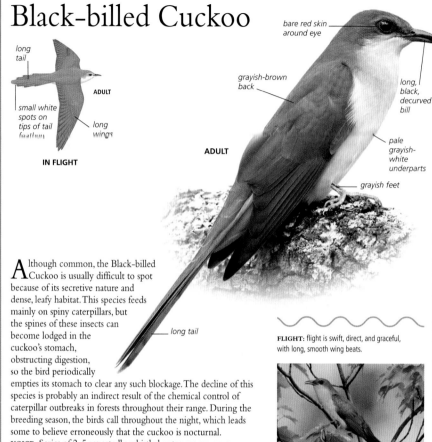

bare red skin around eye

grayish-brown back

long, black, decurved bill

ADULT

pale grayish-white underparts

grayish feet

long tail

Although common, the Black-billed Cuckoo is usually difficult to spot because of its secretive nature and dense, leafy habitat. This species feeds mainly on spiny caterpillars, but the spines of these insects can become lodged in the cuckoo's stomach, obstructing digestion, so the bird periodically empties its stomach to clear any such blockage. The decline of this species is probably an indirect result of the chemical control of caterpillar outbreaks in forests throughout their range. During the breeding season, the birds call throughout the night, which leads some to believe erroneously that the cuckoo is nocturnal.

VOICE Series of 2–5 repeatedly whistled notes, *coo-coo-coo-coo*, with short breaks between series.

NESTING Shallow cup of sticks lined with moss, leaves, grass, and feathers; 2–4 eggs; 1 brood; May–July.

FEEDING Almost exclusively eats caterpillars, especially tent caterpillars and gypsy moths.

FLIGHT: flight is swift, direct, and graceful, with long, smooth wing beats.

SEARCHING FOR FOOD
These cuckoos spend a lot of their time in trees as they search for their favorite hairy caterpillars.

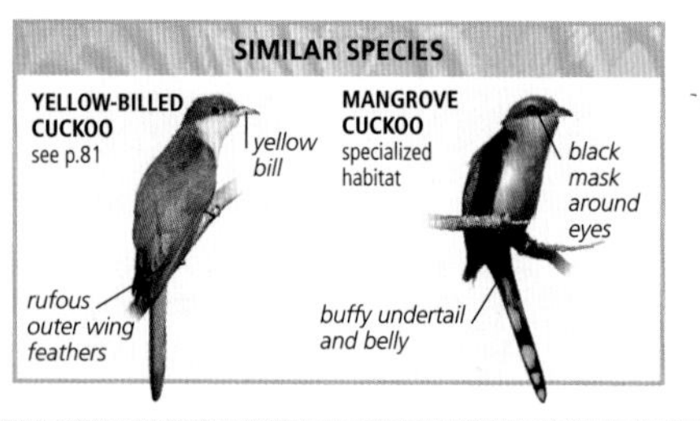
SIMILAR SPECIES
YELLOW-BILLED CUCKOO
see p.81
yellow bill
rufous outer wing feathers
MANGROVE CUCKOO
specialized habitat
black mask around eyes
buffy undertail and belly

OCCURRENCE
Widespread northern and eastern North American species, lives in thickly wooded areas close to water, but can also be found in brushy forest edges and evergreen woods. Winters in South America in evergreen woodlands, scrub, and humid forests.

Length **11–12in (28–31cm)**	Wingspan **16–19in (41–48cm)**	Weight **1$\frac{9}{16}$–2oz (45–55g)**
Social **Solitary**	Lifespan **Up to 5 years**	Status **Declining**

 DATE: ______ TIME: ______ LOCATION: ______

Order **Caprimulgiformes**	Family **Caprimulgidae**	Species ***Chordeiles minor***

Common Nighthawk

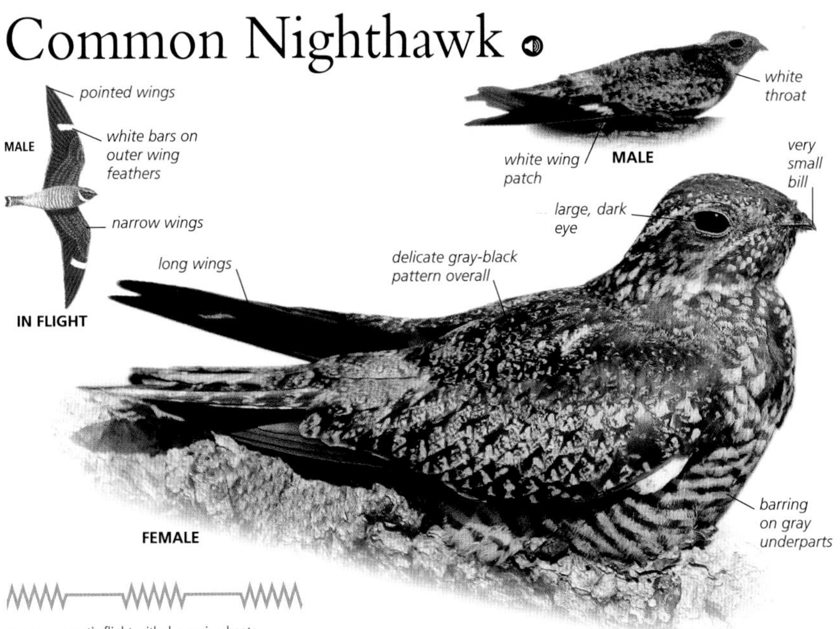
pointed wings
MALE
white bars on outer wing feathers
narrow wings
IN FLIGHT
long wings
white throat
white wing patch
MALE
very small bill
large, dark eye
delicate gray-black pattern overall
barring on gray underparts
FEMALE

FLIGHT: erratic flight with deep wing beats interrupted by banking glides.

Common Nighthawks are easy to spot as they swoop over parking lots, city streets, and athletics fields during the warm summer months. They are more active at dawn and dusk than at night, pursuing insect prey up to 250ft (76m) in the air. The species once took the name Booming Nighthawk, a reference to the remarkable flight display of the male birds, during which they dive rapidly toward the ground, causing their feathers to vibrate and produce a characteristic "booming" sound.

VOICE Nasal *peeent*; also soft clucking noises from both sexes.

NESTING Nests on ground on rocks, wood, leaves, or sand, also on gravel-covered rooftops in urban areas; 2 eggs; 1 brood; May–July.

FEEDING Catches airborne insects, especially moths, mayflies, and beetles, also ants; predominantly active at dusk and dawn.

A RARE SIGHT
Common Nighthawks are seen in flight more often than other caprimulgids, and it is a rare treat to see one resting on a perch.

SIMILAR SPECIES

LESSER NIGHTHAWK
more buffy barring on underside of wings

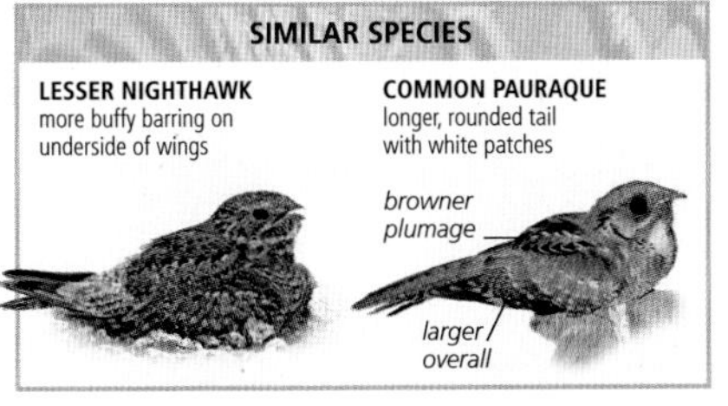

COMMON PAURAQUE
longer, rounded tail with white patches

browner plumage
larger overall

OCCURRENCE
Wide variety of open habitats such as cleared forests, fields, grassland, beaches, and sand dunes; also common in urban areas, including cities. The most common and widespread North American nighthawk, this species also occurs in Central and South America.

Length **9–10in (23–26cm)**	Wingspan **22–24in (56–61cm)**	Weight **2⅞oz (80g)**
Social **Solitary/Flocks**	Lifespan **Up to 9 years**	Status **Threatened**

DATE: ______________ TIME: ______________ LOCATION: ______________________________

Order **Caprimulgiformes**	Family **Caprimulgidae**	Species ***Antrostomus vociferus***

Eastern Whip-poor-will

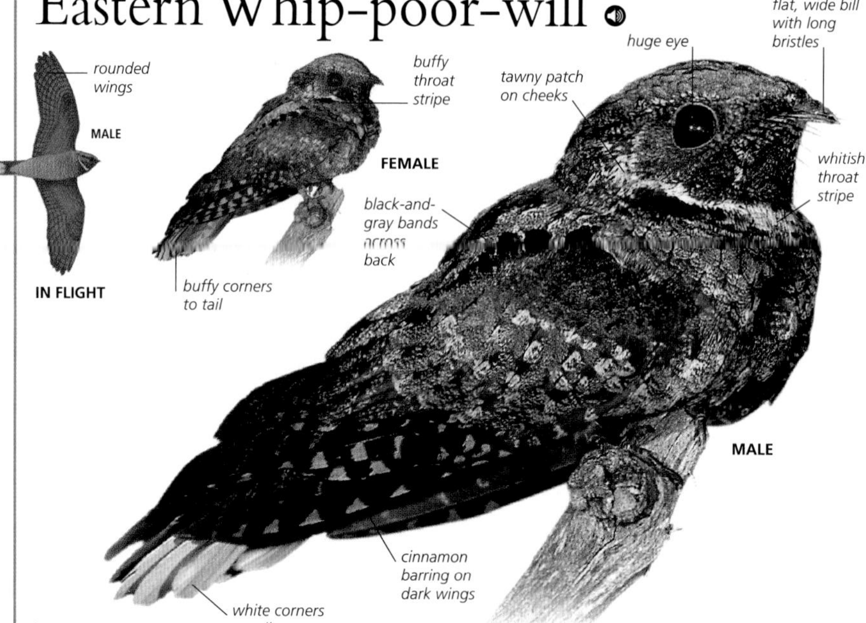
rounded wings
MALE
IN FLIGHT
buffy throat stripe
FEMALE
buffy corners to tail
black-and-gray bands across back
tawny patch on cheeks
huge eye
flat, wide bill with long bristles
whitish throat stripe
MALE
cinnamon barring on dark wings
white corners to tail

As with many of the nightjars, the Eastern Whip-poor-will is heard more often than seen. Its camouflage makes it extremely difficult to spot on the forest floor, and it usually flies away only when an intruder is very close—sometimes within a few feet. This species apparently has an unusual breeding pattern—while the male feeds the first brood until fledging, the female lays eggs for a second brood. Both eggs from one brood may hatch simultaneously during full moon, when there is most light at night, allowing the parents more time to forage for their young.

VOICE Loud, incessant, three-syllable whistle *WHIP-perrr-WIIL.*

NESTING Lays eggs on leaf litter on forest floor, often near overhead plant cover; 2 eggs; 2 broods; April–July.

FEEDING Flies upward quickly from perch to capture passing moths and other insects, such as mosquitoes.

FLIGHT: slow, erratic flight, with alternating bouts of flapping and gliding.

WAITING IN AMBUSH
Like other nightjars, this species waits in ambush for its prey from a perch on the forest floor.

SIMILAR SPECIES

COMMON POORWILL

CHUCK-WILL'S WIDOW
see p.383

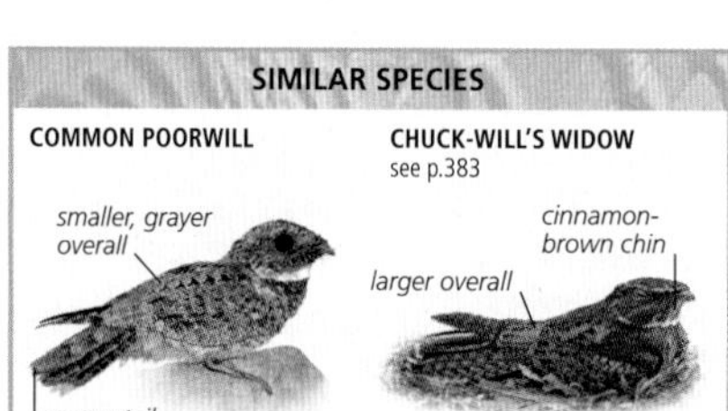
smaller, grayer overall
square tail
cinnamon-brown chin
larger overall

OCCURRENCE
Mixed mature forests with open understory, especially oak and pine forests on dry upland sites. Breeds from southeastern US up to southern Canada.

Length **9–10in (23–26cm)**	Wingspan **17–20in (43–51cm)**	Weight **1$\frac{9}{16}$–2$\frac{1}{4}$oz (45–65g)**
Social **Solitary**	Lifespan **Up to 15 years**	Status **Threatened**

DATE: ______________ TIME: ______________ LOCATION: ______________

Family **Apodidae**

SWIFTS

SWIFTS SPEND VIRTUALLY ALL their daylight hours, and many night hours as well, plying the skies. The most aerial birds in North America—if not the world—swifts eat, drink, court, mate, and even sleep on the wing. Unsurprisingly, swifts also are some of the fastest and most acrobatic flyers of the bird world. Several species have been clocked at over 100mph (160kmh). They feed on insects caught in zooming, zigzagging and dashing pursuits. The family name, based on the Greek *apous*, which means "without feet," originates from the ancient belief that swifts had no feet and lived their entire lives in the air.

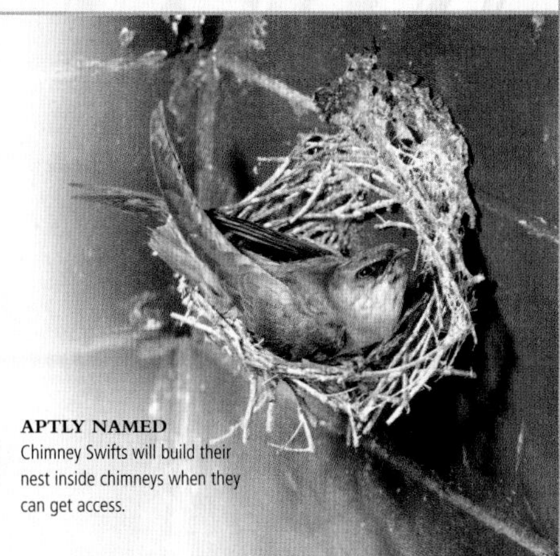

APTLY NAMED
Chimney Swifts will build their nest inside chimneys when they can get access.

Family **Trochilidae**

HUMMINGBIRDS

FOUND ONLY IN THE AMERICAS, hummingbirds are sometimes referred to as the crown jewels of the bird world. The first sight of a glittering hummingbird can be a life-changing experience. The amount of iridescence in their plumages varies from almost none to seemingly every feather. Most North American male hummingbirds have a colorful throat patch called a gorget, but most females lack this gorgeous attribute. Because iridescent colors are structural and not pigment-based, a gorget can often appear blackish until seen at the correct angle towards the light. Hummingbirds are the only birds that can fly backwards, an adaptation that allows them to move easily between flowers. Flying sideways, up, down, and hovering are also within hummingbirds' abilities, and all are achieved by their unique figure-eight, rapid wing strokes and reduced wing bone structure. Their long, thin bills allow them access to nectar in tubular flowers.

AGGRESSIVE MALES
This male Ruby-throated Hummingbird defends his territory from a perch.

Order **Apodiformes**	Family **Apodidae**	Species ***Chaetura pelagica***

Chimney Swift

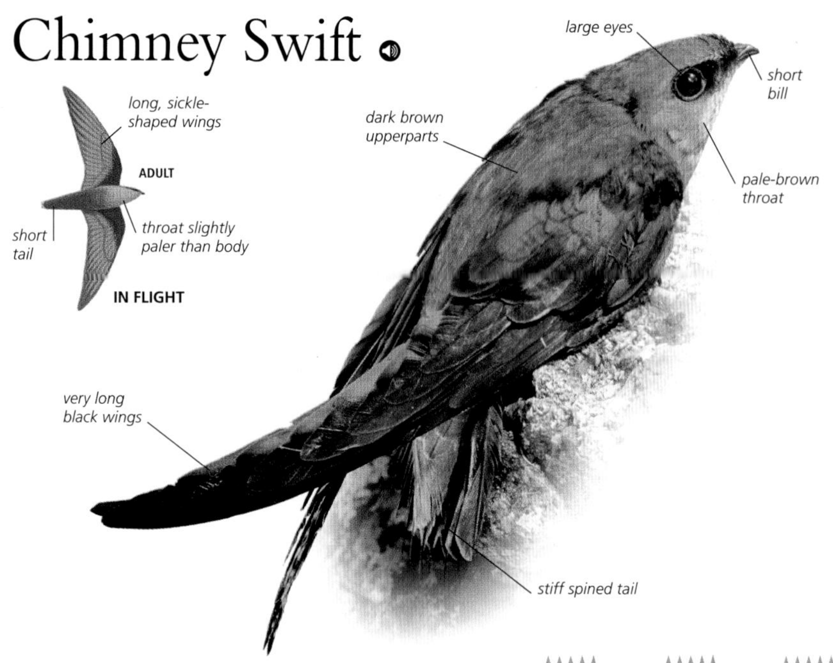
long, sickle-shaped wings
ADULT
short tail
throat slightly paler than body
IN FLIGHT
large eyes
short bill
dark brown upperparts
pale-brown throat
very long black wings
stiff spined tail

Nicknamed "spine-tailed," the Chimney Swift is a familiar summer sight and sound, racing through the skies east of the Rockies, its rolling twitters often heard. This bird does almost everything on the wing—feeding, drinking, and even bathing and copulating. This species has adapted to nest in human structures, including chimneys, although it once nested in tree holes. It remains a common bird, although local populations have declined; and it has expanded its range west and south.

VOICE High, rapid chips and twittering; notes from individuals in a flock run together into a rapid, descending chatter.

NESTING Shallow cup of twigs and saliva attached to inside of chimney or other artificial structure, rarely hollow tree; 4–5 eggs; 1 brood; April–August.

FEEDING Pursues a large variety of small aerial insects.

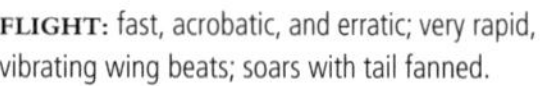

FLIGHT: fast, acrobatic, and erratic; very rapid, vibrating wing beats; soars with tail fanned.

HIGH FLYER
Swifts feed at heights on sunny days, and only feed near the ground when it is cold and cloudy.

SIMILAR SPECIES

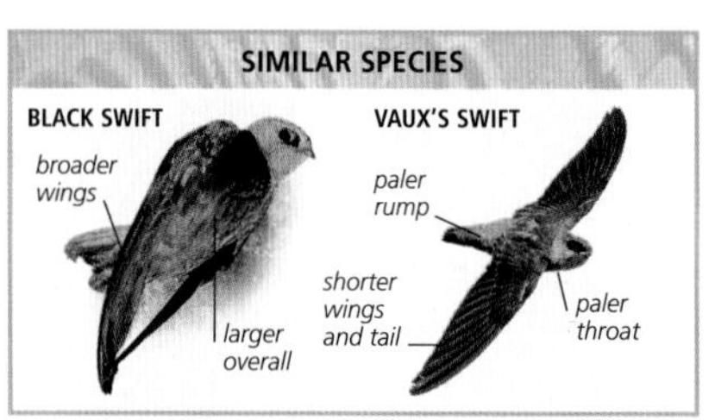
BLACK SWIFT
broader wings
larger overall

VAUX'S SWIFT
paler rump
shorter wings and tail
paler throat

OCCURRENCE
Widespread in eastern North America, over many habitats: urban and suburban areas, small towns; in sparsely populated areas, nests in hollow trees and caves; regular in summer in southern California, present late March to early November. Winters in Amazonian South America.

Length **5in (13cm)**	Wingspan **14in (36cm)**	Weight **⅝–1$^{1}/_{16}$oz (17–30g)**
Social **Flocks**	Lifespan **Up to 15 years**	Status **Threatened**

DATE: ______________ TIME: ______________ LOCATION: ______________

Order **Apodiformes**	Family **Trochilidae**	Species ***Archilochus colubris***

Ruby-throated Hummingbird

MALE
IN FLIGHT (MALE)
dark forked tail
bronzy-green upperparts
pale-tipped crown feathers
greenish speckling on throat
IMMATURE (MALE)
green crown
black face
straight black bill
orange-red throat
white chest
greenish sides and flanks
glittering green upperparts
white chin and throat
FEMALE
white underparts with buff wash on sides and flanks
rounded tail
grayish-white underparts
MALE

The only hummingbird to breed east of the Mississippi River, the Ruby-throated Hummingbird is a welcome addition to gardens throughout its range. It is easily identified in most of its range, though more difficult to distinguish in areas where other species are found, particularly during migration. Males perform a deep diving display for females. Before migration, these birds can add almost 1⁄16oz (2g) of fat to their weight to provide enough fuel for a nonstop 800-mile (1,300-km) flight across the Gulf of Mexico.

VOICE Call a soft, thick *chic*, sometimes doubled; twittered notes in interactions; chase call a fast, slightly buzzy *tsi-tsi-tsi-tsi-tsi-tsi-tsi-tsi*; soft, rattling song very rarely heard.

NESTING Tiny cup of plant down, with bud scales and lichen on the exterior, bound with spider's silk, usually in deciduous trees; 2 eggs; 1–2 broods; April–September.

FEEDING Drinks nectar from many species of flowers; feeds on small insects and spiders, caught aerially or gleaned from foliage.

FLIGHT: swift, forward flight with very fast wing beats; hovers at flowers and darts after insects.

CATCHING THE LIGHT
Although the throat patch often appears all black, the right lighting renders it fiery red.

SIMILAR SPECIES

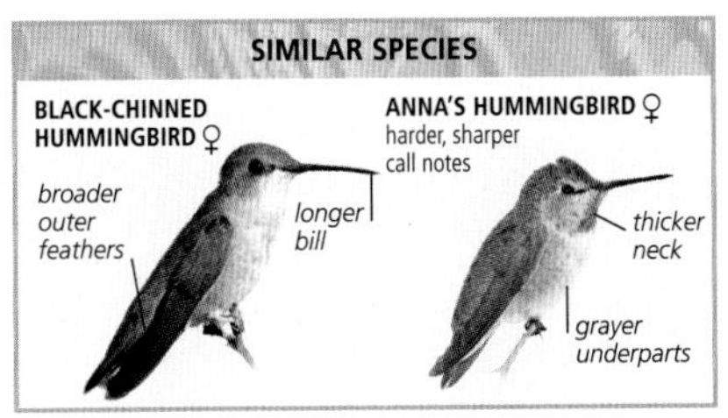
BLACK-CHINNED HUMMINGBIRD ♀
broader outer feathers
longer bill
ANNA'S HUMMINGBIRD ♀
harder, sharper call notes
thicker neck
grayer underparts

OCCURRENCE
Favors a variety of woodlands, and gardens; earliest migrants appear in the south as early as late February; most leave by November; regular in winter in south Florida; small numbers winter elsewhere on the Gulf Coast; vagrant to the West. The bulk of the population migrates to Central America in winter.

Length **3½in (9cm)**	Wingspan **4¼in (11cm)**	Weight **1⁄16–7⁄32oz (2–6g)**
Social **Solitary**	Lifespan **Up to 9 years**	Status **Secure**

DATE: ______________ TIME: ______________ LOCATION: ______________________

RAILS, CRANES, AND RELATIVES

THESE BIRDS OF THE MARSHES AND WETLANDS include many distinctive groups. The Rallidae, or rail family, is a diverse group of small- to medium-sized marsh birds, represented in Canada by two long-billed rails, two short-billed rails, two gallinules (one a rare species in Canada), and a coot. The cranes, or Gruidae, include very large to huge birds, superficially similar to storks and the largest of the herons and egrets. However, genetic and anatomical differences place cranes in a different order from storks, and herons and egrets.

RAILS, GALLINULES, AND COOTS

Rails are mostly secretive, solitary, and inconspicuous in dense marsh vegetation, whereas coots and gallinules are seen on open water. Rails are all somewhat chicken-like birds with stubby tails and short, rounded wings. They look round-bodied from the side but very slender from front to back—the origin of the saying "as thin as a rail." The species in the genus *Rallus* have excellent camouflage, and are noted for their long legs, toes, and bills. They are more often heard than seen. The two short-billed rails are similar, but with shorter necks and stout, stubby bills. Both rails and gallinules walk through wet marsh vegetation, though they can swim well. The gallinules, including the Common Gallinule and the rare Purple Gallinule, are more colorful than rails. They have long, slender toes. The American Coot has broad lobes along the sides of its toes, making it a more proficient swimmer and diver in deeper water.

None has a particularly specialized diet; they eat insects, small crabs, slugs, snails, and plant matter. Breeding pairs of rails keep in close contact in dense vegetation by calling out loudly.

THIN AS A RAIL
This marsh-dwelling Virginia Rail's narrow body enables it to slip easily through reed beds.

CRANES

The two North American species of cranes have long necks, small heads, and short bills. The long plumes on their inner wing feathers form a bustle, cloaking the tail on a standing crane, thereby giving them a different profile than any heron. Cranes fly with their necks straight out, rather than in the tight S-curve that is regularly seen in similar-sized herons. Cranes are long-distance migrants. The western-dwelling Whooping Crane, one of the world's rarest birds, is the tallest bird in North America, standing nearly 5ft (1.5m) high.

CRANE RALLY
Large numbers of Sandhill Cranes gather on feeding grounds in winter; groups arrive in linear or V-formation.

Order **Gruiformes**	Family **Rallidae**	Species ***Coturnicops noveboracensis***

Yellow Rail

dangling legs

white patch on inner wing feathers

ADULT

IN FLIGHT

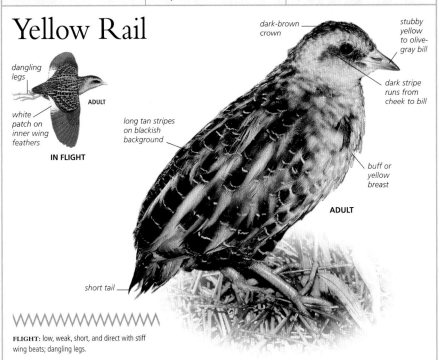

dark-brown crown

stubby yellow to olive-gray bill

dark stripe runs from cheek to bill

long tan stripes on blackish background

buff or yellow breast

ADULT

short tail

FLIGHT: low, weak, short, and direct with stiff wing beats; dangling legs.

Although widespread, the diminutive, secretive, nocturnal Yellow Rail is extremely difficult to observe in its dense, damp, grassy habitat. It is detected mainly by its voice. The Yellow Rail, whose Latin name *noveboracensis* means "of New York," has a small head, almost no neck, a stubby bill, a plump, almost tail-less body, and short legs. The bill of the male turns yellow in the breeding season; for the rest of the year, it is olive-gray like the female's. Although the Yellow Rail tends to dart for cover when disturbed, when it does fly, it reveals a distinctive white patch on its inner wing.

VOICE Two clicking calls followed by three more given by males, usually at night, reminiscent of two pebbles being struck together; also descending cackles, quiet croaking, and soft clucking.

NESTING Small cup of grasses and sedges, on the ground or in a plant tuft above water, concealed by overhanging vegetation; 8–10 eggs; 1 brood; May–June.

FEEDING Plucks seeds, aquatic insects, various small crustaceans, and mollusks (primarily small freshwater snails) from vegetation or ground; forages on the marsh surface or in shallow water, hidden by grass.

CURIOUS LISTENER
Imitating the Yellow Rail's "tick" calls by banging stones together can be an effective way to lure it out into the open.

SIMILAR SPECIES

SORA
see p.92

black streaks on brown upperparts
gray underparts

OCCURRENCE
Breeds in brackish and freshwater marshes and wet sedge meadows in Canada and the north-central US; there is an isolated breeding population in Oregon. Winters predominantly in coastal marshes along the Eastern Seaboard.

Length **7¼in (18.5cm)**	Wingspan **11in (28cm)**	Weight **1¾oz (50g)**
Social **Pairs**	Lifespan **Unknown**	Status **Special Concern**

DATE: ______________ TIME: ______________ LOCATION: ______________

Order **Gruiformes**	Family **Rallidae**	Species ***Rallus elegans***

King Rail

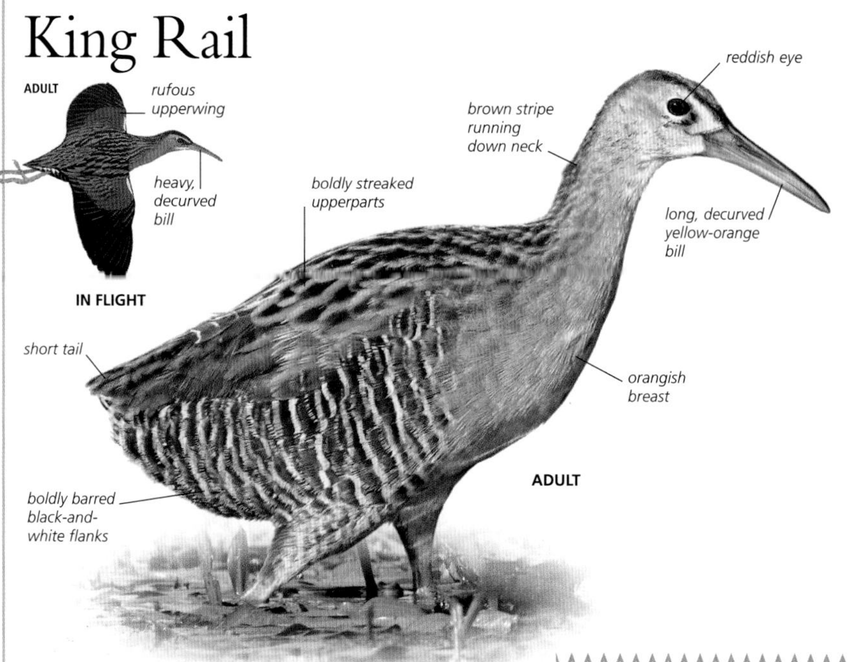
ADULT
rufous upperwing
heavy, decurved bill
IN FLIGHT
brown stripe running down neck
reddish eye
boldly streaked upperparts
long, decurved yellow-orange bill
short tail
orangish breast
ADULT
boldly barred black-and-white flanks

This chicken-like marsh bird is the freshwater version of the Clapper Rail. These two species are known to interbreed where their ranges overlap. A scattered and localized breeder across eastern North America, the King Rail depends on extensive freshwater marshy habitats with tall, emergent reeds and cattails. Concealed by this vegetation, the King Rail is rarely seen and is most often detected by its distinctive calls.

VOICE Male call similar to Clapper Rail but lower; emits a loud *kik kik kik* during breeding season.

NESTING Cup of vegetation, often hidden by bent stems that form a canopy; 6–12 eggs; 2 broods; February–August.

FEEDING Forages in concealed locations for insects, snails, spiders, and crustaceans, such as shrimps, crabs, and barnacles; also fish, frogs, and seeds.

FLIGHT: somewhat clumsy and labored; legs dangling; prefers to run.

LARGEST RAIL
Easily confused with the closely-related Clapper Rail, this is the largest North American rail.

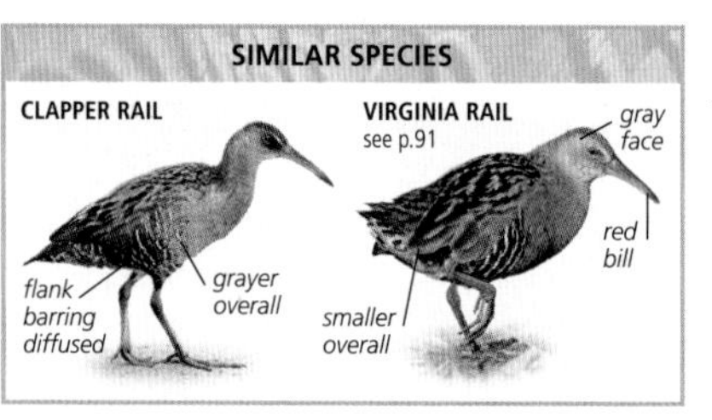
SIMILAR SPECIES
CLAPPER RAIL
VIRGINIA RAIL
see p.91
gray face
red bill
flank barring diffused
grayer overall
smaller overall

OCCURRENCE
Mostly breeds in freshwater marshes in the eastern US and in extreme southern Ontario. Also found throughout the year along the southern coast of the US, including Florida, and in central Mexico and Cuba.

Length **15in (38cm)**	Wingspan **20in (51cm)**	Weight **13oz (375g)**
Social **Pairs**	Lifespan **Unknown**	Status **Endangered**

DATE: ____________ TIME: ____________ LOCATION: ____________

Order **Gruiformes**	Family **Rallidae**	Species ***Rallus limicola***

Virginia Rail

rufous upperwing
ADULT (BREEDING)
dark outer wing feathers
IN FLIGHT
white undertail
streaked, black-and-brown upperparts
gray cheeks
decurved red bill
reddish-brown breast
black-and-white barring on flanks
reddish legs and toes
ADULT (BREEDING)
diffused streaking
dark bill
dark, blotchy breast
ADULT (NONBREEDING)

A smaller version of the King Rail, this freshwater marsh dweller is similar to its other relatives, more often heard than seen. Distributed in a wide range, the Virginia Rail spends most of its time in thick, reedy vegetation, which it pushes aside using its "rail thin" body and flexible vertebrae. Although it spends most of its life walking, it can swim and even dive to escape danger. The Virginia Rail is a partial migrant that leaves its northern breeding grounds in winter.

VOICE Series of pig-like grunting oinks that start loud and sharp, becoming steadily softer; also emits a series of double notes *ka-dik ka-dik*.

NESTING Substantial cup of plant material, concealed by bent-over stems; 5–12 eggs; 1–2 broods; April–July.

FEEDING Actively stalks prey or may wait and dive into water; primarily eats snails, insects, and spiders, but may also eat seeds.

FLIGHT: weak and struggling with outstretched neck and legs trailing behind.

HARD TO SPOT

The secretive Virginia Rail is difficult to spot in its reedy habitat.

SIMILAR SPECIES

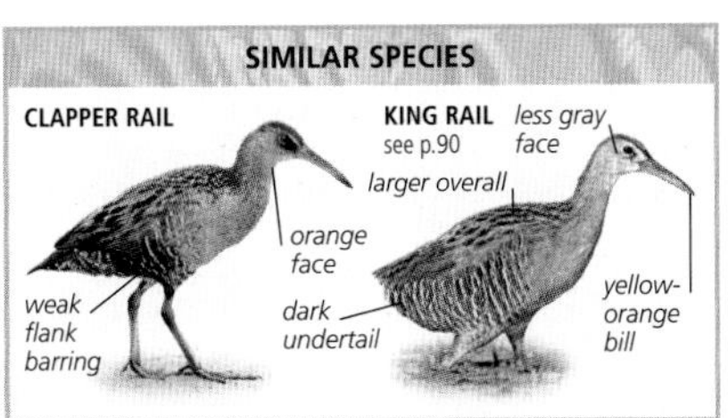
CLAPPER RAIL
orange face
weak flank barring
KING RAIL
see p.90
less gray face
larger overall
dark undertail
yellow-orange bill

OCCURRENCE

Breeds in freshwater habitats across North America, though, it's found throughout the year along the West Coast of the US. In winter, moves to saltwater and freshwater marshes in the southern US, including Florida, and in northern and central Mexico.

Length **9½in (24cm)**	Wingspan **13in (33cm)**	Weight **3oz (85g)**
Social **Pairs**	Lifespan **Unknown**	Status **Secure**

DATE: ____________ TIME: ____________ LOCATION: ____________

Order **Gruiformes**	Family **Rallidae**	Species ***Porzana carolina***

Sora

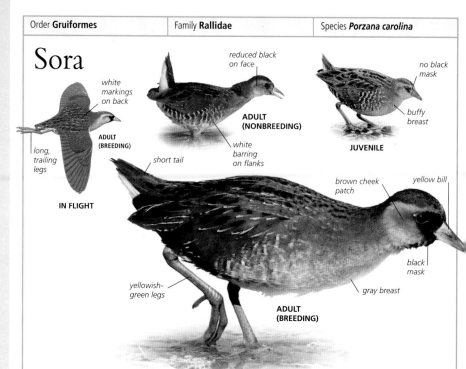

white markings on back
long, trailing legs
ADULT (BREEDING)
IN FLIGHT
reduced black on face
ADULT (NONBREEDING)
white barring on flanks
no black mask
buffy breast
JUVENILE
short tail
brown cheek patch
yellow bill
black mask
yellowish-green legs
gray breast
ADULT (BREEDING)

Despite being the most widely distributed rail in North America, the Sora is rarely seen. It breeds in freshwater marshes and migrates hundreds of miles south in winter, despite its weak and hesitant flight. Although it has long, skinny toes, it swims well, with a characteristichead-bobbing action. The Sora can be spotted walking at the edge of emergent vegetation—its yellow bill and black mask distinguish it from other rails.

VOICE Call a long, high, and loud, descending, horse-like whinny *ko-wee-hee-hee-hee-hee*; has an upslurred whistle.

NESTING Loosely woven basket of marsh vegetation suspended above water or positioned in clumps of vegetation on the water's surface; 8–11 eggs; 1 brood; May–June.

FEEDING Rakes vegetation with feet or pulls with bill in search of seeds of wetland plants, insects, spiders, and snails.

FLIGHT: appears weak, yet strenuous; wing beats hurried and constant.

CHICKEN-LIKE WALK
A rare sight, the Sora walks chicken-like through a marsh, its body in a low crouch.

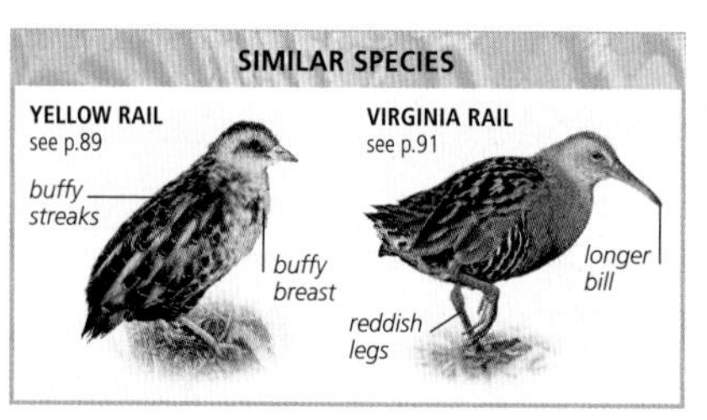
SIMILAR SPECIES
YELLOW RAIL
see p.89
buffy streaks
buffy breast
VIRGINIA RAIL
see p.91
longer bill
reddish legs

OCCURRENCE
Breeds in freshwater marshes with emergent vegetation across most of temperate North America; rarely in salt marshes along the Atlantic Coast. Winters in freshwater, saltwater, and brackish marshes with spartina grass from the southern US to northern South America.

Length **8½in (22cm)**	Wingspan **14in (36cm)**	Weight **2⅝oz (75g)**
Social **Solitary**	Lifespan **Unknown**	Status **Secure**

DATE: ____________ TIME: ____________ LOCATION: ____________

Order **Gruiformes**	Family **Rallidae**	Species ***Gallinula galeata***

Common Gallinule

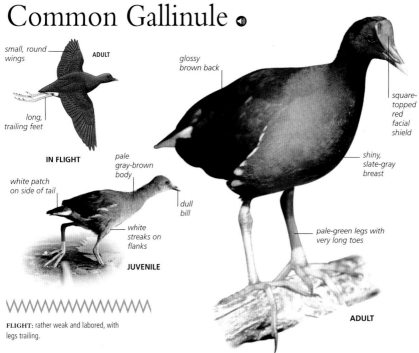

small, round wings
ADULT
long, trailing feet
IN FLIGHT

glossy brown back
square-topped red facial shield
shiny, slate-gray breast
pale-green legs with very long toes
ADULT

pale gray-brown body
white patch on side of tail
dull bill
white streaks on flanks
JUVENILE

FLIGHT: rather weak and labored, with legs trailing.

The Common Gallinule is fairly widespread in southeastern Canada and the eastern US; its distribution is more scattered in the western states. It has similarities in behavior and habitat to both the true rails and the coots. Equally at home on land and water, its long toes allow it to walk easily over floating vegetation and soft mud. When walking or swimming, the Common Gallinule nervously jerks its short tail, revealing its white undertail feathers, and bobs its head.

VOICE A variety of rapid, raucous, cackling phrases and an explosive *krrooo.*

NESTING Bulky platform of aquatic vegetation with growing plants pulled over to conceal it, or close to water; 5–11 eggs, 1–3 broods; May–August, maybe year-round in Florida.

FEEDING Forages mainly on aquatic and terrestrial plants and aquatic vegetation; also eats snails, spiders, and insects.

DUAL HABITAT
A walker and a swimmer, the gallinule is equally at home on land and in water.

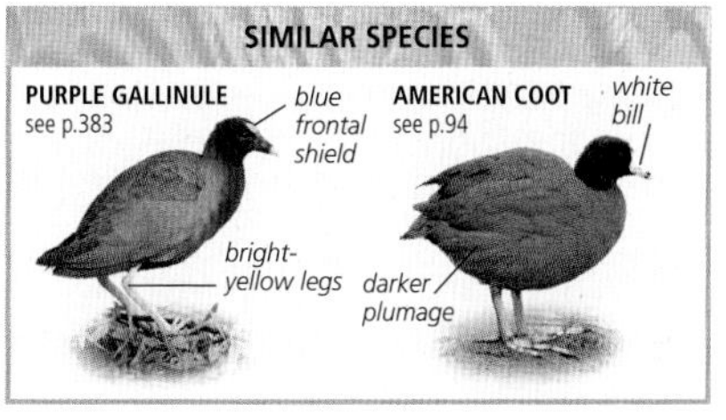
SIMILAR SPECIES
PURPLE GALLINULE
see p.383
blue frontal shield
bright-yellow legs
AMERICAN COOT
see p.94
white bill
darker plumage

OCCURRENCE
Breeds in freshwater habitats in the eastern US and Canada; more localized in the West. Winters in warmer areas with open water, such as the southern US, and Mexico. Also found in Central and South America.

Length **14in (36cm)**	Wingspan **21in (53cm)**	Weight **11oz (325g)**
Social **Pairs**	Lifespan **Up to 10 years**	Status **Secure**

DATE: ____________ TIME: ____________ LOCATION: ____________________

Order **Gruiformes**	Family **Rallidae**	Species ***Fulica americana***

American Coot

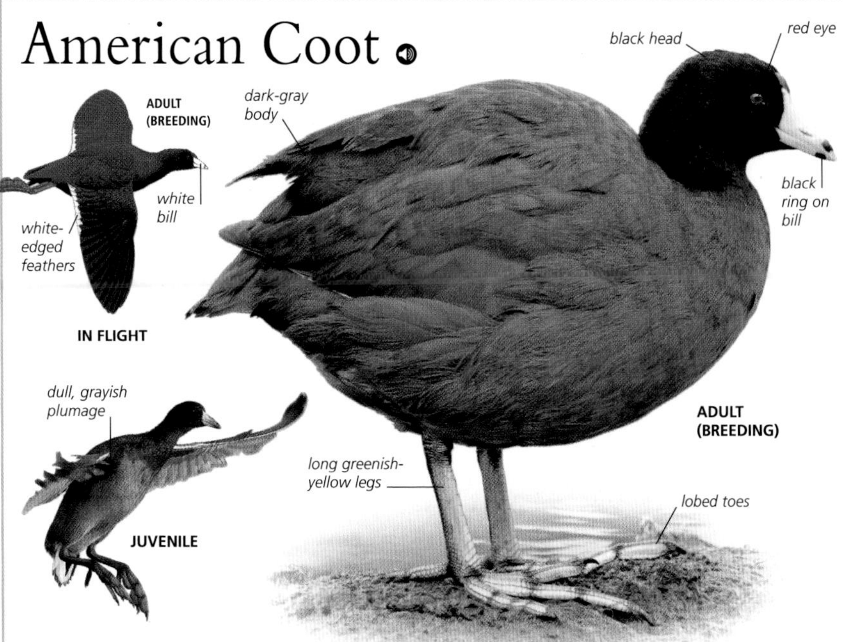

black head
red eye
dark-gray body
ADULT (BREEDING)
white bill
white-edged feathers
IN FLIGHT
black ring on bill
dull, grayish plumage
JUVENILE
long greenish-yellow legs
lobed toes
ADULT (BREEDING)

This duck-like species of rail is the most abundant and widely distributed of North American rails. Its lobed toes make it well adapted to swimming and diving, but they are somewhat of an impediment on land. Its flight is clumsy; it becomes airborne with difficulty, running along the water's surface before taking off. American Coots form l arge flocks on open water in winter, often associating with ducks—an unusual trait for a member of the rail family.

VOICE Various raucous clucks, grunts, and croaks and an explosive *keek*.

NESTING Bulky cup of plant material placed in aquatic vegetation on or near water; 5–15 eggs; 1–2 broods; April–July.

FEEDING Forages on or under shallow water and feeds on land; primarily herbivorous, but also eats snails, insects, spiders, tadpoles, fish, and even carrion.

FLIGHT: low and labored; runs for quite a long distance to take off.

SWIMMING AWAY
The red-headed, baldish-looking American Coot chicks leave the nest a day after hatching.

SIMILAR SPECIES

PURPLE GALLINULE
see p.383

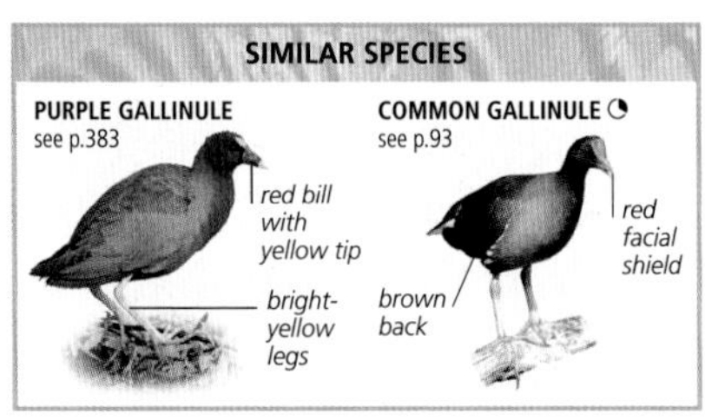

red bill with yellow tip
bright-yellow legs

COMMON GALLINULE
see p.93

red facial shield
brown back

OCCURRENCE
Breeds in open water habitats west of the Appalachians and in Florida. Moves from the northern parts of its range in winter to the southeastern US, where open water persists; also migrates to western and southern Mexico.

Length **15½in (40cm)**	Wingspan **24in (61cm)**	Weight **16oz (450g)**
Social **Flocks**	Lifespan **Up to 22 years**	Status **Secure**

DATE: ____________ TIME: ____________ LOCATION: ____________

Order **Gruiformes**	Family **Gruidae**	Species ***Antigone canadensis***

Sandhill Crane

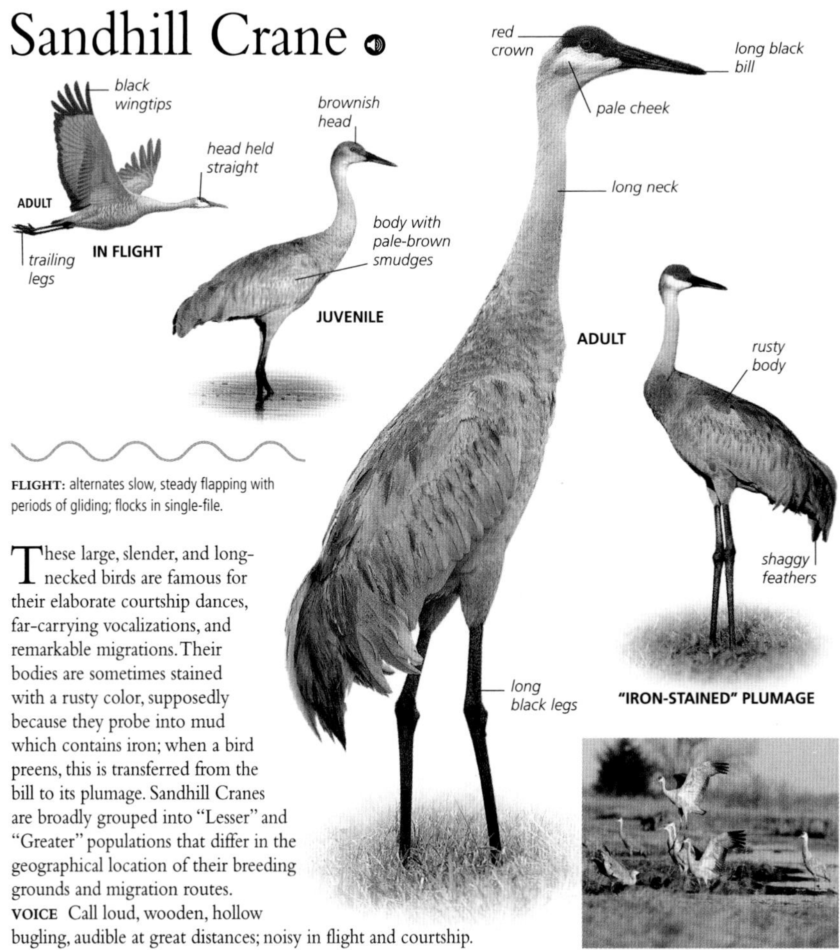
black wingtips
head held straight
ADULT
trailing legs
IN FLIGHT
brownish head
body with pale-brown smudges
JUVENILE
red crown
long black bill
pale cheek
long neck
ADULT
rusty body
shaggy feathers
long black legs
"IRON-STAINED" PLUMAGE

FLIGHT: alternates slow, steady flapping with periods of gliding; flocks in single-file.

These large, slender, and long-necked birds are famous for their elaborate courtship dances, far-carrying vocalizations, and remarkable migrations. Their bodies are sometimes stained with a rusty color, supposedly because they probe into mud which contains iron; when a bird preens, this is transferred from the bill to its plumage. Sandhill Cranes are broadly grouped into "Lesser" and "Greater" populations that differ in the geographical location of their breeding grounds and migration routes.

VOICE Call loud, wooden, hollow bugling, audible at great distances; noisy in flight and courtship.

NESTING Mound of sticks and grasses placed on ground; 1 egg; 1 brood; April–September.

FEEDING Eats shoots, grain; also aquatic mollusks, and insects.

MEMORABLE IMAGE

Its long neck, large wings, and distinctive red crown make it difficult to mistake.

SIMILAR SPECIES

GREAT BLUE HERON see p.178

dark crown

paler legs

WHOOPING CRANE

red on face

all-white plumage

larger overall

OCCURRENCE

Breeds in muskeg (peat bogs), tundra, and forest clearings across northwestern North America, east to Quebec and the Great Lakes; large wintering and migratory flocks, often densely packed, roost in or near marshes. Winters south to northern Mexico.

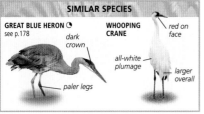

Length **2¾–4ft (0.8–1.2m)**	Wingspan **6–7½ft (1.8–2.3m)**	Weight **7¾–11lb (3.5–5kg)**
Social **Flocks**	Lifespan **Up to 40 years**	Status **Secure**

DATE: ____________ TIME: ____________ LOCATION: ____________

Families **Charadriidae, Scolopacidae, Stercorariidae, Alcidae, Laridae**

SHOREBIRDS, GULLS, AUKS, AND RELATIVES

THE DIVERSE SHOREBIRD, gull, and auk families together form the order Charadriiformes. They are small- to medium-sized, mostly migratory birds, associated with aquatic habitats. Over 100 species are found in North America.

DISTANCE TRAVELER
The Arctic Tern is well known for its long yearly migration of around 25,000 miles (40,000km).

SHOREBIRDS

The various species popularly known as shorebirds belong to several different families. In Eastern Canada, there are the plovers (Charadriidae), and the sandpipers and the phalaropes (Scolopacidae). They have long legs, in proportion to their bodies, and a variety of bills—ranging from short to long, thin, thick, straight, decurved, and recurved.

GULLS

The over 20 species of Canadian gulls in the subfamily Larinae all share a similar stout body shape, sturdy bills, and webbed toes. Nearly all are scavengers. Closely associated with coastal areas, few gulls venture far out to sea. Some species are seen around fishing ports and harbors, or inland, especially in urban areas, landfills, and farm fields.

TERNS

Terns are specialized, long-billed predators that dive for fish. More slender and elegant than gulls, nearly all are immediately recognizable when breeding, due to their black caps and long, pointed bills. The related but differently billed Black Simmer, a vagrant in Canada, also catches fish.

AUKS

Denizens of the northern oceans, these birds come to land only to breed. Most nest in colonies on sheer cliffs overlooking the ocean, but puffins excavate burrows in the ground, and some murrelets nest away from predators high up in treetops far inland.

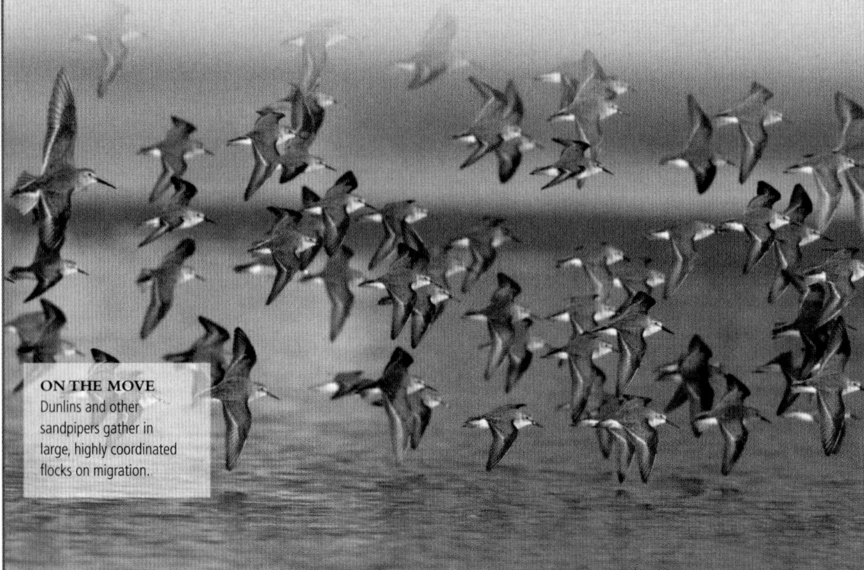

ON THE MOVE
Dunlins and other sandpipers gather in large, highly coordinated flocks on migration.

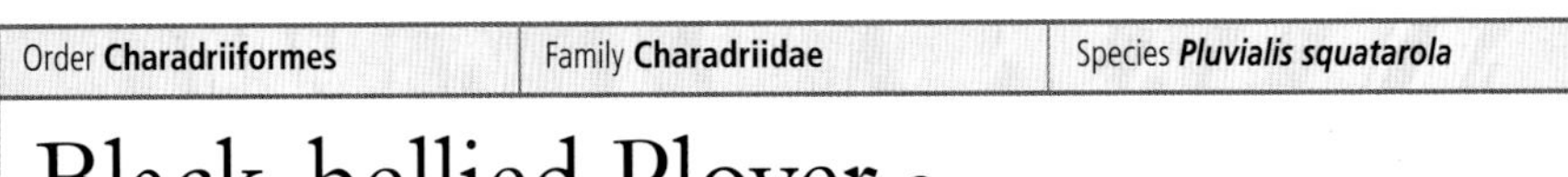

Order **Charadriiformes**	Family **Charadriidae**	Species ***Pluvialis squatarola***

Black-bellied Plover

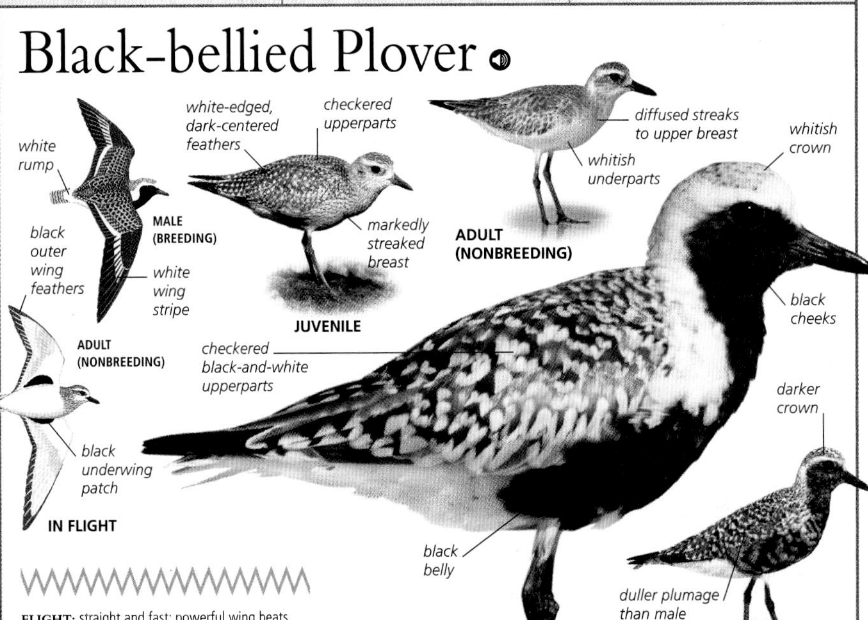
white rump
MALE (BREEDING)
black outer wing feathers
white wing stripe
ADULT (NONBREEDING)
black underwing patch
IN FLIGHT
white-edged, dark-centered feathers
checkered upperparts
markedly streaked breast
JUVENILE
diffused streaks to upper breast
whitish underparts
ADULT (NONBREEDING)
whitish crown
black cheeks
checkered black-and-white upperparts
darker crown
black belly
duller plumage than male
MALE (BREEDING)
FEMALE (MOLTING TO BREEDING PLUMAGE)

FLIGHT: straight and fast; powerful wing beats.

The Black-bellied Plover is the largest and most common of the three North American *Pluvialis* plovers. Its preference for open feeding habitats, its bulky structure, and very upright stance make it a fairly conspicuous species. The Black-bellied Plover's black underwing patches, visible in flight, are present in both its breeding and nonbreeding plumages and distinguish it from the other *Pluvialis* plovers.

VOICE Typical call a three-syllabled, clear, plaintive, whistled *whEE-er-eee*, with middle note lower; flight song of male during breeding softer, with accent on second syllable.

NESTING Shallow depression lined with mosses and lichens in moist to dry lowland tundra; 1–5 eggs; 1 brood; May–July.

FEEDING Forages mainly along coasts in typical plover style: run, pause, and pluck; eats insects, worms, bivalves, and crustaceans.

CASUAL WADING
The Black-bellied Plover wades in shallow water but does most of its foraging in mudflats.

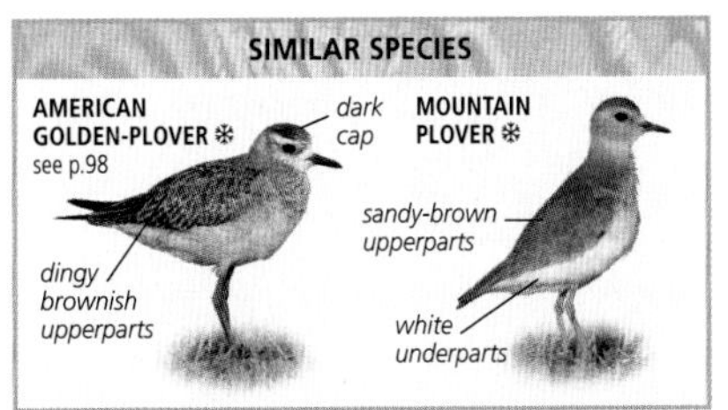
SIMILAR SPECIES
AMERICAN GOLDEN-PLOVER ❄
see p.98
dark cap
dingy brownish upperparts
MOUNTAIN PLOVER ❄
sandy-brown upperparts
white underparts

OCCURRENCE
Breeds in high-Arctic habitats from western Russia across the Bering Sea to Alaska, and east to Baffin Island; winters primarily in coastal areas from southern Canada and the US, south to southern South America. Found inland during migration. Migrates south all the way to South America.

Length **10½–12in (27–30cm)**	Wingspan **29–32in (73–81cm)**	Weight **5–9oz (150–250g)**
Social **Flocks**	Lifespan **Up to 12 years**	Status **Secure**

DATE: ____________ TIME: ____________ LOCATION: ____________

Order **Charadriiformes**	Family **Charadriidae**	Species ***Pluvialis dominica***

American Golden-Plover

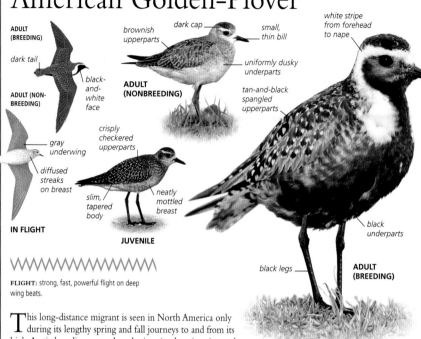

ADULT (BREEDING)
dark tail
black-and-white face
ADULT (NON-BREEDING)
gray underwing
diffused streaks on breast
IN FLIGHT
brownish upperparts
dark cap
small, thin bill
uniformly dusky underparts
ADULT (NONBREEDING)
crisply checkered upperparts
slim, tapered body
neatly mottled breast
JUVENILE
white stripe from forehead to nape
tan-and-black spangled upperparts
black underparts
black legs
ADULT (BREEDING)

FLIGHT: strong, fast, powerful flight on deep wing beats.

This long-distance migrant is seen in North America only during its lengthy spring and fall journeys to and from its high-Arctic breeding grounds and wintering locations in southern South America. An elegant, slender, yet large plover, it prefers inland grassy habitats and plowed fields to coastal mudflats. The American Golden-Plover's annual migration route includes a feeding stop at Labrador, then a 1,550–1,860-mile (2,500–3,000km) flight over the Atlantic Ocean to South America.

VOICE Flight call a whistled two-note *queE-dle*, or *klee-u*, with second note shorter and lower pitched; male flight song a strong, melodious whistled *kid-eek*, or *kid-EEp*.

NESTING Shallow depression lined with lichens in dry, open tundra; 4 eggs; 1 brood; May–July.

FEEDING Forages in run, pause, and pluck sequence on insects, mollusks, crustaceans, and worms; also berries and seeds.

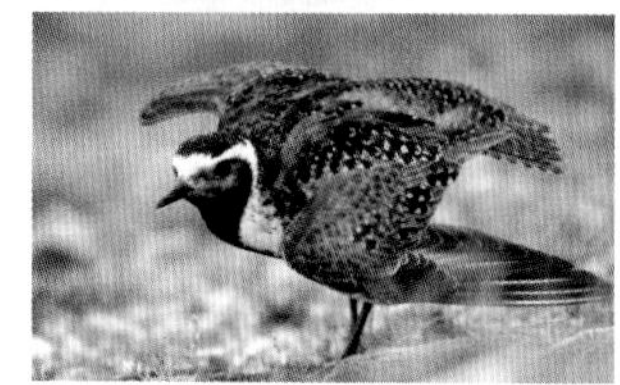

DISTRACTION TECHNIQUE
This breeding American Golden-Plover is feigning an injury to its wing to draw predators away from its chicks or eggs in its nest.

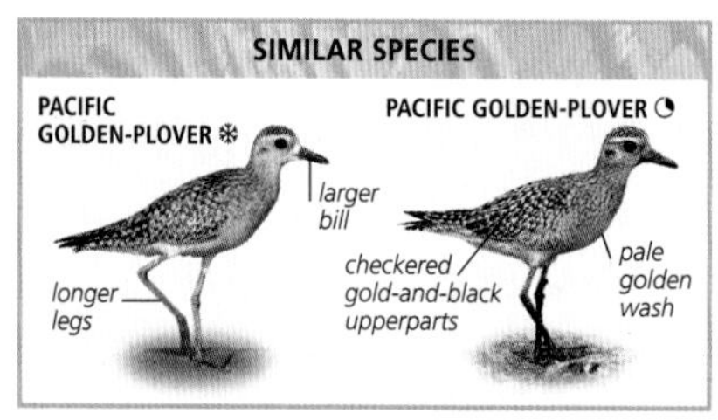
SIMILAR SPECIES
PACIFIC GOLDEN-PLOVER ❄
larger bill
longer legs
PACIFIC GOLDEN-PLOVER ◔
checkered gold-and-black upperparts
pale golden wash

OCCURRENCE
Breeds in Arctic tundra habitats. During migration, it occurs in prairies, tilled farmlands, golf courses, pastures, airports; also mudflats, shorelines, and beaches. In spring, seen in Texas and the Great Plains; in fall, uncommon in northeast Maritimes and New England; scarce along the Pacific Coast.

Length **9½–11in (24–28cm)**	Wingspan **23–28in (59–72cm)**	Weight **4–7oz (125–200g)**
Social **Solitary/Small flocks**	Lifespan **At least 8 years**	Status **Secure**

DATE: __________ TIME: __________ LOCATION: __________

Order **Charadriiformes**	Family **Charadriidae**	Species ***Charadrius vociferus***

Killdeer

long wings
white wing bar
ADULT
reddish-orange tail and rump
IN FLIGHT
brownish upperparts
rufous wash to back and wings
black collar encircling neck
red eye-ring
brownish crown
small, thin black bill
MALE
long tail
second neck band crosses upper breast
white underparts
pinkish legs, sometimes with yellowish tinge

FLIGHT: fast, twisting flight with fluid wing beats.

This loud and vocal shorebird is the most widespread plover in North America, nesting in all southern Canadian provinces and across the US. The Killdeer's piercing call carries for long distances, sometimes causing other birds to fly away in fear of imminent danger. These birds often nest near human habitation, allowing a close observation of their vigilant parental nature with young chicks.

VOICE Flight call a rising, drawn out *deeee*; alarm call a loud, penetrating *dee-ee*, given repetitively; agitated birds also give series of *dee* notes, followed by a rising trill.

NESTING Scrape on ground, sometimes in slight depression; 4 eggs; 1 brood (north), 2–3 broods (south); March–July.

FEEDING Forages in typical plover style: run, pause, and pick; eats a variety of invertebrates, such as worms, snails, grasshoppers, and beetles; also small vertebrates and seeds.

CLEVER MANEUVER

The Killdeer lures intruders away from its nest with a "broken wing" display.

SIMILAR SPECIES

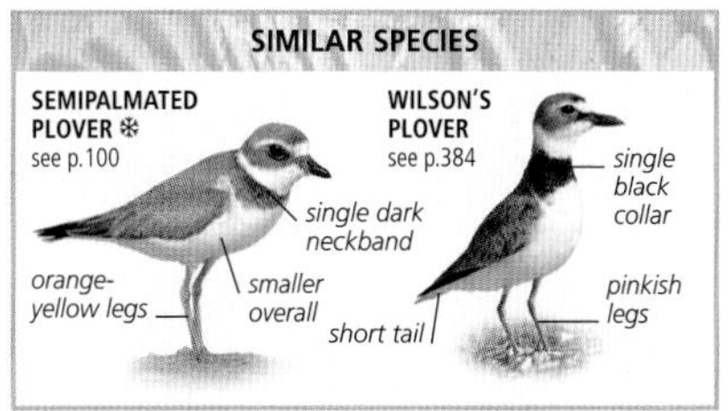
SEMIPALMATED PLOVER ❄
see p.100
single dark neckband
orange-yellow legs
smaller overall
WILSON'S PLOVER
see p.384
single black collar
short tail
pinkish legs

OCCURRENCE

Widespread across Canada and the US, the Killdeer occurs in a wide variety of habitats. These include shorelines, mudflats, lake and river edges, sparsely grassy fields and pastures, golf courses, roadsides, parking lots, flat rooftops, driveways, and other terrestrial habitats.

Length **9–10in (23–26cm)**	Wingspan **23–25in (58–63cm)**	Weight **2¼–3⅛ oz (65–90g)**
Social **Small flocks**	Lifespan **Up to 10 years**	Status **Declining**

DATE: ______ TIME: ______ LOCATION: ______

Order **Charadriiformes**	Family **Charadriidae**	Species ***Charadrius semipalmatus***

Semipalmated Plover

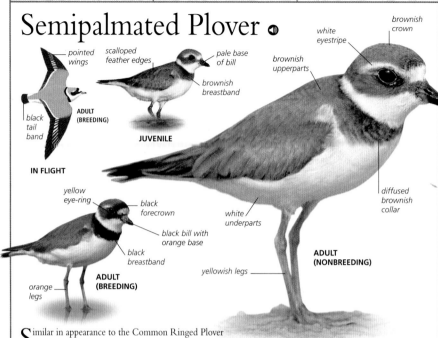

pointed wings
black tail band
ADULT (BREEDING)
IN FLIGHT

scalloped feather edges
pale base of bill
brownish breastband
JUVENILE

white eyestripe
brownish crown
brownish upperparts
diffused brownish collar
white underparts
yellowish legs
ADULT (NONBREEDING)

yellow eye-ring
black forecrown
black bill with orange base
black breastband
orange legs
ADULT (BREEDING)

Similar in appearance to the Common Ringed Plover in Eurasia, the Semipalmated Plover is a small bird with a tapered shape. They are a familiar sight in a wide variety of habitats during migration and in winter, they gather in loose flocks. A casual walk down a sandy beach between fall and spring might awaken up to 100 Semipalmated Plovers, sleeping in slight depressions in the sand, though, flocks of up to 1,000 birds may also be encountered.

VOICE Flight call a whistled abrupt *chu-WEEp*, with soft emphasis on second syllable; courtship display song is quick version of flight call followed by rough *r-r-r-r-r-r-r*, ending with a slurred, descending *yelp*.

NESTING Simple scrape on bare or slightly vegetated ground in Arctic tundra; 3–4 eggs; 1 brood; May–June.

FEEDING Forages in typical plover style: run, pause, and pluck; eats aquatic mollusks, crustaceans, flies, beetles, and spiders.

FLIGHT: straight, fast; with fluttering wing beats.

BY SIGHT AND TOUCH
Semipalmated Plovers locate prey by sight or through the sensitive soles of their feet.

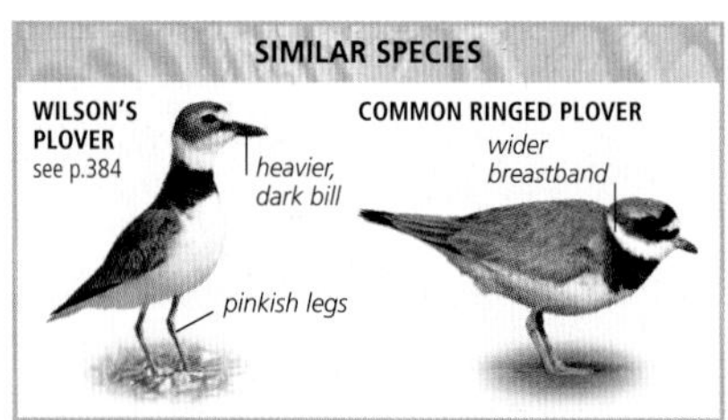
SIMILAR SPECIES
WILSON'S PLOVER
see p.384
heavier, dark bill
pinkish legs
COMMON RINGED PLOVER
wider breastband

OCCURRENCE
Breeding habitat is Arctic or sub-Arctic tundra with well-drained gravel, shale, or other sparsely vegetated ground. During migration, they inhabit mudflats, saltwater marshes, lake edges, tidal areas, and flooded fields. During winter, coastal or near coastal habitats are chosen.

Length **6¾–7½in (17–19cm)**	Wingspan **17–20½in (43–52cm)**	Weight **1 1/16–2½oz (30–70g)**
Social **Solitary/Flocks**	Lifespan **Up to 6 years**	Status **Secure**

DATE: ____________ TIME: ____________ LOCATION: ____________________

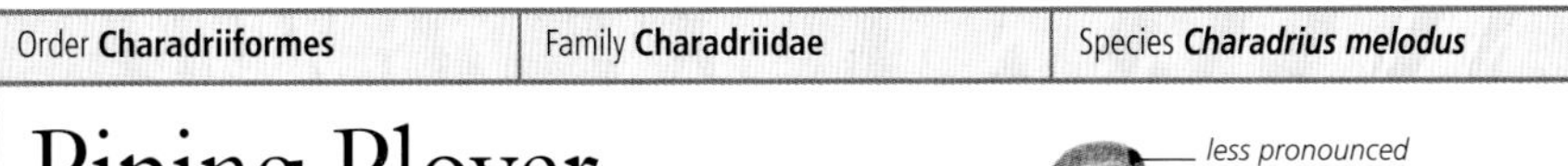
Order **Charadriiformes**
Family **Charadriidae**
Species ***Charadrius melodus***

Piping Plover

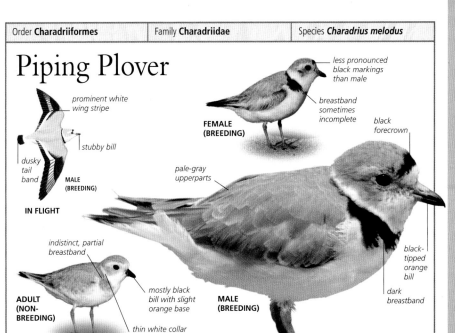

prominent white wing stripe
stubby bill
dusky tail band
MALE (BREEDING)
IN FLIGHT

less pronounced black markings than male
breastband sometimes incomplete
FEMALE (BREEDING)

black forecrown
pale-gray upperparts
black-tipped orange bill
dark breastband
orange legs
MALE (BREEDING)

indistinct, partial breastband
mostly black bill with slight orange base
thin white collar throughout year
ADULT (NON-BREEDING)

FLIGHT: fast, twisting flight; rapid wing beats.

Small and pale, the Piping Plover is at risk due to eroding coastlines, human disturbance, and predation by foxes, raccoons, and cats. With its pale-gray back, it is well camouflaged along beaches or in dunes, but conservation measures, such as fencing off nesting beaches and controlling predators, are necessary to restore populations. Two subspecies of the Piping Plover are recognized; one nests on the Atlantic Coast and the other inland.

VOICE Clear, whistled *peep* call in flight; quiet *peep-lo* during courtship and contact; high-pitched *pipe-pipe-pipe* song.

NESTING Shallow scrape in sand, gravel, dunes, or salt flats; 4 eggs; 1 brood; April–May.

FEEDING Typical run-pause-pluck plover feeding style; diet includes marine worms, insects, and mollusks.

VULNERABLE NESTS
The fragile nature of their preferred nesting sites has led to this species becoming endangered.

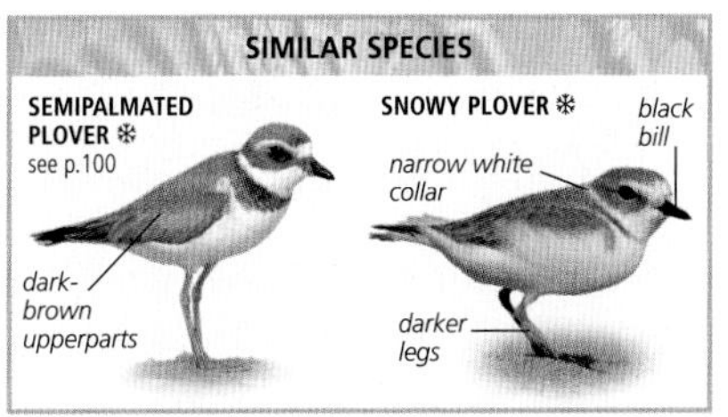
SIMILAR SPECIES
SEMIPALMATED PLOVER ❄
see p.100
dark-brown upperparts
SNOWY PLOVER ❄
black bill
narrow white collar
darker legs

OCCURRENCE
Found along beaches, in saline sandflats, and adjacent mudflats; during winter, found exclusively along the Atlantic and the Gulf Coasts, sandflats, and mudflats. Inland subspecies nest on sand or gravel beaches adjacent to large lakes, rivers, and saline lakes.

Length **6½–7in (17–18cm)**	Wingspan **18–18½in (45–47cm)**	Weight **1⅝–2⅜oz (45–65g)**
Social **Small flocks**	Lifespan **Up to 11 years**	Status **Endangered**

DATE: ____________ TIME: ____________ LOCATION: ____________

Order **Charadriiformes**	Family **Scolopacidae**	Species ***Bartramia longicauda***

Upland Sandpiper

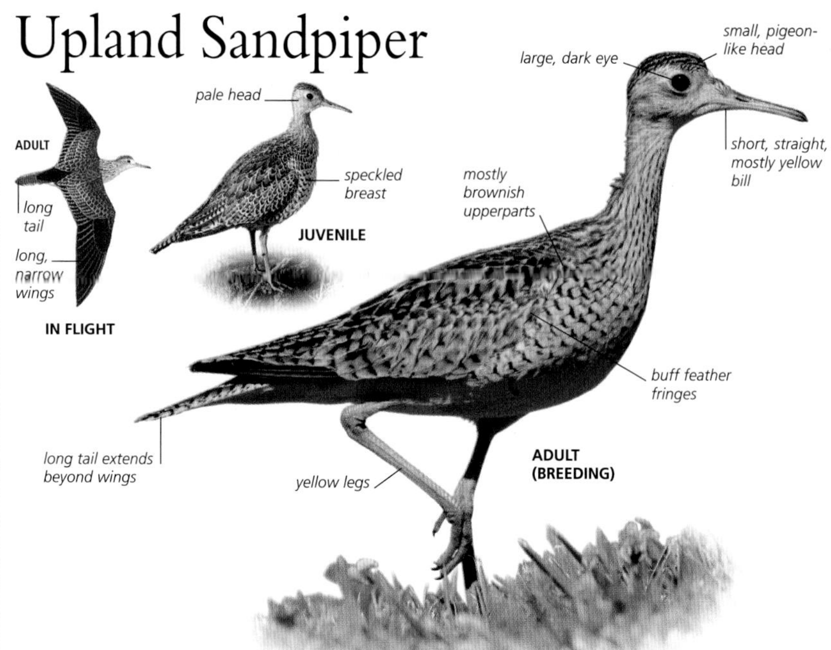

ADULT
long tail
long, narrow wings
IN FLIGHT
pale head
speckled breast
JUVENILE
mostly brownish upperparts
large, dark eye
small, pigeon-like head
short, straight, mostly yellow bill
buff feather fringes
long tail extends beyond wings
yellow legs
ADULT (BREEDING)

Unlike other sandpipers, this graceful bird spends most of its life away from water in grassy habitats. The Upland Sandpiper's coloration helps it camouflage itself in the grasslands, especially while nesting on the ground. It is well known for landing on fence posts and raising its wings while giving its tremulous, whistling call. The bird is currently listed as endangered in many of its breeding states/provinces due to the disappearance of its grassland habitat.

VOICE Flight call a low *qui-pi-pi-pi*; song consists of gurgling notes followed by long, descending "wolf whistle" *whoooleeeeee, wheeeloooo-ooooo*.

NESTING Simple depression in ground among grass clumps; 4 eggs; 1 brood; May.

FEEDING Feeds, with head-bobbing motion, on adult and larval insects, spiders, worms, centipedes; occasionally seeds.

FLIGHT: strong and swift; rapid, fluttering flight in breeding display.

DRY GROUND WADER
A true grassland species, the Upland Sandpiper is rarely found away from these habitats.

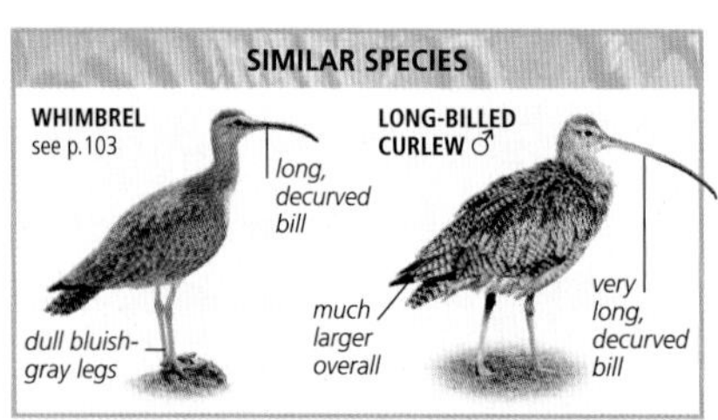

SIMILAR SPECIES
WHIMBREL
see p.103
long, decurved bill
dull bluish-gray legs
LONG-BILLED CURLEW ♂
much larger overall
very long, decurved bill

OCCURRENCE
Breeds in native tallgrass or mixed-grass prairies. Airports make up a large portion of its breeding habitat in the northeast US. During migration and in winter, it prefers shortgrass habitats, such as grazed pastures, turf farms, and cultivated fields.

Length **11–12½in (28–32cm)**	Wingspan **25–27in (64–68cm)**	Weight **4–7oz (150–200g)**
Social **Migrant flocks**	Lifespan **Up to 12 years**	Status **Declining**

 DATE: ______ TIME: ______ LOCATION: ______

Order **Charadriiformes**	Family **Scolopacidae**	Species ***Numenius phaeopus***

Whimbrel

long, pointed wings

ADULT

all-dark rump

coarsely streaked face, neck, and breast

IN FLIGHT

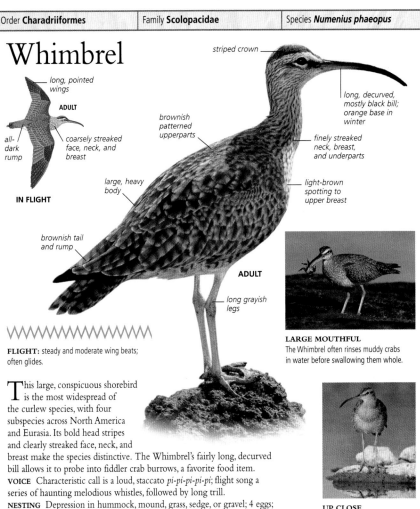

striped crown

long, decurved, mostly black bill; orange base in winter

brownish patterned upperparts

finely streaked neck, breast, and underparts

large, heavy body

light-brown spotting to upper breast

brownish tail and rump

ADULT

long grayish legs

FLIGHT: steady and moderate wing beats; often glides.

LARGE MOUTHFUL
The Whimbrel often rinses muddy crabs in water before swallowing them whole.

This large, conspicuous shorebird is the most widespread of the curlew species, with four subspecies across North America and Eurasia. Its bold head stripes and clearly streaked face, neck, and breast make the species distinctive. The Whimbrel's fairly long, decurved bill allows it to probe into fiddler crab burrows, a favorite food item.

VOICE Characteristic call is a loud, staccato *pi-pi-pi-pi-pi*; flight song a series of haunting melodious whistles, followed by long trill.

NESTING Depression in hummock, mound, grass, sedge, or gravel; 4 eggs; 1 brood; May–August.

FEEDING Probes for crabs, in addition to worms, mollusks, and fish; also eats insects and berries.

UP CLOSE
A close look at the Whimbrel shows this bird's beautiful, fine patterning.

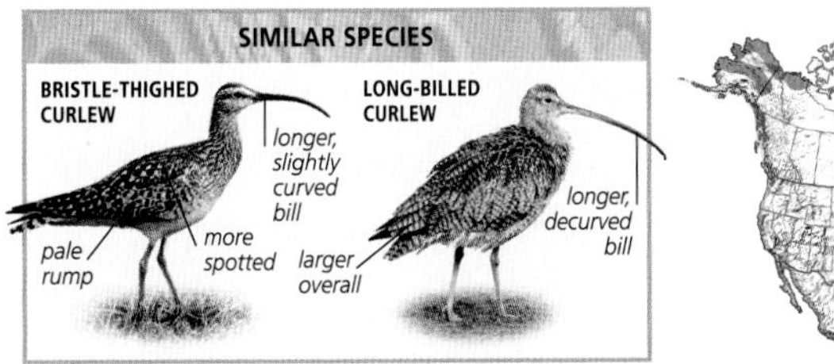
SIMILAR SPECIES
BRISTLE-THIGHED CURLEW
longer, slightly curved bill
pale rump
more spotted
LONG-BILLED CURLEW
longer, decurved bill
larger overall

OCCURRENCE
Several populations breed in northern, sub-Arctic, and low-Arctic regions of North America; during migration and in winter, found mostly in coastal marshes, tidal creeks, flats, and mangroves; also at the inland Salton Sea, California. Winters along rocky coasts in South America.

Length **15½–16½in (39–42cm)**	Wingspan **30–35in (76–89cm)**	Weight **11–18oz (300–500g)**
Social **Flocks**	Lifespan **Up to 19 years**	Status **Secure**

DATE: ____________ TIME: ____________ LOCATION: ____________________

Order **Charadriiformes**	Family **Scolopacidae**	Species ***Limosa haemastica***

Hudsonian Godwit

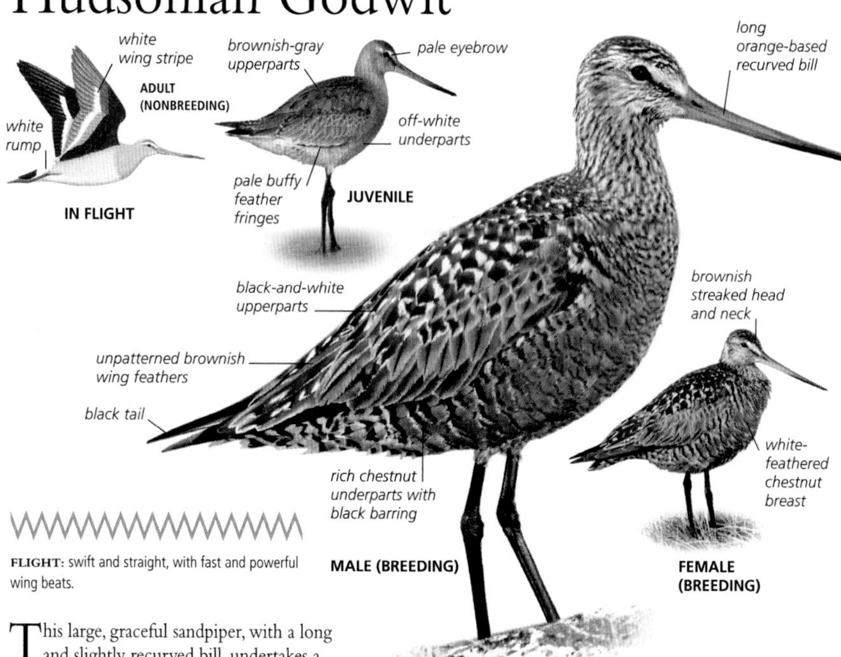

white wing stripe
white rump
ADULT (NONBREEDING)
IN FLIGHT
brownish-gray upperparts
pale eyebrow
off-white underparts
pale buffy feather fringes
JUVENILE
long orange-based recurved bill
black-and-white upperparts
unpatterned brownish wing feathers
black tail
rich chestnut underparts with black barring
MALE (BREEDING)
brownish streaked head and neck
white-feathered chestnut breast
FEMALE (BREEDING)

FLIGHT: swift and straight, with fast and powerful wing beats.

This large, graceful sandpiper, with a long and slightly recurved bill, undertakes a remarkable annual migration from its tundra breeding grounds in Alaska and Canada all the way to extreme southern South America—a distance probably close to 10,000 miles (16,000km) in one direction, with very few stopovers. There are perhaps 50,000–80,000 breeding pairs. Counts in Tierra del Fuego indicate a total of perhaps 30,000 to 40,000 birds wintering there, all found in two areas of tidal mudflats. Between the far North and the far South, North American stops are few, and only in the spring, along a mid-continental central route. Hudsonian Godwits spend six months wintering, two months breeding, and four flying between the two locations.

VOICE Flight call emphatic *peed-wid*; also high *peet* or *kwee*; display song *to-wida to-wida to-wida*, or *to-wit, to-wit, to-wit*.

NESTING Saucer-shaped depression on dry hummock or tussocks under cover; 4 eggs; 1 brood; May–July.

FEEDING Probes in mud for insects, insect grubs, worms, crustaceans, and mollusks; also eats plant tubers in fall.

LONG-HAUL BIRD
Hudsonian Godwits only make a few stops on their long flights to and from South America.

SIMILAR SPECIES

BAR-TAILED GODWIT
more streaks
shorter legs
longer bill

OCCURRENCE
Breeds in the high Arctic, in sedge meadows and bogs in scattered tundra; scarce along the Atlantic Coast in fall, near coastal freshwater reservoirs; but locally common in flooded rice fields, pastures, and reservoirs in spring. Winters in extreme southern Chile and Argentina.

Length **14–16in (35–41cm)**	Wingspan **27–31in (68–78cm)**	Weight **7–12oz (200–350g)**
Social **Flocks**	Lifespan **Up to 29 years**	Status **Vulnerable**

DATE: ____________ TIME: ____________ LOCATION: ____________

Order **Charadriiformes**	Family **Scolopacidae**	Species ***Limosa fedoa***

Marbled Godwit

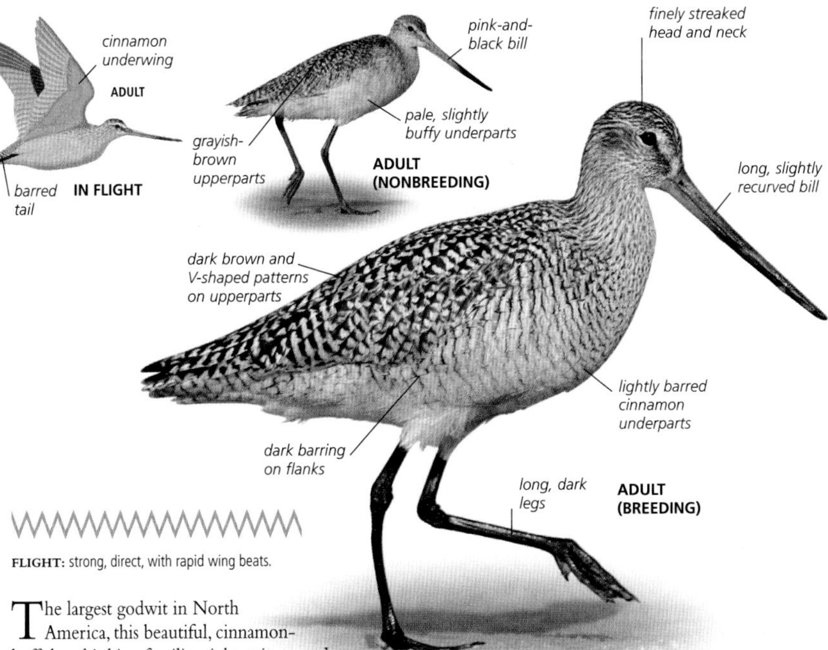
cinnamon underwing
ADULT
barred tail
IN FLIGHT
pink-and-black bill
pale, slightly buffy underparts
grayish-brown upperparts
ADULT (NONBREEDING)
finely streaked head and neck
long, slightly recurved bill
dark brown and V-shaped patterns on upperparts
lightly barred cinnamon underparts
dark barring on flanks
long, dark legs
ADULT (BREEDING)

FLIGHT: strong, direct, with rapid wing beats.

The largest godwit in North America, this beautiful, cinnamon-buff shorebird is a familiar sight at its coastal wintering areas. Its distinctive brown-and-cinnamon plumage and the fact that it chooses open habitats, such as mudflats and floodplains, to feed and roost, make the Marbled Godwit a conspicuous species. A monogamous bird, the Marbled Godwit is also long-lived—the oldest bird recorded was 29 years old.

VOICE Call a nasal *ah-ahk*, and single *ahk*; breeding call, *goddWhit*, *wik-wik*; other calls include *rack-a, karatica*, *ratica*, *ratica*.

NESTING Depression in short grass in Alaska; also nests on vegetation in water; 4 eggs; 1 brood; May–July.

FEEDING Probes mudflats, beaches, short grass for insects, especially grasshoppers; also crustaceans, mollusks, and small fish.

EASILY RECOGNIZED
Its large size and buffy to cinnamon color make this godwit a very distinctive shorebird.

SIMILAR SPECIES

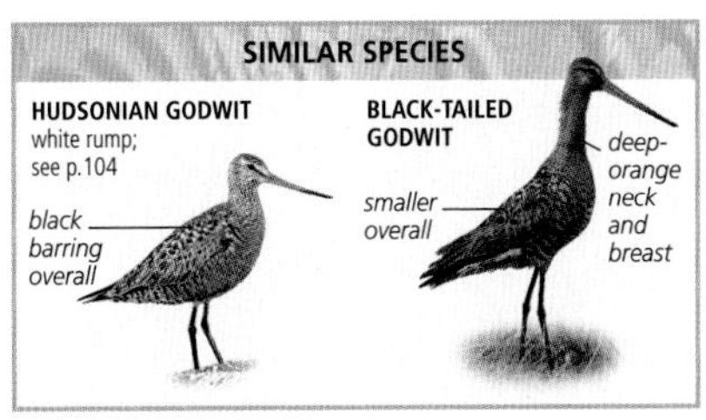
HUDSONIAN GODWIT
white rump;
see p.104
black barring overall
BLACK-TAILED GODWIT
smaller overall
deep-orange neck and breast

OCCURRENCE
Breeds in the grassy marshes of the Great Plains. During migration and in winter, prefers sandy beaches and coastal mudflats with adjoining meadows or prairies in California and the Gulf of Mexico. Also seen on inland wetlands and lake edges.

Length **16½–19in (42–48cm)**	Wingspan **28–32in (70–81cm)**	Weight **10–16oz (275–450g)**
Social **Winter flocks**	Lifespan **Up to 29 years**	Status **Secure**

DATE: ____________ TIME: ____________ LOCATION: ____________

Order **Charadriiformes**	Family **Scolopacidae**	Species ***Arenaria interpres***

Ruddy Turnstone

bold red patches on back and wings

dark flight feathers

ADULT (BREEDING)

IN FLIGHT

black-and-white head and breast pattern

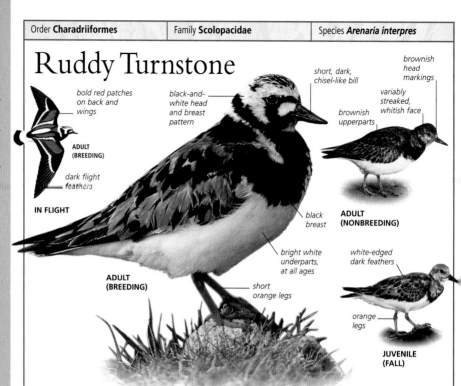

short, dark, chisel-like bill

black breast

bright white underparts, at all ages

short orange legs

ADULT (BREEDING)

brownish head markings

variably streaked, whitish face

brownish upperparts

ADULT (NONBREEDING)

white-edged dark feathers

orange legs

JUVENILE (FALL)

This tame, medium-sized, and stocky sandpiper with a chisel-shaped bill is a common visitor along the shorelines of North and South America. On its high-Arctic breeding grounds, it is bold and aggressive and is able to drive off predators as large as the Glaucous Gull and the Parasitic Jaeger. The Ruddy Turnstone was given its name due to its reddish back color and because of its habit of flipping and overturning items like mollusk shells and pebbles, or digging in the sand and looking for small crustaceans and other marine invertebrates. Two subspecies live in Arctic North America: *A. i. interpres* in northeast Canada and *A. i. morinellas* elsewhere in Canada and Alaska.

VOICE Rapid chatter on breeding ground: *TIT-wooo TIT-woooRITititititit*; flight call a low, rapid *kut-a-kut.*

NESTING Simple scrape lined with lichens and grasses in dry, open areas; 4 eggs; 1 brood; June.

FEEDING Forages along shoreline for crustaceans, insects, including beetles, spiders; also eats plants.

FLIGHT: swift and strong flight, with quick wing beats.

WINTER GATHERINGS

Ruddy Turnstones often congregate in large winter flocks on rocky shorelines.

SIMILAR SPECIES

BLACK TURNSTONE
darker overall
duller legs
no rust color in plumage

OCCURRENCE

Breeds in high-Arctic: wide-open, barren, and grassy habitats and rocky coasts, usually near water. In winter, on sandy or gravel beaches and rocky shorelines, from northern California to South America, and from northern Massachusetts south along the Atlantic and Gulf Coasts.

Length **8–10½in (20–27cm)**	Wingspan **20–22½in (51–57cm)**	Weight **3½–7oz (100–200g)**
Social **Flocks**	Lifespan **Up to 7 years**	Status **Secure**

DATE: ____________ TIME: ____________ LOCATION: ____________

Order **Charadriiformes**	Family **Scolopacidae**	Species ***Calidris canutus***

Red Knot

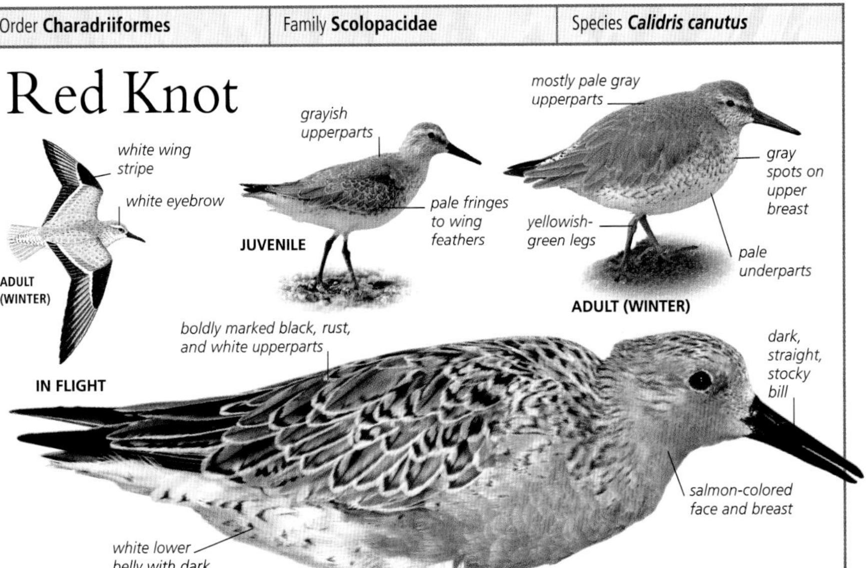

white wing stripe
white eyebrow
ADULT (WINTER)
IN FLIGHT
grayish upperparts
pale fringes to wing feathers
JUVENILE
mostly pale gray upperparts
gray spots on upper breast
yellowish-green legs
pale underparts
ADULT (WINTER)
boldly marked black, rust, and white upperparts
dark, straight, stocky bill
salmon-colored face and breast
white lower belly with dark V-shaped marks
short, dark legs
ADULT (SUMMER)

A substantial, plump sandpiper, the Red Knot is the largest North American shorebird in the genus *Calidris*. There are two North American subspecies—*C. c. rufa* and *C. c. roselaari*. Noted for its extraordinary long-distance migration, *C. c. rufa* flies about 9,300 miles (15,000km) between its high-Arctic breeding grounds and the wintering area in South America, especially in Tierra del Fuego, at the tip of South America. Recent declines have occurred in this population, attributed to overharvesting of horseshoe crab eggs—its critical food source. With the population of *C. c. rufa* having declined from over 100,000 birds in the mid-1980s to below 15,000 today, the Red Knot is now listed as endangered in New Jersey, and faces possible extinction.

VOICE Flight call a soft *kuEEt* or *kuup*; display song eerie *por-meeee por-meeee*, followed by *por-por por-por*.

NESTING Simple scrape in grassy or barren tundra, often lined; 4 eggs; 1 brood; June.

FEEDING Probes mud or sand for insects, plant material, small mollusks, crustaceans, especially small snails, worms, and other invertebrates.

FLIGHT: powerful, swift, direct flight with rapid wing beats.

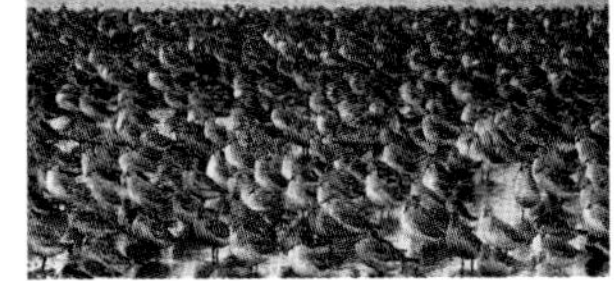

STAGING AREAS
Red Knots form colossal flocks during migration and on their wintering grounds.

SIMILAR SPECIES

BLACK-BELLIED PLOVER
see p.97

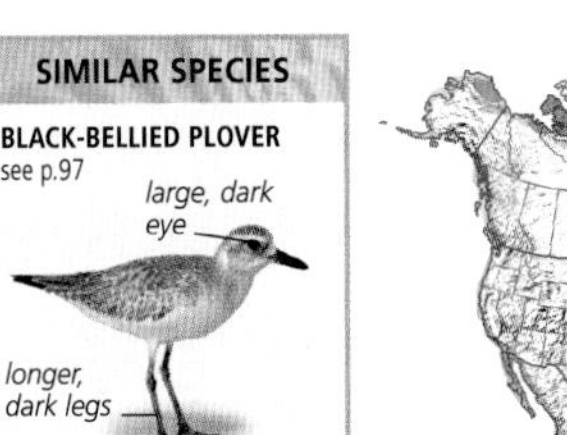

large, dark eye
longer, dark legs

OCCURRENCE
Breeds in flat, barren tundra in the high-Arctic islands and peninsulas. Mostly coastal during migration and winter, preferring sandbars, beaches, and tidal flats, where it congregates in huge flocks.

Length **9–10in (23–25cm)**	Wingspan **23–24in (58–61cm)**	Weight **3⅜–8oz (95–225g)**
Social **Large flocks**	Lifespan **Up to 19 years**	Status **Threatened**

DATE: ______________ TIME: ______________ LOCATION: ______________

Order **Charadriiformes**	Family **Scolopacidae**	Species ***Calidris himantopus***

Stilt Sandpiper

white rump
long, pointed wing
dusky tail band
ADULT (NONBREEDING)
IN FLIGHT

crisp white-and-rust-fringed upperparts
scaly look to upperparts
whitish eyebrow extends behind eye
long dark straight bill
slightly diffused gray streaks to breast and neck
long yellowish legs
JUVENILE (FALL)

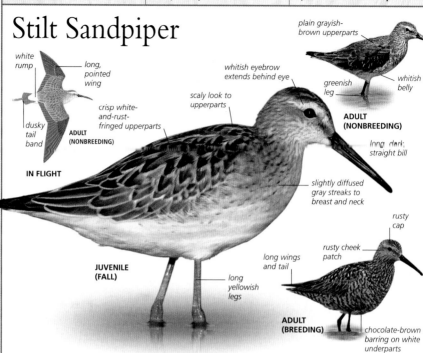

plain grayish-brown upperparts
greenish leg
whitish belly
ADULT (NONBREEDING)

rusty cap
rusty cheek patch
long wings and tail
chocolate-brown barring on white underparts
ADULT (BREEDING)

The slender Stilt Sandpiper is uncommon and unique to North America, where it breeds in several small areas of northern tundra. It favors shallow, freshwater habitats, where it feeds in a distinctive style—walking slowly through belly-deep water with its neck outstretched and bill pointed downward. It either picks at the surface, or submerges itself, keeping its tail raised up all the while. During migration, it forms dense, rapidly moving flocks that sometimes include other sandpiper species.

VOICE Flight or alarm call low, muffled *chuf*; also *krrit* and sharp *kew-it*; display call *xxree-xxree-xxree-xxree-ee-haw, ee-haw.*

NESTING Shallow depression on raised knolls or ridges in tundra; 4 eggs; 1 brood; June.

FEEDING Eats mostly adult and larval insects; also some snails, mollusks, and seeds.

FLIGHT: fast and direct, with rapid beats of its long wings.

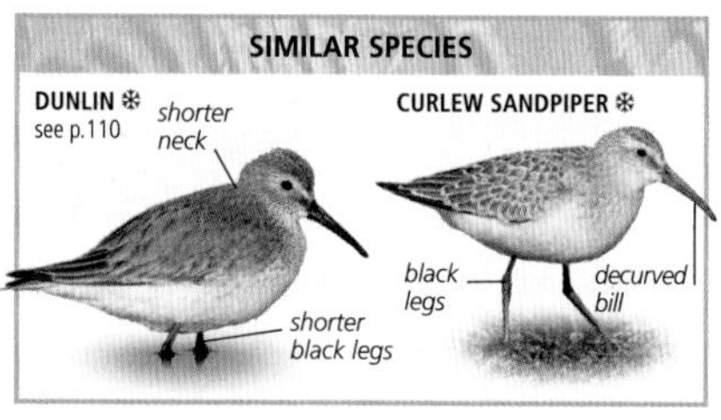
SIMILAR SPECIES
DUNLIN ❄
see p.110
shorter neck
shorter black legs
CURLEW SANDPIPER ❄
black legs
decurved bill

PALE BELOW
Wading through shallow water, this Stilt Sandpiper displays its whitish underparts.

OCCURRENCE
Breeds in moist to wet coastal tundra on well-drained, raised knolls or ridges in Alaska, Yukon, northwestern territories, and the Hudson Bay. During migration and in winter, prefers freshwater habitats, such as flooded fields, marsh pools, reservoirs, and sheltered lagoons to tidal mudflats.

Length **8–9in (20–23cm)**	Wingspan **17–18½in (43–47cm)**	Weight **1¾–2⅛oz (50–60g)**
Social **Pairs/Flocks**	Lifespan **At least 3 years**	Status **Secure**

DATE: ____________ TIME: ____________ LOCATION: ____________

Order **Charadriiformes**	Family **Scolopacidae**	Species ***Calidris alba***

Sanderling

bold white wing stripe
mostly grayish upperparts
ADULT (NONBREEDING)
IN FLIGHT

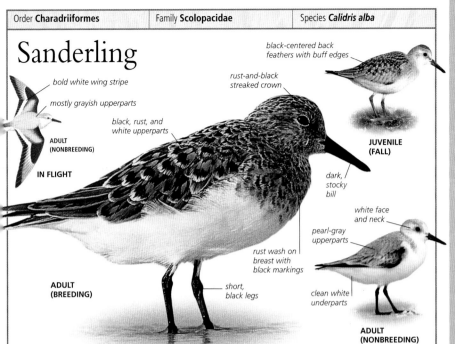

black, rust, and white upperparts
rust-and-black streaked crown
black-centered back feathers with buff edges
JUVENILE (FALL)
dark, stocky bill
white face and neck
pearl-gray upperparts
rust wash on breast with black markings
ADULT (BREEDING)
short, black legs
clean white underparts
ADULT (NONBREEDING)

The Sanderling is among the best-known shorebirds in the world. It breeds in some of the most remote, high-Arctic habitats, from Greenland to Siberia, but occupies just about every temperate and tropical shoreline in the Americas when not breeding. Indeed, its wintering range spans both American coasts, from Canada to Argentina. Feeding in flocks, it is a common sight in winter on sandy beaches. In many places though, the bird is declining rapidly, with pollution of the sea and shore, and the disturbance caused by people using beaches for various recreational purposes being the main causes.

VOICE Flight call squeaky *pweet*, threat call *sew-sew-sew*; display song harsh, buzzy notes and chattering *cher-cher-cher*.

NESTING Small, shallow depression on dry, stony ground; 4 eggs; 1–3 broods; June–July.

FEEDING Probes along the surf-line in sand for insects, small crustaceans, small mollusks, and worms.

FLIGHT: rapid, free-form; birds in flocks twisting and turning as if they were one.

CHASING THE WAVES
The Sanderling scampers after retreating waves to pick up any small creatures stranded by the sea.

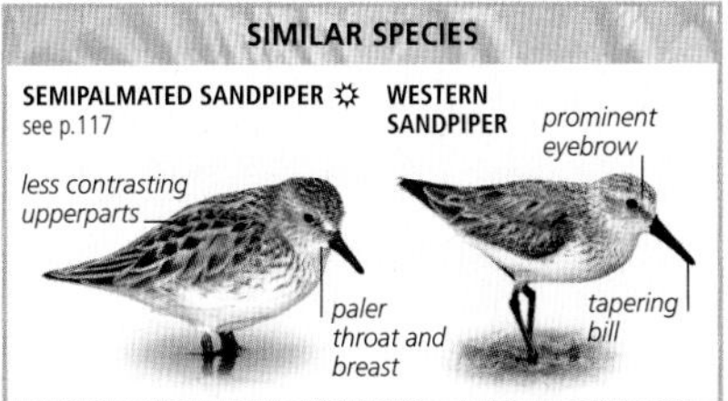
SIMILAR SPECIES
SEMIPALMATED SANDPIPER ☼
see p.117
less contrasting upperparts
paler throat and breast
WESTERN SANDPIPER
prominent eyebrow
tapering bill

OCCURRENCE
Breeds in barren high-Arctic coastal tundra of northernmost Canada, including the islands, north to Ellesmere Island. During winter months and migration, found along all North American coastlines, but especially sandy beaches; inland migrants found along lake and river edges.

Length **7½–8in (19–20cm)**	Wingspan **16–18in (41–46cm)**	Weight **1 7/16–3½oz (40–100g)**
Social **Small flocks**	Lifespan **Up to 10 years**	Status **Declining**

DATE: ____________ TIME: ____________ LOCATION: ____________

Order **Charadriiformes**	Family **Scolopacidae**	Species ***Calidris alpina***

Dunlin

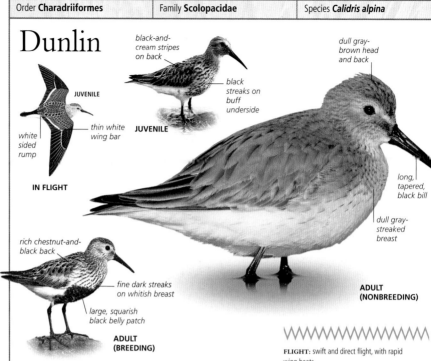

black-and-cream stripes on back
black streaks on buff underside
JUVENILE

JUVENILE
white sided rump
thin white wing bar
IN FLIGHT

dull gray-brown head and back
long, tapered, black bill
dull gray-streaked breast
ADULT (NONBREEDING)

rich chestnut-and-black back
fine dark streaks on whitish breast
large, squarish black belly patch
ADULT (BREEDING)

FLIGHT: swift and direct flight, with rapid wing beats.

The Dunlin is one of the most abundant and widespread of North America's shorebirds, but of the ten officially recognized subspecies, only two breed in Canada: *C. a. arcticola* and *C. a. hudsonia.* The Dunlin is unmistakable in its striking red-backed, black-bellied breeding plumage. In winter, it sports much drabber colors but more than makes up for this by gathering in spectacular flocks—of many thousands of birds—on its favorite coastal mudflats.

VOICE Call accented trill, *drurr-drurr*, that rises slightly, then descends; flight call *jeeezp*; song *wrraah-wrraah*.

NESTING Simple cup lined with grasses, leaves, and lichens in moist to wet tundra; 4 eggs; 1 brood; June–July.

FEEDING Probes for marine, freshwater, terrestrial invertebrates: clams, worms, insect larvae, crustaceans; also plants and small fish.

OLD RED BACK
The Dunlin was once known as the Red-backed Sandpiper due to its distinct breeding plumage.

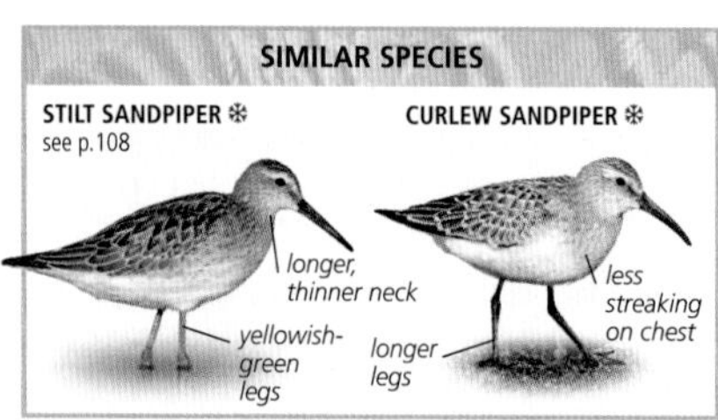
SIMILAR SPECIES
STILT SANDPIPER ❄
see p.108
longer, thinner neck
yellowish-green legs
CURLEW SANDPIPER ❄
less streaking on chest
longer legs

OCCURRENCE
Breeds in Arctic and sub-Arctic moist, wet tundra, often near ponds, with drier islands for nest sites. In migration and winter, prefers coastal areas with extensive mudflats and sandy beaches; also feeds in flooded fields and seasonal inland wetlands.

Length **6½–8½in (16–22cm)**	Wingspan **12½–17½in (32–44cm)**	Weight **1⁹⁄₁₆–2¼oz (45–65g)**
Social **Large flocks**	Lifespan **Up to 24 years**	Status **Declining**

DATE: ____________ TIME: ____________ LOCATION: ____________

Order **Charadriiformes**	Family **Scolopacidae**	Species ***Calidris maritima***

Purple Sandpiper

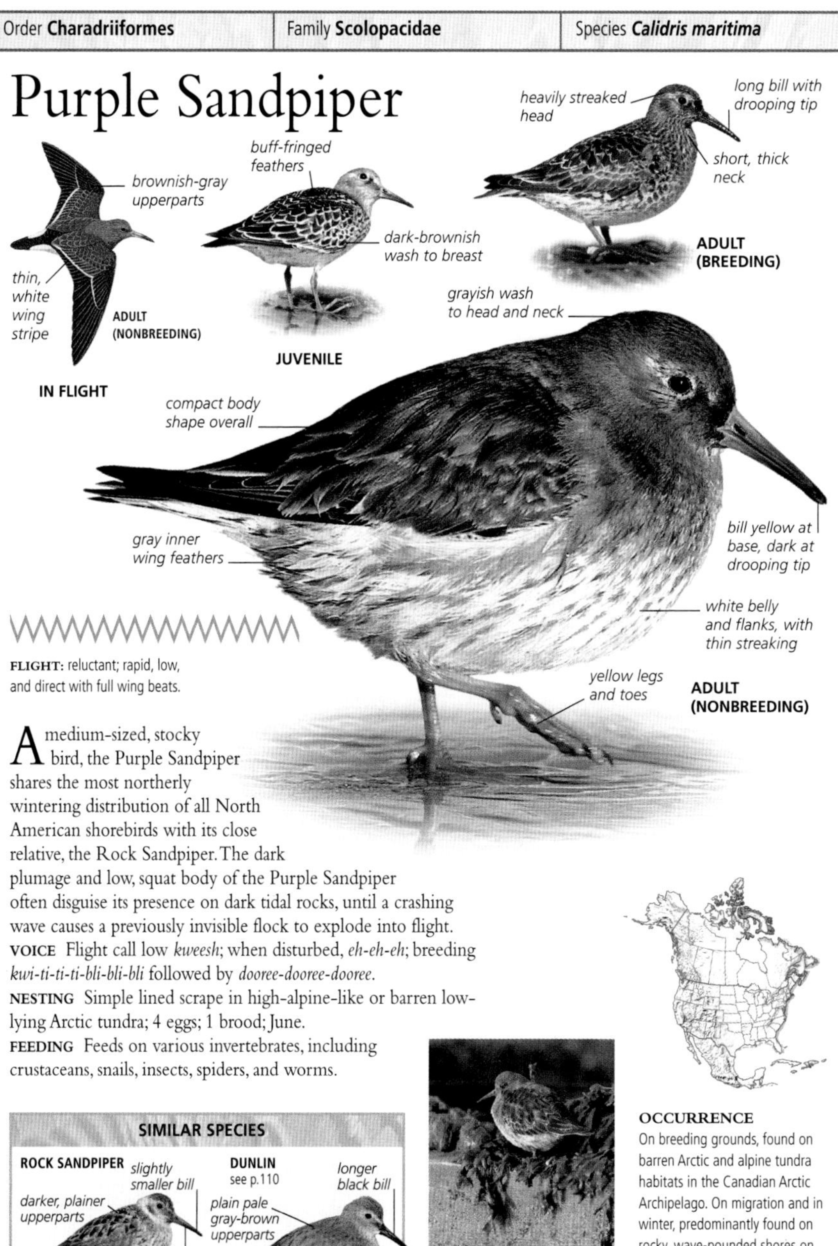

heavily streaked head
long bill with drooping tip
short, thick neck
ADULT (BREEDING)
buff-fringed feathers
brownish-gray upperparts
dark-brownish wash to breast
thin, white wing stripe
ADULT (NONBREEDING)
IN FLIGHT
JUVENILE
grayish wash to head and neck
compact body shape overall
bill yellow at base, dark at drooping tip
gray inner wing feathers
white belly and flanks, with thin streaking
yellow legs and toes
ADULT (NONBREEDING)

FLIGHT: reluctant; rapid, low, and direct with full wing beats.

A medium-sized, stocky bird, the Purple Sandpiper shares the most northerly wintering distribution of all North American shorebirds with its close relative, the Rock Sandpiper. The dark plumage and low, squat body of the Purple Sandpiper often disguise its presence on dark tidal rocks, until a crashing wave causes a previously invisible flock to explode into flight.

VOICE Flight call low *kweesh*; when disturbed, *eh-eh-eh*; breeding *kwi-ti-ti-ti-bli-bli-bli* followed by *dooree-dooree-dooree*.

NESTING Simple lined scrape in high-alpine-like or barren low-lying Arctic tundra; 4 eggs; 1 brood; June.

FEEDING Feeds on various invertebrates, including crustaceans, snails, insects, spiders, and worms.

SIMILAR SPECIES

ROCK SANDPIPER
slightly smaller bill
darker, plainer upperparts
less orange color to base of bill
DUNLIN
see p.110
longer black bill
plain pale gray-brown upperparts

WINTER EXPOSURE
The Purple Sandpiper winters mainly on exposed rocky shores along the Eastern Seaboard.

OCCURRENCE
On breeding grounds, found on barren Arctic and alpine tundra habitats in the Canadian Arctic Archipelago. On migration and in winter, predominantly found on rocky, wave-pounded shores on the Eastern Seaboard.

Length **8–8½in (20–21cm)**	Wingspan **16½–18½in (42–47cm)**	Weight **1¾–3½oz (50–100g)**
Social **Small flocks**	Lifespan **Up to 20 years**	Status **Declining**

DATE: ____________ TIME: ____________ LOCATION: ____________

Order **Charadriiformes**	Family **Scolopacidae**	Species ***Calidris bairdii***

Baird's Sandpiper

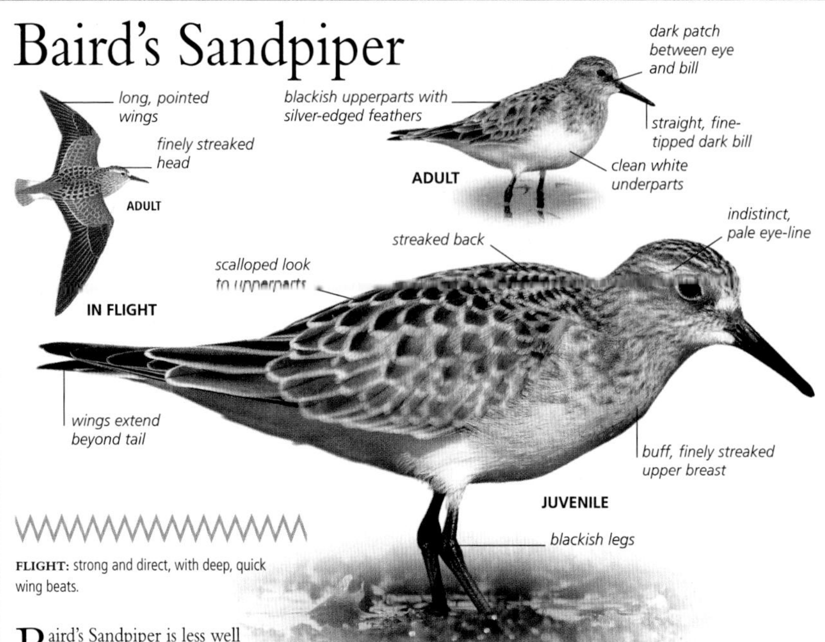

long, pointed wings
finely streaked head
ADULT
IN FLIGHT
blackish upperparts with silver-edged feathers
dark patch between eye and bill
straight, fine-tipped dark bill
clean white underparts
ADULT
indistinct, pale eye-line
streaked back
scalloped look to upperparts
wings extend beyond tail
buff, finely streaked upper breast
JUVENILE
blackish legs

FLIGHT: strong and direct, with deep, quick wing beats.

Baird's Sandpiper is less well known than the other North American *Calidris* sandpipers. It was named in 1861, later than its relatives, by the famous North American ornithologist Elliott Coues, a former surgeon in the US Army, in honor of Spencer Fullerton Baird. Both men were founding members of the AOS (the American Ornithological Society). From its high-Arctic tundra habitat, Baird's Sandpiper moves across North America and the western US into South America, and all the way to Tierra del Fuego—a remarkable biannual journey of 6,000–9,000 miles (9,700–14,500km).

VOICE Flight call a low, dry *preep*; song on Arctic breeding ground: *brraay, brray, brray*, followed by *hee-aaw, hee-aaw, hee-aaw*.

NESTING Shallow depression in coastal or upland tundra; 4 eggs; 1 brood; June.

FEEDING Picks and probes for insects and larvae; also spiders and pond crustaceans.

FEEDING IN FLOCKS
Flocks of this sandpiper rush about in search of food in shallow water and muddy areas.

SIMILAR SPECIES

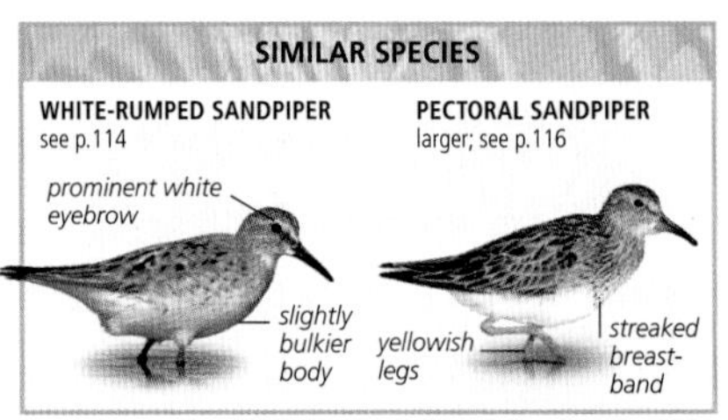

WHITE-RUMPED SANDPIPER
see p.114
prominent white eyebrow
slightly bulkier body
PECTORAL SANDPIPER
larger; see p.116
yellowish legs
streaked breast-band

OCCURRENCE
Breeds in tundra habitats of high-Arctic Alaska and Canada. During migration and winter, inland freshwater habitats: lake and river margins, wet pastures, rice fields; also tidal flats at coastal locations. In winter, common in the high Andes of South America, and sometimes all the way to Tierra del Fuego.

Length **5¾–7¼in (14.5–18.5cm)**	Wingspan **16–18½in (41–47cm)**	Weight **1¹⁄₁₆–2oz (30–55g)**
Social **Flocks**	Lifespan **Unknown**	Status **Secure**

DATE: ______________ TIME: ______________ LOCATION: ______________

Order **Charadriiformes**	Family **Scolopacidae**	Species ***Calidris minutilla***

Least Sandpiper

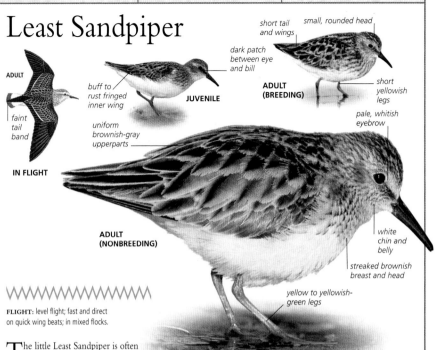

short tail and wings
small, rounded head
dark patch between eye and bill
ADULT (BREEDING)
short yellowish legs
ADULT
faint tail band
IN FLIGHT
buff to rust fringed inner wing
JUVENILE
uniform brownish-gray upperparts
pale, whitish eyebrow
white chin and belly
ADULT (NONBREEDING)
streaked brownish breast and head
yellow to yellowish-green legs

FLIGHT: level flight; fast and direct on quick wing beats; in mixed flocks.

The little Least Sandpiper is often overlooked because of its muted plumage and preference for feeding unobtrusively near vegetative cover. With its brown or brownish-gray plumage, the Least Sandpiper virtually disappears in the landscape when feeding crouched down on wet margins of water bodies. The bird is often found in small to medium flocks, members of which typically are nervous when foraging, and frequently burst into flight, only to alight a short way off.

VOICE Its flight call, *kreeeep*, rises in pitch, often repeated two-syllable *kree-eep*; display call trilled *b-reeee*, *b-reeee*, *b-reeee*.

NESTING Depression in open, sub-Arctic habitat near water; 4 eggs; 1 brood; May–June.

FEEDING Forages for variety of small terrestrial and aquatic prey, especially sand fleas, mollusks, and flies.

FLOCK IN FLIGHT
The narrow pointed wings of the Least Sandpiper allow it to fly fast and level.

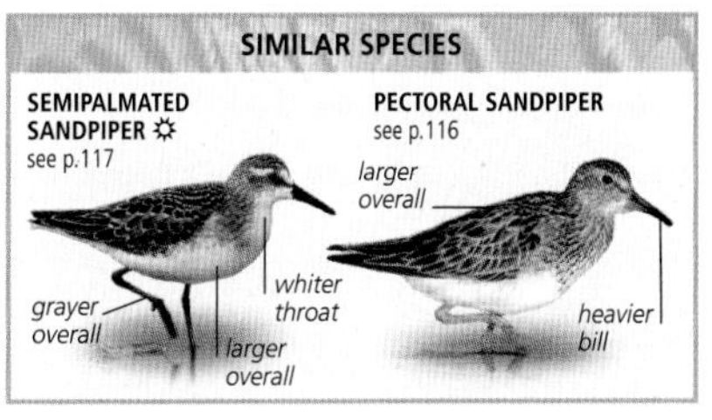
SIMILAR SPECIES
SEMIPALMATED SANDPIPER ☼
see p.117
grayer overall
whiter throat
larger overall
PECTORAL SANDPIPER
see p.116
larger overall
heavier bill

OCCURRENCE
Breeds in wet low-Arctic areas from Alaska and the Yukon to Quebec and Newfoundland. During migration and in winter, uses muddy areas, such as lake shores, riverbanks, flooded fields, and tidal flats. Winters from southern North America south to Peru and Brazil.

Length **4¾in (12cm)**	Wingspan **13–14in (33–35cm)**	Weight **5/16–1oz (9–27g)**
Social **Flocks**	Lifespan **Up to 16 years**	Status **Declining**

DATE: ____________ TIME: ____________ LOCATION: ____________

Order **Charadriiformes**	Family **Scolopacidae**	Species ***Calidris fuscicollis***

White-rumped Sandpiper

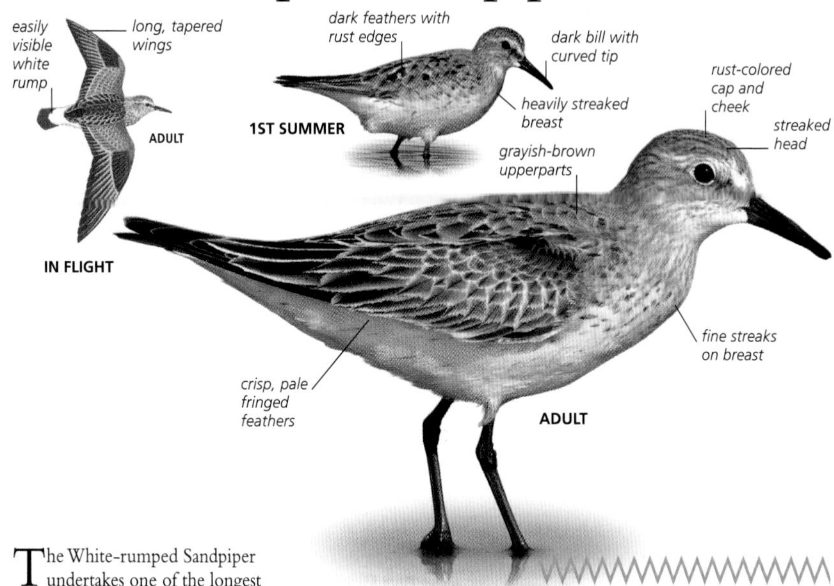
easily visible white rump
long, tapered wings
ADULT
IN FLIGHT
dark feathers with rust edges
dark bill with curved tip
heavily streaked breast
1ST SUMMER
rust-colored cap and cheek
streaked head
grayish-brown upperparts
fine streaks on breast
crisp, pale fringed feathers
ADULT

The White-rumped Sandpiper undertakes one of the longest migrations of any bird in the Western Hemisphere. From its high-Arctic breeding grounds in Alaska and Canada, it migrates in several long jumps to extreme southern South America—about 9,000–12,000 miles (14,500–19,300km), twice a year. Almost the entire population migrates through the central US and Canada in spring, with several stopovers, which are critical to the success of its journey. While associating with other shorebird species during migration and winter, it can be overlooked in the crowd. Its insect-like call and white rump aid identification.

VOICE Call a very high-pitched, insect-like *tzeet*; flight song an insect-like, high-pitched, rattling buzz, interspersed with grunts.

NESTING Shallow depression in usually wet but well-vegetated tundra; 4 eggs; 1 brood; June.

FEEDING Picks and probes for insects, spiders, earthworms, and marine worms; also some plant matter.

FLIGHT: fast, strong, and direct flight with deep wing beats.

WING POWER

Long, narrow wings enable this species to migrate to and from the Arctic and Tierra del Fuego.

SIMILAR SPECIES

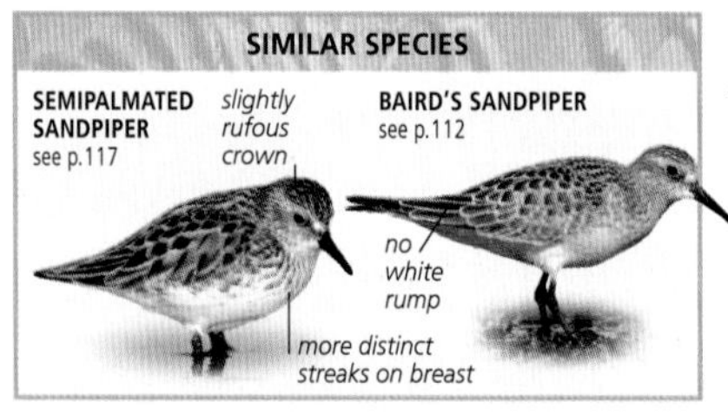
SEMIPALMATED SANDPIPER
see p.117
slightly rufous crown
more distinct streaks on breast
BAIRD'S SANDPIPER
see p.112
no white rump

OCCURRENCE

Breeds in wet but well-vegetated tundra, usually near ponds, lakes, or streams. During migration and winter, grassy areas: flooded fields, grassy lake margins, rivers, ponds, grassy margins of tidal mudflats, and roadside ditches. On wintering grounds, often associates with Baird's Sandpiper.

Length **6–6¾in (15–17cm)**	Wingspan **16–18in (41–46cm)**	Weight **⅞–1¾oz (25–50g)**
Social **Flocks**	Lifespan **Unknown**	Status **Secure**

DATE: ____________ TIME: ____________ LOCATION: ____________

Order **Charadriiformes**	Family **Scolopacidae**	Species ***Calidris subruficollis***

Buff-breasted Sandpiper

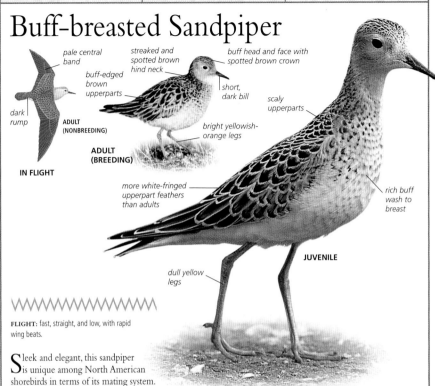

pale central band
dark rump
ADULT (NONBREEDING)
IN FLIGHT

streaked and spotted brown hind neck
buff-edged brown upperparts
buff head and face with spotted brown crown
short, dark bill
bright yellowish-orange legs
ADULT (BREEDING)

scaly upperparts
more white-fringed upperpart feathers than adults
rich buff wash to breast
dull yellow legs
JUVENILE

FLIGHT: fast, straight, and low, with rapid wing beats.

Sleek and elegant, this sandpiper is unique among North American shorebirds in terms of its mating system. On the ground in the Arctic, each male flashes his white underwings to attract females for mating. After mating, the female leaves to perform all nest duties alone, while the male continues to display and mate with other females. Once nesting is over, the Buff-breasted Sandpiper migrates an astonishing 16,000 miles (26,000km) from its breeding grounds to winter in temperate South America.

VOICE Flight call soft, short *gert*, or longer, rising *grriit*.

NESTING Simple depression on well-drained moss or grass hummock; 4 eggs; 1 brood; June.

FEEDING Forages on land for insects, insect larvae, and spiders; occasionally eats seeds.

LANDLUBBER
The Buff-breasted Sandpiper is very much a shorebird of dry land; it doesn't swim or dive.

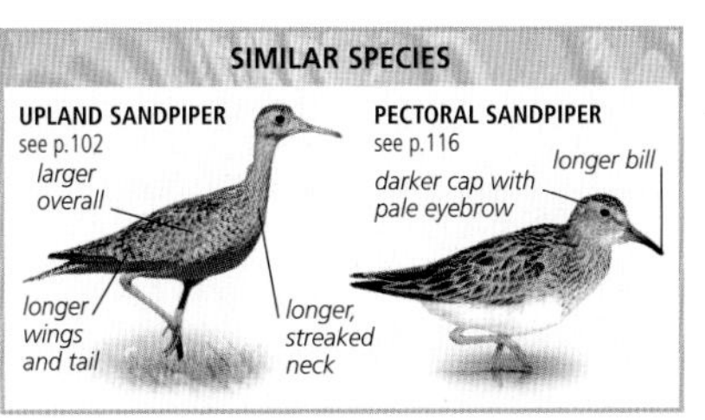
SIMILAR SPECIES
UPLAND SANDPIPER
see p.102
larger overall
longer wings and tail
longer, streaked neck
PECTORAL SANDPIPER
see p.116
darker cap with pale eyebrow
longer bill

OCCURRENCE
Breeds in moist to wet, grassy or sedge coastal tundra; during migration, favors shortgrass areas, such as pastures, sod farms, meadows, rice fields, or agricultural areas. Winters in the Pampas region of South America in short, wet grass habitats.

Length **7$\frac{1}{4}$–8in (18.5–20cm)**	Wingspan **17–18$\frac{1}{2}$in (43–47cm)**	Weight **1$\frac{7}{16}$–3$\frac{3}{8}$oz (40–95g)**
Social **Large flocks**	Lifespan **Unknown**	Status **Special Concern**

DATE: ______________ TIME: ______________ LOCATION: ______________

Order **Charadriiformes**	Family **Scolopacidae**	Species ***Calidris melanotos***

Pectoral Sandpiper

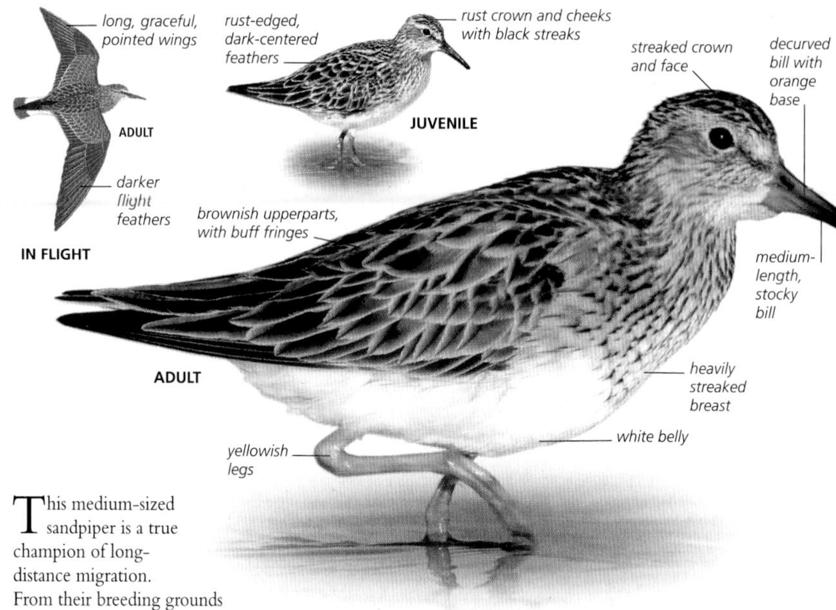
long, graceful, pointed wings
ADULT
darker flight feathers
IN FLIGHT
rust-edged, dark-centered feathers
rust crown and cheeks with black streaks
JUVENILE
streaked crown and face
decurved bill with orange base
brownish upperparts, with buff fringes
medium-length, stocky bill
ADULT
heavily streaked breast
white belly
yellowish legs

This medium-sized sandpiper is a true champion of long-distance migration. From their breeding grounds in the high-Arctic to their wintering grounds on the pampas of southern South America, some birds travel up to 30,000 miles (48,000km) each year. The Pectoral Sandpiper is a promiscuous breeder, with males keeping harems of females in guarded territories. Males mate with as many females as they can attract, with a display that includes a deep, booming call, and flights, but take no part in nest duties. Males migrate earlier than females, with both sexes preferring wet, grassy habitats during migration and in winter.

VOICE Flight call low, trilled *chrrk*; display song deep, hollow hooting: *whoop, whoop, whoop*.

NESTING Shallow depression on ridges in moist to wet sedge tundra; 4 eggs; 1 brood; June.

FEEDING Probes or jabs mud for larvae, and forages for insects and spiders on tundra.

FLIGHT: fast and direct, with rapid, powerful wing beats; flocks zigzag when flushed.

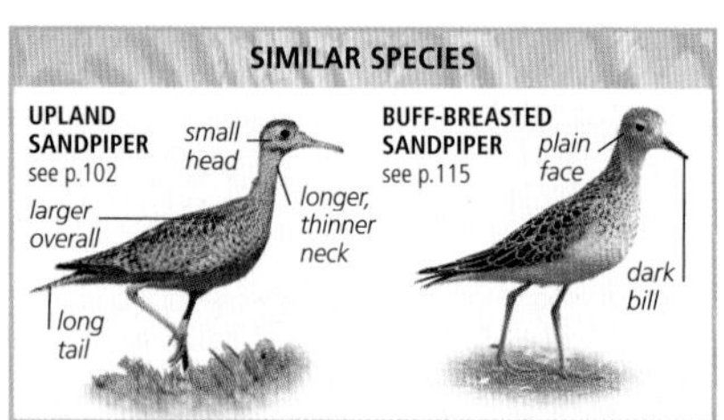
SIMILAR SPECIES
UPLAND SANDPIPER
see p.102
small head
larger overall
longer, thinner neck
long tail
BUFF-BREASTED SANDPIPER
see p.115
plain face
dark bill

LONG JOURNEYS
This species migrates long distances to arrive in southern South America for the winter.

OCCURRENCE
In North America, breeds in northern Alaska, northern Yukon, Northern Territories, and some islands of the Canadian Arctic Archipelago, in wet, grassy tundra, especially near coasts. On migration and in winter favors wet pastures, the grassy margins of ponds and lakes, and salt marshes.

Length **7½–9in (19–23cm)**	Wingspan **16½–19½in (42–49cm)**	Weight **1¾–4oz (50–125g)**
Social **Migrant flocks**	Lifespan **Up to 4½ years**	Status **Secure**

DATE: ____________ TIME: ____________ LOCATION: ____________

Order **Charadriiformes**	Family **Scolopacidae**	Species ***Calidris pusilla***

Semipalmated Sandpiper

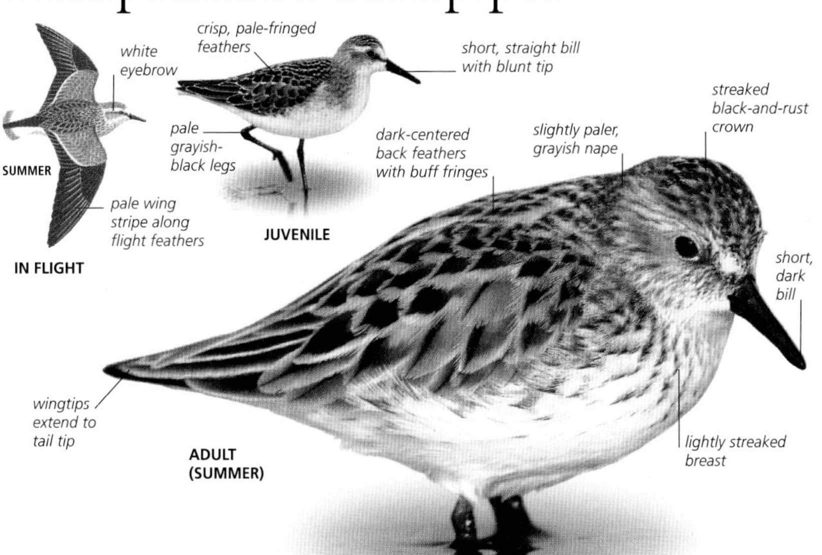

white eyebrow
crisp, pale-fringed feathers
short, straight bill with blunt tip
SUMMER
pale grayish-black legs
pale wing stripe along flight feathers
JUVENILE
IN FLIGHT
dark-centered back feathers with buff fringes
slightly paler, grayish nape
streaked black-and-rust crown
short, dark bill
wingtips extend to tail tip
ADULT (SUMMER)
lightly streaked breast

This is the most abundant of the so-called "peep" *Calidris* sandpipers, especially in the eastern US. Flocks of up to 300,000 birds gather on migration staging areas. As a species, though, it can be hard to identify due to plumage variation between juveniles and breeding adults, and a bill that varies markedly in size and shape from West to East. Semipalmated sandpipers from northeasterly breeding grounds may fly from their northeasterly breeding grounds nonstop to their South American wintering grounds in the fall.

VOICE Flight call *chrrk* or higher, sharper *chit*; display song monotonous, droning trill, often repeated for minutes at a time.

NESTING Shallow, lined scrape in shortgrass habitat; 4 eggs; 1 brood; May–June.

FEEDING Probes mud for aquatic and terrestrial invertebrates, such as mollusks, worms, and spiders.

FLIGHT: fast and direct on narrow, pointed, wings; flies in large flocks in winter.

SLEEPING TOGETHER
Semipalmated Sandpipers form large feeding or resting flocks on migration and in winter.

OCCURRENCE
Breeds in Arctic and sub-Arctic tundra habitats near water; in Alaska, on outer coastal plain. Migrants occur in shallow fresh- or saltwater and open muddy areas with little vegetation, such as intertidal flats or lake shores. Winters in Central and South America, south to Brazil and Peru.

SIMILAR SPECIES

SANDERLING see p.109
more contrasting upperparts; *darker breast*

WESTERN SANDPIPER ❄
puffier head; *usually longer legs*; *usually more pointed bill*

LEAST SANDPIPER ❄ see p.113
yellowish legs; *smaller overall*

Length **$5\frac{1}{4}$–6in (13.5–15cm)**	Wingspan **$13\frac{1}{2}$–15in (34–38cm)**	Weight **$\frac{1}{2}$–$1\frac{7}{16}$oz (14–40g)**
Social **Large flocks**	Lifespan **Up to 12 years**	Status **Secure**

DATE: ____________ TIME: ____________ LOCATION: ____________

Order **Charadriiformes**	Family **Scolopacidae**	Species ***Limnodromus griseus***

Short-billed Dowitcher

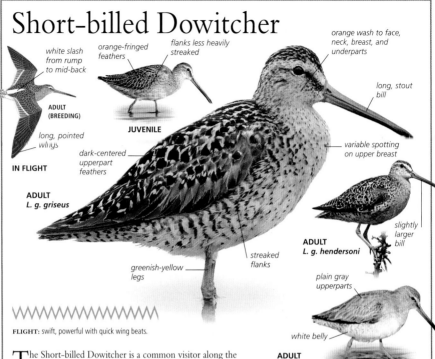

white slash from rump to mid-back

ADULT (BREEDING)

long, pointed wings

IN FLIGHT

orange-fringed feathers

flanks less heavily streaked

JUVENILE

orange wash to face, neck, breast, and underparts

long, stout bill

variable spotting on upper breast

dark-centered upperpart feathers

ADULT
L. g. griseus

streaked flanks

greenish-yellow legs

slightly larger bill

ADULT
L. g. hendersoni

plain gray upperparts

white belly

ADULT (NONBREEDING)

FLIGHT: swift, powerful with quick wing beats.

The Short-billed Dowitcher is a common visitor along the Atlantic, Gulf, and Pacific Coasts. Its remote and bug-infested breeding areas in northern bogs have hindered the study of its breeding behavior until recent years. There are three subspecies (*L. g. griseus*, *L. g. hendersoni*, and *L. g. caurinus*), which differ in plumage, size, and respective breeding areas. Recent knowledge about shape and structure has helped ornithologists distinguish the Short-billed from the Long-billed Dowitcher.

VOICE Flight call low, plaintive *tu-tu-tu*, 3–4 notes; flight song *tu-tu*, *tu-tu*, *toodle-ee*, *tu-tu*, ending with low *anh-anh-anh*.

NESTING Simple depression, typically in sedge hummock; 4 eggs; 1 brood; May–June.

FEEDING Probes in "sewing machine" feeding style, with water up to belly, for aquatic mollusks, crustaceans, and insects.

ORANGE UNDERPARTS
In complete breeding plumage, the Short-billed Dowitcher is orange, even in late afternoon light.

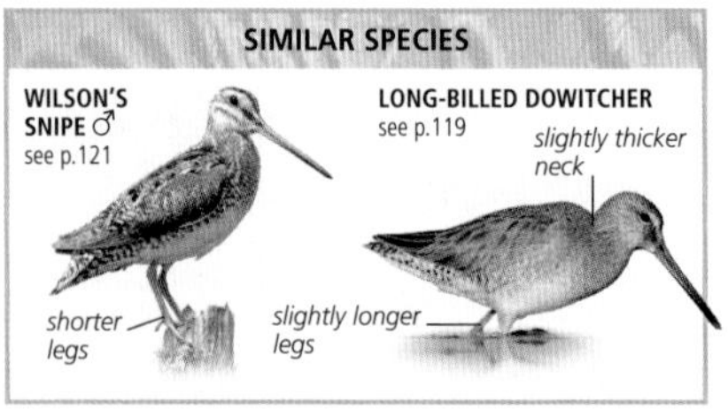
SIMILAR SPECIES
WILSON'S SNIPE ♂
see p.121
shorter legs
LONG-BILLED DOWITCHER
see p.119
slightly thicker neck
slightly longer legs

OCCURRENCE
Breeds mostly in sedge meadows or bogs with interspersed spruce and tamaracks, between sub-Arctic tundra and boreal forest. Migrates south to Central and South America, preferring coastal mudflats, salt marshes, or adjacent freshwater pools.

Length **9–10in (23–25cm)**	Wingspan **18–20in (46–51cm)**	Weight **2½–5½oz (70–155g)**
Social **Pairs/Flocks**	Lifespan **Up to 20 years**	Status **Secure (p)**

Order **Charadriiformes**	Family **Scolopacidae**	Species ***Limnodromus scolopaceus***

Long-billed Dowitcher

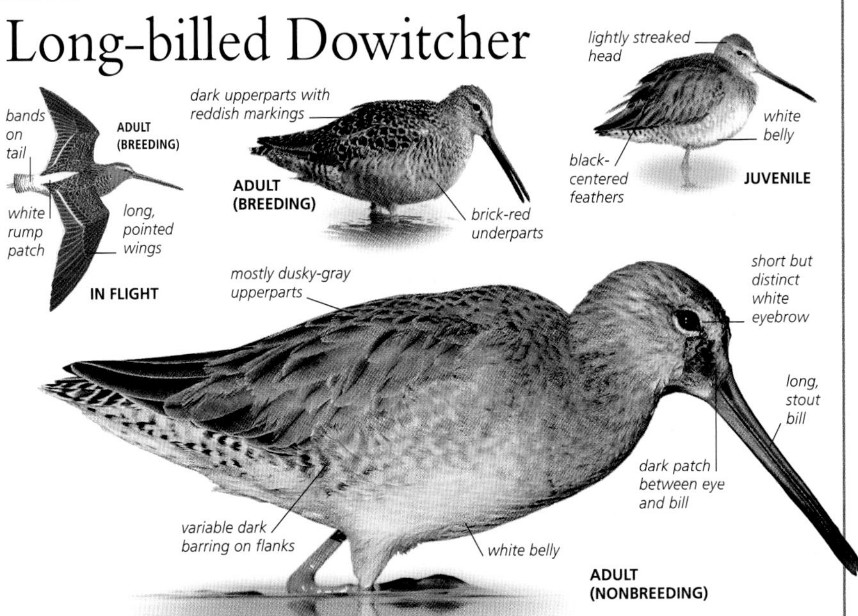

bands on tail
white rump patch
long, pointed wings
ADULT (BREEDING)
IN FLIGHT
dark upperparts with reddish markings
ADULT (BREEDING)
brick-red underparts
lightly streaked head
white belly
black-centered feathers
JUVENILE
mostly dusky-gray upperparts
short but distinct white eyebrow
long, stout bill
dark patch between eye and bill
variable dark barring on flanks
white belly
ADULT (NONBREEDING)

It was not until 1950 that museum and field studies identified two separate species of dowitcher in North America. The Long-billed Dowitcher is usually slightly larger, longer-legged, and heavier in the chest and neck than the Short-billed Dowitcher. The breeding ranges of the two species are separate, but their migration and en route stopover areas overlap. The Long-billed Dowitcher is usually found in freshwater wetlands, and in the fall most of its population is found west of the Mississippi River.

VOICE Flight and alarm call sharp, whistled *keek*, given singly or in series when agitated; song buzzy *pipipipipipi-chi-drrr.*

NESTING Deep sedge or grass-lined depression in sedge or grass; 4 eggs; 1 brood; May–June.

FEEDING Probes wet ground with "sewing-machine" motion for spiders, snails, worms, insects, and seeds.

FLIGHT: swift, direct flier with fast, powerful wing beats.

TOUCHY FEELY
Sensitive touch receptors at the tip of the bird's bill enable it to feel in the mud for food.

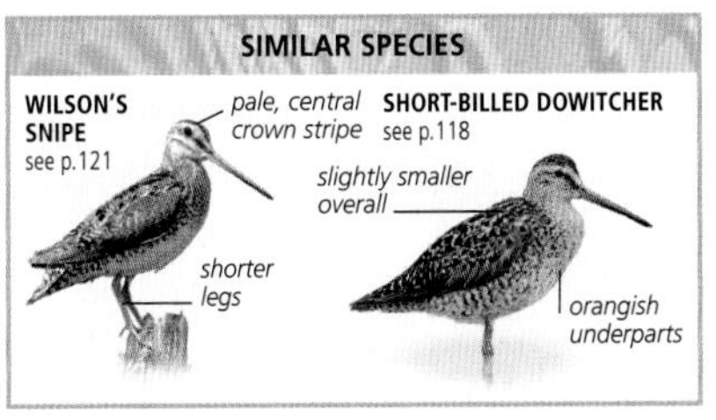

SIMILAR SPECIES
WILSON'S SNIPE
see p.121
pale, central crown stripe
shorter legs
SHORT-BILLED DOWITCHER
see p.118
slightly smaller overall
orangish underparts

OCCURRENCE
Breeds in wet, grassy meadows or coastal sedge tundra near freshwater pools. Migrates to Mexico and Central America, south to Panama, found in freshwater habitats, including ponds, flooded fields, lake shores, also sheltered lagoons, salt marsh pools, and tidal mudflats.

Length **9½–10in (24–26cm)**	Wingspan **18–20½in (46–52cm)**	Weight **3–4oz (85–125g)**
Social **Pairs/Flocks**	Lifespan **Up to 7 years**	Status **Vulnerable**

DATE: ____________ TIME: ____________ LOCATION: ____________

Order **Charadriiformes**	Family **Scolopacidae**	Species ***Scolopax minor***

American Woodcock

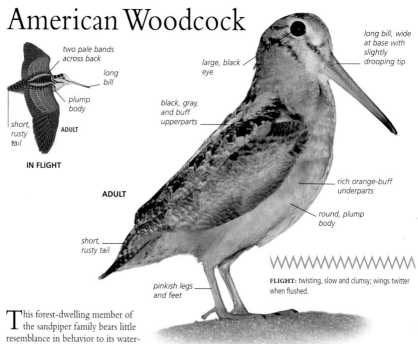

two pale bands across back
long bill
plump body
short, rusty tail
ADULT
IN FLIGHT

large, black eye
long bill, wide at base with slightly drooping tip
black, gray, and buff upperparts
ADULT
rich orange-buff underparts
round, plump body
short, rusty tail
pinkish legs and feet

FLIGHT: twisting, slow and clumsy; wings twitter when flushed.

This forest-dwelling member of the sandpiper family bears little resemblance in behavior to its water-favoring relatives, but slightly resembles Wilson's Snipe and the dowitchers. Although widespread, the American Woodcock is very secretive and seldom seen, except during its twilight courtship displays. It is largely nocturnal, and feeds in mature fields or woodlands. Its noisy, repetitive display flights are a welcome sign of spring in northern breeding areas.

VOICE Low, nasal *peen* call by male during dawn and dusk display; variety of chirping and twittering sounds given by male in display flight, made by air passing through narrow outer wing feathers.

NESTING Shallow depression in existing leaf-and-twig litter in young, mixed-growth woodlands; 4 eggs; 1 brood; January (southern populations) and April (northern populations).

FEEDING Probes deep in damp soil or mud—mostly for earthworms, but also insects, snails, and some plants.

EYES IN THE BACK OF THE HEAD
A foraging woodcock can see frontward and backward at the same time to detect food and predators.

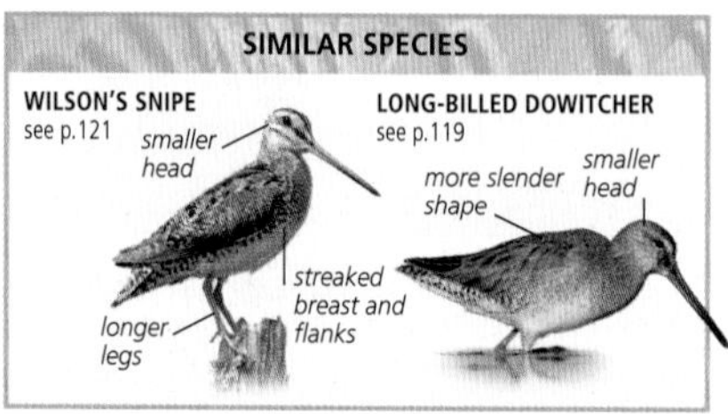
SIMILAR SPECIES
WILSON'S SNIPE
see p.121
smaller head
streaked breast and flanks
longer legs
LONG-BILLED DOWITCHER
see p.119
more slender shape
smaller head

OCCURRENCE
Breeds from southern Canada to the southeastern US states, in damp second-growth forest, overgrown fields, and bogs. In winter, found in similar habitat; also found along marsh edges, swamps, and damp, grassy roadsides in Texas and Florida in the southern US.

Length **10–12in (25–31cm)**	Wingspan **16–20in (41–51cm)**	Weight **4–7oz (125–200g)**
Social **Solitary**	Lifespan **Up to 9 years**	Status **Secure**

DATE: ____________ TIME: ____________ LOCATION: ____________

Order **Charadriiformes**	Family **Scolopacidae**	Species ***Gallinago delicata***

Wilson's Snipe

long, pointed, angled wings

long bill

short tail

ADULT

IN FLIGHT

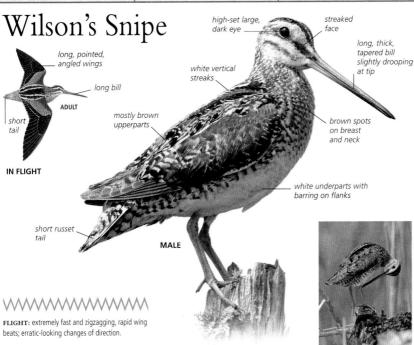

high-set large, dark eye

streaked face

long, thick, tapered bill slightly drooping at tip

white vertical streaks

mostly brown upperparts

brown spots on breast and neck

white underparts with barring on flanks

short russet tail

MALE

FLIGHT: extremely fast and zigzagging, rapid wing beats; erratic-looking changes of direction.

This secretive and well-camouflaged member of the sandpiper family has an unsettled taxonomic history, but is now classified individually. On its breeding grounds, the Wilson's Snipe produces rather eerie sounds during its aerial, mainly nocturnal, display flights. The birds fly up silently from the ground, and then, from about 330ft (100m) up, they descend quickly—their tail feathers spread, producing a unique loud and vibrating sound through modified feathers.

VOICE Alarm and overhead flight call raspy *kraitsch*; perched and low-flying breeding birds give repetitive, monotonous *kup-kup-kup-kup* in alarm or aggression; distinctive winnowing sound during territorial displays.

NESTING Elaborate woven nest lined with fine grass on ground, sedge, or moss; 4 eggs; 1 brood; May–June.

FEEDING Forages in mud or shallow water; probes deep into subsoil; diet includes mostly insect larvae, but also crustaceans, earthworms, and mollusks.

RUSSET TAIL

Wilson's Snipe's russet-colored tail is usually hard to see, but it is evident on this preening bird.

OCCURRENCE

Widespread from Alaska to Quebec and Labrador, south of the tundra zone; breeds in a variety of wetlands, including marshes, bogs, and open areas with rich soil. Winters farther south, where it prefers damp areas with vegetative cover, such as marshes, wet fields, and other bodies of water.

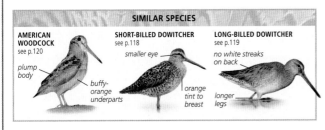

SIMILAR SPECIES

AMERICAN WOODCOCK see p.120

plump body

buffy-orange underparts

SHORT-BILLED DOWITCHER see p.118

smaller eye

orange tint to breast

LONG-BILLED DOWITCHER see p.119

no white streaks on back

longer legs

Length **10–11in (25–28cm)**	Wingspan **17–19in (43–48cm)**	Weight **2⅞–5oz (80–150g)**
Social **Solitary**	Lifespan **Up to 10 years**	Status **Secure**

DATE: ____________ TIME: ____________ LOCATION: ____________________

Order **Charadriiformes**	Family **Scolopacidae**	Species ***Actitis macularius***

Spotted Sandpiper

darker flight feathers
white wing stripe
ADULT (BREEDING)
IN FLIGHT

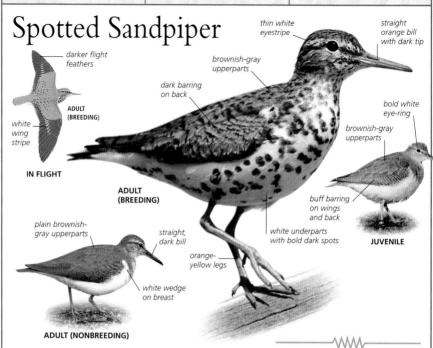

thin white eyestripe
straight orange bill with dark tip
brownish-gray upperparts
dark barring on back
ADULT (BREEDING)
white underparts with bold dark spots
orange-yellow legs

bold white eye-ring
brownish-gray upperparts
buff barring on wings and back
JUVENILE

plain brownish-gray upperparts
straight, dark bill
white wedge on breast
ADULT (NONBREEDING)

One of only two species of the genus *Actitis*, from the Latin meaning "a coastal inhabitant," this small, short-legged sandpiper is the most widespread shorebird in North America. It is characterized by its quick walking pace, as well as by its unique habit of constantly teetering and bobbing its tail and style of flying low over water. Spotted Sandpipers have an unusual mating behavior, in which the females take on an aggressive role—defending territories and mating with three or more males per season.

VOICE Call a clear, ringing note *tee-tee-tee-tee*; flight song a monotonous *cree-cree-cree*.

NESTING Nest cup shaded by or scrape built under herbaceous vegetation; 3 eggs; 1–3 broods; May–June.

FEEDING Eats many items, including adult and larval insects, mollusks, small crabs, and worms.

FLIGHT: mostly shallow, rapidly, stiffly fluttering wing beats, usually low above water.

BEHAVIORAL QUIRKS
This bird "teeters," uniquely raising and lowering its tail while walking along the water's edge.

SIMILAR SPECIES

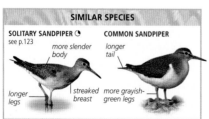

SOLITARY SANDPIPER see p.123
more slender body; longer legs; streaked breast

COMMON SANDPIPER
longer tail; more grayish-green legs

OCCURRENCE
Breeds across North America in a wide variety of grassy, brushy, forested habitats near water, but not high-Arctic tundra. During migration and in winter, found in habitats near freshwater, including lake shores, rivers, streams, beaches, sewage ponds, ditches, seawalls, sometimes estuaries.

Length **7¼–8in (18.5–20cm)**	Wingspan **15–16in (38–41cm)**	Weight **1⁹⁄₁₆–1¾oz (45–50g)**
Social **Small flocks**	Lifespan **Up to 12 years**	Status **Secure**

DATE: ______________ TIME: ______________ LOCATION: ______________________

Order **Charadriiformes**	Family **Scolopacidae**	Species ***Tringa solitaria***

Solitary Sandpiper

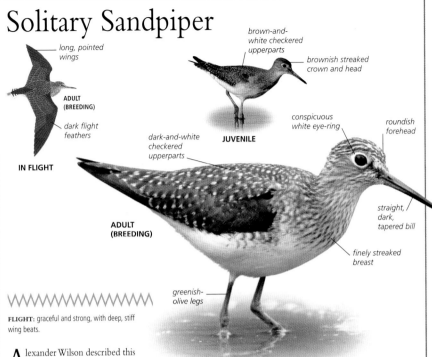

long, pointed wings

ADULT (BREEDING)

dark flight feathers

IN FLIGHT

brown-and-white checkered upperparts

brownish streaked crown and head

JUVENILE

conspicuous white eye-ring

roundish forehead

dark-and-white checkered upperparts

ADULT (BREEDING)

straight, dark, tapered bill

finely streaked breast

greenish-olive legs

FLIGHT: graceful and strong, with deep, stiff wing beats.

Alexander Wilson described this species in 1813, naming it, quite appropriately, "Solitary." This sandpiper seldom associates with other shorebirds as it moves nervously along margins of wetlands. When feeding, the Solitary Sandpiper constantly bobs its head like the Spotted Sandpiper. When disturbed, the Solitary Sandpiper often flies directly upward, and when landing, it keeps its wings upright briefly, flashing the white underneath, before carefully folding them to its body.

VOICE Flight and alarm call a high-pitched *weet-weet-weet* or *pit*; display song a *pit-pit-pit-pit*; *kik-kik-kik*.

NESTING Abandoned nests in trees (a unique behavior for a North American shorebird); 4 eggs; 1 brood; May–June.

FEEDING Eats insects, small crustaceans, snails, and small frogs.

LONE RANGER
This sandpiper is often solitary and is found in quiet, sheltered habitats and along river shores.

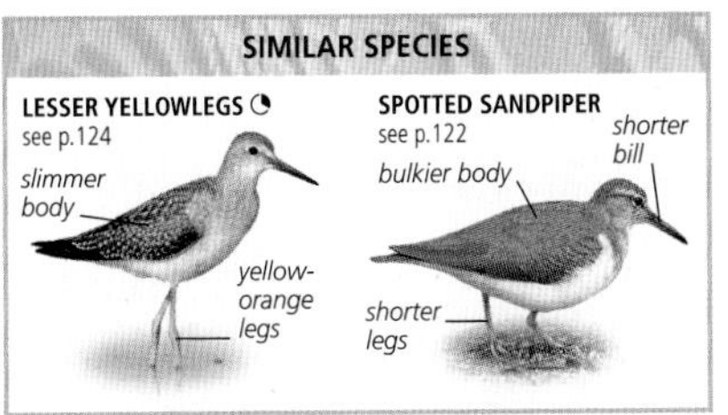
SIMILAR SPECIES
LESSER YELLOWLEGS
see p.124
slimmer body
yellow-orange legs
SPOTTED SANDPIPER
see p.122
bulkier body
shorter bill
shorter legs

OCCURRENCE
Breeds primarily in bogs in northern forests; in winter and during migration, occurs in sheltered pools or muddy areas near forests. Winters from Mexico down to South America, sometimes in tiny pools at high altitude in the Andes; also riverbanks, streams, rain pools, and ditches.

Length **7½–9in (19–23cm)**	Wingspan **22–23in (56–59cm)**	Weight **1 1/16–2¼oz (30–65g)**
Social **Solitary/Small flocks**	Lifespan **Unknown**	Status **Secure**

DATE: ____________ TIME: ____________ LOCATION: ____________________

Order **Charadriiformes**	Family **Scolopacidae**	Species ***Tringa flavipes***

Lesser Yellowlegs

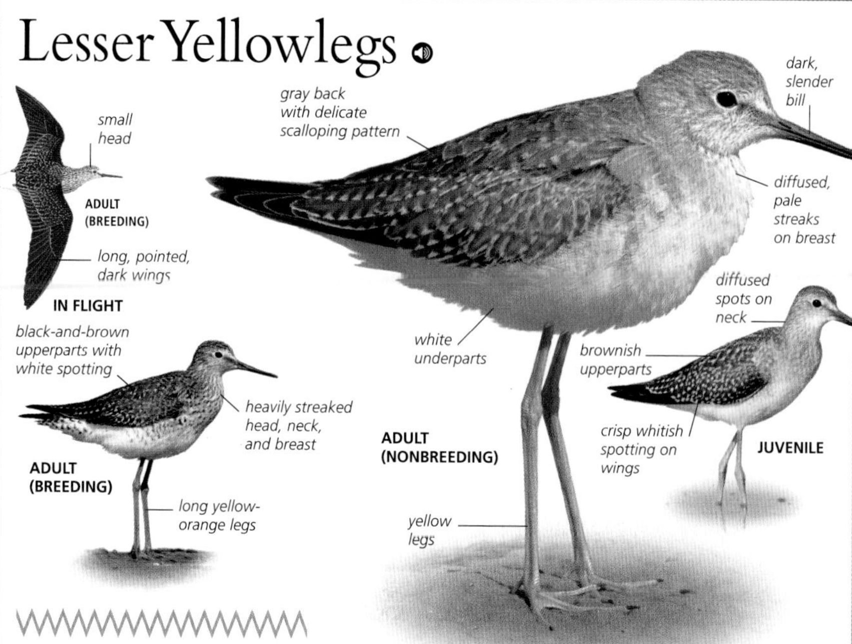
small head
ADULT (BREEDING)
long, pointed, dark wings
IN FLIGHT
black-and-brown upperparts with white spotting
heavily streaked head, neck, and breast
ADULT (BREEDING)
long yellow-orange legs
gray back with delicate scalloping pattern
dark, slender bill
diffused, pale streaks on breast
diffused spots on neck
white underparts
brownish upperparts
ADULT (NONBREEDING)
crisp whitish spotting on wings
JUVENILE
yellow legs

FLIGHT: straight and fast; with gliding and sideways banking; legs trail behind body.

With its smaller head, thinner bill, and smoother body shape, the Lesser Yellowlegs has a more elegant profile than the Greater Yellowlegs. It prefers smaller, freshwater, or brackish pools to open saltwater habitats, and it walks quickly and methodically while feeding. Although this species is a solitary feeder, it is often seen in small to large loose flocks during migration and winter.

VOICE Low, whistled *tu-tu* call; series of *tu* or *cuw* notes when agitated; display song a *pill-e-wee, pill-e-wee, pill-e-wee.*

NESTING Depression in ground or moss, lined with grass and leaves; 4 eggs; 1 brood; May–June.

FEEDING Eats a wide variety of aquatic and terrestrial insects, mollusks, and crustaceans, especially flies and beetles; also seeds.

BALANCING ACT

The Lesser Yellowlegs uses its long, raised wings for balance while feeding in soft mud.

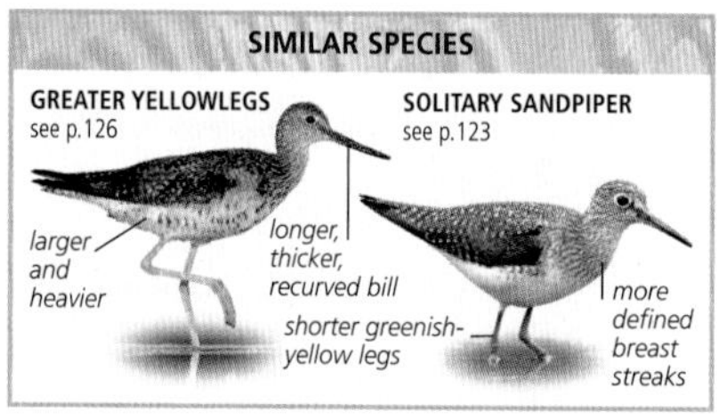
SIMILAR SPECIES
GREATER YELLOWLEGS
see p.126
larger and heavier
longer, thicker, recurved bill
SOLITARY SANDPIPER
see p.123
shorter greenish-yellow legs
more defined breast streaks

OCCURRENCE

Breeds in northerly forest with clearings, and where forest meets tundra. In migration and in winter, uses a wide variety of shallow wetlands, including flooded pastures and agricultural fields, swamps, lake and river shores, tidal creeks, and brackish mudflats. Winters from Mexico to Argentina.

Length **9–10in (23–25cm)**	Wingspan **23–25in (58–64cm)**	Weight **2–3⅜oz (55–95g)**
Social **Flocks**	Lifespan **Up to 5 years**	Status **Secure**

DATE: ____________ TIME: ____________ LOCATION: ____________

Order **Charadriiformes**	Family **Scolopacidae**	Species ***Tringa semipalmata***

Willet

bold black-and-white wing pattern

ADULT (WESTERN WINTER)

unpatterned pale underparts

IN FLIGHT

crisp, thin buff fringes

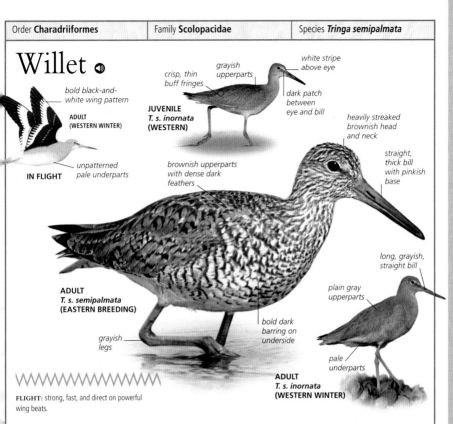

grayish upperparts

white stripe above eye

dark patch between eye and bill

JUVENILE *T. s. inornata* (WESTERN)

heavily streaked brownish head and neck

straight, thick bill with pinkish base

brownish upperparts with dense dark feathers

ADULT *T. s. semipalmata* (EASTERN BREEDING)

grayish legs

bold dark barring on underside

long, grayish, straight bill

plain gray upperparts

pale underparts

ADULT *T. s. inornata* (WESTERN WINTER)

FLIGHT: strong, fast, and direct on powerful wing beats.

The two distinct subspecies of the Willet, Eastern (*T. s. semipalmata*) and Western (*T. s. inornata*), differ in breeding habits, plumage coloration, vocalizations, and migratory habits. The Eastern Willet leaves North America from September to March, whereas the Western Willet winters along the southern North American shorelines south to South America.

VOICE Flight call a loud *kyah-yah*; alarm call a sharp, repeated *kleep*; song an urgent, rapid *pill-will-willet*.

NESTING Depression in vegetated dunes, wetlands, prairies, or salt marshes; 4 eggs; 1 brood; April–June.

FEEDING Picks, probes, or swishes for crustaceans, such as fiddler and mole crabs, aquatic insects, marine worms, small mollusks, and fish.

EXPOSED PERCH
Willets roost on exposed perches at breeding grounds.

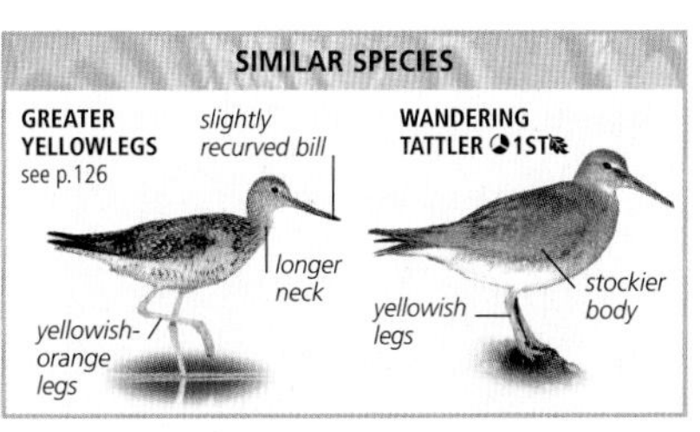
SIMILAR SPECIES
GREATER YELLOWLEGS
see p.126
slightly recurved bill
longer neck
yellowish-orange legs
WANDERING TATTLER 1ST
stockier body
yellowish legs

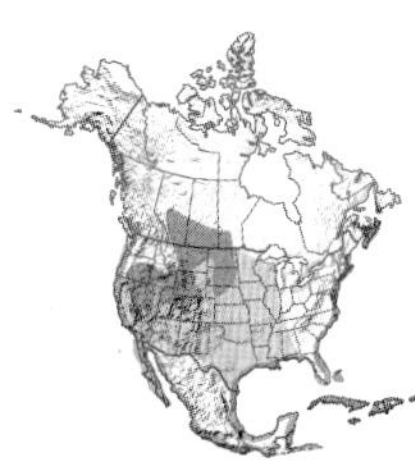

OCCURRENCE
Eastern subspecies breeds in coastal saltwater habitats: salt marshes, barrier islands, beaches, and mangroves; winters in similar habitats. Western subspecies breeds near sparsely vegetated prairie wetlands or adjacent semiarid grasslands; winters in coastal regions.

Length **12½–16½in (32–42cm)**	Wingspan **21½–28½in (54–72cm)**	Weight **7–12oz (200–350g)**
Social **Flocks**	Lifespan **Up to 10 years**	Status **Secure**

DATE: ______________ TIME: ______________ LOCATION: ______________

Order **Charadriiformes**	Family **Scolopacidae**	Species ***Tringa melanoleuca***

Greater Yellowlegs

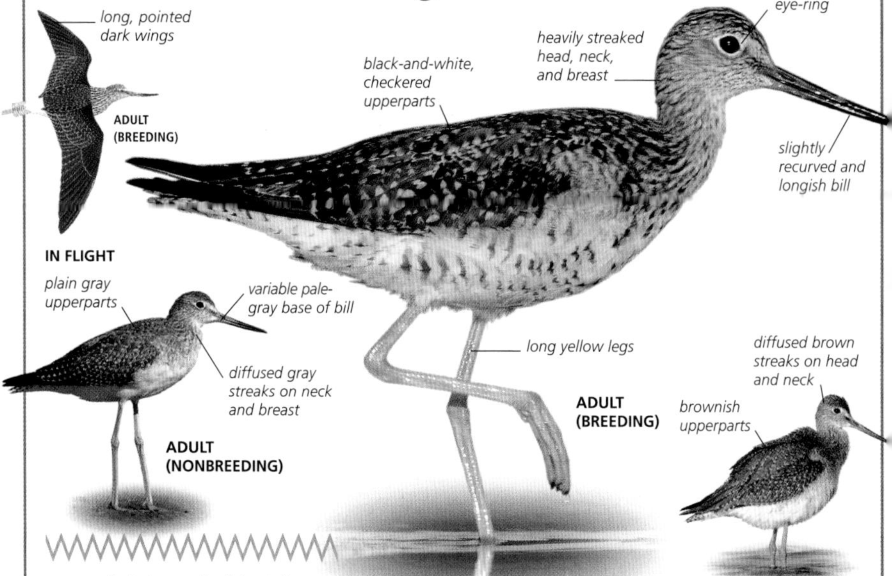

long, pointed dark wings

ADULT (BREEDING)

IN FLIGHT

black-and-white, checkered upperparts

heavily streaked head, neck, and breast

bold white eye-ring

slightly recurved and longish bill

plain gray upperparts

variable pale-gray base of bill

diffused gray streaks on neck and breast

ADULT (NONBREEDING)

long yellow legs

ADULT (BREEDING)

diffused brown streaks on head and neck

brownish upperparts

JUVENILE

FLIGHT: direct, strong, and swift; legs trail behind tail.

This fairly large shorebird often runs frantically in many directions while pursuing small prey. It is one of the first northbound shorebird migrants in the spring, and one of the first to return south in late June or early July. Its plumage, a mixture of brown, black, and white checkered upperparts, and streaked underparts, is more streaked during the breeding season.

VOICE Call a loud, penetrating *tew-tew-tew*; agitated birds make repetitive *keu* notes; song a continuous *too-whee.*

NESTING Simple scrape in moss or peat, usually close to water; 4 eggs; 1 brood; May–June.

FEEDING Picks at the water's surface and mud for small aquatic and terrestrial crustaceans and worms; also eats small fish, frogs, seeds, and berries.

EFFECTIVE METHOD

The Greater Yellowlegs often catches small fish by sweeping its bill sideways through water.

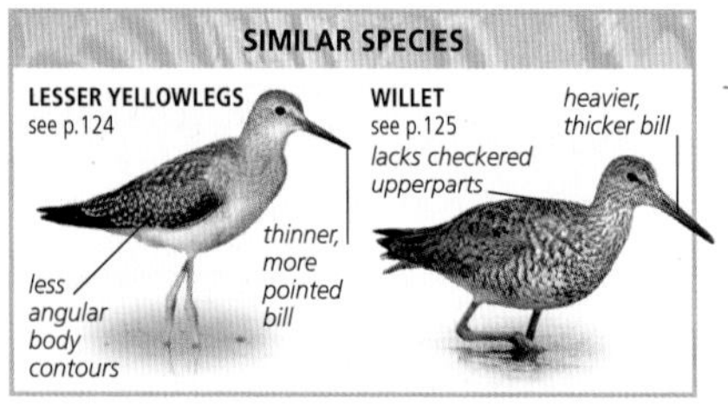
SIMILAR SPECIES
LESSER YELLOWLEGS
see p.124
less angular body contours
thinner, more pointed bill
WILLET
see p.125
lacks checkered upperparts
heavier, thicker bill

OCCURRENCE

Breeds in openings in northerly forests with bogs and wet meadows, a habitat called muskeg. In migration and winter, uses a wide variety of shallow water habitats, including freshwater and saltwater marshes, reservoirs, and tidal mudflats.

Length **11½–13in (29–33cm)**	Wingspan **28–29in (70–74cm)**	Weight **4–8oz (125–225g)**
Social **Solitary/Flocks**	Lifespan **Unknown**	Status **Secure**

DATE: ______________ TIME: ______________ LOCATION: ______________

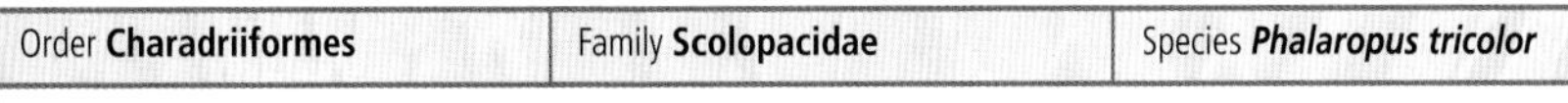
Order **Charadriiformes**
Family **Scolopacidae**
Species ***Phalaropus tricolor***

Wilson's Phalarope

reddish-brown markings on sides of back
FEMALE (BREEDING)
grayish-brown wings
IN FLIGHT
plain gray upperparts
largely white face
yellowish legs
white underparts
white cheek
MOLTING TO 1ST WINTER
plain gray-and-black upperparts
paler head markings
MALE
white eyebrow
fairly long, straight bill
black stripe from bill to nape
gray and reddish-brown back
rust neck and throat
FEMALE (BREEDING)

A truly American phalarope, Wilson's is the largest of the three phalarope species. Unlike its two relatives, it does not breed in the Arctic, but in the shallow wetlands of western North America, and winters mainly in continental habitats of Bolivia and Argentina instead of in the ocean. This species can be found employing the following feeding technique: spinning in shallow water to churn up adult and larval insects, or running in various directions on muddy wetland edges with its head held low to the ground while chasing and picking up insects. Wilson's phalaropes are quite tolerant of humans on their breeding grounds, but they become more wary immediately before migration because they are heavier and more sluggish.

VOICE Flight call a low, nasal *werpf*; also higher, repetitive *emf, emf, emf, emf*, or *luk, luk, luk*.

NESTING Simple scrape lined with grass; 4 eggs; 1 brood; May–June.

FEEDING Eats brine shrimp, various insects, and insect larvae.

FLIGHT: fast and direct with quick wing beats.

ODD ONE OUT

Unlike its two essentially oceanic cousins, Wilson's Phalarope is also found in freshwater habitats.

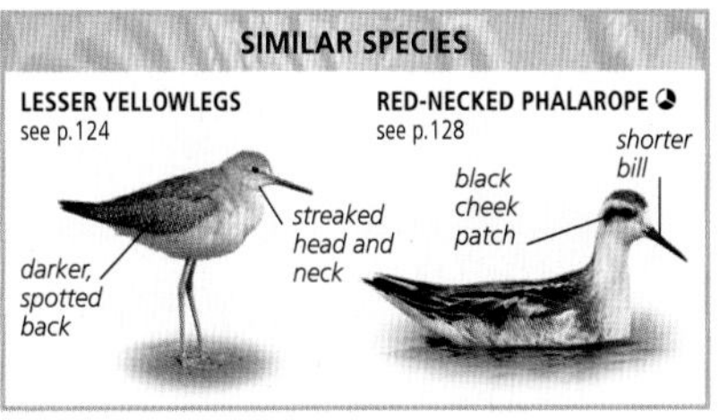
SIMILAR SPECIES
LESSER YELLOWLEGS
see p.124
RED-NECKED PHALAROPE
see p.128
streaked head and neck
darker, spotted back
black cheek patch
shorter bill

OCCURRENCE

Breeds in shallow, grassy wetlands of interior North America; during migration and winter, occurs in salty lakes and saline ponds as well as inland waterbodies. In winter, tens of thousands can be seen in the middle of Titicaca Lake in Bolivia.

Length **8½–9½in (22–24cm)**	Wingspan **15½–17in (39–43cm)**	Weight **1¼–3oz (35–85g)**
Social **Large flocks**	Lifespan **Up to 10 years**	Status **Secure**

DATE: ____________ TIME: ____________ LOCATION: ____________

Order **Charadriiformes**	Family **Scolopacidae**	Species ***Phalaropus lobatus***

Red-necked Phalarope

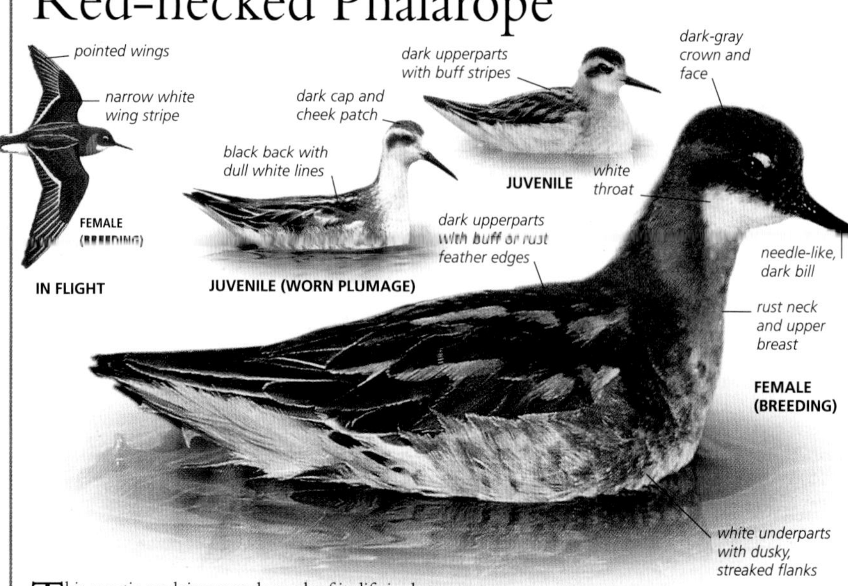
pointed wings
narrow white wing stripe
FEMALE
IN FLIGHT
dark cap and cheek patch
black back with dull white lines
JUVENILE (WORN PLUMAGE)
dark upperparts with buff stripes
JUVENILE
dark-gray crown and face
white throat
dark upperparts with buff or rust feather edges
needle-like, dark bill
rust neck and upper breast
FEMALE (BREEDING)
white underparts with dusky, streaked flanks

This aquatic sandpiper spends much of its life in deep ocean waters feeding on tiny plankton; each year, after nine months at sea, it comes to nest in the Arctic. Its Latin name *lobatus* reflects the morphology of its feet, which are webbed (lobed). Both the Red-necked Phalarope and the Red Phalarope are oceanic birds that are found in large flocks or "rafts" far from shore. However, both species are occasionally found swimming inland in freshwater habitats. Like the other two phalaropes, the Red-necked has a fascinating and unusual reversal of typical sex roles. The female is more brightly colored and slightly larger than the male; she will also pursue the male, compete savagely for him, and will migrate shortly after laying her eggs, leaving him to care for them.

VOICE Flight call a hard, squeaky *pwit* or *kit*; on breeding grounds, vocalizations include variations of flight call notes.

NESTING Depression in wet sedge or grass; 3–4 eggs; 1–2 broods; May–June.

FEEDING Eats plankton; also insects, brine shrimp, and mollusks.

FLIGHT: fast and direct, with rapid wing beats.

SINGLE FATHER
Male phalaropes perform all nesting and rearing duties after the female lays the eggs.

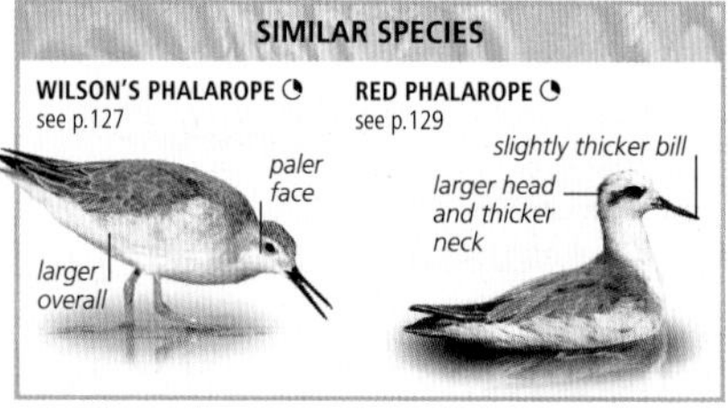
SIMILAR SPECIES
WILSON'S PHALAROPE
see p.127
paler face
larger overall
RED PHALAROPE
see p.129
slightly thicker bill
larger head and thicker neck

OCCURRENCE
Breeds in wet tundra, on raised ridges, or hummocks, but during migration and in winter, occurs far out to sea and away from shores, although sometimes found in a number of freshwater habitats.

Length **7–7½in (18–19cm)**	Wingspan **12½–16in (32–41cm)**	Weight **1¹⁄₁₆–1⁹⁄₁₆oz (30–45g)**
Social **Flocks**	Lifespan **At least 10 years**	Status **Special Concern**

DATE: ______________ TIME: ______________ LOCATION: ______________________

Order **Charadriiformes**	Family **Scolopacidae**	Species ***Phalaropus fulicarius***

Red Phalarope

bold white wing bar
FEMALE (BREEDING)
white rump with black line in center, and white edges
broad, pointed wings
IN FLIGHT
buff feather fringes
scalloped upperparts
dull rust crown with black streaks
brick-red underparts; paler than female
MALE (BREEDING)
black cheek patch and nape
mostly gray upperparts
white neck and head
white underparts
ADULT (NONBREEDING)
bold white cheek patch
black crown
tan, fringed feathers on upperparts
stout, yellow bill with black tip
deep brick-red neck, throat, and underparts
FEMALE (BREEDING)

The Red Phalarope spends more than ten months each year over deep ocean waters. It also migrates across the ocean, which explains why few birds of this species are ever seen inland. Many Red Phalaropes winter in tropical waters, with concentrations in the Humboldt Current off Peru and Chile, and in the Benguela current off southwestern Africa. During migration over Alaskan waters, flocks of Red Phalaropes feed on crustaceans in the mud plumes that are created during foraging by gray and bowhead whales on the ocean floor.

VOICE Flight call a sharp *psip* or *pseet*, often in rapid succession; alarm call a drawn-out, two-syllabled *sweet*.

NESTING Depression on ridge or hummock in coastal sedge; 3–4 eggs; 1 brood; June.

FEEDING Plucks prey from sea; marine crustaceans, fish eggs, larval fish; adult or larval insects.

FLIGHT: direct with rapid wing beats, birds in flocks often synchronize.

DIFFERENT COLOR
In nonbreeding plumage, phalaropes are gray and white.

NO TIES
After mating and laying eggs, females leave the male and play no role in raising the young.

SIMILAR SPECIES

WILSON'S PHALAROPE
more terrestrial; see p.127

RED-NECKED PHALAROPE
see p.129

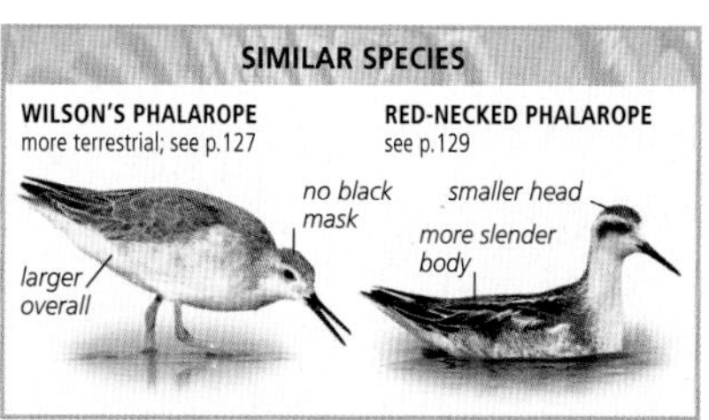

no black mask
larger overall
smaller head
more slender body

OCCURRENCE
Breeds in coastal Arctic tundra; during migration and in winter, occurs in deep ocean waters; small numbers are seen near the shore in coastal California in fall and winter. The Red Phalarope is rare inland.

Length **8–8½in (20–22cm)**	Wingspan **16–17½in (41–44cm)**	Weight **1¼–2⅝oz (35–75g)**
Social **Large flocks**	Lifespan **At least 6 years**	Status **Secure**

DATE: ________ TIME: ________ LOCATION: ________

Order **Charadriiformes**	Family **Stercorariidae**	Species ***Stercorarius pomarinus***

Pomarine Jaeger

ADULT (BREEDING; PALE FORM) — prominent white "flash" in feathers

ADULT (DARK FORM) — white wing flash; dark overall; blunt tail spike

IN FLIGHT

ADULT (NONBREEDING; PALE FORM) — barred flanks; dusky breastband

JUVENILE (FALL; DARK FORM) — all-dark body; deep, barrel breast

ADULT (BREEDING; PALE FORM) — blackish cap; pale-based, thick bill; cream cheeks; gray-brown back; dusky breast-band; twisted, spoon-like central tail feathers

The intimidating Pomarine Jaeger uses its size and strength to overpower larger seabirds, such as gulls and shearwaters, in order to steal their food. Thought to be nomadic during the breeding season, it only nests opportunistically, when populations of lemmings are at their peak to provide food for its young. Although larger and more powerful than the Parasitic Jaeger, the Pomarine Jaeger is not as acrobatic in the air. It is readily driven away from breeding territories by the more dynamic Parasitic Jaeger. Interestingly, research suggests that the Pomarine Jaeger is actually more closely related to the large skuas—such as the Great and the South Polar Skuas—than to other jaegers.

VOICE Nasal *cow-cow-cow* and various sharp, low whistles.

NESTING Shallow, unlined depression on a rise or hummock in open tundra; 2 eggs; 1 brood; June–August.

FEEDING Hunts lemmings and other rodents; eats fish or scavenges refuse from fishing boats during nonbreeding season; often steals fish from other seabirds, such as gulls.

FLIGHT: powerful, deep, quick wing beats, with glides; rapid twists and turns in pursuit of prey.

SIMILAR SPECIES
PARASITIC JAEGER
see p.131
white "necklace"
gray breastband
LONG-TAILED JAEGER ☼
see p.132
extremely long tail
pale breast

OBVIOUS FEATURE
The twisted, spoon-like central tail feathers are clearly visible when the Pomarine Jaeger flies.

OCCURRENCE
Breeds on open tundra in the Canadian Arctic. Migrates north in spring and south in fall, along coasts and also far offshore. Most often seen when brought close to land by gales. Storm-driven birds are very occasionally found inland. More commonly seen on the West Coast than the East Coast; winters far out at sea.

Length **17–20in (43–51cm)**	Wingspan **4ft (1.2m)**	Weight **23–26oz (650–750g)**
Social **Solitary**	Lifespan **Unknown**	Status **Secure**

DATE: ______________ TIME: ______________ LOCATION: ______________

Order **Charadriiformes**	Family **Stercorariidae**	Species ***Stercorarius parasiticus***

Parasitic Jaeger

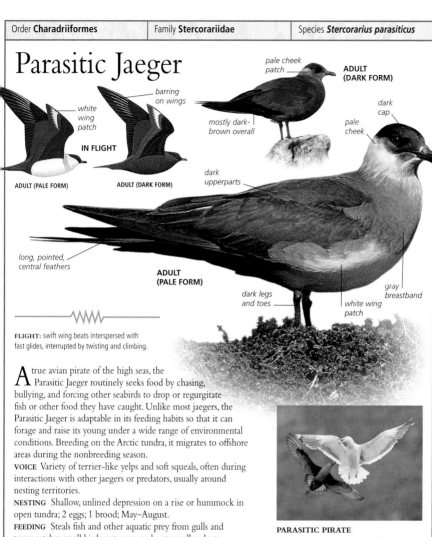

pale cheek patch
ADULT (DARK FORM)
barring on wings
white wing patch
IN FLIGHT
mostly dark-brown overall
dark cap
pale cheek
ADULT (PALE FORM)
ADULT (DARK FORM)
dark upperparts
long, pointed, central feathers
ADULT (PALE FORM)
dark legs and toes
white wing patch
gray breastband

FLIGHT: swift wing beats interspersed with fast glides, interrupted by twisting and climbing.

A true avian pirate of the high seas, the Parasitic Jaeger routinely seeks food by chasing, bullying, and forcing other seabirds to drop or regurgitate fish or other food they have caught. Unlike most jaegers, the Parasitic Jaeger is adaptable in its feeding habits so that it can forage and raise its young under a wide range of environmental conditions. Breeding on the Arctic tundra, it migrates to offshore areas during the nonbreeding season.

VOICE Variety of terrier-like yelps and soft squeals, often during interactions with other jaegers or predators, usually around nesting territories.

NESTING Shallow, unlined depression on a rise or hummock in open tundra; 2 eggs; 1 brood; May–August.

FEEDING Steals fish and other aquatic prey from gulls and terns; catches small birds, eats eggs, or hunts small rodents on breeding grounds.

PARASITIC PIRATE
This Parasitic Jaeger is harrying a gull by pecking at it to make it disgorge its hard-won meal.

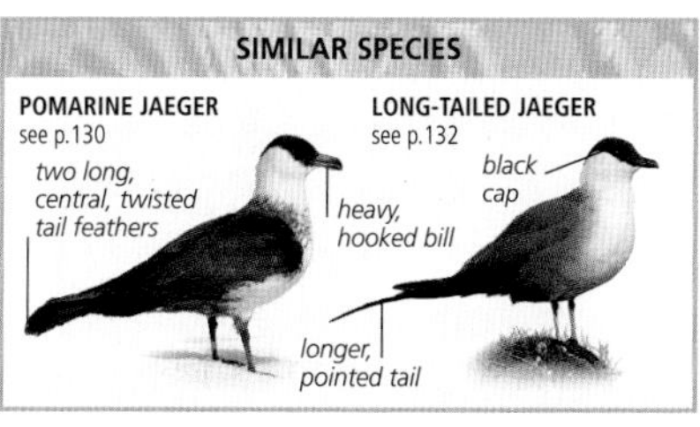
SIMILAR SPECIES
POMARINE JAEGER
see p.130
two long, central, twisted tail feathers
heavy, hooked bill
LONG-TAILED JAEGER
see p.132
black cap
longer, pointed tail

OCCURRENCE
Breeds on tundra in northern Canada and Alaska (breeds farther south than other jaegers); during migration and in winter, uses both nearshore and offshore waters; rarely found inland outside the breeding season.

Length **16–18½in (41–47cm)**	Wingspan **3ft 3in–3½ft (1–1.1m)**	Weight **13–18oz (375–500g)**
Social **Solitary/Small flocks**	Lifespan **Up to 18 years**	Status **Secure**

Order **Charadriiformes**	Family **Stercorariidae**	Species ***Stercorarius longicaudus***

Long-tailed Jaeger

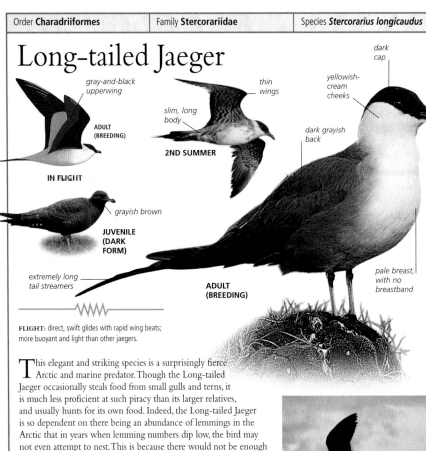

gray-and-black upperwing

ADULT (BREEDING)

IN FLIGHT

slim, long body

thin wings

2ND SUMMER

dark cap

yellowish-cream cheeks

dark grayish back

grayish brown

JUVENILE (DARK FORM)

extremely long tail streamers

ADULT (BREEDING)

pale breast, with no breastband

FLIGHT: direct, swift glides with rapid wing beats; more buoyant and light than other jaegers.

This elegant and striking species is a surprisingly fierce Arctic and marine predator. Though the Long-tailed Jaeger occasionally steals food from small gulls and terns, it is much less proficient at such piracy than its larger relatives, and usually hunts for its own food. Indeed, the Long-tailed Jaeger is so dependent on there being an abundance of lemmings in the Arctic that in years when lemming numbers dip low, the bird may not even attempt to nest. This is because there would not be enough lemmings with which to feed its chicks.

VOICE Calls include a chorus of *kreek*, a loud *kreer* warning call, whistles, and high-pitched, sharp clicks.

NESTING Shallow, unlined depression on a rise or hummock in open tundra; 2 eggs; 1 brood; May–August.

FEEDING Hunts lemmings on tundra breeding grounds; takes fish, beetles, and mayflies from the water's surface; occasionally steals small fish from terns.

DEFENSIVE MOVES

This species protects its territory with angry calls, aggressive swoops, and distraction displays.

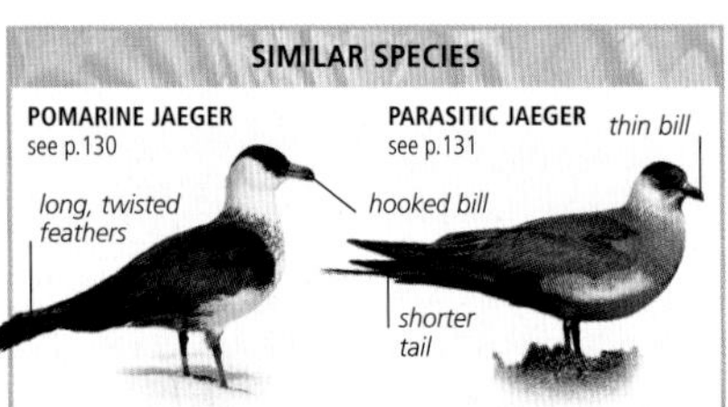
SIMILAR SPECIES
POMARINE JAEGER
see p.130
long, twisted feathers
hooked bill
PARASITIC JAEGER
see p.131
thin bill
shorter tail

OCCURRENCE

Breeds on tundra in northern Canada and Alaska—generally the most northern breeding jaeger; on migration and in winter, uses mostly offshore waters; very rarely seen inland in winter.

Length **19–21in (48–53cm)**	Wingspan **3½ft (1.1m)**	Weight **10–11oz (275–300g)**
Social **Solitary/Flocks**	Lifespan **Up to 8 years**	Status **Secure**

 DATE: ________ TIME: ________ LOCATION: ________

Order **Charadriiformes**	Family **Alcidae**	Species ***Alle alle***

Dovekie

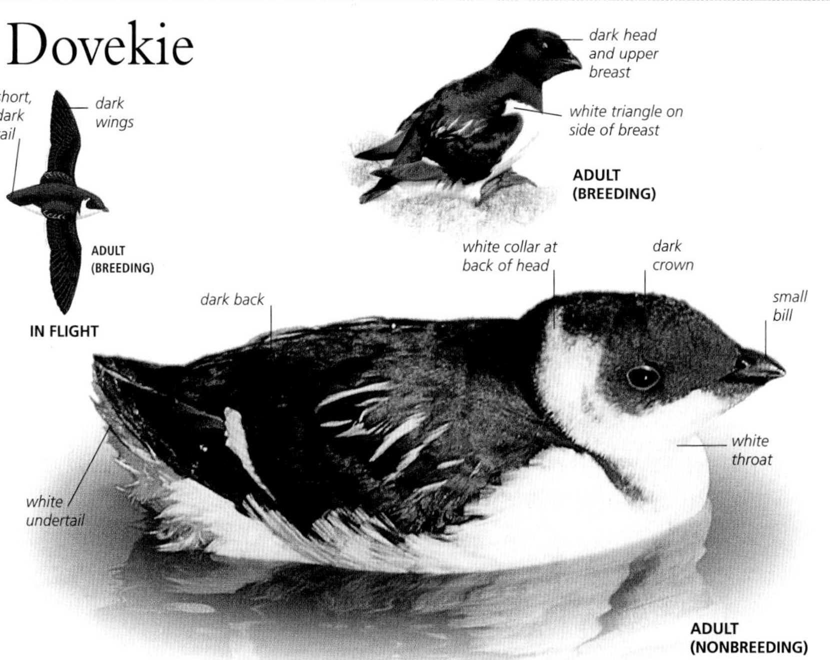
short, dark tail
dark wings
ADULT (BREEDING)
IN FLIGHT
dark head and upper breast
white triangle on side of breast
ADULT (BREEDING)
white collar at back of head
dark crown
small bill
dark back
white throat
white undertail
ADULT (NONBREEDING)

Also known widely as the Little Auk, the stocky and diminutive black-and-white Dovekie is a bird of the high Arctic. Most Dovekies breed in Greenland in large, noisy, crowded colonies (the largest one containing 15–20 million birds), but some breed in northeastern Canada, and others on a few islands in the Bering Sea, off Alaska. On their breeding grounds, both adult and juvenile Dovekies are hunted ruthlessly by Glaucous Gulls, as well as mammalian predators, such as the Arctic Fox. Vast numbers of Dovekies winter on the low-Arctic waters off the Northeastern Seaboard of North America, in immense flocks. Occasionally, severe onshore gales cause entire flocks to become stranded along the East Coast of North America.

VOICE Variety of calls at breeding colony, including high-pitched trilling that rises and falls; silent at sea.

NESTING Pebble nest in crack or crevice in boulder field or rocky outcrop; 1 egg; 1 brood; April–August.

FEEDING Mostly picks tiny crustaceans from just below the sea's surface.

FLIGHT: rapid, whirring wing beats; flies in flocks low over the water's surface.

SOCIABLE LITTLE AUK
After initial squabbles over nest sites, Dovekies in breeding colonies become highly sociable.

SIMILAR SPECIES

BLACK GUILLEMOT ◔
see p.137

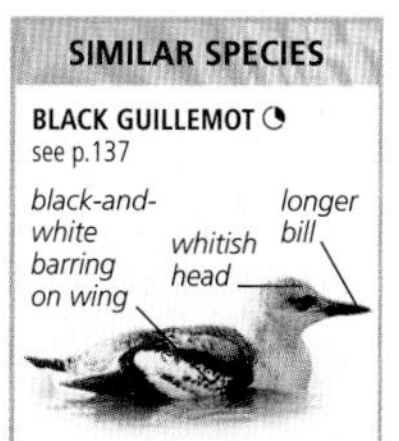
black-and-white barring on wing
whitish head
longer bill

OCCURRENCE
Breeds on islands inside the Arctic Circle; in Greenland, mostly, but also in northeastern Canada and the Bering Sea. Many birds remain just south of the Arctic pack ice throughout the winter; others fly south to winter off the Northeastern Seaboard of North America.

Length **8½in (21cm)**	Wingspan **15in (38cm)**	Weight **6oz (175g)**
Social **Colonies**	Lifespan **Unknown**	Status **Secure**

DATE: ____________ TIME: ____________ LOCATION: ____________

Order **Charadriiformes**	Family **Alcidae**	Species ***Uria aalge***

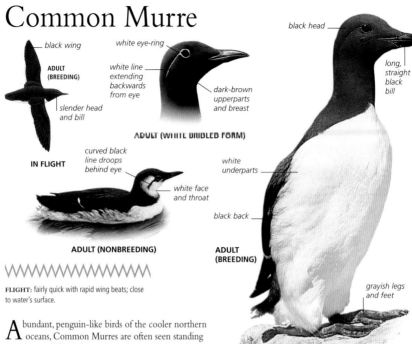

Common Murre

black wing

ADULT (BREEDING)

slender head and bill

IN FLIGHT

white eye-ring

white line extending backwards from eye

dark-brown upperparts and breast

ADULT (WHITE BRIDLED FORM)

curved black line droops behind eye

white face and throat

ADULT (NONBREEDING)

black head

long, straight black bill

white underparts

black back

grayish legs and feet

ADULT (BREEDING)

FLIGHT: fairly quick with rapid wing beats; close to water's surface.

Abundant, penguin-like birds of the cooler northern oceans, Common Murres are often seen standing upright on cliffs. They are strong fliers and adept divers—to a depth of 500ft (150m). Their large nesting colonies, on rocky sea cliff ledges, are so densely packed that incubating adults may touch each other on both sides. Common Murre eggs are pointed at one end—perhaps to reduce the chance of the egg rolling off the ledge, but more likely to help maximize contact with the brood patch. The egg's unique markings could facilitate clutch recognition by the parents.

VOICE Low-pitched, descending call given from cliffs or water, reminiscent of trumpeting elephant.

NESTING Directly on bare rock near shore, on wide cliff ledge, or large crevice; 1 egg; 1 brood; May-July.

FEEDING Pursues small schooling fish, such as herring, sand lance, and haddock; also crustaceans, marine worms, and squid.

BREEDING COLONY
Crowded together, Common Murres are not territorial but will defend a personal space.

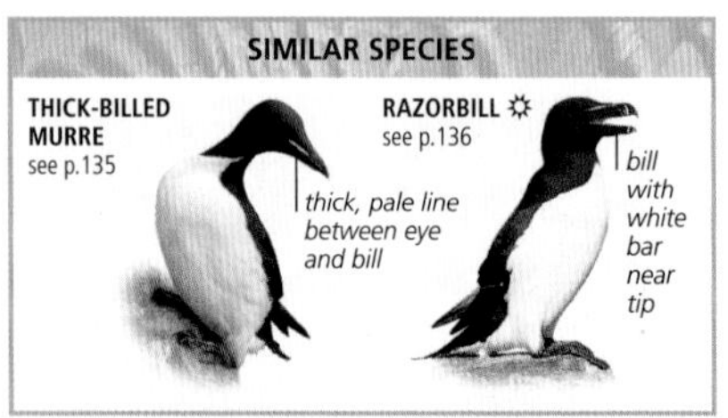
SIMILAR SPECIES
THICK-BILLED MURRE
see p.135
thick, pale line between eye and bill
RAZORBILL ☼
see p.136
bill with white bar near tip

OCCURRENCE
Breeds close to rocky shorelines, nesting on coastal cliff ledges or flat rocks on top of sea stacks on both the East and West Coasts. Found farther offshore during nonbreeding season, spending extended periods on the open ocean and in large bays. Winters at sea.

Length **17½in (44cm)**	Wingspan **26in (65cm)**	Weight **35oz (1kg)**
Social **Colonies**	Lifespan **At least 40 years**	Status **Localized**

DATE: ____________ TIME: ____________ LOCATION: ____________________

Order **Charadriiformes**	Family **Alcidae**	Species ***Uria lomvia***

Thick-billed Murre

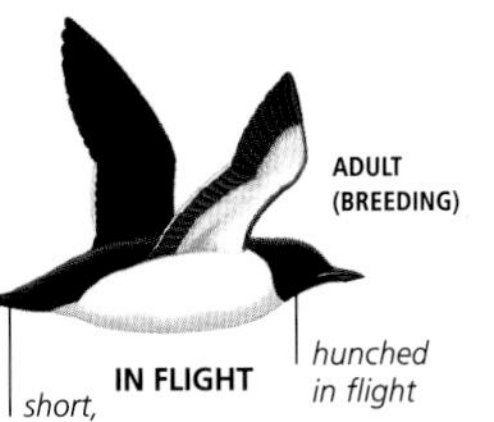

ADULT (BREEDING)
IN FLIGHT
short, black tail
hunched in flight

brownish-black sides of head

white line along bill

white breast and underparts

all-blackish upperparts

ADULT (BREEDING)

reduced or absent white line on bill

more extensive white on throat

ADULT (NONBREEDING)

FLIGHT: near the water's surface with strong, rapid wing beats.

Large and robust, the Thick-billed Murre is one of the most abundant seabirds in the whole of the Northern Hemisphere. Its dense, coastal cliff breeding colonies can be made up of around a million birds each. Chicks leave the colony when they are only about 25 percent of the adult's weight. Their growth is completed at sea, while being fed by the male parent alone. The Thick-billed Murre can dive to a remarkable 600ft (180m) to catch fish and squid.

VOICE Roaring, groaning, insistent sounding *aoorrr*; lower-pitched than the Common Murre.

NESTING Rocky coast or narrow sea cliff ledge in dense colony; 1 egg; 1 brood; March–September.

FEEDING Cod, herring, capelin, and sand lance in summer; also crustaceans, worms, and squid.

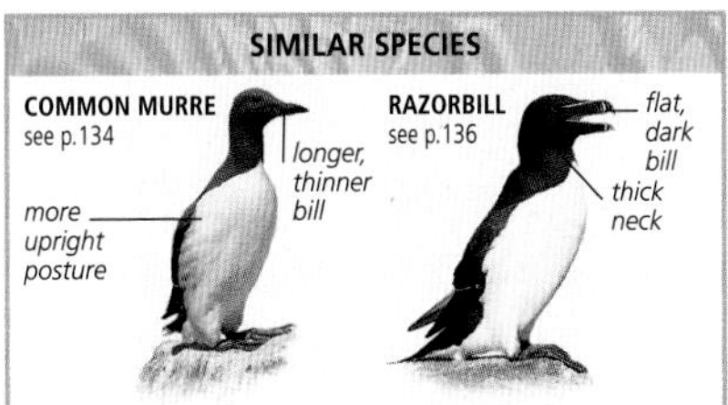

SIMILAR SPECIES
COMMON MURRE
see p.134
longer, thinner bill
more upright posture
RAZORBILL
see p.136
flat, dark bill
thick neck

CLIFF HANGER
Thick-billed Murres breed in dense colonies on steep cliffs, often in very remote areas.

OCCURRENCE
Breeds on rocky shorelines, using the same nest each year. Winters at sea, spending extended periods of time on very cold, deep, and often remote ocean waters and pack ice edges or openings.

Length **18in (46cm)**	Wingspan **28in (70cm)**	Weight **34oz (975g)**
Social **Colonies**	Lifespan **At least 25 years**	Status **Secure**

DATE: ____________ TIME: ____________ LOCATION: ____________

Order **Charadriiformes**	Family **Alcidae**	Species ***Alca torda***

Razorbill

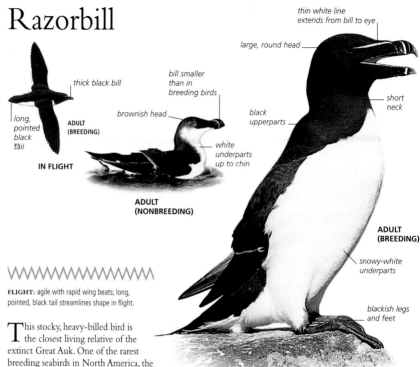

thin white line extends from bill to eye
large, round head
thick black bill
bill smaller than in breeding birds
brownish head
short neck
black upperparts
long, pointed black tail
ADULT (BREEDING)
white underparts up to chin
IN FLIGHT
ADULT (NONBREEDING)
ADULT (BREEDING)
snowy-white underparts
blackish legs and feet

FLIGHT: agile with rapid wing beats; long, pointed, black tail streamlines shape in flight.

This stocky, heavy-billed bird is the closest living relative of the extinct Great Auk. One of the rarest breeding seabirds in North America, the Razorbill is a strong flier and more agile in flight than many related species. Razorbills typically feed at depths of about 20ft (6m), but are sometimes known to dive to depths of more than 450ft (140m). Onshore, Razorbills walk upright like penguins. They carry small fish, initially, to their chick, but later male razorbills escort their flightless young to the sea to feed.

VOICE Deep, guttural, resonant croak, *hey al*.

NESTING Enclosed sites often built in crevices, among boulders, or in abandoned burrows; 1 egg; 1 brood; May–July.

FEEDING Dives for schooling fish, including capelin, herring, and sand lance; also consumes marine worms and crustaceans; sometimes steals fish from other auks.

IN FLIGHT
The razorbill flaps its wings constantly in flight, as they are too small for the bird to glide.

SIMILAR SPECIES
THICK-BILLED MURRE
see p.135
more slender body
thick, pale line between eye and bill
COMMON MURRE ☼
see p.134
slimmer bill
more slender body

OCCURRENCE
Breeds on rocky islands and shorelines, or steep mainland cliffs in northeast North America; most of the world's population breeds in Iceland. Winters south of breeding range on ice-free coastal waters reaching New Jersey and Virginia. Forages in cool, shallower water, near shore.

Length **17in (43cm)**	Wingspan **26in (65cm)**	Weight **26oz (725g)**
Social **Colonies**	Lifespan **At least 30 years**	Status **Localized**

DATE: ____________ TIME: ____________ LOCATION: ____________

Order **Charadriiformes**	Family **Alcidae**	Species ***Cepphus grylle***

Black Guillemot

ADULT (BREEDING)
broad, rounded wings
oval, snowy-white upperwing patch
IN FLIGHT
gray bars in white wing patch
gray cap
gray neck
JUVENILE
thin, straight bill
large white patch
dark belly
scarlet legs and feet
ADULT (BREEDING)
round black body

Black Guillemots, also known as "sea pigeons," are medium-sized auks with distinctive black plumage and white wing patches. Their striking scarlet legs and mouth lining help attract a mate during the breeding season. Like the other two species of the *Cepphus* genus, Black Guillemots prefer shallow, inshore waters to the open ocean. They winter near the shore, sometimes moving into the mouths of rivers.

VOICE Very high-pitched whistles and squeaks given on land and water, near nesting habitat, that resonate like an echo.

NESTING Shallow scrape in soil or pebbles within cave or crevice; site may be reused; 1–2 eggs; 1 brood; May–August.

FEEDING Dives under water near shore to hunt small, bottom-dwelling fish, such as rock eels, sand lance, and sculpin; propels down to depths of 59ft (18m) using partly opened wings, and webbed feet as a rudder; feeds close to nesting islands.

FLIGHT: flies low over the water with very rapid wing beats.

FOOD FOR CHICKS
The birds carry food for the chicks in their bills and often pause near the nest before dashing home.

SIMILAR SPECIES

DOVEKIE ❄
see p.133
smaller
dark back
white patch behind eye
PIGEON GUILLEMOT ☼
dusky underwings in flight
black bar on white wing patch

OCCURRENCE
Primarily an Atlantic species. Breeds in crevices on remote, rocky islands and cliffs that provide protection from predators. At sea, prefers shallow waters, close to rocky coasts. At the end of breeding season, adults and young move closer to shore to avoid pack ice.

Length **13in (33cm)**	Wingspan **21in (53cm)**	Weight **15oz (425g)**
Social **Colonies**	Lifespan **At least 20 years**	Status **Localized**

DATE: ______________ TIME: ______________ LOCATION: ______________________________

Order **Charadriiformes**	Family **Alcidae**	Species ***Fratercula arctica***

Atlantic Puffin

short tail
ADULT (BREEDING)
IN FLIGHT

black back, collar, and underwings
blue-gray, orange, and red stripes on bill
orange legs and feet
ADULT (BREEDING)

dusky-gray face
dull bill
ADULT (NONBREEDING)

gray face
red eye-ring
thick, black line
stocky, rounded body
large, colorful, triangular bill
white breast
ADULT (BREEDING)

With its black-and-white "tuxedo," ungainly upright posture, and enormous, colorful bill, the Atlantic Puffin is often known as the "clown of the sea." It is seen in summer, when large breeding colonies gather on remote, rocky islands. To feed itself and its young, it can dive down to 200ft (60m) with partly-folded wings, essentially "flying" underwater in pursuit of small schooling fish. The Atlantic Puffin is the provincial bird of Newfoundland and Labrador.

VOICE Rising and falling buzzy growl, resembling a chainsaw.

NESTING Underground burrow or deep rock crevice lined with grass and feathers; 1 egg; 1 brood; June–August.

FEEDING Dives deep for capelin, herring, hake, sand lance, and other small fish, which it swallows underwater, or stores as many as 60 small fish, crosswise in its bill, to take back to its chicks.

FLIGHT: swift and direct, with rapid wing beats; often circles breeding islands.

CATCH AND CARRY
When returning to breeding colonies to feed chicks, most birds carry dozens of fish in their bill.

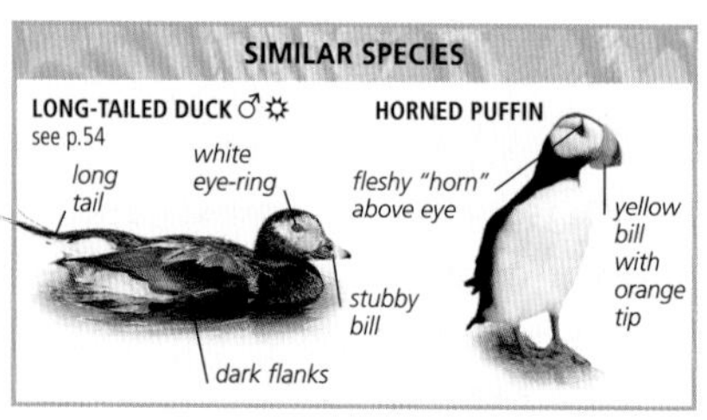
SIMILAR SPECIES
LONG-TAILED DUCK ♂ ☼
see p.54
long tail
white eye-ring
stubby bill
dark flanks
HORNED PUFFIN
fleshy "horn" above eye
yellow bill with orange tip

OCCURRENCE
This northern North Atlantic seabird (found on both sides of the ocean) breeds in colonies on small, rocky, offshore islands, where it excavates nesting burrows or nests under boulders. Between breeding seasons, it heads for the high seas and remains far offshore, favoring cold, open waters.

Length **12½in (32cm)**	Wingspan **21in (53cm)**	Weight **12oz (350g)**
Social **Colonies**	Lifespan **At least 30 years**	Status **Localized**

DATE: ____________ TIME: ____________ LOCATION: ____________

Order **Charadriiformes**	Family **Laridae**	Species ***Rissa tridactyla***

Black-legged Kittiwake

pale outer wing feathers
black "M" pattern wings
pale-gray upperparts
black tip to tail
black bill
black wingtip
ADULT
IN FLIGHT
JUVENILE

yellow bill
white head
pale-gray back feathers
black legs and feet
ADULT

dark neck collar
dark wing bar
JUVENILE

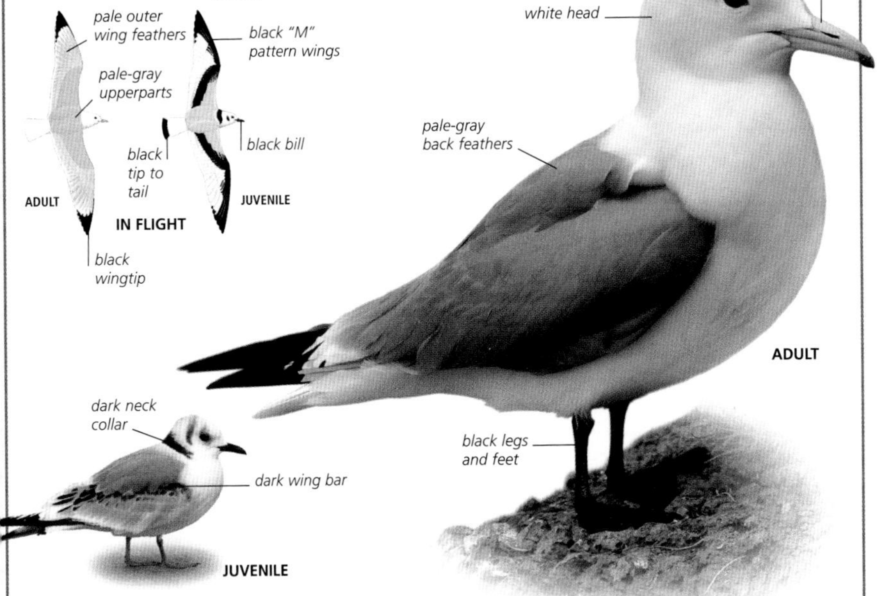

A kittiwake nesting colony is an impressive sight, with, sometimes, thousands of birds lined up along steep cliff ledges overlooking the sea. The ledges are often so narrow that the birds' tails stick out over the edge. Kittiwakes have sharper claws than other gulls, probably to give them a better grip on their ledges. In the late 20th century, the Black-legged Kittiwake population expanded greatly in the Canadian Maritime Provinces, with numbers doubling in the Gulf of St. Lawrence.

VOICE Repeated, nasal *kit-ti-wake, kit-ti-wake* call; vocal near nesting cliffs; usually silent in winter.

NESTING Mound of mud and vegetation on narrow cliff ledge; 1–3 eggs; 1 brood; April–August.

FEEDING Snatches small marine fish and invertebrates from the surface, or dives just below the water's surface; feeds in flocks.

FLIGHT: very stiff-winged; rapid, shallow wing beats; overall more buoyant than most gulls.

LIVING ON THE EDGE
Young and adult kittiwakes pack together tightly on their precariously narrow cliff ledges.

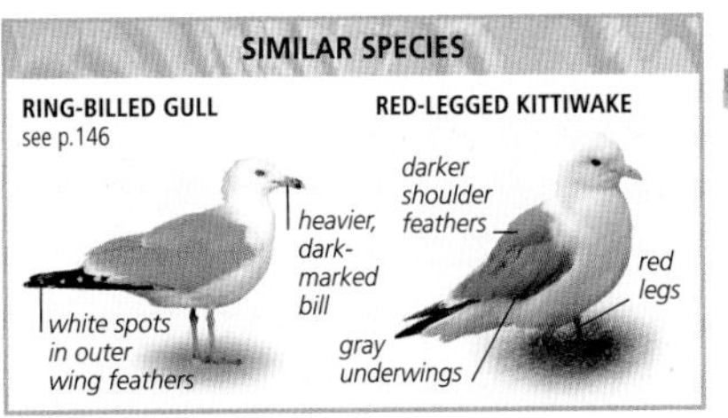
SIMILAR SPECIES
RING-BILLED GULL
see p.146
heavier, dark-marked bill
white spots in outer wing feathers
RED-LEGGED KITTIWAKE
darker shoulder feathers
red legs
gray underwings

OCCURRENCE
Rarely seen far from the ocean; common in summer around sea cliffs, with ledges suitable for nesting, and nearby offshore waters; winters at sea; most likely to be seen from land during and after storms; strays have appeared throughout the interior.

Length **15–16in (38–41cm)**	Wingspan **3ft 1in–4ft (0.95m–1.2m)**	Weight **11–18oz (300–500g)**
Social **Colonies**	Lifespan **Up to 26 years**	Status **Secure**

DATE: ____________ TIME: ____________ LOCATION: ____________________

Order **Charadriiformes**	Family **Laridae**	Species ***Xema sabini***

Sabine's Gull

white triangle on wing
black outer wing feathers
ADULT
JUVENILE
black band on tail
IN FLIGHT

gray hood
red eye-ring
black border
yellow-tipped black bill
gray back
white underparts
black legs
ADULT (BREEDING)

barring on gray-brown back
black bill
JUVENILE

This strikingly patterned gull was discovered in Greenland by the English scientist, Edward Sabine, during John Ross's search for the Northwest Passage in 1818 (it was described in 1819). The distinctive wing pattern and notched tail make it unmistakable in all plumages—only juvenile kittiwakes are superficially similar. Previously thought to be related to the larger, but similarly patterned, Swallow-tailed Gull of the Galapagos, recent research indicates that Sabine's Gull is more closely related to the Ivory Gull. This species breeds in the Arctic and winters at sea, off the coasts of the Americas (south to Peru) and Africa (south to the Cape region).

VOICE Raucous, harsh *kyeer, kyeer, kyeer*; tern-like.

NESTING Shallow depression in marsh or tundra vegetation usually near water, lined with grass or unlined; 3–4 eggs; 1 brood; May–August.

FEEDING Catches aquatic insects from the water's surface while swimming, wading, or flying during breeding season; winter diet mainly includes crustaceans, small fish, and plankton.

FLIGHT: wing beats shallow and stiff; tern-like, buoyant.

STRIKING WING PATTERN
Juvenile Sabine's Gulls have a muted version of the distinctive triangular wing pattern seen in the adults.

SIMILAR SPECIES

BLACK-LEGGED KITTIWAKE
see p.139

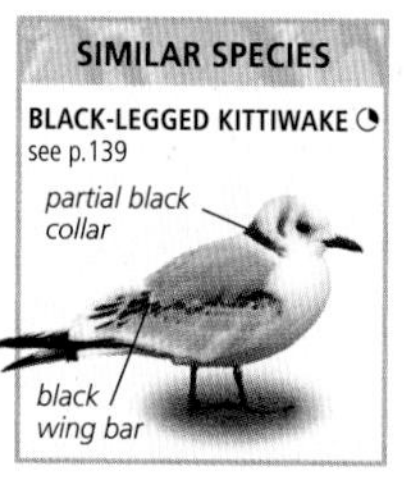
partial black collar
black wing bar

OCCURRENCE
In the summer, breeds near the Arctic Coast and on wet tundra in freshwater and brackish habitats, but also occurs near salt water. Winters far offshore in tropical and subtropical waters; widespread in the Pacific and Atlantic Oceans on migration.

Length **13–14in (33–36 cm)**	Wingspan **2ft 11in–3ft 3in (90–100cm)**	Weight **5–9oz (150–250g)**
Social **Colonies**	Lifespan **At least 8 years**	Status **Secure**

DATE: ____________ TIME: ____________ LOCATION: ____________

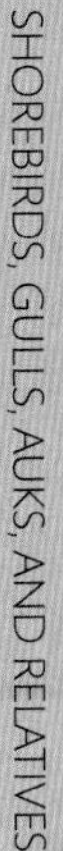

Bonaparte's Gull

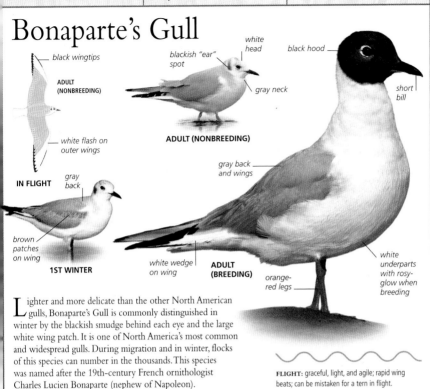

black wingtips

ADULT (NONBREEDING)

white flash on outer wings

IN FLIGHT

blackish "ear" spot

white head

gray neck

ADULT (NONBREEDING)

black hood

short bill

gray back and wings

gray back

brown patches on wing

1ST WINTER

white wedge on wing

ADULT (BREEDING)

orange-red legs

white underparts with rosy-glow when breeding

Lighter and more delicate than the other North American gulls, Bonaparte's Gull is commonly distinguished in winter by the blackish smudge behind each eye and the large white wing patch. It is one of North America's most common and widespread gulls. During migration and in winter, flocks of this species can number in the thousands. This species was named after the 19th-century French ornithologist Charles Lucien Bonaparte (nephew of Napoleon).

FLIGHT: graceful, light, and agile; rapid wing beats; can be mistaken for a tern in flight.

VOICE Harsh *keek, keek*; can be vocal in feeding flocks, *kew, kew, kew.*

NESTING Stick nest of twigs, branches, tree bark, lined with mosses or lichens; usually in conifers 5–20ft (1.5–6m) above ground; also in rushes over water; 1–4 eggs; 1 brood; May–July.

FEEDING Catches insects in flight on breeding grounds; picks crustaceans, mollusks, and small fish from water's surface; also plunge-dives.

TERN-LIKE GULL
Bonaparte's Gulls are very social and, flying in flocks, these pale, delicate birds look like terns.

WHITE UNDERWINGS
In all plumages, Bonaparte's Gull has white underwings, unlike other similar small gulls.

SIMILAR SPECIES

BLACK-HEADED GULL
see p.142
dark outer wing feathers
larger overall
red bill

LITTLE GULL
see p.143
smaller overall
uniform gray upperwing

OCCURRENCE
During breeding season, found in northern forest zone, in lakes, ponds, or bogs; on migration, may be found anywhere where there is water: ponds, lakes, sewage pools, or rivers. Winters on Great Lakes and along the coast; often found in large numbers at coastal inlets.

Length **11–12in (28–30cm)**	Wingspan **35–40in (90–100cm)**	Weight **6–8oz (175–225g)**
Social **Flocks**	Lifespan **Up to 18 years**	Status **Secure**

DATE: ____________ TIME: ____________ LOCATION: ____________

Order **Charadriiformes**	Family **Laridae**	Species ***Chroicocephalus ridibundus***

Black-headed Gull

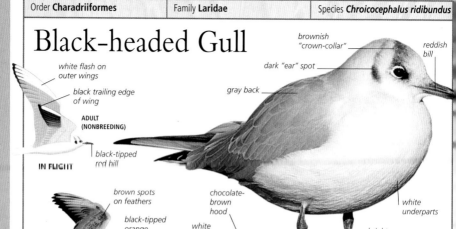

white flash on outer wings
black trailing edge of wing
ADULT (NONBREEDING)
black-tipped red bill
IN FLIGHT
brownish "crown-collar"
reddish bill
dark "ear" spot
gray back
white underparts
bright-red legs
ADULT (NONBREEDING)

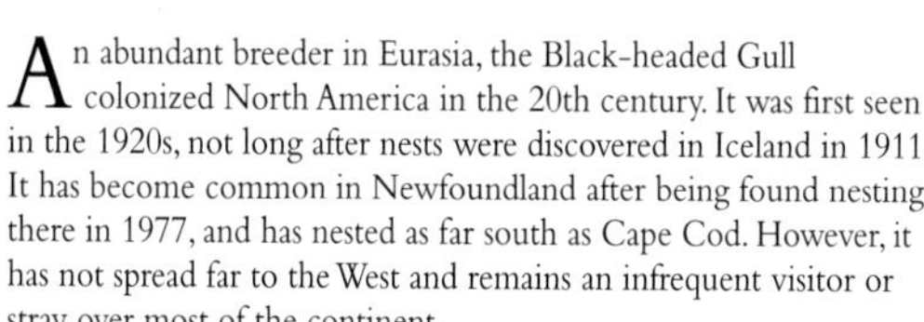
brown spots on feathers
black-tipped orange bill
black tail tip
1ST WINTER
chocolate-brown hood
white nape
very pale gray back
dark-red bill
dark-red legs
ADULT (BREEDING)

An abundant breeder in Eurasia, the Black-headed Gull colonized North America in the 20th century. It was first seen in the 1920s, not long after nests were discovered in Iceland in 1911. It has become common in Newfoundland after being found nesting there in 1977, and has nested as far south as Cape Cod. However, it has not spread far to the West and remains an infrequent visitor or stray over most of the continent.

VOICE Loud laughing (its French name is Laughing Gull) or a chattering *kek kek keeaar*; very vocal at breeding sites.

NESTING Loose mass of vegetation, on ground or on top of other vegetation; may be a large mound in wet areas; 2–3 eggs; 1 brood; April–August.

FEEDING Picks insects, small crustaceans, and mollusks off water's surface while flying or hovering; eats some vegetation; also forages in plowed farm fields; raids garbage dumps.

FLIGHT: graceful, light, and buoyant; agile.

BEAUTIFUL BREEDING PLUMAGE
Most North American birders never see the elegant summer plumage of the Black-headed Gull.

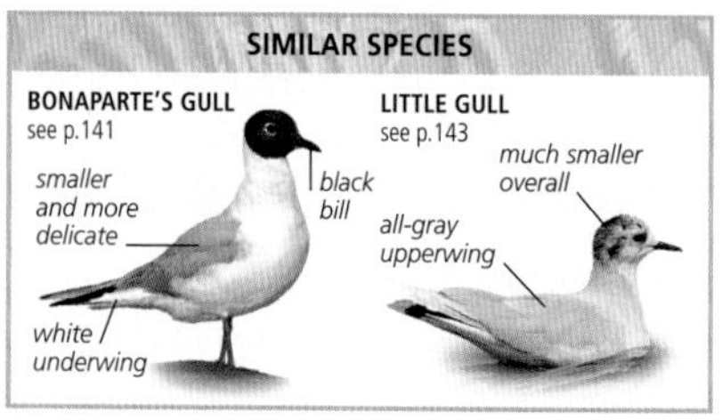
SIMILAR SPECIES
BONAPARTE'S GULL
see p.141
smaller and more delicate
black bill
white underwing
LITTLE GULL
see p.143
much smaller overall
all-gray upperwing

OCCURRENCE
Rare breeder in northeastern North America; singles or a few individuals may be found along the coast, often with Bonaparte's Gulls, at harbors, inlets, bays, rivers, lakes, sewage outlets, or garbage dumps; strays may occur anywhere. One of the most common European gulls.

Length **13½–14½in (34–37cm)**	Wingspan **39–42in (1–1.1m)**	Weight **7–14oz (200–400g)**
Social **Colonies**	Lifespan **Up to 18 years**	Status **Localized**

 DATE: ____________ TIME: ____________ LOCATION: ____________

Order **Charadriiformes**	Family **Laridae**	Species ***Hydrocoloeus minutus***

Little Gull

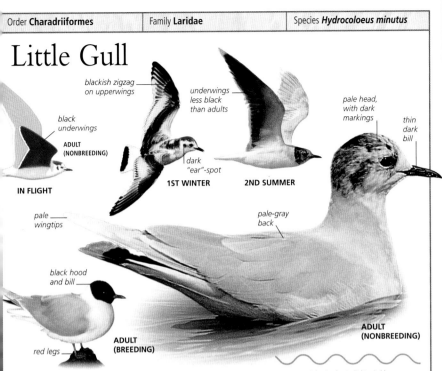

blackish zigzag on upperwings
black underwings
ADULT (NONBREEDING)
IN FLIGHT
dark "ear"-spot
1ST WINTER
underwings less black than adults
2ND SUMMER
pale head, with dark markings
thin dark bill
pale wingtips
pale-gray back
black hood and bill
red legs
ADULT (BREEDING)
ADULT (NONBREEDING)

A Eurasian species distributed from the Baltic to China, the Little Gull is the smallest gull in the world. Whether it is a recent immigrant to North America or has actually been here, unnoticed, in small numbers for many years remains a mystery. It was first recorded in North America in the early 1800s, but a nest was not found until 1962, in Ontario, Canada. Known nesting areas are still few, but winter numbers have been increasing steadily in recent decades.

VOICE Nasal *kek, kek, kek, kek*, reminiscent of a small tern.
NESTING Thick, floating mass of dry cattails, reeds, or other vegetation, in marshes and ponds; 3 eggs; 1 brood; May–August.
FEEDING Seizes prey from the water's surface, while swimming or plunge-diving; typical prey includes flying insects, aquatic invertebrates, such as shrimps, and small fish.

FLIGHT: quick wing beats; light, nimble, and agile.

SIMPLE ELEGANCE
Its long, pale-gray wings with a thin, white border place this bird among the most elegant of gulls.

SIMILAR SPECIES

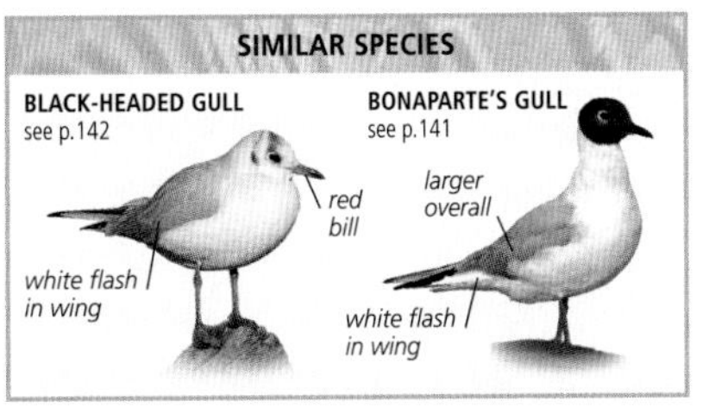
BLACK-HEADED GULL
see p.142
red bill
white flash in wing
BONAPARTE'S GULL
see p.141
larger overall
white flash in wing

OCCURRENCE
Breeds in extensive freshwater marshes in the Hudson Bay and the Great Lakes region, but the full extent of its breeding range in North America is unknown; can appear almost anywhere while migrating. Winters primarily along sea coasts, at sewage outfalls; often with groups of Bonaparte's Gulls.

Length **10–12in (25–30cm)**	Wingspan **23½–26in (60–65cm)**	Weight **3½–5oz (100–150g)**
Social **Colonies**	Lifespan **Up to 6 years**	Status **Secure**

DATE: ____________ TIME: ____________ LOCATION: ____________________

Order **Charadriiformes**	Family **Laridae**	Species ***Leucophaeus atricilla***

Laughing Gull

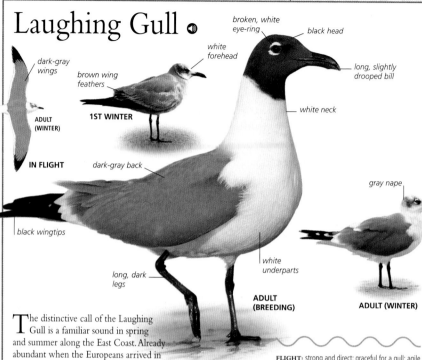

broken, white eye-ring
black head
white forehead
dark-gray wings
brown wing feathers
long, slightly drooped bill
white neck
ADULT (WINTER)
1ST WINTER
IN FLIGHT
dark-gray back
gray nape
black wingtips
white underparts
long, dark legs
ADULT (BREEDING)
ADULT (WINTER)

The distinctive call of the Laughing Gull is a familiar sound in spring and summer along the East Coast. Already abundant when the Europeans arrived in North America, it was greatly reduced in the 19th century by egg collectors and the millinery trade. Its numbers increased in the 1920s, following protection, but declined again due to competition with larger gulls from the North. With the closing of landfills, however, the Laughing Gull population has recovered. It has been known to hybridize with the Ring-billed Gull.

VOICE Typical call strident laugh, *ha...ha...ha...ha...ha*; very vocal in breeding season; quiet in winter.

NESTING Mass of grass on dry land with heavy vegetation, sand, rocks, or salt marshes; 2–4 eggs, 1 brood; April–July.

FEEDING Picks from surface while walking and swimming; feeds on various invertebrates: insects, earthworms, squid, crabs, crab eggs, and larvae; also eats small fish, garbage, and berries.

FLIGHT: strong and direct; graceful for a gull; agile enough to catch flying insects.

DARK WINGTIPS
Unlike many gulls, the Laughing Gull usually shows little or no white in the wingtips.

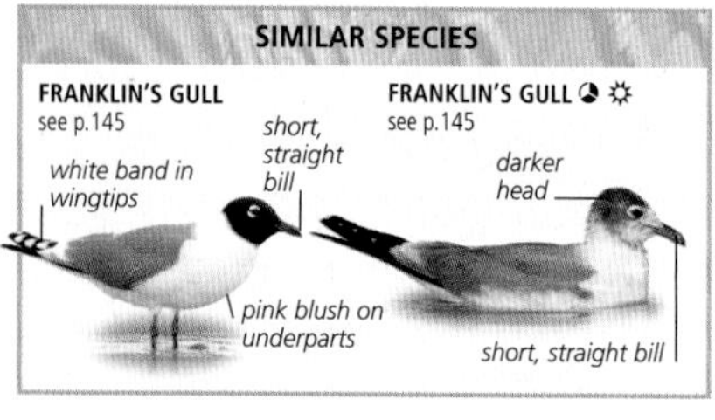

SIMILAR SPECIES
FRANKLIN'S GULL
see p.145
FRANKLIN'S GULL
see p.145
white band in wingtips
short, straight bill
darker head
pink blush on underparts
short, straight bill

OCCURRENCE
During breeding season usually found near salt water. Post-breeders and juveniles wander widely; strays can turn up anywhere, including parking lots. Rare in winter in the northeast. On occasion, they show up as far north as Newfoundland.

Length **15½–18in (39–46cm)**	Wingspan **40–48in (1–1.2m)**	Weight **7–13oz (200–375g)**
Social **Colonial**	Lifespan **Up to 20 years**	Status **Secure**

DATE: ____________ TIME: ____________ LOCATION: ____________

Order **Charadriiformes**	Family **Laridae**	Species ***Leucophaeus pipixcan***

Franklin's Gull

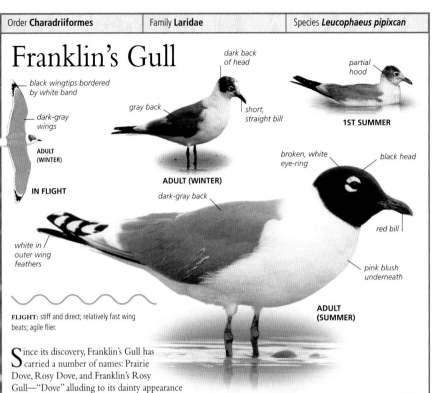

black wingtips bordered by white band
dark-gray wings
ADULT (WINTER)
IN FLIGHT

dark back of head
gray back
short, straight bill
ADULT (WINTER)

partial hood
1ST SUMMER

broken, white eye-ring
black head
dark-gray back
red bill
white in outer wing feathers
pink blush underneath
ADULT (SUMMER)

FLIGHT: stiff and direct; relatively fast wing beats; agile flier.

Since its discovery, Franklin's Gull has carried a number of names: Prairie Dove, Rosy Dove, and Franklin's Rosy Gull—"Dove" alluding to its dainty appearance and "rosy" to the pink blush of its undersides. Its official name honors British Arctic explorer, John Franklin, on whose first expedition, the bird was discovered in 1823. Unlike other gulls, this species has two complete molts each year. As a result, its plumage usually looks fresh and it rarely has the scruffy look of some other gulls.

VOICE Nasal *weeh-a, weeh-a*; shrill *kuk kuk kuk kuk*; extremely vocal around breeding colonies.

NESTING Floating mass of bulrushes or other plants; material added as nest sinks; 2–4 eggs; 1 brood; April–July.

FEEDING Feeds mainly on earthworms and insects, and some seeds during breeding, picked while walking or flying; opportunistic feeder during migration and winter.

PROMINENT EYES
In all plumages, Franklin's Gull has much more prominent white eye-crescents than similar species.

SIMILAR SPECIES
LAUGHING GULL
see p.144
longer, drooped bill
longer legs
LAUGHING GULL
see p.144
smaller eye-rings
longer, drooped bill
longer legs

OCCURRENCE
In summer, a bird of the high prairies; always nests over water. On migration often found in agricultural areas; large numbers frequent plowed fields or follows plows. Winters mainly along the Pacific Coast of South America.

Length **12½–14in (32–36cm)**	Wingspan **2ft 9in–3ft 1in (85–95cm)**	Weight **8–11oz (225–325g)**
Social **Colonial**	Lifespan **At least 10 years**	Status **Declining**

DATE: ____________ TIME: ____________ LOCATION: ____________________

Order **Charadriiformes**	Family **Laridae**	Species ***Larus delawarensis***

Ring-billed Gull

white wing spots

ADULT (BREEDING)

IN FLIGHT

dark eye

mottled-gray back

black-tipped pink bill

white neck

1ST WINTER

heavily mottled back

mottled underparts

pink legs

JUVENILE

fine streaks on head

gray back

olive-yellow legs

ADULT (NONBREEDING)

pale gray back

2ND WINTER

black band on yellow bill

pale eye with red eye-ring

pale-gray back

white markings on outer wing feathers

white underparts

yellowish or greenish legs

ADULT (BREEDING)

FLIGHT: quick, deep wing beats; strong, direct flight, soaring on thermals.

One of the most common birds in North America, the medium-sized Ring-billed Gull is distinguished by the black band on its yellow bill. From the mid-19th to the early 20th century, population numbers crashed due to shooting and habitat loss. Protection allowed the species to make a spectacular comeback, and in the 1990s, there were an estimated 3–4 million birds. It can often be seen scavenging in parking lots at malls and following farmers' tractors.

VOICE Call a slightly nasal and whiny *kee-ow* or *meee-ow*; series of 4–6 *kyaw* notes, higher pitched than Herring Gull.

NESTING Shallow cup of plant matter on ground in open areas, usually near low vegetation; 1–5 eggs; 1 brood; April–August.

FEEDING Picks food while walking; also dips and plunges in water; eats small fish, insects, grain, small rodents; also scavenges.

BLACK WING MARKING
The sharply demarcated black wingtips are prominent from both above and below.

SIMILAR SPECIES
SHORT-BILLED GULL
round head
small bill
darker mantle
SHORT-BILLED GULL 1ST
round head
less distinct streaks
small bill

OCCURRENCE
Breeds in freshwater habitats in the interior of the continent. In winter, switches to mostly saltwater areas and along both the East and West Coasts; also along major river systems and reservoirs. Found year-round near the southern Great Lakes.

Length **17–21½in (43–54cm)**	Wingspan **4–5ft (1.2–1.5m)**	Weight **11–25oz (300–700g)**
Social **Colonies**	Lifespan **Up to 32 years**	Status **Secure**

DATE: ________ TIME: ________ LOCATION: ________

Order **Charadriiformes**	Family **Laridae**	Species ***Larus argentatus***

Herring Gull

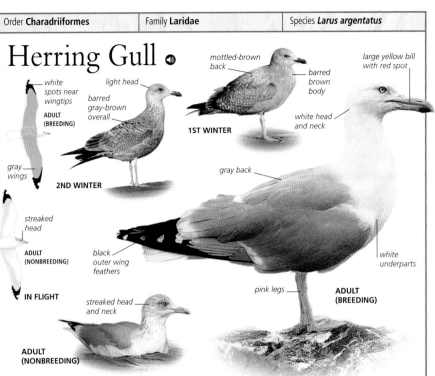

white spots near wingtips
ADULT (BREEDING)
gray wings
light head
barred gray-brown overall
2ND WINTER
mottled-brown back
barred brown body
1ST WINTER
large yellow bill with red spot
white head and neck
gray back
streaked head
ADULT (NONBREEDING)
IN FLIGHT
black outer wing feathers
white underparts
pink legs
ADULT (BREEDING)
streaked head and neck
ADULT (NONBREEDING)

The Herring Gull is the archetypal, large "white-headed" gull that nearly all other gulls are compared with. When people mention "seagulls" they usually refer to the Herring Gull. The term "seagull" is actually misleading because the Herring Gull, like most other gulls, does not commonly go far out to sea—it is a bird of near-shore waters, coasts, lakes, rivers, and inland waterways. Now very common, the Herring Gull was nearly wiped out in the late 19th and early 20th century by plumage hunters and egg collectors.

VOICE Typical call a high-pitched, shrill, repeated *heyaa…heyaa…heyaa…heyaa*; vocal throughout the year.

NESTING Shallow bowl on ground, lined with feathers, vegetation, detritus; 2–4 eggs; 1 brood; April–August.

FEEDING Eats fish, crustaceans, mollusks, worms; eggs and chicks of other seabirds; scavenges carrion, garbage; steals from other birds.

FLIGHT: steady, regular, slow wing beats; also commonly soars and glides.

MASTER SCAVENGER
A common sight near any water body, the Herring Gull is an expert scavenger of carrion and trash.

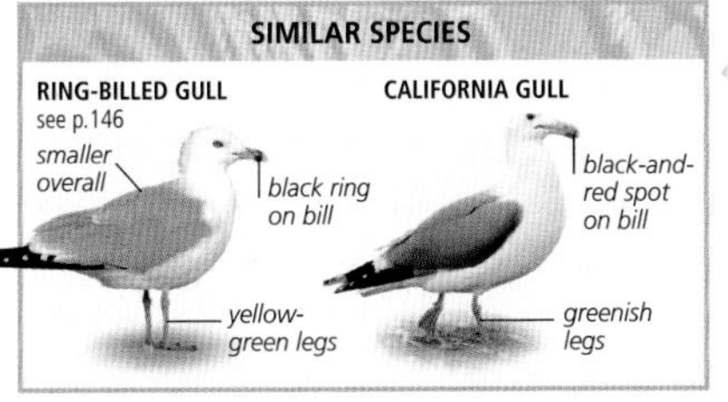
SIMILAR SPECIES
RING-BILLED GULL
see p.146
smaller overall
black ring on bill
yellow-green legs
CALIFORNIA GULL
black-and-red spot on bill
greenish legs

OCCURRENCE
Found throughout North America along coasts and inland on lakes, rivers, and reservoirs; also frequents garbage dumps. Breeds in northeastern US and across Canada. Migrates southward across much of the continent to winter in coastal areas and along lakes and major rivers.

Length **22–26in (56–66cm)**	Wingspan **4–5ft (1.2–1.5m)**	Weight **28–42oz (0.8–1.2kg)**
Social **Colonies**	Lifespan **At least 35 years**	Status **Secure**

DATE: ____________ TIME: ____________ LOCATION: ____________

Order **Charadriiformes**	Family **Laridae**	Species ***Larus glaucoides***

Iceland Gull

gray wingtips

pale-brown plumage

ADULT (WINTER)

1ST WINTER

IN FLIGHT

wingtip white or marked with gray

gray back

markedly streaked head

short, pale-yellow bill with red spot

white belly

pink legs

ADULT (WINTER)
L. g. kumlieni

brown, barred plumage

blackish bill

head mostly white

pale, barred underparts

1ST WINTER

2ND WINTER

Iceland Gulls of the subspecies *kumlieni* (seen in all the images here) are the most familiar form of this species in North America. They breed in the Canadian Arctic and winter farther south. Young birds have a dark tail band and brown streaks on the wingtip, while adults vary from white wingtips to gray with white spots. A darker subspecies, *thayeri*, breeds on Arctic islands west of the *kumlieni*'s range, and has black-and-white wingtips like the Herring Gull and a darker eye. Thayer's Gull was considered to be a different species until 2017, when it was grouped with the Iceland Gull. The "Iceland" form of the gull, *L. g. glaucoides*, breeds in Greenland but is found farther eastward in winter, including in Iceland.

VOICE Call a *clew, clew, clew* or *kak-kak-kak*; vocal around breeding colonies; virtually silent on wintering grounds.

NESTING Loose nest of moss, vegetation, and feathers, usually on narrow rock ledge; 2–3 eggs; 1 brood; May–August.

FEEDING Grabs small fish from surface while in flight; also eats crustaceans, mollusks, carrion, and garbage.

FLIGHT: light and graceful; wings long in proportion to body.

WINGTIP COLOR VARIATION
Some adult Iceland Gulls found in North America have wingtips that are almost pure white.

SIMILAR SPECIES

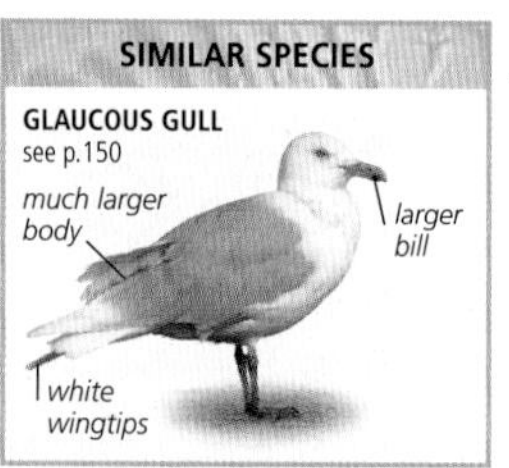

GLAUCOUS GULL
see p.150
much larger body
larger bill
white wingtips

OCCURRENCE
Usually nests on ledges on vertical cliffs overlooking the sea; winters where it finds regions of open water in frozen seas and along coasts. A few wander to open water areas in the interior, such as the Niagara Falls, the Great Lakes and major rivers.

Length **20½–23½in (52–60cm)**	Wingspan **4½–5ft (1.4–1.5m)**	Weight **21–39oz (0.6–1.1kg)**
Social **Colonies**	Lifespan **Up to 33 years**	Status **Secure**

DATE: ______________ TIME: ______________ LOCATION: ______________

Order **Charadriiformes**	Family **Laridae**	Species ***Larus fuscus***

Lesser Black-backed Gull

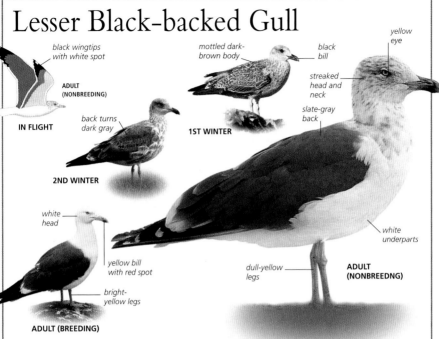

black wingtips with white spot
ADULT (NONBREEDING)
IN FLIGHT
mottled dark-brown body
black bill
1ST WINTER
back turns dark gray
2ND WINTER
yellow eye
streaked head and neck
slate-gray back
white underparts
dull-yellow legs
ADULT (NONBREEDNG)
white head
yellow bill with red spot
bright-yellow legs
ADULT (BREEDING)

This European visitor was first discovered in North America on the New Jersey coast on September 9, 1934 and in New York City a few months later. In recent decades, it has become an annual winter visitor. Nearly all the Lesser Black-backed Gulls found in North America are of the Icelandic and western European subspecies *L. f. graellsii*, with a slate-gray back. Another European subspecies, with a much darker back, has rarely been reported in North America, but it is probably only a matter of time before it nests there.

VOICE A *kyow…yow…yow…yow* call, similar to that of Herring Gull; also a deeper and throaty, repeated *gah-gah-gah-gah*.

NESTING Scrape on ground lined with dry lichens, dry grass, and feathers; 3 eggs; 1 brood; April–September.

FEEDING Eats mollusks, crustaceans, and various insects; also scavenges carrion and garbage.

FLIGHT: powerful and direct; regular wing beats; long wings make it appear graceful.

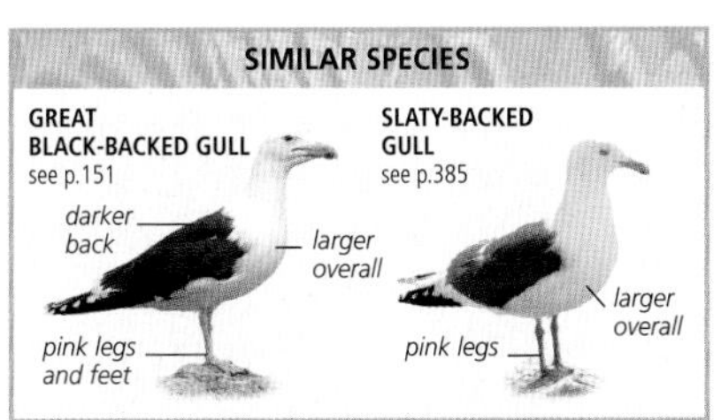
SIMILAR SPECIES
GREAT BLACK-BACKED GULL
see p.151
darker back
larger overall
pink legs and feet
SLATY-BACKED GULL
see p.385
larger overall
pink legs

EXCITING FIND
In recent years, gull enthusiasts and birdwatchers have found these birds visiting from Europe.

OCCURRENCE
Regular and increasingly common winter visitor to eastern North America, usually along the coast, but also in the interior; wherever gulls commonly concentrate such as harbors, lakeshores, landfills, and around fishing boats.

Length **20½–26in (52–67cm)**	Wingspan **4¼–5ft (1.3–1.5m)**	Weight **22–35oz (625g–1kg)**
Social **Colonies**	Lifespan **Up to 26 years**	Status **Secure**

DATE: ____________ TIME: ____________ LOCATION: ____________

Order **Charadriiformes**	Family **Laridae**	Species ***Larus hyperboreus***

Glaucous Gull

ADULT (WINTER)

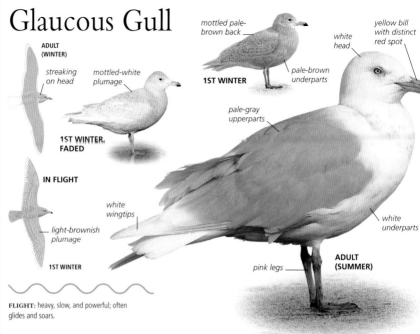

streaking on head

mottled-white plumage

1ST WINTER, FADED

mottled pale-brown back

pale-brown underparts

1ST WINTER

white head

yellow bill with distinct red spot

pale-gray upperparts

IN FLIGHT

white wingtips

light-brownish plumage

1ST WINTER

white underparts

pink legs

ADULT (SUMMER)

FLIGHT: heavy, slow, and powerful; often glides and soars.

The Glaucous Gull is the largest of the "white-winged" gulls. Its bulky, pale shape is immediately apparent in a group of gulls as it appears like a large white spectre among its smaller, darker cousins. In the southern part of its US winter range, pale juveniles are encountered more frequently than adults. In the Arctic, successful pairs of Glaucous Gulls maintain the bonds with their mates for years, often returning to the same nest site year after year.

VOICE Similar to that of the Herring Gull, but slightly harsher and deeper; hoarse, nasal *ku-ku-ku*.

NESTING Shallow cup, lined with vegetation on ground, at edge of tundra pools, on cliffs and ledges and islands; 1–3 eggs; 1 brood; May–July.

FEEDING Eats fish, crustaceans, mollusks; also eggs and chicks of waterfowl, small seabirds, and small mammals.

NORTHERN VISITOR
This large gull is an uncommon visitor over most of North America during the winter months.

SIMILAR SPECIES

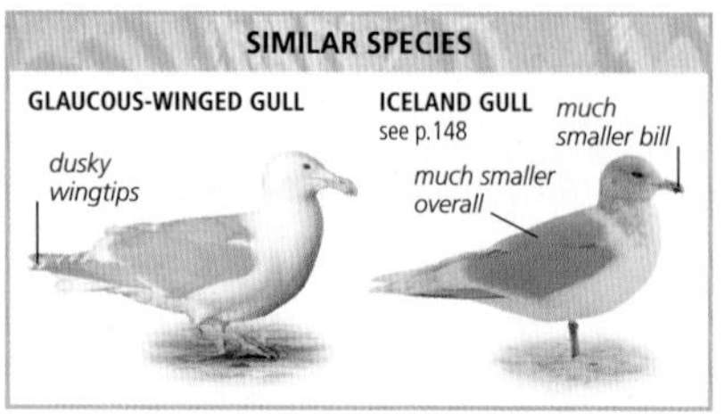
GLAUCOUS-WINGED GULL
dusky wingtips
ICELAND GULL
see p.148
much smaller bill
much smaller overall

OCCURRENCE
Breeds along the high-Arctic coast, rarely inland; winters along the northern Atlantic and Pacific Coasts and the Great Lakes; frequently seen at the Niagara Falls. Strays, usually juveniles, can occur inland anywhere where concentrations of gulls are found, such as landfill sites and dumps.

Length **26–30in (65–75cm)**	Wingspan **5–6ft (1.5–1.8m)**	Weight **2¾–6lb (1.2–2.7kg)**
Social **Colonies**	Lifespan **Up to 21 years**	Status **Secure**

 DATE: ____________ TIME: ____________ LOCATION: ____________

Order **Charadriiformes**	Family **Laridae**	Species ***Larus marinus***

Great Black-backed Gull

large white spot on wingtips
ADULT (BREEDING)
IN FLIGHT
white head with faint streaks
ADULT (NONBREEDING)
white underwings
ADULT (BREEDING)
red eye-ring
white head and neck
yellow bill with red spot
black upperparts
white tips to outer feathers
white underparts
ADULT (BREEDING)
pale-pink legs and feet
whitish head
black bill
speckled back
1ST WINTER

The largest gull in North America, the Great Black-backed Gull is known for its bullying dispostion. In breeding colonies, it is especially aggressive in the morning and early evening, and after the chicks hatch; adults dive at ground predators and strike them with their wings and feet. For other birds, there are advantages and disadvantages to this behavior: while eiders nesting in Great Black-backed gull colonies might suffer low predation from other predators, they lose many of their ducklings to the predatory gulls.

VOICE Low, growling flight call, often repeated, low-pitched *heyaa… heyaa…heyaa…heyaa*, similar to the Herring Gull.

NESTING Shallow bowl on ground, lined with vegetation, feathers, and trash; 2–3 eggs; 1 brood; April–August.

FEEDING Scavenges and hunts fish, marine invertebrates, small mammals, eggs, chicks, adult seabirds, and waterfowl.

FLIGHT: heavy lumbering with deep wing beats.

SOLITARY BIRDS
While all gulls are social animals, the Great Black-backed Gull is the most solitary.

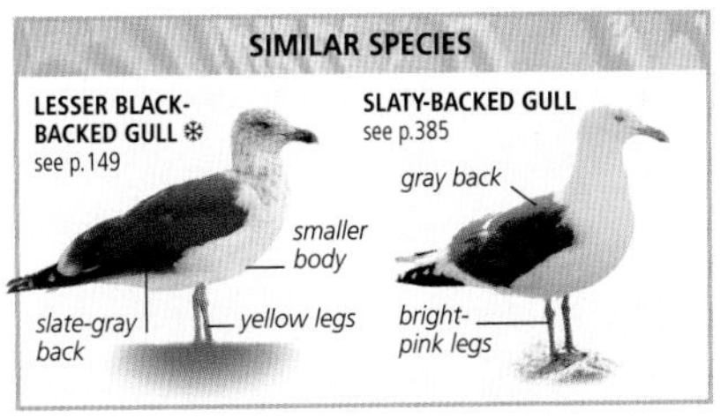
SIMILAR SPECIES
LESSER BLACK-BACKED GULL ❄
see p.149
slate-gray back
smaller body
yellow legs
SLATY-BACKED GULL
see p.385
gray back
bright-pink legs

OCCURRENCE
Breeds on natural and artificial islands, barrier beaches, salt marshes, sand dunes; during winter, found along the coast, near shore water, major rivers, landfills, and harbors; in all seasons, often found together with Herring Gulls and Ring-billed Gulls. Also occurs in Europe.

Length **28–31in (71–79cm)**	Wingspan **5–5¼ft (1.5–1.6m)**	Weight **2¾–4½lb (1.3–2kg)**
Social **Pairs/Colonies**	Lifespan **Up to 27 years**	Status **Secure**

DATE: ____________ TIME: ____________ LOCATION: ____________________

Order **Charadriiformes**	Family **Laridae**	Species ***Hydroprogne caspia***

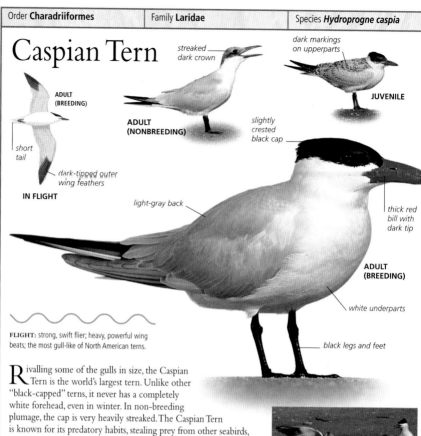

Caspian Tern

streaked dark crown

dark markings on upperparts

ADULT (BREEDING)

JUVENILE

ADULT (NONBREEDING)

slightly crested black cap

short tail

dark-tipped outer wing feathers

IN FLIGHT

light-gray back

thick red bill with dark tip

ADULT (BREEDING)

white underparts

black legs and feet

FLIGHT: strong, swift flier; heavy, powerful wing beats; the most gull-like of North American terns.

Rivalling some of the gulls in size, the Caspian Tern is the world's largest tern. Unlike other "black-capped" terns, it never has a completely white forehead, even in winter. In non-breeding plumage, the cap is very heavily streaked. The Caspian Tern is known for its predatory habits, stealing prey from other seabirds, as well as snatching eggs and eating the chicks of gulls and other terns. It is aggressive in defending its nesting territory, giving hoarse alarm calls, and rhythmically opening and closing its beak in a threatening display to intruders.

VOICE Hoarse, deep *kraaa, kraaa*; also barks at intruders; male's wings vibrate loudly in courtship flight.

NESTING Shallow scrape on ground; 2–3 eggs; 1 brood; May–August.

FEEDING Plunges into water to snatch fish, barnacles, and snails.

AGRESSIVE BIRDS

The Caspian Tern is one of the most aggressive terns, though, actual physical contact is rare.

SIMILAR SPECIES

ELEGANT TERN smaller overall; thin orange-yellow bill

ROYAL TERN thinner orange bill; slender build

OCCURRENCE

Found in a variety of aquatic habitats, freshwater and marine; rare offshore; breeds on interior lakes, salt marshes, and on coastal barrier islands; winters on and near the coast. May be seen on marshes and wetlands during migration.

Length **18½–21½in (47–54cm)**	Wingspan **4¼–5ft (1.3–1.5m)**	Weight **19–27oz (525–775g)**
Social **Colonies/Pairs**	Lifespan **Up to 30 years**	Status **Secure**

DATE: ____________ TIME: ____________ LOCATION: ____________

Order **Charadriiformes**	Family **Laridae**	Species ***Chlidonias niger***

Black Tern

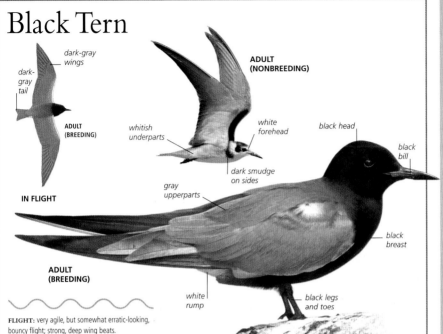

dark-gray wings
dark-gray tail
ADULT (BREEDING)
IN FLIGHT

ADULT (NONBREEDING)
whitish underparts
white forehead
dark smudge on sides

black head
black bill
gray upperparts
black breast
white rump
black legs and toes
ADULT (BREEDING)

FLIGHT: very agile, but somewhat erratic-looking, bouncy flight; strong, deep wing beats.

The Black Tern is a small, elegant, marsh-dwelling tern that undergoes a remarkable change in appearance from summer to winter—more so than any other regularly occurring North American tern. The Black Tern's breeding plumage can cause the bird to be confused with the closely related White-winged Tern, which is an accidental visitor to North America. The Black Tern's nonbreeding plumage is much paler than its breeding plumage—the head turns white with irregular black streaks, and the neck, breast, and belly become whitish gray.

VOICE Call nasal and harsh *krik*, *kip*, or *kik*; most vocal during breeding, but calls throughout the year.

NESTING Shallow cup on top of floating mass of vegetation, sometimes on top of muskrat lodges; usually 3 eggs; 1 brood; May–August.

FEEDING Picks prey off water's surface or vegetation; rarely plunge-dives; in summer, feeds mainly on insects, caught from the air or ground, also freshwater fish; in winter, eats mainly small sea fish.

FLOATING NEST
A floating nest is a dry place to lay eggs and raise chicks in a watery environment.

SIMILAR SPECIES

SOOTY TERN ◔

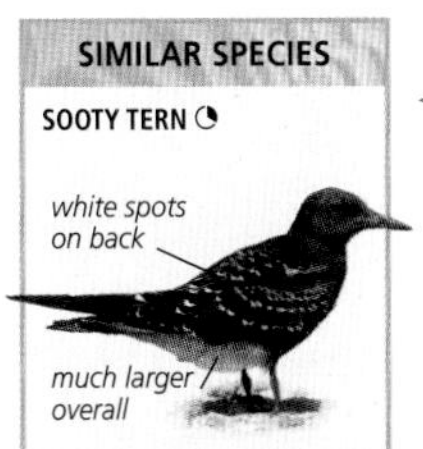
white spots on back
much larger overall

OCCURRENCE
Freshwater marshes in summer, but nonbreeding-plumaged birds—probably young—occasionally seen along the coast. During migration, can be found almost anywhere near water. Winters in the marine coastal waters of Central and South America.

Length **9–10in (23–26cm)**	Wingspan **25–35in (63–88cm)**	Weight **1¾–2½oz (50–70g)**
Social **Colonies**	Lifespan **Up to 9 years**	Status **Vulnerable**

DATE: ____________ TIME: ____________ LOCATION: ____________

Order **Charadriiformes**	Family **Laridae**	Species ***Sterna dougallii***

Roseate Tern

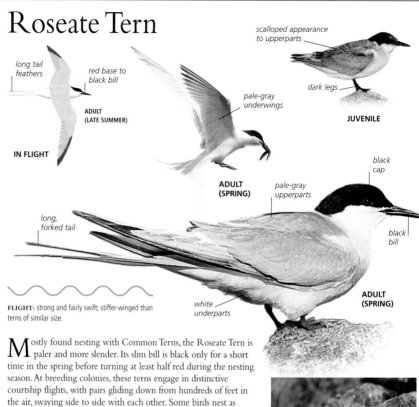

long tail feathers

red base to black bill

ADULT (LATE SUMMER)

IN FLIGHT

pale-gray underwings

ADULT (SPRING)

scalloped appearance to upperparts

dark legs

JUVENILE

black cap

pale-gray upperparts

long, forked tail

black bill

white underparts

ADULT (SPRING)

FLIGHT: strong and fairly swift; stiffer-winged than terns of similar size.

Mostly found nesting with Common Terns, the Roseate Tern is paler and more slender. Its slim bill is black only for a short time in the spring before turning at least half red during the nesting season. At breeding colonies, these terns engage in distinctive courtship flights, with pairs gliding down from hundreds of feet in the air, swaying side to side with each other. Some birds nest as trios—two females and a male—all taking part in incubating the eggs and raising the young.

VOICE Most common calls *keek* or *ki-rik* given in flight and around nesting colony.

NESTING Simple scrape, often under vegetation or large rocks; adds twigs and dry grass during incubation; 1–3 eggs; 1 brood; May–August.

FEEDING Catches small fish with its bill by diving from a height of 3–20ft (1–6m); carries whole fish to young.

GRACEFUL COURTSHIP
Roseate Tern pairs engage in elegant, graceful courtship displays before mating.

SIMILAR SPECIES

SANDWICH TERN ☼
yellow-tipped bill
larger overall

COMMON TERN ☼
shorter tail; see p.155
darker gray overall

OCCURRENCE
Breeds almost exclusively in coastal areas in the northeast from Long Island, New York, to Nova Scotia, with another small population in the outer Florida Keys. Typically nests on beaches and offshore islands. Not often seen far from breeding sites.

Length **13–16in (33–41cm)**	Wingspan **28in (70cm)**	Weight **3–5oz (85–150g)**
Social **Colonies**	Lifespan **Up to 26 years**	Status **Endangered**

DATE: ____________ TIME: ____________ LOCATION: ____________

Order **Charadriiformes**	Family **Laridae**	Species ***Sterna hirundo***

Common Tern

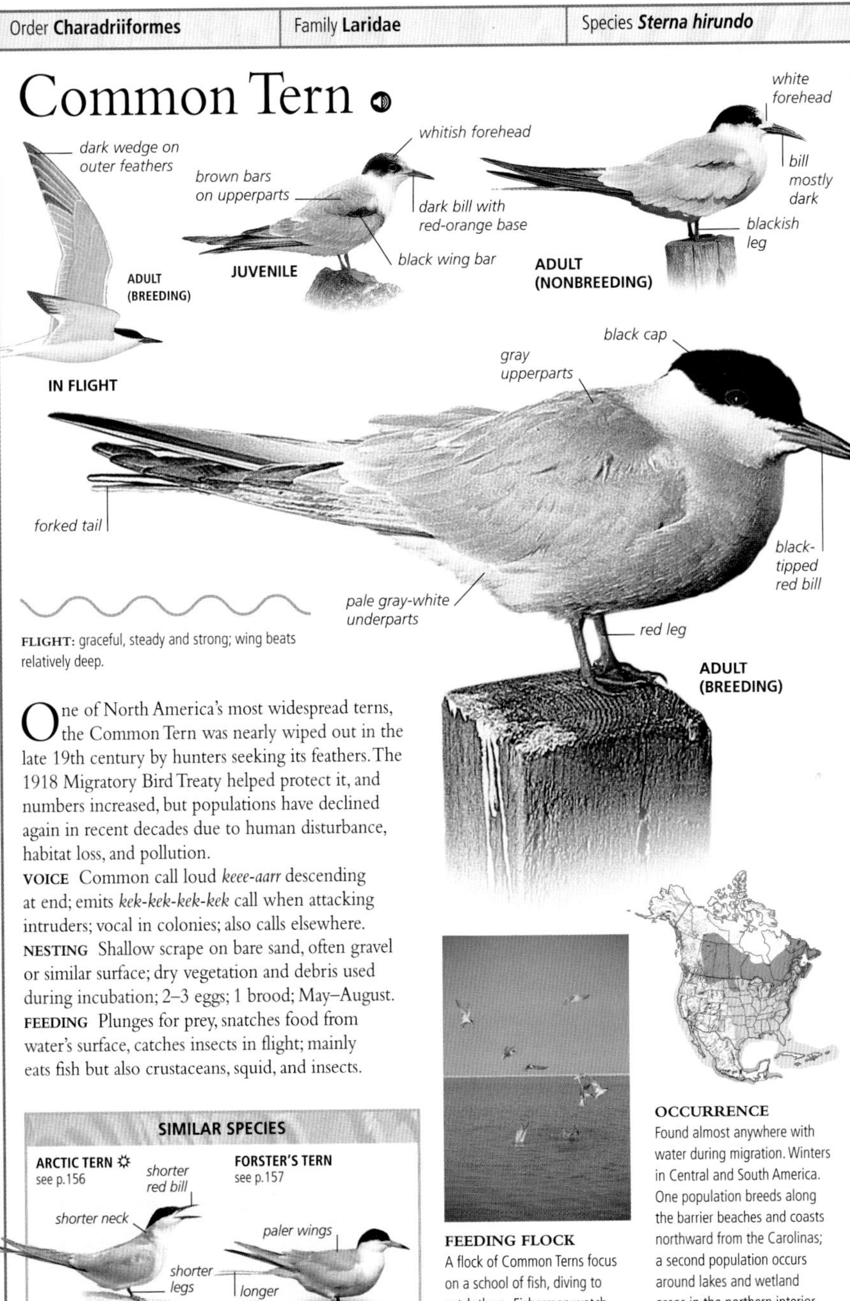
dark wedge on outer feathers
ADULT (BREEDING)
IN FLIGHT
brown bars on upperparts
whitish forehead
dark bill with red-orange base
black wing bar
JUVENILE
white forehead
bill mostly dark
blackish leg
ADULT (NONBREEDING)
black cap
gray upperparts
forked tail
black-tipped red bill
pale gray-white underparts
red leg
ADULT (BREEDING)

FLIGHT: graceful, steady and strong; wing beats relatively deep.

One of North America's most widespread terns, the Common Tern was nearly wiped out in the late 19th century by hunters seeking its feathers. The 1918 Migratory Bird Treaty helped protect it, and numbers increased, but populations have declined again in recent decades due to human disturbance, habitat loss, and pollution.

VOICE Common call loud *keee-aarr* descending at end; emits *kek-kek-kek-kek* call when attacking intruders; vocal in colonies; also calls elsewhere.

NESTING Shallow scrape on bare sand, often gravel or similar surface; dry vegetation and debris used during incubation; 2–3 eggs; 1 brood; May–August.

FEEDING Plunges for prey, snatches food from water's surface, catches insects in flight; mainly eats fish but also crustaceans, squid, and insects.

SIMILAR SPECIES

ARCTIC TERN ☼ see p.156

shorter red bill
shorter neck
shorter legs

FORSTER'S TERN see p.157

paler wings
longer tail

FEEDING FLOCK
A flock of Common Terns focus on a school of fish, diving to catch them. Fishermen watch for such flocks to locate fish.

OCCURRENCE
Found almost anywhere with water during migration. Winters in Central and South America. One population breeds along the barrier beaches and coasts northward from the Carolinas; a second population occurs around lakes and wetland areas in the northern interior.

Length **12–14in (31–35cm)**	Wingspan **30–31in (75–80cm)**	Weight **3⅜–5oz (95–150g)**
Social **Colonies**	Lifespan **Up to 26 years**	Status **Vulnerable**

DATE: ______________ TIME: ______________ LOCATION: ______________

Order **Charadriiformes**	Family **Laridae**	Species ***Sterna paradisaea***

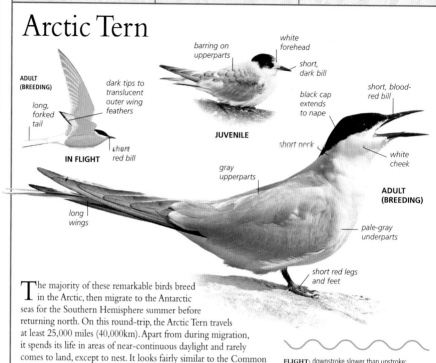

Arctic Tern

ADULT (BREEDING)
long, forked tail
dark tips to translucent outer wing feathers
short red bill
IN FLIGHT

barring on upperparts
white forehead
short, dark bill
JUVENILE

black cap extends to nape
short, blood-red bill
short neck
white cheek
gray upperparts
long wings
pale-gray underparts
short red legs and feet
ADULT (BREEDING)

The majority of these remarkable birds breed in the Arctic, then migrate to the Antarctic seas for the Southern Hemisphere summer before returning north. On this round-trip, the Arctic Tern travels at least 25,000 miles (40,000km). Apart from during migration, it spends its life in areas of near-continuous daylight and rarely comes to land, except to nest. It looks fairly similar to the Common Tern, but the Arctic Tern has a comparatively smaller bill, shorter legs, and a shorter neck.

FLIGHT: downstroke slower than upstroke; buoyant and elegant with regular wing beats.

VOICE Descending *keeyaar* call; nearly all calls similar to Common Tern's, but higher-pitched and harsher.
NESTING Shallow scrape on bare ground or low vegetation in open areas; 2 eggs; 1 brood; May–August.
FEEDING Mostly plunge-dives for small fish and crustaceans, including crabs and shrimps; will also take prey from surface, sometimes catches insects in flight.

FEEDING THE YOUNG
Both parents feed chicks—males bring more food than females, especially right after hatching.

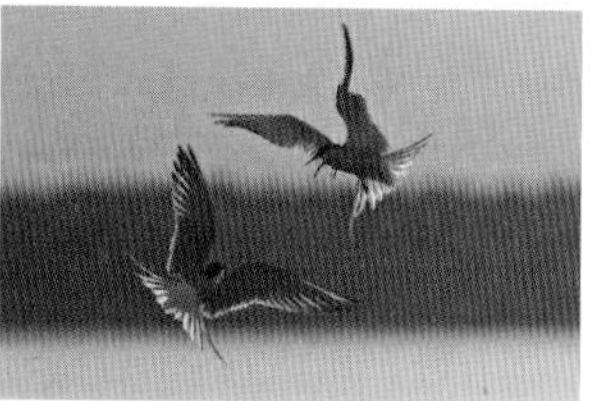

TRANSLUCENT FEATHERS
The translucent outer wing feathers of the Arctic Tern are evident on these two flying birds.

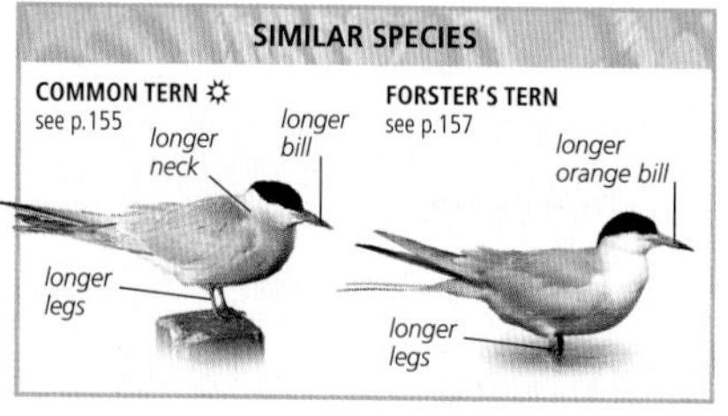
SIMILAR SPECIES
COMMON TERN ☼
see p.155
longer neck
longer bill
longer legs
FORSTER'S TERN
see p.157
longer orange bill
longer legs

OCCURRENCE
Breeds in far north, mostly in open, unforested areas near water and along the coast; generally migrates far offshore. Spends more time away from land than other northern terns. Winters on edge of pack ice in Antarctica.

Length **11–15½in (28–39cm)**	Wingspan **26–30in (65–75cm)**	Weight **3⅛–4oz (90–125g)**
Social **Colonies**	Lifespan **Up to 34 years**	Status **Vulnerable**

DATE: ____________ TIME: ____________ LOCATION: ____________

Order **Charadriiformes**	Family **Laridae**	Species ***Sterna forsteri***

Forster's Tern

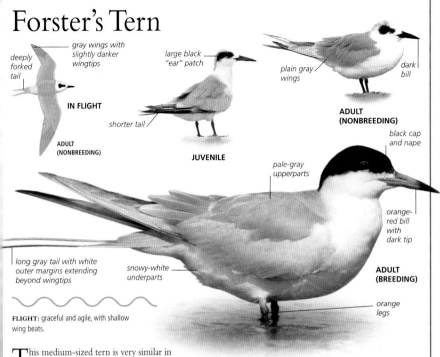

deeply forked tail

gray wings with slightly darker wingtips

IN FLIGHT

ADULT (NONBREEDING)

large black "ear" patch

shorter tail

JUVENILE

plain gray wings

dark bill

ADULT (NONBREEDING)

black cap and nape

pale-gray upperparts

orange-red bill with dark tip

long gray tail with white outer margins extending beyond wingtips

snowy-white underparts

ADULT (BREEDING)

orange legs

FLIGHT: graceful and agile, with shallow wing beats.

This medium-sized tern is very similar in appearance to the Common Tern. The features that differentiate it from the Common Tern are its lighter outer wing feathers and longer tail. Early naturalists could not tell the two species apart until 1834, when English botanist Thomas Nuttall made the distinction. He named this tern after Johann Reinhold Forster, a naturalist who accompanied the English explorer Captain Cook on his epic second voyage (1772–75).

VOICE Harsh, descending *kyerr*; more nasal than Common Tern.

NESTING Shallow scrape in mud or sand, but occasionally nests on top of muskrat lodge or on old grebe nest; sometimes constructs raft of floating vegetation; 2–3 eggs; 1 brood; May–August.

FEEDING Catches fish and crustaceans with shallow plunge-diving, often only head submerges; also catches insects in flight.

BLACK EARS

With its black "ear" patch, Forster's Tern is more distinctive in nonbreeding than breeding plumage.

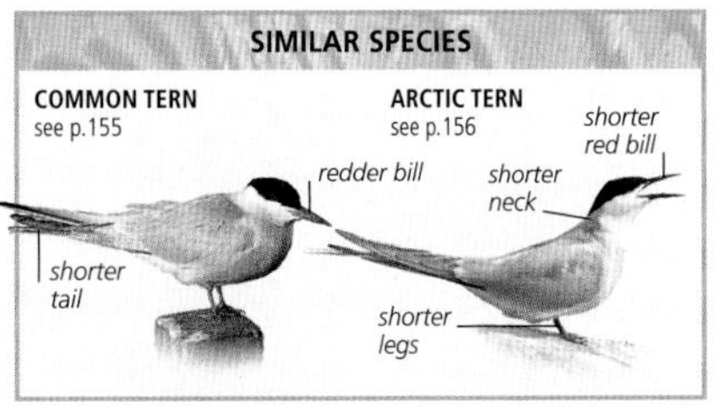
SIMILAR SPECIES
COMMON TERN
see p.155
redder bill
shorter tail
ARCTIC TERN
see p.156
shorter red bill
shorter neck
shorter legs

OCCURRENCE

Breeds in prairie provinces and southern Ontario, in freshwater and saltwater marshes with large stretches of open water. Winters on both coasts and across the southern US states, unlike the Common Tern, which primarily winters in South America.

Length **13–14in (33–36cm)**	Wingspan **29–32in (73–82cm)**	Weight **4–7oz (125–190g)**
Social **Colonies**	Lifespan **Up to 16 years**	Status **Secure**

DATE: ______________ TIME: ______________ LOCATION: ______________

Family **Gaviidae**

LOONS

WORLDWIDE THERE ARE only five species of loons, comprising a single genus (*Gavia*), a single family (the Gaviidae), and a single order (the Gaviiformes). The five species are limited to the Northern Hemisphere, where they are found in both northern North America and northern Eurasia. One feature of loons is that their legs are positioned so far to the rear of their body that they must shuffle on their bellies when they step out of the water onto land. Not surprisingly, therefore, loons are almost entirely aquatic birds. In summer, they are found on rivers, lakes, and ponds, where they nest close to the water's edge. After breeding, they occur along coasts, often after flying hundreds of miles away from their freshwater breeding grounds. Excellent swimmers and divers, loons are unusual among birds in that their bones are less hollow than those of other groups. Consequently, they can expel air from their lungs and compress their body feathers until they slowly sink beneath the surface. They can remain submerged like this for several minutes. A loon's wings are relatively small in proportion to its body weight. This means that they have to run a long way across the surface of the water, flapping energetically, before they can get airborne. Once in the air, they keep on flapping and can fly at up to 60mph (95kmh).

PROVIDING FOR THE FUTURE
A Red-throated Loon gives a fish to its chick to gulp down headfirst and whole.

Families **Diomedeidae, Oceanitidae, Hydrobatidae, Procellariidae**

TUBENOSES

THE TUBENOSES ARE DIVIDED INTO several families, but all are characterized by the tubular nostrils for which the order is named. These nostrils help to get rid of excess salt, and may enhance their sense of smell.

STORM-PETRELS

The smallest tubenoses in North American waters, the storm-petrels (families Oceanitidae and Hydrobatidae) are also the most agile fliers. They often patter or "dance" as they fly low to the surface of the ocean in search of small fish, squid, and crustaceans. Storm-petrels spend most of their lives flying over the open sea, only visiting land in the breeding season, when they form huge colonies.

SHEARWATERS AND PETRELS

Shearwaters and gadfly petrels (family Procellariidae) are smaller than albatrosses (found only in western Canada). Like their larger relatives, they are excellent gliders, but their lighter weight and proportionately shorter wings mean that they use more powered flight than albatrosses. They range over all the world's oceans. With its far more numerous islands, the Pacific Ocean is home to a greater variety of these seabirds than the Atlantic. During and after storms are the best times to look for these birds from land or boats, as this is when they drift away from the deep sea due to wind and waves.

OLD BIRD
The Northern Fulmar is one of the longest-lived birds, with a lifespan of up to 50 years.

Order **Gaviiformes**	Family **Gaviidae**	Species ***Gavia stellata***

Red-throated Loon

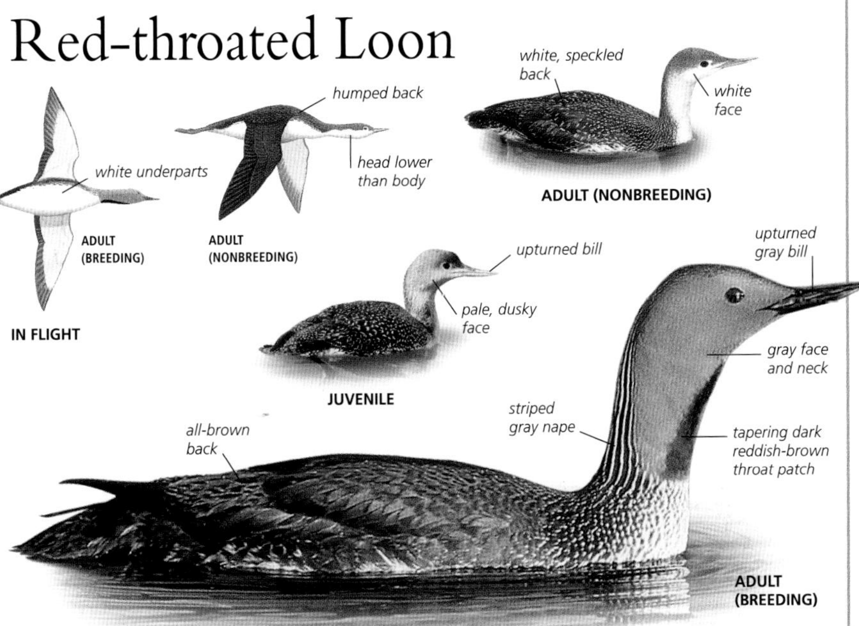
white, speckled back
white face
humped back
white underparts
head lower than body
ADULT (NONBREEDING)
ADULT (BREEDING)
ADULT (NONBREEDING)
IN FLIGHT
upturned bill
pale, dusky face
JUVENILE
upturned gray bill
gray face and neck
striped gray nape
all-brown back
tapering dark reddish-brown throat patch
ADULT (BREEDING)

Even when seen from a distance, this elegant loon is almost unmistakable, with a pale, slim body, upward-tilted head, and a thin, upturned bill. Unlike other loons, the Red-throated Loon can leap straight into the air from both land and water, although most of the time it needs a "runway." The Red-throated Loon has an elaborate breeding ritual—side by side, a pair of birds races upright across the surface of water. Downy chicks climb onto the parents' back only when very young.

VOICE High gull-like or even cat-like wail and low goose-like growl; vocal on breeding grounds, otherwise silent.

NESTING Scrape, with mud and vegetation added during incubation, placed at water's edge in coastal and lake bays, shallow ponds, often at high altitudes; 2 eggs; 1 brood; April–July.

FEEDING Mainly eats fish; also spiders, crustaceans, and mollusks; flies long distances from shallow ponds when food is scarce.

FLIGHT: very direct; fast, with constant wing beats; head held lower than other loons.

TAKING OFF

While this bird is using the water's surface to take off, it can leap directly into flight from water or land.

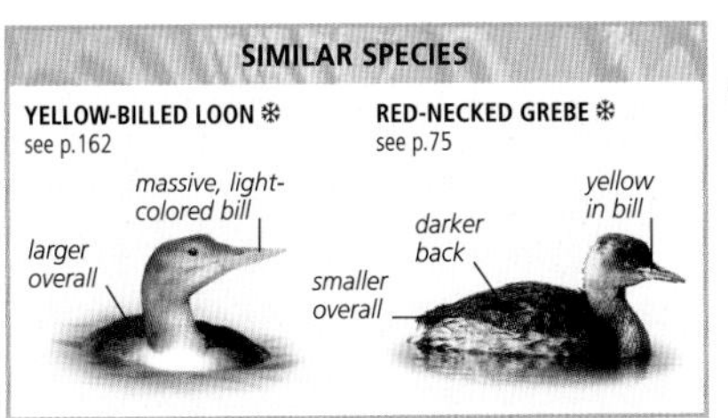
SIMILAR SPECIES
YELLOW-BILLED LOON ❄
see p.162
massive, light-colored bill
larger overall
RED-NECKED GREBE ❄
see p.75
yellow in bill
darker back
smaller overall

OCCURRENCE

Lives in open areas within northern boreal forest, muskeg, and tundra; in Canadian Arctic Archipelago, sometimes in areas almost devoid of vegetation. Winters on the Great Lakes, and both coasts southward to Florida and northern Mexico.

Length **24–27in (61–69cm)**	Wingspan **3½ft (1.1m)**	Weight **3¼lb (1.5kg)**
Social **Solitary/Loose flocks**	Lifespan **Up to 23 years**	Status **Declining**

DATE: ____________ TIME: ____________ LOCATION: ____________

Order **Gaviiformes**	Family **Gaviidae**	Species ***Gavia pacifica***

Pacific Loon

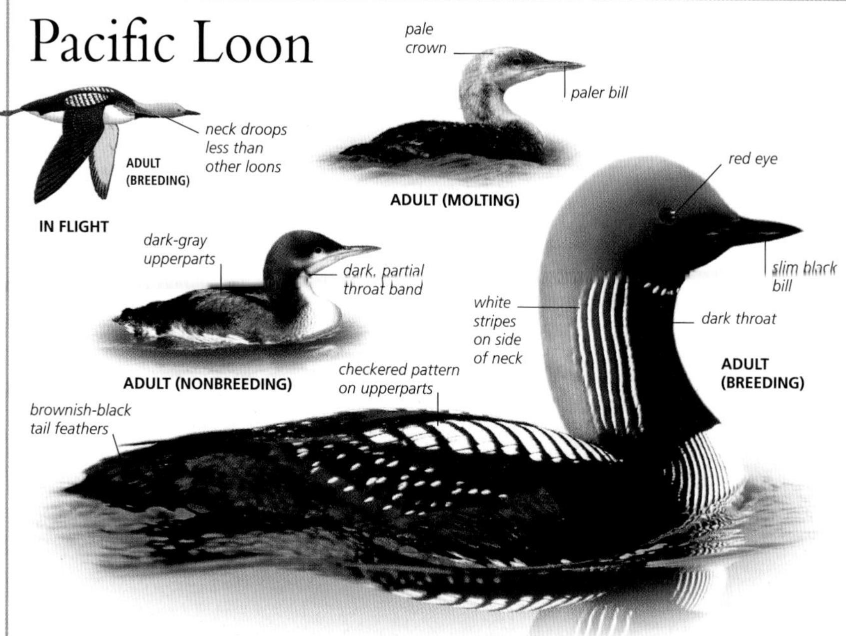
pale crown
paler bill
neck droops less than other loons
ADULT (BREEDING)
IN FLIGHT
ADULT (MOLTING)
red eye
dark-gray upperparts
dark, partial throat band
slim black bill
white stripes on side of neck
dark throat
ADULT (BREEDING)
ADULT (NONBREEDING)
checkered pattern on upperparts
brownish-black tail feathers

Although the Pacific Loon's breeding range is about a third of that of the Common Loon, it is believed to be the most abundant loon species in North America. It shares its habitat in northern Alaska with the nearly identical, but slightly larger and darker Arctic Loon. It is a conspicuous migrant along the Pacific Coast in spring, but disappears to its remote breeding grounds in summer. The Pacific Loon is an expert diver and swimmer, capable of remaining underwater for sustained periods of time, usually in pursuit of fish. However, on its terrestrial nesting site, its chicks are vulnerable to a number of mammalian predators.

VOICE Deep, barking *kowk*; high-pitched wail, croaks, and growls when breeding; makes a yelping noise when diving.

NESTING Simple scrape in flat area close to water, vegetation and mud added during incubation; 1–2 eggs; 1 brood; June–July.

FEEDING Eats fish, aquatic insects, and mollusks in breeding lake or nearby waters; may dip or dive, depending on the depth.

FLIGHT: swift and direct with constant wing beats; humped back, but head in line with body.

LEVEL GROUND

As loons cannot take off from land, nest sites need to be on flat land close to the water.

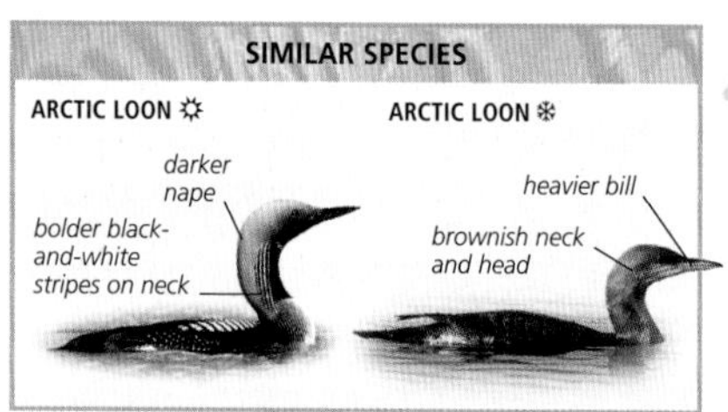
SIMILAR SPECIES
ARCTIC LOON ☼
ARCTIC LOON ❄
darker nape
bolder black-and-white stripes on neck
heavier bill
brownish neck and head

OCCURRENCE

Breeds across Arctic and sub-Arctic North America, from Alaska and northern Canadian provinces to Hudson Bay and on some islands of the Canadian Arctic; in tundra lakes and muskeg. Winters on the Pacific Coast, with small numbers in the Great Lakes and along the Atlantic Coast from Quebec to Florida. Vagrant elsewhere.

Length **23–29in (58–74cm)**	Wingspan **2¾–4¼ft (0.9–1.3m)**	Weight **2½–5½lb (1–2.5kg)**
Social **Flocks**	Lifespan **Up to 25 years**	Status **Secure**

DATE: ______________ TIME: ______________ LOCATION: ______________

Order **Gaviiformes**	Family **Gaviidae**	Species ***Gavia immer***

Common Loon

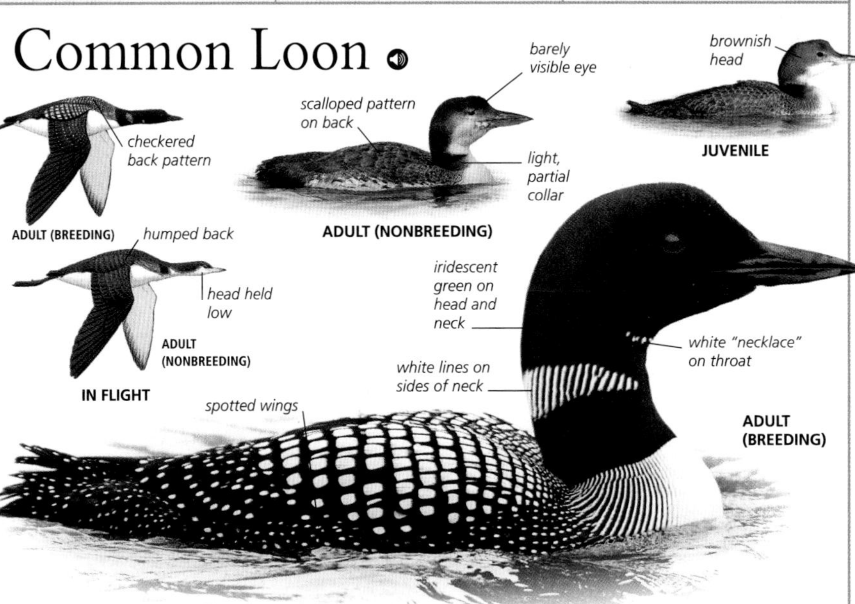
barely
visible eye
brownish
head
JUVENILE
scalloped pattern
on back
checkered
back pattern
light,
partial
collar
ADULT (BREEDING)
humped back
ADULT (NONBREEDING)
head held
low
ADULT
(NONBREEDING)
IN FLIGHT
iridescent
green on
head and
neck
white "necklace"
on throat
white lines on
sides of neck
spotted wings
ADULT
(BREEDING)

The Common Loon has the largest range of all loons in North America and is the only species to nest in a few of the northern states. It is slightly smaller than the Yellow-billed Loon but larger than the other three loons. It can remain underwater for well over 10 minutes, although it usually stays submerged for 40 seconds to 2 minutes while fishing, or a few more minutes if it is being pursued. Evidence shows that, occasionally, it interbreeds with its closest relative, the Yellow-billed Loon, in addition to the Arctic and Pacific Loons. The Common Loon is the provincial bird of Ontario.

VOICE Most recognized call a 3–10 note falsetto yodel, rising, then fading; other calls similar in quality.

NESTING Simple scrape in large mound of vegetation, a few feet from open water; 2 eggs; 1 brood; April–June.

FEEDING Feeds primarily on fish underwater; also eats crustaceans, mollusks, amphibians, leeches, insects, and aquatic plants.

FLIGHT: fast, direct, with constant wing beats; head and neck held just above belly.

COZY RIDE
Downy Common Loon chicks climb up the backs of male and female adults for a safe ride.

BATHING RITUAL
Common Loons often shake their wings after bathing.

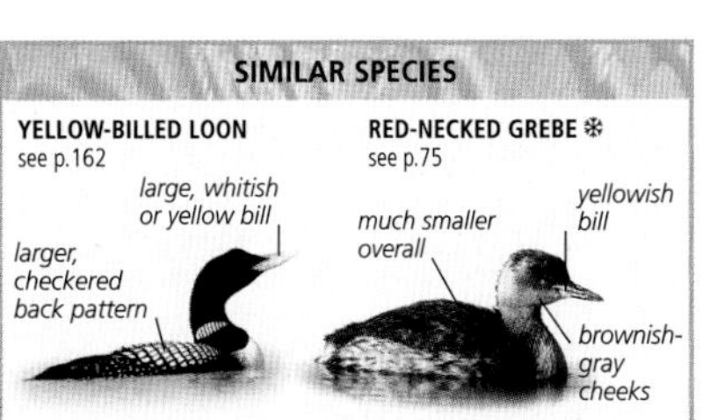
SIMILAR SPECIES
YELLOW-BILLED LOON
see p.162
large, whitish
or yellow bill
larger,
checkered
back pattern
RED-NECKED GREBE
see p.75
much smaller
overall
yellowish
bill
brownish-
gray
cheeks

OCCURRENCE
Breeds across North America—Canada and south to the northern US. Winters on large, ice-free lakes in Canada and the US, and along the Pacific and Atlantic Coasts, south to Baja California and Florida.

Length **26–36in (66–91cm)**	Wingspan **4¼–5ft (1.3–1.5m)**	Weight **4½–18lb (2–8kg)**
Social **Family groups**	Lifespan **Up to 30 years**	Status **Vulnerable**

DATE: ____________ TIME: ____________ LOCATION: ____________________

Order **Gaviiformes**	Family **Gaviidae**	Species ***Gavia adamsii***

Yellow-billed Loon

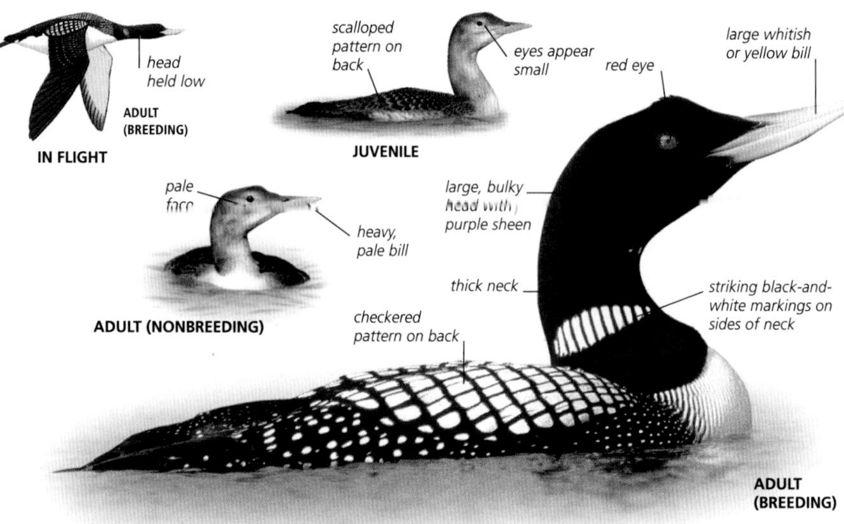
head
held low
ADULT
(BREEDING)
IN FLIGHT
scalloped
pattern on
back
eyes appear
small
JUVENILE
red eye
large whitish
or yellow bill
pale
face
heavy,
pale bill
ADULT (NONBREEDING)
large, bulky
head with
purple sheen
thick neck
striking black-and-
white markings on
sides of neck
checkered
pattern on back
ADULT
(BREEDING)

The largest of the loons, the Yellow-billed Loon has the most restricted range and smallest global population. About three-quarters of the estimated 16,000–30,000 birds live in North America, and unsustainable levels of harvesting have caused recent declines. It makes the most of the short nesting season, arriving at its breeding grounds already paired and breeding immediately, although extensive ice formation can prevent it from breeding in some years. Yellow-billed Loons have more rugged proportions than other loons; their feet, for example, extend further away from their bodies.

VOICE Tremulous call much like Common Loon's, but louder, harsher, and even more "mournful"; yodels, wails, and "laughs."

NESTING Depression in mass of mud and vegetation, on shores of tundra lakes and ponds, and on river islands at high altitudes; 1–2 eggs; 1 brood; June–July.

FEEDING Dives underwater to catch small fish; also eats crustaceans, worms, and some vegetation.

FLIGHT: rapid and direct; head and neck held lower than body.

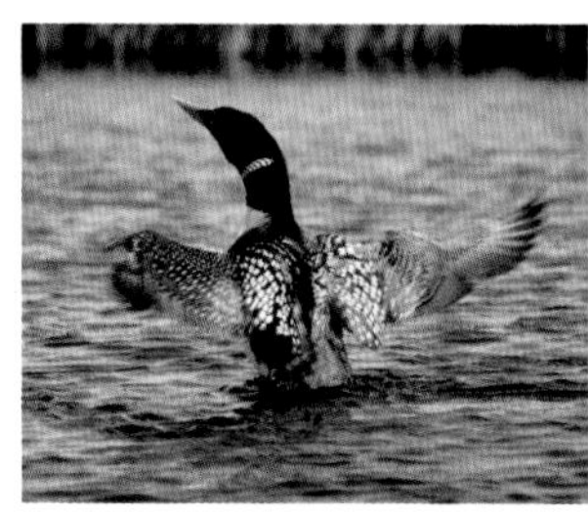

BOLDLY PATTERNED
The adult Yellow-billed Loon is strikingly patterned, like a checkerboard.

SIMILAR SPECIES

COMMON LOON ❄ see p.161
dark crown and pale cheeks; heavy, dark bill

RED-NECKED GREBE ❄ see p.75
shorter bill, yellowish at base; smaller overall

OCCURRENCE
Breeds from extreme northern edge of Alaska to eastern Northwest Territories and Nunavut. Also breeds in northern Siberia. Winters along the Pacific Coast of Alaska and British Columbia, and has been sighted in a number of US states.

Length **30–36in (77–92cm)**	Wingspan **4–5ft (1.2–1.5m)**	Weight **8¾–14lb (4–6.5kg)**
Social **Solitary/Pairs/Family groups**	Lifespan **Up to 30 years**	Status **Vulnerable**

DATE: ______ TIME: ______ LOCATION: ______

Order **Procellariiformes**	Family **Oceanitidae**	Species ***Oceanites oceanicus***

Wilson's Storm-Petrel

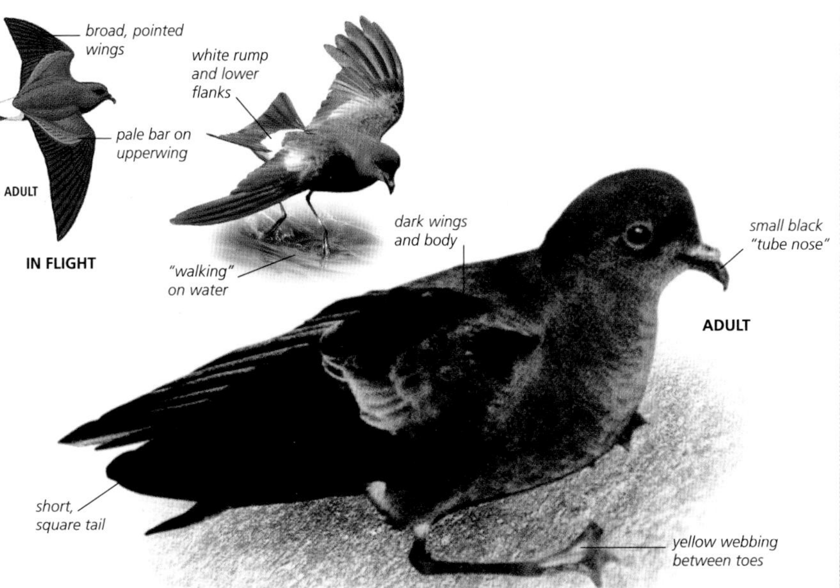

broad, pointed wings
white rump and lower flanks
pale bar on upperwing
ADULT
IN FLIGHT
"walking" on water
dark wings and body
small black "tube nose"
ADULT
short, square tail
yellow webbing between toes

Named after Alexander Wilson, often called the "father of North American ornithology," Wilson's Storm-Petrel is the quintessential small oceanic petrel. It is an extremely abundant species and breeds in the many millions on the Antarctic Peninsula and islands in Antarctica. After breeding, many move north to spend the summer off the Atlantic Coast of North America. Here, they are a familiar sight to fishermen and birders at sea. By August, they can be seen lingering, but by October they have flown south.

VOICE At sea, soft rasping notes; at breeding sites, a variety of *coos*, *churrs*, and twitters during the night.

NESTING Mostly in rock crevices; also burrows where there is peaty soil; 1 egg; 1 brood; November–March.

FEEDING Patters on the water's surface, legs extended, picking up tiny crustaceans; also carrion, oil droplets, and cetacean feces.

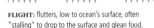

FLIGHT: flutters, low to ocean's surface, often "stalling" to drop to the surface and glean food.

FEEDING FLOCK
While flying, this bird "walks" on water, simultaneously picking food from the surface.

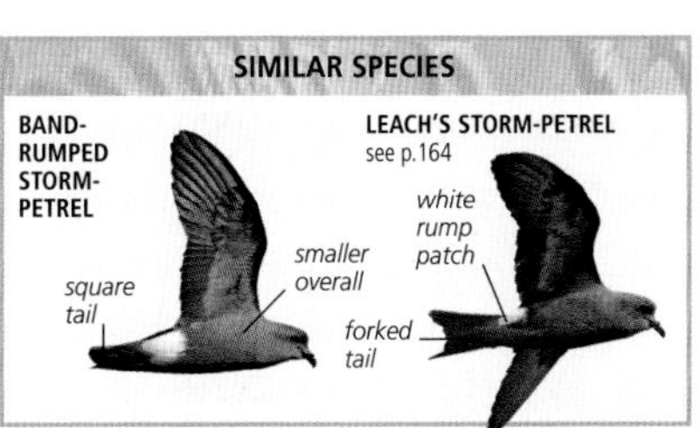

SIMILAR SPECIES
BAND-RUMPED STORM-PETREL
square tail
smaller overall
LEACH'S STORM-PETREL
see p.164
white rump patch
forked tail

OCCURRENCE
Breeds on the Antarctic Peninsula, many sub-Antarctic islands, and islands in the Cape Horn Archipelago. April–September or October, moves north, and is abundant off the coasts of Atlantic Canada and the US in July–September. With inshore winds, can often be seen from land.

Length **6¾in (17cm)**	Wingspan **16in (41cm)**	Weight **$1\frac{1}{16}$–$1\frac{7}{16}$oz (30–40g)**
Social **Flocks**	Lifespan **Up to 10 years**	Status **Secure**

DATE: ____________ TIME: ____________ LOCATION: ____________

Order **Procellariiformes**	Family **Hydrobatidae**	Species ***Hydrobates leucorhus***

Leach's Storm-Petrel

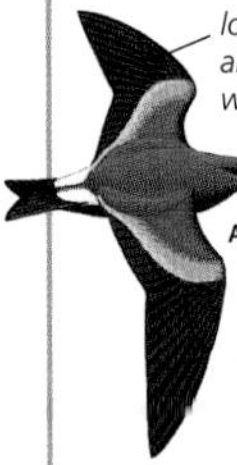

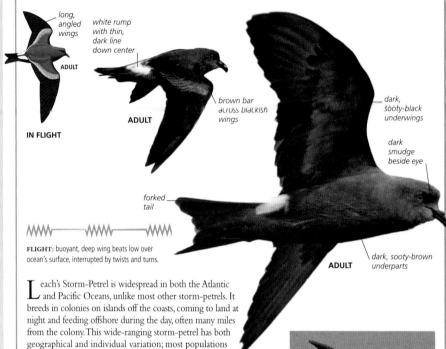

long, angled wings

ADULT

IN FLIGHT

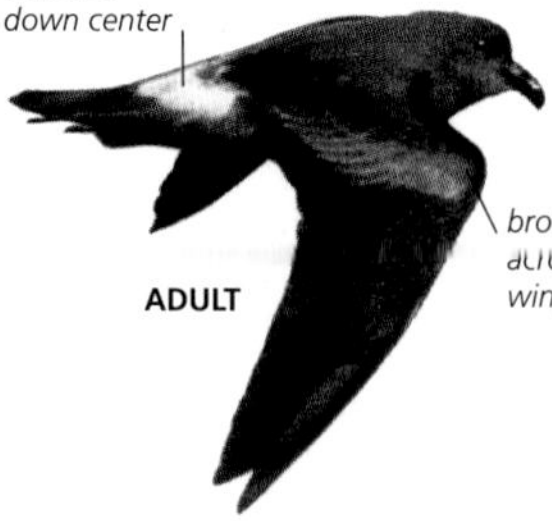

white rump with thin, dark line down center

brown bar across blackish wings

ADULT

dark, sooty-black underwings

dark smudge beside eye

forked tail

dark, sooty-brown underparts

ADULT

FLIGHT: buoyant, deep wing beats low over ocean's surface, interrupted by twists and turns.

Leach's Storm-Petrel is widespread in both the Atlantic and Pacific Oceans, unlike most other storm-petrels. It breeds in colonies on islands off the coasts, coming to land at night and feeding offshore during the day, often many miles from the colony. This wide-ranging storm-petrel has both geographical and individual variation; most populations show a white rump, but others have a dark rump that is the same color as the rest of the body. Leach's Storm-Petrel and the very similar, endangered, Townsend's Storm-Petrel (*H. socorroensis*) were thought to be a single species until they were split in 2016. The latter is identified only by its breeding location and smaller size.

VOICE At nesting sites, often from burrows, calls are long series of soft purring and chattering sounds.

NESTING Underground burrow on island free of predators such as rats; 1 egg; 1 brood; May–November.

FEEDING Gleans small crustaceans and small fish from the water's surface while in flight.

BALANCING ACT
Leach's Storm-Petrel will often balance itself with its wings while walking.

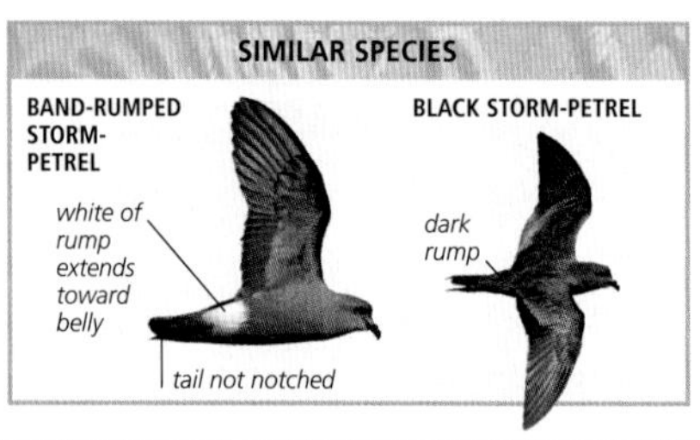
SIMILAR SPECIES
BAND-RUMPED STORM-PETREL
white of rump extends toward belly
tail not notched
BLACK STORM-PETREL
dark rump

OCCURRENCE
Breeds on islands in the Pacific Ocean from Alaska and the Aleutian Islands south to California; in the Atlantic Ocean, from Newfoundland to Maine. After breeding, it wanders widely on both oceans, keeping well out of sight of land.

Length **7–8½in (18–22cm)**	Wingspan **17½–19in (45–48cm)**	Weight **1⁹⁄₁₆–1¾oz (45–50g)**
Social **Colonies**	Lifespan **Up to 36 years**	Status **Secure**

DATE: __________ TIME: __________ LOCATION: __________

Northern Fulmar

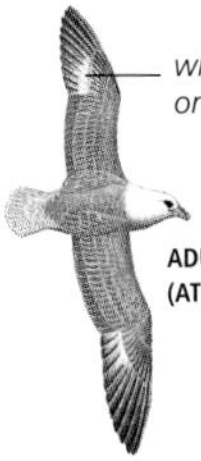

white patch on wing

ADULT (ATLANTIC FORM)

IN FLIGHT

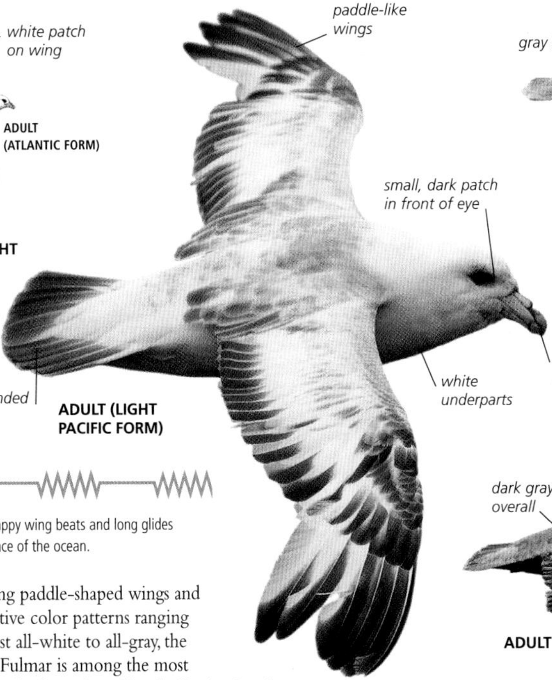

paddle-like wings

small, dark patch in front of eye

thick yellow bill

white underparts

short, rounded gray tail

ADULT (LIGHT PACIFIC FORM)

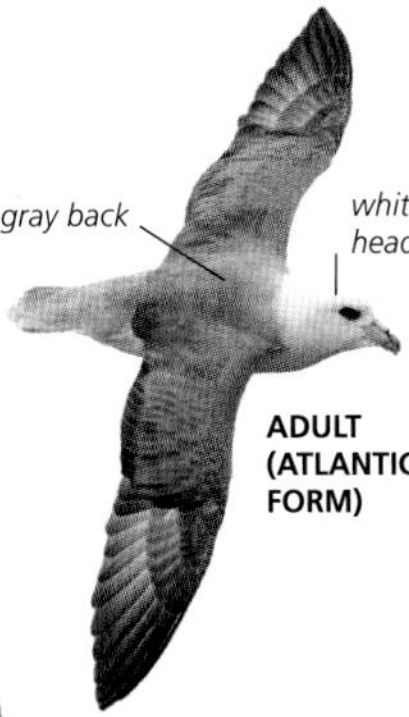

gray back

white head

ADULT (ATLANTIC FORM)

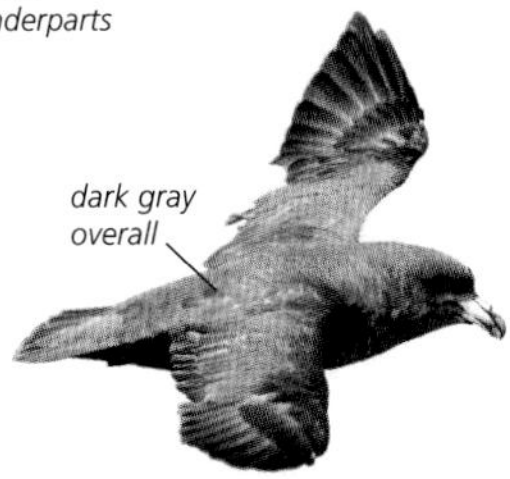

dark gray overall

ADULT (DARK PACIFIC FORM)

FLIGHT: snappy wing beats and long glides near the surface of the ocean.

Possessing paddle-shaped wings and distinctive color patterns ranging from almost all-white to all-gray, the Northern Fulmar is among the most common seabirds in places like the Bering Sea. It breeds at high latitudes, then disperses south to offshore waters on both coasts of the continent. The Northern Fulmar can often be seen in large mixed flocks containing albatrosses, shearwaters, and petrels. Fulmars often follow boats, eager to pounce on the offal thrown overboard by fishermen.

VOICE Mostly silent at sea; occasionally utters cackles and grunts.

NESTING Scrape in rock or soil on edge of cliff; 1 egg; 1 brood; May–October.

FEEDING Picks fish and offal from the surface of the ocean; also dives underwater to catch fish.

FEEDING FRENZY
Large numbers of Northern Fulmars compete for the offal discarded by fishing trawlers.

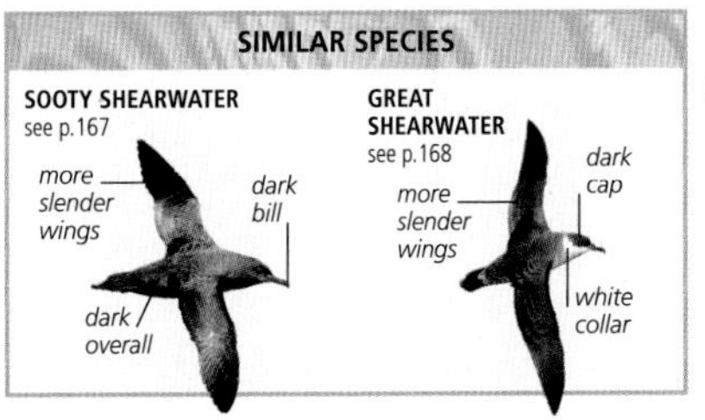
SIMILAR SPECIES
SOOTY SHEARWATER
see p.167
more slender wings
dark bill
dark overall
GREAT SHEARWATER
see p.168
dark cap
more slender wings
white collar

OCCURRENCE
Breeds on remote, high, coastal cliffs in Alaska and northern Canada; winters at sea in offshore Pacific and Atlantic waters, generally farther north than most other seabirds. Breeds in Europe, to Greenland, Svalbard; also parts of Russia.

Length **17½–19½in (45–50cm)**	Wingspan **3¼–3½ft (1–1.1m)**	Weight **16–35oz (0.45–1kg)**
Social **Flocks**	Lifespan **Up to 50 years**	Status **Secure**

DATE: ______________ TIME: ______________ LOCATION: ______________________

Order **Procellariiformes**	Family **Procellariidae**	Species ***Calonectris diomedea***

Cory's Shearwater

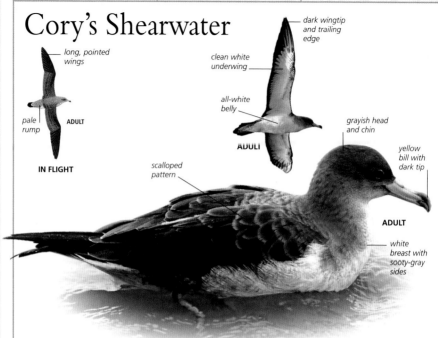

long, pointed wings
pale rump
ADULT
IN FLIGHT

dark wingtip and trailing edge
clean white underwing
all-white belly
ADULT

grayish head and chin
yellow bill with dark tip
scalloped pattern
ADULT
white breast with sooty-gray sides

Close studies of Cory's Shearwaters off the Atlantic Coast suggest the presence of two forms. The more common form, *C. d. borealis*, nests in the eastern Atlantic and is chunkier, with less white in the underwing. The other form, *C. d. diomedea*, breeds in the Mediterranean, has a more slender build (including a thinner bill), and has more extensive white under the wing. Cory's Shearwater has a distinctive, relatively languid flight style that is different from the other shearwaters regularly found in North American waters.

VOICE Mostly silent at sea; descending, lamb-like bleating.
NESTING Nests in burrow or rocky crevice; 1 egg; 1 brood; May–September.
FEEDING Dives into water or picks at surface for small schooling fish, and marine invertebrates, such as squid.

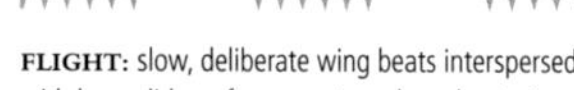

FLIGHT: slow, deliberate wing beats interspersed with long glides; often arcs strongly on bent wings.

LAZY FLIERS
In calm weather, Cory's Shearwaters look heavy and fly low, swooping higher in strong winds.

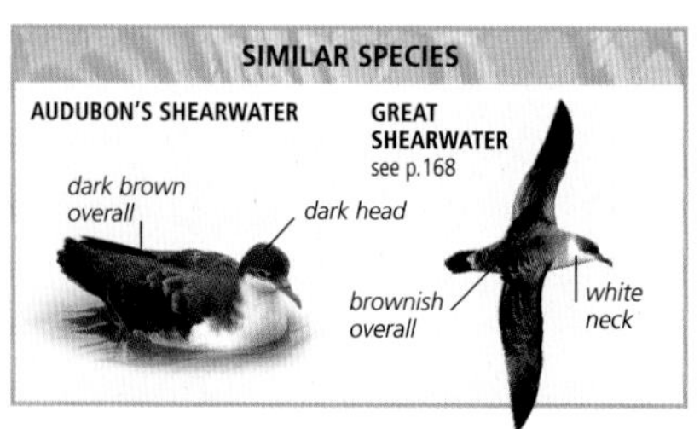
SIMILAR SPECIES
AUDUBON'S SHEARWATER
dark brown overall
dark head
GREAT SHEARWATER
see p.168
brownish overall
white neck

OCCURRENCE
This species breeds in the Mediterranean and on islands of the eastern Atlantic, including the Azores, the Salvages, Madeira, and the Canaries. When nonbreeding, Cory's Shearwaters disperse widely over the Atlantic Ocean, including off the east coast of Canada.

Length **18in (46cm)**	Wingspan **3½ft (1.1m)**	Weight **28oz (800g)**
Social **Flocks**	Lifespan **Unknown**	Status **Secure**

DATE: ______________ TIME: ______________ LOCATION: ______________

Order **Procellariiformes**	Family **Procellariidae**	Species ***Ardenna grisea***

Sooty Shearwater

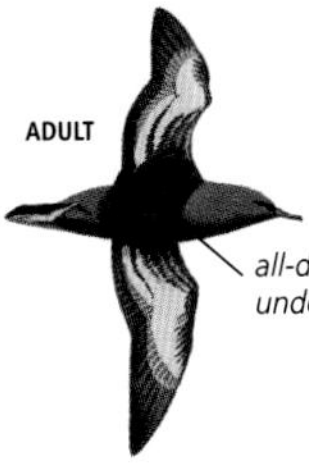

ADULT

all-dark underparts

IN FLIGHT

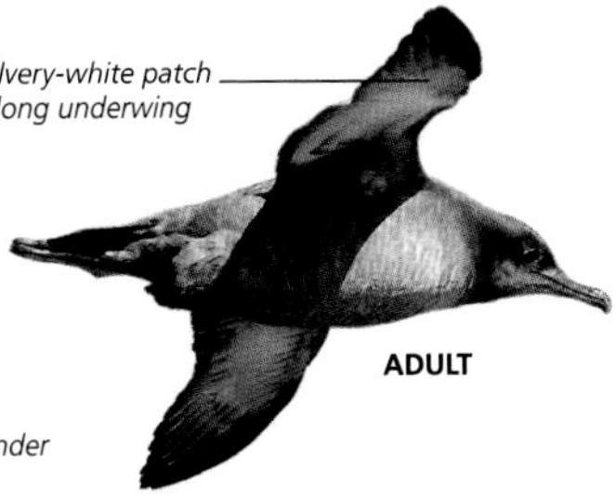

silvery-white patch along underwing

ADULT

long, slender wings

ADULT

all-dark upperparts

sooty head

long, hooked bill

FLIGHT: rapid, stiff wing beats, interspersed with glides; arcs up highly in strong winds.

Sooty Shearwaters are extremely long-distance migrants, with both the Atlantic and Pacific populations undergoing lengthy circular migrations. Pacific birds, in particular, travel as far as 300 miles (480km) per day and an extraordinary 45,000 miles (72,500km) or more per year. Huge flocks of this species are often seen off the coast of California. It is fairly easy to identify off the East Coast of North America, as it is the only all-dark shearwater found there.

VOICE Silent at sea; occasionally gives varied, agitated vocalizations when feeding,very loud calls at breeding colonies.

NESTING In burrow or rocky crevice; 1 egg; 1 brood; October–May.

FEEDING Dives and picks at surface for small schooling fish and mollusks, such as squid.

HUGE FLOCKS
Sooty Shearwaters are often found in "rafts" numbering many thousands of birds.

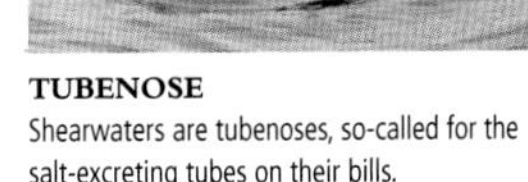

TUBENOSE
Shearwaters are tubenoses, so-called for the salt-excreting tubes on their bills.

SIMILAR SPECIES

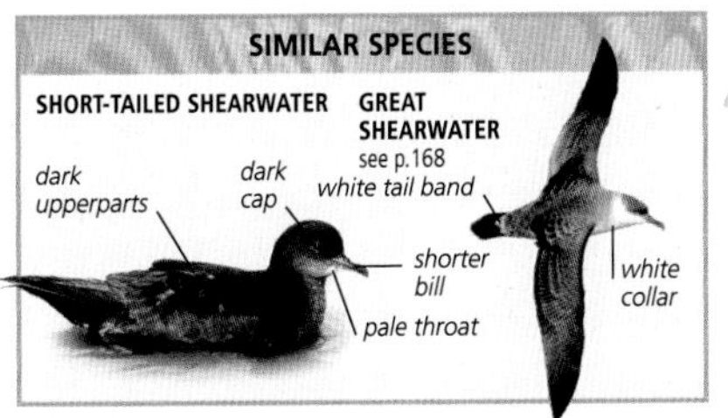
SHORT-TAILED SHEARWATER
dark upperparts
dark cap
shorter bill
pale throat
GREAT SHEARWATER
see p.168
white tail band
white collar

OCCURRENCE
Sooty Shearwaters breed on islands in the Southern Ocean and nearby waters, some colonies numbering thousands of pairs. Postbreeding movements take them north into the Pacific and the Atlantic Oceans, on 8-shaped migrations.

Length **18in (46cm)**	Wingspan **3ft 3in (1m)**	Weight **27oz (775g)**
Social **Flocks**	Lifespan **Unknown**	Status **Secure**

DATE: ________ TIME: ________ LOCATION: ________

Order **Procellariiformes**	Family **Procellariidae**	Species ***Ardenna gravis***

Great Shearwater

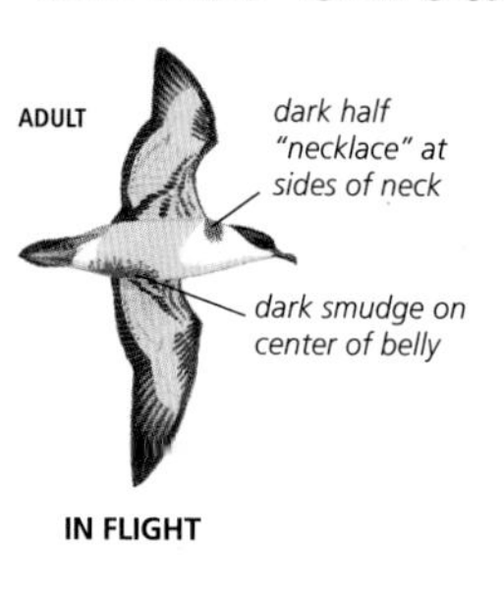
ADULT
dark half "necklace" at sides of neck
dark smudge on center of belly
IN FLIGHT

darker outer wing feathers

brownish upperwings

white collar

dark cap

thin white band on rump

thin black bill

ADULT

A common species in North Atlantic waters, from northern Canada to Florida, the Great Shearwater is similar in size to Cory's Shearwater and the birds scavenge together for scraps around fishing boats. However, their plumages and flight styles are quite different. While Cory's Shearwater has slow, labored wing beats and glides high on broad, bowed, swept-back wings, Great Shearwaters keep low, flapping hurriedly between glides on straight, narrow wings. The brown smudges on the belly (not always visible) and paler underwings of the Great Shearwater also help distinguish the species.

VOICE Silent at sea; descending, lamb-like bleating at breeding sites.

NESTING Digs deep burrow in peaty or boggy soil; 1 egg; 1 brood; September–March.

FEEDING Feeds either from the surface, picking up items, such as fish and squid, or makes shallow dives with open wings.

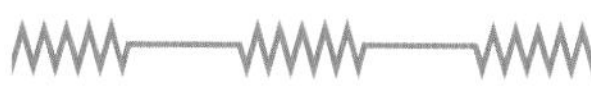

FLIGHT: fast, stiff wing beats interspersed with gliding; arcs high in windy conditions.

WHITE COLLAR
The Great Shearwater's white collar is highly visible between its black cap and sooty back.

SIMILAR SPECIES

BLACK-CAPPED PETREL
large white rump
white forehead

MANX SHEARWATER
see p.169
darker plumage
smaller overall

OCCURRENCE
Nests on just a few islands in the middle of the South Atlantic. Total population probably well over 200 million. Postbreeding birds make a very long, 8-shaped migration around the Atantic, spending late July–September in North Atlantic waters, usually offshore.

Length **18in (46cm)**	Wingspan **3½ft (1.1m)**	Weight **30oz (850g)**
Social **Flocks**	Lifespan **At least 25 years**	Status **Secure**

 DATE: ______________ TIME: ______________ LOCATION: ______________

Order **Procellariiformes**	Family **Procellariidae**	Species ***Puffinus puffinus***

Manx Shearwater

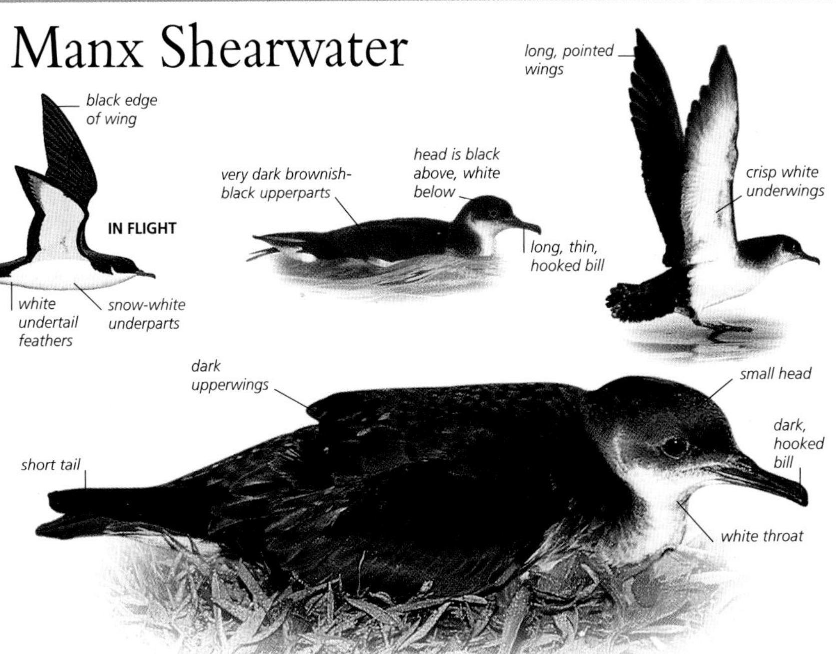
black edge of wing
IN FLIGHT
white undertail feathers
snow-white underparts
very dark brownish-black upperparts
head is black above, white below
long, thin, hooked bill
long, pointed wings
crisp white underwings
dark upperwings
small head
dark, hooked bill
short tail
white throat

Most shearwaters are little known because of their nocturnal and oceanic ways, but the Manx is an exception. It is common in the British Isles, and ornithologists have been studying it there for decades. Long-term banding programs revealed one bird that flew over 3,000 miles (4,800km) from Massachusetts to its nesting burrow in Wales in just 12½ days, and another that was captured 56 years after it was first banded, making its accumulated migration-only mileage around 600,000 miles (1,000,000km).

VOICE Usually silent at sea, but at breeding sites, produces loud and raucous series of cries, *kah-kah-kah-kah-kah-HOWW*.

NESTING In burrow, in peaty soil, or rocky crevice; 1 egg; 1 brood; April–October.

FEEDING Dives into water, often with open wings and stays underwater, or picks at surface for small schooling fish and squid.

FLIGHT: rapid, stiff wing beats interspersed with glides; arcs high in strong winds.

PITTER-PATTER

Unlike gulls, shearwaters have to patter along the surface with their feet to achieve lift-off speed.

SIMILAR SPECIES

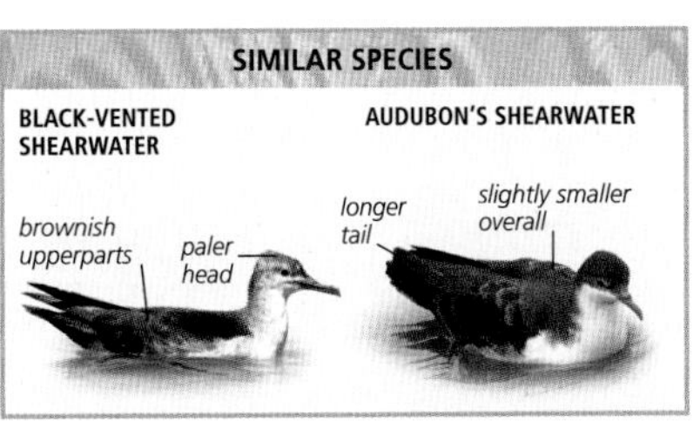
BLACK-VENTED SHEARWATER
brownish upperparts
paler head
AUDUBON'S SHEARWATER
longer tail
slightly smaller overall

OCCURRENCE

Breeds on many islands in the eastern North Atlantic; restricted to islands off Newfoundland in North America. Regularly occurs off the East Coast, as far south as Florida. Rare in Gulf of Mexico and off the West Coast. Rarely seen from shore; cold-water shearwater.

Length **13½in (34cm)**	Wingspan **33in (83cm)**	Weight **14–20oz (400–575g)**
Social **Migrant flocks**	Lifespan **Up to 55 years**	Status **Secure**

DATE: ______________ TIME: ______________ LOCATION: ______________________________

Families **Sulidae, Phalacrocoracidae**

GANNETS AND CORMORANTS

UNTIL RECENTLY, GANNETS AND CORMORANTS were grouped with pelicans under the order Pelicaniformes. Now, they are a part of the order Suliformes, which also includes frigatebirds, boobies, and anhingas. Only gannets and cormorants are found in Canada.

HALF AND HALF
This Northern Gannet shows the distinctive mottled black-and-white plumage of an immature bird.

GANNETS

Gannets are large white seabirds with yellowish heads, long bills, and black-tipped wings. They are fish-eaters that hunt by diving from heights of up to 98ft (30m) into the water. Gannets breed in colonies, usually on islands and coasts, and lay one egg per season. These birds take five years to become fully mature—first-year birds are dark overall, and gradually show more white through subsequent moultings.

CORMORANTS

With 36 species worldwide, cormorants are medium to large waterbirds—some are marine, others are freshwater. They have broad and long wings, rounded tails, short and strong legs, and hook-tipped bills that are often tilted upwards while swimming. In flight, the neck is extended but noticeably kinked. When hunting for fish, cormorants dive from the surface of the water, rolling smoothly under or with a noticeable forward leap; they then swim underwater with closed wings, using their webbed toes for propulsion. Cormorants are able to fill their hollow wing feathers with water for ballast, which they later drain with wings outspread while perched. Most cormorants are dark birds, apart from some distinctive facial patterns on areas of bare skin, which become more colorful in spring. Many of these birds nest on cliff ledges, while some prefer trees, and yet others are happy to use both cliffs and trees. There is one flightless cormorant species in the Galápagos.

DARK PLUMAGE
Grooming for this Double-crested Cormorant includes spreading its wings to dry them in the sun.

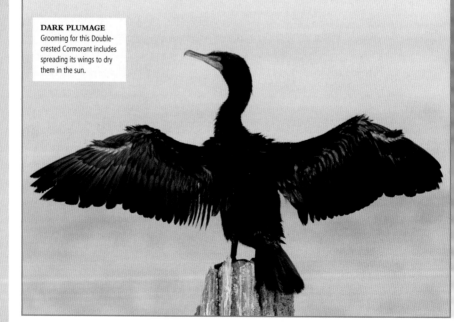

Order **Suliformes**	Family **Sulidae**	Species ***Morus bassanus***

Northern Gannet

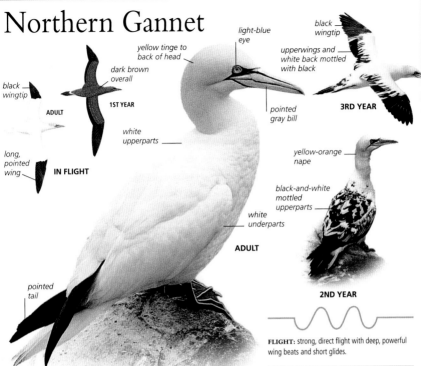

black wingtip
ADULT
long, pointed wing
IN FLIGHT
dark brown overall
1ST YEAR
yellow tinge to back of head
light-blue eye
pointed gray bill
white upperparts
white underparts
pointed tail
ADULT
black wingtip
upperwings and white back mottled with black
3RD YEAR
yellow-orange nape
black-and-white mottled upperparts
2ND YEAR

FLIGHT: strong, direct flight with deep, powerful wing beats and short glides.

The Northern Gannet is known for its spectacular headfirst dives during frantic, voracious foraging for surface-schooling fish in flocks of hundreds to thousands. In North America, this bird nests in just six locations in northeastern Canada. It was the first species to have its total world population estimated—there were 83,000 birds in 1939. Numbers have since increased.

VOICE Loud landing call by both sexes *arrrr, arrah*, or *urrah rah rah*; hollow groan *oh-ah* uttered during takeoff; *krok* call at sea.

NESTING Large pile of mud, seaweed, and rubbish, glued with guano, on bare rock or soil; 1 egg; 1 brood; April–November.

FEEDING Plunge-dives headfirst into water and often swims underwater to catch fish; eats mackerel, herring, capelin, and cod.

NESTING SITE
Northern Gannets prefer to nest in huge, noisy colonies on isolated rock stacks or cliffs.

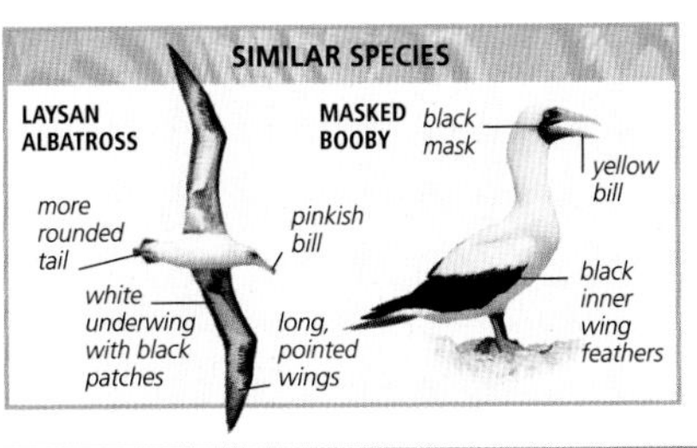
SIMILAR SPECIES
LAYSAN ALBATROSS
more rounded tail
white underwing with black patches
pinkish bill
MASKED BOOBY
black mask
yellow bill
long, pointed wings
black inner wing feathers

OCCURRENCE
Breeds on isolated rock stacks, on small, uninhabited islands in the eastern North Atlantic, or on steep, inaccessible cliffs in marine areas of northeast North America; during migration and in winter, can be found in the waters of the continental shelf of the Gulf and the Atlantic Coasts.

Length **2¾–3½ft (0.8–1.1m)**	Wingspan **5½ft (1.7m)**	Weight **5–8lb (2.2–3.6kg)**
Social **Flocks**	Lifespan **Up to 20 years**	Status **Localized**

DATE: ________ TIME: ________ LOCATION: ________

Order **Suliformes**	Family **Phalacrocoracidae**	Species ***Nannopterum auritum***

Double-crested Cormorant

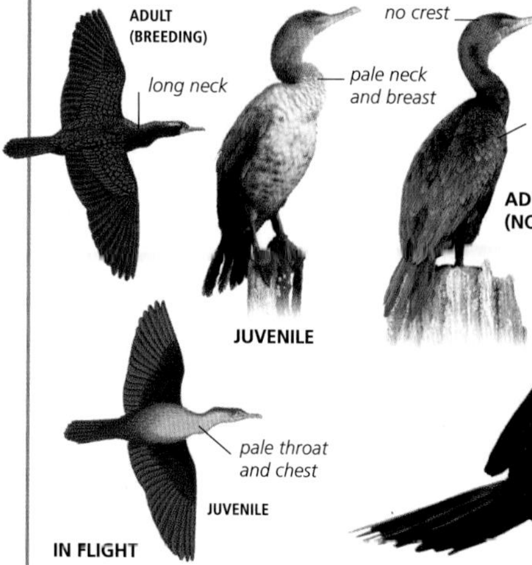

white crest
bluish eye
orange facial skin
black overall
black underparts
ADULT *N. a. auritum* (NORTHEASTERN BREEDING)
blackish crest
ADULT *N. a. cincinatus* (WESTERN; BREEDING)

ADULT (BREEDING)
long neck

JUVENILE
pale neck and breast

no crest
browner plumage overall
ADULT (NONBREEDING)

pale throat and chest
JUVENILE
IN FLIGHT

FLIGHT: regular wing beats, occasional glides; over water, flies close to the surface; often soars.

This species is the most widespread of the North American cormorants. It often flies high over land in V-shaped flocks, but is mostly seen swimming in the water with its head and neck visible, or resting on trees and rocks, sometimes with its wings spread to drain and dry its feathers. While fishing, it dives from the surface of the water and chases fish underwater, using its webbed toes for propulsion.

VOICE Deep grunt-like calls while nesting, roosting, and fishing; *t-t-t-t* call before taking off and *urg-urg-urg* before landing; prolonged *arr-r-r-r-r-t-t* while mating, and *eh-hr* as threat.

NESTING Nests of twigs and sticks, seaweed, and trash, lined with grass; built on ground, cliffs, or in trees usually in colonies; 3-5 eggs; 1 brood; April–August.

FEEDING Pursues slow-moving or schooling fish; feeds on insects, crustaceans, amphibians, and, rarely, on voles and snakes.

DRYING OFF
Typical of cormorants, this species perches with wings spread to drain and dry its feathers.

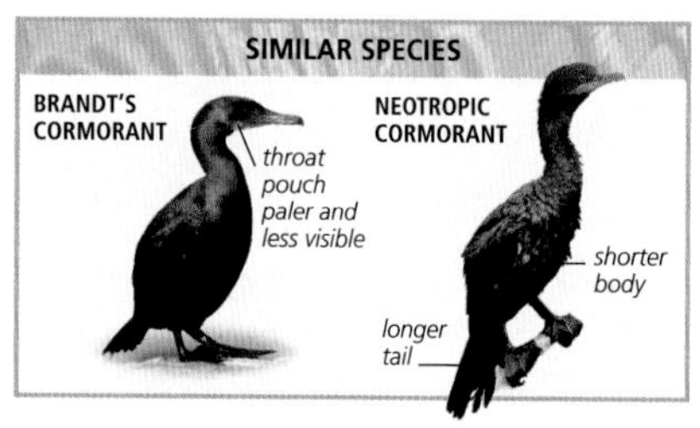
SIMILAR SPECIES
BRANDT'S CORMORANT
throat pouch paler and less visible
NEOTROPIC CORMORANT
shorter body
longer tail

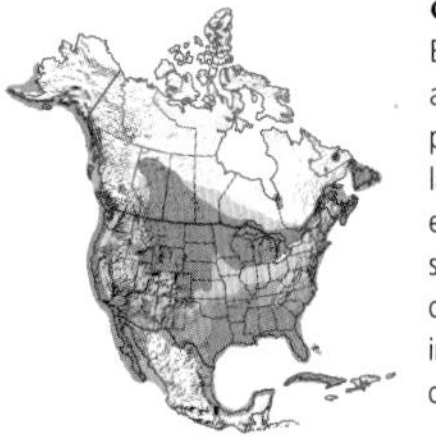

OCCURRENCE
Breeds in a wide range of aquatic habitats, including ponds, artificial and natural lakes, slow-moving rivers, estuaries, lagoons, and seashores; winters on coastlines and sandbars in coastal inlets; roosts near catfish farms in some areas.

Length **28–35in (70–90cm)**	Wingspan **3½–4ft (1.1–1.2m)**	Weight **2¾–5½lb (1.2–2.5kg)**
Social **Flocks**	Lifespan **Up to 18 years**	Status **Secure**

 DATE: ______________ TIME: ______________ LOCATION: ______________

Order **Suliformes**	Family **Phalacrocoracidae**	Species ***Phalacrocorax carbo***

Great Cormorant

JUVENILE

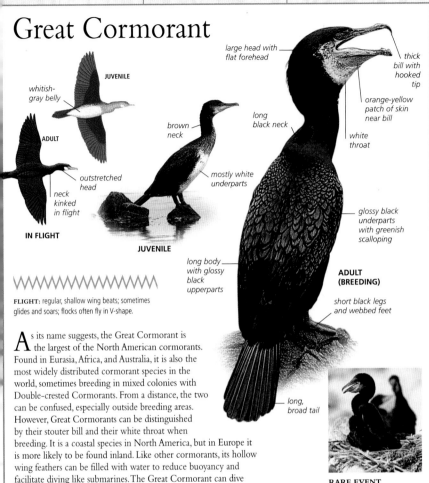

whitish-gray belly

ADULT

outstretched head

neck kinked in flight

IN FLIGHT

brown neck

mostly white underparts

JUVENILE

large head with flat forehead

thick bill with hooked tip

orange-yellow patch of skin near bill

long black neck

white throat

glossy black underparts with greenish scalloping

long body with glossy black upperparts

ADULT (BREEDING)

short black legs and webbed feet

long, broad tail

FLIGHT: regular, shallow wing beats; sometimes glides and soars; flocks often fly in V-shape.

As its name suggests, the Great Cormorant is the largest of the North American cormorants. Found in Eurasia, Africa, and Australia, it is also the most widely distributed cormorant species in the world, sometimes breeding in mixed colonies with Double-crested Cormorants. From a distance, the two can be confused, especially outside breeding areas. However, Great Cormorants can be distinguished by their stouter bill and their white throat when breeding. It is a coastal species in North America, but in Europe it is more likely to be found inland. Like other cormorants, its hollow wing feathers can be filled with water to reduce buoyancy and facilitate diving like submarines. The Great Cormorant can dive to depths of 115ft (35m) to catch prey.

VOICE Deep, guttural calls at nesting and roosting site; otherwise silent.

NESTING Mound of seaweed, sticks, and debris added to previous year's nest, built on cliff ledges and flat tops of rocks above high-water mark on islands; 3–5 eggs; 1 brood; April–August.

FEEDING Dives to pursue fish and small crustaceans; smaller prey swallowed underwater, while larger prey brought to surface.

RARE EVENT
Great Cormorants usually nest on sea cliffs; tree breeding is rare in North America.

SIMILAR SPECIES

DOUBLE-CRESTED CORMORANT
see p.172

thinner bill
black throat

OCCURRENCE
Breeds on cliff ledges of islands along rocky coasts, in the northeast US and Maritimes of Canada; feeds in protected inshore waters. Winters in shallow coastal waters similar to breeding habitat, but not restricted to rocky shoreline; winter habitat extends to the Carolinas in the US.

Length **33–35in (84–90cm)**	Wingspan **4¼–5¼ft (1.3–1.6m)**	Weight **5¾–8¼lb (2.6–3.7kg)**
Social **Colonies**	Lifespan **Up to 14 years**	Status **Secure**

DATE: ____________ TIME: ____________ LOCATION: ____________

Families **Pelecanidae, Ardeidae, Threskiornithidae**

PELICANS, HERONS, IBISES, AND RELATIVES

THESE RELATED WATERBIRDS exploit a diversity of water and waterside habitats in different ways, from plunge-diving in the ocean to wading at the edge of mangroves and freshwater marshes, from scooping up fish to hunting with stealth and patience from overhanging branches.

PELICANS

Pelicans are large fish-eating birds, bulky but buoyant on water. Brown Pelicans, vagrants in Canada, dive headfirst to catch fish, while White Pelicans work together to herd fish into shallow bays, and scoop them up in their large, flexible bill pouches beneath their long bills.

HERONS, EGRETS, AND BITTERNS

The long toes of these waterside birds enable them to walk on wet mud and wade among reed stems. Some herons and egrets roost in trees. Their toes also aid their balance as they lean forward in search of fish and catch prey in their long, pointed bills. Herons and egrets have slender, feathered necks with a distinct kink that gives a lightning forward thrust when catching prey. Herons are known to use bait to catch fish. Most herons and egrets make bulky nests in treetop colonies, whereas bitterns nest on the ground in marshes. Unlike storks and cranes, they all fly with their heads withdrawn into their shoulders.

POISED AND READY
This Green Heron is ready to make a strike for its prey.

IBISES

Waterside or dry-land birds, ibises are long-legged and walk with great strides. They have long, decurved bills that are adapted to picking insects, worms, small mollusks, and crustaceans from wet mud. Ibises often fly in long lines or V-formations.

DANCING ON AIR
The Great Egret's courtship display often involves spreading its wings and leaping in a kind of aerial dance.

Order **Pelecaniformes**	Family **Pelecanidae**	Species ***Pelecanus erythrorhynchos***

American White Pelican

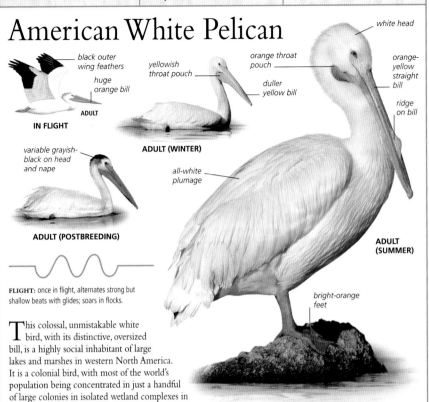

black outer wing feathers
huge orange bill
ADULT
IN FLIGHT

yellowish throat pouch
duller yellow bill
ADULT (WINTER)

variable grayish-black on head and nape
ADULT (POSTBREEDING)

white head
orange throat pouch
orange-yellow straight bill
ridge on bill
all-white plumage
bright-orange feet
ADULT (SUMMER)

FLIGHT: once in flight, alternates strong but shallow beats with glides; soars in flocks.

This colossal, unmistakable white bird, with its distinctive, oversized bill, is a highly social inhabitant of large lakes and marshes in western North America. It is a colonial bird, with most of the world's population being concentrated in just a handful of large colonies in isolated wetland complexes in deserts and prairies. The American White Pelican forms foraging flocks, which beat their wings in coordinated movements to herd fish into shallow water, where they can be caught more easily.

VOICE Usually silent except around nesting colonies; around the nest, young and adults exchange various grunts and hisses.

NESTING Depression in the ground, both sexes incubate; 1–2 eggs; 1 brood; April–August.

FEEDING Mainly gulps down small fish, occasionally eats small amphibians, and crayfish.

LARGE COLONIES
The White Pelican is highly social and is usually seen feeding or roosting in large groups.

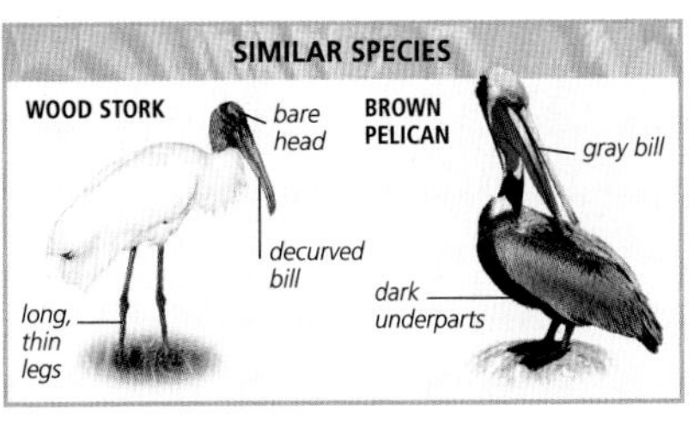
SIMILAR SPECIES
WOOD STORK
bare head
decurved bill
long, thin legs
BROWN PELICAN
gray bill
dark underparts

OCCURRENCE
Breeds on islands in freshwater lakes in south-central Canada, mountainous areas of the western US, and in coastal northeast Mexico; an early spring migrant, often returning to breeding grounds in early March. Winters in coastal regions from California and Texas to Mexico and Central America.

Length **4¼–5½ft (1.3–1.7m)**	Wingspan **7¾–9½ft (2.4–2.9m)**	Weight **12–20lb (5.5–9kg)**
Social **Colonies**	Lifespan **Up to 26 years**	Status **Vulnerable**

DATE: ______________ TIME: ______________ LOCATION: ______________________________

Order **Pelecaniformes**	Family **Ardeidae**	Species ***Botaurus lentiginosus***

American Bittern

trailing legs
dark outer wing feathers
ADULT
IN FLIGHT

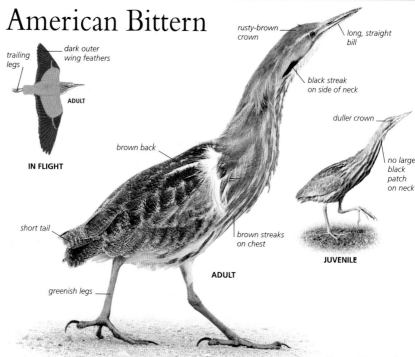

rusty-brown crown
long, straight bill
black streak on side of neck
brown back
short tail
brown streaks on chest
greenish legs
ADULT

duller crown
no large black patch on neck
JUVENILE

The American Bittern's camouflaged plumage and secretive behavior help it to blend into its thick reed habitat. It is heard much more often than it is seen; its call is unmistakable and has given rise to many evocative colloquial names, such as "thunder pumper."

FLIGHT: steady, deep, slightly stiff wing beats; usually flies relatively low and direct.

VOICE Deep, resonant *pump-er-unk, pump-er-unk*; calls mainly at dawn, dusk, and night time, but also during the day in the early mating season.

NESTING Platform or mound constructed of available marsh vegetation, usually over shallow water; 2–7 eggs; 1 brood; April–August.

FEEDING Stands still or moves slowly, then strikes downward with bill to catch prey; eats fish, insects, crustaceans, snakes, amphibians, and small mammals.

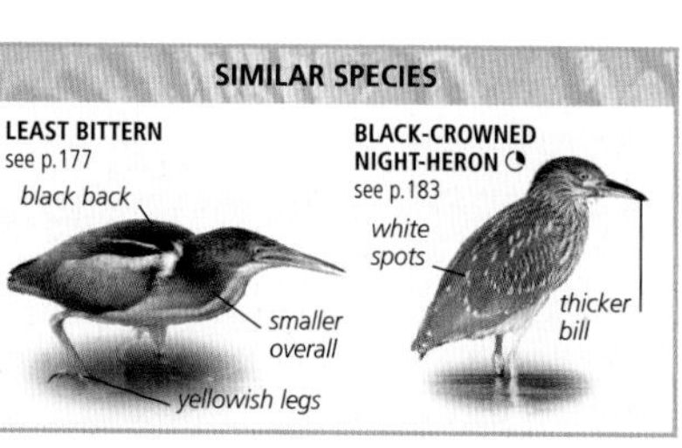
SIMILAR SPECIES
LEAST BITTERN
see p.177
black back
smaller overall
yellowish legs
BLACK-CROWNED NIGHT-HERON
see p.183
white spots
thicker bill

LOOK STRAIGHT
Even with the bill pointed straight upward, a bittern can still see in front of it.

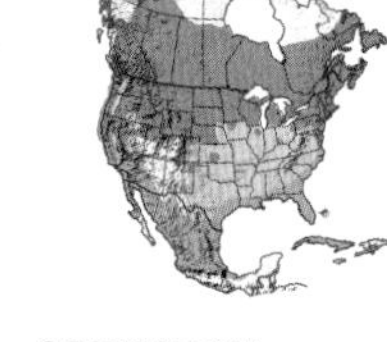

OCCURRENCE
Breeds in heavily vegetated freshwater wetlands across the northern US and southern Canada; also occasionally in estuarine wetlands; winters in southern and coastal wetlands where temperatures stay above freezing; can appear in any wetland habitat during migration.

Length **23½–31in (60–80cm)**	Wingspan **3½–4¼ft (1.1–1.3m)**	Weight **13–20oz (375–575g)**
Social **Solitary**	Lifespan **At least 8 years**	Status **Declining**

DATE: ____________ TIME: ____________ LOCATION: ____________

Order **Pelecaniformes**	Family **Ardeidae**	Species ***Ixobrychus exilis***

Least Bittern

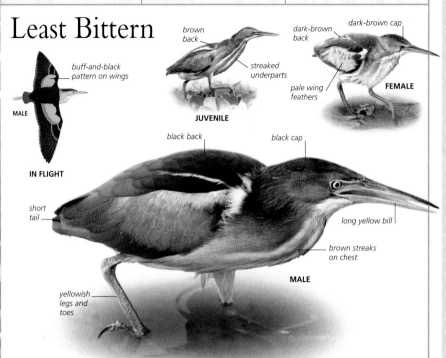

buff-and-black pattern on wings

MALE

IN FLIGHT

brown back

streaked underparts

JUVENILE

dark-brown back

dark-brown cap

pale wing feathers

FEMALE

black back

black cap

short tail

long yellow bill

brown streaks on chest

MALE

yellowish legs and toes

The smallest heron in North America, the Least Bittern is also one of the most colorful, but its secretive nature makes it easy to overlook in its densely vegetated marsh habitat. A dark color form, which was originally described in the 1800s as a separate species named Cory's Bittern, has rarely been reported in recent decades.

VOICE Soft *ku, ku, ku, ku, ku* display call; year-round, a loud *kak, kak, kak.*

NESTING Platform of marsh vegetation with sticks and stems added, usually within 30ft (9m) of open water; 2–7 eggs; 1 brood; April–August.

FEEDING Feeds on small fish, insects including dragonflies; also crustaceans; clings quietly to vegetation before striking prey, or stalks slowly.

FLIGHT: rapid wing beats; weak, direct flight; flies low, around top of vegetation.

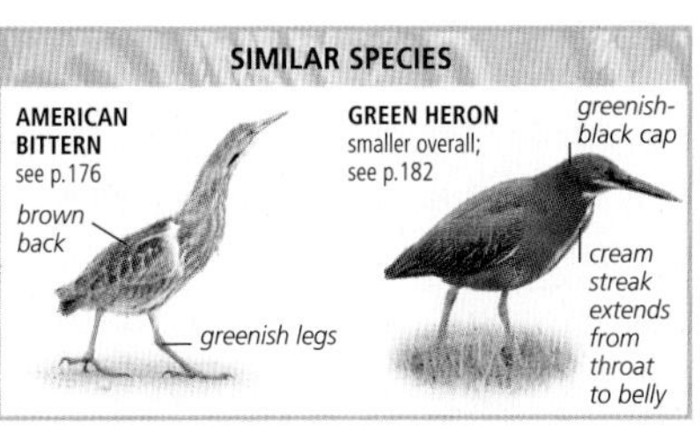
SIMILAR SPECIES
AMERICAN BITTERN
see p.176
brown back
greenish legs
GREEN HERON
smaller overall; see p.182
greenish-black cap
cream streak extends from throat to belly

REED CREEPER
With its small, thin body, this species easily creeps through dense reeds in search of prey.

OCCURRENCE
Breeds in summer in lowland freshwater marshes; less commonly in brackish and rarely in saltwater marshes; frequents similar habitat on migration; winters in brackish and saltwater marshes. Wide distribution in the Americas, south to Argentina.

Length **11–14in (28–36cm)**	Wingspan **15½–18in (40–46cm)**	Weight **2⅝–3⅜oz (75–95g)**
Social **Solitary/Small flocks**	Lifespan **Unknown**	Status **Threatened**

Order **Pelecaniformes**	Family **Ardeidae**	Species ***Ardea herodias***

Great Blue Heron

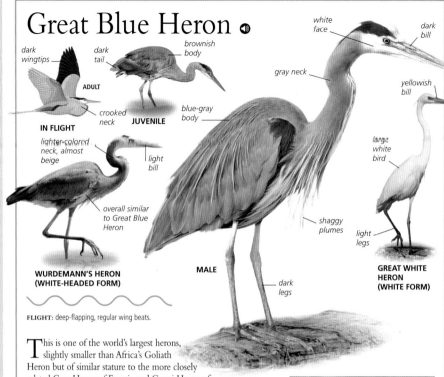

dark wingtips
ADULT
crooked neck
IN FLIGHT
dark tail
brownish body
JUVENILE
lighter-colored neck, almost beige
light bill
overall similar to Great Blue Heron
WURDEMANN'S HERON (WHITE-HEADED FORM)
white face
dark bill
gray neck
blue-gray body
shaggy plumes
dark legs
MALE
yellowish bill
large white bird
light legs
GREAT WHITE HERON (WHITE FORM)

FLIGHT: deep-flapping, regular wing beats.

This is one of the world's largest herons, slightly smaller than Africa's Goliath Heron but of similar stature to the more closely related Gray Heron of Eurasia and Cocoi Heron of South America. It is a common inhabitant of a variety of North American waterbodies, from marshes to swamps, as well as along sea coasts. Its majestic flight is wonderful to behold, especially when it migrates or makes local movements between feeding and roosting sites.

VOICE Mostly silent; gives a loud, barking squawk or *crank* in breeding colonies or when disturbed.

NESTING Nest of twigs and branches; usually in colonies, but also singly; in trees, often over water, but also over ground; 2–4 eggs; 1–2 broods; February–August.

FEEDING Catches prey, sometimes spearing with quick jab of bill; primarily fish but also ducklings, frogs, muskrats, and even mice in fields.

LOFTY ABODE
Great Blue Herons nest in small colonies in trees, and often roost in them.

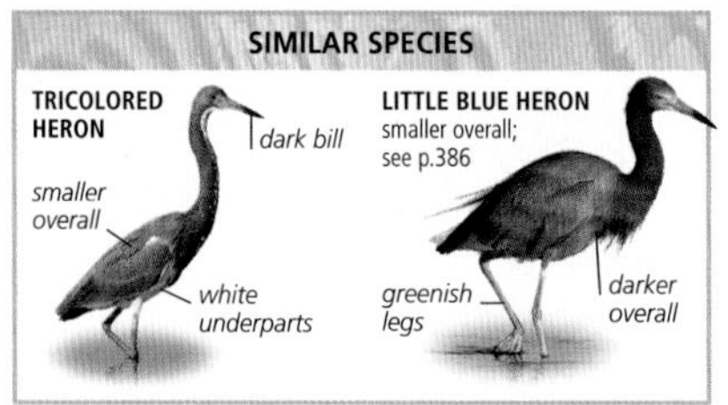
SIMILAR SPECIES
TRICOLORED HERON
dark bill
smaller overall
white underparts
LITTLE BLUE HERON
smaller overall; see p.386
greenish legs
darker overall

OCCURRENCE
Across southern Canada and the US in wetlands, such as marshes, lake edges, and along rivers and swamps; also in marine habitats, especially tidal grass flats. The Great White Heron is primarily found in marine habitats in southern Florida.

Length **2¾–4¼ft (0.9–1.3m)**	Wingspan **5¼–6½ft (1.6–2m)**	Weight **4¾–5½lb (2.1–2.5kg)**
Social **Solitary/Flocks**	Lifespan **Up to 20 years**	Status **Secure**

DATE: ______________ TIME: ______________ LOCATION: ______________

Order **Pelecaniformes**	Family **Ardeidae**	Species ***Ardea alba***

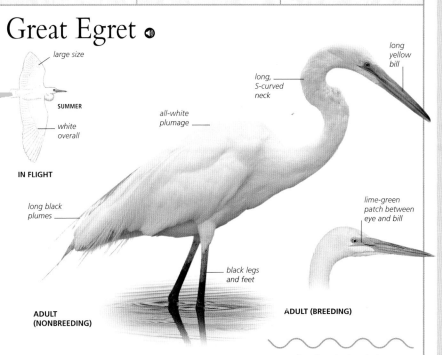

Great Egret

large size

SUMMER

white overall

IN FLIGHT

long, S-curved neck

long yellow bill

all-white plumage

long black plumes

black legs and feet

ADULT (NONBREEDING)

lime-green patch between eye and bill

ADULT (BREEDING)

FLIGHT: flies with regular, deep wing beats.

This large white heron is found on every continent except Antarctica. When feeding, the Great Egret apparently prefers to forage alone rather than in flocks. It maintains space around itself, and will defend a territory of 10ft (3m) in diameter from other wading birds, especially Great Blue Herons. This territory "moves" with the bird as it feeds. In years of scarce food supplies, a chick may kill a sibling, permitting the survival of at least one bird.

VOICE Largely vocal during courtship and breeding; otherwise, *kraak* or *cuk-cuk-cuk* when disturbed or in a combative encounter.

NESTING Nest of twigs in trees, over land or water; 2–4 eggs; 1 brood; March–July.

FEEDING Catches prey with quick thrust of bill; feeds on aquatic prey, primarily fish, also crustaceans.

TREE PERCHES

Great Egrets nest in trees and regularly perch in them when not feeding.

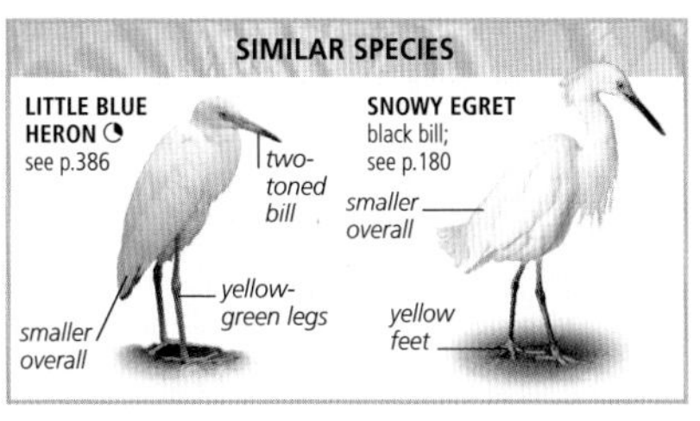
SIMILAR SPECIES
LITTLE BLUE HERON
see p.386
two-toned bill
yellow-green legs
smaller overall
SNOWY EGRET
black bill;
see p.180
smaller overall
yellow feet

OCCURRENCE

Breeds in trees over water or on islands; forages in freshwater and marine wetlands from marshes and ponds to rivers. Migratory over much of its North American range; more southerly populations resident. Range has expanded northward into Canada. Distance migrated depends on severity of winter.

Length **3¼ft (1m)**	Wingspan **6ft (1.8m)**	Weight **1¾–3¼lb (0.8–1.5kg)**
Social **Solitary**	Lifespan **Up to 25 years**	Status **Secure**

DATE: ____________ TIME: ____________ LOCATION: ____________

Order **Pelecaniformes**	Family **Ardeidae**	Species ***Egretta thula***

Snowy Egret

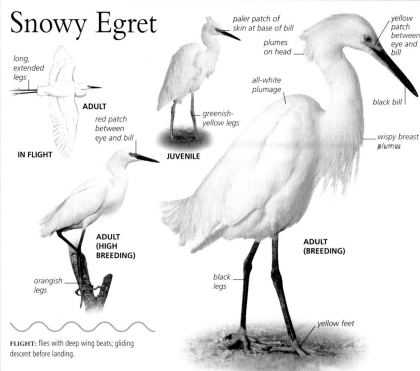

long, extended legs
ADULT
IN FLIGHT

red patch between eye and bill
ADULT (HIGH BREEDING)
orangish legs

paler patch of skin at base of bill
greenish-yellow legs
JUVENILE

plumes on head
yellow patch between eye and bill
all-white plumage
black bill
wispy breast plumes
ADULT (BREEDING)
black legs
yellow feet

FLIGHT: flies with deep wing beats; gliding descent before landing.

A New World species, the Snowy Egret is similar to an Old World species, the Little Egret. It is very adaptable in estuarine and freshwater habitats. When foraging, it uses a wide variety of behaviors, including wing-flicking, foot-stirring, and foot-probing to get its prey moving, making it easier to capture.

VOICE High-pitched *aargaarg* when flushed; low-pitched *arg* and *raah* aggressive calls; *aarg* call during attacks and pursuits.

NESTING Small sticks, branches, and rushes over water or on land; also on ground, in shrubs, mangroves, and other trees; 3–5 eggs; 1 brood; March–August.

FEEDING Feeds on aquatic prey, from invertebrates, such as insects, shrimp, and prawns, to small fish, amphibians, and snakes.

WIDESPREAD SPECIES
Snowy Egrets feed in a wide variety of wetland habitats, using different foraging techniques.

SIMILAR SPECIES

GREAT EGRET
see p.179

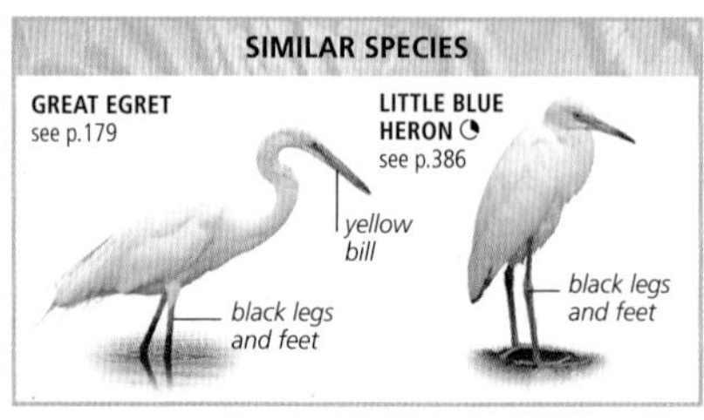
yellow bill
black legs and feet

LITTLE BLUE HERON ◔
see p.386

black legs and feet

OCCURRENCE
Found in a wide variety of wetlands throughout North and South America: from mangroves in Florida to marshlands in New England and the western US. Highly adaptable and widely found. Sites of breeding colonies may change from year to year within a set range.

Length **24in (62cm)**	Wingspan **3½ft (1.1cm)**	Weight **12oz (350g)**
Social **Solitary**	Lifespan **Up to 22 years**	Status **Declining**

DATE: ________ TIME: ________ LOCATION: ________

Order **Pelecaniformes**	Family **Ardeidae**	Species ***Bubulcus ibis***

Cattle Egret

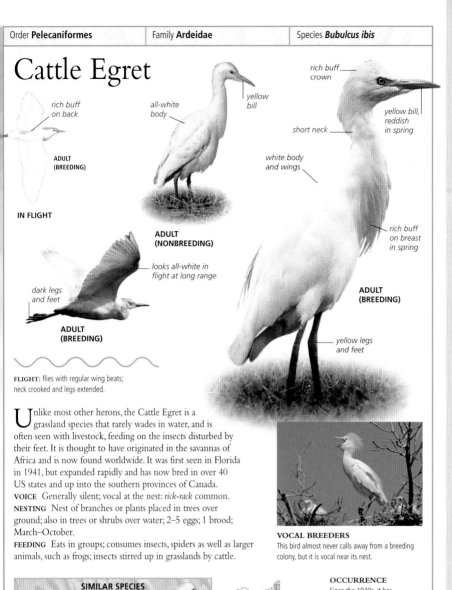

rich buff on back

ADULT (BREEDING)

IN FLIGHT

all-white body

yellow bill

ADULT (NONBREEDING)

rich buff crown

yellow bill, reddish in spring

short neck

white body and wings

rich buff on breast in spring

ADULT (BREEDING)

yellow legs and feet

looks all-white in flight at long range

dark legs and feet

ADULT (BREEDING)

FLIGHT: flies with regular wing beats; neck crooked and legs extended.

Unlike most other herons, the Cattle Egret is a grassland species that rarely wades in water, and is often seen with livestock, feeding on the insects disturbed by their feet. It is thought to have originated in the savannas of Africa and is now found worldwide. It was first seen in Florida in 1941, but expanded rapidly and has now bred in over 40 US states and up into the southern provinces of Canada.

VOICE Generally silent; vocal at the nest: *rick-rack* common.

NESTING Nest of branches or plants placed in trees over ground; also in trees or shrubs over water; 2–5 eggs; 1 brood; March–October.

FEEDING Eats in groups; consumes insects, spiders as well as larger animals, such as frogs; insects stirred up in grasslands by cattle.

VOCAL BREEDERS
This bird almost never calls away from a breeding colony, but it is vocal near its nest.

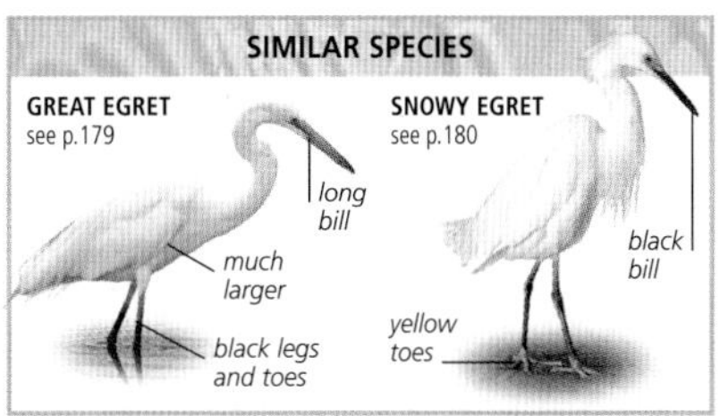
SIMILAR SPECIES
GREAT EGRET
see p.179
long bill
much larger
black legs and toes
SNOWY EGRET
see p.180
black bill
yellow toes

OCCURRENCE
Since the 1940s, it has expanded to many habitats in much of North America, primarily in grasslands and prairies, but also wetland areas. In tropical regions, the Cattle Egrets flock around the cattle feeding in shallow wetlands.

Length **20in (51cm)**	Wingspan **31in (78cm)**	Weight **13oz (375g)**
Social **Colonies**	Lifespan **Up to 17 years**	Status **Secure**

DATE: ______________ TIME: ______________ LOCATION: ______________________________

Order **Pelecaniformes**	Family **Ardeidae**	Species ***Butorides virescens***

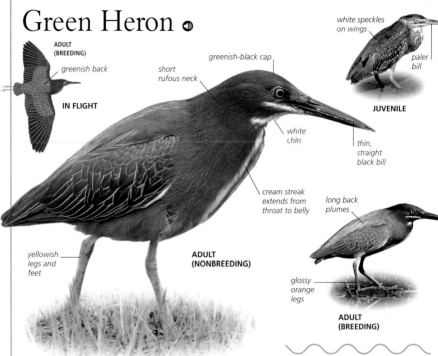

Green Heron

ADULT (BREEDING)

greenish back

IN FLIGHT

greenish-black cap

short rufous neck

white speckles on wings

paler bill

JUVENILE

white chin

thin, straight black bill

cream streak extends from throat to belly

long back plumes

yellowish legs and feet

ADULT (NONBREEDING)

glossy orange legs

ADULT (BREEDING)

A small, solitary, and secretive bird of dense thicketed wetlands, the Green Heron can be difficult to observe. This dark, crested heron is most often seen flying away from a perceived threat, emitting a loud squawk. While the Green Heron of North and Central America has now been recognized as a separate species, it was earlier grouped with what is now the Striated Heron (*B. striata*), which is found in the tropics and subtropics throughout the world.

VOICE Squawking *keow* when flying from disturbance.

NESTING Nest of twigs often in bushes or trees, frequently over water but also on land; 1–2 broods; 3–5 eggs; March–July.

FEEDING Mainly fish, but also frogs, insects, and spiders; lays insects and other items on the water's surface as bait to attract fish.

FLIGHT: direct, a bit plodding, and usually over short distances.

READY TO STRIKE

Green Herons usually catch their prey by lunging forward and downward with their whole body.

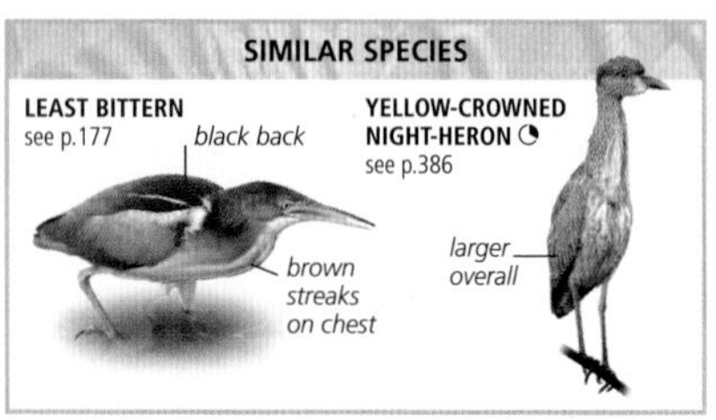
SIMILAR SPECIES
LEAST BITTERN
see p.177
black back
brown streaks on chest
YELLOW-CROWNED NIGHT-HERON
see p.386
larger overall

OCCURRENCE

An inhabitant of swampy thickets, but occasionally dry land close to water. Found across much of the lower half of North America, but missing in the plains, the Rocky Mountains, and the western deserts that do not provide appropriate wetlands. Winters in coastal wetlands.

Length **14½–15½in (37–39cm)**	Wingspan **25–27in (63–68cm)**	Weight **7–9oz (200–250g)**
Social **Solitary/Pairs/Small flocks**	Lifespan **Up to 10 years**	Status **Secure**

DATE: ______ TIME: ______ LOCATION: ______

Order **Pelecaniformes**	Family **Ardeidae**	Species ***Nycticorax nycticorax***

Black-crowned Night-Heron

gray wings
heavily speckled back and wings
ADULT
JUVENILE
broad, rounded wings
IN FLIGHT
long white head plumes
black back
white spots on brown back
pale lower bill
JUVENILE
black crown
short, thick bill
short neck
ADULT
yellow legs; red in spring

FLIGHT: strong, steady flight; wing beats faster than larger herons and egrets; glides into landing.

The Black-crowned Night-Heron is chunky and squat. It is also one of the most common and widespread herons in North America and in the world. However, as its name suggests, it is mainly active at twilight and at night, and thus, is mostly seen roosting along a shoreline. Its distinctive barking call can be heard at night—even at the center of large cities.

VOICE Loud, distinctive *quark* or *wok*, often given in flight and around colonies.

NESTING Large stick nests built usually 20–40ft (6–12m) up in trees; 3–5 eggs; 1 brood; November–August.

FEEDING Feeds primarily on aquatic animals, such as fish, crustaceans, insects, and mollusks; also eggs and chicks of colonial birds, such as egrets, ibises, and terns.

LONG PLUMES
In breeding plumage, the plumes of the male of this species are longer than the female's.

SIMILAR SPECIES

YELLOW-CROWNED NIGHT-HERON *gray neck*
see p.386
black-and-white head

GREEN HERON *rufous neck*
smaller overall; see p.182
thinner bill

OCCURRENCE
Widespread; can be found wherever there are waterbodies, such as lakes, ponds, and streams; generally absent from higher elevations. Colonies often on islands or in marshes; colony sites may be used for decades. In winter, found in areas where water remains open.

Length **23–26in (58–65cm)**	Wingspan **3½–4ft (1.1–1.2m)**	Weight **1½–2½lb (0.7–1kg)**
Social **Colonies**	Lifespan **Up to 21 years**	Status **Secure**

DATE: ____________ TIME: ____________ LOCATION: ____________

Order **Pelecaniformes**	Family **Threskiornithidae**	Species ***Plegadis falcinellus***

Glossy Ibis

outstretched neck
trailing legs
ADULT (BREEDING)
IN FLIGHT

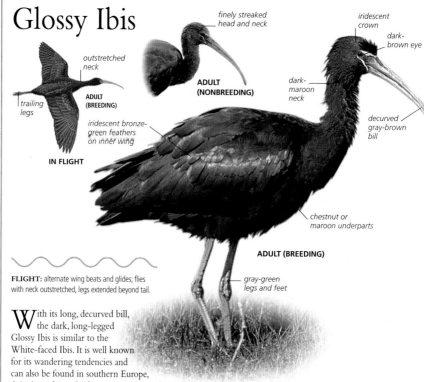

finely streaked head and neck
ADULT (NONBREEDING)

iridescent crown
dark-brown eye
dark-maroon neck
decurved gray-brown bill
iridescent bronze-green feathers on inner wing
chestnut or maroon underparts
ADULT (BREEDING)
gray-green legs and feet

FLIGHT: alternate wing beats and glides; flies with neck outstretched, legs extended beyond tail.

With its long, decurved bill, the dark, long-legged Glossy Ibis is similar to the White-faced Ibis. It is well known for its wandering tendencies and can also be found in southern Europe, Asia, Australia, and Africa. Despite being found in the US in the mid-19th century, the Glossy Ibis was not discovered nesting in Florida until 1886. Confined to Florida until the mid-20th century, it then started spreading northward, eventually as far as southern Ontario and across into Nova Scotia.

VOICE Crow-like croak; subdued nasal chatter in flocks; mostly silent.

NESTING Platform of twigs and reeds in trees, shrubs, or reeds, on ground or over water; 3–4 eggs; 1 brood; April–July.

FEEDING Forages by feel, puts bill in soil and mud to catch prey, including snails, insects, leeches, frogs, and crayfish.

MARSH FEEDER
The Glossy Ibis regularly feeds in shallow pools and along the waterways of coastal marshes.

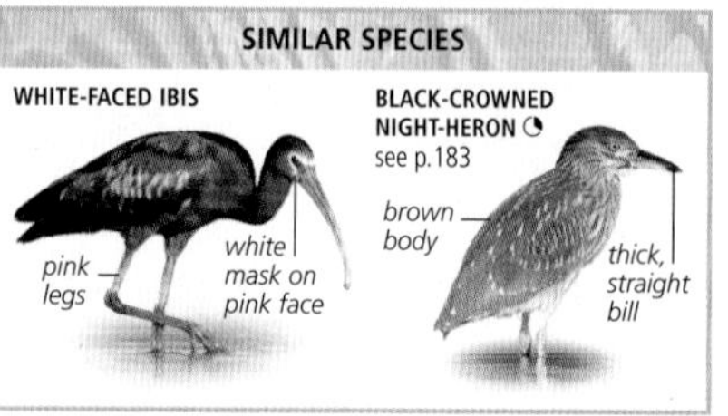
SIMILAR SPECIES
WHITE-FACED IBIS
pink legs
white mask on pink face
BLACK-CROWNED NIGHT-HERON
see p.183
brown body
thick, straight bill

OCCURRENCE
Common from New England south to Florida, but has spread north into the eastern provinces. Occurs in brackish and freshwater marshes and in flooded or plowed fields; feeds with other waders in inland freshwater wetlands as well as coastal lagoons and estuaries.

Length **23in (59cm)**	Wingspan **36in (92cm)**	Weight **13oz (375g)**
Social **Flocks/Colonies**	Lifespan **Up to 20 years**	Status **Secure (p)**

DATE: ____________ TIME: ____________ LOCATION: ____________

Family **Cathartidae**

NEW WORLD VULTURES

NEW WORLD VULTURES are not related to Old World vultures, although they look somewhat similar, having long, broad wings with "fingered" tips. Their heads and necks are more or less bare, which helps prevent meat and bacteria from collecting in their feathers when they feed on carcasses. Their bills are large and hooked to tear flesh, but their feet are unspecialized, with short claws, and are not used for capturing prey. All the birds in this group have exceptional eyesight and find their food by sight while soaring high over open ground. The Turkey Vulture, a common sight in many areas, also has a keen sense of smell, which it can use to find dead animals in dense woodland.

WEAK TOOL
In spite of its sharp beak, the Turkey Vulture cannot always break the skin of carcasses. Thus, it must wait for another predator to tear open the skin or for the carcass to rot and soften.

Families **Pandionidae, Accipitridae**

HAWKS, EAGLES, AND RELATIVES

THESE DIURNAL BIRDS OF PREY include several loosely related groups. All have hooked bills and large eyes, but their shapes and lifestyles are varied.

OSPREY

The sole member of the Pandionidae family, the Osprey catches fish in a headlong dive from a hover. Its feet have long, curved claws and toes equipped with sharp spicules to provide extra grip for slippery fish.

HAWKS AND EAGLES

The Accipitridae family covers a range of raptors with much variation in shape, size, and habitat. Graceful, long-winged harriers are medium-sized birds that feed in open spaces or over marshes. Huge, powerful eagles of mountains and open country have long, broad wings and feathered legs. "Sea-eagles," such as the Bald Eagle, have massive bills and long wings but somewhat short tails and bare legs. Sea-eagles feed on fish as well as birds, mammals, and carrion.

Bird-eating hawks (in the genus *Accipiter*) have rounded wings and slender tails, and long claws for catching prey with their feet. Soaring hawks (in the genus *Buteo*) are more like small eagles, with smaller but powerful bills and feet. Some are more widespread than eagles, and are found in a broader range of habitats.

DOUBLE SHOT
With lots of fish running in a tight school, this Osprey has the strength and skill to catch two with one dive.

Order **Cathartiformes**	Family **Cathartidae**	Species ***Cathartes aura***

Turkey Vulture

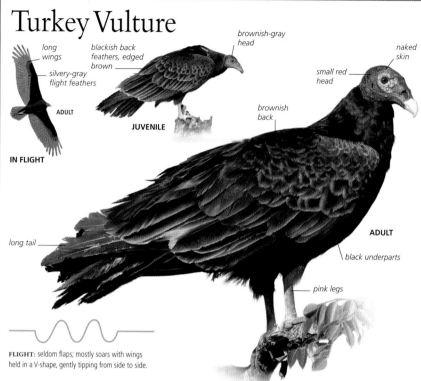

long wings
silvery-gray flight feathers
ADULT
IN FLIGHT

blackish back feathers, edged brown
brownish-gray head
JUVENILE

naked skin
small red head
brownish back
long tail
ADULT
black underparts
pink legs

FLIGHT: seldom flaps; mostly soars with wings held in a V-shape, gently tipping from side to side.

The most widely distributed vulture in North America, the Turkey Vulture is found in most of the US and has expanded its range into southern Canada from coast to coast. It possesses an excellent sense of smell and uses it to locate carcasses sometimes hidden from view. The Turkey Vulture's habit of defecating down its legs, which it shares with the Wood Stork, may serve to cool it or to kill bacteria with its ammonia content.

VOICE Silent, but will hiss at intruders; also grunts.

NESTING Dark recesses, such as under large rocks or stumps, on rocky ledges in caves, and crevices, in mammal burrows and hollow logs, and abandoned buildings; 1–3 eggs; 1 brood; March–August.

FEEDING Feeds on a wide range of wild and domestic carrion, mostly mammals, but also birds, reptiles, amphibians, and fish; occasionally takes live prey, such as nestlings or trapped birds.

SOAKING UP THE SUN
Turkey Vultures often spread their wings to sun themselves and increase their body temperature.

SIMILAR SPECIES

BLACK VULTURE
see p.386
shorter tail
all-black body

OCCURRENCE
Generally forages and migrates over mixed farmland and forest but also beaches; prefers to nest in forested or partly forested hillsides; roosts in large trees, such as cottonwoods, on rocky outcrops, and on power line transmission towers; some winter in urban areas and near landfills. Also widespread in the Caribbean, and in Central and South America.

Length **25–32in (64–81cm)**	Wingspan **5½–6ft (1.7–1.8m)**	Weight **4½lb (2kg)**
Social **Flocks**	Lifespan **At least 17 years**	Status **Secure**

DATE: ______________ TIME: ______________ LOCATION: ______________

Order **Accipitriformes**	Family **Pandionidae**	Species ***Pandion haliaetus***

Osprey

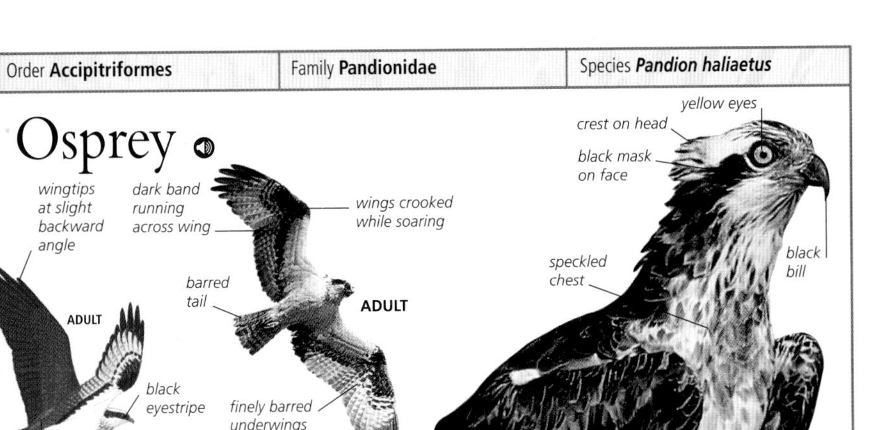

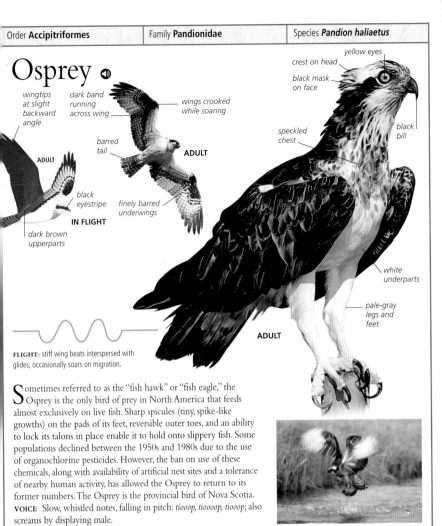

wingtips at slight backward angle
dark band running across wing
wings crooked while soaring
barred tail
ADULT
ADULT
black eyestripe
finely barred underwings
IN FLIGHT
dark brown upperparts
yellow eyes
crest on head
black mask on face
black bill
speckled chest
white underparts
pale-gray legs and feet
ADULT

FLIGHT: stiff wing beats interspersed with glides; occasionally soars on migration.

Sometimes referred to as the "fish hawk" or "fish eagle," the Osprey is the only bird of prey in North America that feeds almost exclusively on live fish. Sharp spicules (tiny, spike-like growths) on the pads of its feet, reversible outer toes, and an ability to lock its talons in place enable it to hold onto slippery fish. Some populations declined between the 1950s and 1980s due to the use of organochlorine pesticides. However, the ban on use of these chemicals, along with availability of artificial nest sites and a tolerance of nearby human activity, has allowed the Osprey to return to its former numbers. The Osprey is the provincial bird of Nova Scotia.

VOICE Slow, whistled notes, falling in pitch: *tiooop, tioooop, tiooop*; also screams by displaying male.

NESTING Twig nest on tree, rock pinnacles, and a wide variety of artificial structures; 1–4 eggs; 1 brood; March–August.

FEEDING Dives as deep as 3ft (90cm) to catch fish.

IMPROVING AERODYNAMICS
Once caught, a fish is held with its head pointing forward, reducing drag as the bird flies.

SIMILAR SPECIES

BALD EAGLE (2ND YEAR) see p.193
no crook in wings during flight
paler tail

GOLDEN EAGLE see p.188
dark-brown head
brown feathered legs

OCCURRENCE
Breeds in a wide variety of habitats: northern forests, near shallow reservoirs, along freshwater rivers and large lakes, estuaries and salt marshes, coastal deserts, and desert saltflat lagoons. Migrates through and winters in similar habitats.

Length **21–23in (53–58cm)**	Wingspan **5–6ft (1.5–1.8m)**	Weight **3–4½lb (1.4–2kg)**
Social **Solitary/Pairs**	Lifespan **Up to 25 years**	Status **Secure**

DATE: ______________ TIME: ______________ LOCATION: ______________________________

Order **Accipitriformes**	Family **Accipitridae**	Species ***Aquila chrysaetos***

Golden Eagle

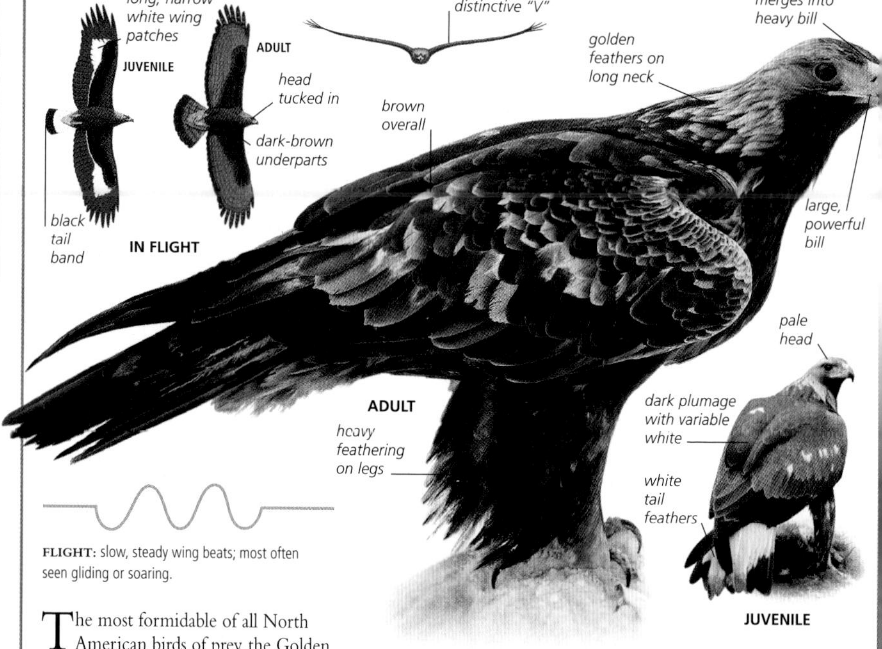

long, narrow white wing patches
JUVENILE
black tail band
ADULT
head tucked in
dark-brown underparts
IN FLIGHT
holds wings in distinctive "V"
brown overall
golden feathers on long neck
flat, broad head merges into heavy bill
large, powerful bill
ADULT
heavy feathering on legs
pale head
dark plumage with variable white
white tail feathers
JUVENILE

FLIGHT: slow, steady wing beats; most often seen gliding or soaring.

The most formidable of all North American birds of prey, the Golden Eagle is more numerous in the western part of Canada. It defends large territories ranging from 8–12 square miles (20–30 square kilometers), containing up to 14 nest sites. Although it appears sluggish, it is amazingly swift and agile, and employs a variety of hunting techniques to catch specific prey. Shot and poisoned by ranchers and trappers, it is unfortunately also faced with dwindling habitat and food sources due to human development.

VOICE High-pitched far-carrying yelps and deep liquid babbling notes.

NESTING Large pile of sticks and vegetation on cliffs, in trees, and on artificial structures; 1–3 eggs; 1 brood; April–August.

FEEDING Eats mammals, such as hares, rabbits, ground squirrels, prairie dogs, marmots, foxes, and coyotes; also large birds.

POWER AND STRENGTH
With its sharp talons and strong wings, legs, and feet, the Golden Eagle can take prey as large as a coyote.

SIMILAR SPECIES
BALD EAGLE
see p.193
dark-brown overall
large head and bill
FERRUGINOUS HAWK (DARK FORM)
no golden tinge
smaller overall

OCCURRENCE
In North America, occurs mostly in grasslands, wetlands, and rocky areas; breeds south to Mexico, in open and semi-open habitats from sea level to 12,000ft (3,500m) including tundra, shrublands, grasslands, coniferous forests, and farmland, areas close to streams or rivers; winters in open habitat.

Length **28–33in (70–84cm)**	Wingspan **6–7¼ft (1.8–2.2m)**	Weight **6½–13lb (3–6kg)**
Social **Solitary/Pairs**	Lifespan **Up to 39 years**	Status **Declining (p)**

DATE: ______________ TIME: ______________ LOCATION: ______________

Order **Accipitriformes**	Family **Accipitridae**	Species ***Circus hudsonius***

Northern Harrier

MALE
black wingtips
wings held in V-shape
white rump
FEMALE
dark barring on silver-gray underwings
IN FLIGHT
bluish-gray head
dark bill with yellow skin near bluish base
bluish-gray upperparts
reddish underparts
JUVENILE
white ring around owl-like face
brown upperparts
white underparts with reddish-brown markings
gray uppertail with light undertail feathers
MALE
FEMALE

Found nearly all over North America, the Northern Harrier is most often seen flying buoyantly low in search of food. A white rump, V-shaped wings, and tilting flight make this species easily identifiable. The blue-gray males are strikingly different from the dark-brown females. The bird's most recognizable characteristic is its owl-like face, which contains stiff feathers to help channel in sounds from prey. Northern Harriers are highly migratory throughout their range.

VOICE Call given by both sexes in rapid succession at nest: *kek* becomes more high-pitched when intruders are spotted.

NESTING Platform of sticks on ground in open, wet field; 4–6 eggs; 1 brood; April–September.

FEEDING Mostly hunts rodents like mice and muskrats; also birds, frogs, reptiles; occasionally takes larger prey, such as rabbits.

FLIGHT: low and slow with lazy flaps, alternating with buoyant, brusquely tilting glides.

WATERY DWELLING
To avoid predators, Northern Harriers prefer to raise their young on wet sites in tall, dense vegetation.

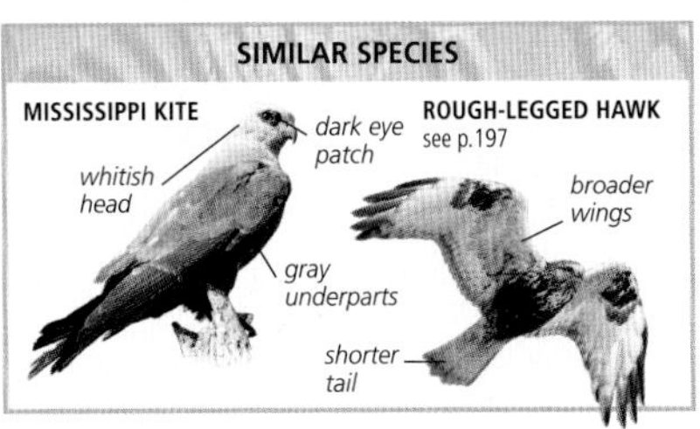
SIMILAR SPECIES
MISSISSIPPI KITE
whitish head
dark eye patch
gray underparts
ROUGH-LEGGED HAWK
see p.197
broader wings
shorter tail

OCCURRENCE
Breeds in a variety of open wetlands: marshes, meadows, pastures, and fallow fields across most of North America; winters in open habitats like deserts, coastal sand dunes, cropland, grasslands, and marshy and riverside areas.

Length **18–20in (46–51cm)**	Wingspan **3½–4ft (1.1–1.2m)**	Weight **11–26oz (300–750g)**
Social **Solitary/Pairs/Colonies**	Lifespan **Up to 16 years**	Status **Secure**

DATE: ______________ TIME: ______________ LOCATION: ______________

Order **Accipitriformes**	Family **Accipitridae**	Species ***Accipiter striatus***

Sharp-shinned Hawk

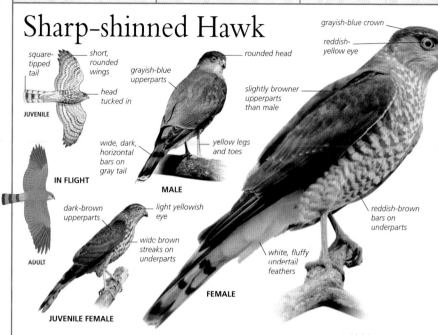

square-tipped tail
short, rounded wings
head tucked in
JUVENILE
IN FLIGHT
ADULT
grayish-blue upperparts
rounded head
wide, dark, horizontal bars on gray tail
yellow legs and toes
MALE
dark-brown upperparts
light yellowish eye
wide brown streaks on underparts
JUVENILE FEMALE
grayish-blue crown
reddish-yellow eye
slightly browner upperparts than male
reddish-brown bars on underparts
white, fluffy undertail feathers
FEMALE

This small and swift hawk is quite adept at capturing birds, occasionally even taking species larger than itself. The Sharp-shinned Hawk's short, rounded wings and long tail allow it to make abrupt turns and lightning-fast dashes in thick woods and dense, shrubby terrain. With needle-like talons, long, spindle-thin legs, and long toes, this hawk is well adapted to snatching birds in flight. The prey is plucked before being consumed or fed to the nestlings.

VOICE High-pitched, repeated *kiu kiu kiu* call; sometimes makes squealing sound when disturbed at nest.

NESTING Sturdy nest of sticks lined with twigs or pieces of bark; sometimes an old crow or squirrel nest; 3–4 eggs; 1 brood; March–June.

FEEDING Catches small birds, such as sparrows and wood warblers, on the wing, or takes them unaware while perched; often frequents feeders to catch songbirds.

FLIGHT: rapid, direct, and strong; nimble enough to maneuver in dense forest; soars during migration.

HUNTING BIRDS
A Sharp-shinned Hawk pauses on the ground with a freshly captured sparrow in its talons.

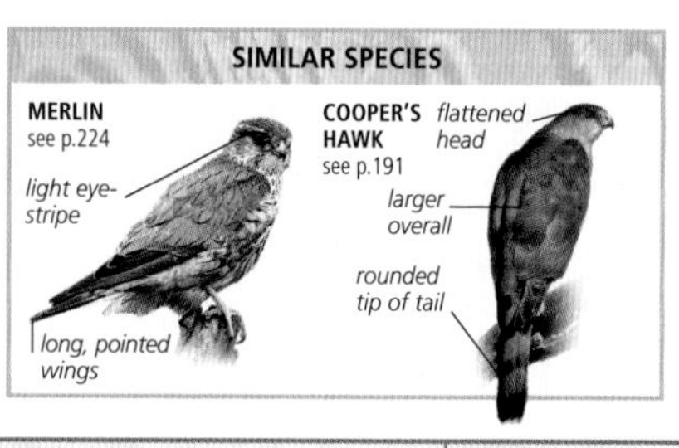
SIMILAR SPECIES
MERLIN
see p.224
light eye-stripe
long, pointed wings
COOPER'S HAWK
see p.191
flattened head
larger overall
rounded tip of tail

OCCURRENCE
Deep coniferous forests and mixed hardwood-conifer woodlands across North America from the tree limit in northern Canada to the Gulf states. During fall migration, sometimes seen in flocks of hundreds of individuals. Winters in Central America, from Guatemala to Panama.

Length **11in (28 cm)**	Wingspan **23in (58cm)**	Weight **3½–6oz (100–175g)**
Social **Solitary/Flocks**	Lifespan **At least 10 years**	Status **Secure**

DATE: ______________ TIME: ______________ LOCATION: ______________

Order **Accipitriformes**	Family **Accipitridae**	Species ***Accipiter cooperii***

Cooper's Hawk

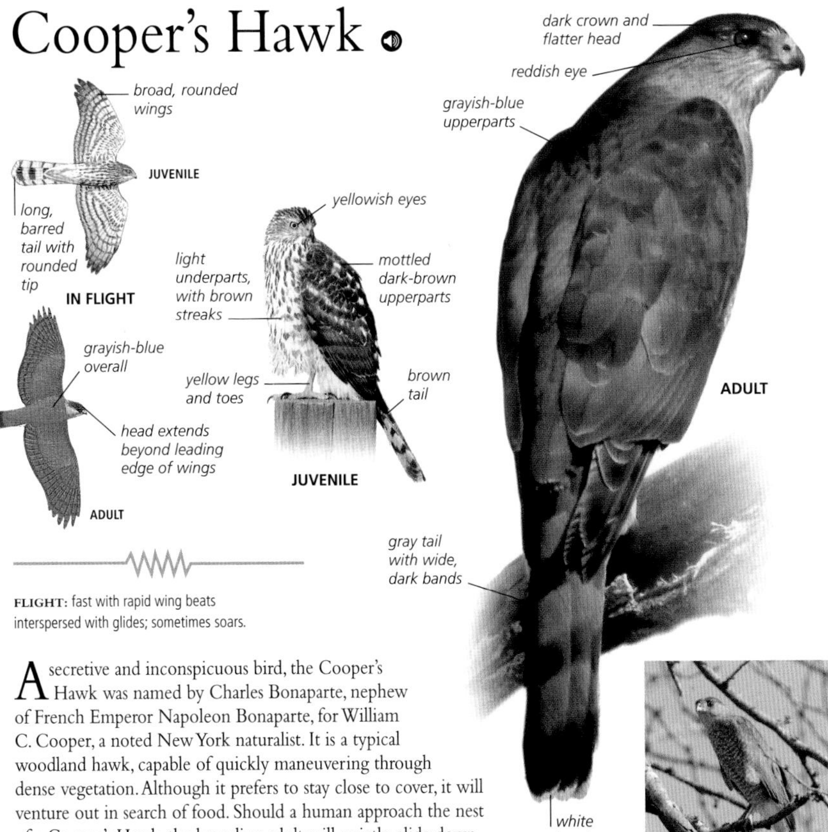

broad, rounded wings
JUVENILE
long, barred tail with rounded tip
IN FLIGHT
grayish-blue overall
head extends beyond leading edge of wings
ADULT
yellowish eyes
light underparts, with brown streaks
mottled dark-brown upperparts
yellow legs and toes
brown tail
JUVENILE
dark crown and flatter head
reddish eye
grayish-blue upperparts
ADULT
gray tail with wide, dark bands
white band at tip of tail

FLIGHT: fast with rapid wing beats interspersed with glides; sometimes soars.

A secretive and inconspicuous bird, the Cooper's Hawk was named by Charles Bonaparte, nephew of French Emperor Napoleon Bonaparte, for William C. Cooper, a noted New York naturalist. It is a typical woodland hawk, capable of quickly maneuvering through dense vegetation. Although it prefers to stay close to cover, it will venture out in search of food. Should a human approach the nest of a Cooper's Hawk, the brooding adult will quietly glide down and away from the nest tree rather than attack the intruder.

VOICE Most common call a staccato *ca-ca-ca-ca*; other vocalizations include as many as 40 different calls.

NESTING Medium-sized, stick nest, usually in a large deciduous tree; 4–5 eggs; 1 brood; April–May.

FEEDING Catches birds from robins to pigeons; larger females can capture grouse; also eats chipmunks, small squirrels, and even bats.

DENSE BARRING
This hawk has characteristic fine reddish-brown, horizontal barring on its undersides.

SIMILAR SPECIES

NORTHERN HARRIER ♀ see p.189
larger overall
whitish underparts

SHARP-SHINNED HAWK see p.190
square-tipped tail
smaller, rounder head

OCCURRENCE
Breeds in woodlands across southern Canada and most of the US, south to Mexico. Prefers mature deciduous woods and also conifers in winter. Winters mostly in the US, south through Central America.

Length **15½–17½in (40–45cm)**	Wingspan **28–34in (70–86cm)**	Weight **13–19oz (375–525g)**
Social **Solitary/Pairs**	Lifespan **At least 10 years**	Status **Secure**

DATE: ____________ TIME: ____________ LOCATION: ____________________

Order **Accipitriformes**	Family **Accipitridae**	Species ***Accipiter gentilis***

Northern Goshawk

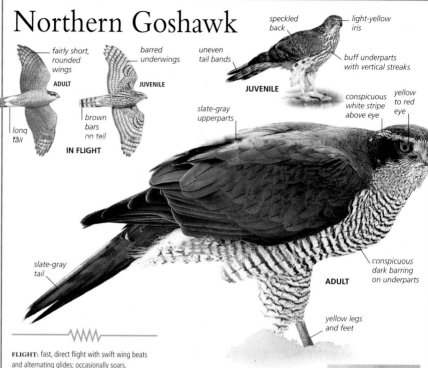

fairly short, rounded wings
ADULT
long tail
barred underwings
JUVENILE
brown bars on tail
IN FLIGHT
speckled back
light-yellow iris
uneven tail bands
buff underparts with vertical streaks
JUVENILE
slate-gray upperparts
conspicuous white stripe above eye
yellow to red eye
slate-gray tail
conspicuous dark barring on underparts
ADULT
yellow legs and feet

FLIGHT: fast, direct flight with swift wing beats and alternating glides; occasionally soars.

The powerful and agile Northern Goshawk is secretive by nature and not easily observed, even in regions where it is common. It has few natural enemies, but will defend its territories, nests, and young fiercely by repeatedly diving and screaming at intruders that get too close. Spring hikers and turkey-hunters occasionally discover Northern Goshawks by wandering into their territory and are driven off by the angry occupants.

VOICE Loud, high-pitched *gek-gek-gek* when agitated.

NESTING Large stick structures lined with bark and plant matter in the mid- to lower region of trees; 1–3 eggs; 1 brood; May–June.

FEEDING Sits and waits on perch before diving rapidly; preys on birds as large as grouse and pheasants; also mammals, including hares and squirrels.

OCCASIONAL SOARER
A juvenile Northern Goshawk takes advantage of a thermal, soaring during migration.

SIMILAR SPECIES
GYRFALCON (GRAY FORM)
see p.225
longer, pointed wings
no streaks on underparts
COOPER'S HAWK
see p.191
brownish upperparts
even tail bands
streaked underparts

OCCURRENCE
Breeds in deep deciduous, coniferous, and mixed woodlands in northern North America, from the tundra–taiga border, south to California, northern Mexico, and Pennsylvania in the eastern US, absent from east-central US. Likes to nest in monoculture forests.

Length **21in (53cm)**	Wingspan **3½ft (1.1m)**	Weight **2–3lb (0.9–1.4kg)**
Social **Solitary/Pairs**	Lifespan **Up to 20 years**	Status **Secure**

DATE: ______________ TIME: ______________ LOCATION: ______________________

Order **Accipitriformes**	Family **Accipitridae**	Species ***Haliaeetus leucocephalus***

Bald Eagle

JUVENILE
ADULT
dark head, jutting out
white head
white tail
brown body
IN FLIGHT
white belly and underwings mottled brown
dark-brown eyes
2ND YEAR
all-white head with yellow eyes
yellow hooked bill
dark brown overall
dark bill starting to turn yellow at base
1ST YEAR
dark eyestripe on whitish face
4TH YEAR
dark chocolate-brown overall
long, wedge-shaped white tail
yellow legs and feet
ADULT

FLIGHT: slow, powerful wing beats; soars and glides on broad, wide wings held at a right angle.

The Bald Eagle, although an opportunist, prefers to scavenge on carrion and steal prey from other birds, including Ospreys. It was nearing extinction due to bounties and reproductive failure caused by DDT. Declared endangered in 1967, its populations have rebounded to high numbers, especially on the coasts. The Bald Eagle was selected, by an act of Congress in 1782, as the national emblem of the US.

VOICE Surprisingly high-pitched voice, 3–4 notes followed by a rapidly descending series.

NESTING Huge stick nest, usually in tallest tree; 1–3 eggs; 1 brood; March–September.

FEEDING Favors carrion, especially fish, also eats birds, mammals, reptiles; steals fish from Osprey.

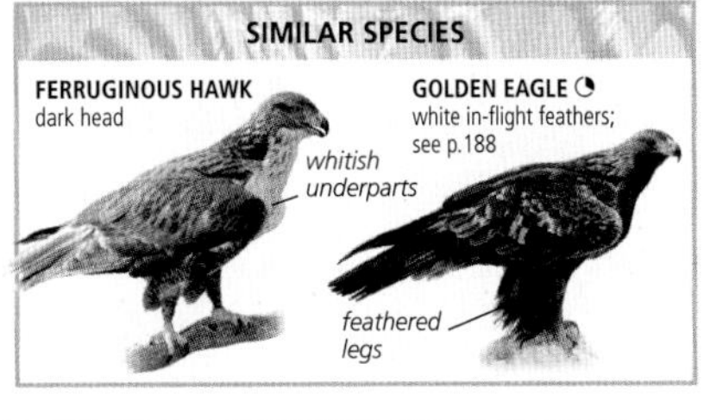

SIMILAR SPECIES
FERRUGINOUS HAWK
dark head
whitish underparts
GOLDEN EAGLE
white in-flight feathers;
see p.188
feathered legs

SUBSTANTIAL ABODE
Bald eagles make the largest stick nest of all raptors; it can weigh up to two tons.

OCCURRENCE
Widespread across Canada and much of the US. Breeds in forested areas near water; also shoreline areas ranging from undeveloped to relatively well-developed with marked human activity; winters along major river systems and in coastal areas and occasionally even in arid regions of the southwest US.

Length **28–38in (71–96cm)**	Wingspan **6½ft (2m)**	Weight **6½–14lb (3–6.5kg)**
Social **Solitary/Pairs**	Lifespan **Up to 28 years**	Status **Secure**

DATE: ____________ TIME: ____________ LOCATION: ____________________

Order **Accipitriformes**	Family **Accipitridae**	Species ***Buteo lineatus***

Red-shouldered Hawk

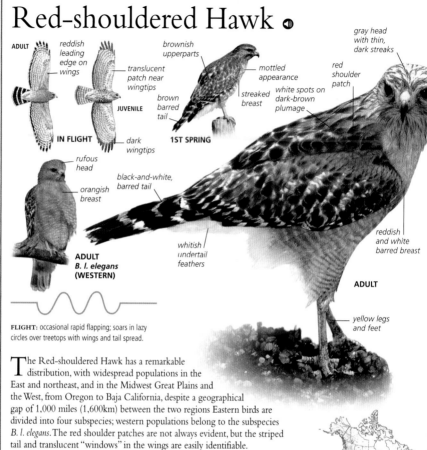

ADULT
reddish leading edge on wings
translucent patch near wingtips
JUVENILE
IN FLIGHT
dark wingtips
brownish upperparts
mottled appearance
streaked breast
brown barred tail
1ST SPRING
gray head with thin, dark streaks
red shoulder patch
white spots on dark-brown plumage
rufous head
orangish breast
black-and-white, barred tail
ADULT
B. l. elegans
(WESTERN)
whitish undertail feathers
reddish and white barred breast
ADULT
yellow legs and feet

FLIGHT: occasional rapid flapping; soars in lazy circles over treetops with wings and tail spread.

The Red-shouldered Hawk has a remarkable distribution, with widespread populations in the East and northeast, and in the Midwest Great Plains and the West, from Oregon to Baja California, despite a geographical gap of 1,000 miles (1,600km) between the two regions Eastern birds are divided into four subspecies; western populations belong to the subspecies *B. l. elegans.* The red shoulder patches are not always evident, but the striped tail and translucent "windows" in the wings are easily identifiable.

VOICE Call a whistled *kee-aah*, accented on first syllable, descending on second.

NESTING Platform of sticks, dried leaves, bark, moss, and lichens in trees not far from water; 3–4 eggs; 1 brood; March–July.

FEEDING Catches mice, chipmunks, and voles; also snakes, toads, frogs, crayfish, and small birds.

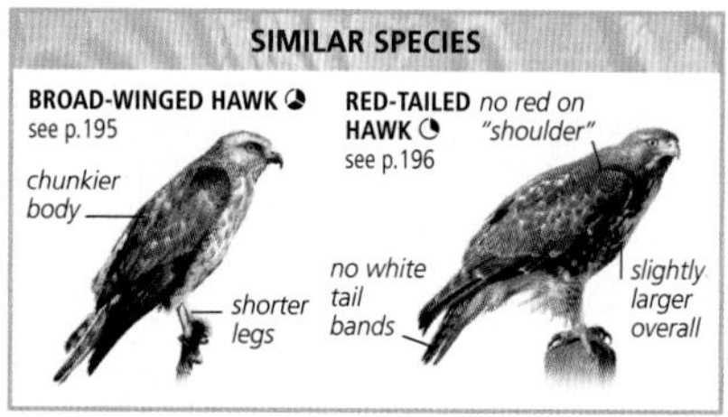
SIMILAR SPECIES
BROAD-WINGED HAWK
see p.195
chunkier body
shorter legs
RED-TAILED HAWK
see p.196
no red on "shoulder"
no white tail bands
slightly larger overall

CHESTNUT WING
When seen from below, the reddish forewing of this adult hawk is clearly visible.

OCCURRENCE
Eastern populations breed in woodlands and forest, deciduous or mixed, whereas those in the West occur in oak woodlands and eucalyptus groves. Lives in mangroves in Florida; found in suburban green spaces. Eastern birds migrate to Mexico.

Length **17–24in (43–61cm)**	Wingspan **3–3½ft (0.9–1.1m)**	Weight **17–27oz (475–775g)**
Social **Solitary/Flocks**	Lifespan **Up to 18 years**	Status **Declining (p)**

DATE: ____________ TIME: ____________ LOCATION: ____________

Order **Accipitriformes**	Family **Accipitridae**	Species ***Buteo platypterus***

Broad-winged Hawk

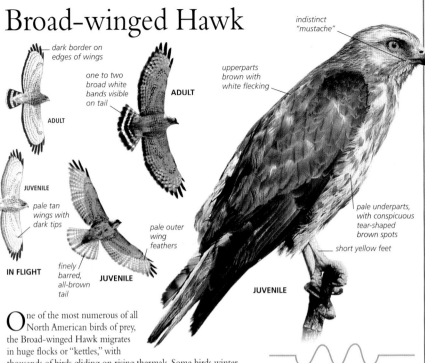

dark border on edges of wings

ADULT

one to two broad white bands visible on tail

ADULT

upperparts brown with white flecking

indistinct "mustache"

JUVENILE

pale tan wings with dark tips

IN FLIGHT

finely barred, all-brown tail

JUVENILE

pale outer wing feathers

pale underparts, with conspicuous tear-shaped brown spots

short yellow feet

JUVENILE

One of the most numerous of all North American birds of prey, the Broad-winged Hawk migrates in huge flocks or "kettles," with thousands of birds gliding on rising thermals. Some birds winter in Florida, but the majority average about 70 miles (110km) a day to log more than 4,000 miles (6,500km) before ending up in Brazil, Bolivia, and even some of the Caribbean islands. Compared to its two cousins, the Red-shouldered and Red-tailed Hawks, the Broad-winged Hawk is slightly smaller, but stockier. Adults are easily identified by a broad white-and-black band on their tails. Broad-winged Hawks have two color forms, the light one being more common than the dark, sooty-brown one.

VOICE High-pitched *peeoweee* call, first note shorter and higher-pitched.

NESTING Platform of fresh twigs or dead sticks, often on old squirrel, hawk, or crow nest in tree; 2–3 eggs; 1 brood; April–August.

FEEDING Eats small mammals, toads, frogs, snakes, grouse chicks, insects, and spiders; crabs in winter.

FLIGHT: circles above forest canopy with wings and tail spread; short flights from branch to branch.

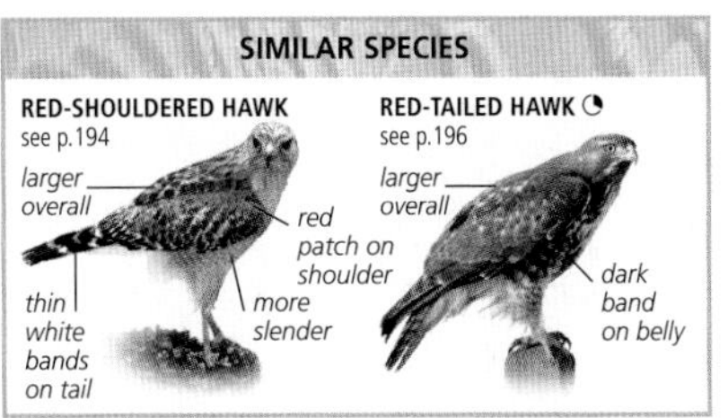
SIMILAR SPECIES
RED-SHOULDERED HAWK
see p.194
larger overall
red patch on shoulder
thin white bands on tail
more slender
RED-TAILED HAWK
see p.196
larger overall
dark band on belly

WATCHING FOR PREY
From an elevated perch, this hawk scans for vertebrate prey, such as rodents.

OCCURRENCE
Breeds across Canada (but not the Rockies) and in the eastern US (not west of the 100th meridian), in forested areas with deciduous, conifers, and mixed trees, with clearings and water nearby. Concentrations of migrants can be seen at bottlenecks, such as the Isthmus of Tehuantepec, Mexico and Panama.

Length **13–17in (33–43cm)**	Wingspan **32–39in (81–100cm)**	Weight **10–19oz (275–550g)**
Social **Flocks**	Lifespan **Up to 14 years**	Status **Secure**

Order **Accipitriformes**	Family **Accipitridae**	Species ***Buteo jamaicensis***

Red-tailed Hawk

pale belly

rufous tail

dark leading edge to wings

ADULT

light-brown tail

pale outer wing feathers

JUVENILE

IN FLIGHT

very dark plumage with white spots

HARLAN'S HAWK

brown overall

streaked belly band

brown tail

JUVENILE

brownish eye

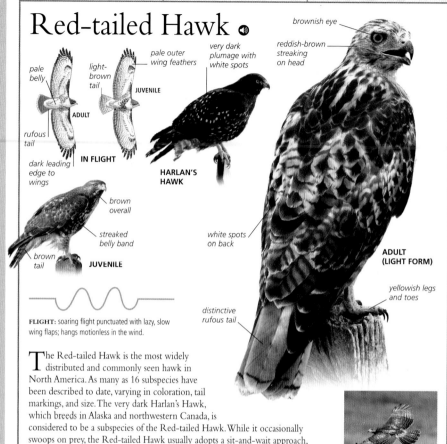

reddish-brown streaking on head

white spots on back

ADULT (LIGHT FORM)

yellowish legs and toes

distinctive rufous tail

FLIGHT: soaring flight punctuated with lazy, slow wing flaps; hangs motionless in the wind.

The Red-tailed Hawk is the most widely distributed and commonly seen hawk in North America. As many as 16 subspecies have been described to date, varying in coloration, tail markings, and size. The very dark Harlan's Hawk, which breeds in Alaska and northwestern Canada, is considered to be a subspecies of the Red-tailed Hawk. While it occasionally swoops on prey, the Red-tailed Hawk usually adopts a sit-and-wait approach, usually from a vantage point like a tree or a hydro or fence pole.

VOICE Call *kee-eee-arrr* that rises then descends over a period of 2–3 seconds.

NESTING Large platform of sticks, twigs on top of tall tree, cliff, building, ledge, or billboard; 2 eggs; 1 brood; February–September.

FEEDING Captures small mammals, such as voles, mice, and rats; birds including pheasant, quail; small reptiles; carrion also eaten.

FLYING HIGH
A Red-tailed Hawk soaring over an open field is a very common sight in North America.

SIMILAR SPECIES

FERRUGINOUS HAWK (LIGHT FORM)
larger bill
larger overall
mostly white underparts

ROUGH-LEGGED HAWK (DARK FORM)
see p.197
dark band on white tail

OCCURRENCE
Breeds and forages in open areas in wide range of habitats and altitudes: scrub desert, grasslands, agricultural fields and pastures, coniferous and deciduous woodlands, and tropical rainforest. Prefers areas with tall perch sites; can be found in suburban woodlots.

Length **18–26in (46–65cm)**	Wingspan **3½–4¼ft (1.1–1.3m)**	Weight **1½–3¼lb (0.7–1.5kg)**
Social **Solitary/Pairs**	Lifespan **Up to 21 years**	Status **Secure**

DATE: ____________ TIME: ____________ LOCATION: ____________

Order **Accipitriformes**	Family **Accipitridae**	Species ***Buteo lagopus***

Rough-legged Hawk

dark wingtips
dark wrist patches
ADULT
dark tail band
IN FLIGHT

bold black patch

FEMALE
black trailing edge
one line before tail tip

pale head

short, broad head
MALE
barred underparts
thin bands near tail tip

JUVENILE
black belly
white tail with faint black band at tip

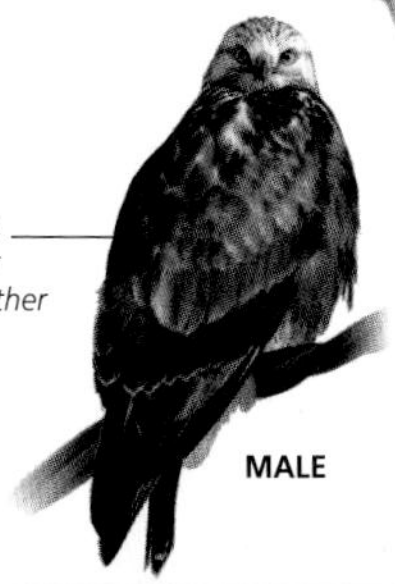

plain gray, brown, or frosty feather edges
MALE

FLIGHT: strong wing beats; usually soars on thermals; frequently hovers in one spot.

The Rough-legged Hawk is known for its extensive variation in plumage—some individuals are almost completely black, whereas others are much paler, very nearly cream or white. The year-to-year fluctuation in numbers of breeding pairs in a given region strongly suggests that this species is nomadic, moving about as a response to the availability of its rodent prey.

VOICE Wintering birds silent; breeding birds utter loud, cat-like mewing or thin whistles, slurred downward when alarmed.

NESTING Bulky mass of sticks, lined with grasses, sedges, feathers and fur from prey, constructed on cliff ledge; 2–6 eggs; 1 brood; April–August.

FEEDING Hovers in one spot over fields in search of prey; lemmings and voles in spring and summer; mice and shrews in winters; variety of birds, ground squirrels, and rabbits year-round.

ABUNDANT FOOD SUPPLY
When small mammals are abundant, these hawks produce large broods on cliff ledges in the tundra.

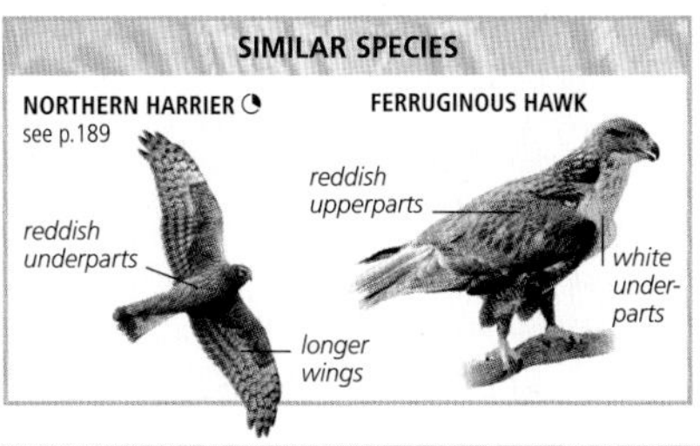
SIMILAR SPECIES
NORTHERN HARRIER
see p.189
reddish underparts
longer wings
FERRUGINOUS HAWK
reddish upperparts
white under-parts

OCCURRENCE
Breeds in rough, open country with low crags and cliffs, in high sub-Arctic and Arctic regions; found on the edge of extensive forest or forest clearings, and in treeless tundra, uplands, and alpine habitats. Winters in open areas with fields, marshes, and rough grasslands.

Length **19–20in (48–51cm)**	Wingspan **4¼–4½ft (1.3–1.4m)**	Weight **1½–3lb (0.7–1.4kg)**
Social **Solitary**	Lifespan **Up to 18 years**	Status **Secure**

DATE: ____________ TIME: ____________ LOCATION: ____________

OWLS

PARTLY BECAUSE OF THEIR nocturnal habits and eerie cries, owls have fascinated humans throughout history. They are placed in the order Strigiformes, and two families are represented in North America: the Barn Owl belongs to the family Tytonidae, while the rest of the owl species belong to the Strigidae. Most owls are active primarily at night and have developed adaptations for living in low-light environments. Their large eyes are sensitive enough to see in the dark and face forward to maximize binocular vision. Since the eyes are fixed in their sockets, a flexible neck helps owls turn the head almost 270° toward a direction of interest.

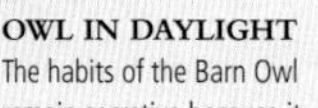

OWL IN DAYLIGHT
The habits of the Barn Owl remain secretive because it is not often seen in daylight.

Ears are offset on each side of the head to help identify the source of a sound. Some species have "ear" tufts, which are used for camouflage and communication, not for hearing. Many owls have serrations on the forward edges of their flight feathers to cushion airflow, so their flight is silent while stalking prey. All North American owls are predatory to some degree, and they inhabit most areas of the continent. The western Burrowing Owl is unique in that it hunts during the day and nests underground.

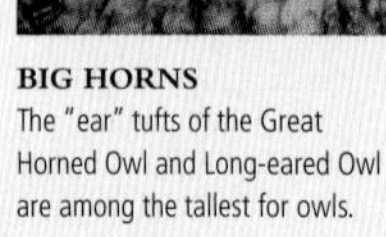

BIG HORNS
The "ear" tufts of the Great Horned Owl and Long-eared Owl are among the tallest for owls.

SNOW SWOOP
The Great Gray Owl can hunt by sound alone, allowing it to locate and capture prey hidden even beneath a thick snow cover.

Order **Strigiformes**	Family **Tytonidae**	Species ***Tyto alba***

Barn Owl

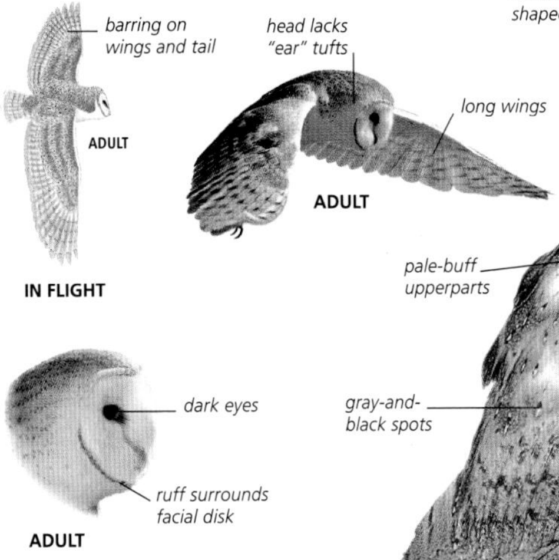

relatively small eyes

rounded, heart-shaped facial disc

barring on wings and tail

head lacks "ear" tufts

long wings

ADULT

ADULT

IN FLIGHT

pale-buff upperparts

white underparts

dark eyes

gray-and-black spots

ruff surrounds facial disk

ADULT

feathered legs

FLIGHT: irregular bursts of flapping, interspersed with short glides, banking, doubling back, fluttering.

Aptly named, the Barn Owl inhabits old sheds, sheltered rafters, and empty buildings in rural fields. With its affinity for human settlement, and 32 subspecies, this owl has an extensive range covering every continent except Antarctica. Although widespread, the Barn Owl is secretive. Primarily nocturnal, it can fly undetected until its screeching call pierces the air. The Barn Owl has expanded its range northward into the southern parts of provinces where winter weather is more mild.

VOICE Typical call loud, raspy, screeching shriek, *shkreee,* often given in flight; also clicking sounds associated with courtship.

NESTING Unlined cavity in tree, cave, building, hay bale, or nest box; 5–7 eggs; 1–2 broods; March–September.

FEEDING Hunts on the wing for small rodents, such as mice; research reveals it can detect the slightest rustle made by prey even in total darkness.

NOCTURNAL HUNTER
The Barn Owl hunts at night for small rodents, but may be seen before sunset feeding its young.

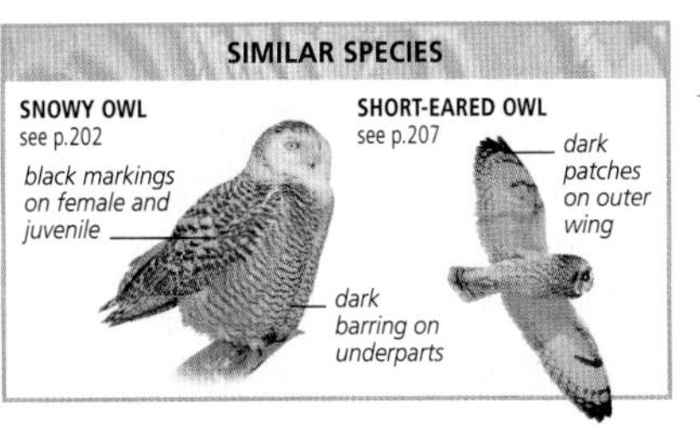
SIMILAR SPECIES
SNOWY OWL
see p.202
black markings on female and juvenile
dark barring on underparts
SHORT-EARED OWL
see p.207
dark patches on outer wing

OCCURRENCE
In North America, breeds from the northwestern and northeastern US south to Mexico. Small Canadian range in southern Ontario and British Columbia. Resident in all except very north of range. Prefers open habitats, such as desert, grassland, and fields, wherever prey and suitable nest sites are available.

Length **12½–15½in (32–40cm)**	Wingspan **3ft 3in (100cm)**	Weight **14–25oz (400–700g)**
Social **Solitary**	Lifespan **Up to 8 years**	Status **Declining**

DATE: ______________ TIME: ______________ LOCATION: ______________________________

Order **Strigiformes**	Family **Strigidae**	Species ***Megascops asio***

Eastern Screech-Owl

dark-gray bars on short, rounded wings
ADULT
streaked underparts
IN FLIGHT
short tail

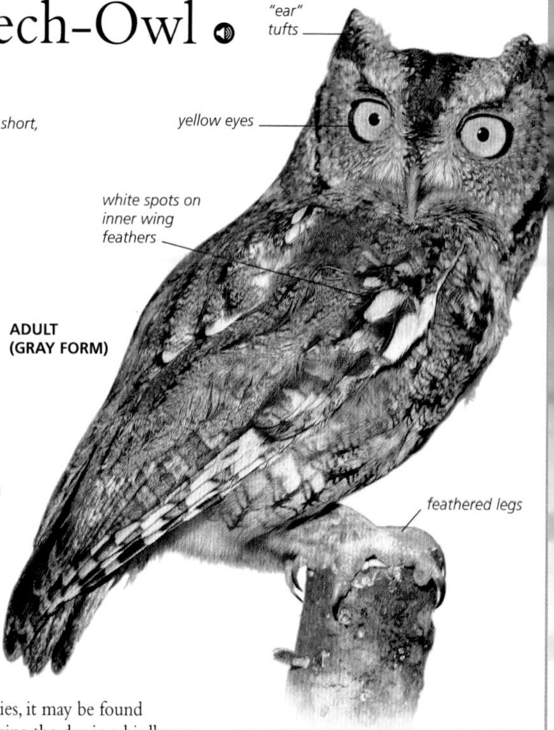

"ear" tufts
yellow eyes
white spots on inner wing feathers
ADULT (GRAY FORM)
feathered legs

FLIGHT: direct, purposeful flight; straight with steady wing beats, typically below tree cover.

This widespread little owl has adapted to suburban areas, and its distinctive call is a familiar sound across the eastern US and southern Canada at almost any time of the year. Although it is an entirely nocturnal species, it may be found roosting in a birdhouse or tree cavity during the day in a birdhouse or tree cavity. With gray and red color morphs, this species shows considerable plumage variation. The relatively high mortality rate of Eastern Screech-Owls, especially juveniles, is caused in part by predation by Great Horned Owls and collisions with motor vehicles.

VOICE Most familiar call a descending whinny—often used in movie soundtracks; also an even trill; occasional barks and screeches; female higher-pitched than male.

NESTING No nest; lays eggs in cavity in tree, woodpecker hole, rotted snag, nest box; 2–6 eggs; 1 brood; March–August.

FEEDING Captures prey with toes; eats insects, earthworms, rodents, songbirds, crayfish, small fish, frogs, snakes, and lizards.

STANDING OUT
The striking red color morph of the Eastern Screech-Owl is less common than the gray.

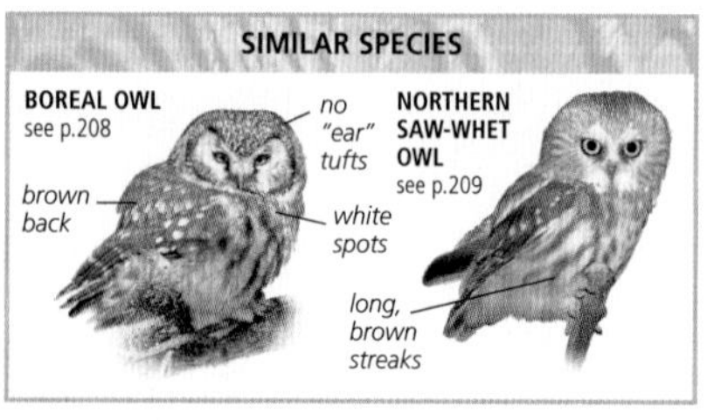
SIMILAR SPECIES
BOREAL OWL
see p.208
no "ear" tufts
brown back
white spots
NORTHERN SAW-WHET OWL
see p.209
long, brown streaks

OCCURRENCE
In the US and southern Canada, breeds in a variety of different lowland wooded areas east of the Rockies. Also breeds south to northeast Mexico. Can be found in suburban and urban parks and gardens; usually avoids mountain forests.

Length **6½–10in (16–25cm)**	Wingspan **19–24in (48–61cm)**	Weight **5–7oz (150–200g)**
Social **Solitary**	Lifespan **Up to 13 years**	Status **Secure**

DATE: ______________ TIME: ______________ LOCATION: ______________

Order **Strigiformes**	Family **Strigidae**	Species ***Bubo virginianus***

Great Horned Owl

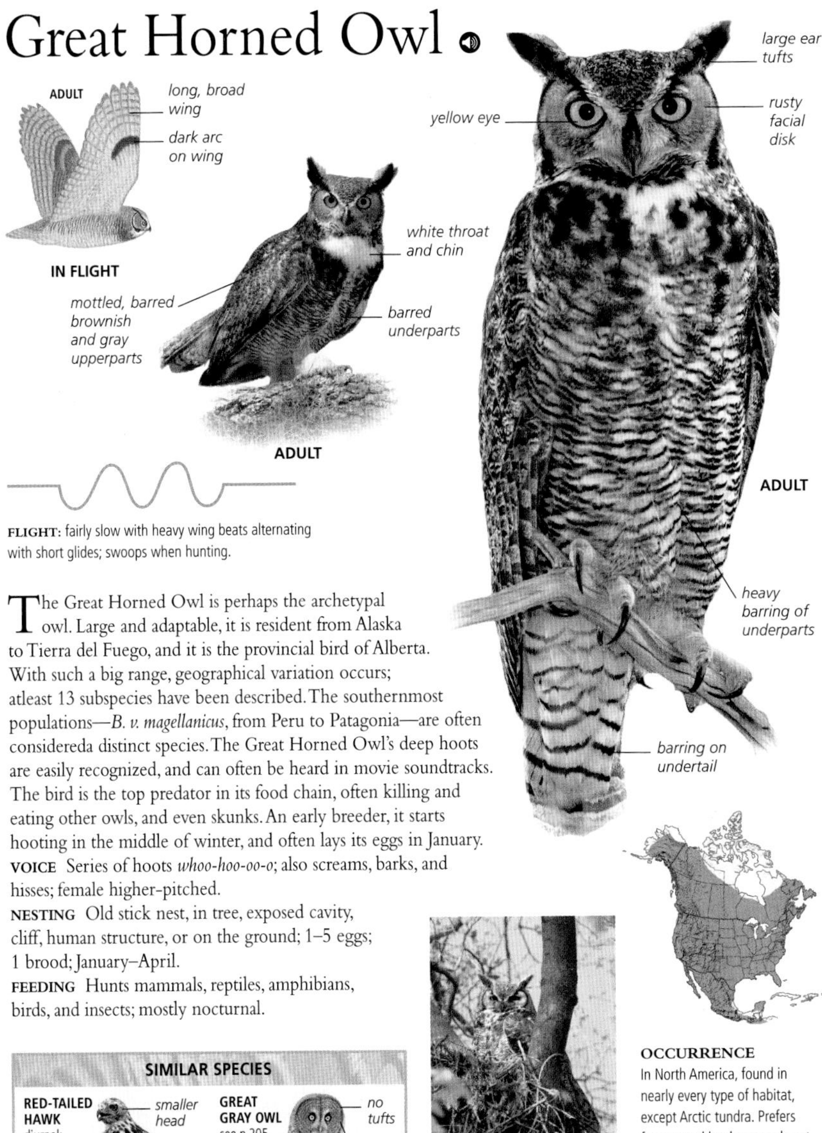
ADULT
long, broad wing
dark arc on wing
IN FLIGHT
mottled, barred brownish and gray upperparts
white throat and chin
barred underparts
ADULT
yellow eye
large ear tufts
rusty facial disk
ADULT
heavy barring of underparts
barring on undertail

FLIGHT: fairly slow with heavy wing beats alternating with short glides; swoops when hunting.

The Great Horned Owl is perhaps the archetypal owl. Large and adaptable, it is resident from Alaska to Tierra del Fuego, and it is the provincial bird of Alberta. With such a big range, geographical variation occurs; atleast 13 subspecies have been described. The southernmost populations—*B. v. magellanicus*, from Peru to Patagonia—are often considereda distinct species. The Great Horned Owl's deep hoots are easily recognized, and can often be heard in movie soundtracks. The bird is the top predator in its food chain, often killing and eating other owls, and even skunks. An early breeder, it starts hooting in the middle of winter, and often lays its eggs in January.

VOICE Series of hoots *whoo-hoo-oo-o*; also screams, barks, and hisses; female higher-pitched.

NESTING Old stick nest, in tree, exposed cavity, cliff, human structure, or on the ground; 1–5 eggs; 1 brood; January–April.

FEEDING Hunts mammals, reptiles, amphibians, birds, and insects; mostly nocturnal.

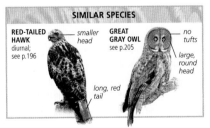

SIMILAR SPECIES

RED-TAILED HAWK diurnal; see p.196
smaller head
long, red tail

GREAT GRAY OWL see p.205
no tufts
large, round head

RECYCLING
The Great Horned Owl breeds in old stick nests constructed by other large birds like crows.

OCCURRENCE
In North America, found in nearly every type of habitat, except Arctic tundra. Prefers fragmented landscapes: desert, swamp, prairie, woodland, and urban areas. Rare only in the Appalachian Mountains in the East and in the Sonoran and Mojave Deserts in the West.

Length **18–25in (46–63cm)**	Wingspan **3–5ft (0.9–1.6m)**	Weight **1⅞–5½lb (0.9–2.5kg)**
Social **Solitary**	Lifespan **Up to 28 years**	Status **Secure**

DATE: ____________ TIME: ____________ LOCATION: ____________

Order **Strigiformes**	Family **Strigidae**	Species ***Bubo scandiacus***

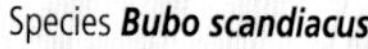

Snowy Owl

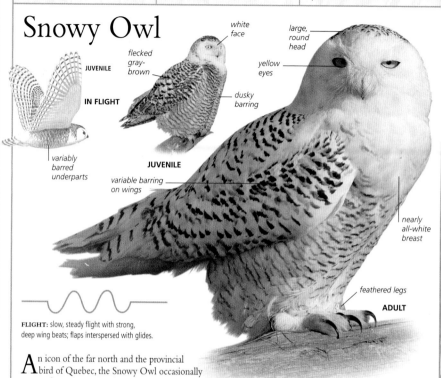

white face
large, round head
flecked gray-brown
yellow eyes
JUVENILE
IN FLIGHT
dusky barring
variably barred underparts
JUVENILE
variable barring on wings
nearly all-white breast
feathered legs
ADULT

FLIGHT: slow, steady flight with strong, deep wing beats; flaps interspersed with glides.

An icon of the far north and the provincial bird of Quebec, the Snowy Owl occasionally appears far to the south of its usual range, making an eye-catching addition to the local landscape. This is a bird of the open tundra, where it hunts from headlands or hummocks and nests on the ground. In such a harsh environment, the Snowy Owl largely depends on lemmings for prey. It is fiercely territorial, and will valiantly defend its young in the nest even against larger animals, such as the Arctic Fox.

VOICE Deep hoots, doubled or given in a short series, usually by male; also rattles, whistles, and hisses.

NESTING Scrape on a mound in short vegetation or dirt, with no lining; 3–12 eggs; 1 brood; May–September.

FEEDING Mostly hunts lemmings, but takes whatever other small mammals, birds, and occasionally fish, it can find.

SNOWY MALE
Some adult males display no barring at all and have entirely pure white plumage.

SIMILAR SPECIES
BARN OWL
see p.199
black eyes
golden brown
SHORT-EARED OWL
see p.207
mottled-brown markings
larger overall

OCCURRENCE
Breeds in the tundra of Eurasia and northern North America, north to Ellesmere Island; North American birds winter south to the Great Plains. In some years, many North American birds winter south of their normal range, including in dunes, marshes, and airfields, as far south as Florida and California.

Length **20–27in (51–68cm)**	Wingspan **4¼–5¼ft (1.3–1.6m)**	Weight **3½–6½lb (1.6–2.9kg)**
Social **Solitary**	Lifespan **Up to 9 years**	Status **Vulnerable**

 DATE: ____________ TIME: ____________ LOCATION: ____________

Order **Strigiformes**	Family **Strigidae**	Species ***Surnia ulula***

Northern Hawk Owl

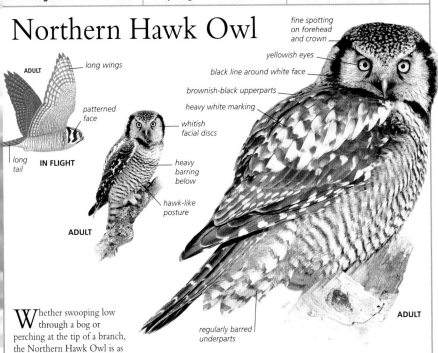

fine spotting on forehead and crown
yellowish eyes
black line around white face
brownish-black upperparts
heavy white marking
regularly barred underparts
ADULT

ADULT *long wings*
patterned face
long tail **IN FLIGHT**

whitish facial discs
heavy barring below
hawk-like posture
ADULT

Whether swooping low through a bog or perching at the tip of a branch, the Northern Hawk Owl is as falcon-like as it is owl-like, being streamlined, a powerful flier, and an active daytime hunter. It is patchily distributed across the northern North American forests far from most human settlements, so is seldom seen—and is not well studied—on its breeding grounds. In winter, though, the bird is somewhat nomadic, and is occasionally seen south of its breeding range for a few days or weeks in southern Canada and the northern US.

VOICE Ascending, whistled, drawn-out trill; also chirps, screeches, and yelps.

NESTING Cavities, hollows, broken-off branches, old stick nests, nest boxes; 3–13 eggs; 1 brood; April–August.

FEEDING Swoops like a falcon from an elevated perch to pounce on prey; preys mainly on rodents in summer, and on grouse and ptarmigan in winter.

FLIGHT: powerful, deep wing beats; glides; highly maneuverable, occasionally soars.

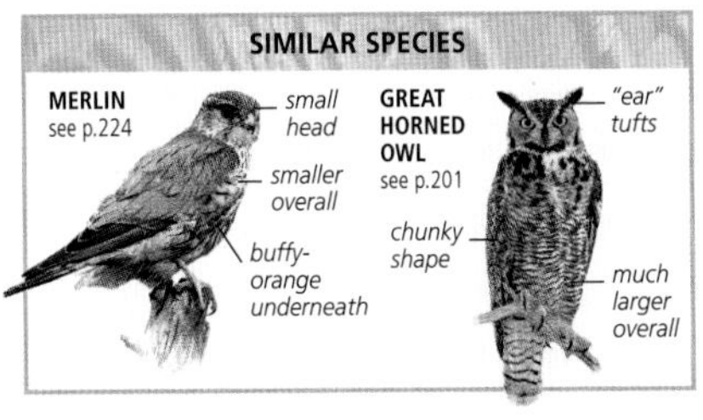
SIMILAR SPECIES
MERLIN
see p.224
small head
smaller overall
buffy-orange underneath
GREAT HORNED OWL
see p.201
"ear" tufts
chunky shape
much larger overall

KEEN-EYED OWL
The Northern Owl hunts mainly by sight, swooping on prey spotted from a high perch.

OCCURRENCE
Breeds across the forests of northern Canada, from Alaska to Quebec and Newfoundland, in sparse woodland or mixed conifer forest with swamps, bogs, burned areas, or storm damage. In winter, occasionally moves south to southern Canada, Great Lakes region, and New England.

Length **14–17½in (36–44cm)**	Wingspan **31in (80cm)**	Weight **11–12oz (300–350g)**
Social **Family groups**	Lifespan **Up to 10 years**	Status **Secure**

DATE: ____________ TIME: ____________ LOCATION: ____________________

Order **Strigiformes**	Family **Strigidae**	Species ***Strix varia***

Barred Owl

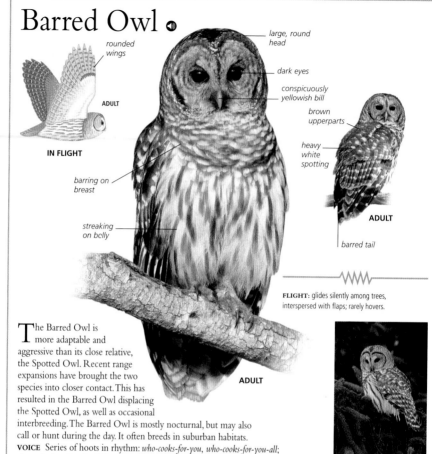

rounded wings

ADULT

IN FLIGHT

large, round head

dark eyes

conspicuously yellowish bill

brown upperparts

heavy white spotting

ADULT

barred tail

barring on breast

streaking on belly

ADULT

FLIGHT: glides silently among trees, interspersed with flaps; rarely hovers.

The Barred Owl is more adaptable and aggressive than its close relative, the Spotted Owl. Recent range expansions have brought the two species into closer contact. This has resulted in the Barred Owl displacing the Spotted Owl, as well as occasional interbreeding. The Barred Owl is mostly nocturnal, but may also call or hunt during the day. It often breeds in suburban habitats.

VOICE Series of hoots in rhythm: *who-cooks-for-you, who-cooks-for-you-all*; also pair duetting (at different pitches), cawing, cackling, and guttural sounds.

NESTING No nest; lays eggs in broken-off branches, cavities, old stick nests; 1–5 eggs; 1 brood; January–September.

FEEDING Perches quietly and waits to spot prey below, then pounces; eats small mammals, birds, amphibians, reptiles, insects, and spiders.

WOODED HABITATS
The Barred Owl is very much at home in deep woodlands, including coniferous forests.

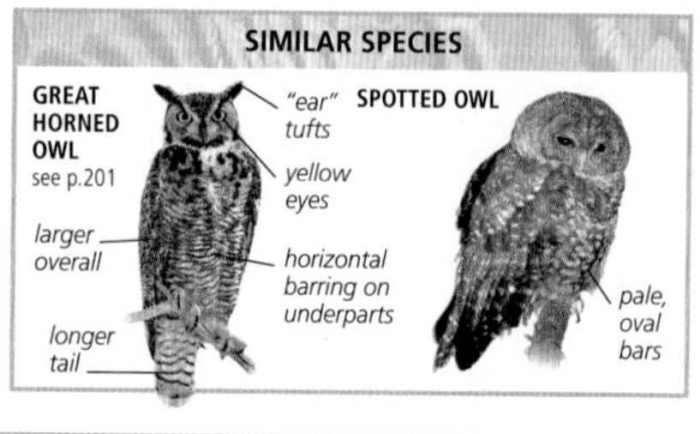
SIMILAR SPECIES
GREAT HORNED OWL
see p.201
"ear" tufts
yellow eyes
larger overall
horizontal barring on underparts
longer tail
SPOTTED OWL
pale, oval bars

OCCURRENCE
Widespread, though not evenly so, across North America from British Columbia across to the Maritimes and much of the eastern US. Found in a variety of wooded habitats—from cypress swamps in the south to conifer rainforest in the northwest—and in mixed hardwoods.

Length **17–19½in (43–50cm)**	Wingspan **3½ft (1.1m)**	Weight **17–37oz (475–1,050g)**
Social **Solitary**	Lifespan **Up to 18 years**	Status **Secure**

DATE: ______ TIME: ______ LOCATION: ______

Order **Strigiformes**	Family **Strigidae**	Species ***Strix nebulosa***

Great Gray Owl

long wings
round facial pattern
long tail
ADULT

long wings
ADULT
IN FLIGHT

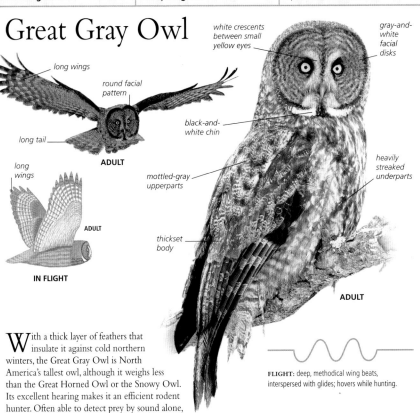

white crescents between small yellow eyes
gray-and-white facial disks
black-and-white chin
mottled-gray upperparts
heavily streaked underparts
thickset body
ADULT

With a thick layer of feathers that insulate it against cold northern winters, the Great Gray Owl is North America's tallest owl, although it weighs less than the Great Horned Owl or the Snowy Owl. Its excellent hearing makes it an efficient rodent hunter. Often able to detect prey by sound alone, it will even plunge through deep snow, or into a burrow, to snatch unseen prey. This bird is primarily nocturnal, but may also hunt by daylight, usually at dawn or dusk. The Great Gray Owl is the provincial bird of Manitoba.

VOICE Slow series of deep hoots, evenly spaced; also variety of hisses and chattering noises around nest site.

NESTING Reuses old eagle or hawk nests, broken-off trees; 2–5 eggs; 1 brood; March–July.

FEEDING Eats rodents and other small mammals; waits to pounce from perch or hunts in flight.

FLIGHT: deep, methodical wing beats, interspersed with glides; hovers while hunting.

SIMILAR SPECIES

GREAT HORNED OWL
see p.201
"ear" tufts
barring on belly
BARRED OWL
see p.204
dark eyes
barring on breast

MAKESHIFT NEST
The Great Gray Owl often utilizes hollow snags as nesting sites, besides reusing deserted nests.

OCCURRENCE
In North America, resident across northern forests from Alaska to Quebec, south to Montana and Wyoming. Also resident in Eurasia from Scandinavia to the Russian Far East. Found in taiga, and muskeg, and in fir, spruce, and pine forests.

Length **24–33in (61–84cm)**	Wingspan **4½ft (1.4m)**	Weight **1½–3¾lb (0.7–1.7kg)**
Social **Solitary**	Lifespan **Up to 14 years**	Status **Secure**

DATE: ____________ TIME: ____________ LOCATION: ____________

Order **Strigiformes**	Family **Strigidae**	Species ***Asio otus***

Long-eared Owl

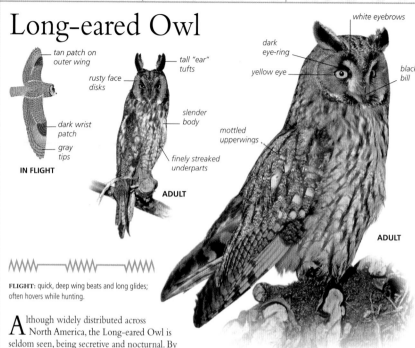

tan patch on outer wing
dark wrist patch
gray tips
IN FLIGHT

tall "ear" tufts
rusty face disks
slender body
finely streaked underparts
ADULT

white eyebrows
dark eye-ring
yellow eye
black bill
mottled upperwings
ADULT

FLIGHT: quick, deep wing beats and long glides; often hovers while hunting.

Although widely distributed across North America, the Long-eared Owl is seldom seen, being secretive and nocturnal. By day, it roosts high up and out of sight in thick cover. Only at nightfall does it fly out to hunt on the wing over open areas, patrolling for small mammals. Its wing feathers, like those of many other owls, have sound-suppressing structures that allow it to fly almost silently, so it can hear the slightest rustle on the ground below.

VOICE Evenly spaced *hooo* notes, continuously repeated, about 3 seconds apart, typically 10–50 per series, sometimes more; barks when alarmed.

NESTING Old stick nests of ravens, crows, magpies, and hawks; 2–7 eggs; 1 brood; March–July.

FEEDING Preys mainly on mice and other small rodents, occasionally small birds.

OWL ON THE WING
In flight, this bird's "ear" tufts are flattened back and not visible, but the face and underwing markings are clearly revealed.

SIMILAR SPECIES

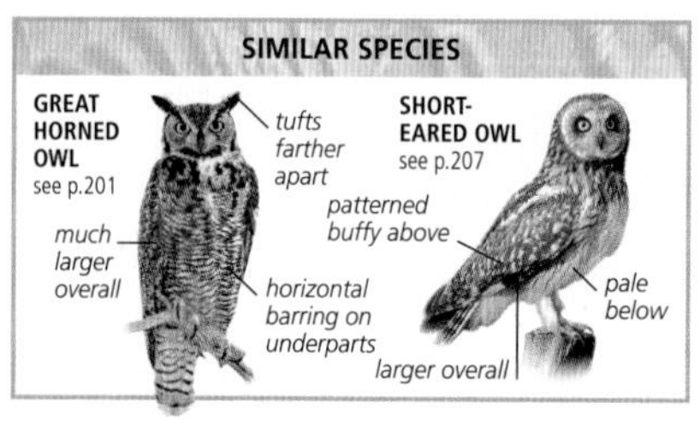
GREAT HORNED OWL
see p.201
tufts farther apart
much larger overall
horizontal barring on underparts
SHORT-EARED OWL
see p.207
patterned buffy above
pale below
larger overall

OCCURRENCE
Breeds in old nests, especially in dense stands of cottonwood, willow, juniper, and conifers by open areas suitable for hunting. Occasionally uses old nests in tree holes, cliffs, or on ground in dense vegetation; in winter, up to 100 birds in roosts. Northern birds move south for winter; some western birds resident.

Length **14–15½in (35–40cm)**	Wingspan **34–39in (86–98cm)**	Weight **8–15oz (225–425g)**
Social **Solitary/Winter flocks**	Lifespan **Up to 27 years**	Status **Secure**

DATE: ____________ TIME: ____________ LOCATION: ____________

Order **Strigiformes**	Family **Strigidae**	Species ***Asio flammeus***

Short-eared Owl

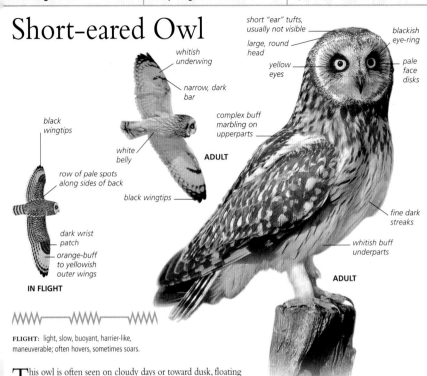

short "ear" tufts, usually not visible
blackish eye-ring
large, round head
yellow eyes
pale face disks
whitish underwing
narrow, dark bar
complex buff marbling on upperparts
black wingtips
white belly
ADULT
row of pale spots along sides of back
black wingtips
fine dark streaks
dark wrist patch
whitish buff underparts
orange-buff to yellowish outer wings
ADULT
IN FLIGHT

FLIGHT: light, slow, buoyant, harrier-like, maneuverable; often hovers, sometimes soars.

This owl is often seen on cloudy days or toward dusk, floating above and patrolling low back and forth over open fields, looking and listening for prey, sometimes with Northern Harriers. Although territorial in the breeding season, it sometimes winters in communal roosts of up to 200 birds, occasionally alongside Long-eared Owls. About 10 subspecies are widely distributed across five continents and numerous island groups, including the Greater Antilles, the Galápagos, the Falklands, and Hawaii. Unlike other North American owls, the Short-eared Owl builds its own nest on the ground.

VOICE Usually silent; male courtship call a rapid *hoo hoo hoo*, often given during display flights; about 16 notes in 3 seconds; also barking, *chee-oww*.

NESTING Scrape lined with grass and feathers on ground; 4–7 eggs; 1–2 broods; March–June.

FEEDING Eats small mammals and some birds.

LOOKOUT POST
Perched on a branch, a Short-eared Owl keeps a wary eye on any intruder on its territory.

SIMILAR SPECIES

NORTHERN HARRIER see p.189

gray upperparts
whitish underparts
long tail

LONG-EARED OWL see p.206

"ear" tufts
rusty face disks

OCCURRENCE
Breeds in open areas, including prairie, grasslands, tundra, fields, and marshes, across northern North America, from Alaska, the Yukon, and British Columbia to Quebec, and Newfoundland, south to the western and central prairies, and east to New England. Northern populations move south in the winter.

Length **13½–16in (34–41cm)**	Wingspan **2¾–3½ft (0.9–1.1m)**	Weight **11–13oz (325–375g)**
Social **Solitary/Winter flocks**	Lifespan **Up to 13 years**	Status **Vulnerable**

DATE: ____________ TIME: ____________ LOCATION: ____________________

Order **Strigiformes**	Family **Strigidae**	Species ***Aegolius funereus***

Boreal Owl

ADULT
rounded wings
IN FLIGHT
white-and-brown streaked underparts
finely spotted crown
black border around face
ADULT
usually flat-topped head, with fine white spots
yellow eyes
pale bill
short tail
ADULT

FLIGHT: quick, strong wing beats; adept at maneuvering; glides down to attack prey.

The female Boreal Owl is much bigger than the male. Males will mate with two or three females in years when voles and other small rodents are abundant. The Boreal Owl roosts on an inconspicuous perch by day and hunts at night, detecting its prey by sound. In the US and Canada, it is elusive and rarely seen since it breeds at high elevations in isolated western mountain ranges. White spotting on the crown, a grayish bill, and a black facial disk distinguish the Boreal Owl from the Northern Saw-whet Owl.

VOICE Prolonged series of whistles, usually increasing in volume and intensity toward the end; also screeches and hisses; can be heard from afar.

NESTING Natural and woodpecker-built tree cavities, also nest boxes; 3–6 eggs; 1 brood; March–July.

FEEDING Mainly eats small mammals, occasionally birds and insects; pounces from elevated perch; sometimes stores prey.

WARM-UP ROUTINE
Boreal Owls are known to use body warmth to thaw frozen prey.

SIMILAR SPECIES

NORTHERN PYGMY-OWL
black streaks on belly
longer tail

NORTHERN SAW-WHET OWL
see p.209
lacks dark frame to facial disk
dark bill

OCCURRENCE
Breeds in northern forests from Alaska to Newfoundland and Quebec, south into the Rockies to Colorado and New Mexico. Largely sedentary, but irregular movements take place south of the breeding range, southward to New England and New York.

Length **8½–11in (21–28cm)**	Wingspan **21½–24in (54–62cm)**	Weight **3⅜–8oz (90–225g)**
Social **Solitary**	Lifespan **Up to 11 years**	Status **Secure**

DATE: ____________ TIME: ____________ LOCATION: ____________

Order **Strigiformes**	Family **Strigidae**	Species ***Aegolius acadicus***

Northern Saw-whet Owl

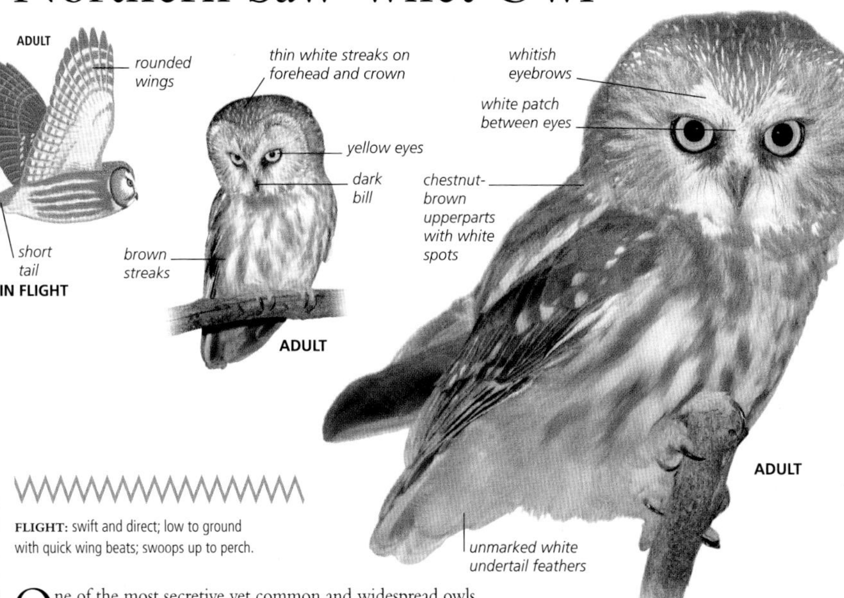
ADULT
rounded wings
short tail
IN FLIGHT
thin white streaks on forehead and crown
yellow eyes
dark bill
brown streaks
ADULT
whitish eyebrows
white patch between eyes
chestnut-brown upperparts with white spots
unmarked white undertail feathers
ADULT

FLIGHT: swift and direct; low to ground with quick wing beats; swoops up to perch.

One of the most secretive yet common and widespread owls in North America, the Northern Saw-whet Owl is much more often heard than seen. Strictly nocturnal, it is concealed as it sleeps by day in thick vegetation, usually in conifers. Although the same site may be used for months if it remains undisturbed, it is never an easy bird to locate. Like most owls, it is elusive, even though it sometimes roosts in large garden trees. When it is discovered, the Northern Saw-whet Owl "freezes," and relies on its camouflage rather than flying off. At night it watches intently from a perch, before swooping down to snatch its prey.

VOICE Long series of rapid whistling notes on a constant pitch similar to the sharpening or "whetting" of a saw.

NESTING Unlined cavity in tree, usually old woodpecker hole or nest box; 4–7 eggs; 1 brood; March–July.

FEEDING Hunts from elevated perch; eats small mammals, including mice and voles; also eats insects and small birds.

TRACKED MOVEMENTS
Scientists frequently use nets to live-trap these owls to affix leg bands to track movements.

SIMILAR SPECIES

ELF OWL
gray back
darker face
smaller overall
BOREAL OWL
see p.208
spotted crown
black facial border

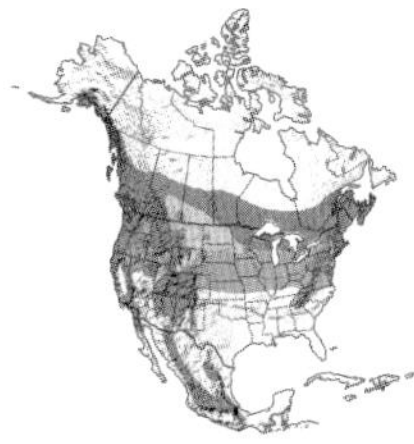

OCCURRENCE
Breeds from Alaska and British Columbia to Maritimes; in the West, south to Mexico; in the East, south to Appalachians; coniferous and mixed deciduous forests, swampy forests, wooded wetlands, bogs. Winters in south to central states, in open woodlands, pine plantations, shrubby areas.

Length **7–8½in (18–21cm)**	Wingspan **16½–19in (42–48cm)**	Weight **3½oz (100g)**
Social **Solitary**	Lifespan **Up to 10 years**	Status **Secure**

DATE: ______________ TIME: ______________ LOCATION: ______________

Family **Alcedinidae**

KINGFISHERS

KINGFISHERS ARE PRIMARILY a tropical family that apparently originated in the Australasian region. There are approximately 90 species of kingfishers in the world, and most have large heads with long, pointed bills, short legs, stubby tails, and bright plumage. Three species are found in North America, but only one, the Belted Kingfisher, is widespread and found in Canada. Like most species of kingfishers, Belted Kingfishers are large-headed and large-billed but have comparatively short legs and toes. Although lacking the array of bright blues, greens, and reds associated with their tropical and European counterparts, Belted Kingfishers are striking birds, distinguished by shaggy head crests, breastbands, and white underparts. The females of the species are more brightly colored than the males, sporting chestnut-colored belly bands. While they also eat amphibians, reptiles, insects, and crustaceans, Belted Kingfishers are primarily fish-eaters. They will frequent a favorite perch along a waterway for hunting, or hover if no perch is available, and plunge headfirst into the water to catch their prey. After catching a fish, they routinely stun their prey by beating it against a perch before turning the fish around so that it can be eaten head first. Mating pairs dig a burrow in a bank about 3–6ft (1–2m) long. The female lays 6–7 eggs; both adults share the task of incubating the eggs and feeding the young. Parents entice the young to leave the burrow by perching outside with a fish in their bill and calling to them. It usually takes a week for the fledglings to be able to capture live fish. Migration depends on the availability of open water—kingfishers will stay in an area year-round if they have access to fishing grounds.

FISH DINNER
A female Belted Kingfisher, distinguished by her rust-colored belly band, uses its large bill to catch and hold slippery prey.

DULL MALE
Unlike many birds, the male Belted Kingfisher is not as colorful as the female.

Order **Coraciiformes**	Family **Alcedinidae**	Species ***Megaceryle alcyon***

Belted Kingfisher

MALE
large head
single blue breastband
barred tail
IN FLIGHT
bluish-gray head with shaggy crest
long, thick, powerful bill
white collar
bluish-slate upperparts
white belly
MALE
prominent crest
chestnut band across belly
chestnut flanks
FEMALE
double crest
white collar
single dark breastband
JUVENILE MALE

FLIGHT: strongly flaps its wings and then glides after two or three beats; frequently hovers.

Its stocky body, double-pointed crest, large head, and contrasting white collar distinguish the Belted Kingfisher from other species in its range. This kingfisher's loud and far-carrying, angry rattles are heard more often than the bird is seen. Interestingly, it is one of the few birds in North America in which the female is more colorful than the male. The Belted Kingfisher can be found in a large variety of aquatic habitats, both coastal and inland, vigorously defending its territory, all year round.

VOICE Harsh mechanical rattle given in flight or from a perch; sometimes emits screams or trill-like warble during breeding.

NESTING Unlined chamber in subterranean burrow 3–6ft (1–2m) deep, excavated in earthen bank usually over water, but sometimes in ditches, sand, or gravel pits; 6–7 eggs; 1 brood; March–July.

FEEDING Plunge-dives from branches or wires to catch a wide variety of fish near the surface, including sticklebacks and trout; also takes crustaceans, such as crayfish.

SIMILAR SPECIES

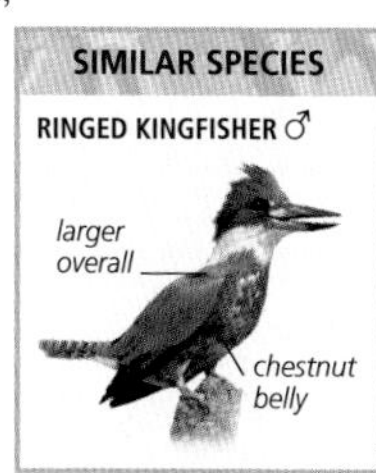

SIMILAR SPECIES
RINGED KINGFISHER ♂
larger overall
chestnut belly

CATCH OF THE DAY
The female's chestnut belly band and flanks are clearly visible here as she perches with her catch.

OCCURRENCE
Breeds and winters around clear, open waters of streams, rivers, lakes, estuaries, and protected marine shorelines, where perches are available and prey is visible. Avoids water with emergent vegetation. Northern populations migrate south to Mexico, Central America, and the West Indies.

Length **11–14in (28–35cm)**	Wingspan **19–23in (48–58cm)**	Weight **5–6oz (150–175g)**
Social **Solitary**	Lifespan **At least 4 years**	Status **Secure**

DATE: ____________ TIME: ____________ LOCATION: ____________

Family **Picidae**

WOODPECKERS

Woodpeckers are found throughout North America except in the tundra. They are adapted to gripping upright tree trunks, using the tail as a support or prop. Most woodpeckers have two toes facing forward and two facing backward for an extra-strong grip on wooden surfaces. Unlike nuthatches, they do not perch upside-down but can cling to the underside of angled branches. They have striking plumage patterns with simple, bold colors. Many proclaim their territory by instrumental rather than vocal means, hammering the bill against a hard surface—even metal—to give a brief but rapid "drumroll." The bill is also used for chipping into bark and excavating deep nestholes in solid wood. Sapsuckers make rows or rings of small holes on tree trunks, allowing sap to ooze freely: they feed on the sap and also on the insects that are attracted to it. Some species of woodpeckers, especially flickers, feed on the ground, probing inside ant nests for larvae and catching them with their long, sticky tongues.

BALANCING ACT
The Yellow-bellied Sapsucker rests its stiff tail against a tree to maintain its balance.

RED ALERT
With its crimson head, the Red-headed Woodpecker is an instantly recognizable bird in North America.

COMMON BIRD
The Northern Flicker can be found across the entire North American continent.

Order **Piciformes**	Family **Picidae**	Species ***Melanerpes erythrocephalus***

Red-headed Woodpecker

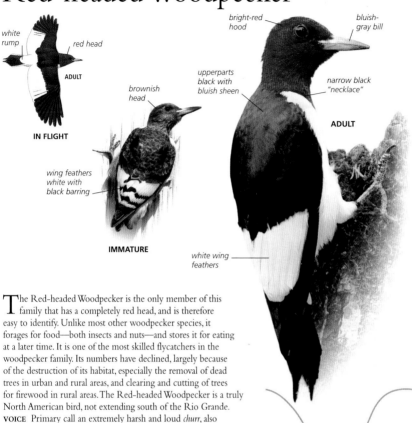

white rump
red head
ADULT
IN FLIGHT

brownish head
wing feathers white with black barring
IMMATURE

bright-red hood
bluish-gray bill
upperparts black with bluish sheen
narrow black "necklace"
ADULT
white wing feathers

The Red-headed Woodpecker is the only member of this family that has a completely red head, and is therefore easy to identify. Unlike most other woodpecker species, it forages for food—both insects and nuts—and stores it for eating at a later time. It is one of the most skilled flycatchers in the woodpecker family. Its numbers have declined, largely because of the destruction of its habitat, especially the removal of dead trees in urban and rural areas, and clearing and cutting of trees for firewood in rural areas. The Red-headed Woodpecker is a truly North American bird, not extending south of the Rio Grande.

VOICE Primary call an extremely harsh and loud *churr*, also produces breeding call and alarm; no song; active drummer.

NESTING Excavates cavity in dead wood; 3–5 eggs; 1–2 broods; May–August.

FEEDING Forages in flight, on ground, and in trees; feeds on a variety of insects, spiders, nuts, seeds, berries, and fruit; in rare cases, small mammals, such as mice.

WORK IN PROGRESS
The Red-headed Woodpecker excavates its breeding cavities in tree trunks and stumps.

FLIGHT: strong flapping; undulation not as marked as in other woodpecker species.

OCCURRENCE
Breeds in a variety of habitats, especially open deciduous woodlands, including riverine areas, orchards, municipal parks, agricultural areas, forest edges, and forests affected by fire. Uses the same habitats during the winter as in the breeding season.

Length **8½–9½in (22–24cm)**	Wingspan **16–18in (41–46cm)**	Weight **2–3oz (55–85g)**
Social **Solitary**	Lifespan **At least 10 years**	Status **Endangered**

Order **Piciformes** | Family **Picidae** | Species ***Melanerpes carolinus***

Red-bellied Woodpecker

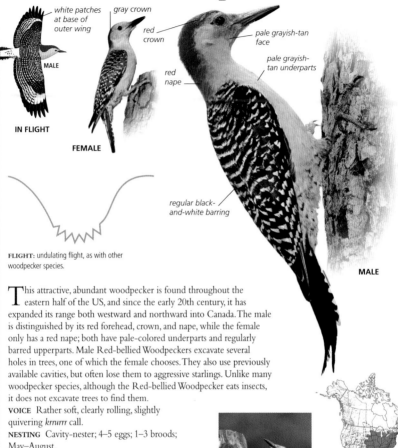

white patches at base of outer wing

MALE

IN FLIGHT

gray crown

FEMALE

red crown

pale grayish-tan face

pale grayish-tan underparts

red nape

regular black-and-white barring

MALE

FLIGHT: undulating flight, as with other woodpecker species.

This attractive, abundant woodpecker is found throughout the eastern half of the US, and since the early 20th century, it has expanded its range both westward and northward into Canada. The male is distinguished by its red forehead, crown, and nape, while the female only has a red nape; both have pale-colored underparts and regularly barred upperparts. Male Red-bellied Woodpeckers excavate several holes in trees, one of which the female chooses. They also use previously available cavities, but often lose them to aggressive starlings. Unlike many woodpecker species, although the Red-bellied Woodpecker eats insects, it does not excavate trees to find them.

VOICE Rather soft, clearly rolling, slightly quivering *krrurrr* call.

NESTING Cavity-nester; 4–5 eggs; 1–3 broods; May–August.

FEEDING Eats insects, fruit, seeds, acorns, and other nuts; in winter, eats mainly vegetable matter.

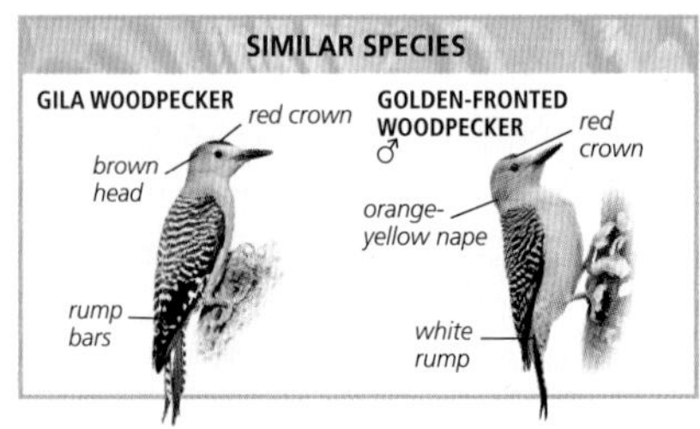
SIMILAR SPECIES
GILA WOODPECKER
red crown
brown head
rump bars
GOLDEN-FRONTED WOODPECKER ♂
red crown
orange-yellow nape
white rump

SUBURBAN SPECIES These birds can be seen and heard on tree trunks in suburban and urban woods.

OCCURRENCE
Resident in southeastern Canada and the eastern and southeastern US, where it breeds in a wide range of habitats; found in forests, swamps, suburban wooded areas, open woodlands, and parks. Winter habitats resemble the breeding areas.

Length **9–10½in (23–27cm)**	Wingspan **16in (41cm)**	Weight **2½oz (70g)**
Social **Solitary/Pairs**	Lifespan **Up to 12 years**	Status **Secure**

DATE: __________ TIME: __________ LOCATION: __________

Order **Piciformes**	Family **Picidae**	Species ***Sphyrapicus varius***

Yellow-bellied Sapsucker

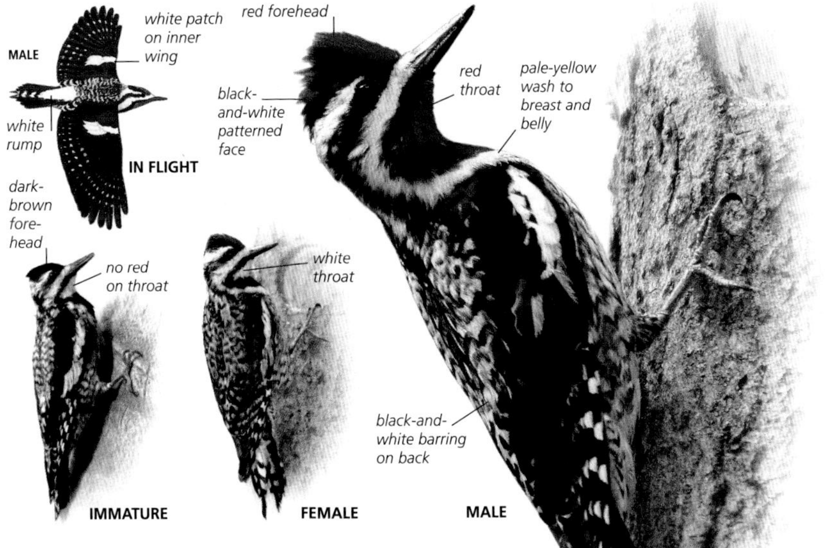

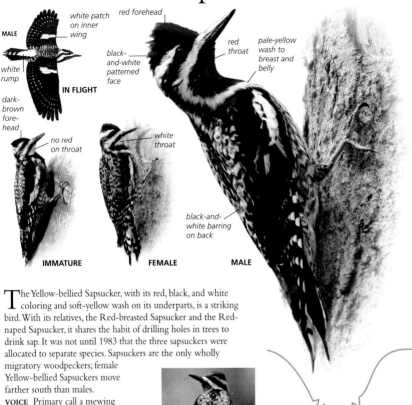

MALE
white patch on inner wing
white rump
IN FLIGHT
dark-brown forehead
no red on throat
IMMATURE
white throat
FEMALE
red forehead
black-and-white patterned face
red throat
pale-yellow wash to breast and belly
black-and-white barring on back
MALE

The Yellow-bellied Sapsucker, with its red, black, and white coloring and soft-yellow wash on its underparts, is a striking bird. With its relatives, the Red-breasted Sapsucker and the Red-naped Sapsucker, it shares the habit of drilling holes in trees to drink sap. It was not until 1983 that the three sapsuckers were allocated to separate species. Sapsuckers are the only wholly migratory woodpeckers; female Yellow-bellied Sapsuckers move farther south than males.

VOICE Primary call a mewing *wheer-wheer-wheer.*

NESTING Cavities in dead trees; 5–6 eggs; 1 brood; May–June.

FEEDING Drinks sap; eats ants and other small insects; feeds on the inner bark of trees, also a variety of fruit.

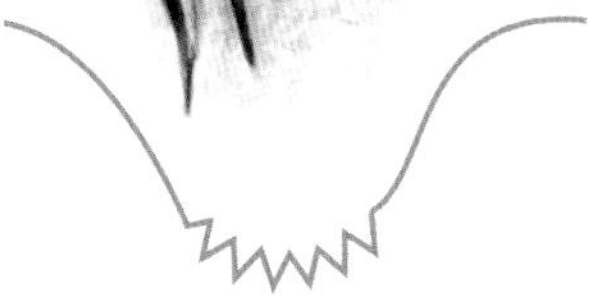

FLIGHT: typical woodpecker, undulating flight pattern with intermittent flapping and gliding.

STRIKING SPECIES

The Yellow-bellied Sapsucker's white rump and black-and-white forked tail are clearly evident here.

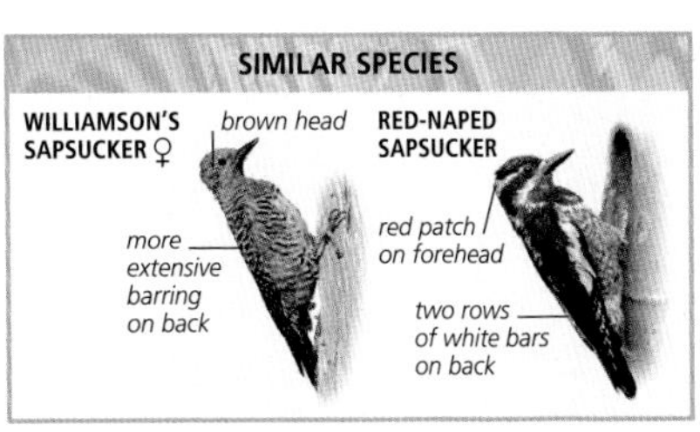
SIMILAR SPECIES
WILLIAMSON'S SAPSUCKER ♀
brown head
more extensive barring on back
RED-NAPED SAPSUCKER
red patch on forehead
two rows of white bars on back

OCCURRENCE

Breeds in eastern Alaska, Canada, and south to the Appalachians. Prefers either deciduous forests or mixed deciduous-coniferous forests; prefers young forests. In winter, it is found in open wooded areas in southeastern states, Caribbean islands, and Central America.

Length **8–9in (20–23cm)**	Wingspan **16–18in (41–46cm)**	Weight **1¾oz (50g)**
Social **Solitary/Pairs**	Lifespan **Up to 7 years**	Status **Secure**

DATE: ____________ TIME: ____________ LOCATION: ____________________

Order **Piciformes**	Family **Picidae**	Species ***Picoides dorsalis***

American Three-toed Woodpecker

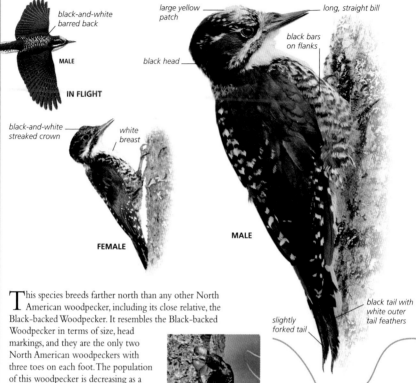

black-and-white barred back

MALE

IN FLIGHT

black-and-white streaked crown

white breast

FEMALE

large yellow patch

long, straight bill

black bars on flanks

black head

MALE

black tail with white outer tail feathers

slightly forked tail

This species breeds farther north than any other North American woodpecker, including its close relative, the Black-backed Woodpecker. It resembles the Black-backed Woodpecker in terms of size, head markings, and they are the only two North American woodpeckers with three toes on each foot. The population of this woodpecker is decreasing as a result of habitat loss. These woodpeckers require mature forests with old and dead trees; western birds frequent burned forests.

VOICE Call notes *queep*, *quip*, or *pik*; generally quiet, likened to the Yellow-bellied Sapsucker.

NESTING Excavates cavity mainly in dead or dying wood, sometimes in live wood; 4 eggs; 1 brood; May–July.

FEEDING Flakes off bark and eats insects underneath, mainly the larvae of bark beetles.

FLIGHT: undulating flight with rapid wing beats typical of other woodpeckers.

COLOR VARIATION

The streaks on this species' back are highly variable; some populations have nearly all-white backs.

SIMILAR SPECIES

BLACK-BACKED WOODPECKER shorter call; see p.217

solid black back

OCCURRENCE

Breeds in mature northern coniferous forests from Alaska to eastern Canada and south through the Rockies. Since it is largely nonmigratory, this is also the winter habitat for most populations, although it is found in more open areas in winter.

Length **8–9in (20–23cm)**	Wingspan **15in (38cm)**	Weight **2¼–2½oz (65–70g)**
Social **Solitary/Pairs**	Lifespan **Unknown**	Status **Vulnerable**

DATE: ______________ TIME: ______________ LOCATION: ______________

Order **Piciformes**	Family **Picidae**	Species ***Picoides arcticus***

Black-backed Woodpecker

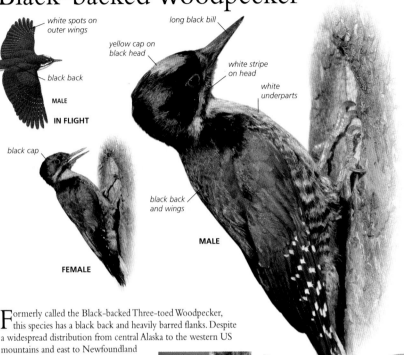

white spots on outer wings

black back

MALE

IN FLIGHT

black cap

FEMALE

long black bill

yellow cap on black head

white stripe on head

white underparts

black back and wings

MALE

Formerly called the Black-backed Three-toed Woodpecker, this species has a black back and heavily barred flanks. Despite a widespread distribution from central Alaska to the western US mountains and east to Newfoundland and the northeastern US, this bird is difficult to find. It often occurs in areas with burned forest, eating wood-boring beetles that occur after outbreaks of fire. This diet is very restrictive, and the species is greatly affected by forestry programs, which prevent the spread of fire. Although it overlaps geographically with the American Three-toed Woodpecker, the two are rarely found together in the same locality.

FLIGHT: typical undulating flight of woodpeckers.

FREQUENT MOVING

This bird excavates a new nest cavity each year, rarely returning in subsequent years.

VOICE Main call a single *pik*.

NESTING Cavity excavated in tree; 3–4 eggs; 1 brood; May–July.

FEEDING Eats beetles, especially larvae of wood-boring beetles, by flaking off bark.

SIMILAR SPECIES

AMERICAN THREE-TOED WOODPECKER
see p.216

black-and-white barred upperparts

OCCURRENCE

Inhabitant of northerly and mountainous coniferous forests that require fire for renewal. Breeding occurs soon after sites are burned as new colonies are attracted to the habitat. Occasional irruptive movements into the Great Lakes region and the Maritimes in response to outbreaks of wood-boring beetles.

Length **9–9½in (23–24cm)**	Wingspan **15–16in (38–41cm)**	Weight **2½oz (70g)**
Social **Pairs**	Lifespan **Up to 10 years**	Status **Secure**

DATE: ____________ TIME: ____________ LOCATION: ____________

Order **Piciformes** | Family **Picidae** | Species ***Dryobates pubescens***

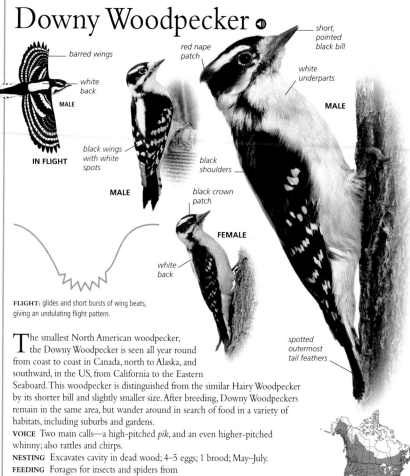

Downy Woodpecker

barred wings

white back

MALE

IN FLIGHT

black wings with white spots

MALE

red nape patch

short, pointed black bill

white underparts

MALE

black shoulders

black crown patch

FEMALE

white back

spotted outermost tail feathers

FLIGHT: glides and short bursts of wing beats, giving an undulating flight pattern.

The smallest North American woodpecker, the Downy Woodpecker is seen all year round from coast to coast in Canada, north to Alaska, and southward, in the US, from California to the Eastern Seaboard. This woodpecker is distinguished from the similar Hairy Woodpecker by its shorter bill and slightly smaller size. After breeding, Downy Woodpeckers remain in the same area, but wander around in search of food in a variety of habitats, including suburbs and gardens.

VOICE Two main calls—a high-pitched *pik*, and an even higher-pitched whinny; also rattles and chirps.

NESTING Excavates cavity in dead wood; 4–5 eggs; 1 brood; May–July.

FEEDING Forages for insects and spiders from the bark in live and dead trees, but also eats fruit, seeds, and other vegetable matter, depending on the season, frequents feeders.

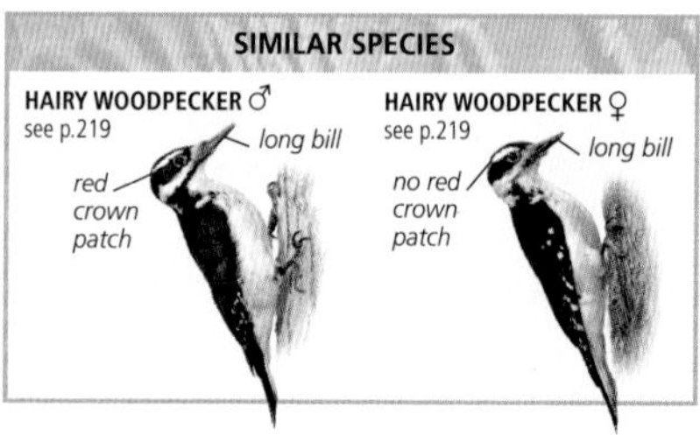
SIMILAR SPECIES
HAIRY WOODPECKER ♂
see p.219
long bill
red crown patch
HAIRY WOODPECKER ♀
see p.219
long bill
no red crown patch

SUET LOVERS
Downy Woodpeckers will feed on suet provided in feeders during the winter.

OCCURRENCE
Breeds in a wide variety of habitats, including deciduous and mixed deciduous-coniferous woodlands, parks, wooded suburban areas, and areas near rivers. Along with using nature's bounty of dead trees, it also uses human-made objects, such as fence posts. Resident, but local movements occur.

Length **6–7in (15–18cm)**	Wingspan **10–12in (25–30cm)**	Weight **1¹⁄₁₆oz (30g)**
Social **Solitary/Flocks**	Lifespan **Up to 11 years**	Status **Secure**

DATE: ______________ TIME: ______________ LOCATION: ______________

Order **Piciformes**	Family **Picidae**	Species ***Dryobates villosus***

Hairy Woodpecker

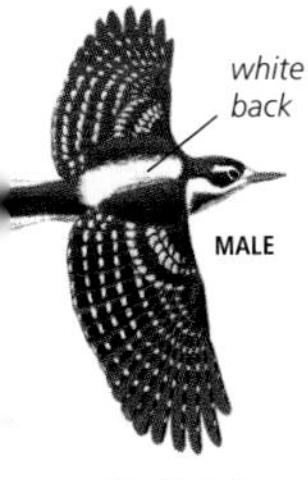

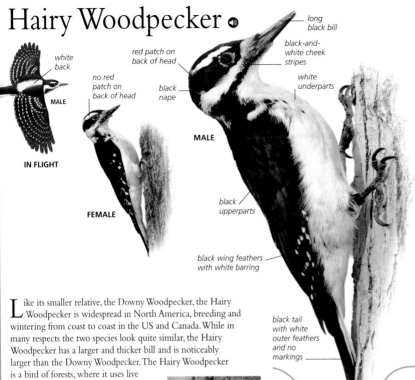

white back
MALE
IN FLIGHT

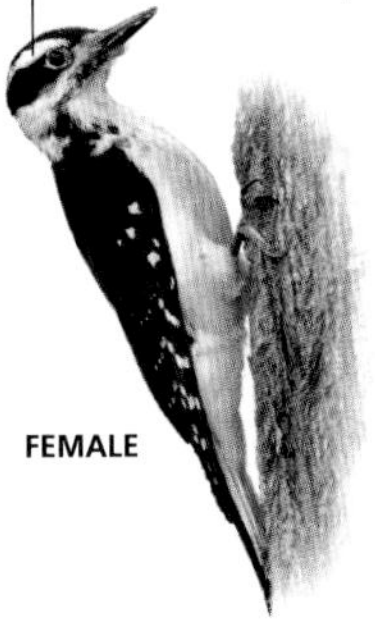

no red patch on back of head
FEMALE

red patch on back of head
black nape
long black bill
black-and-white cheek stripes
white underparts
MALE
black upperparts
black wing feathers with white barring
black tail with white outer feathers and no markings

Like its smaller relative, the Downy Woodpecker, the Hairy Woodpecker is widespread in North America, breeding and wintering from coast to coast in the US and Canada. While in many respects the two species look quite similar, the Hairy Woodpecker has a larger and thicker bill and is noticeably larger than the Downy Woodpecker. The Hairy Woodpecker is a bird of forests, where it uses live tree trunks for nesting and foraging.

VOICE Call a bold, grating, sharp *Peek,* similar to that of the Downy Woodpecker, but lower in pitch, and louder. Drumming a rather loud, even series of taps.

NESTING Excavates cavity in live trees; 4 eggs; 1 brood; May–July.

FEEDING Eats mainly insects and their larvae; also nuts and seeds; frequents bird feeders.

FLIGHT: undulating; short glides alternating with wing beats.

HOME SWEET HOME

The Hairy Woodpecker is generally found in forests and prefers mature woodland areas, using both deciduous and coniferous trees.

SIMILAR SPECIES

DOWNY WOODPECKER ♂
see p.218
shorter bill
white markings on outer wing feathers

DOWNY WOODPECKER ♀
see p.218
shorter bill
white markings on outer wing feathers

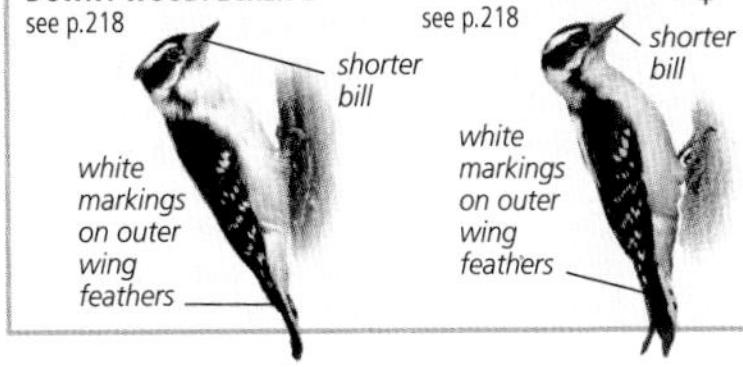

OCCURRENCE

Breeds primarily in forests, both deciduous and coniferous, but also in more open woodlands, swamps, suburban parks, and wooded areas. Resident in North America all year round, though in the far north of its range it may move south for the winter.

Length **9–9½in (23–24cm)**	Wingspan **15–16in (38–41cm)**	Weight **2½oz (70g)**
Social **Solitary/Winter flocks**	Lifespan **At least 16 years**	Status **Secure**

DATE: ____________ TIME: ____________ LOCATION: ____________

Order **Piciformes**	Family **Picidae**	Species ***Colaptes auratus***

Northern Flicker

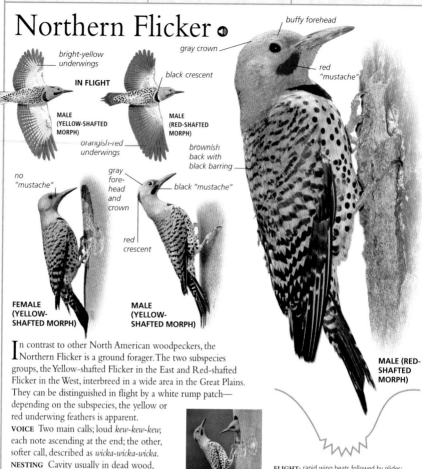

bright-yellow underwings
IN FLIGHT
black crescent
MALE (YELLOW-SHAFTED MORPH)
MALE (RED-SHAFTED MORPH)
orangish-red underwings
buffy forehead
gray crown
red "mustache"
brownish back with black barring
no "mustache"
gray forehead and crown
black "mustache"
red crescent
FEMALE (YELLOW-SHAFTED MORPH)
MALE (YELLOW-SHAFTED MORPH)
MALE (RED-SHAFTED MORPH)

In contrast to other North American woodpeckers, the Northern Flicker is a ground forager. The two subspecies groups, the Yellow-shafted Flicker in the East and Red-shafted Flicker in the West, interbreed in a wide area in the Great Plains. They can be distinguished in flight by a white rump patch—depending on the subspecies, the yellow or red underwing feathers is apparent.

VOICE Two main calls; loud *kew-kew-kew,* each note ascending at the end; the other, softer call, described as *wicka-wicka-wicka.*

NESTING Cavity usually in dead wood, but sometimes in live wood; 6–8 eggs; 1 brood; May–June.

FEEDING Unusual ground-feeder, eating ants in breeding season and fruits in winter.

FLIGHT: rapid wing beats followed by glides; fewer undulations than most woodpeckers.

SHARING CHORES
The Northern Flicker nests in tree cavities, where parents take turns incubating eggs.

SIMILAR SPECIES

GILDED FLICKER
cinnamon crown
paler brown back

FEET ON THE GROUND
Unlike other woodpeckers, flickers can be found foraging for ants on the ground.

OCCURRENCE
A common species found in woodland in every part of the US, the southern half of Canada, and north into Alaska. During breeding season, prefers open woodlands and forest edge; also suburbs. Little is known about this bird's winter habitat.

Length **12–13in (31–33cm)**	Wingspan **19–21in (48–53cm)**	Weight **4oz (125g)**
Social **Solitary**	Lifespan **9 years**	Status **Secure**

DATE: ______________ TIME: ______________ LOCATION: ______________

Order **Piciformes**	Family **Picidae**	Species ***Dryocopus pileatus***

Pileated Woodpecker

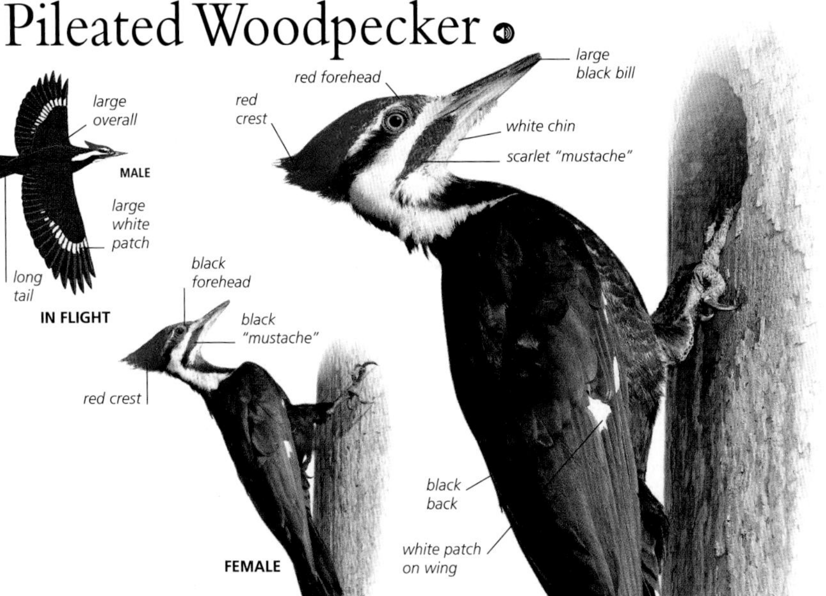
large overall
MALE
large white patch
long tail
IN FLIGHT
black forehead
black "mustache"
red crest
FEMALE
red forehead
red crest
large black bill
white chin
scarlet "mustache"
black back
white patch on wing
MALE

The largest woodpecker in North America, the Pileated Woodpecker is instantly recognizable by its spectacular large, tapering bright-red crest. A mated pair of Pileated Woodpeckers defends their breeding territory all year—even if one bird dies, the other does not desert the territory. Indeed, a pair may live in the same dead tree every year, but will hammer out a new nest cavity with their powerful bills each season. Their abandoned squarish nest cavities created by the Pileated Woodpecker are sometimes reused by other birds, and occasionally inhabited by mammals.

VOICE Two primary calls, both high-pitched and quite loud—*yuck-yuck-yuck*, and *yuka-yuka-yuka*.

NESTING Excavates cavity, usually in dead tree; 3–5 eggs; 1 brood; May–July.

FEEDING Bores deep into trees and peels off large strips of bark to extract carpenter ants and beetle larvae; also digs on ground and on fallen logs, and opportunistically eats fruit and nuts.

FLIGHT: slow, deep wing beats, with occasional undulation when wings briefly folded.

EASY PICKINGS
Pileated woodpeckers occasionally visit feeders to supplement their diet.

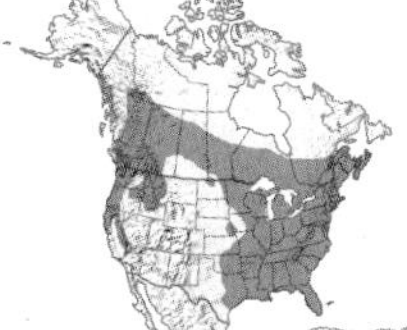

OCCURRENCE
Resident throughout eastern North America, across central Canada to the Pacific Northwest, in deciduous and coniferous forest and woodlands; also found in swampy areas. In some areas, chooses young forests with dead trees but in other places, old-growth conifers.

Length **16–18in (41–46cm)**	Wingspan **26–30in (66–76cm)**	Weight **10oz (275g)**
Social **Pairs**	Lifespan **Up to 10 years**	Status **Secure**

DATE: ____________ TIME: ____________ LOCATION: ____________________

Family **Falconidae**

FALCONS

RECENTLY SEPARATED FROM other diurnal birds of prey, such as eagles and hawks, falcons and caracaras form a distinctive group of raptors. Caracaras are found in the New World but not in Canada, while falcons have a worldwide distribution, with a much larger number of species.

Falcons are known for their speed and agility inflight, but paradoxically, spend long periods perched on a rock ledge or tree branch. The larger, bird-hunting species, such as the Peregrine Falcon, draw attention to their presence by creating panic among other birds when they fly over, ready to chase prey as large as ducks and pigeons. Falcons include birds that catch and eat insects on the wing, those that hover in one place searching for small prey below, and yet others that are more dramatic aerial hunters. Falcons in dramatic pursuits, or in high-speed "stoops" from above, seize birds up to their own size. Large species, such as the Gyrfalcon, may kill prey bigger than themselves. Falcons are distinguished from bird-eating hawks belonging to the genus *Accipiter* by their dark eyes. They also have a notch, or tooth, on the upper mandible, possibly to help them to dispatch and dismember their prey. Unlike the Accipiters, they do not build nests, but many falcons use abandoned nests of other birds and some lay eggs on a bare ledge or in an unlined cavity.

ARCTIC GIANT
The Arctic-dwelling Gyrfalcon is the largest of the falcons.

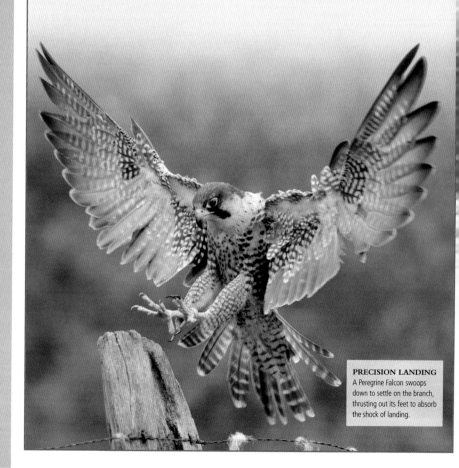

PRECISION LANDING
A Peregrine Falcon swoops down to settle on the branch, thrusting out its feet to absorb the shock of landing.

Order **Falconiformes**	Family **Falconidae**	Species ***Falco sparverius***

American Kestrel

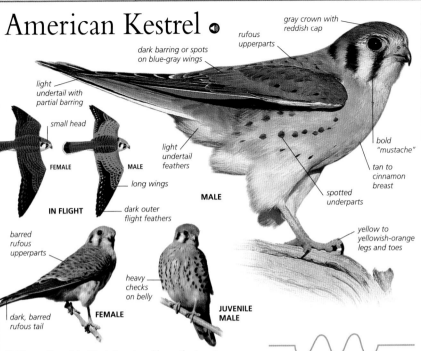

gray crown with reddish cap
rufous upperparts
dark barring or spots on blue-gray wings
light undertail with partial barring
small head
FEMALE
MALE
light undertail feathers
bold "mustache"
tan to cinnamon breast
long wings
MALE
spotted underparts
IN FLIGHT
dark outer flight feathers
yellow to yellowish-orange legs and toes
barred rufous upperparts
heavy checks on belly
dark, barred rufous tail
FEMALE
JUVENILE MALE

The smallest of the North American falcons, the American Kestrel features long pointed wings, a "tooth and notch" bill structure, and the dark-brown eyes typical of falcons, though, kestrels have shorter toes than other falcons, possibly because they take less birds and/or because it facilitates diving into long grass for insects and mammals. Male and female American Kestrels show differences in plumage, and also in size: females are slightly larger.

VOICE Common call a high-pitched *killy-killy-killy*.

NESTING Natural cavities, crevices, holes in dead trees, woodpeckers' holes, crevices in barns, artificial nest boxes, and buildings; 4–5 eggs; 1 brood; April–June.

FEEDING Mostly insectivorous—eats grasshoppers and beetles, among others; also takes small birds, rodents, amphibians, and reptiles; eats lizards in the West.

FLIGHT: delicate and almost mothlike; frequently hover in one place, searching for prey.

HIGH FLIER
A male American Kestrel hovers over a field, its sharp eyes scanning the ground for insects and rodents.

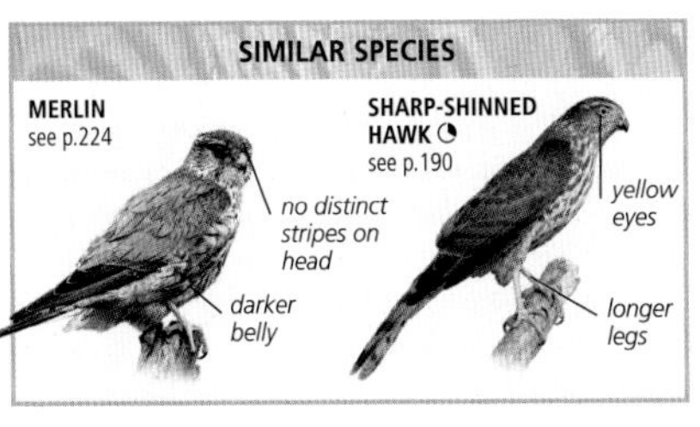
SIMILAR SPECIES
MERLIN
see p.224
no distinct stripes on head
darker belly
SHARP-SHINNED HAWK
see p.190
yellow eyes
longer legs

OCCURRENCE
From near the northern tree line in Alaska and Canada south, east, and west throughout most of North America. Occurs also in Central and South America. Habitat ranges from semi-open tree groves to grasslands, cultivated and fallow farmland, and open desert.

Length **9in (23cm)**	Wingspan **22in (56cm)**	Weight **3½–4oz (100–125g)**
Social **Family groups**	Lifespan **10–15 years**	Status **Secure**

Order **Falconiformes**	Family **Falconidae**	Species ***Falco columbarius***

Merlin

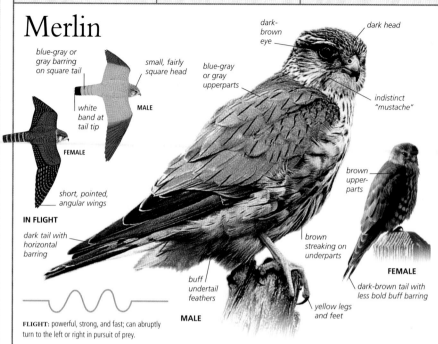

blue-gray or gray barring on square tail
small, fairly square head
white band at tail tip
MALE
FEMALE
short, pointed, angular wings
IN FLIGHT
dark-brown eye
dark head
blue-gray or gray upperparts
indistinct "mustache"
brown upperparts
dark tail with horizontal barring
brown streaking on underparts
FEMALE
buff undertail feathers
dark-brown tail with less bold buff barring
yellow legs and feet
MALE

FLIGHT: powerful, strong, and fast; can abruptly turn to the left or right in pursuit of prey.

Merlins are small, fast-flying falcons that were formerly known as "pigeon hawks" because their shape and flight are similar to those strong fliers. Merlins can overtake and capture a wide variety of prey, but mostly small birds. They can turn on a dime and use their long, thin middle toes, typical of falcons, to pluck birds from the air after launching a direct attack. The smaller males are different in color. Both males and females show geographical color variations.

VOICE Male call a high-pitched *ki-ki-ki-ki*; female call a low-pitched *kek-ek-ek-ek-ek*.

NESTING Small scrapes on ground in open country, or abandoned nests of other species, such as crows, in forested areas and more recently in suburban green spaces; 4–6 eggs; 1 brood; April–June.

FEEDING Catches small birds in midair, and occasionally birds as large as doves; also feeds on small mammals, including bats.

ABOUT TO ROUSE

An adult female Merlin sits on a moss-covered rock, about to "rouse," or fluff out and shake her feathers.

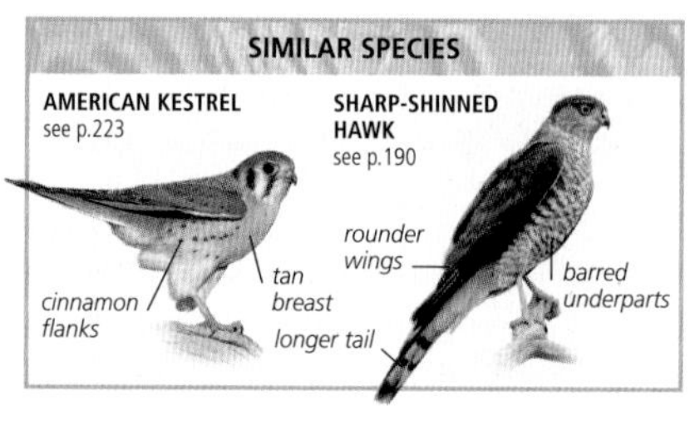
SIMILAR SPECIES
AMERICAN KESTREL
see p.223
cinnamon flanks
tan breast
SHARP-SHINNED HAWK
see p.190
rounder wings
barred underparts
longer tail

OCCURRENCE

In North America, breeds throughout Alaska and Canada. Highly migratory; winters throughout the US south to northern South America. Merlins can be seen hunting along coastlines, over marshlands and open fields, and in desert areas.

Length **10in (25cm)**	Wingspan **24in (61cm)**	Weight **5–7oz (150–200g)**
Social **Pairs/Family groups**	Lifespan **10–15 years**	Status **Secure**

DATE: ____________ TIME: ____________ LOCATION: ____________

Order **Falconiformes**	Family **Falconidae**	Species ***Falco rusticolus***

Gyrfalcon

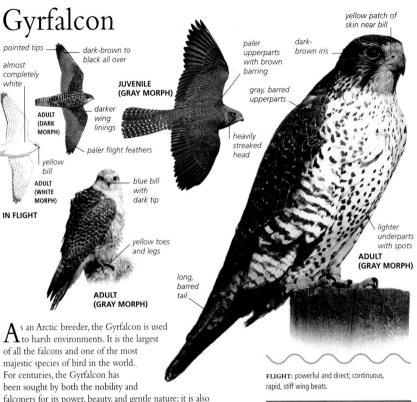

pointed tips
dark-brown to black all over
almost completely white
darker wing linings
paler flight feathers
yellow bill
ADULT (DARK MORPH)
ADULT (WHITE MORPH)
IN FLIGHT
JUVENILE (GRAY MORPH)
paler upperparts with brown barring
heavily streaked head
blue bill with dark tip
yellow toes and legs
ADULT (GRAY MORPH)
yellow patch of skin near bill
dark-brown iris
gray, barred upperparts
lighter underparts with spots
long, barred tail
ADULT (GRAY MORPH)

As an Arctic breeder, the Gyrfalcon is used to harsh environments. It is the largest of all the falcons and one of the most majestic species of bird in the world. For centuries, the Gyrfalcon has been sought by both the nobility and falconers for its power, beauty, and gentle nature; it is also the official bird of the Northwest Territories. It uses its speed to pursue prey in a "tail chase," sometimes striking its quarry on the ground, but also in flight. Three forms are known, ranging from almost pure-white to gray and blackish.

VOICE Loud, harsh *KYHa-KYHa-KYHa.*

NESTING Scrape on cliff or old Common Ravens' nests; 2–7 eggs; 1 brood; April–July.

FEEDING Feeds mostly on large birds, such as ptarmigan, pigeons, grouse; may also hunt mammals, such as Arctic hare.

FLIGHT: powerful and direct; continuous, rapid, stiff wing beats.

SNOWY PLUMAGE
A Gyrfalcon stands on an Arctic hillside. From a distance, it might be mistaken for a patch of snow.

SIMILAR SPECIES

PRAIRIE FALCON light brown-spotted underparts; light sandy-brown upperparts; light, barred underparts

PEREGRINE FALCON see p.226 dark "hood" on head; smaller overall

OCCURRENCE
Breeds in Alaska and Arctic Canada. In winter, some birds move south as far as the northern US. A truly Arctic species, it is found in the most barren regions of the tundra, high mountains and foothills of the tundra, and Arctic and sub-Arctic evergreen forests and woodlands. Not common outside its breeding range.

Length **22in (56cm)**	Wingspan **4ft (1.2m)**	Weight **2¾–4lb (1.2–1.8kg)**
Social **Solitary/Pairs**	Lifespan **Up to 30 years**	Status **Localized**

DATE: ____________ TIME: ____________ LOCATION: ____________

Order **Falconiformes**	Family **Falconidae**	Species ***Falco peregrinus***

Peregrine Falcon

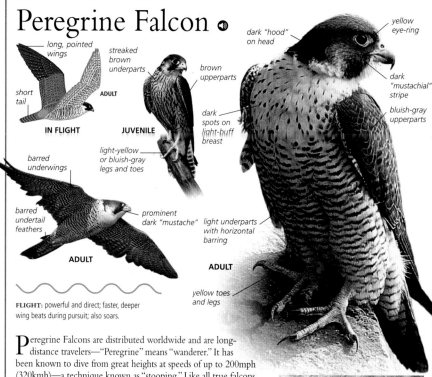

long, pointed wings
short tail
ADULT
IN FLIGHT

streaked brown underparts
brown upperparts
JUVENILE
light-yellow or bluish-gray legs and toes

barred underwings
barred undertail feathers
prominent dark "mustache"
ADULT

dark "hood" on head
yellow eye-ring
dark "mustachial" stripe
bluish-gray upperparts
dark spots on light-buff breast
light underparts with horizontal barring
ADULT
yellow toes and legs

FLIGHT: powerful and direct; faster, deeper wing beats during pursuit; also soars.

Peregrine Falcons are distributed worldwide and are long-distance travelers—"Peregrine" means "wanderer." It has been known to dive from great heights at speeds of up to 200mph (320kmh)—a technique known as "stooping." Like all true falcons, this species has a pointed "tooth" on its upper beak and a "notch" on the lower one, and it instinctively bites the neck of captured prey to kill it. From the 1950s to the 1980s, its breeding ability was reduced by the insecticide DDT, which resulted in thin eggshells that could easily be crushed by the parent. Peregrines were then bred in captivity, and later released into the wild. Their status is now secure.

VOICE Sharp *kak, kak, kak* when alarmed.

NESTING Shallow scrape on cliff or building (nest sites are used year after year); 2–5 eggs; 1 brood; March–June.

FEEDING Dives on birds from jays to ducks in flight; feeds on pigeons and migratory birds in cities, and occasionally mammals.

PARENTAL CARE
An adult Peregrine gently feeds a hatchling bits of meat; the remaining egg is not likely to hatch.

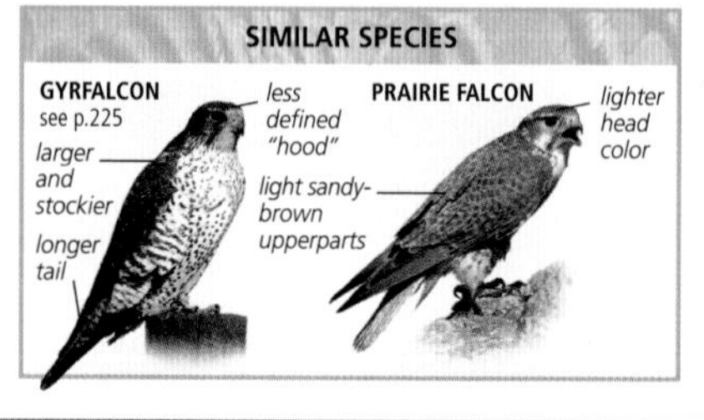
SIMILAR SPECIES
GYRFALCON
see p.225
larger and stockier
longer tail
less defined "hood"
PRAIRIE FALCON
lighter head color
light sandy-brown upperparts

OCCURRENCE
A variety of habitats across northern North America, ranging from open valleys to cities with tall buildings. Peregrines prefer to inhabit cliffs along sea coasts, in addition to inland mountain ranges, but also occur in open country, such as scrubland and salt marshes.

Length **16in (41cm)**	Wingspan **3¼–3½ft (1–1.1m)**	Weight **22–35oz (620g–1kg)**
Social **Solitary/Pairs**	Lifespan **Up to 20 years**	Status **Secure**

DATE: ____________ TIME: ____________ LOCATION: ____________

NEW WORLD FLYCATCHERS

BIRDS POPULARLY KNOWN AS "flycatchers" occur in many parts of the world; however, several different families of songbird have this name. With the exception of some Old World species that may stray into Alaska, the North American species are all members of a single family—the Tyrant Flycatchers (Tyrannidae). With about 400 species, this is the largest bird family in the New World. The North American species are uniform in appearance, with only a hint of the family's diversity found in Central and South America. Most are drab-colored olive-green or gray birds, sometimes with yellow on the underparts, but an exception is the Scissor-tailed Flycatcher, seen on rare occasions in Canada. The members of the genus *Empidonax* include some of the most difficult birds to identify in North America; they are best distinguished by their songs. Typical flycatcher feeding behavior is to sit on a branch or exposed perch and sally forth to catch flying insects. Tyrannid flycatchers are found across North America, except in the Arctic regions. Most are found in wooded habitats, though the kingbirds (genus *Tyrannus*) prefer woodland edges and deserts. Nearly all flycatchers are long-distance migrants and spend the winter in Central and South America.

KEEPING WATCH
This Alder Flycatcher is on the alert to spot a potential meal.

ERECT STANCE
A large-headed look and erect posture are typical of this Eastern Phoebe.

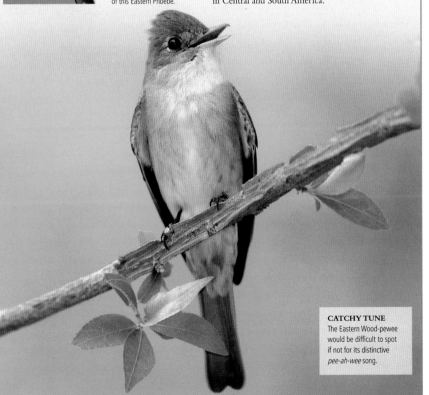

CATCHY TUNE
The Eastern Wood-pewee would be difficult to spot if not for its distinctive *pee-ah-wee* song.

Order **Passeriformes**	Family **Tyrannidae**	Species ***Myiarchus crinitus***

Great Crested Flycatcher

ADULT

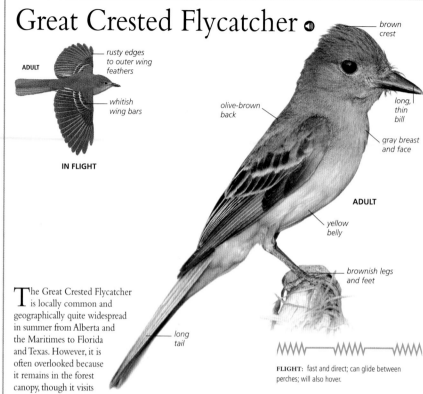

rusty edges to outer wing feathers

whitish wing bars

IN FLIGHT

brown crest

long, thin bill

olive-brown back

gray breast and face

ADULT

yellow belly

brownish legs and feet

long tail

FLIGHT: fast and direct; can glide between perches; will also hover.

The Great Crested Flycatcher is locally common and geographically quite widespread in summer from Alberta and the Maritimes to Florida and Texas. However, it is often overlooked because it remains in the forest canopy, though it visits the ground for food and nest material. Its presence is usually given away by its loud, sharp, double-syllabled notes. It lines its nest with shed snakeskins like other *Myiarchus* flycatchers, possibly to reduce predation by flying squirrels.

VOICE Principal call is a loud, abrupt *purr-it* given by both sexes; male song is a repeated *whee-eep*, occasionally *wheeyer*.

NESTING In deep cavity, usually woodpecker hole, lined with leaves, bark, trash, and snakeskins; 4–6 eggs; 1 brood; May–July.

FEEDING Picks flying insects, moths, and caterpillars mainly from leaves and branches in the canopy; also small berries and fruit.

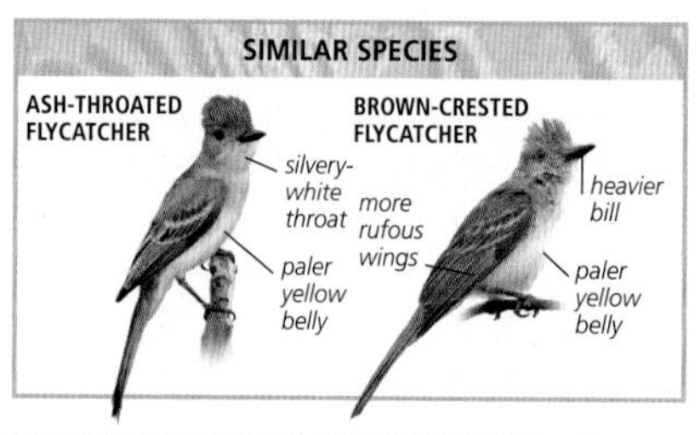
SIMILAR SPECIES
ASH-THROATED FLYCATCHER
silvery-white throat
paler yellow belly
BROWN-CRESTED FLYCATCHER
more rufous wings
heavier bill
paler yellow belly

TRICOLORED SPECIES
Viewed from the front, the eastern Great Crested Flycatcher is tricolored.

OCCURRENCE
Widespread in eastern North America, from Alberta to the Maritimes in Canada, and, in the US, south to Texas and Florida. Migrates to Mexico, Central America, and northern South America. Breeds in deciduous and mixed woodlands with clearings.

Length **7–8in (18–20cm)**	Wingspan **13in (33cm)**	Weight **$\frac{7}{8}$–1$\frac{7}{16}$oz (25–40g)**
Social **Solitary**	Lifespan **Up to 13 years**	Status **Secure**

DATE: ____________ TIME: ____________ LOCATION: ____________

Order **Passeriformes**	Family **Tyrannidae**	Species ***Tyrannus verticalis***

Western Kingbird

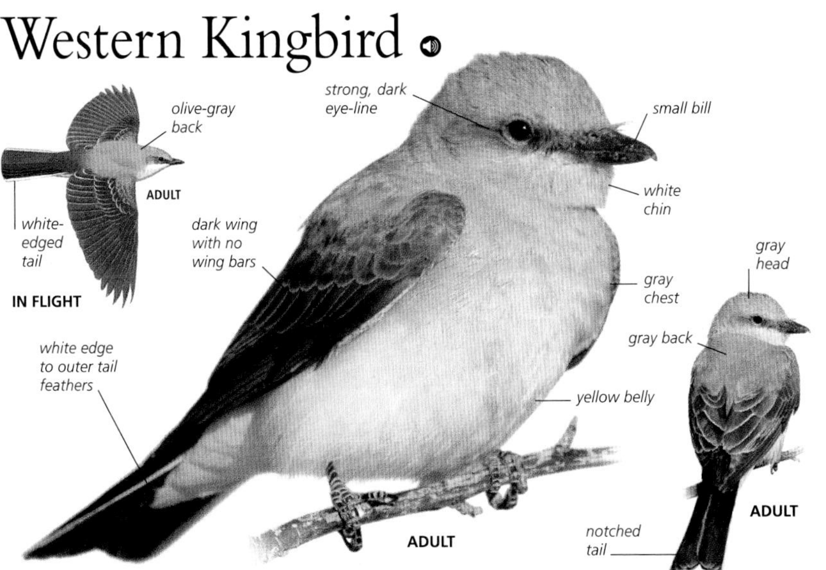
olive-gray back
ADULT
white-edged tail
IN FLIGHT
dark wing with no wing bars
white edge to outer tail feathers
strong, dark eye-line
small bill
white chin
gray chest
yellow belly
ADULT
gray head
gray back
notched tail
ADULT

A conspicuous summer breeder in the US and lower parts of the western provinces, the Western Kingbird occurs in open habitats in much of western North America. The white outer edges on its outer tail feathers distinguish it from other kingbirds. Its population has expanded eastward over the last 100 years. A large, loosely defined territory is defended against other kingbirds when breeding begins in spring; a smaller core area is defended as the season progresses.

VOICE Calls include *whit*, *pwee-t*, and chatter; song, regularly repeated sharp *kip* notes and high-pitched notes.

NESTING Open, bulky cup of grass, rootlets, and twigs in tree, shrub, or utility pole; 2–7 eggs; 1 brood; April–July.

FEEDING Feeds on insects and fruit.

FLIGHT: agile, fast, direct, flapping flight; flies to catch insects; hovers to pick bugs on vegetation.

FENCE POST
A favorite place for the Western Kingbird to perch and look around is on fenceposts.

QUENCHING THIRST
An immature Western Kingbird drinks at the edge of a shallow pool of water.

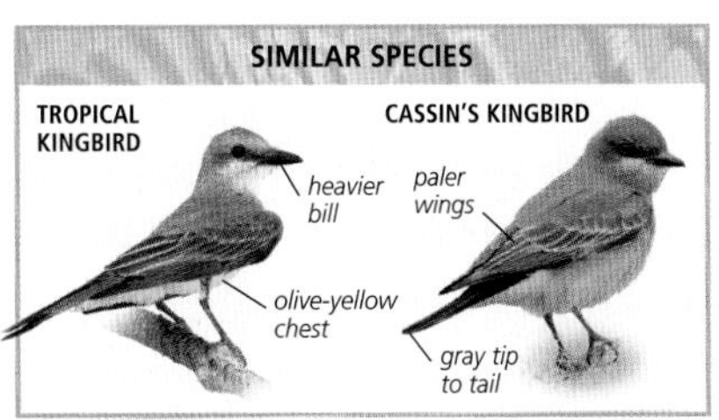
SIMILAR SPECIES
TROPICAL KINGBIRD
heavier bill
olive-yellow chest
CASSIN'S KINGBIRD
paler wings
gray tip to tail

OCCURRENCE
Widespread in southwestern Canada and the western US, in open habitats, such as grasslands, prairie, desert shrub, pastures, and cropland, near elevated perches; particularly near water. Winters in similar habitats and in tropical forest and shrubbery from Mexico to Costa Rica.

Length **8–9in (20–23cm)**	Wingspan **15–16in (38–41cm)**	Weight **1¼–1$\frac{9}{16}$oz (35–45g)**
Social **Solitary**	Lifespan **Up to 6 years**	Status **Secure**

DATE: ______________ TIME: ______________ LOCATION: ______________

Order **Passeriformes**	Family **Tyrannidae**	Species ***Tyrannus tyrannus***

Eastern Kingbird

ADULT
white-tipped tail
white throat
IN FLIGHT
dark crown and cheeks, almost black
dark eyes
faint gray "necklace"
white throat and underparts
relatively short, thick bill
slate-gray back
pale edges to wing feathers
ADULT
black legs and toes
white belly
white undertail feathers
black tail with white tip
ADULT

The Eastern Kingbird is a tame and widely distributed bird. It is a highly territorial species and is known for its aggressive behavior toward potential predators, particularly crows and hawks, which it pursues relentlessly. It is able to identify and remove the eggs of the Brown-headed Cowbird when they are laid in its nest. The Eastern Kingbird is generally monogamous and pairs will return to the same territory in subsequent years. This species winters in tropical South America, where it forages for fruit in the treetops of evergreen forests.

VOICE Principal call is a loud, metallic *chatter-zeer*; song is a rapid, electric *kdik-kdik-kdik-pika-pika-pika-kzeeeer.*

NESTING Open cup of twigs, roots, stems in hawthorn, elm, stump, fence, or post; 2–5 eggs; 1 brood; May–August.

FEEDING Catches flying insects from elevated perch or gleans insects from foliage; eats berries and fruit, except in spring.

FLIGHT: strong, direct, and very agile with vigorous, rapid wing beats; hovers and sails.

WHITE-TIPPED
The white-tipped tails of these two Eastern Kingbirds are conspicuous as they sit on a budding twig.

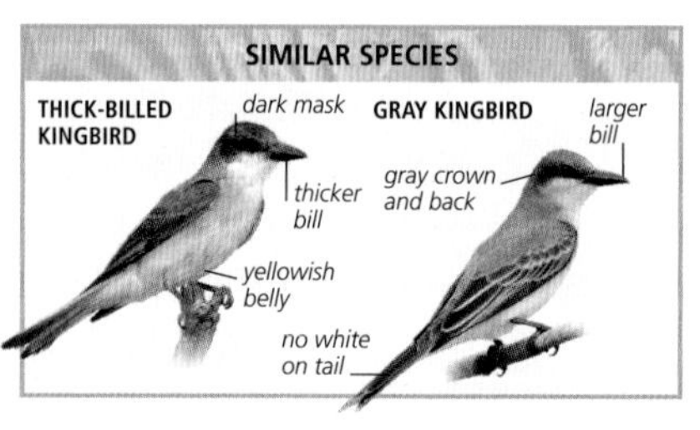
SIMILAR SPECIES
THICK-BILLED KINGBIRD
dark mask
thicker bill
yellowish belly
GRAY KINGBIRD
larger bill
gray crown and back
no white on tail

OCCURRENCE
Breeds across much of North America in a variety of open habitats, including urban areas, parks, golf courses, fields with scattered shrubs, beaver ponds, and along forest edges. Long-distance migrant; winters in South America, south to Argentina.

Length **7–9in (18–23cm)**	Wingspan **13–15in (33–38cm)**	Weight **1¹⁄₁₆–2oz (30–55g)**
Social **Solitary/Pairs**	Lifespan **Up to 7 years**	Status **Secure**

DATE: ____________ TIME: ____________ LOCATION: ____________

Order **Passeriformes**	Family **Tyrannidae**	Species ***Contopus cooperi***

Olive-sided Flycatcher

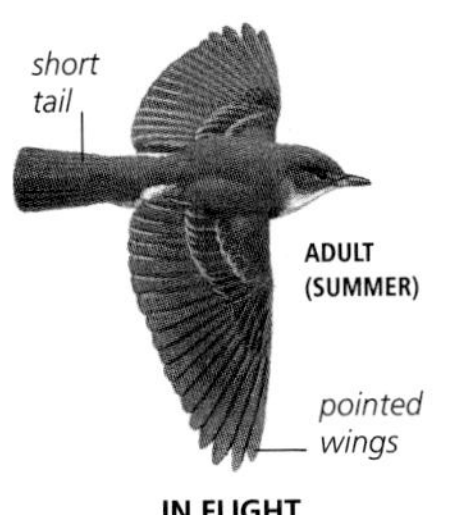
short tail
ADULT (SUMMER)
pointed wings

IN FLIGHT

large, dark head

lower base of bill often dull orange

brownish-gray back

dull-white throat

brownish-olive flanks

white belly

ADULT (SUMMER)

FLIGHT: fast and direct, with deep, rapid wing beats; turns sharply to chase prey.

The Olive-sided Flycatcher is identified by its distinctive song, relatively large size, and contrasting belly and flank colors, which make its underside appear like a vest with the buttons undone. Both members of a breeding pair are known to defend their territory aggressively. This flycatcher undertakes a long journey from northern parts of North America to winter in Panama and the Andes.

VOICE Call an evenly spaced *pip-pip-pip*; song a loud 3-note whistle: *quick-THREE-BEERS* or *whip-WEE-DEER*.

NESTING Open cup of twigs, rootlets, lichens; 2–5 eggs; 1 brood; May–August.

FEEDING Sits and waits for prey to fly past its perch before swooping after it; eats flying insects, such as bees, wasps, and flying ants.

BUILDING THE NEST
The female Olive-sided Flycatcher usually constructs the nest on her own.

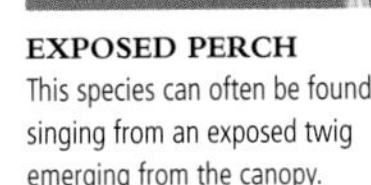

EXPOSED PERCH
This species can often be found singing from an exposed twig emerging from the canopy.

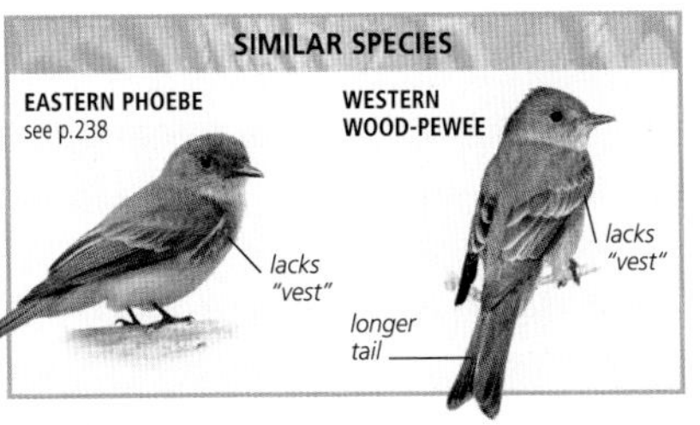
SIMILAR SPECIES
EASTERN PHOEBE
see p.238
lacks "vest"
WESTERN WOOD-PEWEE
lacks "vest"
longer tail

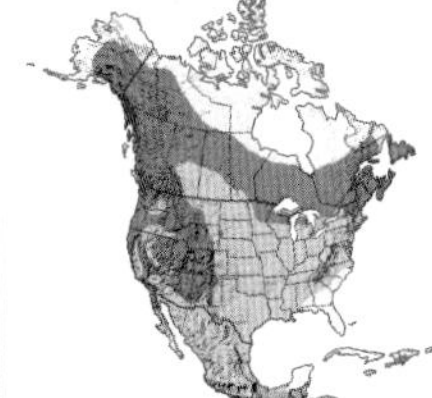

OCCURRENCE
Breeds in mountainous, northern coniferous forests at edges or openings around ponds, bogs, and meadows where standing dead trees occur. Also found in post-fire forests with abundant stumps. Winters in forest edges with tall trees and stumps.

Length **7–8in (18–20cm)**	Wingspan **13in (33cm)**	Weight **1¹⁄₁₆–1¼oz (30–35g)**
Social **Solitary**	Lifespan **Up to 7 years**	Status **Declining**

DATE: ______________ TIME: ______________ LOCATION: ______________________________

Order **Passeriformes**	Family **Tyrannidae**	Species ***Contopus virens***

Eastern Wood-Pewee

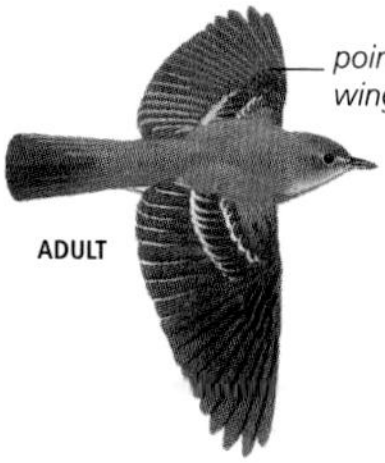

pointed wings

ADULT

IN FLIGHT

slightly ragged crest

partial eye-ring

yellow lower mandible

pale gray

pale throat

thin white wing bars

yellowish wash on underparts

thin white edges to wing feathers

ADULT

FLIGHT: flies out from perch to catch flying insects; direct, steady wing beats.

The Eastern Wood-Pewee is found in many types of woodland in the eastern US and southeastern Canada. The male is slightly larger than the female, but their plumage is practically identical. Recent population declines in this species have been attributed to heavy browsing by White-tailed Deer. This has been compounded by the Eastern Wood-Pewee's susceptibility to brood parasitism by Brown-headed Cowbirds.

VOICE Call terse *chip*; song slurred *pee-ah-wee*, plaintive *wee-ooo*, or *wee-ur*, and slurred *ah di dee*.

NESTING Shallow cup of grass, lichens on horizontal limbs; 2–4 eggs; 1 brood; May–September.

FEEDING Consumes mainly flying insects, such as flies, beetles, and bees; occasionally forages for insects on foliage on the ground.

SEARCHING FOR PREY
Holding its tail perfectly still, this Wood-Pewee is perched upright, scanning for prey.

COLORATION
The Eastern Wood-Pewee has yellowish underparts and a yellow lower mandible.

SIMILAR SPECIES

WESTERN WOOD-PEWEE range barely overlaps

dark-gray back

WILLOW FLYCATCHER tendency to wag tail; see p.236

smaller size

stronger eye-ring

lighter breast and head

OCCURRENCE
Widely distributed in the eastern US and adjacent Canadian provinces. Breeds in deciduous and coniferous forests, often near clearings or edges; uses waterside areas in the Midwest, less so in the East. Late-arriving migrant. Winters in shrubby, second-growth forests of South America.

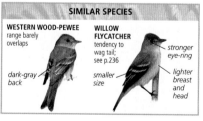

Length **6in (15cm)**	Wingspan **9–10in (23–26cm)**	Weight **3/8–11/16oz (10–19g)**
Social **Solitary**	Lifespan **Up to 7 years**	Status **Special Concern**

DATE: ______________ TIME: ______________ LOCATION: ______________

Order **Passeriformes**	Family **Tyrannidae**	Species ***Empidonax flaviventris***

Yellow-bellied Flycatcher

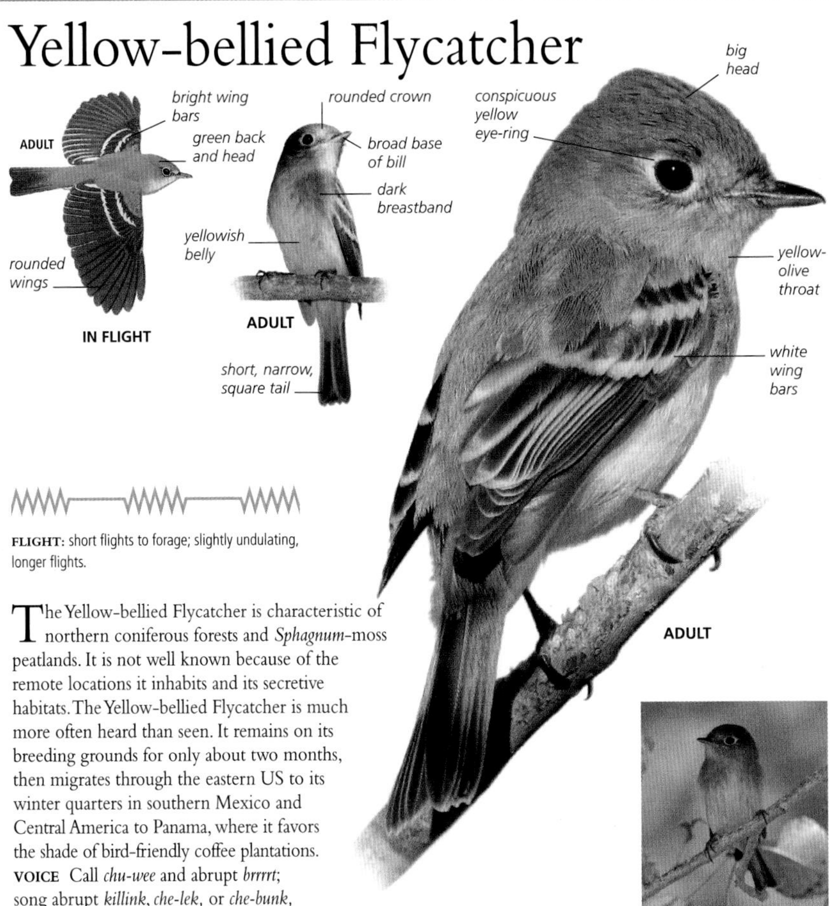
big head
conspicuous yellow eye-ring
rounded crown
broad base of bill
dark breastband
bright wing bars
green back and head
ADULT
rounded wings
IN FLIGHT
yellowish belly
ADULT
short, narrow, square tail
yellow-olive throat
white wing bars
ADULT

FLIGHT: short flights to forage; slightly undulating, longer flights.

The Yellow-bellied Flycatcher is characteristic of northern coniferous forests and *Sphagnum*-moss peatlands. It is not well known because of the remote locations it inhabits and its secretive habitats. The Yellow-bellied Flycatcher is much more often heard than seen. It remains on its breeding grounds for only about two months, then migrates through the eastern US to its winter quarters in southern Mexico and Central America to Panama, where it favors the shade of bird-friendly coffee plantations.

VOICE Call *chu-wee* and abrupt *brrrrt*; song abrupt *killink*, *che-lek*, or *che-bunk*, with variations.

NESTING Cup of moss, twigs, and needles on or near ground, often in a bog; 3–5 eggs; 1 brood; June–July.

FEEDING Catches insects in the air or gleans mosquitoes, midges, and flies from foliage; sometimes eats berries and seeds.

WELL HIDDEN
These birds, subtly patterned with pale yellow and green, have excellent camouflage in foliage.

SIMILAR SPECIES

ACADIAN FLYCATCHER see p.234
larger bill; larger overall; lacks olive on breast; longer, wider tail

LEAST FLYCATCHER distinctive call; see p.237
darker lower mandible; distinct, pale throat patch

OCCURRENCE
Breeds from Alaska to Quebec, Newfoundland, and the northeast US (New England) in boreal forests and bogs dominated by spruce trees. Winters in Mexico and Central America to Panama, in lowland forests, second-growth, and riverside habitats.

Length **5½in (14cm)**	Wingspan **8in (20cm)**	Weight **9/32–½oz (8–15g)**
Social **Solitary**	Lifespan **At least 4 years**	Status **Secure**

DATE: ____________ TIME: ____________ LOCATION: ____________

Order **Passeriformes**	Family **Tyrannidae**	Species ***Empidonax virescens***

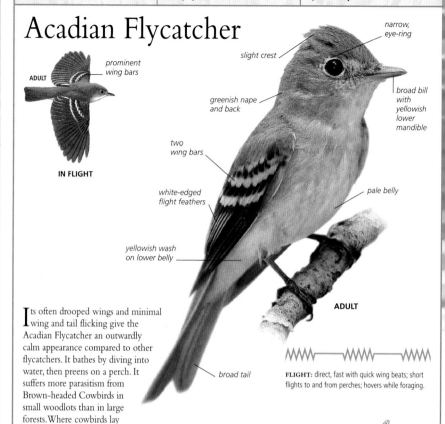

Acadian Flycatcher

ADULT

prominent wing bars

IN FLIGHT

slight crest

narrow, eye-ring

broad bill with yellowish lower mandible

greenish nape and back

two wing bars

white-edged flight feathers

pale belly

yellowish wash on lower belly

broad tail

ADULT

FLIGHT: direct, fast with quick wing beats; short flights to and from perches; hovers while foraging.

Its often drooped wings and minimal wing and tail flicking give the Acadian Flycatcher an outwardly calm appearance compared to other flycatchers. It bathes by diving into water, then preens on a perch. It suffers more parasitism from Brown-headed Cowbirds in small woodlots than in large forests. Where cowbirds lay their eggs in the flycatcher's nest, they displace the flycatcher's young.

VOICE Contact call soft *peet,* one of many calls; territorial song *tee-chup, peet-sah* or *flee-sick*, loud and "explosive" sounding.

NESTING Shallow open cup in tree fork or shrub near water; 3 eggs; 2 broods; May–August.

FEEDING Takes insects from undersides of leaves, also catches them in the air and occasionally on the ground; eats berries.

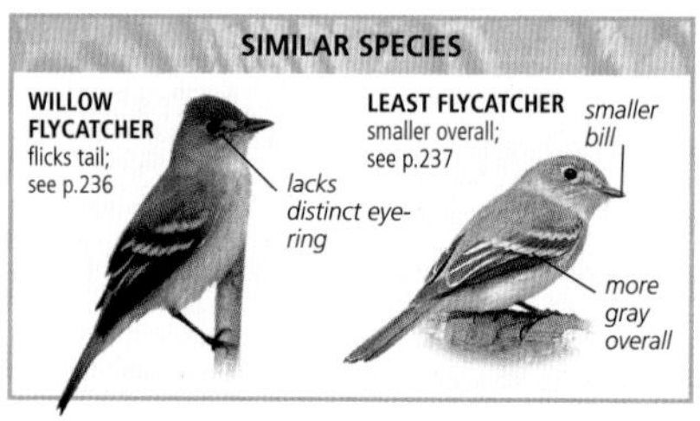
SIMILAR SPECIES
WILLOW FLYCATCHER
flicks tail;
see p.236
lacks distinct eye-ring
LEAST FLYCATCHER
smaller overall;
see p.237
smaller bill
more gray overall

TOP PERFORMER

This flycatcher is seen typically perched on a treetop from where it sings forcefully.

OCCURRENCE

Breeds in the eastern US and southern Ontario in mature deciduous forests associated with water; prefers large undisturbed tracts. Winters in Nicaragua, Costa Rica, and Panama, and in South America along the Andes from Venezuela and Colombia to Ecuador, in tropical forests and woodlands with evergreen trees.

Length **6in (15cm)**	Wingspan **9in (23cm)**	Weight **3/8–1/2oz (11–14g)**
Social **Solitary**	Lifespan **Up to 10 years**	Status **Endangered**

DATE: ____________ TIME: ____________ LOCATION: ____________________

Order **Passeriformes**	Family **Tyrannidae**	Species ***Empidonax alnorum***

Alder Flycatcher

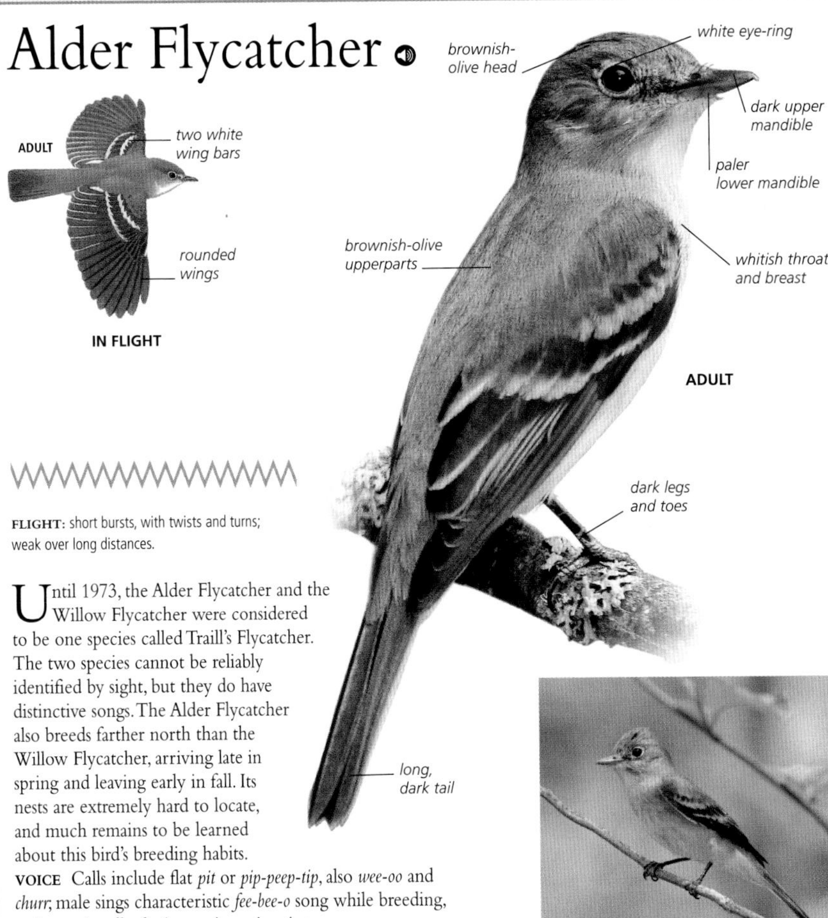
ADULT
two white wing bars
rounded wings
IN FLIGHT
brownish-olive head
white eye-ring
dark upper mandible
paler lower mandible
brownish-olive upperparts
whitish throat and breast
ADULT
dark legs and toes
long, dark tail

FLIGHT: short bursts, with twists and turns; weak over long distances.

Until 1973, the Alder Flycatcher and the Willow Flycatcher were considered to be one species called Traill's Flycatcher. The two species cannot be reliably identified by sight, but they do have distinctive songs. The Alder Flycatcher also breeds farther north than the Willow Flycatcher, arriving late in spring and leaving early in fall. Its nests are extremely hard to locate, and much remains to be learned about this bird's breeding habits.

VOICE Calls include flat *pit* or *pip-peep-tip*, also *wee-oo* and *churr*; male sings characteristic *fee-bee-o* song while breeding, and occasionally during spring migration.

NESTING Coarse and loosely structured nest low in fork of deciduous shrub; 3–4 eggs; 1 brood; June–July.

FEEDING Mostly eats insects, caught mainly in flight, but some gleaned from foliage; eats fruit in winter.

ON THE ALERT
Attentive to potential meals, an Alder Flycatcher will swiftly pursue prey as soon as it flies by.

SIMILAR SPECIES

ACADIAN FLYCATCHER see p.234
longer, deeper bill; greener back

WILLOW FLYCATCHER see p.236
slightly longer bill; fainter eye-ring

OCCURRENCE
Breeds at low density across northern North America, in wet shrubby habitats with alder or willow thickets, often close to streams. Winters at low elevations in South America, in tropical second-growth forest and forest edges.

Length **5¾in (14.5cm)**	Wingspan **8½in (22cm)**	Weight **½oz (14g)**
Social **Solitary**	Lifespan **At least 3 years**	Status **Secure**

DATE: ____________ TIME: ____________ LOCATION: ____________

Order **Passeriformes**	Family **Tyrannidae**	Species ***Empidonax traillii***

Willow Flycatcher

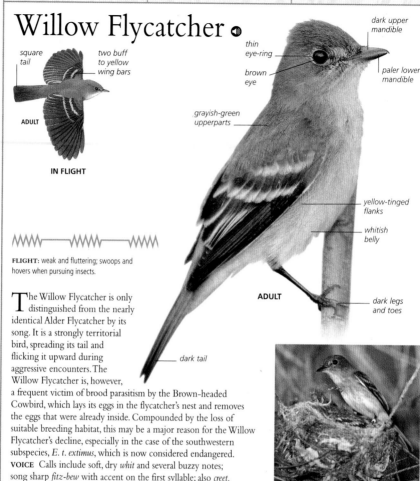

square tail
two buff to yellow wing bars
ADULT
IN FLIGHT

dark upper mandible
thin eye-ring
brown eye
paler lower mandible
grayish-green upperparts
yellow-tinged flanks
whitish belly
ADULT
dark legs and toes
dark tail

FLIGHT: weak and fluttering; swoops and hovers when pursuing insects.

The Willow Flycatcher is only distinguished from the nearly identical Alder Flycatcher by its song. It is a strongly territorial bird, spreading its tail and flicking it upward during aggressive encounters. The Willow Flycatcher is, however, a frequent victim of brood parasitism by the Brown-headed Cowbird, which lays its eggs in the flycatcher's nest and removes the eggs that were already inside. Compounded by the loss of suitable breeding habitat, this may be a major reason for the Willow Flycatcher's decline, especially in the case of the southwestern subspecies, *E. t. extimus*, which is now considered endangered.

VOICE Calls include soft, dry *whit* and several buzzy notes; song sharp *fitz-bew* with accent on the first syllable; also *creet*.

NESTING Rather loose and untidy cup in base of shrub near water; 3–4 eggs; 1 brood; May–August.

FEEDING Eats insects, mostly caught in flight; eats fruit in winter.

UNEVEN WORKLOAD
Although both parents feed their young, the female Willow Flycatcher does so the most.

SIMILAR SPECIES

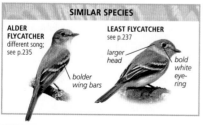

ALDER FLYCATCHER different song; see p.235
bolder wing bars

LEAST FLYCATCHER see p.237
larger head
bold white eye-ring

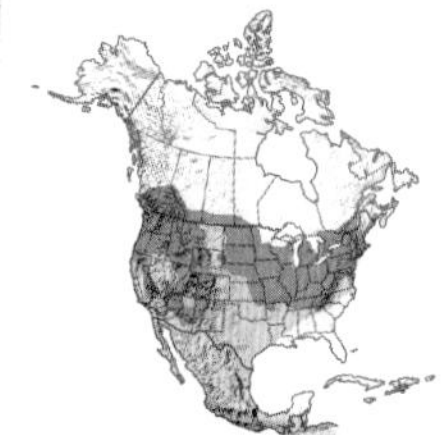

OCCURRENCE
Breeds from southern Canada to the eastern and southwestern US, mainly in willow thickets and other moist shrubby areas along watercourses. On winter grounds, it favors lighter woodland, shrubby clearings, and brush near water in coastal areas.

Length **5–6¾in (13–17cm)**	Wingspan **7½–9½in (19–24cm)**	Weight **⅜–9/16oz (11–16g)**
Social **Solitary**	Lifespan **Up to 11 years**	Status **Declining**

DATE: ____________ TIME: ____________ LOCATION: ____________

Order **Passeriformes**	Family **Tyrannidae**	Species ***Empidonax minimus***

Least Flycatcher

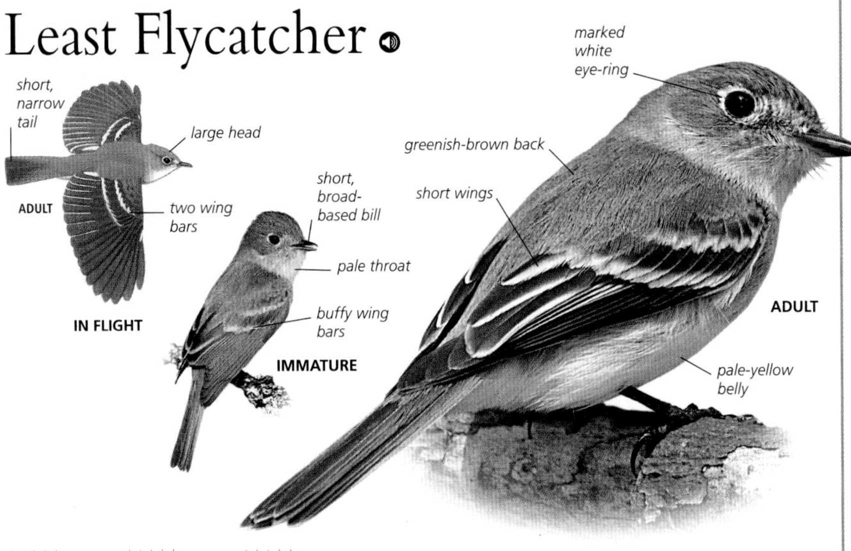
short, narrow tail
large head
ADULT
two wing bars
IN FLIGHT
short, broad-based bill
pale throat
buffy wing bars
IMMATURE
marked white eye-ring
greenish-brown back
short wings
ADULT
pale-yellow belly

FLIGHT: direct, short forays with rapid wing beats to catch prey; sometimes hovers briefly.

The smallest eastern member of the *Empidonax* genus is a solitary bird and is very aggressive toward intruders encroaching upon its breeding territory, including other species of flycatchers. This combative behavior reduces the likelihood of acting as unwitting host parents to eggs laid by the Brown-headed Cowbird. The Least Flycatcher is very active, and frequently flicks its wings and tail upward. It is common in the eastern US and across Canada in mixed and deciduous woodland, especially at the edges. It spends a short time—up to only two months—on its northern breeding grounds before migrating south. Adults molt in winter, while the young molt before and during fall migration.

VOICE Call soft, short *whit*; song frequent, persistent, characteristic *tchebeck*, sings during spring migration and breeding season.

NESTING Compact cup of tightly woven bark strips and plant fibers in fork of deciduous tree; 3–5 eggs; 1 brood; May–July.

FEEDING Feeds principally on insects, such as flies, midges, beetles, ants, butterflies, and larvae; occasionally eats berries and seeds.

YELLOW TINGE
The subtle yellow tinge to its underparts and white undertail feathers are evident here.

SIMILAR SPECIES

WILLOW FLYCATCHER see p.236
larger body; longer bill

ALDER FLYCATCHER see p.235
larger overall; wider tail

OCCURRENCE
Breeds in coniferous and mixed deciduous forests across North America, east of Rockies to the East Coast; occasionally in conifer groves or wooded wetlands, often near openings or edges. Winters in Central America in varied habitat from second-growth evergreen woodland to arid scrub.

Length **5¼in (13.5cm)**	Wingspan **7¾in (19.5cm)**	Weight **9/32–7/16oz (8–13g)**
Social **Solitary**	Lifespan **Up to 6 years**	Status **Secure**

DATE: ______________ TIME: ______________ LOCATION: ______________________________

Order **Passeriformes**	Family **Tyrannidae**	Species ***Sayornis phoebe***

Eastern Phoebe

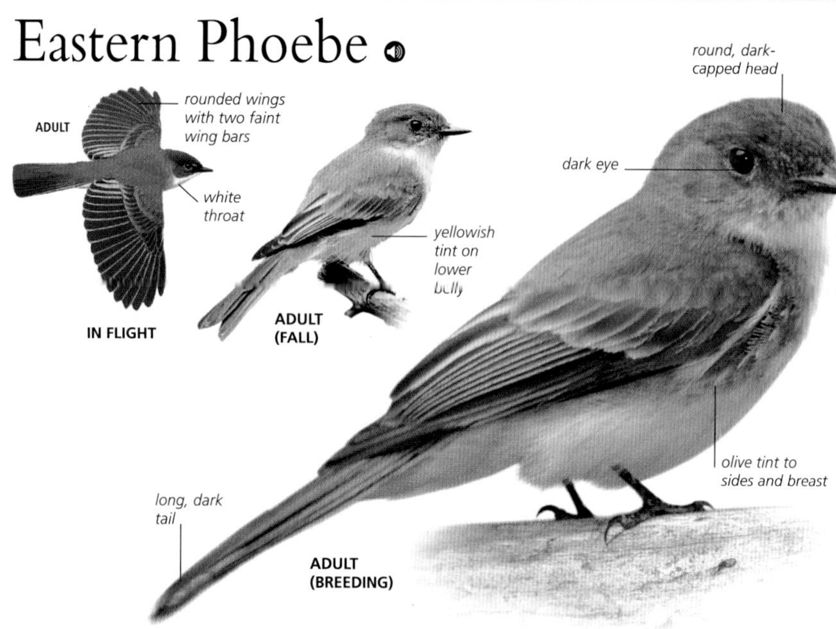

ADULT
rounded wings with two faint wing bars
white throat
IN FLIGHT
yellowish tint on lower belly
ADULT (FALL)
round, dark-capped head
dark eye
olive tint to sides and breast
long, dark tail
ADULT (BREEDING)

The Eastern Phoebe is an early spring migrant that tends to nest under bridges, culverts, and on buildings, in addition to rocky outcroppings. Not shy, it is also familiar because of its *fee-bee* vocalization and constant tail wagging. By tying a thread on the leg of several Eastern Phoebes, ornithologist John James Audubon established that individuals return from the south to a previously used nest site. Although difficult to tell apart, males tend to be slightly larger and darker than females.

VOICE Common call a clear, weak *chip*; song an emphatic *fee-bee* or *fee-b-be-bee*.

NESTING Open cup of mud, moss, and leaves, almost exclusively on artificial structures; 3–5 eggs; 2 broods; April–July.

FEEDING Feeds mainly on flying insects; also consumes small fruit from fall through winter.

FLIGHT: direct, with steady wing beats; hovers occasionally; approaches nest with a low swoop.

PALE EDGES
Perched on a twig, a male shows off the pale margins of his wing feathers.

LIGHTER FEMALE
They are difficult to distinguish, but the female is slightly lighter-colored overall than the male.

SIMILAR SPECIES

EASTERN WOOD-PEWEE lacks tail-wag; see p.232
distinct wing bars

WILLOW FLYCATCHER flicks tail upwards; see p.236
often has eye-ring
more distinct wing bars
smaller overall

OCCURRENCE
Found in open woodland and along deciduous or mixed forest edges, in gardens and parks, near water. Breeds across Canada from the Northwest Territories south of the tundra belt and in the eastern half of the US. Winters in the southeast US and Mexico.

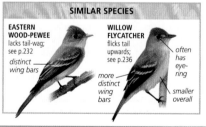

Length **5½–7in (14–17cm)**	Wingspan **10½in (27cm)**	Weight **$^{11}/_{16}$oz (20g)**
Social **Solitary**	Lifespan **Up to 9 years**	Status **Secure**

DATE: ______________ TIME: ______________ LOCATION: ______________

Family **Vireonidae**

VIREOS

VIREOS ARE A FAMILY of songbirds restricted to the New World, with 15 species occurring in Canada and the United States. The classification of vireos has long been problematic—traditionally they were associated with warblers, but recent molecular studies suggest that they are actually related to crow-like birds. Vireo plumage is drab, often predominantly greenish or grayish above and whitish below, augmented by eye-rings, "spectacles," eyestripes, and wing bars. Most vireos have a preference for broad-leaved habitats, where they move about deliberately, hopping and climbing as they slowly forage for their prey. Because they are mainly insect-eaters, most are mid- to long-distance migrants, retreating to warmer climes in winter, when insects are dormant. Vireos are most often detected by the male's loud and clear territorial song, which is repetitive and persistent.

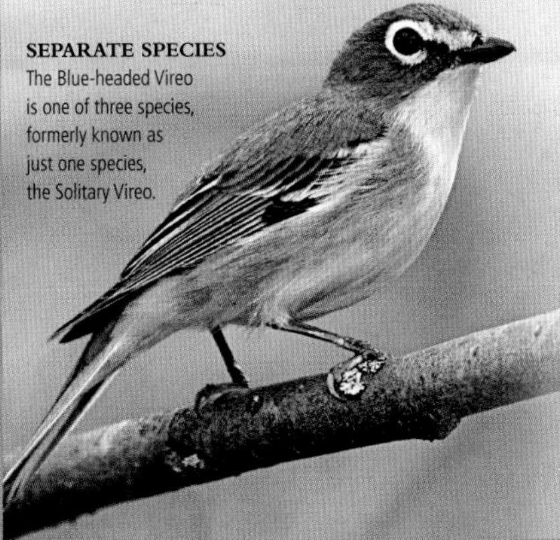

SEPARATE SPECIES
The Blue-headed Vireo is one of three species, formerly known as just one species, the Solitary Vireo.

KEEN SONGSTER
The White-eyed Vireo sings almost continuously, even on the hottest days of summer.

Family **Corvidae**

JAYS AND CROWS

ALTHOUGH JAYS AND CROWS belong to a highly diverse family, the corvids, most members share some important characteristics. They are remarkably social, some species even breed cooperatively, but at the same time they can be quiet and stealthy. Always the opportunists, corvids use strong bills and toes to obtain a varied, omnivorous diet. Ornithologists have shown that ravens, magpies, jays, and crows are among the most intelligent birds. They exhibit self-awareness when looking into mirrors, can make tools, and successfully tackle difficult counting and problem-solving. As a rule, most corvid plumage comes in shades of blue, black, and/or white. The plumage of adult corvids does not vary by season. Corvidae are part of an ancient bird lineage (Corvoidea) that originated in Australasia. Crows and jays were among the birds most affected by the spread of West Nile virus in the early 2000s, but most populations seem to have recovered quickly.

BRAINY BIRD
Common Ravens are one of the smartest birds, known for their problem-solving skills.

Order **Passeriformes**	Family **Laniidae**	Species ***Lanius ludovicianus***

Loggerhead Shrike

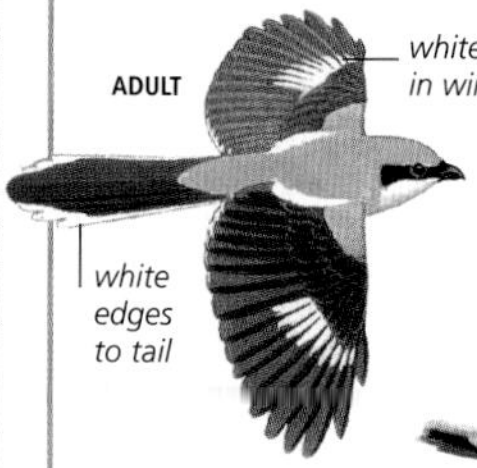

ADULT
white flash in wings
white edges to tail
IN FLIGHT

black wings
pale undertail feathers
IMMATURE

gray crown
hooked bill
black mask
unstreaked gray underparts
rounded tail
ADULT

FLIGHT: fast with rapid wing beats, sometimes interspersed with glides; swoops from perches.

While formally regarded as a songbird, the Loggerhead Shrike, with its prominent black face mask, has a hooked bill and behaves like a small bird of prey. It sits atop posts or tall trees, swooping down to catch prey on the ground. It has the unusual habit of then impaling its prey on thorns, barbed wire, or sharp twigs, which is the reason for the nickname "butcher bird." Unfortunately, Loggerhead Shrike numbers are declining, possibly because of human alteration of its habitat and/or food resources.

VOICE Quiet warbles, trills, and harsh notes; song harsh notes singly or in series: *chaa chaa chaa*.

NESTING Open cup of vegetation, placed in thorny tree; 5 eggs; 1 brood; March–June.

FEEDING Kills large insects and small vertebrates—rodents, birds, reptiles—with its powerful bill.

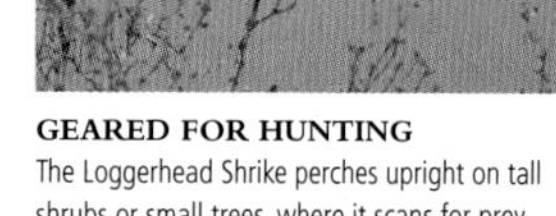

GEARED FOR HUNTING
The Loggerhead Shrike perches upright on tall shrubs or small trees, where it scans for prey.

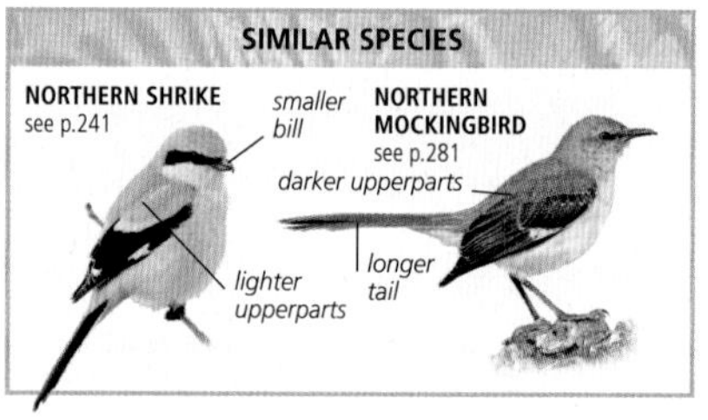
SIMILAR SPECIES
NORTHERN SHRIKE
see p.241
smaller bill
lighter upperparts
NORTHERN MOCKINGBIRD
see p.281
darker upperparts
longer tail

OCCURRENCE
Found in semi-open country with scattered perches, but its distribution is erratic, occurring in relatively high densities in certain areas, but absent from seemingly suitable habitat. Occurs in congested residential areas in some regions (south Florida), but generally favors fairly remote habitats.

Length **9in (23cm)**	Wingspan **12in (31cm)**	Weight **1¼–2⅛oz (35–60g)**
Social **Solitary**	Lifespan **Unknown**	Status **Declining**

DATE: ______________ TIME: ______________ LOCATION: ______________

Order **Passeriformes**	Family **Laniidae**	Species ***Lanius borealis***

Northern Shrike

ADULT

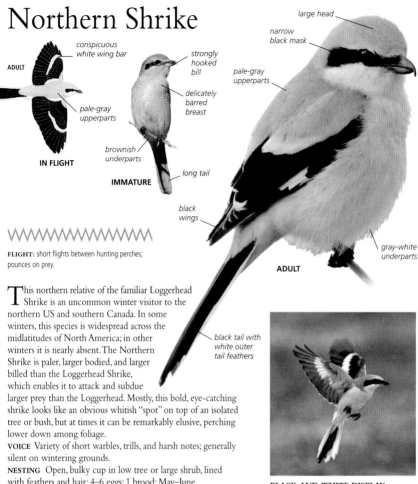

conspicuous white wing bar

pale-gray upperparts

IN FLIGHT

strongly hooked bill

delicately barred breast

brownish underparts

long tail

IMMATURE

large head

narrow black mask

pale-gray upperparts

black wings

gray-white underparts

black tail with white outer tail feathers

ADULT

FLIGHT: short flights between hunting perches; pounces on prey.

This northern relative of the familiar Loggerhead Shrike is an uncommon winter visitor to the northern US and southern Canada. In some winters, this species is widespread across the midlatitudes of North America; in other winters it is nearly absent. The Northern Shrike is paler, larger bodied, and larger billed than the Loggerhead Shrike, which enables it to attack and subdue larger prey than the Loggerhead. Mostly, this bold, eye-catching shrike looks like an obvious whitish "spot" on top of an isolated tree or bush, but at times it can be remarkably elusive, perching lower down among foliage.

VOICE Variety of short warbles, trills, and harsh notes; generally silent on wintering grounds.

NESTING Open, bulky cup in low tree or large shrub, lined with feathers and hair; 4–6 eggs; 1 brood; May–June.

FEEDING Swoops down on prey, such as rodents, small birds, and insects, which it impales on thorns or pointed branches.

BLACK-AND-WHITE DISPLAY
The Northern Shrike flashes its distinctive black-and-white markings while in flight.

SIMILAR SPECIES

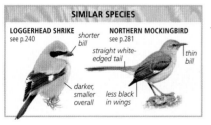

LOGGERHEAD SHRIKE
see p.240

shorter bill

darker, smaller overall

NORTHERN MOCKINGBIRD
see p.281

straight white-edged tail

thin bill

less black in wings

OCCURRENCE
Breeds in sub-Arctic coniferous forests, across Canada and Alaska. Winters in more southerly open country with sufficient perches. Avoids built-up and residential districts, but spends much time perching on fence posts and roadside signs.

Length **10in (25cm)**	Wingspan **14in (35cm)**	Weight **1¾–2⅝oz (50–75g)**
Social **Solitary**	Lifespan **Unknown**	Status **Vulnerable**

DATE: ______________ TIME: ______________ LOCATION: ______________________________

Order **Passeriformes**	Family **Vireonidae**	Species ***Vireo griseus***

White-eyed Vireo

two wing bars
ADULT
short tail
IN FLIGHT

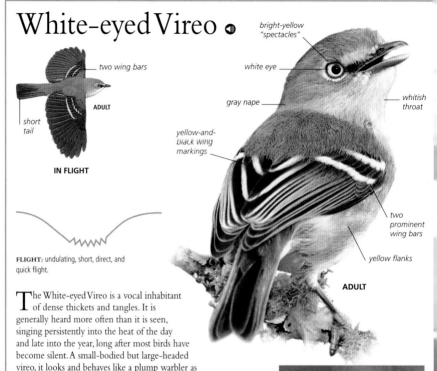

bright-yellow "spectacles"
white eye
gray nape
whitish throat
yellow-and-black wing markings
two prominent wing bars
yellow flanks
ADULT

FLIGHT: undulating, short, direct, and quick flight.

The White-eyed Vireo is a vocal inhabitant of dense thickets and tangles. It is generally heard more often than it is seen, singing persistently into the heat of the day and late into the year, long after most birds have become silent. A small-bodied but large-headed vireo, it looks and behaves like a plump warbler as it forages actively in shrubbery. It is heavily parasitized by the Brown-headed Cowbird, and as many as half of the White-eyed Vireo's offsprings do not survive.

VOICE Call a raspy, angry scold; male's song a highly variable and complex repertoire of over a dozen distinct songs.

NESTING Deep cup in dense vegetation, outer layer composed of coarse material, lined with finer fibers, often near water, suspended from twigs by the rim; 3–5 eggs; 2 broods; March–July.

FEEDING Hops from branch to branch pursuing bees, flies, beetles, and bugs, plucking them from leaves or sallying out to snatch them in the air; feeds primarily on fruit in winter.

WHITE EYE, WHITE WING BARS
The White-eyed Vireo's distinctive markings ensure that it is highly conspicuous.

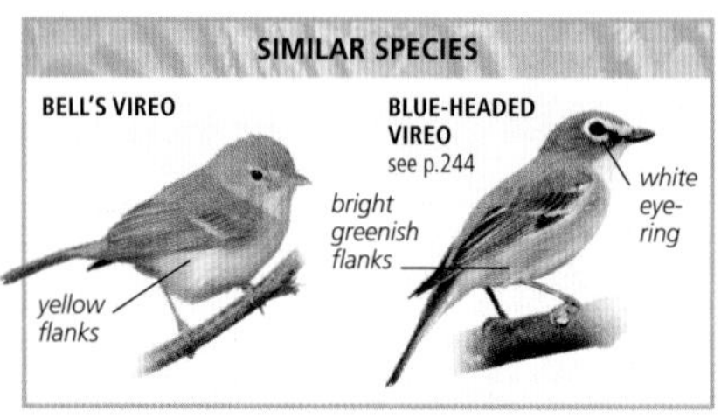
SIMILAR SPECIES
BELL'S VIREO
yellow flanks
BLUE-HEADED VIREO
see p.244
bright greenish flanks
white eye-ring

OCCURRENCE
A common breeder in dense brush and scrub across the eastern US and southern Ontario, from Texas to the Great Lakes region and southern New England. Retreats to southern states of the US, the Atlantic slope of Mexico, Cuba, and the Bahamas in winter.

Length **5in (13cm)**	Wingspan **7½in (19cm)**	Weight **⅜oz (10g)**
Social **Solitary**	Lifespan **Up to 7 years**	Status **Secure**

DATE: ______ TIME: ______ LOCATION: ______

Order **Passeriformes**	Family **Vireonidae**	Species ***Vireo flavifrons***

Yellow-throated Vireo

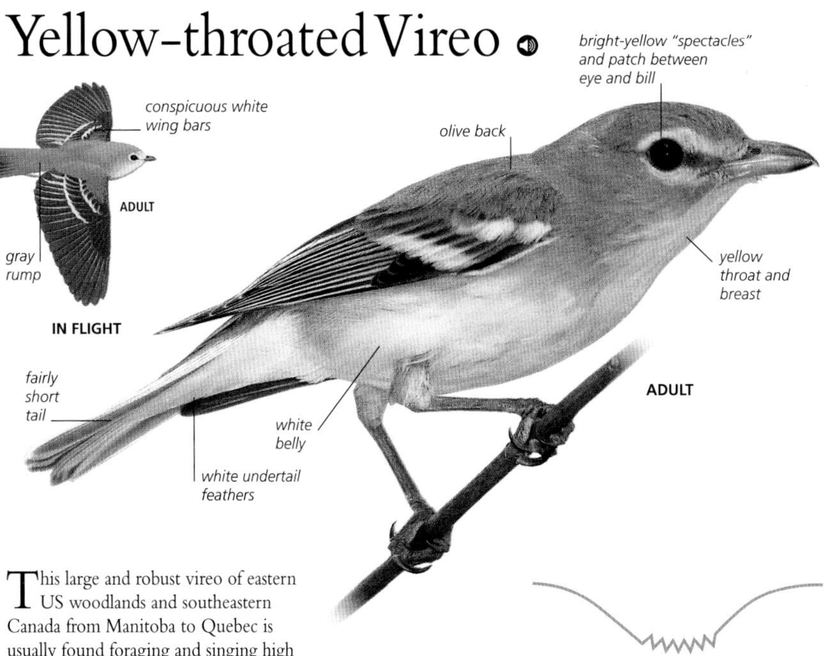
bright-yellow "spectacles" and patch between eye and bill
conspicuous white wing bars
olive back
ADULT
gray rump
IN FLIGHT
yellow throat and breast
fairly short tail
ADULT
white belly
white undertail feathers

This large and robust vireo of eastern US woodlands and southeastern Canada from Manitoba to Quebec is usually found foraging and singing high in the canopy. It is distinctly patterned, with a bright-yellow throat, breast, and "spectacles," and a white belly and flanks. The fragmentation of forests, spraying of insecticides, and cowbird parasitism have led to regional declines in Yellow-throated Vireo populations, but the bird's range, as a whole, has actually expanded.

VOICE Scolding, hoarse, rapid calls; male song a slow, repetitive, two- or three-note phrase, separated by long pauses.

NESTING Rounded cup of plant and animal fibers bound with spider webs, usually located toward the top of a large tree and hung by the rim; 3–5 eggs; 1 brood; April–July.

FEEDING Forages high in trees, picking insects from the branches; also eats fruit when available.

FLIGHT: direct, but jerky, alternating rapid wing beats with brief pauses.

CANOPY SINGER
The Yellow-throated Vireo sings from the very tops of tall trees.

HIGH FORAGER
This bird finds much of its food in the peeling bark of mature trees.

SIMILAR SPECIES

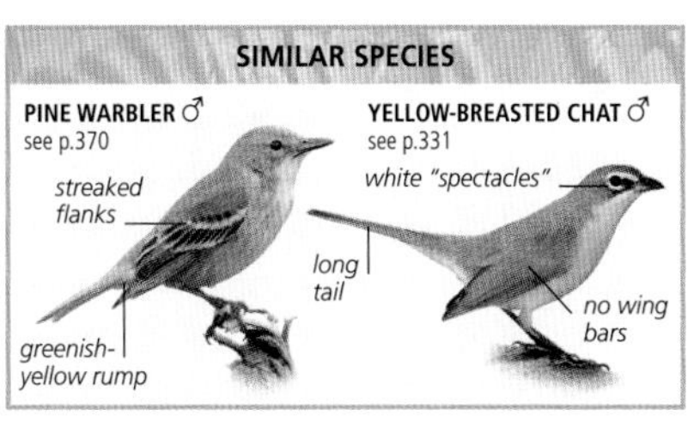
PINE WARBLER ♂
see p.370
streaked flanks
greenish-yellow rump
YELLOW-BREASTED CHAT ♂
see p.331
white "spectacles"
long tail
no wing bars

OCCURRENCE
Breeds in extensive mature deciduous and mixed woodlands in the eastern half of the US, and extreme southern Canada. Winters mainly from southern Mexico to northern South America, primarily in wooded areas.

Length **5½in (14cm)**	Wingspan **9½in (24cm)**	Weight **⅝oz (18g)**
Social **Solitary/Pairs**	Lifespan **Up to 6 years**	Status **Secure**

DATE: ____________ TIME: ____________ LOCATION: ____________

Order **Passeriformes**	Family **Vireonidae**	Species ***Vireo solitarius***

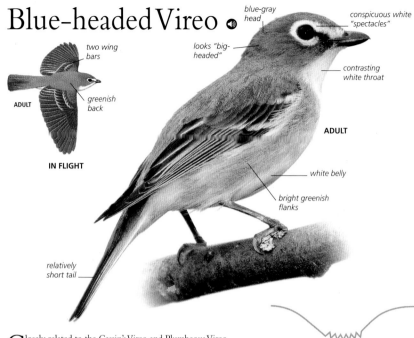

Blue-headed Vireo

blue-gray head

conspicuous white "spectacles"

looks "big-headed"

contrasting white throat

two wing bars

greenish back

ADULT

IN FLIGHT

ADULT

white belly

bright greenish flanks

relatively short tail

Closely related to the Cassin's Vireo and Plumbeous Vireo, the fairly common Blue-headed Vireo is the brightest and most colorful of the three. Its blue-gray, helmeted head, adorned with striking white "spectacles" around its dark eyes, also helps to distinguish it from other vireos in its range. This stocky and slow-moving bird is heard more often than it is seen in its forest breeding habitat. However, during migration it can be more conspicuous, and it is the first vireo to return in spring.

VOICE Call a harsh, scolding chatter; male's song a series of rich, sweet, high phrases of two to six notes slurred together.

NESTING Shallow, rounded cup loosely constructed of animal and plant fibers, lined with finer material and suspended from twigs by the rim; 3–5 eggs; 2 broods; May–July.

FEEDING Gleans insects from branches and leaves, usually high in shrubs and trees; often makes short sallies after prey.

FLIGHT: slow, heavy, undulating flight with a series of deep wing beats followed by short pauses.

SPECTACLED VIREO
Its rather thick head with conspicuous "spectacles" and gray color are distinctive field marks.

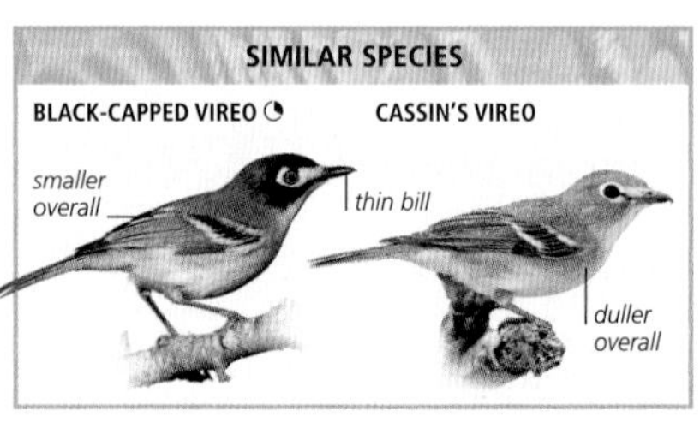
SIMILAR SPECIES
BLACK-CAPPED VIREO
CASSIN'S VIREO
smaller overall
thin bill
duller overall

OCCURRENCE
Breeds in large tracts of undisturbed coniferous and mixed forests with a rich understory, largely across eastern North America. It winters in woodlands across the southeastern US from Virginia to Texas, as well as in Mexico and northern Central America to Costa Rica.

Length **5½in (14in)**	Wingspan **9½in (24cm)**	Weight **9/16oz (16g)**
Social **Solitary/Pairs**	Lifespan **Up to 7 years**	Status **Secure**

DATE: ______________ TIME: ______________ LOCATION: ______________

Order **Passeriformes**	Family **Vireonidae**	Species ***Vireo philadelphicus***

Philadelphia Vireo

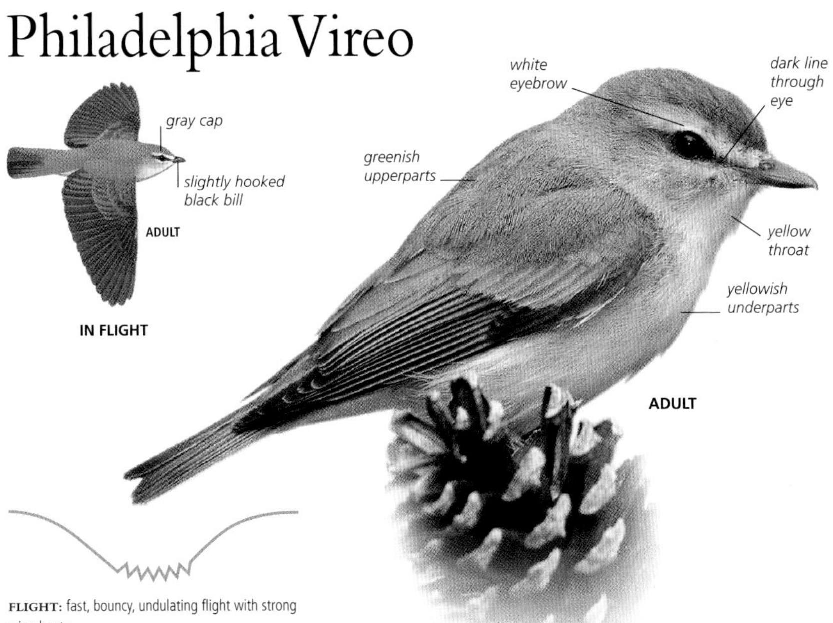
gray cap
slightly hooked black bill
ADULT
IN FLIGHT
white eyebrow
dark line through eye
greenish upperparts
yellow throat
yellowish underparts
ADULT

FLIGHT: fast, bouncy, undulating flight with strong wing beats.

Despite being widespread, the Philadelphia Vireo remains rather poorly studied. It shares its breeding habitat with the similar-looking, but larger and more numerous, Red-eyed Vireo, and, interestingly, it modifies its behavior to avoid competition. It is the most northerly breeding vireo, with its southernmost breeding range barely reaching the US. Its scientific and English names derive from the fact that the bird was first discovered near Philadelphia in the mid-19th century.

VOICE Song a series of two- and four-note phrases, remarkably similar to the song of the Red-eyed Vireo.

NESTING Rounded cup of plant fibers bound by spider webs, hanging between forked twigs that narrows at the rim; 3–5 eggs; 1–2 broods; June–August.

FEEDING Gleans caterpillars, bees, flies, and bugs from leaves; usually forages high in trees, moving with short hops and flights.

DISTINGUISHED APPEARANCE
The Philadelphia Vireo's gentle expression and pudgy appearance help separate it from its neighbor, the Red-eyed Vireo.

SIMILAR SPECIES

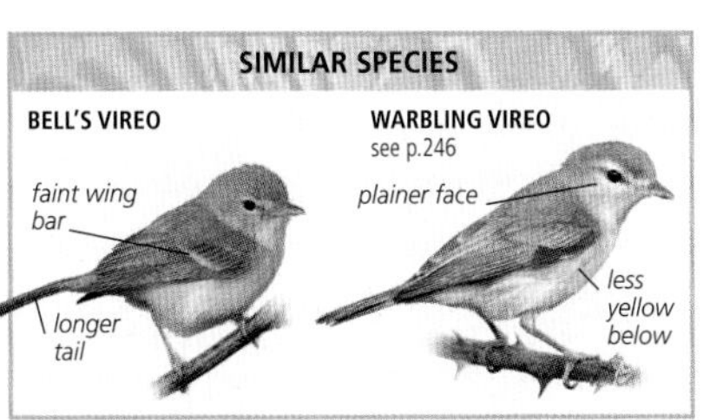
BELL'S VIREO
faint wing bar
longer tail
WARBLING VIREO
see p.246
plainer face
less yellow below

OCCURRENCE
Breeds in deciduous woodlands, mixed woodlands, and woodland edges, in a wide belt across Canada, reaching the Great Lakes and northern New England. The Philadelphia Vireo winters from Mexico to Panama and northern Colombia.

Length **5¼in (13.5cm)**	Wingspan **8in (20cm)**	Weight **7/16oz (12g)**
Social **Solitary/Pairs**	Lifespan **Up to 8 years**	Status **Secure**

DATE: ____________ TIME: ____________ LOCATION: ____________

Order **Passeriformes**	Family **Vireonidae**	Species ***Vireo gilvus***

Warbling Vireo

pale brownish crown contrasts with darker back
grayish-green upperparts
blackish bill
ADULT
ADULT (FALL)
IN FLIGHT
white eyebrow
grayish behind eye
pale patch between eye and bill
grayish overall
yellowish flanks
ADULT

FLIGHT: fast and undulating; rapid wing beats followed by brief, closed-winged glides.

Widely distributed across North America, this rather drab vireo is better known for its cheerful warbling song than for its plumage. Coincidentally, its thin bill and longish tail give this rather active vireo a somewhat warbler-like appearance. Eastern and Western Warbling Vireos are quite different and may, in fact, be separate species. Eastern birds are heavier and have a larger bill. Of all the vireos, the Warbling Vireo is most likely to breed in human developments, such as city parks, suburbs, and orchards.

VOICE Harsh, raspy scold call; male's persistent song a high, rapid, and highly variable warble.

NESTING Rough cup placed high in a deciduous tree, hung from the rim between forked twigs; 3–5 eggs; 2 broods; March–July.

FEEDING Gleans a variety of insects, including grasshoppers, aphids, and beetles from leaves; eats fruit in winter.

PLAIN-LOOKING SONGSTER
The Warbling Vireo makes up for its plain appearance by its colorful voice, full of rounded notes and melodious warbles.

SIMILAR SPECIES

BELL'S VIREO
faint wing bar
longer tail
PHILADELPHIA VIREO
see p.245
dark line extends to bill
no wing bar
shorter bill
yellow on breast and throat

OCCURRENCE
Extensive distribution across most of temperate North America, from Alaska to western, central, and eastern North America. Breeds in deciduous and mixed forests, particularly near water. Winters in southern Mexico and Central America.

Length **5½in (14cm)**	Wingspan **8½in (21cm)**	Weight **7/16oz (12g)**
Social **Solitary/Pairs**	Lifespan **Up to 13 years**	Status **Secure**

DATE: ______________ TIME: ______________ LOCATION: ______________

Order **Passeriformes**	Family **Vireonidae**	Species ***Vireo olivaceus***

Red-eyed Vireo

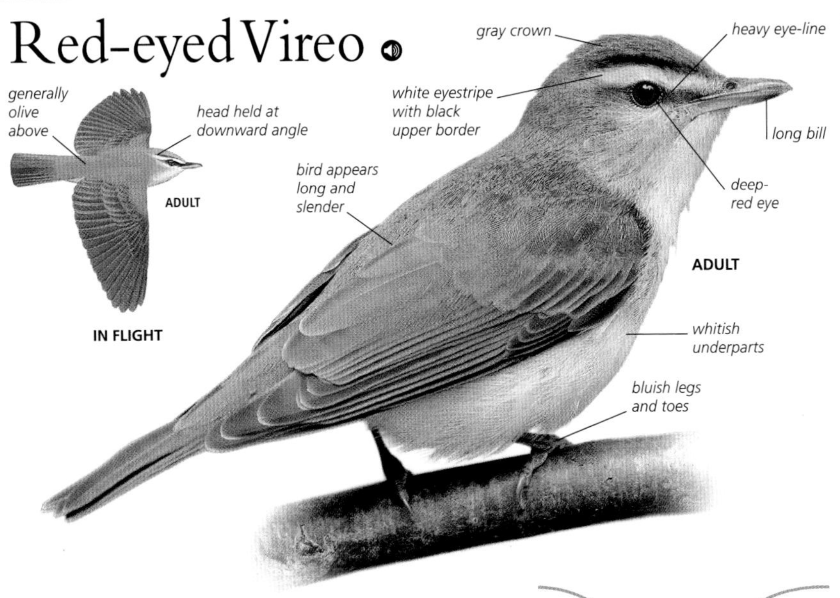

generally olive above
head held at downward angle
ADULT
IN FLIGHT
gray crown
heavy eye-line
white eyestripe with black upper border
long bill
bird appears long and slender
deep-red eye
ADULT
whitish underparts
bluish legs and toes

FLIGHT: fast, strong, and undulating with the body angled upwards.

Probably the most common songbird of northern and eastern North America, the Red-eyed Vireo is perhaps the quintessential North American vireo, although it is heard far more often than it is seen. It sings persistently and monotonously all day long and late into the season, long after other species have stopped singing. It generally stays high in the canopy of the deciduous and mixed woodlands where it breeds. The entire population migrates to central South America in winter. To reach their Amazonian winter habitats, Red-eyed Vireos migrate in fall (August–October) through Central America, Caribbean Islands, and northern South America to Educador, Peru, and Brazil.

VOICE Nasal mewing call; male song consists of slurred short, robin-like, three-note phrases.

NESTING Open cup nest hanging on horizontal fork of tree branch; built with plant fibers bound with spider's web; exterior is sometimes decorated with lichen; 3–5 eggs; 1 brood; May–July.

FEEDING Gleans insects from leaves, hopping methodically in the canopy and sub-canopy of deciduous trees; during fall and winter, primarily feeds on fruit.

HOPPING BIRD
The Red-eyed Vireo's primary form of locomotion is hopping; at ground level and in trees.

SIMILAR SPECIES

BLACK-WHISKERED VIREO
faint black "mustache"
duller green upperparts

BROWN EYES
Immature Red-eyed Vireos have brown eyes, but those of the adult birds are red.

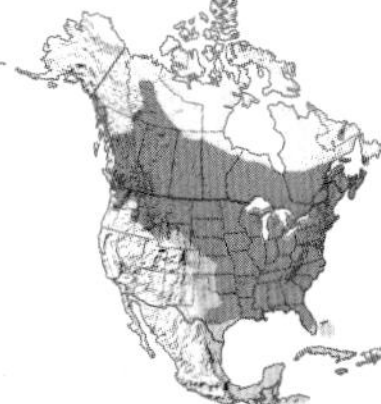

OCCURRENCE
Breeds across North America from the Yukon and British Columbia east to the Canadian Maritimes, and from Washington to the eastern and southeastern US. Inhabits canopy of deciduous forests and pine hardwood forests.

Length **6in (15cm)**	Wingspan **10in (25cm)**	Weight **⅝oz (17g)**
Social **Solitary/Pairs**	Lifespan **Up to 10 years**	Status **Secure**

DATE: ____________ TIME: ____________ LOCATION: ____________

Order **Passeriformes**	Family **Corvidae**	Species ***Perisoreus canadensis***

Canada Jay

ADULT

IN FLIGHT

long tail with white corners

dark-gray upperparts

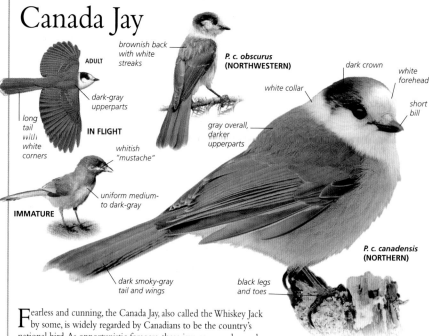

brownish back with white streaks

P. c. obscurus (NORTHWESTERN)

whitish "mustache"

uniform medium- to dark-gray

IMMATURE

dark crown

white forehead

white collar

short bill

gray overall, darker upperparts

P. c. canadensis (NORTHERN)

dark smoky-gray tail and wings

black legs and toes

Fearless and cunning, the Canada Jay, also called the Whiskey Jack by some, is widely regarded by Canadians to be the country's national bird. As opportunistic foragers, these jays commonly perch on the hands and heads of campers, hikers, and skiers, looking for handouts. This tough, non-migratory bird, capable of incubating its eggs at -30°C (-22°F), relies on cold fall and winter temperatures to preserve its food items, storing them under tree bark above the snow with sticky saliva. While numbers are stable across the country, a long-studied population in Algonquin Park has seen its breeding population halved in recent years, likely due to global warming causing its stored food to rot.

VOICE Mostly silent, but also produces variety of odd clucks and screeches; sometimes Blue Jay-like *jay!* and eerie warning whistles, including bisyllabic *whee-oo* or *ew*.

NESTING Bulky platform of sticks with cocoons on south side of coniferous tree; 2–5 eggs; 1 brood; February–May.

FEEDING Forages for insects and berries; also raids birds' nests.

FLIGHT: hollow-sounding wing beats followed by slow, seemingly awkward, rocking glides.

BUILT FOR COLD

The Canada Jay's short extremities and dense, fluffy plumage are perfect for long, harsh winters.

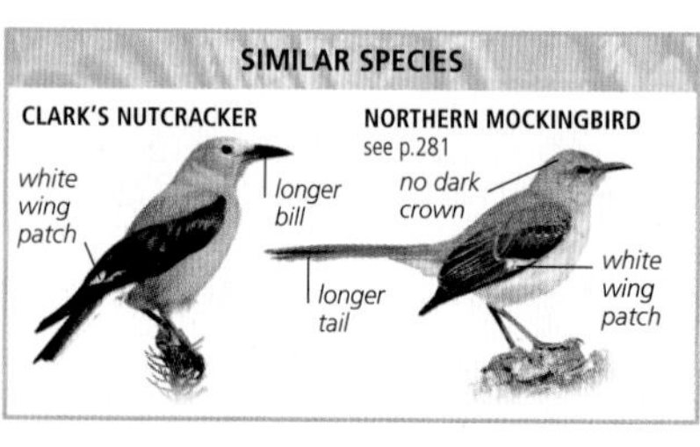
SIMILAR SPECIES
CLARK'S NUTCRACKER
white wing patch
longer bill
NORTHERN MOCKINGBIRD
see p.281
no dark crown
longer tail
white wing patch

OCCURRENCE

Northerly forests, especially lichen-festooned areas with firs and spruces. Found in coniferous forests across northern North America from Alaska to Newfoundland, the Maritimes, and north New York and New England; south to the western mountains.

Length **10–11½in (25–29cm)**	Wingspan **18in (46cm)**	Weight **2⅛–2⅞oz (60–80g)**
Social **Family groups**	Lifespan **Up to 10 years**	Status **Secure**

DATE: ____________ TIME: ____________ LOCATION: ____________

Order **Passeriformes**	Family **Corvidae**	Species ***Cyanocitta cristata***

Blue Jay

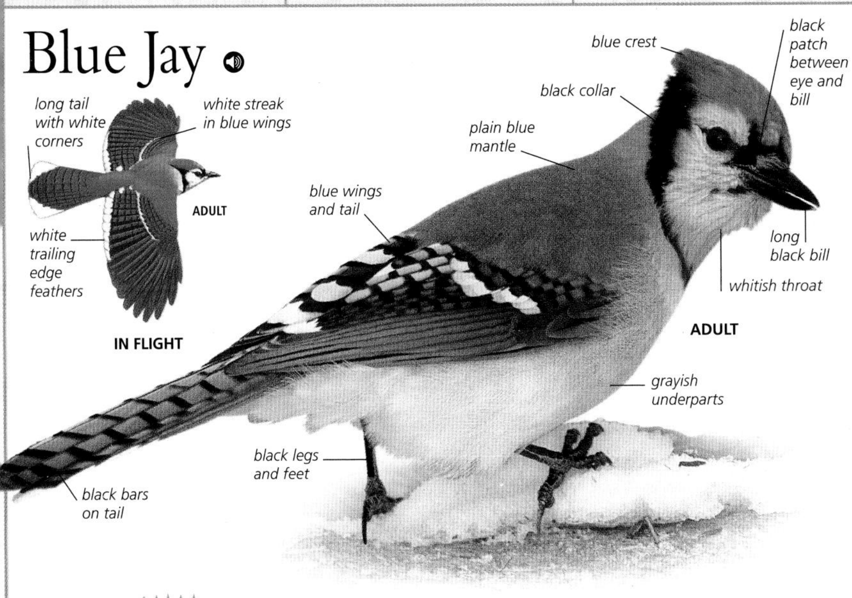
long tail with white corners
white streak in blue wings
ADULT
white trailing edge feathers
IN FLIGHT
blue crest
black patch between eye and bill
black collar
plain blue mantle
blue wings and tail
long black bill
whitish throat
ADULT
grayish underparts
black legs and feet
black bars on tail

FLIGHT: bursts of flapping followed by long glides on flat wings.

The Blue Jay is common in rural and suburban backyards across Canada and the eastern US. Beautiful as it is, the Blue Jay has a darker side. It often raids the nests of smaller birds for eggs and nestlings. Although usually thought of as a nonmigratory species, some Blue Jays undertake impressive migrations, with loose flocks sometimes numbering in the hundreds visible overhead in spring and fall. The Blue Jay is the provincial bird of Prince Edward Island.

VOICE Harsh, screaming *jay! jay!;* other common call an odd ethereal, chortling *queedle-ee-dee;* soft clucks when feeding. Known to mimic hawks.

NESTING Cup of strong twigs at variable height in trees or shrubs; 3–6 eggs; 1 brood; March–July.

FEEDING Eats insects, acorns, small vertebrates, such as lizards, rodents, bird eggs, birds, tree frogs; fruit and seeds.

UNIQUE FEATURES
The Blue Jay is unique among American jays, in having white patches on its wings and tail.

VERSATILE BIRD
Blue Jays are true omnivores, eating almost anything they can find. They are also excellent imitators of other bird calls.

SIMILAR SPECIES

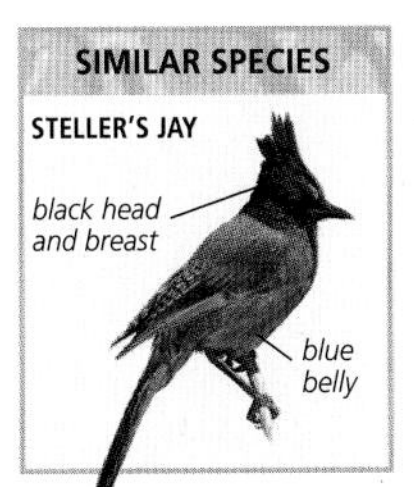
STELLER'S JAY
black head and breast
blue belly

OCCURRENCE
Native to eastern deciduous, coniferous, and mixed woodlands, but also at home in suburban vegetation; found extensively in backyards. The Blue Jay is especially fond of oak trees and their acorns.

Length **9½–12in (24–30cm)**	Wingspan **16in (41cm)**	Weight **2¼–3½oz (65–100g)**
Social **Small flocks**	Lifespan **Up to 7 years**	Status **Secure**

DATE: ______________ TIME: ______________ LOCATION: ______________________________

Order **Passeriformes**	Family **Corvidae**	Species ***Pica hudsonia***

Black-billed Magpie

large white patches on outer wings
white shoulder feathers
ADULT
IN FLIGHT
black back and head
blue-green iridescence to wings and tail
thick black bill
black breast
ADULT
white belly
long, dark tail

Loud, flashy, and conspicuous, the Black-billed Magpie is abundant in the northwestern quarter of the continent, from Alaska to the interior of the US. It has adapted to suburbia, confidently strutting across front lawns in some places. Until recently, it was considered to be the same species as the Eurasian Magpie (*P. pica*), but even though they look nearly identical, scientific evidence points instead to a close relationship with the other North American magpie, the Yellow-billed Magpie. Its long tail enables it to make rapid changes in direction in flight. The male will also use his tail to perform a variety of displays while courting a female. Black-billed Magpies are rarely found in large flocks, but they form them sometimes in fall.

VOICE Common call a questioning, nasal *ehnk*; also raspy *shenk, shenk, shenk*, usually in series.

NESTING Large, domed, often made of thorny sticks; 5–8 eggs; 1 brood; March–June.

FEEDING Omnivorous; forages on ground, mainly for insects, worms, seeds and carrion; even picks ticks from mammals.

FLIGHT: direct, with slow, steady, and often shallow wing beats; occasional shallow glides.

IRIDESCENT SHEEN
In bright sunlight, beautiful iridescent blues, greens, golds, and purples appear on the wings and tail.

SIMILAR SPECIES

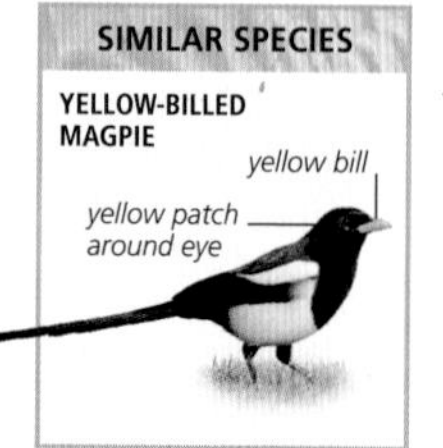
YELLOW-BILLED MAGPIE
yellow bill
yellow patch around eye

OCCURRENCE
Found in open habitats, foothills, and plains of the western US and Canada; nests in streamside vegetation; persecution has made it wary and restricted to wilderness in some areas, but in others it has adapted to suburbs of towns and cities.

Length **17–19½in (43–50cm)**	Wingspan **25in (63cm)**	Weight **6–7oz (175–200g)**
Social **Small flocks**	Lifespan **Up to 15 years**	Status **Secure**

DATE: ________ TIME: ________ LOCATION: ________

Order **Passeriformes**	Family **Corvidae**	Species ***Corvus brachyrhynchos***

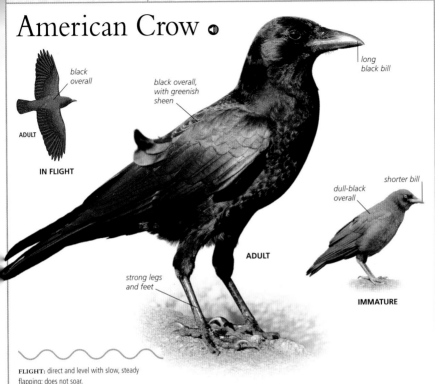

American Crow

black overall

ADULT

IN FLIGHT

black overall, with greenish sheen

long black bill

shorter bill

dull-black overall

ADULT

strong legs and feet

IMMATURE

FLIGHT: direct and level with slow, steady flapping; does not soar.

One of the most widespread and familiar of North American birds, the highly intelligent American Crow is common in almost all habitats—from wilderness to urban centers. Like most birds with large ranges, there is substantial geographical variation in this species. Birds are black across the whole continent, but size and bill shape vary from region to region. The birds of the coastal Pacific Northwest (*C. b. hesperis*), are on average smaller and have a lower-pitched voice; Floridian birds (*C. b. pascuus*) are more solitary and warier than most.

VOICE Call a loud, familiar *caw!*; immature birds' call higher-pitched.

NESTING Stick base with finer inner cup; 3–7 eggs; 1 brood; April–June.

FEEDING Feeds omnivorously on fruit, carrion, garbage, insects, spiders; raids nests.

LOOKING AROUND
Extremely inquisitive, American Crows are always on the look-out for food or something of interest.

SIMILAR SPECIES

COMMON RAVEN
see p.252

larger, decurved bill
much larger overall
shaggy throat feathers

OCCURRENCE
Often seen converging on favored roosting areas; most numerous in relatively open areas with widely spaced, large trees; has become abundant in some cities; a partial migrant, some populations are more migratory than others.

Length **15½–19½in (39–49cm)**	Wingspan **3ft (1m)**	Weight **15–22oz (425–625g)**
Social **Social**	Lifespan **Up to 15 years**	Status **Secure**

DATE: ____________ TIME: ____________ LOCATION: ____________

Order **Passeriformes**	Family **Corvidae**	Species ***Corvus corax***

Common Raven

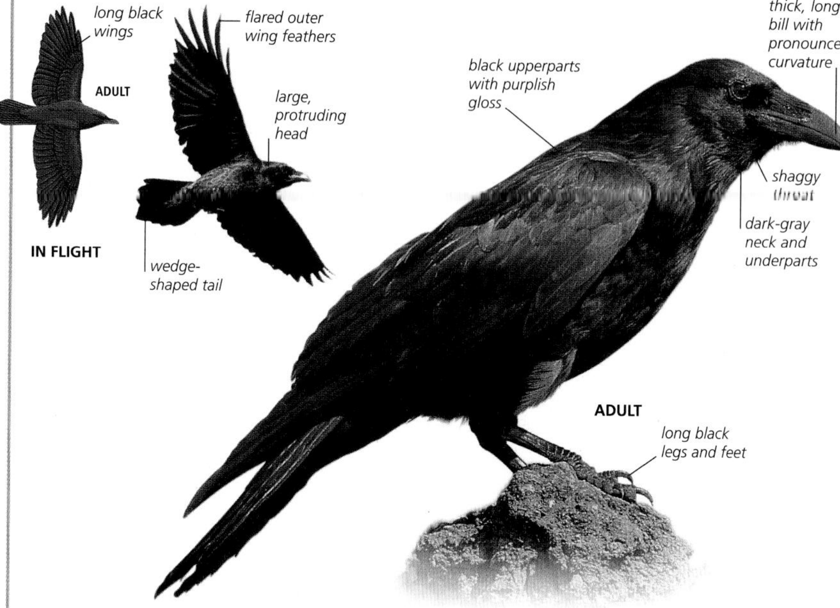
long black wings
ADULT
flared outer wing feathers
large, protruding head
IN FLIGHT
wedge-shaped tail
black upperparts with purplish gloss
thick, long bill with pronounced curvature
shaggy throat
dark-gray neck and underparts
ADULT
long black legs and feet

The Common Raven is twice the size of the American Crow, a bird of indigenous legends, literature, and scientific wonder. Its Latin name, *Corvux corax*, means "crow of crows." Ravens are perhaps the most intelligent of all birds on the planet: they learn quickly, adapt to new circumstances with remarkable mental agility, and communicate with each other through an array of vocal and motional behaviors. The Common Raven is the official bird of the Yukon Territory.

VOICE Varied vocalizations, including hoarse, rolling *krruuk*, twangy peals, guttural clicks, and resonant *bonks*.

NESTING Platform of sticks with fine inner material on trees, cliffs, or artificial structure; 4–5 eggs; 1 brood; March–June.

FEEDING Feeds omnivorously on carrion, small crustaceans, fish, rodents, fruit, grain, and garbage; also raids nests and kill rabbits.

FLIGHT: slow, steady, and direct; can also be quite acrobatic; commonly soars.

SHARING INFORMATION
Ravens in flocks can communicate information about food sources.

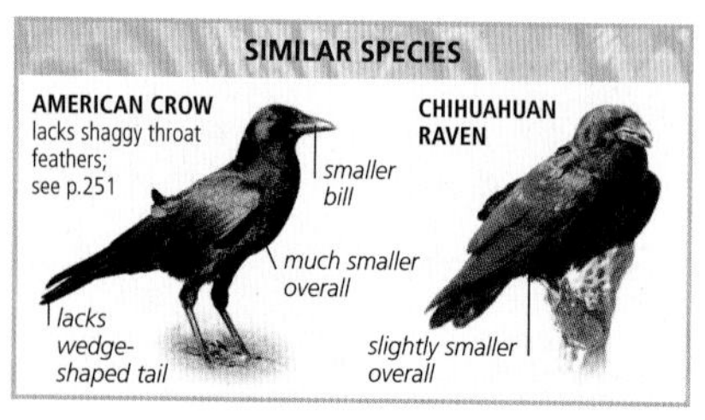
SIMILAR SPECIES
AMERICAN CROW
lacks shaggy throat feathers;
see p.251
smaller bill
much smaller overall
lacks wedge-shaped tail
CHIHUAHUAN RAVEN
slightly smaller overall

OCCURRENCE
Found in almost every kind of habitat, including tundra, mountainous areas, northern forest, woodlands, prairies, arid regions, coasts, and around human settlements; has recently recolonized areas on southern edge of range, from which it was once expelled by humans.

Length **23½–27in (60–69cm)**	Wingspan **4½ft (1.4m)**	Weight **2½–3¼lb (1–1.5kg)**
Social **Solitary/Pairs/Small flocks**	Lifespan **Up to 15 years**	Status **Secure**

DATE: ______________ TIME: ______________ LOCATION: ______________

Family **Paridae**

CHICKADEES AND TITMICE

CHICKADEES AND TITMICE may be some of the most well-known and widespread birds in North America. Once considered to be in the same genus, recent genetic studies have placed titmice and chickadees in different genera.

CHICKADEES

Chickadees are readily distinguished from titmice by their smooth-looking dark caps and black bibs. The name "chickadee" is derived from the common calls of several species. Highly social outside the breeding season and generally tolerant of people, these energetic little birds form flocks in winter. Some species, such as the Black-capped Chickadee, can lower their body temperature to survive the cold, but others, like the similar-looking Carolina Chickadee (a vagrant species in Canada), have a high winter mortality rate. Most species eat a combination of insects and plant material.

TITMICE

Titmice are distinguished from chickadees by their crests; most, like the familiar Tufted Titmouse, also have plain throats. Like chickadees, titmice are highly territorial and insectivorous during the breeding season, then become gregarious seed-eaters afterward. At that time, they often form mixed-species flocks with other small birds, like kinglets, as they move through woodlands searching for food. Titmice are nonmigratory.

TAME BIRDS
Black-capped Chickadees have distinctive black-and-white markings and are often very tame.

Family **Hirundinidae**

SWALLOWS

SWALLOWS ARE A COSMOPOLITAN family of birds with species found nearly everywhere, except in the polar regions and some of the largest deserts. However, during migration they fly over some of the world's harshest deserts, including the Sahara and the Atacama. Most species have relatively short, notched tails, but some have elongated outer tail feathers. Among these latter species, females appear to prefer males with the longest tails as mates. The Bank Swallow and the Barn Swallow, which are also found across Eurasia, are the most widespread. All North American swallows are migratory, and most of them winter in Central and South America, where they feed on flying insects that occur year-round. They are all superb fliers, and skilled at aerial pursuit and capture of flying insects. They are sometimes confused with swifts, which belong to a different family and order, and have a different style of flight. Swallows have relatively shorter, broader wings and less stiff wing beats.

SURFACE SKIMMER
This Tree Swallow flies low over fresh water to catch insects as they emerge into the air.

Order **Passeriformes**	Family **Paridae**	Species ***Poecile atricapillus***

Black-capped Chickadee

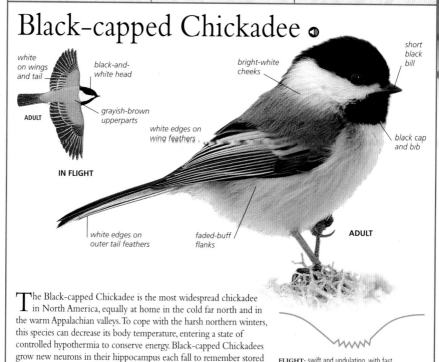

white on wings and tail
black-and-white head
grayish-brown upperparts
ADULT
IN FLIGHT
white edges on wing feathers
bright-white cheeks
short black bill
black cap and bib
white edges on outer tail feathers
faded-buff flanks
ADULT

FLIGHT: swift and undulating, with fast wing beats.

The Black-capped Chickadee is the most widespread chickadee in North America, equally at home in the cold far north and in the warm Appalachian valleys. To cope with the harsh northern winters, this species can decrease its body temperature, entering a state of controlled hypothermia to conserve energy. Black-capped Chickadees grow new neurons in their hippocampus each fall to remember stored seed locations. There is some variation in appearance according to geographical location, with northern birds being slightly larger and possessing brighter white wing edgings than southern birds. Although it is a nonmigratory species, flocks occasionally travel south of their traditional range in large numbers in winter. The Black-capped Chickadee is the provincial bird of New Brunswick.

VOICE Raspy *tsick-a-dee-dee-dee* call; song loud, clear whistle *bee-bee* or *bee-bee-be*, first note higher in pitch.

NESTING Cavity in rotting tree stump, lined with hair, fur, feathers, plant fibers; 6–8 eggs; 1 brood; April–June.

FEEDING Forages for insects and their eggs, and spiders in trees and bushes; mainly seeds in winter; may take seeds from an outstretched hand.

ROUGH-EDGED BIB
The Black-capped Chickadee has a smaller bib than the Chestnut-backed Chickadee.

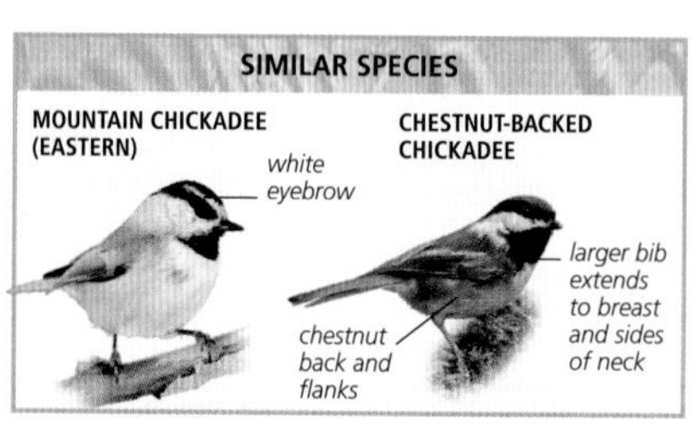

SIMILAR SPECIES
MOUNTAIN CHICKADEE (EASTERN)
white eyebrow
CHESTNUT-BACKED CHICKADEE
larger bib extends to breast and sides of neck
chestnut back and flanks

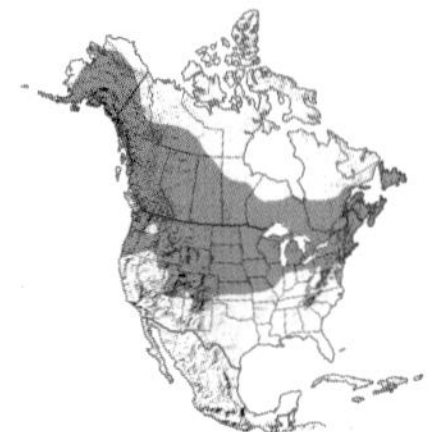

OCCURRENCE
Variety of wooded habitats, from vast forests in the far north to small woodlands in urban parks and suburbs. In years of poor seed crops in northern parts of the range, large numbers migrate sometimes as far south as Texas.

Length **5¼in (13.5cm)**	Wingspan **8½in (22cm)**	Weight **⅜oz (11g)**
Social **Mixed flocks**	Lifespan **Up to 12 years**	Status **Secure**

DATE: ____________ TIME: ____________ LOCATION: ____________

Order **Passeriformes**	Family **Paridae**	Species ***Poecile hudsonicus***

Boreal Chickadee

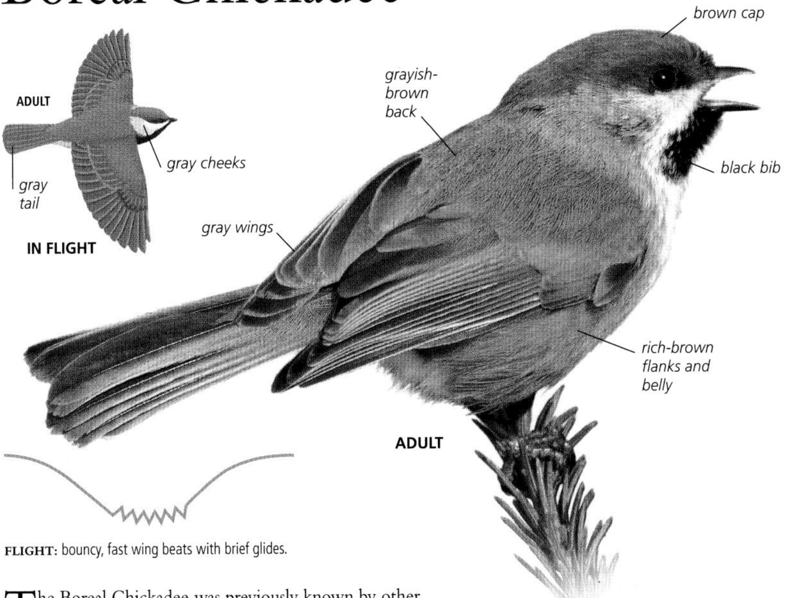
brown cap
grayish-brown back
black bib
ADULT
gray cheeks
gray tail
IN FLIGHT
gray wings
rich-brown flanks and belly
ADULT

FLIGHT: bouncy, fast wing beats with brief glides.

The Boreal Chickadee was previously known by other names, including Hudsonian Chickadee, referring to its northern range, and the Brown-capped Chickadee, due to its appearance. In the past, this species made large, irregular journeys south of its usual range during winters of food shortage, but this pattern of invasions has not occurred in recent decades. Its back color is an interesting example of geographic variation—grayish in the West and brown in the central and eastern portions of its range.

VOICE Call a low-pitched, buzzy, lazy *tsee-day-day*; also a high-pitched trill, *dididididididi*; no whistled song.

NESTING Cavity lined with fur, hair, plant down; in natural, excavated, or old woodpecker hole; 4–9 eggs; 1 brood; May–June.

FEEDING Gleans insects, conifer seeds; hoards larvae and seeds in bark crevices in fall in preparation for winter.

IDENTIFICATION TIP
A grayish-brown back or flank helps distinguish a Boreal Chickadee from a Black-capped Chickadee.

SIMILAR SPECIES

CHESTNUT-BACKED CHICKADEE *narrow white cheeks*; *chestnut sides*

ACROBATIC FORAGER
This acrobatic feeder is able to cling on to conifer needles as it searches for insects and spiders.

OCCURRENCE
Found across the vast northern spruce-fir forests, from Alaska to Newfoundland, and from the treeline at the tundra south to the northeastern and northwestern states. The southern edge of the range appears to be retracting for unknown reasons.

Length **5½in (14cm)**	Wingspan **8½in (21cm)**	Weight **⅜oz (10g)**
Social **Flocks**	Lifespan **Up to 5 years**	Status **Secure**

DATE: ____________ TIME: ____________ LOCATION: ____________________

Order **Passeriformes**	Family **Paridae**	Species ***Baeolophus bicolor***

Tufted Titmouse

ADULT

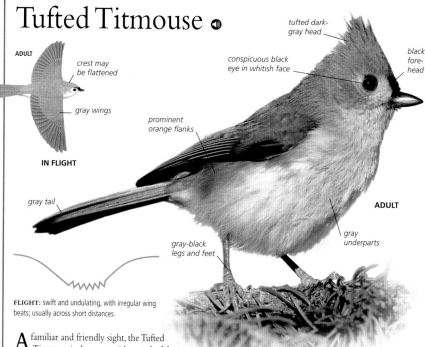

crest may be flattened

gray wings

IN FLIGHT

tufted dark-gray head

conspicuous black eye in whitish face

black fore-head

prominent orange flanks

gray tail

ADULT

gray underparts

gray-black legs and feet

FLIGHT: swift and undulating, with irregular wing beats; usually across short distances.

A familiar and friendly sight, the Tufted Titmouse is the most widespread of the North American titmice, and one of the two largest and most fearless; this lack of fear, particularly around people, has enabled it to adapt very well to human habitations. In the last century, its range has expanded significantly northward up to southern Canada, probably due to the increased numbers of bird feeders, which allow the Tufted Titmouse to survive the cold northern winters.

VOICE Call a loud, harsh *pshurr, pshurr, pshurr,* song a ringing, far-carrying *peto peto peto,* sometimes shortened to *peer peer peer.*

NESTING Tree cavities, old woodpecker holes, and nest boxes, lined with damp leaves, moss, grass, hair; 5–6 eggs; 1 brood; March–May.

FEEDING Forages actively in trees and shrubs for insects, spiders, and their eggs; in winter, eats corn kernels, seeds, and small fruit; can split an acorn by hammering it with its bill.

COLOR VARIATION
The orange on the flanks varies between bright on freshly molted feathers and dull on worn adults.

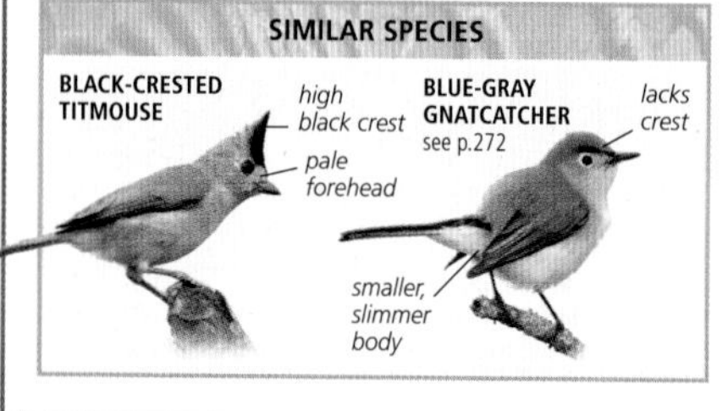
SIMILAR SPECIES
BLACK-CRESTED TITMOUSE
high black crest
pale forehead
BLUE-GRAY GNATCATCHER
see p.272
lacks crest
smaller, slimmer body

OCCURRENCE
Lives year-round in areas of large and small deciduous and coniferous woodlands in the eastern half of the US and southeastern Canada. It has flourished in parks and gardens and can often be found using nest boxes in suburban backyards.

Length **6½in (16cm)**	Wingspan **10in (25cm)**	Weight **$^{11}/_{16}$oz (20g)**
Social **Mixed flocks**	Lifespan **Up to 13 years**	Status **Secure**

DATE: ______________ TIME: ______________ LOCATION: ______________

Order **Passeriformes**	Family **Alaudidae**	Species ***Eremophila alpestris***

Horned Lark

brown wings

ADULT

IN FLIGHT

variable brown on upperparts

muted facial markings

ADULT (POSTBREEDING)

tiny "horns"

bold black-and-yellow face

dark streaks on reddish-brown upperparts

streaked upperparts

IMMATURE

black tail with narrow white edges to outer feathers

white underparts

short legs

ADULT (BREEDING)

FLIGHT: undulating, with wings folded in after every few beats.

The Horned Lark is a bird of open country, especially places with extensive bare ground. The species is characteristic of arid, alpine, and Arctic regions; in these areas, it flourishes in the bleakest of habitats imaginable, from sun-scorched, arid lakes in the Great Basin to windswept tundra above the timberline. In some places, the only breeding bird species are the Horned Lark and the equally resilient Common Raven. In Europe and Asia, this species is known as the Shore Lark.

VOICE Flight call a sharp *sweet* or *soo-weet*; song, either in flight or from the ground, pleasant, musical tinkling series, followed by *sweet... swit... sweet... s'sweea'weea'witta'swit.*

NESTING In depression in bare ground, somewhat sheltered by grass or low shrubs, lined with plant matter; 2–5 eggs; 1–3 broods; March–July.

FEEDING Survives exclusively on seeds of grasses and sedges in winter; eats mostly insects in summer.

GROUND FORAGER
With its short legs bent under its body, an adult looks for insects and seeds.

SIMILAR SPECIES
SPRAGUE'S PIPIT
shorter wings
shorter tail
EURASIAN SKYLARK
streaked crest
streaked overall

VERY VOCAL
The Horned Lark is a highly vocal bird, singing from the air, the ground, or low shrubs.

OCCURRENCE
Breeds widely, in any sort of open, even barren habitat with extensive bare ground, especially shortgrass prairies and deserts. Winters wherever there are snow-free openings, including places along beaches and roads. Winters from southern Canada southward to Florida and Mexico.

Length **7in (18cm)**	Wingspan **12in (30cm)**	Weight **1$\frac{1}{16}$oz (30g)**
Social **Winter flocks**	Lifespan **Up to 8 years**	Status **Secure**

DATE: ____________ TIME: ____________ LOCATION: ________________________

Order **Passeriformes**	Family **Hirundinidae**	Species ***Riparia riparia***

Bank Swallow

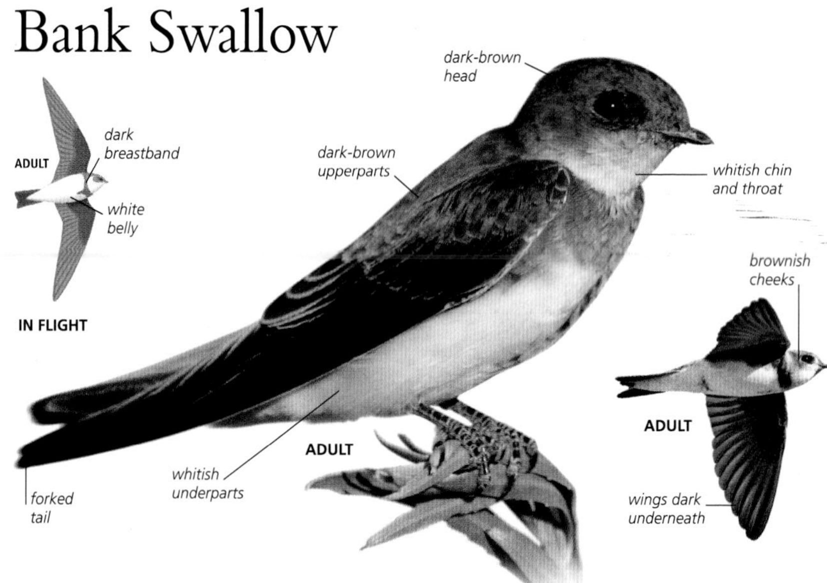
dark-brown head
ADULT
dark breastband
white belly
IN FLIGHT
dark-brown upperparts
whitish chin and throat
brownish cheeks
ADULT
ADULT
forked tail
whitish underparts
wings dark underneath

The Bank Swallow, known in the UK as the Sand Martin, is the slimmest and smallest of North American swallows. As its scientific name *riparia* (meaning "riverbanks") and common name suggest, the Bank Swallow nests in the banks and bluffs of rivers, streams, and lakes. It also favors sand and gravel quarries in the East. It is widely distributed across North America, breeding from south of the tundra–taiga line down to the central US. The nesting colonies can range from as few as 10 pairs to as many as 2,000, which are quite noisy when all the birds are calling or coming in to feed the young.

VOICE Call a soft *brrrrr* or *breee* often issued in pairs; song a harsh twittering or continuous chatter.

NESTING Burrow in soft, sandy bank containing a flat platform of grass, feathers, and twigs; 2–6 eggs; 1 brood; April–August.

FEEDING Catches insects, such as flies, moths, dragonflies, and bees in flight, but occasionally skims aquatic insects or their larvae off the water or terrestrial insects from the ground.

FLIGHT: fast, frantic, butterfly-like flight with glides, twists, and turns; shallow, rapid wing beats.

WAITING FOR MOM
Hungry youngsters still expect to be fed, even when they're ready to fledge.

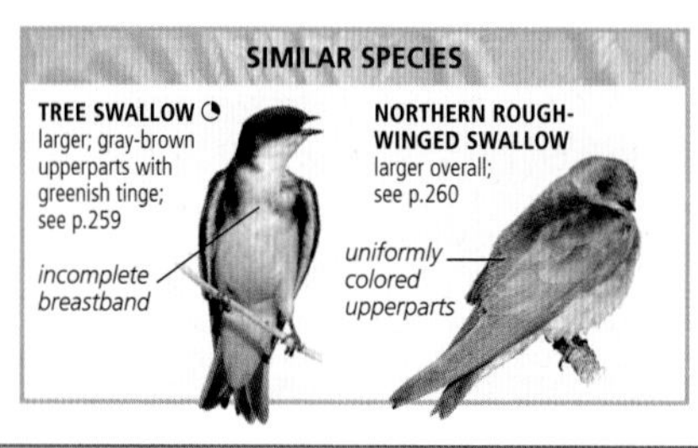
SIMILAR SPECIES
TREE SWALLOW
larger; gray-brown upperparts with greenish tinge; see p.259
incomplete breastband
NORTHERN ROUGH-WINGED SWALLOW
larger overall; see p.260
uniformly colored upperparts

OCCURRENCE
Widespread in North America. Breeds in lowland habitats associated with rivers, streams, lakes, reservoirs, and coasts, as well as in sand and gravel quarries. Often prefers artificial sites; winters in grasslands, open farm habitat, and freshwater areas in South America.

Length **4¾–5½in (12–14cm)**	Wingspan **10–11in (25–28cm)**	Weight **$\frac{3}{8}$–$\frac{11}{16}$oz (10–19g)**
Social **Colonies**	Lifespan **Up to 9 years**	Status **Threatened**

Order **Passeriformes**	Family **Hirundinidae**	Species ***Tachycineta bicolor***

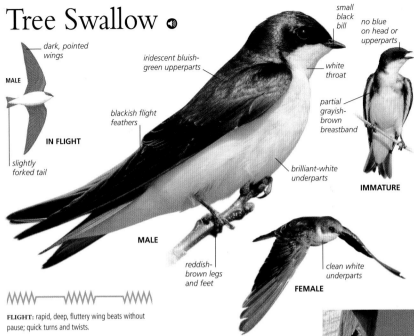

Tree Swallow

dark, pointed wings

MALE

IN FLIGHT

slightly forked tail

iridescent bluish-green upperparts

blackish flight feathers

small black bill

white throat

brilliant-white underparts

MALE

reddish-brown legs and feet

no blue on head or upperparts

partial grayish-brown breastband

IMMATURE

clean white underparts

FEMALE

FLIGHT: rapid, deep, fluttery wing beats without pause; quick turns and twists.

One of the most common North American swallows, the Tree Swallow is found from coast to coast in the upper half of the continent all the way up to Alaska. As its Latin name *bicolor* suggests, it has iridescent bluish-green upperparts and white underparts. Immature birds can be confused with the smaller Bank Swallow, which has a more complete breastband. The Tree Swallow lives in a variety of habitats, but its hole-nesting habit makes it completely dependent on abandoned woodpecker cavities in dead trees and on artificial "housing," such as nest boxes. The size of the population fluctuates according to the availability of the nesting sites.

VOICE Ranges from variable high, chirping notes to chatters and soft trills; also complex high and clear two-note whistle phrases.

NESTING Layer of fine plant matter in abandoned woodpecker hole or nest box, lined with feathers; 4–6 eggs; 1 brood; May–July.

FEEDING Swoops after flying insects from dawn to dusk; also takes bayberries.

KEEPING LOOKOUT
This species uses artificial nest boxes, which the males defend as soon as they arrive.

SIMILAR SPECIES
BANK SWALLOW
paler brown rump;
see p.258
distinct dusky breastband
VIOLET-GREEN SWALLOW
white flank patch
white eye patch
violet-green upperparts

OCCURRENCE
Typically breeds close to water in open habitat, such as fields, marshes, lakes, and swamps, especially those with standing dead wood for cavity-nesting. Hundreds of thousands of birds winter in tall marsh vegetation.

Length **5–6in (13–15cm)**	Wingspan **12–14in (30–35cm)**	Weight **⅝–⅞oz (17–25g)**
Social **Large flocks**	Lifespan **Up to 11 years**	Status **Secure**

DATE: ____________ TIME: ____________ LOCATION: ____________

Order **Passeriformes**	Family **Hirundinidae**	Species ***Stelgidopteryx serripennis***

Northern Rough-winged Swallow

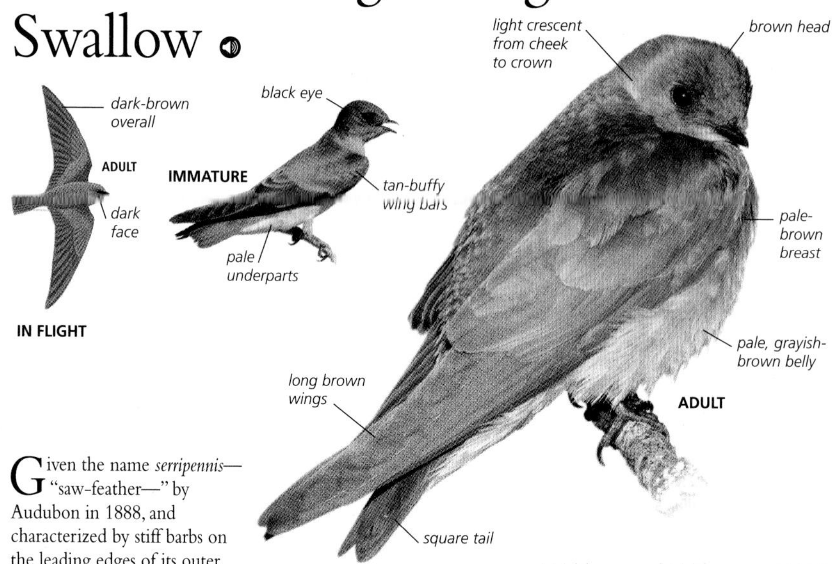

dark-brown overall
ADULT
dark face
IN FLIGHT
black eye
IMMATURE
tan-buffy wing bars
pale underparts
light crescent from cheek to crown
brown head
pale-brown breast
pale, grayish-brown belly
long brown wings
ADULT
square tail

Given the name *serripennis*—"saw-feather—" by Audubon in 1888, and characterized by stiff barbs on the leading edges of its outer wing feathers, this species is otherwise somewhat drab in color and aspect. The Northern Rough-winged Swallow has a broad distribution in North America, being found across southern Canada and throughout the US. With no obvious discernible markings, this brown-backed, dusky-throated swallow can be spotted hunting insects over water. In size and habit, the Northern Rough-winged Swallow shares many similarities with the Bank Swallow, including breeding habits and color, but the latter's notched tail and smaller size make it easy to tell them apart.

VOICE Steady repetition of short, rapid *brrrt* notes inflected upward; sometimes a buzzy *jee-jee-jee* or high-pitched *brzzzzzt*.

NESTING Loose cup of twigs and straw in a cavity or burrow in a bank, such as road cuts; 4–7 eggs; 1 brood; May–July.

FEEDING Captures flying insects, including flies, wasps, bees, damselflies, and beetles in the air; more likely to feed over water and at lower altitudes than other swallows.

FLIGHT: slow, deliberate wing beats; short to long glides; long, straight flight, ends in steep climb.

JUST A BROWN BIRD
This swallow is brownish above and pale grayish below, with a brown smudge on its neck.

SIMILAR SPECIES

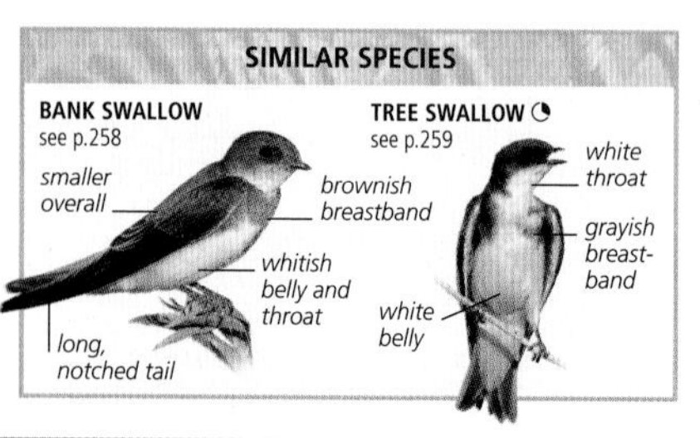

BANK SWALLOW
see p.258
smaller overall
brownish breastband
whitish belly and throat
long, notched tail
TREE SWALLOW
see p.259
white throat
grayish breast-band
white belly

OCCURRENCE
In North America, widespread from coast to coast. Nests at a wide variety of altitudes, prefers exposed banks of clay, sand, or gravel, such as gorges, shale banks, and gravel pits. Forages along watercourses where aerial insects are plentiful. Breeds south to Costa Rica. Winters in Central America.

Length **4¾–6in (12–15cm)**	Wingspan **11–12in (28–30cm)**	Weight **⅜–⅝oz (10–18g)**
Social **Solitary**	Lifespan **At least 5 years**	Status **Secure**

DATE: ___________ TIME: ___________ LOCATION: ___________

Order **Passeriformes**	Family **Hirundinidae**	Species ***Progne subis***

Purple Martin

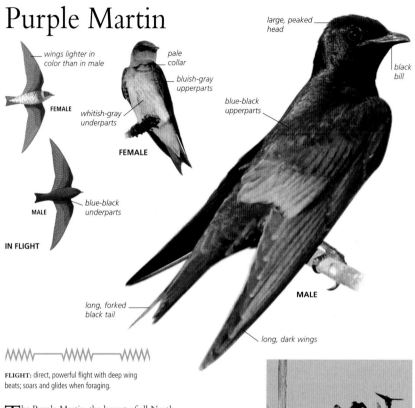

wings lighter in color than in male

FEMALE

blue-black underparts

MALE

IN FLIGHT

pale collar

bluish-gray upperparts

whitish-gray underparts

FEMALE

large, peaked head

black bill

blue-black upperparts

MALE

long, forked black tail

long, dark wings

FLIGHT: direct, powerful flight with deep wing beats; soars and glides when foraging.

The Purple Martin, the largest of all North American swallows, is one of the most popular of all backyard birds. Thousands of people have become devoted to the Purple Martin populations in their local areas; in the eastern half of the continent, especially, the Purple Martin now depends almost entirely on specially built "apartment-style" birdhouses for nest sites. In the west, this glossy-blue swallow is a more localized bird, although common in some areas. Here, it nests principally in old woodpecker holes.

VOICE Alarm call a *zwrack* or *zweet*; other calls are a variety of rolling, bubbling sounds; song a series of gurgles, chortles, and croaking phrases.

NESTING Loose mat of vegetation and mud in birdhouse compartments, rarely in natural cavities; 4 eggs; 1 brood; April–August.

FEEDING Captures flying insects at 150–500ft (45–150m) in the air; sometimes gleans insects from foliage or the ground.

FLOCK TOGETHER
Purple Martins are social birds; they breed in colonies and roost in flocks, as shown.

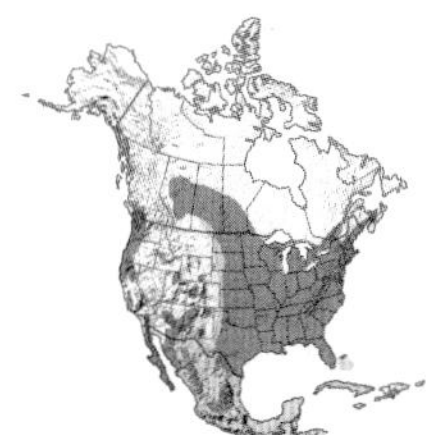

OCCURRENCE
In North America, eastern birds found almost exclusively in towns and cities where nest boxes are provided; western populations occur in more rural areas, such as mountain and coastal forests where woodpecker holes are abundant; also uses saguaro cactus for nesting in the Southwest.

Length **7–8in (18–20cm)**	Wingspan **15–16in (38–41cm)**	Weight **$1\frac{7}{16}$–$2\frac{1}{8}$oz (40–60g)**
Social **Large flocks/Colonies**	Lifespan **Up to 13 years**	Status **Secure**

DATE: ____________ TIME: ____________ LOCATION: ____________

Order **Passeriformes**	Family **Hirundinidae**	Species ***Hirundo rustica***

Barn Swallow

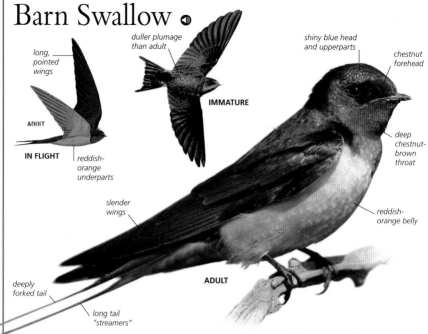

long, pointed wings
ADULT
IN FLIGHT
reddish-orange underparts
duller plumage than adult
IMMATURE
shiny blue head and upperparts
chestnut forehead
deep chestnut-brown throat
reddish-orange belly
slender wings
ADULT
deeply forked tail
long tail "streamers"

The most widely distributed and abundant swallow in the world, the Barn Swallow is found just about everywhere in North America south of the Arctic timberline. Originally a cave-nester before Europeans settlers came to the New World, the Barn Swallow readily adapted to nesting under the eaves of houses, under bridges, and inside buildings, such as barns. It is now rare to find this elegant swallow breeding in a natural site. Steely-blue upperparts, reddish underparts, and a deeply forked tail identify the Barn Swallow. North American breeders have deep, reddish-orange underparts, but birds from Eurasia are white-bellied.

VOICE High-pitched, squeaky *chee-chee* call; song a long series of chatty, pleasant *churrs,* squeaks, chitterings, and buzzes.

NESTING Deep cup of mud and grass-stems attached to vertical surfaces or on ledges; 4–6 eggs; 1–2 broods; May–September.

FEEDING Snatches flying insects, such as flies, mosquitoes, wasps, and beetles in the air at lower altitudes than other swallows; sometimes eats wild berries and seeds.

FLIGHT: bursts of straight flight; close to the ground; weaves left and right, with sharp turns.

WELL PROTECTED
Whether in a barn or other structure, a Barn Swallow nest is protected from wind and rain.

SIMILAR SPECIES

TREE SWALLOW ♂
see p.259

lacks forked tail and dark breast band
white underparts

OCCURRENCE
Breeds across North America, except in the tundra zone; south as far as central Mexico. Found in most habitats, but prefers agricultural regions, towns, and highway overpasses; migrates over coastal marshes; winters near sugarcane fields, grain fields, and marshes.

Length **6–7½in (15–19cm)**	Wingspan **11½–13in (29–33cm)**	Weight **$\frac{5}{8}$–$\frac{11}{16}$oz (17–20g)**
Social **Small colonies/flocks**	Lifespan **Up to 8 years**	Status **Threatened**

DATE: ______________ TIME: ______________ LOCATION: ______________

Order **Passeriformes**	Family **Hirundinidae**	Species ***Petrochelidon pyrrhonota***

Cliff Swallow

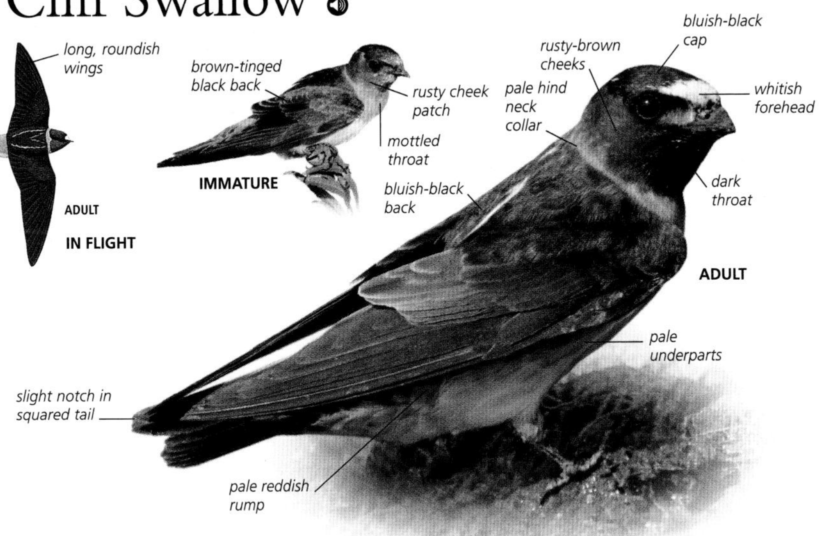

long, roundish wings
ADULT
IN FLIGHT
brown-tinged black back
rusty cheek patch
mottled throat
IMMATURE
rusty-brown cheeks
bluish-black cap
pale hind neck collar
whitish forehead
bluish-black back
dark throat
ADULT
pale underparts
slight notch in squared tail
pale reddish rump

The Cliff Swallow is one of North America's most social land birds, sometimes nesting in colonies of over 3,500 pairs, especially in the western US. It is more locally distributed across the east. It can be distinguished from other North American swallows by its square tail and orange rump, but it resembles its close relative, the Cave Swallow, in color, pattern, and in affixing its mud nests to the sides of highway culverts, bridges, and buildings. The considerable increase in such structures has allowed the species to expand its range from the west to breed almost everywhere, except in dense forests and desert habitats.

VOICE Gives *purr* and *churr* calls when alarmed; song a low, squeaky, 6-second twitter given in flight and near nests.

NESTING Domed nests of mud pellets on cave walls, buildings, culverts, bridges, and dams; 3–5 eggs; 1–2 broods; April–August.

FEEDING Catches flying insects (often swarming varieties) while on the wing; sometimes forages on the ground; ingests grit to aid digestion.

FLIGHT: strong, fast wing beats; glides more often but less acrobatically than other swallows.

GATHERING MUD
The Cliff Swallow gathers wet mud from puddles, pond edges, and streamsides to build its nests.

SIMILAR SPECIES

CAVE SWALLOW
brighter orange cheek
paler overall

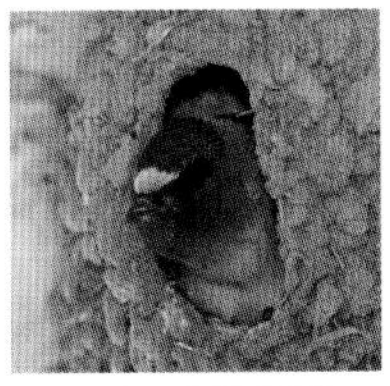

INDIVIDUAL HOMES
In a Cliff Swallow colony, each nest has a single opening.

OCCURRENCE
Breeds almost anywhere in North America from Alaska to Mexico, except deserts, tundra, and unbroken forest; prefers concrete or cliff walls, culverts, buildings, and undersides of piers on which to affix mud nests; feeds over grasslands, marshes, lakes, and reservoirs. Migrates to South America.

Length **5in (13cm)**	Wingspan **11–12in (28–30cm)**	Weight **11/16–1¼oz (20–35g)**
Social **Colonies**	Lifespan **Up to 11 years**	Status **Secure**

DATE: ______________ TIME: ______________ LOCATION: ______________________

Family **Sittidae**

NUTHATCHES

COMMON WOODLAND BIRDS, NUTHATCHES are easily recognized by their distinctive shape and characteristic feeding techniques, and often located by loud squeaky calls. They are tree-dwellers, feeding around branches and nesting in small holes. Nuthatches are plump-bodied, short-tailed but large-headed birds, with strong, pointed bills and short legs, strong toes and arched claws. Unlike woodpeckers and creepers, which mostly climb in an upward direction, they do not need to use the tail as a prop when exploring a tree's bark. These birds rely solely on their strong and secure grip to hop and shuffle in all directions, frequently hanging upside down. They feed on spiders and also probe for insects and their larvae in the cracks of tree bark. They also eat seeds and nuts, which they may wedge into a crevice and break open with noisy taps of the bill—hence, the name "nuthatch."

ACROBATIC POSE
Downward-facing nuthatches, such as this White-breasted Nuthatch, often lift their heads in a characteristic pose.

Family **Troglodytidae**

WRENS

WITH ONE EXCEPTION, THE EURASIAN WREN, wrens are North American songbirds. They are sharp-billed birds with short- or medium-length tails that are frequently cocked upward. Wrens are intricately patterned, mostly with dark bars and streaks, and pale spots on buff-and-rusty backgrounds. Their family name, *Troglodytidae,* derives from a Greek word for "cave-dweller"—while they do not really inhabit caves, the description is apt as some North American species, such as the Winter Wren, forage deep inside thick cover of all kinds, from scrub to upturned tree roots and overgrown stumps, or in dense growth inside ditches. The aptly named Marsh Wrens are found in marshes and Sedge Wrens in sedge meadows. Wrens are often best located by their calls, which are fairly loud for such small birds. Some wren species sing precisely synchronized duets.

COCKED TAIL
As they sing, Winter Wrens often hold their tails upward, in a near-vertical position.

Order **Passeriformes**	Family **Regulidae**	Species ***Corthylio calendula***

Ruby-crowned Kinglet

red patch on crown

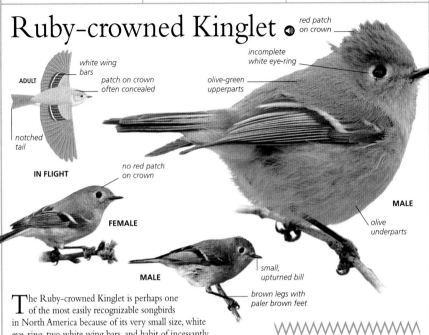

incomplete white eye-ring

olive-green upperparts

white wing bars

ADULT

patch on crown often concealed

notched tail

IN FLIGHT

no red patch on crown

FEMALE

MALE

olive underparts

MALE

small, upturned bill

brown legs with paler brown feet

FLIGHT: short bursts of rapid wing beats, but overall quick and direct flight.

The Ruby-crowned Kinglet is perhaps one of the most easily recognizable songbirds in North America because of its very small size, white eye-ring, two white wing bars, and habit of incessantly flicking its wings while foraging. This bird is renowned for its loud, complex song and for laying up to 12 eggs in a clutch—probably the highest of any North American songbird. Despite local declines resulting from logging and forest fires, the Ruby-crowned Kinglet is common across the continent. It will sometimes join mixed-species flocks in winter with nuthatches and titmice.

VOICE Call a low, husky *jidit*; song, remarkably loud for such a small bird, begins with 2–3 high, clear notes *tee* or *zee* followed by 5–6 lower *tu* or *turr* notes, and ends with ringing galloping notes *tee-da-leet, tee-da-leet, tee-da-leet*.

NESTING Globular or elongated nest hanging from or on large branch with an enclosed or open cup, made of mosses, feathers, lichens, spider's silk, bark, hair, and fur; 5–12 eggs; 1 brood; May–October.

FEEDING Gleans a wide variety of insects, spiders, and their eggs among the leaves on the outer tips of higher, smaller branches; eats fruit and seeds; often hovers to catch prey.

CONCEALED COLOR
This bird's red patch is often concealed unless the bird is agitated or excited.

SIMILAR SPECIES

HUTTON'S VIREO
larger head
stouter bill
heavier overall

ALWAYS FLICKING
Ruby-crowned Kinglets are easily identified by their habit of constantly flicking their wings.

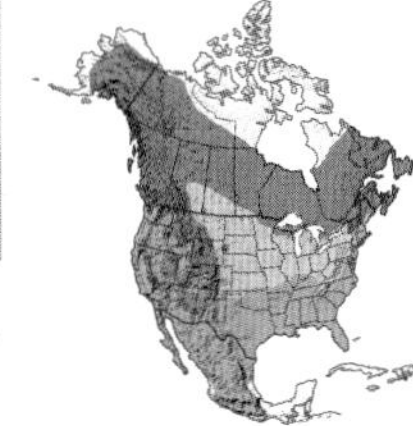

OCCURRENCE
Within the northerly forest zone, breeds near water in black spruce and tamarack forests, muskegs, forests with mixed conifers and northern hardwoods; in the mountainous West, spruce-fir, lodgepole pine, and Douglas fir forests. Winters in a broad range of forests, thickets, and borders.

Length **3½–4¼in (9–11cm)**	Wingspan **6–7in (15–18cm)**	Weight **3/16–3/8oz (5–10g)**
Social **Winter flocks**	Lifespan **Up to 5 years**	Status **Secure**

DATE: ____________ TIME: ____________ LOCATION: ____________

Order **Passeriformes**	Family **Regulidae**	Species ***Regulus satrapa***

Golden-crowned Kinglet

orange-and-yellow patch on crown, with black border

yellow crown patch, with black border

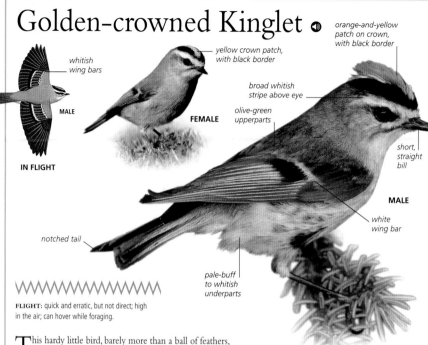

whitish wing bars

MALE

FEMALE

IN FLIGHT

broad whitish stripe above eye

olive-green upperparts

short, straight bill

MALE

white wing bar

notched tail

pale-buff to whitish underparts

FLIGHT: quick and erratic, but not direct; high in the air; can hover while foraging.

This hardy little bird, barely more than a ball of feathers, breeds in northern and mountainous coniferous forests in North America. Other unconnected populations are residents of high-elevation forests in Mexico and Guatemala. Planting of spruce trees has been quite beneficial to the Golden-crowned Kinglet, allowing it to expand its range southward into the US Midwest.

VOICE Call a thin, high-pitched and thread-like *tsee* or *see see*; song a series of high-pitched ascending notes for two seconds; complex song *tsee-tsee-tsee-tsee-teet-leetle*, followed by brief trill.

NESTING Deep, cup-shaped nest with rims arching inward, made of moss, lichen, and bark, and lined with finer strips of the same; 8–9 eggs; 1–2 broods; May–August.

FEEDING Gleans flies, beetles, mites, spiders, and their eggs from tips of branches, under bark, tufts of conifer needles; eats seeds and persimmon fruit.

CONIFER CONNOISSEUR
This bird particularly favors coniferous forests for foraging for insects and seeds.

SIMILAR SPECIES

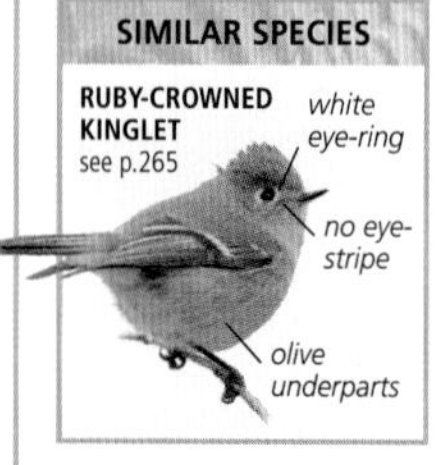
RUBY-CROWNED KINGLET
see p.265
white eye-ring
no eye-stripe
olive underparts

HIGHER VOICE
The Golden-crowned has a higher-pitched and less musical song than the Ruby-crowned.

OCCURRENCE
Breeds in remote northern and subalpine spruce or fir forests, mixed coniferous–deciduous forests, single-species stands, and pine plantations; winters in a wide variety of habitats—coniferous and deciduous forests, pine groves, low-lying hardwood forests, swamps, and urban and suburban habitats.

Length **3¼–4¼in (8–11cm)**	Wingspan **5½–7in (14–18cm)**	Weight **5/32–9/32oz (4–8g)**
Social **Solitary/Pairs**	Lifespan **Up to 5 years**	Status **Secure**

DATE: ______ TIME: ______ LOCATION: ______

Order **Passeriformes**	Family **Bombycillidae**	Species ***Bombycilla garrulus***

Bohemian Waxwing

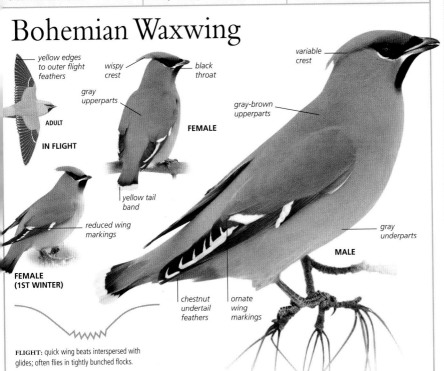

yellow edges to outer flight feathers

ADULT

IN FLIGHT

wispy crest

black throat

gray upperparts

FEMALE

yellow tail band

reduced wing markings

FEMALE (1ST WINTER)

variable crest

gray-brown upperparts

gray underparts

MALE

chestnut undertail feathers

ornate wing markings

FLIGHT: quick wing beats interspersed with glides; often flies in tightly bunched flocks.

The Bohemian Waxwing is the wilder and rarer of the two waxwing species in North America. It breeds mainly in Alaska and western Canada. The species is migratory, but the extent of its wintertime movement is notoriously variable, depending on the availability of wild fruit. In most winters, relatively few Bohemian Waxwings visit the lower 48 states, but in special "irruption" years, tens of thousands may reach as far south as Colorado.

VOICE Call actually a dull trill, but effect of hundreds of birds calling at the same time is remarkable; flocks vocalize constantly.

NESTING Dishevelled cup of sticks and grasses, placed in tree; 4–6 eggs; number of broods unknown; June–July.

FEEDING Catches insects on the wing in summer; flocks devour berries of native and exotic trees and shrubs throughout the year.

STRIKING TAIL

The Bohemian Waxwing's yellow tail band and chestnut undertail are evident here.

SIMILAR SPECIES

CEDAR WAXWING see p.268

plainer wing markings

warmer tones overall

CEDAR WAXWING ◔ see p.268

unmarked wings

smaller overall

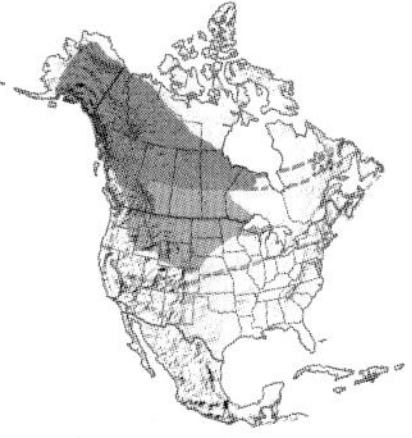

OCCURRENCE

Breeds in sub-Arctic coniferous forest, favoring disturbed areas, such as beaver ponds and logging sites. Flocks gather at forest edges, hedges, and residential areas in winter. Hundreds or thousands of birds appear in an area, then disappear once food is depleted.

Length **8½in (21cm)**	Wingspan **14½in (37cm)**	Weight **1⁹⁄₁₆–2½oz (45–70g)**
Social **Flocks**	Lifespan **Up to 12 years**	Status **Localized**

DATE: __________ TIME: __________ LOCATION: __________

Order **Passeriformes**	Family **Bombycillidae**	Species ***Bombycilla cedrorum***

Cedar Waxwing

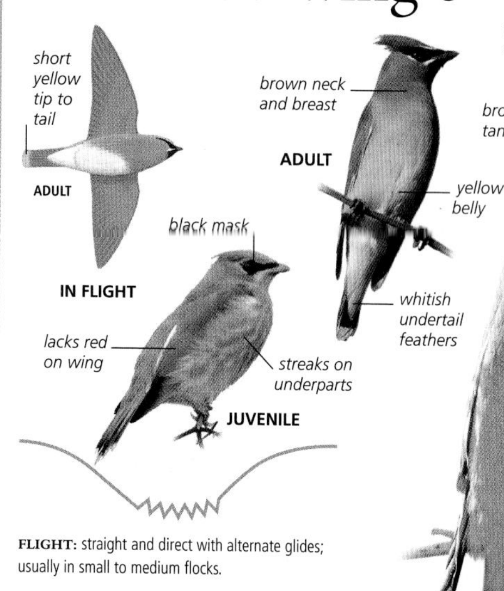
short yellow tip to tail
ADULT
IN FLIGHT
brown neck and breast
ADULT
yellow belly
whitish undertail feathers
black mask
lacks red on wing
streaks on underparts
JUVENILE
wispy crest
white bars on face
brownish-tan back
black "bandit" mask
ADULT
waxy red tips on inner wing

FLIGHT: straight and direct with alternate glides; usually in small to medium flocks.

Flocks of Cedar Waxwings, a nomadic species with a beautifully sculpted plumage, wander about North America looking for sugary fruits, their favorite food. Common in a specific location one year, they may disappear the next and occur elsewhere. Northern breeders tend to be more migratory and nomadic than southern ones, wintering as far south as South America. The waxy red feather tips might function as status signals for mate selection. They can often be heard and identified by their high-pitched calls, long before the flock settles to feed.

VOICE Basic vocalization a shrill trill: *shr-r-r-r-r-r* or *tre-e-e-e-e-e,* which appears to serve the function of both call note and song.

NESTING Open cup placed in fork of tree, often lined with grasses, plant fibers; 3–5 eggs; 1–2 broods; June–August.

FEEDING Eats in flocks at trees and shrubs with ripe berries throughout the year; also catches flying insects in summer.

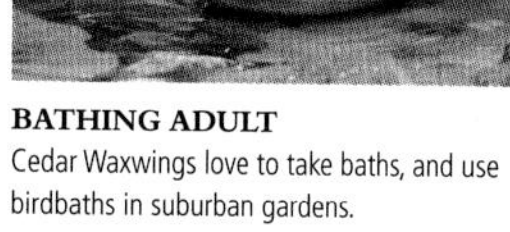

BATHING ADULT
Cedar Waxwings love to take baths, and use birdbaths in suburban gardens.

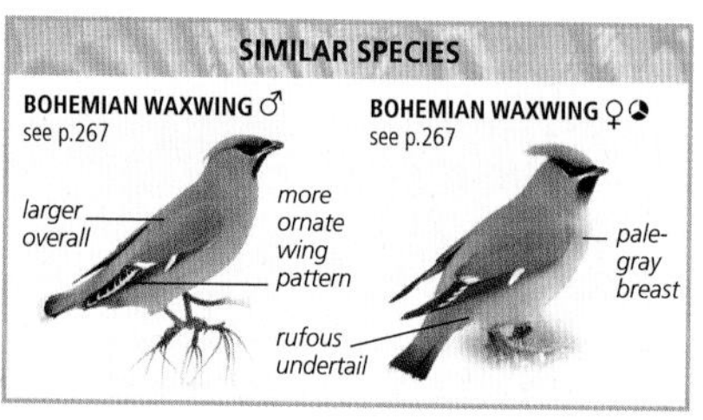
SIMILAR SPECIES
BOHEMIAN WAXWING ♂
see p.267
larger overall
more ornate wing pattern
BOHEMIAN WAXWING ♀
see p.267
pale-gray breast
rufous undertail

OCCURRENCE
Breeds in woodlands across the northern US and southern Canada, especially near streams and clearings. Winters where trees and shrubs have ripe fruits, especially in Mexico and South America. Spends a lot of time in treetops, but sometimes comes down to shrub level.

Length **7½in (19cm)**	Wingspan **12in (30cm)**	Weight **1¹⁄₁₆–1¼oz (30–35g)**
Social **Flocks**	Lifespan **Up to 7 years**	Status **Secure**

DATE: ____________ TIME: ____________ LOCATION: ____________

Order **Passeriformes**	Family **Sittidae**	Species ***Sitta canadensis***

Red-breasted Nuthatch

rounded wings
MALE
white bands on tail
IN FLIGHT
slightly muted head pattern
dark blue-gray crown and eyestripe
pale-orange underparts
FEMALE
bold black-and-white head pattern
pointed, chisel-like bill
black eyestripe
blue-gray upperparts
white cheeks
short blue-gray tail, with black side feathers
rusty underparts
compact body shape
MALE

FLIGHT: short, swift dashes across forest clearings; irregular, undulating motion.

This inquisitive nuthatch, with its distinctive black eyestripe, breeds in conifer forests across North America. The bird inhabits mountains in the West; in the East, it is found in lowlands and hills. However, sometimes it breeds in conifer groves away from its core range. Each fall, birds move from their main breeding grounds, but the extent of this exodus varies from year to year, depending on population cycles and food availability.

VOICE Call a one-note tooting sound, often repeated, with strong nasal yet musical quality: *aaank*, *enk*, *ink*, rather like a horn.

NESTING Excavates cavity in pine tree; nest of grass lined with feathers, with sticky pine resin applied to entrance; 5–7 eggs, 1 brood; May–July.

FEEDING Probes bark for beetle grubs; also eats insect larvae found on conifer needles; seeds in winter.

TASTY GRUB
This nuthatch has just extracted its dinner from the bark of a tree, a favorite foraging habitat.

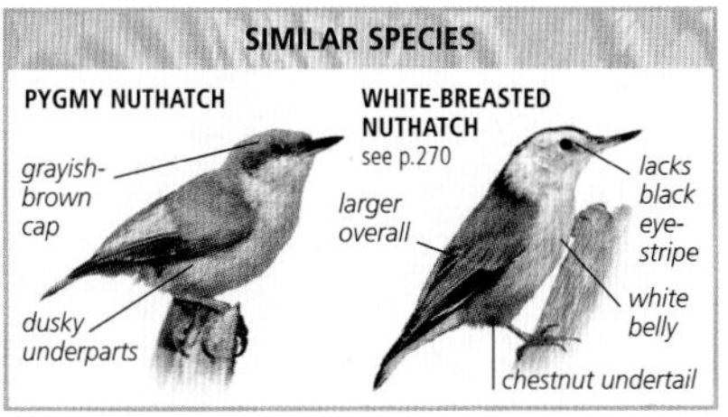
SIMILAR SPECIES
PYGMY NUTHATCH
grayish-brown cap
dusky underparts

WHITE-BREASTED NUTHATCH
see p.270
larger overall
lacks black eye-stripe
white belly
chestnut undertail

OCCURRENCE
Found year-round in coniferous and mixed hardwood forests. During breeding season, absent from southeastern pine forests, except in the Appalachians. In the West, shares its habitat with the Pygmy Nuthatch, but ranges to higher elevations.

Length **4¼in (11cm)**	Wingspan **8½in (22cm)**	Weight **⅜–⁷⁄₁₆oz (10–13g)**
Social **Solitary/Pairs**	Lifespan **Up to 7 years**	Status **Secure**

DATE: ______________ TIME: ______________ LOCATION: ______________________________

Order **Passeriformes**	Family **Sittidae**	Species ***Sitta carolinensis***

White-breasted Nuthatch

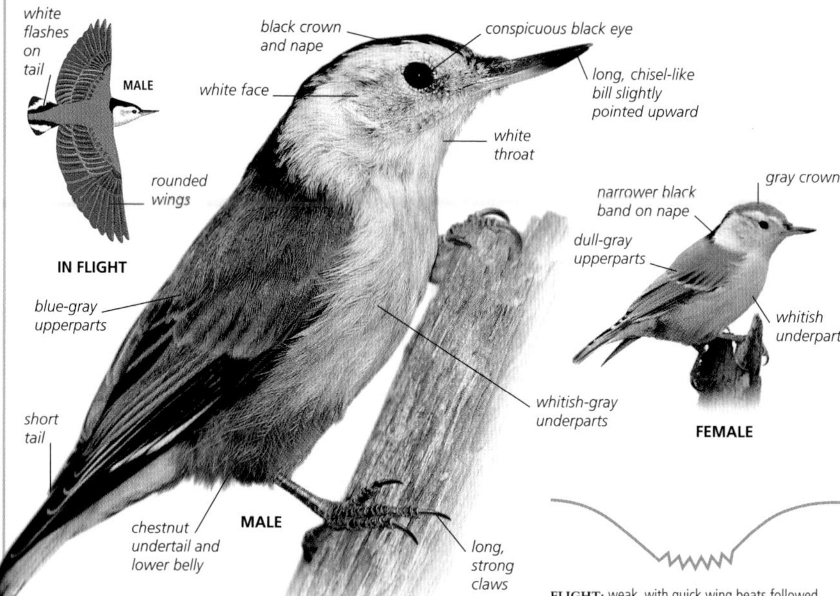
white flashes on tail
MALE
rounded wings
IN FLIGHT
black crown and nape
conspicuous black eye
white face
long, chisel-like bill slightly pointed upward
white throat
blue-gray upperparts
short tail
chestnut undertail and lower belly
MALE
long, strong claws
whitish-gray underparts
gray crown
narrower black band on nape
dull-gray upperparts
whitish underparts
FEMALE

FLIGHT: weak, with quick wing beats followed by glide; often short, from tree to tree.

The amiable White-breasted Nuthatch inhabits woodlands across the US and southern Canada, but often visits bird feeders in winter. The largest of our nuthatches, it spends more time probing furrows and crevices on trunks and boughs than other nuthatches do. It walks irregularly on trees: forward, backward, upside-down, or horizontally. Of the 11 subspecies in its Canada-to-Mexico range, five occur in Canada and in the US. They differ in call notes and, to a lesser extent, in plumage.

VOICE Calls vary geographically: eastern birds nasal *yank yank*; interior birds stuttering *st't't't't*; Pacific-slope birds tremulous *yiiiirk*; song of all populations a mellow *tu tu tu tu*, like a flicker, but softer.

NESTING Tree cavity, once used by woodpeckers, lined with grass and hair, adds mud to cavity opening; 5–9 eggs, 1 brood; April–June.

FEEDING Scours bark methodically for insects, such as beetle larvae.

UNUSUAL DESCENT
Nuthatches are unusual in that they routinely descend branches and trunks headfirst.

SIMILAR SPECIES

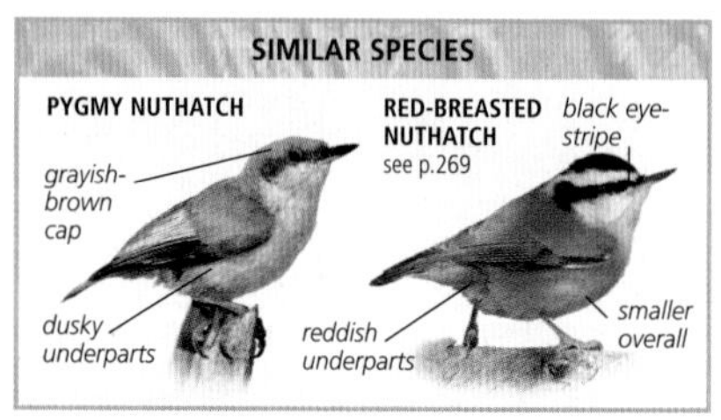
PYGMY NUTHATCH
grayish-brown cap
dusky underparts
RED-BREASTED NUTHATCH
see p.269
black eye-stripe
reddish underparts
smaller overall

OCCURRENCE
More liberal than other nuthatches in the use of forest types; overlaps with the smaller species in coniferous forest ranges, but also common in broadleaf deciduous or mixed forests; weakly migratory: little movement in most falls, but moderate departures from breeding grounds in some years.

Length **5¾in (14.5cm)**	Wingspan **11in (28cm)**	Weight **$^{11}/_{16}$–⅞oz (19–25g)**
Social **Solitary/Pairs**	Lifespan **Up to 9 years**	Status **Secure**

DATE: ____________ TIME: ____________ LOCATION: ____________

Order **Passeriformes**	Family **Certhiidae**	Species ***Certhia americana***

Brown Creeper

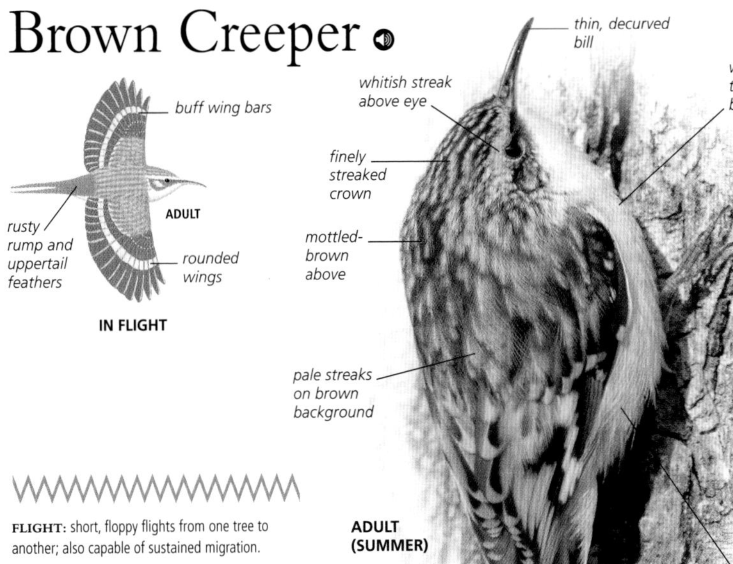

buff wing bars
ADULT
rusty rump and uppertail feathers
rounded wings
IN FLIGHT
thin, decurved bill
whitish streak above eye
white chin, throat, and breast
finely streaked crown
mottled-brown above
pale streaks on brown background
ADULT (SUMMER)
rusty tint to belly and undertail
long, forked tail

FLIGHT: short, floppy flights from one tree to another; also capable of sustained migration.

Although distinctive, widespread, and fairly common, the Brown Creeper is one of the most understated of the forest birds, with its soft vocalizations and cryptic plumage. As it forages, it hops up a tree trunk, then flies down to another tree, starts again from near the ground, hops up, and so on. These birds have adapted to habitat changes in the northeast and their numbers have increased in regenerating forests. Mid- and southwestern populations, by contrast, have declined because forest cutting has reduced their breeding habitat. The Brown Creeper is a partial migrant—some individuals move south in the fall, and head north in the spring; others remain close to their breeding grounds.

VOICE High-pitched and easily overlooked call a buzzy *zwisss*, flight call an abrupt *tswit*; song a wheezy jumble of thin whistles and short buzzes.

NESTING Unique hammock-shaped nest, behind piece of peeling bark; 5–6 eggs, 1 brood; May–July.

FEEDING Probes bark for insects, especially larvae, eggs, pupae, and aphids.

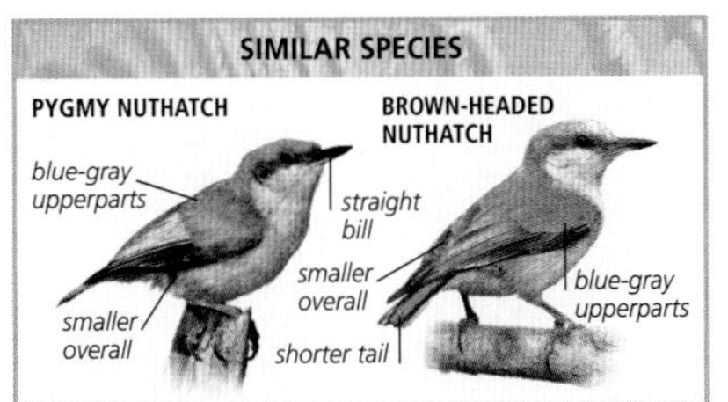

SIMILAR SPECIES
PYGMY NUTHATCH
blue-gray upperparts
straight bill
smaller overall
BROWN-HEADED NUTHATCH
smaller overall
blue-gray upperparts
shorter tail

STRONG TAIL
The Brown Creeper uses its stiff forked tail to prop itself against the trunk of this tree.

OCCURRENCE
The only North American creeper, it breeds in a variety of forests, particularly fairly moist coniferous or mixed hardwood forests, also large stands with snags and standing dead trees. In winter, it is seen in small groves without coniferous trees; also in residential districts or suburbs.

Length **5¼in (13.5cm)**	Wingspan **8in (20cm)**	Weight **¼–⅜oz (7–10g)**
Social **Solitary**	Lifespan **At least 5 years**	Status **Secure**

DATE: ____________ TIME: ____________ LOCATION: ____________________________

Order **Passeriformes**	Family **Polioptilidae**	Species ***Polioptila caerulea***

Blue-gray Gnatcatcher

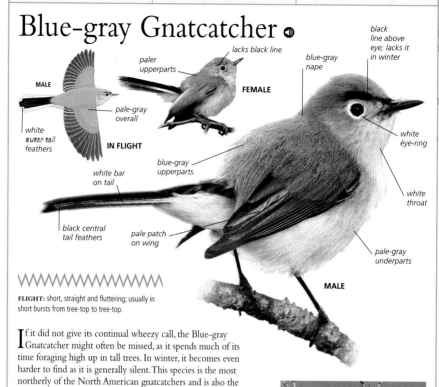

MALE
white outer tail feathers
pale-gray overall
IN FLIGHT
paler upperparts
lacks black line
FEMALE
blue-gray nape
black line above eye; lacks it in winter
white eye-ring
blue-gray upperparts
white bar on tail
white throat
black central tail feathers
pale patch on wing
pale-gray underparts
MALE

FLIGHT: short, straight and fluttering; usually in short bursts from tree-top to tree-top.

If it did not give its continual wheezy call, the Blue-gray Gnatcatcher might often be missed, as it spends much of its time foraging high up in tall trees. In winter, it becomes even harder to find as it is generally silent. This species is the most northerly of the North American gnatcatchers and is also the only one to migrate. It can exhibit aggressive behavior and is capable of driving off considerably larger birds than itself. The range of the Blue-gray Gnatcatcher appears to be expanding and populations are increasing.

VOICE Call soft, irregular *zhee, zhee*, uttered constantly while foraging; song soft combination of short notes and nasal wheezes.

NESTING Cup of plant fibers, spider webs, mosses; usually high on branch; lined with soft plant material; 4–5 eggs; 1–2 broods; April–June.

FEEDING Forages for small insects and spiders by acrobatically flitting from twig to twig, while constantly twitching its long tail.

LISTEN CLOSELY
The complex song is rather faint; it is heard best when the bird is singing on a low perch.

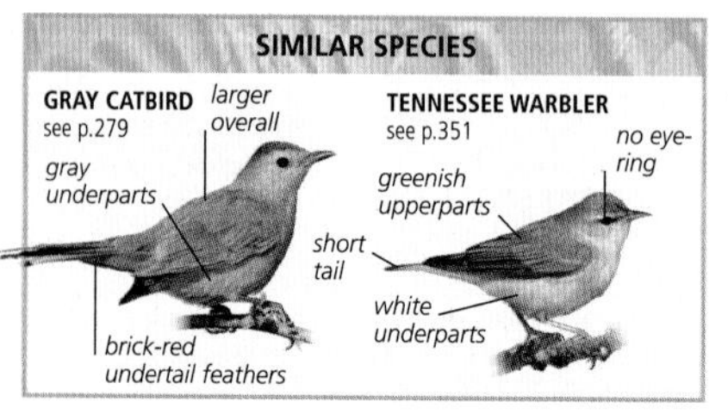
SIMILAR SPECIES
GRAY CATBIRD
see p.279
larger overall
gray underparts
brick-red undertail feathers
TENNESSEE WARBLER
see p.351
no eye-ring
greenish upperparts
short tail
white underparts

OCCURRENCE
In eastern North America, breeds in deciduous or pine woodlands; in the West, in scrubby habitats, often near water. Winters in brushy habitats in the southern US, Mexico, and Central America. Also breeds in Mexico, Belize, and the Bahamas.

Length **4¼in (11cm)**	Wingspan **6in (15cm)**	Weight **7/32oz (6g)**
Social **Solitary/Flocks**	Lifespan **At least 4 years**	Status **Secure**

Order **Passeriformes**	Family **Troglodytidae**	Species ***Troglodytes aedon***

House Wren

plain brown crown

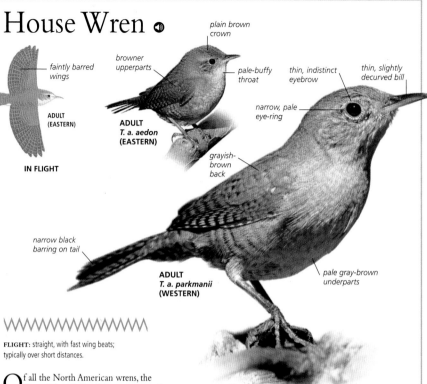

faintly barred wings

browner upperparts

pale-buffy throat

thin, indistinct eyebrow

thin, slightly decurved bill

narrow, pale eye-ring

ADULT (EASTERN)

ADULT *T. a. aedon* (EASTERN)

IN FLIGHT

grayish-brown back

narrow black barring on tail

pale gray-brown underparts

ADULT *T. a. parkmanii* (WESTERN)

FLIGHT: straight, with fast wing beats; typically over short distances.

Of all the North American wrens, the House Wren is the plainest, yet one of the most familiar and endearing, especially when making its home in a backyard nest box. However, it can be a fairly aggressive species, driving away nearby nesting birds of its own species and others by destroying nests, puncturing eggs, and even killing young. In the 1920s, distraught bird-lovers mounted a campaign calling for the eradication of House Wrens, though the campaign did not last long as most were in favor of letting nature take its course.

VOICE Call a sharp *chep* or *cherr*; song opens with several short notes, followed by a bubbly explosion of extending spluttering notes.

NESTING Cup lined with soft material on stick platform in natural or constructed cavities, such as nest boxes; 5–8 eggs; 2–3 broods; April–July.

FEEDING Forages for insects and spiders in trees and shrubs, gardens, and yards.

SIMILAR SPECIES

WINTER WREN see p.274

dark-brown overall
shorter tail
heavily barred flanks

NESTING MATERIAL
This small bird has brought an unusually large twig to its nest inside an old woodpecker hole.

OCCURRENCE
Breeds in cities, towns, parks, farms, yards, gardens, and woodland edges. Rarely seen during migration period (late July to early October). Winters south of its breeding range, from the southern US to Mexico, in woodlands, shrubby areas, and weedy fields. Nests, or is resident, as far south as Tierra del Fuego.

Length **4½in (11.5cm)**	Wingspan **6in (15cm)**	Weight **⅜oz (11g)**
Social **Solitary**	Lifespan **Up to 9 years**	Status **Secure**

DATE: ____________ TIME: ____________ LOCATION: ____________________

Order **Passeriformes**	Family **Troglodytidae**	Species ***Troglodytes hiemalis***

Winter Wren

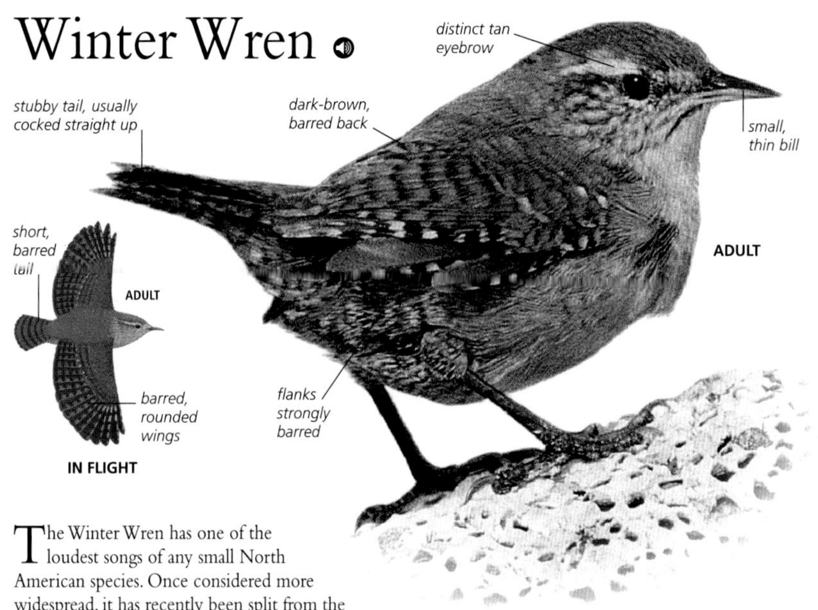
distinct tan eyebrow
stubby tail, usually cocked straight up
dark-brown, barred back
small, thin bill
ADULT
short, barred tail
ADULT
barred, rounded wings
flanks strongly barred
IN FLIGHT

The Winter Wren has one of the loudest songs of any small North American species. Once considered more widespread, it has recently been split from the Pacific Wren, which occupies much of the western fringe of the continent. It is a bird of low undergrowth and tangled roots, often foraging in the upturned roots and broken branches of fallen trees, appearing mouse-like as it creeps amid the shadows. It frequently appears in full view, gives a few harsh, scolding calls, then dives back out of sight into the low cover. It can survive periods of intense cold and even snow cover by finding insects and spiders in bark crevices and soil-encrusted roots. Several Winter Wrens may roost together in small cavities for warmth.

VOICE Call a double *chek-chek* or *chimp-chimp*; song a loud, extremely long, complex series of warbles, trills, and single notes.

NESTING Well-hidden in a cavity near ground with dead wood and crevices; nest a messy mound lined with feathers; 4–7 eggs; 1–2 broods; April–July.

FEEDING Forages for insects in low, dense undergrowth, often in wet areas along streams; sometimes thrusts its head into water to capture prey.

FLIGHT: fast and direct, with rapid beats of its short, broad wings.

VOCAL VIRTUOSO
The Winter Wren is a skulker, but in the breeding season singing males show up on lower perches.

SIMILAR SPECIES

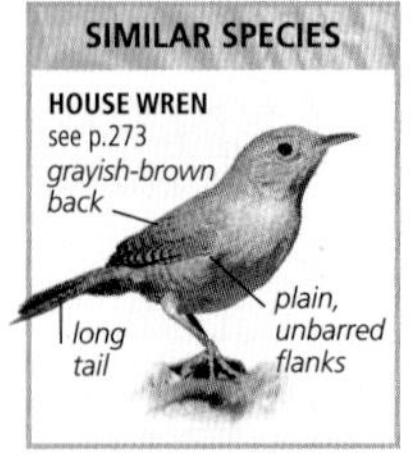
HOUSE WREN
see p.273
grayish-brown back
long tail
plain, unbarred flanks

NERVOUS REACTION
When alarmed, this wren cocks its tail almost vertically before escaping into a mossy thicket.

OCCURRENCE
Breeds in northerly and mountain forests dominated by evergreen trees with a dense understory, fallen trees, and banks of streams. In the Appalachians, breeds in treeless areas with grass near cliffs. Northernmost birds migrate south to winter in woodlands, brush piles, tangles, and secluded spots.

Length **4in (10cm)**	Wingspan **5½in (14cm)**	Weight **5/16oz (9g)**
Social **Solitary/Family groups**	Lifespan **At least 4 years**	Status **Secure**

DATE: ______________ TIME: ______________ LOCATION: ______________

Order **Passeriformes**	Family **Troglodytidae**	Species ***Cistothorus stellaris***

Sedge Wren

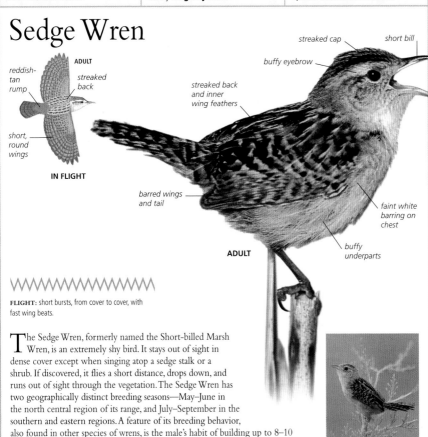

ADULT
reddish-tan rump
streaked back
short, round wings
IN FLIGHT
streaked cap
short bill
buffy eyebrow
streaked back and inner wing feathers
barred wings and tail
faint white barring on chest
buffy underparts
ADULT

FLIGHT: short bursts, from cover to cover, with fast wing beats.

The Sedge Wren, formerly named the Short-billed Marsh Wren, is an extremely shy bird. It stays out of sight in dense cover except when singing atop a sedge stalk or a shrub. If discovered, it flies a short distance, drops down, and runs out of sight through the vegetation. The Sedge Wren has two geographically distinct breeding seasons—May–June in the north central region of its range, and July–September in the southern and eastern regions. A feature of its breeding behavior, also found in other species of wrens, is the male's habit of building up to 8–10 unlined "dummy" nests before the female builds the better-concealed, real nest.

VOICE Call a loud *chap*; song a dry, staccato two-part chatter: *cha cha cha cha ch'ch'ch ch'ch'ch'ch'*.

NESTING Globular, woven structure of sedges with side entrance; lined with plant matter, down, and hair; 4–8 eggs; 1–2 broods; May–August.

FEEDING Forages for spiders and insects, such as grasshoppers, flies, mosquitoes, and bugs, close to or on ground in cover of sedges and grass.

LOOK CLOSELY
Close study is necessary to appreciate the Sedge Wren's subtle patterning, which is plainer than the Marsh Wren's.

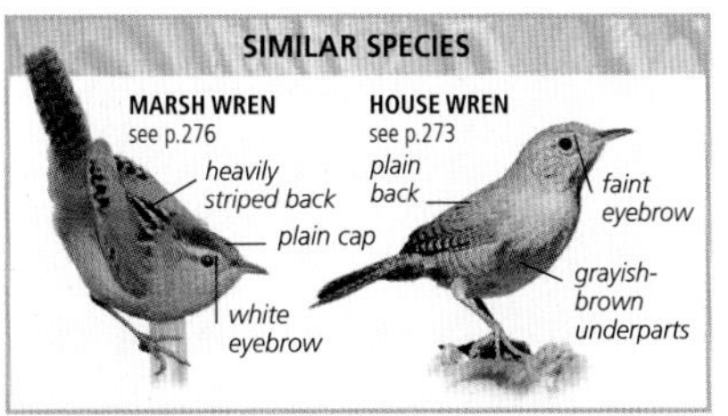
SIMILAR SPECIES
MARSH WREN
see p.276
heavily striped back
plain cap
white eyebrow
HOUSE WREN
see p.273
plain back
faint eyebrow
grayish-brown underparts

OCCURRENCE
In North America, breeds in wet meadows and sedge marshes with low water levels. Widely distributed in the Americas from the Canadian prairies east to Quebec, and from the northern US to the south central states. Winters from Texas to Florida in drier habitats including grassy fields and coastal-plain prairies.

Length **4in (10cm)**	Wingspan **5½–6in (14–15.5cm)**	Weight **5⁄16oz (9g)**
Social **Loose colonies**	Lifespan **Unknown**	Status **Secure**

DATE: ____________ TIME: ____________ LOCATION: ____________

Order **Passeriformes**	Family **Troglodytidae**	Species ***Cistothorus palustris***

Marsh Wren

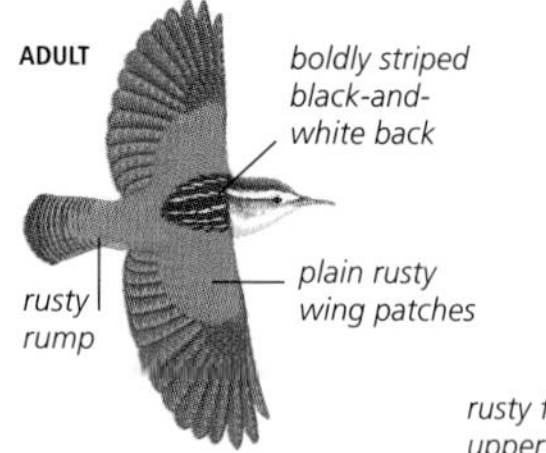
ADULT
boldly striped black-and-white back
rusty rump
plain rusty wing patches
IN FLIGHT

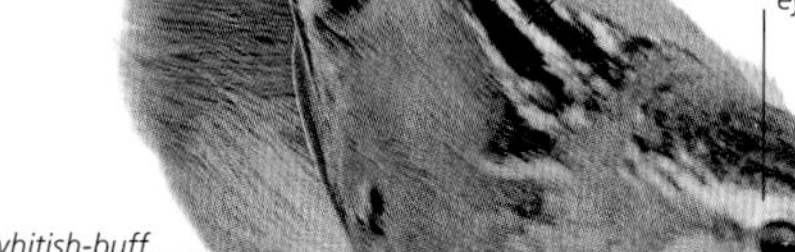
barred tail feathers
heavily streaked
white back
rusty flanks and uppertail feathers
whitish eyebrow
brown cap
dull whitish-buff underparts
long bill
ADULT

FLIGHT: straight, with rapid wing beats over short distances, from one reed patch to another.

The Marsh Wren, a common resident of saltwater and freshwater marshes, is known for singing loudly through both day and night. The males perform fluttery, aerial courtship flights while singing, and are polygamous, mating with two or more females. Like the Sedge Wren, the male builds several "dummy" nests before his mate constructs one herself. The Marsh Wren nests in taller vegetation than the Sedge Wren and over deeper water. Eastern and Western Marsh Wrens differ in voice and behavior, and some ornithologists classify them as separate species.

VOICE Calls a low *chek* and a raspy *churr*; song a loud *chuk chuk chuk*, then fast *tih-tih-tih-rih-tih-tih*, an enthusiastic singer.

NESTING Oblong structure with side entrance, woven of reeds and lined with soft materials; 4–5 eggs; 2 broods; March–July.

FEEDING Forages acrobatically for insects, such as mosquitoes, dragonflies, and beetles, within dense clusters of cattails and reeds.

DELICATELY PERCHED
This wren perches on vertical reeds and often holds itself up by spreading its legs across two stalks.

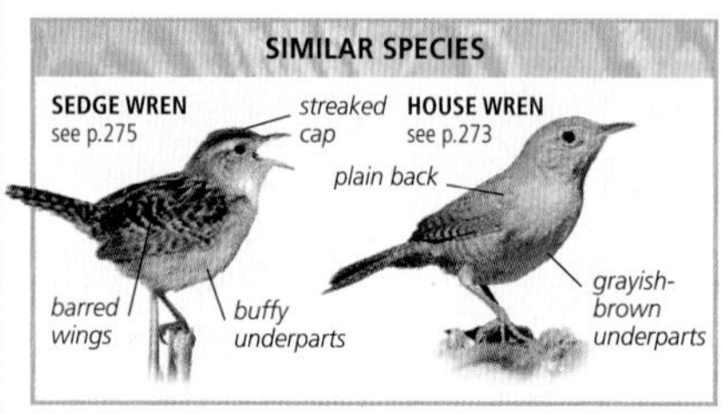
SIMILAR SPECIES
SEDGE WREN
see p.275
streaked cap
barred wings
buffy underparts
HOUSE WREN
see p.273
plain back
grayish-brown underparts

OCCURRENCE
Breeds from Canada down to the mountains of the western US as well as the central and the northeastern US states. Inhabits freshwater and saltwater marshes with tall vegetation, above water, sometimes more than 3ft (1m) deep. It is irregularly distributed in its range. Winters in grassy marshes.

Length **5in (13cm)**	Wingspan **6in (15cm)**	Weight **3/8oz (11g)**
Social **Loose colonies**	Lifespan **Unknown**	Status **Localized**

 DATE: ______________ TIME: ______________ LOCATION: ______________

Order **Passeriformes**	Family **Troglodytidae**	Species ***Thryothorus ludovicianus***

Carolina Wren

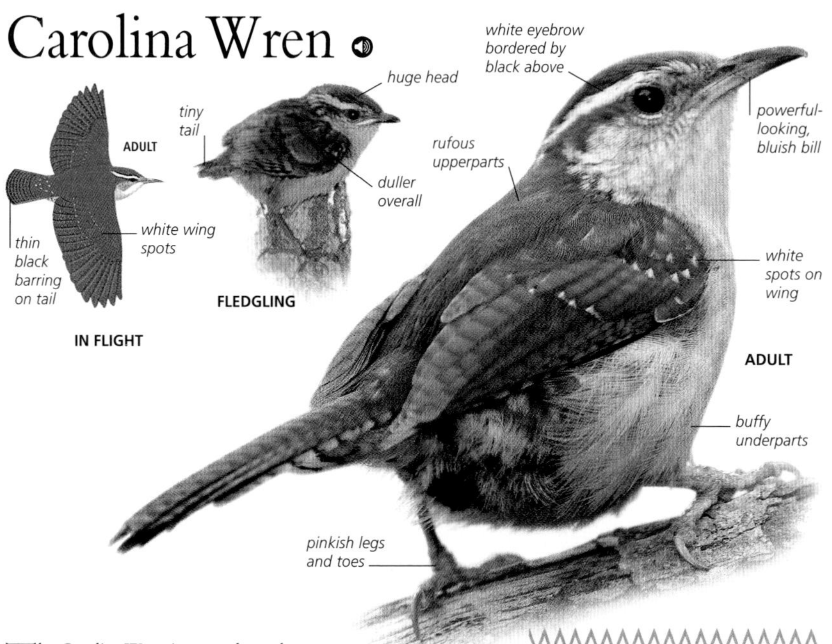

huge head
white eyebrow bordered by black above
tiny tail
ADULT
powerful-looking, bluish bill
rufous upperparts
duller overall
white wing spots
thin black barring on tail
white spots on wing
FLEDGLING
IN FLIGHT
ADULT
buffy underparts
pinkish legs and toes

The Carolina Wren is a popular and common backyard bird in most of its range. It is rarely still, often flicking its tail and looking around nervously. Extremely harsh winters at the northernmost fringe of the Carolina Wren's range in New England and southeastern Canada can cause a sudden decline in numbers, as food resources are covered for long periods by ice and heavy snow. At such times, survival may depend on human help for food and shelter.

VOICE Calls variable; often a sharp *chlip* or long, harsh chatter; song a loud, long, fast *whee'dle-dee whee'dle-dee whee'dle-dee.*

NESTING Cup of weeds, twigs, leaves in natural or human-made cavity; 4–8 eggs; 2–3 broods; April–July.

FEEDING Forages for insects in shrubs and on ground; in winter, favorite foods are peanut butter or suet at a feeder.

FLIGHT: fast and straight over short distances, with rapid wing beats.

DISTINCTIVE BORDER
A unique feature of this wren, not always noticed but visible here, is the black border on the eyebrow.

TIRELESS SINGER
Unlike many birds, the male Carolina Wren sings all year long, even on cold winter days.

SIMILAR SPECIES

BEWICK'S WREN dull-brown or gray upperparts
longer tail

OCCURRENCE
Breeds in a variety of bushy woodland habitats, such as thickets, parks with shrubby undergrowth, suburban yards with dense, low trees or bushes, and gardens; from northeastern Mexico to the Great Lakes and up into southeastern Canada. A separate population can be found from Mexico to Nicaragua.

Length **5¼ in (13.5cm)**	Wingspan **7½ in (19cm)**	Weight **¹¹⁄₁₆ oz (19g)**
Social **Pairs/Family groups**	Lifespan **At least 9 years**	Status **Secure**

DATE: ______ TIME: ______ LOCATION: ______

Families **Mimidae, Sturnidae**

THRASHERS

THE FAMILY NAME FOR THRASHERS, mockingbirds, and catbirds, Mimidae, is derived from the Latin word for "to imitate" or mimic. Perhaps no other word better describes the dozen or so thrashers of North America. They are well known for their ability to mimic the songs of other species and incorporate phrases into their own complex song sequences. In appearance, they are superficially thrush-like, but thrashers are more elongated and have longer, somewhat more decurved bills, and generally longer legs and tails. While mockingbirds may be bold, brash, and conspicuous—they are often found on open perches—thrashers are more reclusive, tending to forage deep within thickets or low vegetation, hopping on their strong feet, and digging into the leaf layer to find food with their bills.

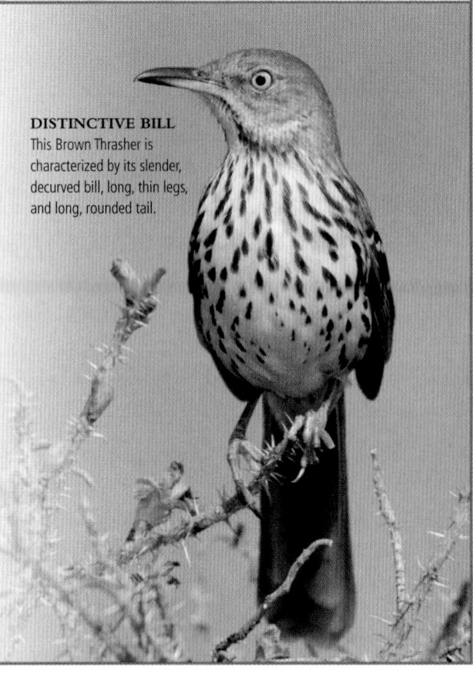

DISTINCTIVE BILL
This Brown Thrasher is characterized by its slender, decurved bill, long, thin legs, and long, rounded tail.

Families **Muscicapidae, Turdidae**

THRUSHES AND CHATS

THRUSHES, CHATS (wheatears and bluethroats), and their relatives are small- to medium-sized birds. Many are forest species but feed mostly on the ground, while others, such as the Northern Wheatear, are birds of the open countryside. Many thrushes have a plain brown upperside and a spotted underside, but make up for their lack of color with their beautiful flute-like songs. Some, however, are brightly colored and strongly patterned: the American Robin is one of the most familiar birds. The smaller bluebirds are renowned for their bright blues while the North American solitaire is a much grayer species.

GROUND BIRDS
Though they perch to sing, thrushes, including this Gray-cheeked Thrush, spend a lot of their time on or near the ground.

Order **Passeriformes**	Family **Mimidae**	Species ***Dumetella carolinensis***

Gray Catbird

gray overall

ADULT

long black tail

IN FLIGHT

dark-gray to black head

straight blackish bill

gray upperparts

large black eye

gray underparts

bright brick-red undertail feathers

ADULT

In addition to the feline-like, mewing calls that earned it its common name, the Gray Catbird not only has an extraordinarily varied vocal repertoire, but it can also sing two notes simultaneously. It has been reported to imitate the vocalizations of over 40 bird species, at least one frog species, and several sounds produced by machines and electronic devices. Despite their shy, retiring nature, Gray Catbirds tolerate human presence and will rest in shrubs in suburban and urban lots. Another fascinating skill is the Gray Catbird's ability to recognize and remove eggs of the brood parasite, the Brown-headed Cowbird.

VOICE *Mew* call, like a young kitten; song a long, complex series of unhurried, often grouped notes, sometimes interspersed with whistles and squeaks.

NESTING Large, untidy cup of woven twigs, grass, and hair lined with finer material; 3–4 eggs; 1–2 broods; May–August.

FEEDING Feeds on a wide variety of berries and insects, usually whatever is most abundant in season.

FLIGHT: short flights between habitat patches with constant, medium-speed wing beats.

ANGLED ATTITUDE
Between bouts of feeding, a Gray Catbird often rests with its body and tail at a 50-degree angle.

LARGE BLACK EYES
Peering from the foliage, but often hidden, a Gray Catbird investigates its surroundings.

SIMILAR SPECIES

NORTHERN MOCKINGBIRD
see p.281
white wing patch
longer tail edged in white
lighter gray
TOWNSEND'S SOLITAIRE
see p.284
tan patches
shorter bill
white eye-ring

OCCURRENCE
Breeds in mixed young to mid-aged forests with abundant undergrowth, from British Columbia east to the Maritimes and Newfoundland, and in the US diagonally west-east from Washington State to New Mexico, east to the Gulf Coast, north to New England. Northern population migratory.

Length **8–9½in (20–24cm)**	Wingspan **10–12in (25–30cm)**	Weight **1¼–2⅛oz (35–60g)**
Social **Solitary/Pairs**	Lifespan **Up to 11 years**	Status **Secure**

DATE: ____________ TIME: ____________ LOCATION: ______________________

Order **Passeriformes**	Family **Mimidae**	Species ***Toxostoma rufum***

Brown Thrasher

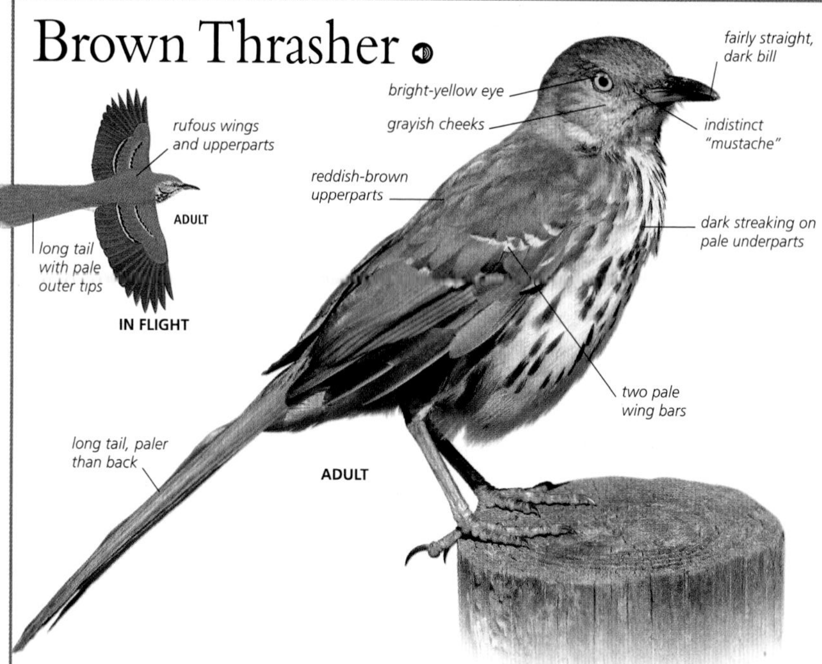
fairly straight, dark bill
bright-yellow eye
grayish cheeks
indistinct "mustache"
rufous wings and upperparts
reddish-brown upperparts
ADULT
dark streaking on pale underparts
long tail with pale outer tips
IN FLIGHT
two pale wing bars
long tail, paler than back
ADULT

The Brown Thrasher is usually difficult to view clearly because it keeps to dense underbrush. Like most other thrashers, this species prefers running or hopping to flying. When nesting, it can recognize and remove the eggs of brood parasites like the Brown-headed Cowbird. The current population decline is most likely the result of fragmentation of large, wooded habitats into patches, which lack the forest interior habitat this species needs.

VOICE Calls varied, including rasping sounds; song a long series of musical notes, sometimes imitating other species; repeats phrase twice before moving on to the next one.

NESTING Bulky cup of twigs close to ground, lined with leaves, grass, bark; 3–5 eggs; 1 brood; April–July.

FEEDING Mainly insects (especially beetles) and worms gathered from leaf litter on the forest floor; will peck at cultivated grains, nuts, berries, and fruit.

FLIGHT: slow and heavy with deep wing beats; below treetops, especially in and around ground.

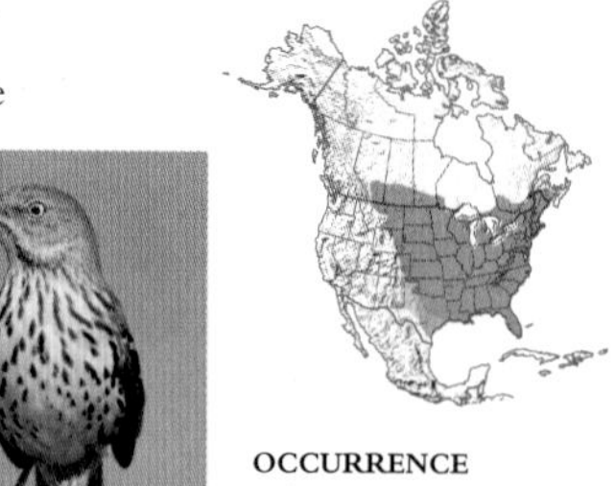

STREAKED BREAST
Displaying its heavily streaked underparts, this Brown Thrasher is perched and ready to sing.

OCCURRENCE
Widespread across central and eastern North America, from Canada to Texas and Florida, in a variety of densely wooded habitats, particularly those with thick undergrowth, but will also use woodland edges, hedges, and riverside trees. A partial migrant, it winters in the southern part of its range.

SIMILAR SPECIES

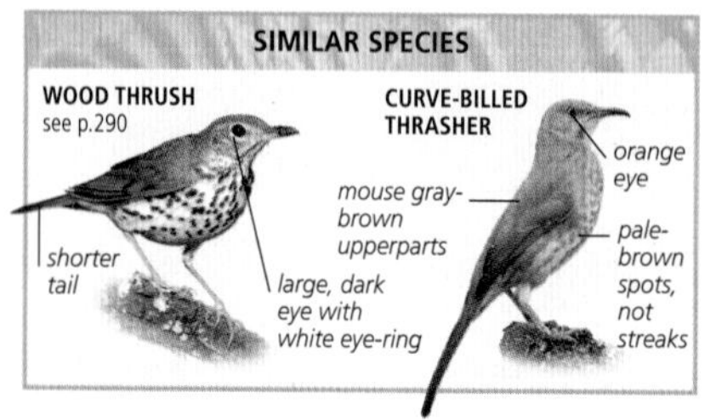
WOOD THRUSH
see p.290
shorter tail
large, dark eye with white eye-ring
CURVE-BILLED THRASHER
mouse gray-brown upperparts
orange eye
pale-brown spots, not streaks

Length **10–12in (25–30cm)**	Wingspan **11–14in (28–36cm)**	Weight **$2\frac{1}{8}$–$2\frac{7}{8}$oz (60–80g)**
Social **Solitary/Flocks**	Lifespan **Up to 13 years**	Status **Declining**

DATE: ______________ TIME: ______________ LOCATION: ______________

Order **Passeriformes**	Family **Mimidae**	Species ***Mimus polyglottos***

Northern Mockingbird

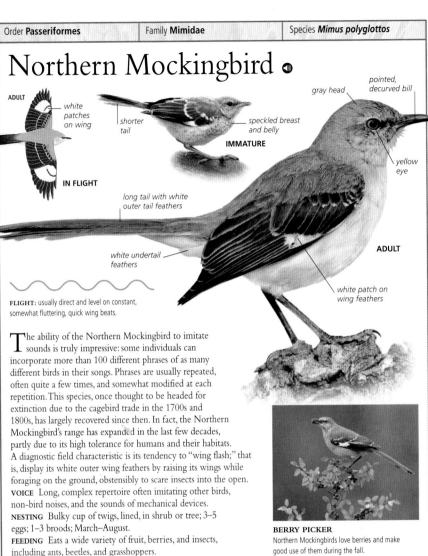

ADULT
white patches on wing
IN FLIGHT

shorter tail
speckled breast and belly
IMMATURE

gray head
pointed, decurved bill
yellow eye
long tail with white outer tail feathers
white undertail feathers
ADULT
white patch on wing feathers

FLIGHT: usually direct and level on constant, somewhat fluttering, quick wing beats.

The ability of the Northern Mockingbird to imitate sounds is truly impressive: some individuals can incorporate more than 100 different phrases of as many different birds in their songs. Phrases are usually repeated, often quite a few times, and somewhat modified at each repetition. This species, once thought to be headed for extinction due to the cagebird trade in the 1700s and 1800s, has largely recovered since then. In fact, the Northern Mockingbird's range has expanded in the last few decades, partly due to its high tolerance for humans and their habitats. A diagnostic field characteristic is its tendency to "wing flash;" that is, display its white outer wing feathers by raising its wings while foraging on the ground, obstensibly to scare insects into the open.

VOICE Long, complex repertoire often imitating other birds, non-bird noises, and the sounds of mechanical devices.

NESTING Bulky cup of twigs, lined, in shrub or tree; 3–5 eggs; 1–3 broods; March–August.

FEEDING Eats a wide variety of fruit, berries, and insects, including ants, beetles, and grasshoppers.

BERRY PICKER
Northern Mockingbirds love berries and make good use of them during the fall.

SIMILAR SPECIES

LOGGERHEAD SHRIKE
see p.240
brown mask
black wings

CLARK'S NUTCRACKER
white patch low on wing
darker gray belly
whiter sides to tail

OCCURRENCE
Widespread in the US from coast to coast, primarily along edges of disturbed habitats, including young forests and especially suburban and urban areas with shrubs or hedges. Breeding range has extended into southern Canada.

Length **8½–10in (22–25cm)**	Wingspan **13–15in (33–38cm)**	Weight **1$\frac{9}{16}$–2oz (45–55g)**
Social **Pairs**	Lifespan **Up to 20 years**	Status **Secure**

DATE: ____________ TIME: ____________ LOCATION: ____________

Order **Passeriformes**	Family **Sturnidae**	Species ***Sturnus vulgaris***

European Starling

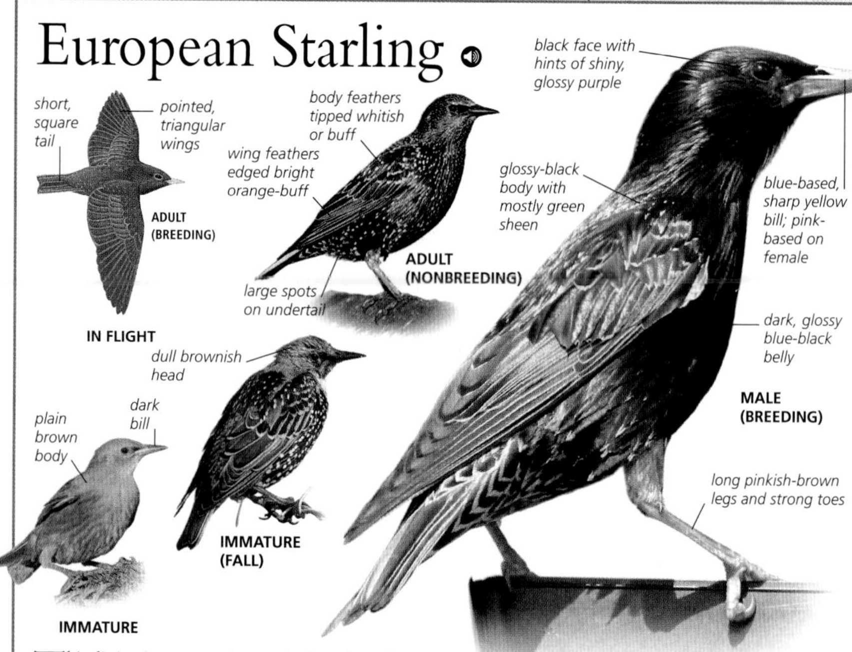

short, square tail
pointed, triangular wings
ADULT (BREEDING)
IN FLIGHT
body feathers tipped whitish or buff
wing feathers edged bright orange-buff
large spots on undertail
ADULT (NONBREEDING)
black face with hints of shiny, glossy purple
glossy-black body with mostly green sheen
blue-based, sharp yellow bill; pink-based on female
dark, glossy blue-black belly
MALE (BREEDING)
long pinkish-brown legs and strong toes
dull brownish head
dark bill
plain brown body
IMMATURE (FALL)
IMMATURE

This distinctive non-native species is perhaps the most successful bird in North America—and probably the most maligned. In the 1890s, 60 to 100 European Starlings were successfully released in New York City's Central Park to become the ancestors of the 200 million birds now living in North America. This adaptable and aggressive bird competes with native species for nest sites, and usually wins—even against larger species such as the Northern Flicker and the American Kestrel.

VOICE Highly varied; gives whooshing *sssssheer*, often in flight; also whistled *wheeeooo*; song an elaborate pulsing series with slurred whistles and clicking notes; imitates other birds and various noises.

NESTING Natural or artificial cavity of any sort; 4–6 eggs; 1–2 broods; March–July.

FEEDING Omnivorous; picks at anything that might be edible; eats insects and berries; raids berry crops and vineyards; visits bird feeders and trashcans; often feeds on grubs in lawns.

FLIGHT: individuals fly in direct, buzzy manner; flocks bunch up tightly in flight.

INSECT EATER
Despite its parents' omnivorous diet, the nestlings are fed almost exclusively on insects and larvae.

SIMILAR SPECIES

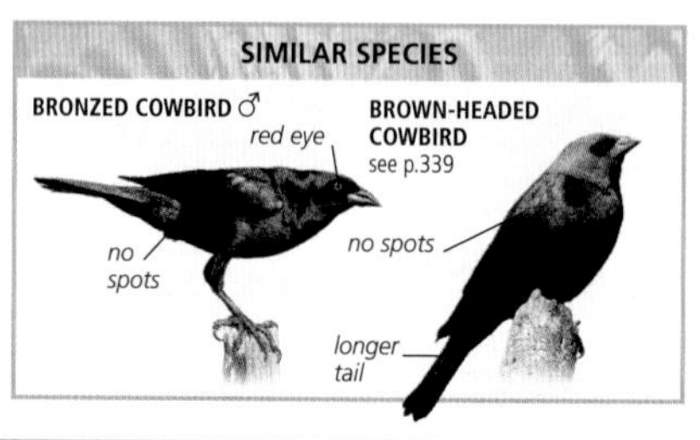

BRONZED COWBIRD ♂
red eye
no spots
BROWN-HEADED COWBIRD
see p.339
no spots
longer tail

OCCURRENCE
In North America from southern Canada to the US-Mexico border; also Puerto Rico and other Caribbean islands. Common to abundant in cities, towns, and farmlands; also occurs in relatively "wild" settings far from human habitation. Forms flocks at all times, huge in winter.

Length **8½in (21cm)**	Wingspan **16in (41cm)**	Weight **2⅝– 3⅜oz (75–95g)**
Social **Colonies**	Lifespan **Up to 17 years**	Status **Secure**

DATE: ______________ TIME: ______________ LOCATION: ______________

Order **Passeriformes**	Family **Turdidae**	Species ***Sialia sialis***

Eastern Bluebird

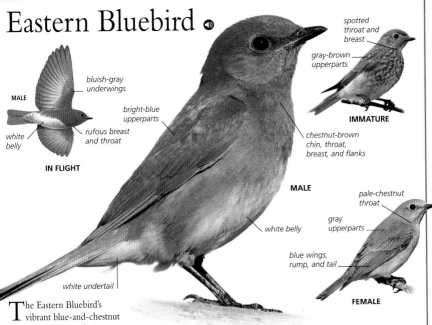

MALE
bluish-gray underwings
white belly
rufous breast and throat
IN FLIGHT

bright-blue upperparts
white undertail
chestnut-brown chin, throat, breast, and flanks
white belly
MALE

spotted throat and breast
gray-brown upperparts
IMMATURE

pale-chestnut throat
gray upperparts
blue wings, rump, and tail
FEMALE

The Eastern Bluebird's vibrant blue-and-chestnut body is a beloved sight in eastern North America, especially after the remarkable comeback of the species in the past 30 years. After much of the bird's habitat was eliminated by agriculture in the mid-20th century, nest boxes were designed and constructed for the bluebirds to provide alternatives to their traditional nesting sites in tree cavities. The Eastern Bluebird's mating system involves males seeking (or not minding) multiple partners.

VOICE Main song a melodious series of soft, whistled notes; *churr-wi* or *churr-li*; songs for mating and asserting territoriality.

NESTING Cavity-nester, in trees or artificial boxes; nest lined with grass, weeds, and twigs; uses old nests of other species; 3–7 eggs; 2 broods; February–September.

FEEDING Feeds on insects, like grasshoppers and caterpillars in breeding season; in winter, also takes fruit and plants.

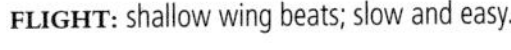

FLIGHT: shallow wing beats; slow and easy.

HOME DELIVERY
A female bluebird delivers food to a nest box.

SIMILAR SPECIES
WESTERN BLUEBIRD ♀
brownish back
grayish throat
MOUNTAIN BLUEBIRD ♀
gray-brown head and body

OCCURRENCE
Found in eastern Canada and the eastern US, where it lives in clearings and woodland edges; occupies multiple open habitats in rural, urban, and suburban areas: woodlands, plains, orchards, parks, and spacious lawns. Breeds and winters across the eastern half of North America.

Length **6–8in (15–20cm)**	Wingspan **10–13in (25–33cm)**	Weight **1¹⁄₁₆oz (30g)**
Social **Flocks**	Lifespan **8–10 years**	Status **Secure**

DATE: ______________ TIME: ______________ LOCATION: ______________________________

Order **Passeriformes**	Family **Turdidae**	Species ***Myadestes townsendi***

Townsend's Solitaire

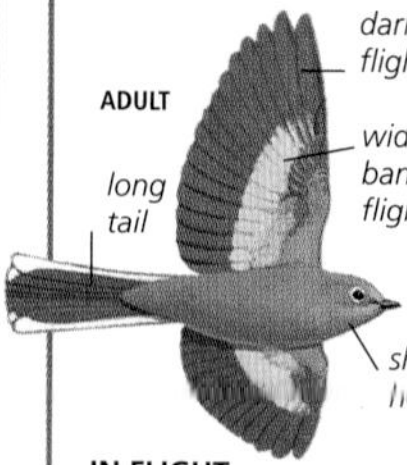

ADULT
dark-gray outer flight feathers
wide buff bands on flight feathers
long tail
short head
IN FLIGHT

plain gray
upright posture
ADULT
black legs and feet

large black eye
white eye-ring
short black bill
gray upperparts and head
paler underparts
ADULT
pale chestnut-tan patches
long, dark tail with white outer feathers

spotted back
heavily spotted breast
IMMATURE
long tail

The rather shy Townsend's Solitaire inhabits most of western North America, especially high-elevation coniferous forests of the Sierras and the Rockies. Its drab-gray plumage, with a chestnut-tan wing pattern, remains the same throughout the year, and the sexes look alike. From a perch high on a branch, Townsend's Solitaire darts after flying insects and snaps its bill shut after catching its prey, unlike other thrushes.

VOICE Calls are single-note, high-pitched whistles; sings all year, but especially when establishing territories; main song robin-like, full of rolled or trilled sounds interspersed with squeaky notes.

NESTING Cup of pine needles, dry grass, weed stems, and bark on ground or under overhang; 4 eggs; 1–2 broods; May–August.

FEEDING Forages for a wide variety of insects and spiders during breeding season; feeds on fruit and berries after breeding, particularly junipers.

FLIGHT: unhurried motion, usually over short distances, with slow, steady wing beats.

JUNIPER-LOVER
Solitaires love the berry-like cones of junipers, which they eat to supplement their winter diet.

SIMILAR SPECIES
MOUNTAIN BLUEBIRD ♀
dull bluish back
blue in wings and tail
short tail

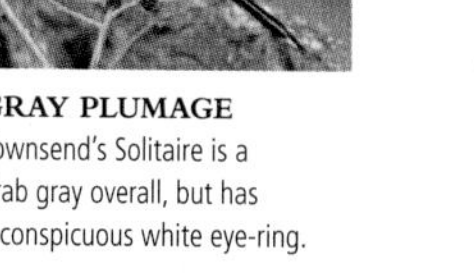

GRAY PLUMAGE
Townsend's Solitaire is a drab gray overall, but has a conspicuous white eye-ring.

OCCURRENCE
During breeding season, found in open conifer forests along steep slopes or areas with landslides; during winter, at lower elevations, in open woodlands where junipers are abundant. Partial-migrant, northern populations move south, as far as central Mexico, in winter.

Length **8–8½in (20–22cm)**	Wingspan **13–14½in (33–37cm)**	Weight **1¹⁄₁₆–1¼oz (30–35g)**
Social **Solitary**	Lifespan **Up to 5 years**	Status **Secure**

DATE: ______________ TIME: ______________ LOCATION: ______________

Order **Passeriformes**	Family **Turdidae**	Species ***Catharus fuscescens***

Veery

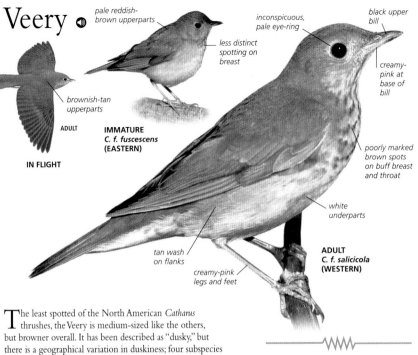

pale reddish-brown upperparts

less distinct spotting on breast

brownish-tan upperparts

ADULT

IN FLIGHT

IMMATURE
C. f. fuscescens
(EASTERN)

inconspicuous, pale eye-ring

black upper bill

creamy-pink at base of bill

poorly marked brown spots on buff breast and throat

white underparts

tan wash on flanks

creamy-pink legs and feet

ADULT
C. f. salicicola
(WESTERN)

The least spotted of the North American *Catharus* thrushes, the Veery is medium-sized like the others, but browner overall. It has been described as "dusky," but there is a geographical variation in duskiness; four subspecies have been described to reflect this. Eastern birds (*C. f. fuscescens*) are ruddier than their western relatives (*C. f. salicicola*). The Veery is a long-distance migrant, spending the northern winter months in central Brazil, in a variety of tropical habitats.

VOICE A series of descending *da-vee-ur, vee-ur, veer, veer*, somewhat bitonal, sounding like the name Veery; call a rather soft *veer*.

NESTING Cup of dead leaves, bark, weed stems, and moss on or near ground; 4 eggs; 1–2 broods; May–July.

FEEDING Forages on the ground for insects, spiders, snails; eats fruit and berries after breeding.

FLIGHT: rapid and straight, with intermittent hops and glides; makes long hops when on ground.

DAMP DWELLINGS
The Veery breeds in damp habitats, such as moist wooded areas or in trees near or in swamps.

OCCURRENCE
In summer, mainly found in damp deciduous forests, preferring the canopy, but in some places habitat near rivers preferred. In winter, choice of habitat flexible; found in tropical broadleaf evergreen forest, on forest edges, in open woodlands, and in second-growth areas regenerating after fires or clearing.

SIMILAR SPECIES

GRAY-CHEEKED THRUSH see p.286
gray face
bold black-brown breast spots

BICKNELL'S THRUSH see p.287
bold brown breast spots
olive-brown upperparts

SWAINSON'S THRUSH see p.288
buffy-colored face
bold brown-black breast spots

Length **7in (18cm)**	Wingspan **11–11½in (28–29cm)**	Weight **1¹⁄₁₆–2oz (28–54g)**
Social **Pairs**	Lifespan **Up to 10 years**	Status **Declining**

DATE: ____________ TIME: ____________ LOCATION: ____________________

Order **Passeriformes**	Family **Turdidae**	Species ***Catharus minimus***

Gray-cheeked Thrush

ADULT

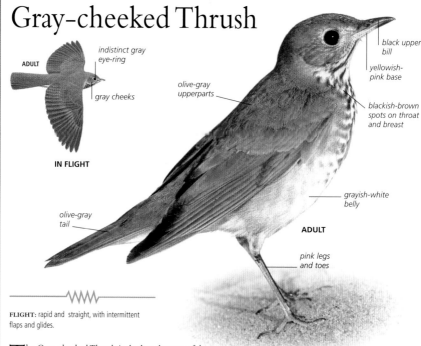

indistinct gray eye-ring

gray cheeks

IN FLIGHT

olive-gray upperparts

black upper bill

yellowish-pink base

blackish-brown spots on throat and breast

grayish-white belly

olive-gray tail

ADULT

pink legs and toes

FLIGHT: rapid and straight, with intermittent flaps and glides.

The Gray-cheeked Thrush is the least known of the five North American *Catharus* thrushes because it breeds in remote areas of northern Canada and Alaska. In fact, most of the existing information on this species is a result of research on the Bicknell's Thrush, which was considered to be a subspecies of the Gray-cheeked Thrush until 1993. During migration, the Gray-cheeked Thrush is more likely to be heard in flight at night than seen on the ground by birdwatchers.

VOICE Call a thin *kweer*, sometimes two notes; song flute-like, somewhat nasal, several notes ending on a lower pitch.

NESTING Cup of grass, twigs, moss, dead leaves, and mud, placed near ground in shrubbery; 4 eggs; 1 brood; May–July.

FEEDING Forages for insects, including beetles, ants, spiders, earthworms, and fruit.

FEEDING HABITAT
A Gray-cheeked Thrush hops across the forest floor looking for prey.

SIMILAR SPECIES

BICKNELL'S THRUSH see p.287

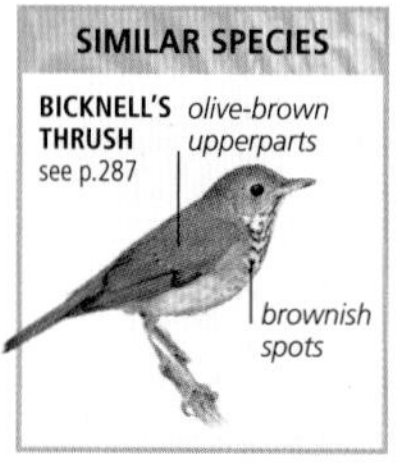
olive-brown upperparts
brownish spots

TREETOP SINGER
This bird is most likely to be seen in the evening, singing from treetops on its nesting grounds.

OCCURRENCE
On breeding grounds, occupies densely vegetated areas with small shrubs; preference for spruce forests in northern Canada and Alaska. During migration, favors wooded areas with dense understory. In winter, prefers forested areas and secondary succession woodlands.

Length **6½–7in (16–18cm)**	Wingspan **11½–13½in (29–34cm)**	Weight **7/8–1 1/16oz (26–30g)**
Social **Mixed flocks**	Lifespan **Up to 7 years**	Status **Secure**

DATE: ____________ TIME: ____________ LOCATION: ____________

Order **Passeriformes**	Family **Turdidae**	Species ***Catharus bicknelli***

Bicknell's Thrush

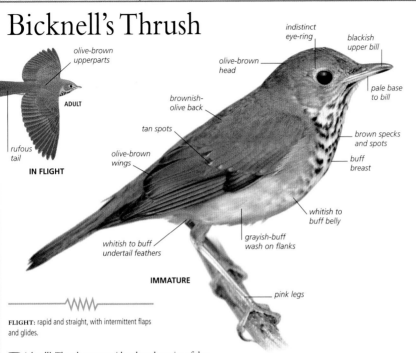

olive-brown upperparts
ADULT
rufous tail
IN FLIGHT

indistinct eye-ring
blackish upper bill
olive-brown head
pale base to bill
brownish-olive back
tan spots
brown specks and spots
olive-brown wings
buff breast
whitish to buff belly
whitish to buff undertail feathers
grayish-buff wash on flanks
IMMATURE
pink legs

FLIGHT: rapid and straight, with intermittent flaps and glides.

Bicknell's Thrush was considered a subspecies of the Gray-cheeked Thrush until 1993, when it was shown to be a distinct species with a slight difference in color, song, habitat, and migration. In the field, it is best distinguished from the Gray-cheeked Thrush by its song, which is less full and lower in pitch. Bicknell's Thrush breeds only in dwarf conifer forests on mountaintops in eastern Canada and the adjacent northeastern US, usually above 3,000ft (1,000m). Habitat loss threatens this species on its wintering grounds in Cuba, Hispaniola, and Puerto Rico. Males and females mate with multiple partners in a single season; because of this, males may care for the young in multiple nests.

VOICE Call *pheeuw*, one or two notes; complicated flute-like song of about four parts, ending with rising pitch; males sing, especially during flight; females rarely sing; song varies among populations.

NESTING Cup of moss and evergreen twigs, near ground; 3–4 eggs; 1 brood; June–August.

FEEDING Feeds mainly on caterpillars and insects; in addition, fruit during migration and possibly in winter.

MOUNTAIN-TOP BREEDING
This species breeds in high-elevation woodland areas, especially in conifers.

SIMILAR SPECIES

GRAY-CHEEKED THRUSH
see p.286

olive-gray brown
grayish face

OCCURRENCE
Restricted to dense spruce or fir forest at or near the treeline, at 3,000ft (1,000m), often in disturbed areas undergoing successional changes. During migration, found in a variety of habitats, such as woodlots and beaches. In winter, strong preference for wet mountainous Caribbean forests.

Length **6½–7in (16–18cm)**	Wingspan **12in (30cm)**	Weight **$\frac{7}{8}$–$1\frac{1}{16}$oz (26–30g)**
Social **Solitary/Small flocks**	Lifespan **Up to 8 years**	Status **Threatened**

DATE: ______________ TIME: ______________ LOCATION: ______________________

Order **Passeriformes**	Family **Turdidae**	Species ***Catharus ustulatus***

Swainson's Thrush

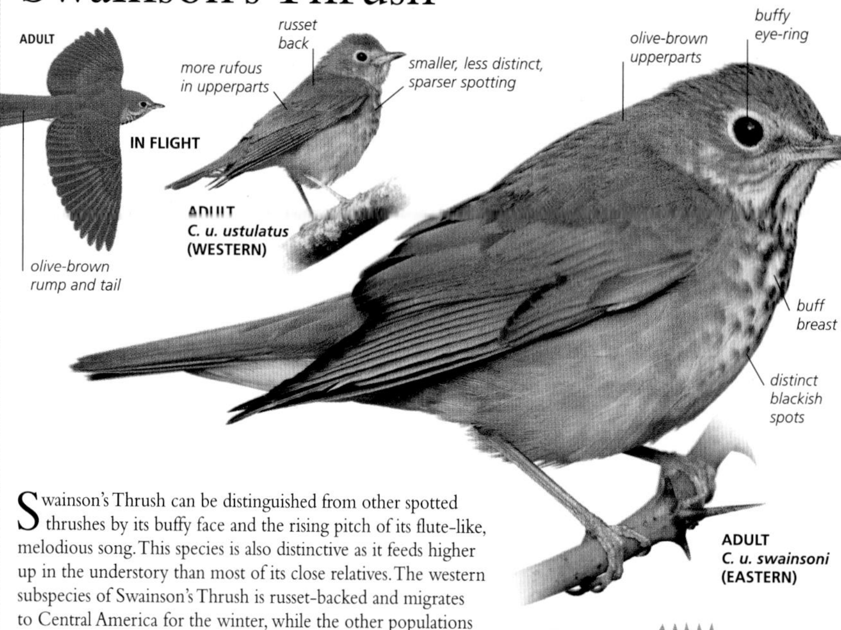
ADULT
IN FLIGHT
olive-brown rump and tail
russet back
more rufous in upperparts
smaller, less distinct, sparser spotting
ADULT *C. u. ustulatus* (WESTERN)
olive-brown upperparts
buffy eye-ring
buff breast
distinct blackish spots
ADULT *C. u. swainsoni* (EASTERN)

Swainson's Thrush can be distinguished from other spotted thrushes by its buffy face and the rising pitch of its flute-like, melodious song. This species is also distinctive as it feeds higher up in the understory than most of its close relatives. The western subspecies of Swainson's Thrush is russet-backed and migrates to Central America for the winter, while the other populations are olive-backed and winter in South America.

VOICE Single-note call *whit or whooit*; main song delivered by males, several phrases, each one spiraling upward; flute-like song is given during breeding and migration.

NESTING Open cup of twigs, moss, dead leaves, bark, and mud, on branches near trunks of small trees or in shrubs; 3–4 eggs; 1–2 broods; April–July.

FEEDING Forages in the air, using fly-catching methods to capture a wide range of insects during breeding season; berries during migration and in winter.

FLIGHT: rapid and straight, with intermittent flaps and glides.

DISTINCTIVE SONG
This bird's song distinguishes it from other thrushes.

TREE-DWELLER
Shy and retiring, Swainson's Thrush feeds in trees more than other *Catharus* thrushes.

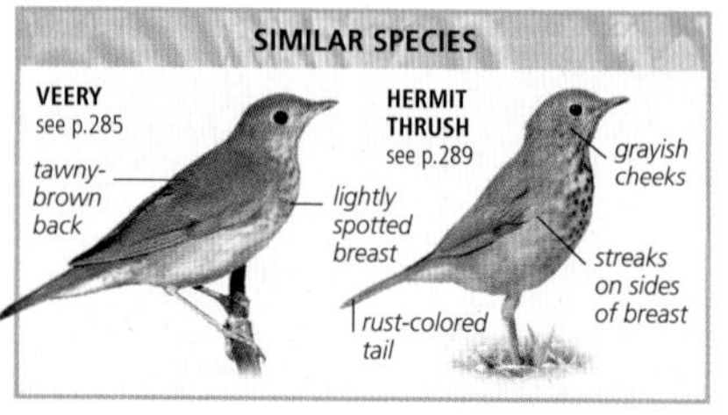
SIMILAR SPECIES
VEERY
see p.285
tawny-brown back
lightly spotted breast
HERMIT THRUSH
see p.289
grayish cheeks
streaks on sides of breast
rust-colored tail

OCCURRENCE
Breeds mainly in coniferous forests, especially spruce and fir, except in California, where it prefers deciduous riverside woodlands and damp meadows with shrubbery. During spring and fall migrations, dense understory is preferred. Winter habitat is mainly old-growth forest.

Length **6½–7½in (16–19cm)**	Wingspan **11½–12in (29–31cm)**	Weight **⅞–1⁹⁄₁₆oz (25–45g)**
Social **Pairs/Flocks**	Lifespan **Up to 11 years**	Status **Declining**

DATE: ______________ TIME: ______________ LOCATION: ______________

Order **Passeriformes** | Family **Turdidae** | Species ***Catharus guttatus***

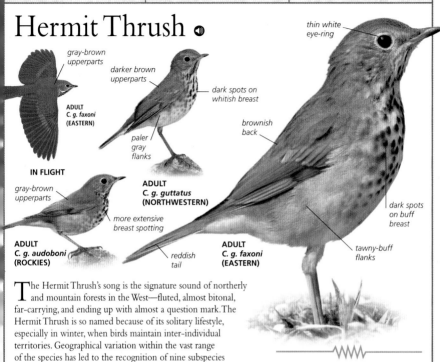

Hermit Thrush

gray-brown upperparts

ADULT
C. g. faxoni
(EASTERN)

IN FLIGHT

darker brown upperparts

dark spots on whitish breast

paler gray flanks

ADULT
C. g. guttatus
(NORTHWESTERN)

gray-brown upperparts

more extensive breast spotting

ADULT
C. g. audoboni
(ROCKIES)

thin white eye-ring

brownish back

dark spots on buff breast

tawny-buff flanks

reddish tail

ADULT
C. g. faxoni
(EASTERN)

The Hermit Thrush's song is the signature sound of northerly and mountain forests in the West—fluted, almost bitonal, far-carrying, and ending up with almost a question mark. The Hermit Thrush is so named because of its solitary lifestyle, especially in winter, when birds maintain inter-individual territories. Geographical variation within the vast range of the species has led to the recognition of nine subspecies (three are shown here). It winters in the southern US, Mexico, Guatemala, and El Salvador.

FLIGHT: rapid and straight, with intermittent flaps and glides.

VOICE Calls *tchek*, soft, dry; song flute-like, ethereal, falling, repetitive, and varied; several phrases delivered on a different pitch.

NESTING Cup of grasses, mosses, twigs, leaves, mud, hair, on ground or in low tree branches; 4 eggs; 1–2 broods; May–July.

FEEDING Mainly forages on ground for insects, larvae, earthworms, and snails; in winter, also eats fruit.

URBAN VISITOR
This thrush is frequently seen in wooded areas in urban and suburban parks.

OCCURRENCE
Occurs in coniferous forests and mixed conifer-deciduous woodlands; prefers to nest along the edges of a forest interior, like a bog location. Found in forests and other open woodlands during winter. During migration, found in many wooded habitats.

SIMILAR SPECIES

VEERY
see p.285
tawny-brown back
lightly spotted breast

BICKNELL'S THRUSH
see p.287
olive-brown back
yellow base of bill

SWAINSON'S THRUSH
see p.288
olive-brown upperparts

Length **6–7in (15–18cm)**	Wingspan **10–11in (25–28cm)**	Weight **7/8 –1 1/16oz (25–30g)**
Social **Solitary**	Lifespan **Up to 9 years**	Status **Secure**

DATE: ____________ TIME: ____________ LOCATION: ____________________

Order **Passeriformes**	Family **Turdidae**	Species ***Hylocichla mustelina***

Wood Thrush

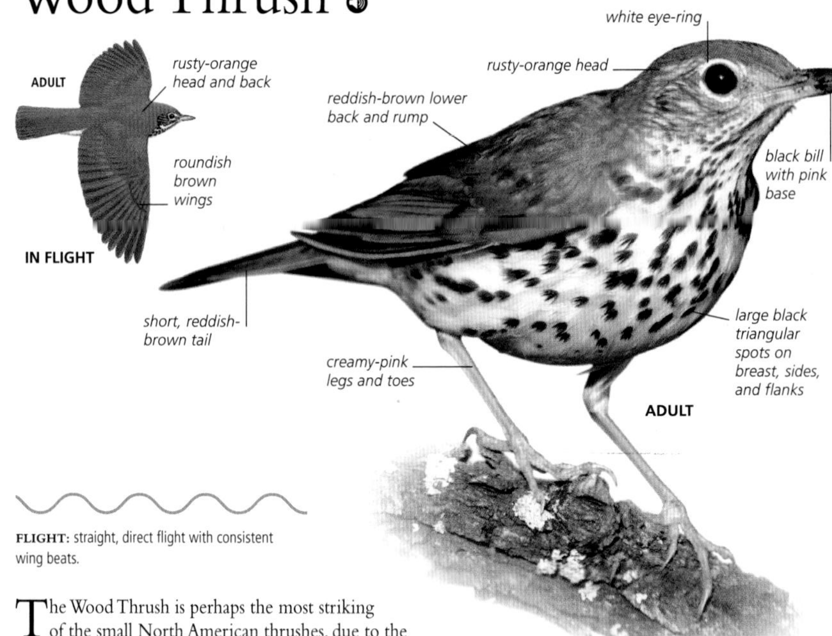
ADULT
rusty-orange head and back
roundish brown wings
IN FLIGHT
white eye-ring
rusty-orange head
reddish-brown lower back and rump
black bill with pink base
short, reddish-brown tail
creamy-pink legs and toes
large black triangular spots on breast, sides, and flanks
ADULT

FLIGHT: straight, direct flight with consistent wing beats.

The Wood Thrush is perhaps the most striking of the small North American thrushes, due to the black spots that cover its underparts and its rufous head and back. In the breeding season, its flute-like song echoes through the northeastern hardwood forests and suburban forested areas. Wood Thrush populations have fallen over the past 30 years, largely due to forest destruction and fragmentation. Sadly, this decline has been exacerbated by the Wood Thrush's susceptibility to brood parasitism by the Brown-headed Cowbird.

VOICE Rapid *pip-pippipip* or *rhuu-rhuu*; a three-part flute-like song—first part indistinct, second part loudest, third part trilled; males have variations of all three parts; mainly before sunrise.

NESTING Cup-shaped nest made with dried grass and weeds in trees or shrubs; 3–4 eggs; 1–2 broods; May–July.

FEEDING Forages in leaf litter, mainly for worms, beetles, moths, and caterpillars; eats fruit after breeding season.

STUNNING SOLOIST
The Wood Thrush can often be seen singing its melodious songs from a conspicuous perch.

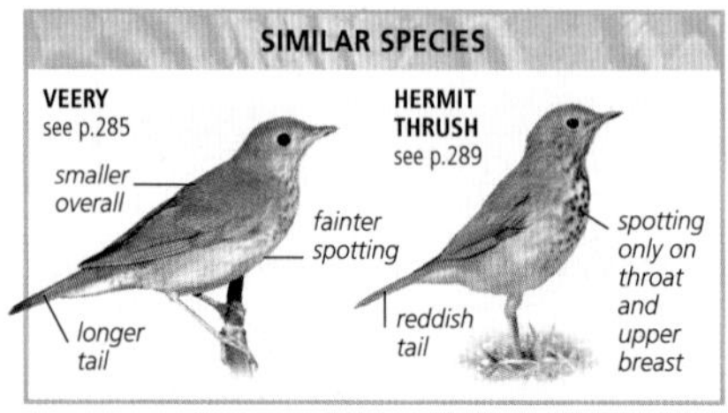
SIMILAR SPECIES
VEERY
see p.285
smaller overall
fainter spotting
longer tail
HERMIT THRUSH
see p.289
spotting only on throat and upper breast
reddish tail

OCCURRENCE
Hardwood forests in the East, from Texas and Florida to Minnesota and the Canadian Maritimes. Breeds in interior and at edges of deciduous and mixed forests; needs dense understory, shrubbery, and moist soil. Winters from eastern Mexico south through Central America to Panama.

Length **7½–8½in (19–21cm)**	Wingspan **12–13½in (30–34cm)**	Weight **$1\frac{7}{16}$–$1\frac{3}{4}$ oz (40–50g)**
Social **Pairs/Flocks**	Lifespan **Up to 9 years**	Status **Threatened**

DATE: ____________ TIME: ____________ LOCATION: ____________

Order **Passeriformes**	Family **Turdidae**	Species ***Turdus migratorius***

American Robin

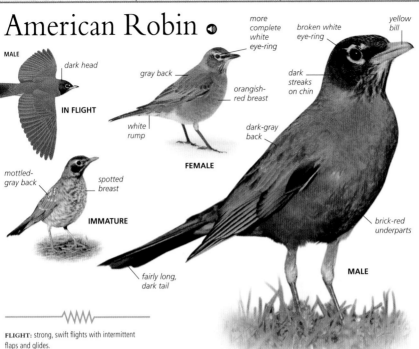

MALE
dark head
IN FLIGHT

gray back
more complete white eye-ring
orangish-red breast
white rump
FEMALE

mottled-gray back
spotted breast
IMMATURE

broken white eye-ring
yellow bill
dark streaks on chin
dark-gray back
brick-red underparts
fairly long, dark tail
MALE

FLIGHT: strong, swift flights with intermittent flaps and glides.

The American Robin, the largest and most abundant of the North American thrushes, is probably the most familiar bird on the continent. Its presence on suburban lawns is an early sign of spring. Unlike other species, it has adapted and prospered in human-altered habitats. It breeds across all of Canada and the US, and it winters across the US, migrating out of most of Canada in the fall. The decision to migrate is largely governed by changes in the availability of food. As the breeding season approaches, it is the males that sing first, either late in winter or early spring. The bird's brick-red breast—more vivid in males than in females—is its most distinguishing feature.

VOICE Calls a high-pitched *tjip* and a multi-note, throaty *tjuj-tjuk*; primary song a melodious *cheer-up, cheer-up, cheer-wee*, one of the first birds to be heard during dawn chorus, and one of the last to cease singing in the evening.

NESTING Substantial cup of grass, weeds, twigs, occasional garbage in tree or shrub, in the fork of a tree, or on the branch of a tree; 4 eggs; 2–3 broods; April–July.

FEEDING Forages in leaf litter, mainly for earthworms and small insects; mostly consumes fruit in the winter season.

SIMILAR SPECIES

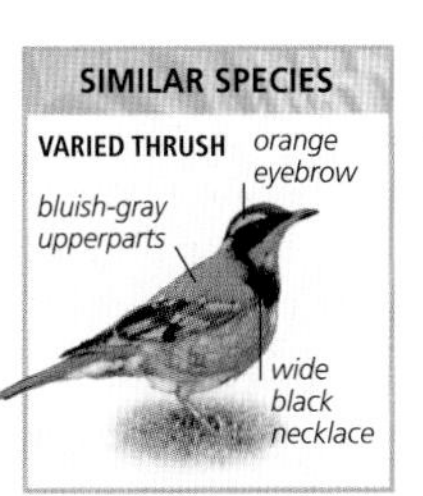
VARIED THRUSH
orange eyebrow
bluish-gray upperparts
wide black necklace

SEASONAL DIET
Robins are particularly dependent on the availability of fruit during the winter months.

OCCURRENCE
Breeding habitat a mix of forest, woodland, suburban gardens, lawns, municipal parks, and farms. A partial migrant, these robins tend to be found in woodlands where berry-bearing trees are present. Nonmigrating populations' winter habitat is similar to breeding habitat.

Length **8–11in (20–28cm)**	Wingspan **12–16in (30–41cm)**	Weight **2⅝oz (75g)**
Social **Flocks**	Lifespan **Up to 13 years**	Status **Secure**

DATE: ____________ TIME: ____________ LOCATION: ____________

Order **Passeriformes**	Family **Muscicapidae**	Species ***Oenanthe oenanthe***

Northern Wheatear

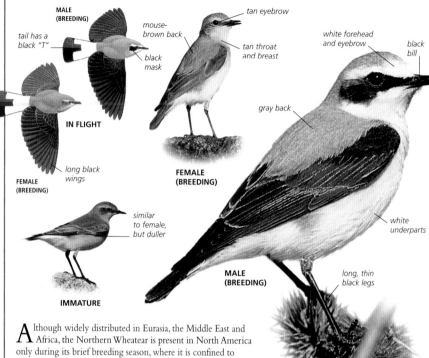

MALE (BREEDING)
tail has a black "T"
black mask
mouse-brown back
tan eyebrow
tan throat and breast
white forehead and eyebrow
black bill
IN FLIGHT
FEMALE (BREEDING)
long black wings
FEMALE (BREEDING)
gray back
similar to female, but duller
white underparts
IMMATURE
MALE (BREEDING)
long, thin black legs

Although widely distributed in Eurasia, the Middle East and Africa, the Northern Wheatear is present in North America only during its brief breeding season, where it is confined to Alaska and northeastern Canada. The two subspecies that breed in North America, the larger *O. o. leucorhoa* in the Northeast and *O. o. oenanthe* in the Northwest, migrate to wintering grounds in sub-Saharan Africa. The Northern Wheatear can be distinguished by its black-and-white tail, which bobs when the bird walks.

VOICE Multiple calls, a sharp *tuc* or *tek* common; three types of songs—territorial, conversational, and perched—consisting of mixtures of sweet and harsh notes; imitates other species.

NESTING Under rocks or in abandoned burrows; nests have coarse outer foundation, with cradle and cup within of finer material; 5–6 eggs; 1 brood; June–July.

FEEDING Eats insects, but also takes berries; diet in North America not well known.

FLIGHT: undulating when flying long distances; fluttering from perch to perch.

KEEP YOUR DISTANCE
Northern Wheatears are highly territorial, so neighbors get a scolding if they come too close.

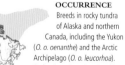

OCCURRENCE
Breeds in rocky tundra of Alaska and northern Canada, including the Yukon (*O. o. oenanthe*) and the Arctic Archipelago (*O. o. leucorhoa*). Both subspecies winter in Africa, *O. o. oenanthe* by flying across Asia, *O. o. leucorhoa* by flying across the Atlantic.

Length **5½–6in (14–15cm)**	Wingspan **10¾in (27cm)**	Weight **½oz (14g)**
Social **Solitary/Flocks**	Lifespan **Up to 7 years**	Status **Secure**

DATE: ____________ TIME: ____________ LOCATION: ____________

Family **Passeridae**

OLD WORLD SPARROWS

THESE SMALL, SHORT-LEGGED, short-billed, principally seed-eating birds were introduced to North America from Europe and Asia, and their name has carried over to many unrelated New World species. House and Tree Sparrows are small and finch-like, but always unstreaked below. Male and female House Sparrows differ in appearance, while Tree Sparrows of both sexes are more like the male House Sparrow, with pale cheeks and a black bib. House Sparrows are familiar urban and suburban birds, always associated with buildings, parks, or farmsteads.

FEEDING FRENZY
House Sparrows feed their chicks on caterpillars, visiting the nest scores of times each day.

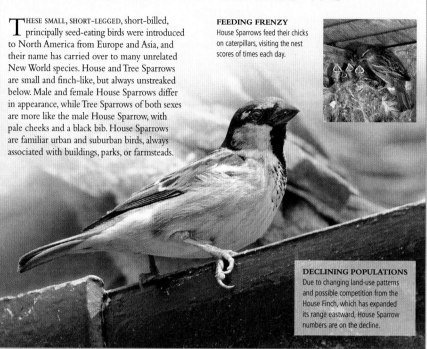

DECLINING POPULATIONS
Due to changing land-use patterns and possible competition from the House Finch, which has expanded its range eastward, House Sparrow numbers are on the decline.

Family **Motacillidae**

PIPITS

THIS GROUP OF ground-dwelling songbirds occurs across most of the world, although only two are found in Canada, and only one—the American Pipit—is Canada-wide. The two species of pipit that breed in North America also winter there. They inhabit open, treeless country, walking rather than hopping on the ground. They are more likely to be seen in their widespread wintering areas than in their remote breeding range.

COUNTRY-LOVERS
Pipits, such as this American Pipit, live in open country, including beaches, dunes, and tundra.

Order **Passeriformes**	Family **Passeridae**	Species ***Passer domesticus***

House Sparrow

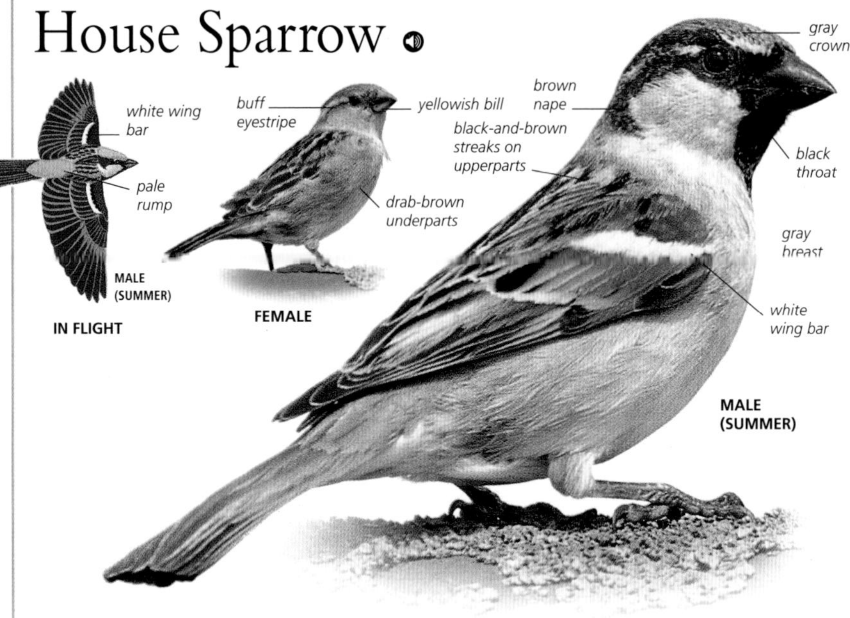
white wing bar
pale rump
MALE (SUMMER)
IN FLIGHT
buff eyestripe
yellowish bill
drab-brown underparts
FEMALE
gray crown
brown nape
black-and-brown streaks on upperparts
black throat
gray breast
white wing bar
MALE (SUMMER)

This is the familiar "sparrow" of towns, cities, suburbs, and farms. The House Sparrow is not one of the American or New World Sparrows—family Passerellidae—more commonly known in North America; rather it is a member of the Eurasian family, Passeridae. It was first introduced in Brooklyn, New York in 1850. From this modest beginning, and with the help of several other introductions up until the late 1860s, this hardy, and aggressive bird eventually spread right through the North American continent. In a little more than 150 years, the House Sparrow has evolved and shows the same sort of geographic variation as some widespread native birds. It is pale in the arid southwest US, and darker in wetter regions.

VOICE Variety of calls, including a cheery chirp, a dull *jurv* and a rough *jigga*; song consists of *chirp* notes repeated endlessly.

NESTING Untidy mass of dried vegetable material in either natural or artificial cavities; 3–5 eggs; 2–3 broods; April–August.

FEEDING Mostly seeds; sometimes gleans insects and fruit.

FLIGHT: fast and bouncing, with rapid wing beats; short wings and tail give it a portly profile.

APTLY NAMED
House Sparrows are often seen near human structures—fences, roofs, curbs, and streetlights.

SIMILAR SPECIES

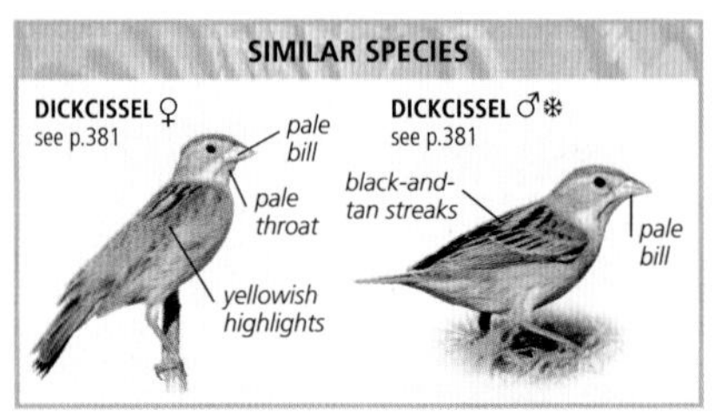
DICKCISSEL ♀
see p.381
pale bill
pale throat
yellowish highlights
DICKCISSEL ♂ ❄
see p.381
black-and-tan streaks
pale bill

OCCURRENCE
Flourishes in the downtown sections of cities and anywhere near human habitations, including agricultural outbuildings in remote areas of the continent. Also found in Mexico, Central and South America, the West Indies, Eurasia, southern Africa, Australia, and New Zealand.

Length **6in (15.5cm)**	Wingspan **9½in (24cm)**	Weight **⅝–1¹⁄₁₆oz (18–30g)**
Social **Flocks**	Lifespan **Up to 7 years**	Status **Declining**

 DATE: ______ TIME: ______ LOCATION: ______

Order **Passeriformes**	Family **Motacillidae**	Species ***Anthus rubescens***

American Pipit

ADULT

IN FLIGHT

white outer tail feathers

gray cheek with buffy eyestripes

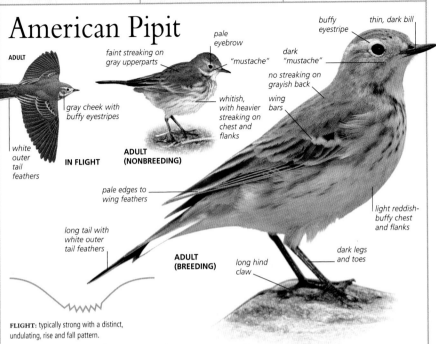

faint streaking on gray upperparts

pale eyebrow

"mustache"

whitish, with heavier streaking on chest and flanks

ADULT (NONBREEDING)

buffy eyestripe

thin, dark bill

dark "mustache"

no streaking on grayish back

wing bars

pale edges to wing feathers

light reddish-buffy chest and flanks

long tail with white outer tail feathers

ADULT (BREEDING)

long hind claw

dark legs and toes

FLIGHT: typically strong with a distinct, undulating, rise and fall pattern.

The American Pipit is divided into four subspecies, three of which breed in North America, and the fourth in Siberia. In its nonbreeding plumage, the American Pipit is a drab-looking, brownish-gray bird that forages for insects along water and shores, or in cultivated fields with short stems. In the breeding season, molting transforms it into a beauty—with gray upperparts and reddish underparts. American Pipits are known for pumping their tails up and down. When breeding, males display by rising into the air, then flying down with wings open and singing. Its migration takes the American Pipit as far south as Guatemala.

VOICE Alarm call a *tzeeep*; song repeated *tzwee-tzooo* from the air.

NESTING Cup in shallow depression on ground, outer frame of grass, lined with fine grass and hair; 4–6 eggs; 1 brood; June–July.

FEEDING Picks insects; also eats seeds during migration.

WINTER DRAB

Foraging in short vegetation, this bird is almost the same color as its surroundings.

SIMILAR SPECIES
HORNED LARK
see p.257
less white on tail edge
less streaking on throat and chest
SPRAGUE'S PIPIT
heavy streaking on back
pale cheeks and throat
pale legs

OCCURRENCE

Breeds in the Arctic tundra in the north, and alpine tundra in the Rockies; also breeds on treeless mountaintops in Maine and New Hampshire. Winters in open coastal areas and harvested agricultural fields across the US. Some North American migrants fly to Asia for the winter.

Length **6–8in (15–20cm)**	Wingspan **10–11in (25–28cm)**	Weight **$^{11}/_{16}$oz (20g)**
Social **Flocks**	Lifespan **Up to 6 years**	Status **Secure**

DATE: ________ TIME: ________ LOCATION: ________

Family **Fringillidae**

FINCHES

FINCHES IN THE FAMILY FRINGILLIDAE COMPRISE a family of seed-eating birds, of which 16 species can be found in North America. They vary in size and shape from the small and fragile-looking redpolls to the robust and chunky Evening Grosbeak. Finch colors range from whitish with some pink (redpolls) to gold (American Goldfinch), bright-red (crossbills), and yellow, white, and black (Evening Grosbeak). However, irrespective of body shape, size, and color, all have conical bills with razor-sharp edges. Finches do not crush seeds. Instead, they cut open the hard hull, then seize the seed inside with their tongue and swallow it. The bills of conifer-loving crossbills are crossed at the tip, a unique arrangement that permits them to open tough-hulled pine cones. Roughly 50 percent of crossbills are "left-billed" and 50 percent "right-billed"—lefties are right-footed, and vice versa. Most finches are social. Although they breed in pairs, post-nesting finches form flocks, some of which are huge. Most finch populations fluctuate in size, synchronized with seed production and abundance, which can lead to periodic irruptions in the south. All finches are vocal, calling constantly while flying, and singing in the spring. Calls are usually sharp, somewhat metallic sounds, although the American Goldfinch's tinkling calls are sweeter. Songs can be quite musical, clear-sounding melodies, like that of the Purple Finch. Finches make open cup-shaped nests of grasses and lichens, in trees or shrubs, and are remarkably adept at hiding them.

CROSSBILL
Perched on a pine tree branch, a female Red Crossbill grinds a seed in her bill to break open the hull and reach the fat-rich kernel inside.

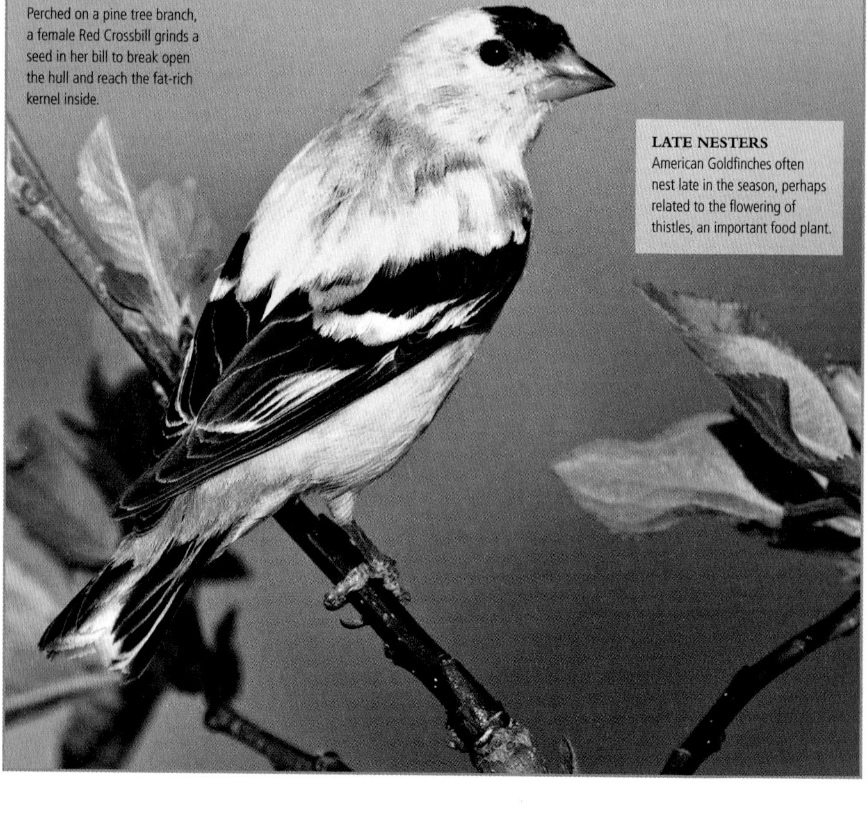

NOT REALLY PURPLE
The inaccurately named Purple Finch actually has a lovely wine-red coloration.

LATE NESTERS
American Goldfinches often nest late in the season, perhaps related to the flowering of thistles, an important food plant.

Order **Passeriformes**	Family **Fringillidae**	Species ***Coccothraustes vespertinus***

Evening Grosbeak

conspicuous yellow eyebrow
black wingtips
very dark gray head and shoulders
yellow rump
MALE
large white wing patches
huge yellowish-white bill
large white wing patch
MALE
IN FLIGHT
large grayish bill
black outer wing feathers
mustard-yellow underparts
grayish wing patch
short, square tail
FEMALE

There is no mistaking a noisy, boisterous winter flock of husky gold-and-black Evening Grosbeaks when they descend upon a feeder. The bird's outsized yellow bill seems to be made as much for threatening would-be rivals as it is designed for efficiently cracking sunflower seeds. In the breeding season, by contrast, the Evening Grosbeak is secretive and seldom seen, neither singing loudly nor displaying ostentatiously and nesting high in a tree. Once a bird of western North America, it has extended its range eastward in the past 200 years, and now nests as far east as Newfoundland. This is partly due to the planting of ornamental box elders, which provides year-round seeds, as well as outbreaks of insects like the spruce budworm.

VOICE Call descending *feeew*; also buzzy notes and beeping chatter.

NESTING Loose, grass-lined twig cup, usually on conifer branch; 3–4 eggs; 1–2 broods; May–July.

FEEDING Eats seeds of pines and other conifers, maple, and box elder seeds; also insects and their larvae, particularly spruce budworm.

FLIGHT: undulating, with dips between bouts of wing beats, may hover briefly.

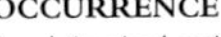

SIMILAR SPECIES

PINE GROSBEAK ♀ see p.298

AMERICAN GOLDFINCH ♂ see p.306

stubby bill
wing bars
gray underparts
white rump
short pinkish bill

CAPABLE BILL
This bird's extremely robust bill can deal with all kinds of winter fruits and seeds.

OCCURRENCE
Breeds in mixed conifer and spruce forests from the Rocky Mountain region to eastern Canada, and on mountain ranges south to Mexico. Winters in coniferous or deciduous woodlands, often in suburban locations; may move south from northern range, depending on food supply.

Length **6½–7in (16–18cm)**	Wingspan **12–14in (30–36cm)**	Weight **2–2½oz (55–70g)**
Social **Flocks**	Lifespan **Up to 15 years**	Status **Special Concern**

DATE: ______________ TIME: ______________ LOCATION: ______________

Order **Passeriformes**	Family **Fringillida**	Species ***Pinicola enucleator***

Pine Grosbeak

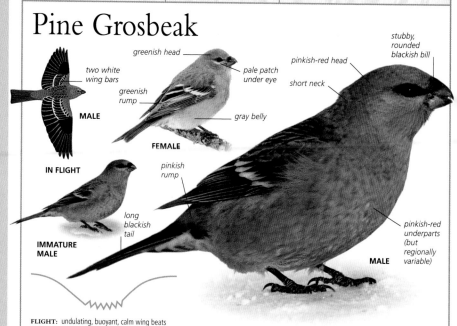

two white wing bars
MALE
IN FLIGHT
greenish head
pale patch under eye
greenish rump
gray belly
FEMALE
IMMATURE MALE
pinkish rump
long blackish tail
stubby, rounded blackish bill
pinkish-red head
short neck
pinkish-red underparts (but regionally variable)
MALE

FLIGHT: undulating, buoyant, calm wing beats interrupted by glides.

The largest member of the family Fringillidae in North America, and easily distinguished by the male's unmistakable thick, stubby bill, the Pine Grosbeak is a resident of boreal forests across Canada and Alaska and some mountain ranges in the western US. In winter, northern birds occasionally move south into the northern US. Due to extensive color variation of individual plumages, the age and sex of the bird are not always easily determined.

VOICE Contact calls of eastern birds *tee-tew*, or *tee-tee-tew*; western forms give more complex *tweedle*; warbling song.

NESTING Well-hidden, open cup nest usually in spruce or larch trees; 2–5 eggs, 1 brood; June–July.

FEEDING Eats spruce buds, maple seeds, and mountain ash berries throughout the year; consumes insects in summer.

FRUIT-LOVER
This species can often be seen hanging from branches, gorging on ripe fruit.

SIMILAR SPECIES
RED CROSSBILL
see p.303
brownish wings
mandibles crossed
WHITE-WINGED CROSSBILL
see p.304
mandibles crossed
white bars on wing

OCCURRENCE
Found in the boreal zone from Alaska to Newfoundland in Canada, and in California, the Southwest, and the Rockies in the US. Occurs in open, northerly coniferous forests in summer, usually near fresh water. Winters throughout its breeding range, but may move southward to southern Canada and the northeastern US.

Length **8–10in (20–25cm)**	Wingspan **13in (33cm)**	Weight **2–2½oz (55–70g)**
Social **Flocks**	Lifespan **Up to 10 years**	Status **Secure**

DATE: ____________ TIME: ____________ LOCATION: ____________

Order **Passeriformes**	Family **Fringillidae**	Species ***Haemorhous mexicanus***

House Finch

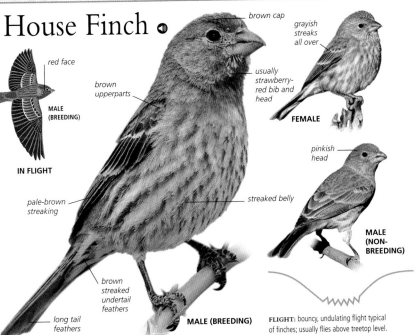

red face
MALE (BREEDING)
IN FLIGHT
brown cap
brown upperparts
usually strawberry-red bib and head
pale-brown streaking
streaked belly
brown streaked undertail feathers
long tail feathers
MALE (BREEDING)
grayish streaks all over
FEMALE
pinkish head
MALE (NON-BREEDING)

FLIGHT: bouncy, undulating flight typical of finches; usually flies above treetop level.

Historically, the House Finch was a western bird, and was first reported in the eastern side of the US on Long Island, New York City in 1941. These birds are said to have originated from the illegal bird trade. The population of the eastern birds started expanding in the 1960s; by the late 1990s, their population had expanded westward to link up with the original western population. The male House Finch is distinguished from the Purple and Cassin's Finches by its brown streaked underparts, while the females have plainer faces and generally blurrier streaking. The former also has a heavier, triangular bill.

VOICE Call note *queet*; varied jumble of notes, often starting with husky notes to whistled and burry notes, and ending with a long *wheeerr*.

NESTING Females build nests from grass stems, thin twigs, and thin weeds in trees and on artificial structures; 1–6 eggs; 2–3 broods; March–August.

FEEDING Eats, almost exclusively, vegetable matter, such as buds, fruit, and seeds; readily comes to feeders.

RED IN THE FACE
The breeding male House Finch can be identified by its stunning strawberry-red plumage.

SIMILAR SPECIES

PURPLE FINCH
see p.300
pinkish neck
whitish underparts

CASSIN'S FINCH
reddish head
white underparts

OCCURRENCE
Found in urban, suburban, and settled areas; in the West, also in wilder areas, such as prairies, desert grasslands, and chaparral, particularly near people; in the East, almost exclusively in settled areas, including the centers of large cities. Resident, some birds migrate after breeding.

Length **5–6in (12.5–15cm)**	Wingspan **8–10in (20–25cm)**	Weight **$^{9}/_{16}$–1oz (16–27g)**
Social **Flocks**	Lifespan **Up to 12 years**	Status **Secure**

DATE: ______________ TIME: ______________ LOCATION: ______________________________

Order **Passeriformes**	Family **Fringillidae**	Species ***Haemorhous purpureus***

Purple Finch

pinkish-red body

MALE

rounded brownish wings

IN FLIGHT

pale-brown overall

lightly streaked overall

darker, streaked wings

FEMALE

brownish, conical bill

brown stripe between eye and bill

raspberry-red crown

pink-and-brown streaked upperparts

pink rump and upper tail

MALE

whitish belly with rosy patches

One of three difficult-to-distinguish members of the genus *Haemorhous* in North America, the Purple Finch is best known as a visitor to winter feeding stations. The western subspecies (*californicus*) is slightly darker and duller than the eastern form (*purpureus*). Only moderately common, the raspberry-red males pose less of an identification challenge than the brown-streaked females. Even on their breeding grounds in open and mixed coniferous forest, Purple Finches are more often heard than seen.

VOICE Flight call single, rough *pikh*; songs rich series of notes, up and down in pitch.

NESTING Cup of sticks and grasses on a conifer branch; 4 eggs; 2 broods; May–July.

FEEDING Eats buds, seeds, and flowers of deciduous trees; insects and caterpillars in summer; also seeds and berries.

FLIGHT: rapid wing beats, alternating with downward glides.

RASPBERRY TINTED
On a lichen-covered branch this male's delicate coloring is quite striking.

OCCURRENCE
Breeds in northern mixed conifer and hardwood forests in all Canadian provinces, the Yukon and Northwest Territories, where it is partially migratory. Resident from Baja California north along the Pacific Coast and the Cascade Mountains to Washington and a small part of southern British Columbia.

SIMILAR SPECIES

HOUSE FINCH ♀ western; see p.299
thinner streaks

CASSIN'S FINCH ♀
more marked facial patterning

RED-WINGED BLACKBIRD ♀ see p.338
larger overall
heavily streaked
darker overall

Length **4¾–6in (12–15cm)**	Wingspan **8½–10in (22–26cm)**	Weight **11/16–1 1/16oz (20–30g)**
Social **Flocks**	Lifespan **Up to 14 years**	Status **Declining**

DATE: ______ TIME: ______ LOCATION: ______

Order **Passeriformes**	Family **Fringillidae**	Species ***Acanthis flammea***

Common Redpoll

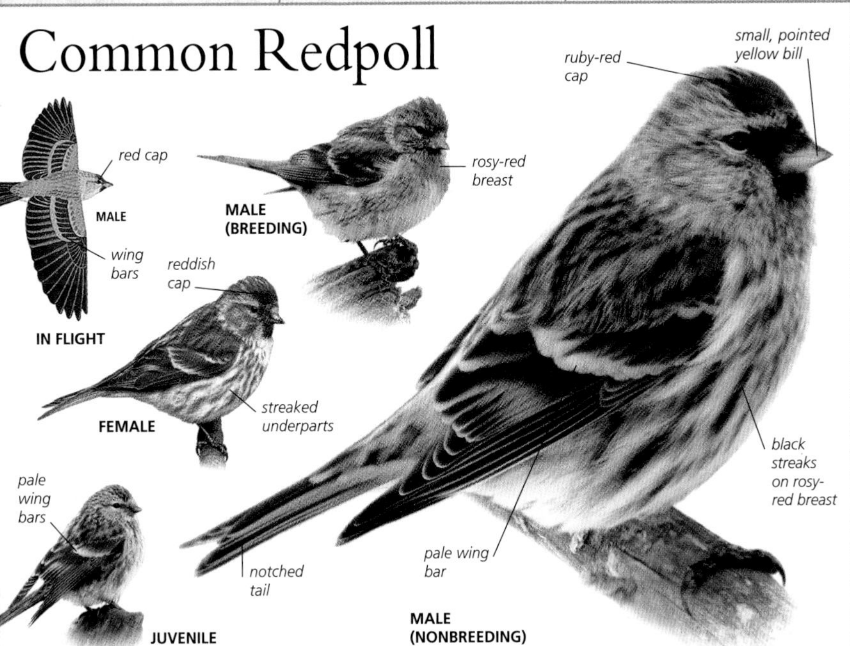
red cap
MALE
wing bars
IN FLIGHT
rosy-red breast
MALE (BREEDING)
reddish cap
FEMALE
streaked underparts
pale wing bars
JUVENILE
ruby-red cap
small, pointed yellow bill
black streaks on rosy-red breast
notched tail
pale wing bar
MALE (NONBREEDING)

Every other year, spruce, birch, and other trees in the northern forest zone fail to produce a good crop of seeds, forcing the Common Redpoll to look for food farther south than usual—as far south as the northern US states. The Common Redpoll is oddly tame around people and is easily attracted to winter feeders. The degree of whiteness in its plumage varies greatly among individuals, based on sex and age. Recent DNA studies suggest that Common, Hoary, and Lesser Redpolls are one and the same species.

VOICE Flight call dry *zit-zit-zit-zit* and rattling *chirr*; also high *too-ee* call while perched; song series of rapid trills.

NESTING Cup of small twigs in spruces, larches, willows, alders; 4–6 eggs; 1–2 broods; May–June.

FEEDING Feeds on small seeds from conifers, sedge, birch, willow, alder; also insects and spiders.

FLIGHT: deeply undulating, with dips between bouts of wing beats.

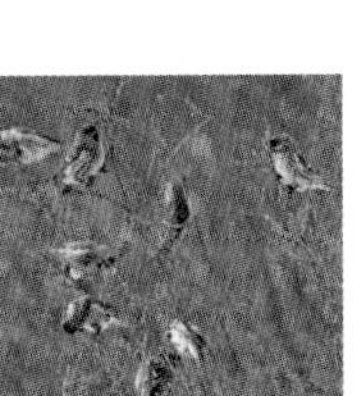

FRIENDLY FLOCK
Common Redpolls are only weakly territorial, sometimes even nesting close together.

OCCURRENCE
Mainly in extreme northern North America from Alaska to Quebec and Labrador, in low forest, sub-Arctic, and shrubby tundra habitats. More southerly winter appearances typically occur every other year, rarely south of the northern US, from Dakota east to New York and New England.

SIMILAR SPECIES

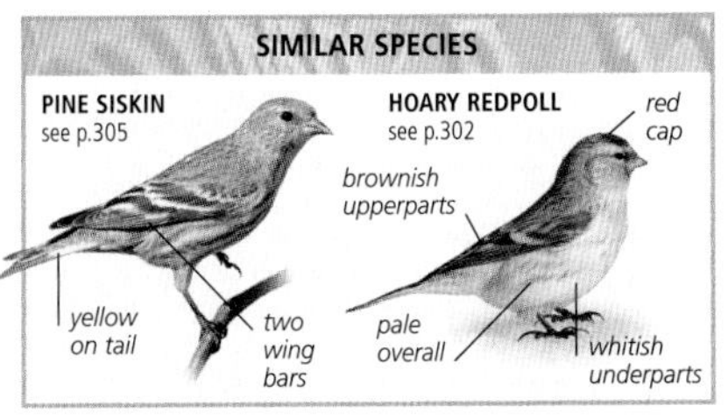
PINE SISKIN
see p.305
yellow on tail
two wing bars
HOARY REDPOLL
see p.302
red cap
brownish upperparts
pale overall
whitish underparts

Length **4¾–5½in (12–14cm)**	Wingspan **6½–6¾in (16–17cm)**	Weight **3/8–11/16oz (11–19g)**
Social **Flocks**	Lifespan **Up to 10 years**	Status **Secure**

DATE: ______________ TIME: ______________ LOCATION: ______________________________

Order **Passeriformes**	Family **Fringillidae**	Species ***Acanthis hornemanni***

Hoary Redpoll

pale upperparts
MALE
creamy-white wing bars
IN FLIGHT
white rump
small pinkish-red patch on forehead
lightly streaked breast
FEMALE
whitish belly
pinkish-red forehead
streaked neck
small conical bill
MALE
white uppertail feathers
notched tail
pink wash on breast
faint streaks
creamy-white undertail feathers

When a flock of redpolls settles at a feeding station, one or more may stand out as exceptionally white-breasted, somewhat fluffier, and with a stubbier bill. These may be Hoary Redpolls, a distinct species from the rest of the redpoll group. This bird of the high Arctic has two recognized subspecies—*A. h. exilipes* and *A. h. hornemanni*. These close relatives of the Common Redpoll often breed in the same areas, but do not interbreed. However, recent DNA studies may see the Hoary Redpoll lumped in with the Common Redpoll in the near future. Their chattering flocks buzz rapidly over trees and fields and are tame around humans.

VOICE Flight calls dry *zit-zit-zit-zit* and rattling *chirr*; also high *too-ee* call while perched; song series of rapid trills.

NESTING Lined cup of twigs, grasses in scrubby trees; 4–6 eggs; 1–2 broods; May-July.

FEEDING Eats seeds, insects, and spiders; in winter, prefers niger thistle seed.

FLIGHT: flurries of energetic wing beats alternating with glides.

GROUND FEEDER
Seeds that fall from trees or bird feeders onto the snow provide a good meal for the Hoary Redpoll.

SIMILAR SPECIES

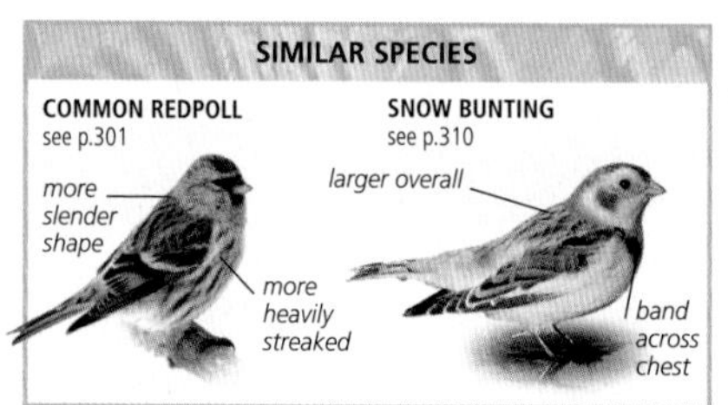
COMMON REDPOLL
see p.301
more slender shape
more heavily streaked
SNOW BUNTING
see p.310
larger overall
band across chest

OCCURRENCE
Breeds in the high Arctic, including the Canadian Arctic Archipelago; prefers low trees of the open tundra; winters within the boreal forest belt from the Canadian Maritimes and northern New England westward to Alaska.

Length **5–5½in (12.5–14cm)**	Wingspan **8½–9¼in (21–23.5cm)**	Weight **7/16–11/16oz (12–20g)**
Social **Flocks**	Lifespan **Up to 5 years**	Status **Secure**

DATE: ________ TIME: ________ LOCATION: ________

Order **Passeriformes**	Family **Fringillidae**	Species ***Loxia curvirostra***

Red Crossbill

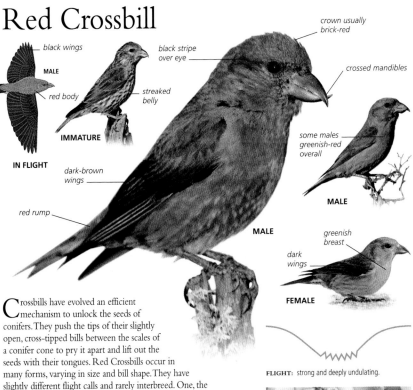

crown usually brick-red
black wings
MALE
red body
IN FLIGHT
black stripe over eye
crossed mandibles
streaked belly
IMMATURE
some males greenish-red overall
MALE
dark-brown wings
red rump
MALE
greenish breast
dark wings
FEMALE

Crossbills have evolved an efficient mechanism to unlock the seeds of conifers. They push the tips of their slightly open, cross-tipped bills between the scales of a conifer cone to pry it apart and lift out the seeds with their tongues. Red Crossbills occur in many forms, varying in size and bill shape. They have slightly different flight calls and rarely interbreed. One, the Cassia Crossbill, is treated as a separate species, *Loxia sinesciuris*. Other forms are nomadic, but this species remains in a tiny part of Idaho all year, feeding on lodgepole pine. It is nearly impossible to identify the different forms of the Red Crossbill other than by voice or DNA.

VOICE Common call *jit* repeated 2–5 times; song complex, continuous warbling of notes, whistles, and buzzes.

NESTING Cup nest on lateral conifer branch; 3–5 eggs; 2 broods; can breed year-round.

FEEDING Feeds on pine seeds; also insects and larvae, particularly aphids; also other seeds.

FLIGHT: strong and deeply undulating.

PROCESSING SEEDS
The Red Crossbill manipulates seeds with its tongue before swallowing them.

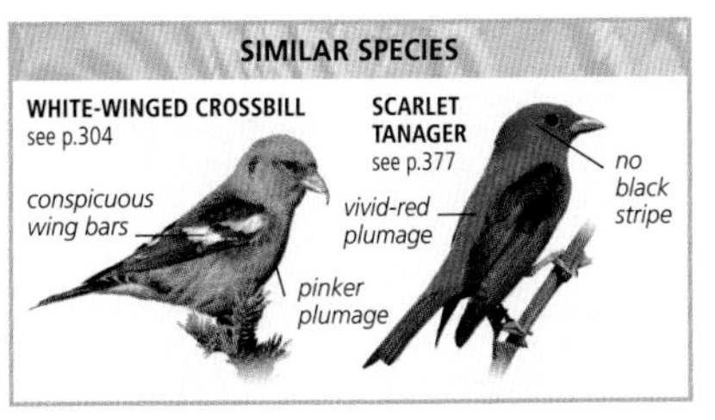
SIMILAR SPECIES
WHITE-WINGED CROSSBILL
see p.304
conspicuous wing bars
pinker plumage
SCARLET TANAGER
see p.377
vivid-red plumage
no black stripe

OCCURRENCE
Range covers coniferous or mixed-coniferous and deciduous forests from Newfoundland to British Columbia and southern Alaska; also mountain forests in the Rockies, south to Mexico; irregular movements, depending on the availability of pine cones.

Length **5–6¾in (13–17cm)**	Wingspan **10–10½in (25–27cm)**	Weight **⅞–1¼oz (25–35g)**
Social **Flocks**	Lifespan **Up to 10 years**	Status **Declining**

DATE: ______________ TIME: ______________ LOCATION: ______________

Order **Passeriformes**	Family **Fringillidae**	Species ***Loxia leucoptera***

White-winged Crossbill

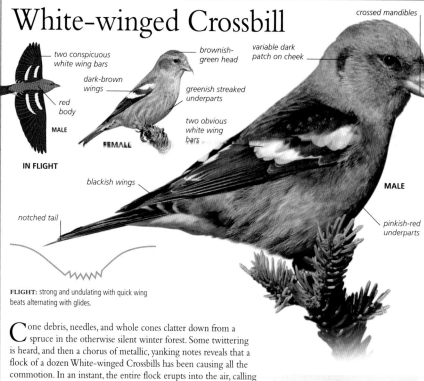

two conspicuous white wing bars
red body
MALE
IN FLIGHT
dark-brown wings
brownish-green head
greenish streaked underparts
FEMALE
variable dark patch on cheek
crossed mandibles
two obvious white wing bars
blackish wings
notched tail
MALE
pinkish-red underparts

FLIGHT: strong and undulating with quick wing beats alternating with glides.

Cone debris, needles, and whole cones clatter down from a spruce in the otherwise silent winter forest. Some twittering is heard, and then a chorus of metallic, yanking notes reveals that a flock of a dozen White-winged Crossbills has been causing all the commotion. In an instant, the entire flock erupts into the air, calling loudly in flight, only to disappear completely in the distance. Few other creatures of the northerly forest go about their business with such determined energy, and no others accent a winter woodland with hot-pink and magenta—the colors of the White-winged Crossbill's head and breast.

VOICE Calls are sharp, chattering *plik*, or deeper *tyoop*, repeated in series of 3–7 notes; song melodious trilling.

NESTING Open cup nest, usually high on end of a spruce branch; 3–5 eggs; 2 broods; July, January–February.

FEEDING Eats seeds from small-coned conifers; spruces, firs, and larches; feeds on insects when available.

EATING SNOW
The White-winged Crossbill frequently eats snow to provide essential moisture.

SIMILAR SPECIES

PINE GROSBEAK see p.298
blunt bill
longer tail

RED CROSSBILL see p.303
no wing bars
redder plumage

OCCURRENCE
Nomadic; most common in the spruce zone of Canada and Alaska but has bred as far south as Colorado in the West; in the East, from Quebec and Newfoundland southward to New York and New England.

Length **5½–6in (14–15cm)**	Wingspan **10–10½in (26–27cm)**	Weight **$^{11}/_{16}$–$1^{1}/_{16}$oz (20–30g)**
Social **Flocks**	Lifespan **Up to 10 years**	Status **Secure**

DATE: ____________ TIME: ____________ LOCATION: ____________

Order **Passeriformes**	Family **Fringillidae**	Species ***Spinus pinus***

Pine Siskin

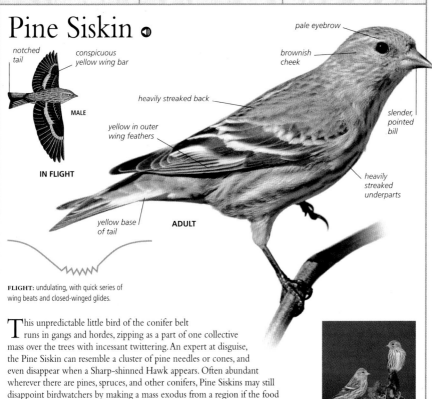

notched tail
conspicuous yellow wing bar
MALE
IN FLIGHT

pale eyebrow
brownish cheek
heavily streaked back
yellow in outer wing feathers
slender, pointed bill
heavily streaked underparts
yellow base of tail
ADULT

FLIGHT: undulating, with quick series of wing beats and closed-winged glides.

This unpredictable little bird of the conifer belt runs in gangs and hordes, zipping as a part of one collective mass over the trees with incessant twittering. An expert at disguise, the Pine Siskin can resemble a cluster of pine needles or cones, and even disappear when a Sharp-shinned Hawk appears. Often abundant wherever there are pines, spruces, and other conifers, Pine Siskins may still disappoint birdwatchers by making a mass exodus from a region if the food supply is not to their liking. A vicious fighter at feeding tables, nomadic by nature, with high energy and fearlessness, the Pine Siskin is a fascinating species.

VOICE Rising *toooeeo*, mostly when perched; also raspy *chit-chit-chit* in flight.

NESTING Shallow cup of grass and lichens near the end of a conifer branch; 3–4 eggs; 1–2 broods; February–August.

FEEDING Eats conifer seeds; gleans insects and spiders; also seen feeding on roadsides, lawns, and weed fields.

FOREST DWELLER
The streaked Pine Siskin inhabits northern and western coniferous forests.

QUARRELSOME
A bird warns off a neighbor at a food source, displaying its yellow wing stripe.

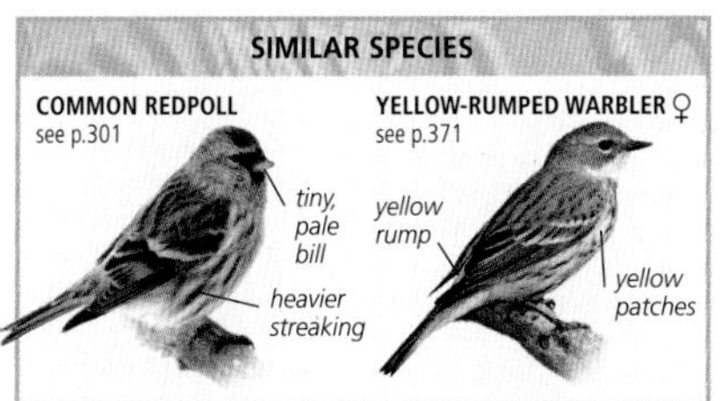
SIMILAR SPECIES
COMMON REDPOLL
see p.301
tiny, pale bill
heavier streaking
YELLOW-RUMPED WARBLER ♀
see p.371
yellow rump
yellow patches

OCCURRENCE
Widespread across North America; occurs in coniferous and mixed coniferous forests, but also seen in parkland and suburbs. In some winters, it may appear south of its regular breeding range to Missouri and Tennessee, also Mexico. Prefers open areas to continuous forest.

Length **$4\frac{1}{4}$–$5\frac{1}{2}$in (11–14cm)**	Wingspan **7–9in (18–23cm)**	Weight **$\frac{7}{16}$–$\frac{5}{8}$oz (12–18g)**
Social **Flocks**	Lifespan **Up to 10 years**	Status **Secure**

DATE: ______________ TIME: ______________ LOCATION: ______________

Order **Passeriformes**	Family **Fringillidae**	Species ***Spinus tristis***

American Goldfinch

MALE (BREEDING)

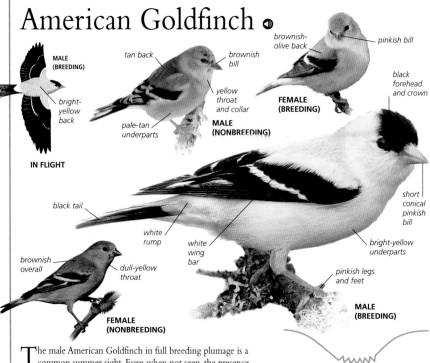

bright-yellow back

IN FLIGHT

tan back

brownish bill

yellow throat and collar

pale-tan underparts

MALE (NONBREEDING)

brownish-olive back

pinkish bill

FEMALE (BREEDING)

black forehead and crown

short conical pinkish bill

black tail

white rump

white wing bar

bright-yellow underparts

pinkish legs and feet

MALE (BREEDING)

brownish overall

dull-yellow throat

FEMALE (NONBREEDING)

The male American Goldfinch in full breeding plumage is a common summer sight. Even when not seen, the presence of goldfinches in an area is quickly given away by the sound of the birds calling in flight. If there are weed seeds around, goldfinches will find them, whether they are out in the fields or on the feeding table. When a male performs his courtship songs, often singing them while circling his female, he does justice to the nickname "American canary."

VOICE Loud, rising *pter-yee* by males; 3–5-note *tit-tse-tew-tew* by both sexes, usually in flight; song complex warbling.

NESTING Open cup nest of grass, usually shaded from above; 4–5 eggs; 1–2 broods; July–September, a very late-nesting species tied to the flowering of thistle plants.

FEEDING Feeds mainly on seeds from annual plants, birch, and alder; some insects; prefers sunflower and thistle seed at feeders.

FLIGHT: deeply undulating; wing beats alternating with closed-wing dips.

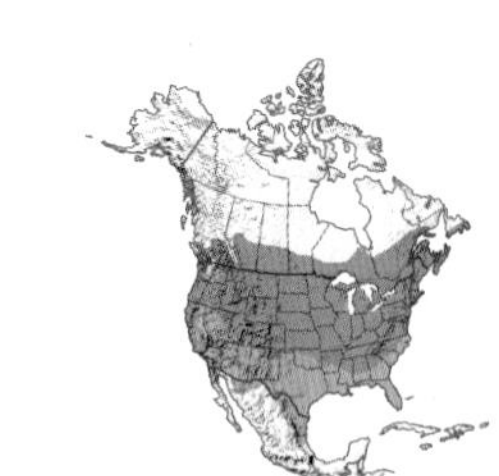

OCCURRENCE

In low shrubs, deciduous woodlands, farmlands, orchards, suburbs, and gardens across much of North America, from southern Canada to California and Georgia; in winter south to Northern Mexico and Florida; winter habitats similar to those used at other times.

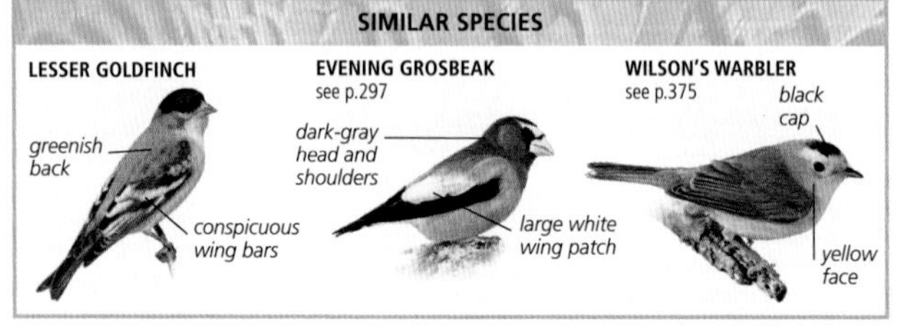
SIMILAR SPECIES
LESSER GOLDFINCH
greenish back
conspicuous wing bars
EVENING GROSBEAK
see p.297
dark-gray head and shoulders
large white wing patch
WILSON'S WARBLER
see p.375
black cap
yellow face

Length **4¼–5in (11–13cm)**	Wingspan **7–9in (18–23cm)**	Weight **3/8–11/16oz (11–20g)**
Social **Small flocks**	Lifespan **Up to 11 years**	Status **Secure**

DATE: ____________ TIME: ____________ LOCATION: ____________

Family **Calcariidae**

LONGSPURS AND SNOW BUNTINGS

Four species of longspurs, the Snow Bunting, and McKay's Bunting all generally forage on bare or open ground, from tundra and mountain tops to open prairies, often in flocks. Their short blackish legs help give longspurs a long, low shape on the ground. Their calls provide useful clues for identification as they fly. Snow Buntings have distinctive white bands on their wings.

CHANGING COLORS
Snow Buntings are well camouflaged against exposed rocks and snow throughout the year. Brown edges on the feathers in winter wear off, so they become pristine black and white in spring.

Family **Passerellidae**

NEW WORLD SPARROWS

New world sparrows are more akin to Old World buntings than other sparrows, but, as with robins, familiar names were given to quite different birds by early European settlers and have stayed with us. New World sparrows are rounded but long-tailed, and have small conical or triangular bills that are adapted to feed on grass seeds. While some birds are distinctive, especially the more brightly patterned males, many are small, "streaky-brown" species that present considerable identification difficulties. Range, habitat, behavior, and voice are all often used together as a suite of characteristics for identification. Not only are the species much alike, but studies conducted in recent years have revealed different relationships between them, with some subspecies being split as separate species and others being grouped together. Nevertheless, their neat, subtle patterns make even the duller species worth studying: the exquisite streaking of a Lincoln's Sparrow, for example, repays close observation.

TYPICAL SPECIES
A White-crowned Sparrow shows the typical stout beak of New World sparrows.

Order **Passeriformes**	Family **Calcariidae**	Species ***Calcarius lapponicus***

Lapland Longspur

thin white edge to tail
MALE (BREEDING)
black face
IN FLIGHT
streaked crown
black streak on throat
FEMALE (BREEDING)
white eye-line
thick yellowish bill
bright-rufous nape
rich buffy hood
thick streaking on flanks
ADULT (NONBREEDING)
rusty wing panel
white underparts
black flanks
MALE (BREEDING)

FLIGHT: deeply undulating, with birds often calling in troughs as they flap.

One of the most numerous breeding birds of the Arctic tundra, the Lapland Longspur is found in huge flocks over open habitats of Canada's southern prairies and in the US in the winter. They can be seen on gravel roads and in barren countryside immediately following heavy snowfalls. The longspurs and the Snow Bunting were formerly part of the Emberizidae family but are now placed in a distinct family of their own. This species is known as the Lapland Bunting in Great Britain and Ireland.

VOICE Flight call a dry rattle, *tyew*, unlike other longspurs; song a series of thin tinklings and whistles, often in flight.

NESTING Cup of grass and sedges placed in depression on ground next to a clump of vegetation; 4–6 eggs; 1 brood; May–July.

FEEDING Eats insects during breeding season; seeds in winter.

CONSPICUOUS SPECIES
This longspur is one of the most conspicuous breeding birds in the Arctic tundra.

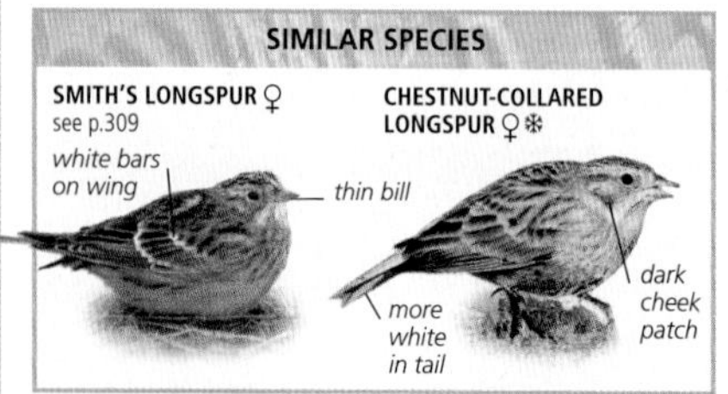

SIMILAR SPECIES
SMITH'S LONGSPUR ♀
see p.309
white bars on wing
thin bill
CHESTNUT-COLLARED LONGSPUR ♀ ❄
more white in tail
dark cheek patch

OCCURRENCE
Breeds in tundra right across Arctic North America and Eurasia. Winters in open grasslands and barren fields, and on beaches across the northern and central US and parts of southern Canada.

Length **6½in (16cm)**	Wingspan **10½–11½in (27–29cm)**	Weight **⅞–1¹⁄₁₆oz (25–30g)**
Social **Large flocks**	Lifespan **Up to 5 years**	Status **Secure**

DATE: ____________ TIME: ____________ LOCATION: ____________

Order **Passeriformes**	Family **Calcariidae**	Species ***Calcarius pictus***

Smith's Longspur

MALE (BREEDING)
white outer tail feathers
white cheek patch
relatively long wings
IN FLIGHT
rich buff color overall
wings extend past tail
fine breast streaks
FEMALE (FALL)
white shoulder
black-and-white "helmet"
thin bill
orange collar
rich pumpkin-colored underparts
MALE (BREEDING)
white undertail feathers

With its pumpkin-colored breast and black-and-white "helmet," Smith's Longspur in its breeding colors contrasts strongly with its drab winter plumage. On both its remote breeding grounds in the Arctic, and its restricted range of shortgrass prairie in winter, this bird hides on the ground at all times, making it very hard to spot. Smith's Longspur migrates through the Great Plains to reach its wintering grounds, but on the return journey it swings east, giving it an elliptical migration path. This species breeds communally: males mate with several females who, in turn, mate with other males.

VOICE Flight call a mechanical, dry, sharp rattle; also a nasal *nief* when squabbling; song a series of thin, sweet whistles.

NESTING Concealed cup of sedges, lined with feathers, placed in hummock on ground; 3–5 eggs; 1 brood; June–July.

FEEDING Eats mainly seeds and insects; migrants may rely heavily upon introduced foxtail grass.

FLIGHT: deeply undulating, with birds often calling in troughs as they flap.

LINEBACK LONGSPUR
On his breeding or spring staging grounds, the male sports a striking black-and-white "helmet."

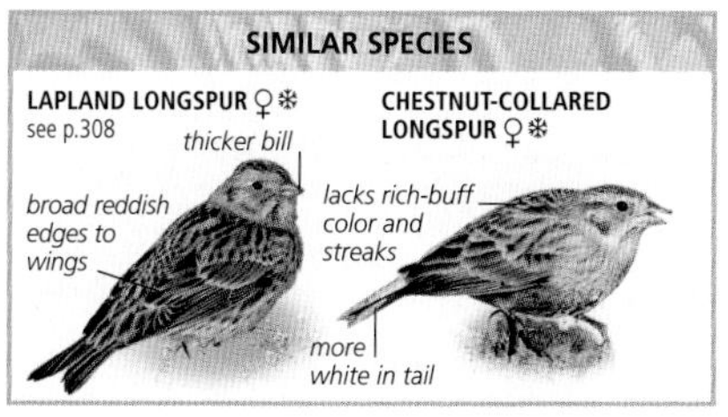
SIMILAR SPECIES
LAPLAND LONGSPUR ♀ ❄
see p.308
thicker bill
broad reddish edges to wings
CHESTNUT-COLLARED LONGSPUR ♀ ❄
lacks rich-buff color and streaks
more white in tail

OCCURRENCE
Breeds along the tundra-taiga timberline from northern Alaska southeast to northern Ontario; also mountainous southeastern Alaska and southwestern Yukon. Migrant birds are found in shortgrass prairie. Winters in various open areas with shortgrass in Kansas, Texas, and Arkansas.

Length **6–6½in (15–16cm)**	Wingspan **10–11½in (25–29cm)**	Weight **⅞–1¹⁄₁₆oz (25–30g)**
Social **Large flocks**	Lifespan **Up to 5 years**	Status **Secure**

DATE: ______________ TIME: ______________ LOCATION: ______________________________

Order **Passeriformes**	Family **Calcariidae**	Species ***Plectrophenax nivalis***

Snow Bunting

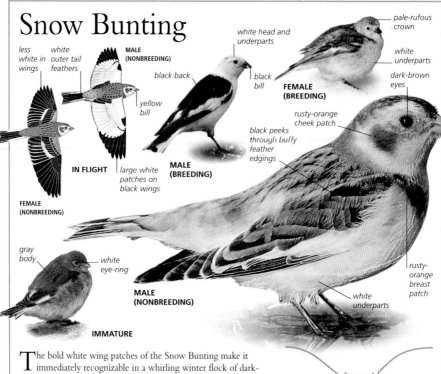

less white in wings
white outer tail feathers
MALE (NONBREEDING)
yellow bill
IN FLIGHT
large white patches on black wings
FEMALE (NONBREEDING)
black back
white head and underparts
black bill
MALE (BREEDING)
pale-rufous crown
white underparts
FEMALE (BREEDING)
dark-brown eyes
rusty-orange cheek patch
black peeks through buffy feather edgings
gray body
white eye-ring
MALE (NONBREEDING)
rusty-orange breast patch
white underparts
IMMATURE

The bold white wing patches of the Snow Bunting make it immediately recognizable in a whirling winter flock of dark-winged longspurs and larks. In winter, heavy snowfall forces flocks onto roadsides, where they can be seen more easily. To secure and defend the best territories, some of the males of this remarkably hardy species arrive as early as April in their barren high-Arctic breeding grounds. The Snow Bunting is very similar in appearance to the rare and localized McKay's Bunting. Although McKay's Bunting generally has less black on the back, in the wings, and on the tail, the two species cannot always be conclusively identified. This is especially true since Snow and McKay's Buntings sometimes interbreed, producing hybrids.

VOICE Flight call a musical, liquid rattle, also *tyew* notes and short buzz; song a pleasant series of squeaky and whistled notes.

NESTING Bulky cup of grass and moss, lined with feathers, and placed in sheltered rock crevice; 3–6 eggs; 1 brood; June–August.

FEEDING Eats seeds (sedge in the Arctic), flies and other insects, and buds on migration.

FLIGHT: deeply undulating; flocks "roll" along as birds at back overtake those in front.

ROCKY GROUND
About the only perches in the Snow Bunting's barren breeding grounds are large boulders.

SIMILAR SPECIES

McKAY'S BUNTING
mostly white tail, back, and wings

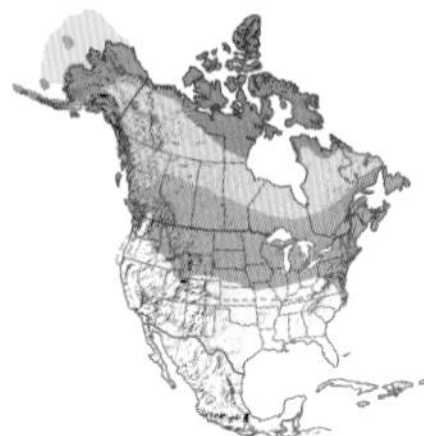

OCCURRENCE
Breeds in rocky areas, usually near sparsely vegetated tundra, right across the Arctic. North American birds winter in open country and on shores across the whole of southern Canada and the northern US, and in southern and western coastal areas of Alaska.

Length **6½–7in (16–18cm)**	Wingspan **12½–14in (32–35cm)**	Weight **1¼–2oz (35–55g)**
Social **Large flocks**	Lifespan **At least 4 years**	Status **Declining**

DATE: ____________ TIME: ____________ LOCATION: ____________

Order **Passeriformes**	Family **Passerellidae**	Species ***Ammodramus savannarum***

Grasshopper Sparrow

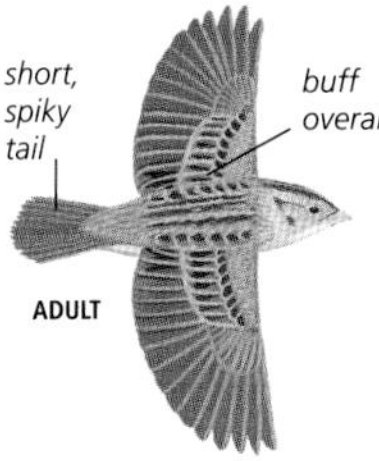

short, spiky tail

buff overall

ADULT

IN FLIGHT

large head

fairly long bill

pale eyebrow

reddish-and-dark spots on upperparts

white eye-ring

buff breast, sides, and flanks

yellow at bend of wing

ADULT
A. s. perpallidus
(WESTERN)

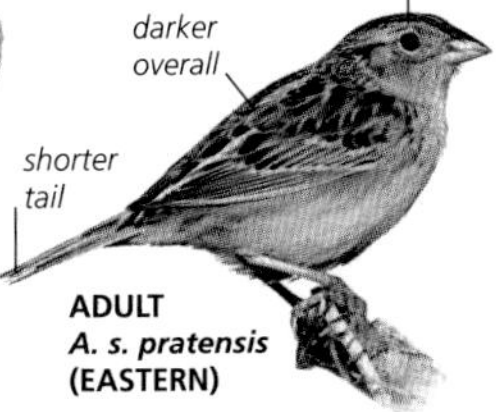

darker crown

darker overall

shorter tail

ADULT
A. s. pratensis
(EASTERN)

FLIGHT: low and weak, with spiky tail pointed down; much flapping.

A Grasshopper Sparrow singing briefly atop a weed is usually the first glimpse people get of this secretive bird—it is more often heard than seen. The bird is small, with a large head, spiky tail, and plain breast. It is one of the few North American sparrows that has two completely different songs. While it does eat grasshoppers, its common name derives from its song, which resembles the sounds grasshoppers make. It varies geographically, with about 12 subspecies.

VOICE Sharp *tik* call; flight call a long, high *tseeee*; song an insect-like trill *tik'-tok-TREEEE*, or series of quick buzzes.

NESTING Cup of grass placed in clump of grass; 3–6 eggs; 1–2 broods; April–August.

FEEDING Forages on ground for seeds and insects.

YELLOW PATCH
The pale crown stripe and the small yellow patch at the bend of its wings are visible here.

SIMILAR SPECIES

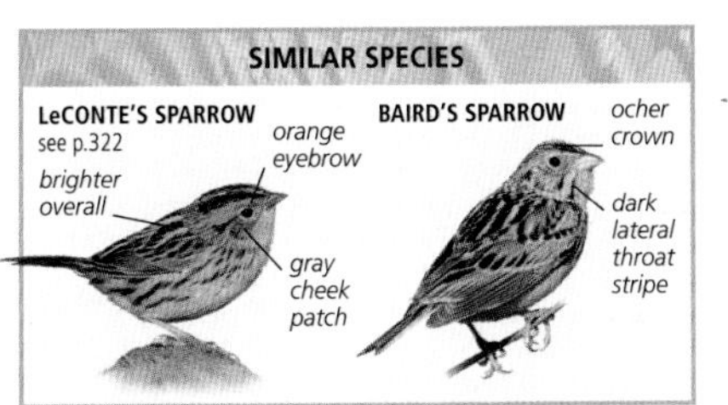
LeCONTE'S SPARROW
see p.322
orange eyebrow
brighter overall
gray cheek patch
BAIRD'S SPARROW
ocher crown
dark lateral throat stripe

OCCURRENCE
Breeds in short grassland, pastures, and even mown areas across much of the US and southern Canada. Locally distributed in the Southwest, also patchily through the central US. Winters in similar habitats from the southern US to Colombia; also found in the West Indies.

Length **5in (13cm)**	Wingspan **8in (20cm)**	Weight **½–¹¹⁄₁₆oz (15–20g)**
Social **Solitary/Flocks**	Lifespan **Up to 7 years**	Status **Declining**

DATE: ____________ TIME: ____________ LOCATION: ____________

Order **Passeriformes**	Family **Passerellidae**	Species ***Spizella passerina***

Chipping Sparrow

bright-rufous crown
blackish bill
white eyebrow
black eye-line
rusty cast to crown
pinkish bill
pale underparts
ADULT
IN FLIGHT
ADULT (WINTER)
ADULT (BREEDING)
heavily streaked, especially on breast
IMMATURE
gray underparts
cleft tail

The Chipping Sparrow is a common, trusting bird, which breeds in backyards across most of North America. While they are easily identifiable in the summer, "Chippers" molt into a drab, nonbreeding plumage during fall, at which point they are easily confused with the Clay-colored and Brewer's Sparrows they flock with. Most reports of this species across the north in winter are actually of the larger American Tree Sparrow. In the winter, Chipping Sparrows can be easily recognized as they lack their bright rusty crown and are restricted to the south.

VOICE Call a sharp *tsip*; flight call a sharp, thin *tsiiit*; song an insect-like trill of *chip* notes, variable in duration and quality.

NESTING Nest cup usually placed well off the ground in tree or shrub; 3–5 eggs; 1–2 broods; April–August.

FEEDING Eats seeds of grasses and annuals, plus some fruit; when breeding, also eats insects and other invertebrates.

FLIGHT: slightly undulating, often to open perch when flushed.

BACKYARD BIRD
Chipping Sparrows are a very common sight in gardens and backyards all across the continent.

SIMILAR SPECIES
CLAY-COLORED SPARROW
see p.313
heavy streaks
BREWER'S SPARROW
streaked crown
partial "necklace"
pale underparts

OCCURRENCE
Found in a wide variety of habitats: open forest, woodlands, grassy, park-like areas, shorelines, and backyards. Breeds in North America south of the Arctic timberline and in Mexico, and in Central America, as far south as Nicaragua. Winters from southern states to Nicaragua.

Length **5½in (14cm)**	Wingspan **8½in (21cm)**	Weight **⅜–½oz (10–15g)**
Social **Large flocks**	Lifespan **Up to 9 years**	Status **Secure**

Order **Passeriformes**	Family **Passerellidae**	Species ***Spizella pallida***

Clay-colored Sparrow

bold dark cheek stripes
white crown stripe
unstreaked gray nape
bold, dark-brown streaks on upperparts
white wing bars
long tail
thick white eyebrow
brown rump
ADULT
IN FLIGHT
very pale buffy wash across breast
whitish-gray underparts
ADULT
notched tail

FLIGHT: slightly undulating, often flies to open perch when flushed.

The little Clay-colored Sparrow is best known for its mechanical, buzzy song. This bird spends much of its foraging time away from the breeding habitat; consequently, males' territories are quite small, allowing for dense breeding populations. Clay-colored Sparrows have shifted their breeding range eastward and northward over the last century, most likely because of changes in land practices. During the nonbreeding season, they form large flocks in open country, associating with other *Spizella* sparrows, especially Chipping and Brewer's.

VOICE Call a sharp *tsip*; flight call a short, rising *sip*; song a series of 2–7 mechanical buzzes on one pitch.

NESTING Cup of grass placed just off the ground in shrub or small tree; 3–5 eggs; 1–2 broods; May–August.

FEEDING Forages on or low to the ground for seeds and insects.

CHRISTMAS PRESENT
The Clay-colored Sparrow is fond of short conifers for breeding, so Christmas tree farms form a perfect habitat.

SIMILAR SPECIES

CHIPPING SPARROW ❄
see p.312
grayish rump
dark stripe through eye
grayer breast
BREWER'S SPARROW
streaked nape
lacks bold crown stripe

OCCURRENCE
Breeds in open habitats: prairies, shrubland, forest edges, and Christmas tree farms along the US/Canadian border and northward to the southern Northwest Territories. Winters in a large variety of brushy, weedy areas from south Texas to Mexico. Migration takes it to the Great Plains.

Length **5½in (14cm)**	Wingspan **7½in (19cm)**	Weight **⅜–½oz (10–15g)**
Social **Large flocks**	Lifespan **Up to 5 years**	Status **Secure**

DATE: ____________ TIME: ____________ LOCATION: ____________

Order **Passeriformes**	Family **Passerellidae**	Species ***Spizella pusilla***

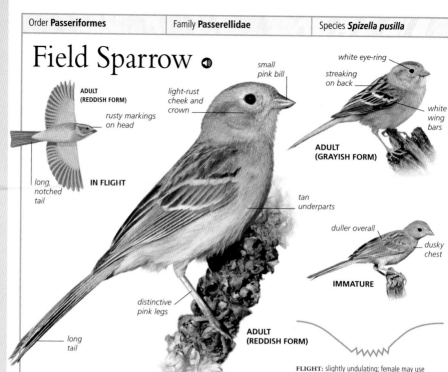

Field Sparrow

ADULT (REDDISH FORM)

rusty markings on head

long, notched tail

IN FLIGHT

light-rust cheek and crown

small pink bill

white eye-ring

streaking on back

white wing bars

ADULT (GRAYISH FORM)

tan underparts

duller overall

dusky chest

IMMATURE

distinctive pink legs

long tail

ADULT (REDDISH FORM)

FLIGHT: slightly undulating; female may use moth-like flight to approach the nest.

The distinctive accelerating trilling song of the Field Sparrow is a characteristic sound of shrubby fields and scrubby areas in southeastern Canada and the eastern US. The bird's bright-pink bill, plain "baby face," and white eye-ring make this sparrow one of the easiest to identify. The Field Sparrow has a brighter plumage in the East, and drabber plumage in the interior part of its range. Although quite dissimilar at first glance, the Black-chinned Sparrow may in fact be the Field Sparrow's closest relative, sharing its pink bill, relatively unpatterned plumage, and its song.

VOICE Call a sharp *tsik*; flight call a strongly descending *tsiiiu*; song a series of sweet, downslurred whistles accelerating to a rapid trill.

NESTING Grass cup placed on or just above ground in grass or bush; 3–5 eggs; 1–3 broods; March–August.

FEEDING Eats seeds; also insects, insect larvae, and spiders in the summer.

FAMILIAR SONG
Male Field Sparrows sing their familiar and distinctive song throughout the summer.

SIMILAR SPECIES

WHITE-CROWNED SPARROW see p.318

larger body

pale crown stripe

AMERICAN TREE SPARROW see p.316

lacks bold white eye-ring

central black breast spot

OCCURRENCE
Breeds in overgrown fields, woodland edges, roadsides, and other shrubby, overgrown areas; occasionally in orchards and parks in southeastern Canada, west to the Dakotas, east to New England. Winters in similar habitats in the southern US. Casual in Atlantic Canada and on the Pacific Coast.

Length **5½in (14cm)**	Wingspan **8in (20cm)**	Weight **⅜–½oz (11–15g)**
Social **Solitary/Flocks**	Lifespan **Up to 6 years**	Status **Declining**

DATE: ____________ TIME: ____________ LOCATION: ____________

Order **Passeriformes**	Family **Passerellidae**	Species ***Passerella iliaca***

Fox Sparrow

ADULT (RED)

dark-rufous overall

IN FLIGHT

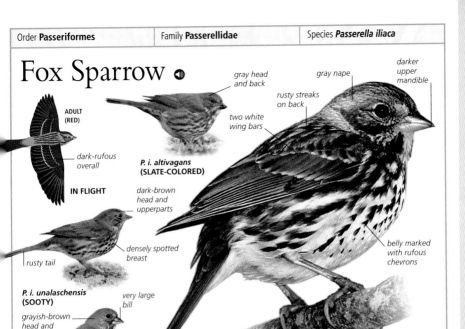

gray head and back

P. i. altivagans (SLATE-COLORED)

dark-brown head and upperparts

densely spotted breast

rusty tail

P. i. unalaschensis (SOOTY)

very large bill

grayish-brown head and upperparts

fine streaks on throat

rusty wings and tail

P. i. stephensi (THICK-BILLED)

gray nape

darker upper mandible

rusty streaks on back

two white wing bars

belly marked with rufous chevrons

long rusty tail

ADULT (RED)

Larger, more robust, and more colorful than its close relatives, the Fox Sparrow is a beautiful species. When it appears in backyards, its presence can be detected by its foraging habits; it crouches low in leaf litter, and hops to disturb leaves, under which it finds seeds or insects. It varies considerably over its huge range, from thick-billed birds in the Sierras to dark ones in the Northwest, and distinctive red Fox Sparrows in taiga forest from Newfoundland to Alaska.

VOICE Call is sharp, dry *tshak* or *tshuk*; flight call a high-pitched *tzeep!*; song is complex and musical with trills and whistles.

NESTING Dense cup of grasses or moss lined with fine material; usually placed low in shrub; 2–5 eggs; 1 brood; April–July.

FEEDING Forages for insects, seeds, and fruit.

FLIGHT: alternates wing beats and glides; straight and fluttery, from cover to cover.

FOXY RED

The Fox Sparrow gets its name from the rusty coloration of the eastern "red" birds.

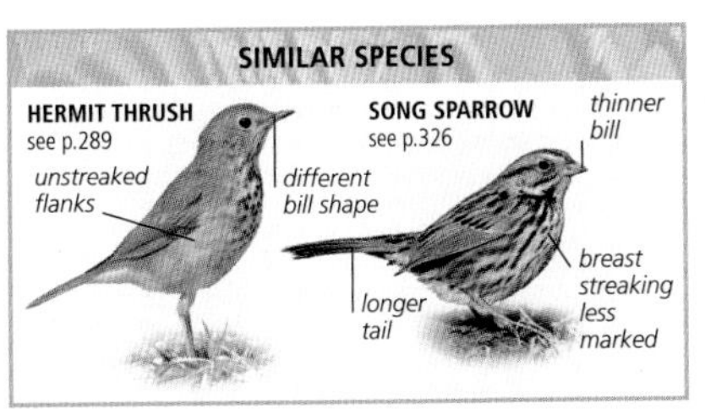
SIMILAR SPECIES
HERMIT THRUSH
see p.289
unstreaked flanks
different bill shape
SONG SPARROW
see p.326
thinner bill
longer tail
breast streaking less marked

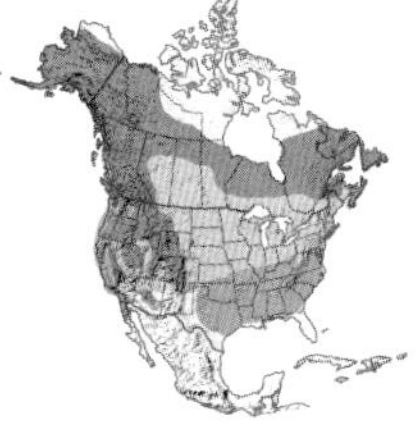

OCCURRENCE

Encompasses the entire boreal forest zone, from Alaska in the West to Quebec, Labrador, and Newfoundland in the East. In the West, it occurs in coastal and near-coast thickets within coniferous or mixed woodlands. Winters in the Pacific West, south to Baja California; also from Texas to Massachusetts.

Length **6–7½in (15–19cm)**	Wingspan **10½–11½in (27–29cm)**	Weight **⅞–1$\frac{9}{16}$oz (25–45g)**
Social **Solitary/Small flocks**	Lifespan **Up to 9 years**	Status **Secure**

DATE: ____________ TIME: ____________ LOCATION: ____________

Order **Passeriformes**	Family **Passerellidae**	Species ***Spizelloides arborea***

American Tree Sparrow

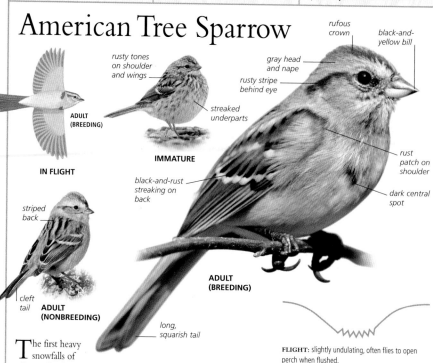

rufous crown
black-and-yellow bill
gray head and nape
rusty stripe behind eye
rust patch on shoulder
dark central spot
black-and-rust streaking on back
long, squarish tail
ADULT (BREEDING)

rusty tones on shoulder and wings
streaked underparts
IMMATURE

ADULT (BREEDING)
IN FLIGHT

striped back
cleft tail
ADULT (NONBREEDING)

The first heavy snowfalls of winter often bring large flocks of American Tree Sparrows to bird feeders. This bird is commonly mistaken for the smaller Chipping Sparrow, but the two species look quite dissimilar in the winter. The American Tree Sparrow is larger and has a central breast spot and a bicolored bill. A highly social, vocal, and misnamed species, noisy winter flocks numbering in the hundreds can be found feeding in weedy fields and along the roadsides of the northern US and southern Canada.

VOICE Call a bell-like *teedle-ee*; flight call a thin, slightly descending *tsiiiu*; song *seee seee di-di-di di-di-di dyew dyew*.

NESTING Nest cup on ground concealed within thicket; 4–6 eggs; 1 brood; June–July.

FEEDING Feeds on seeds, berries, and a variety of insects.

FLIGHT: slightly undulating, often flies to open perch when flushed.

WINTER HABITATS
In winter, this species frequents barren habitats, like old fields and roadsides, as well as feeders.

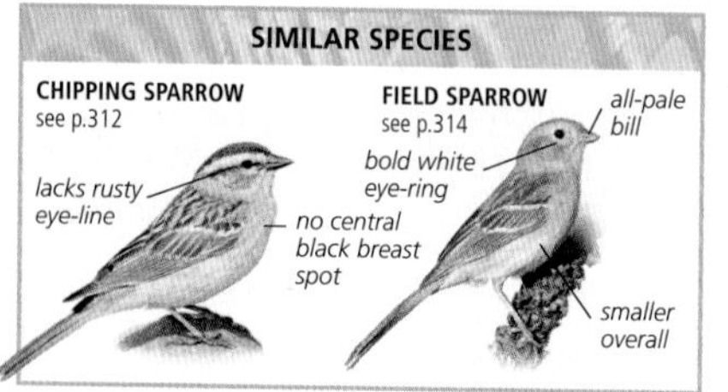
SIMILAR SPECIES
CHIPPING SPARROW
see p.312
lacks rusty eye-line
no central black breast spot
FIELD SPARROW
see p.314
all-pale bill
bold white eye-ring
smaller overall

OCCURRENCE
Breeds in scrubby thickets of birch and willows in the area between taiga and tundra across Alaska and north Canada. Nonbreeders choose open, grassy, brushy habitats. Winters across south Canada and the northern US. Casual to the Pacific Coast and the southern US.

Length **6¼in (16cm)**	Wingspan **9½in (24cm)**	Weight **7/16–7/8oz (13–25g)**
Social **Flocks**	Lifespan **Up to 11 years**	Status **Secure**

DATE: ____________ TIME: ____________ LOCATION: ____________

Order **Passeriformes**	Family **Passerellidae**	Species ***Junco hyemalis***

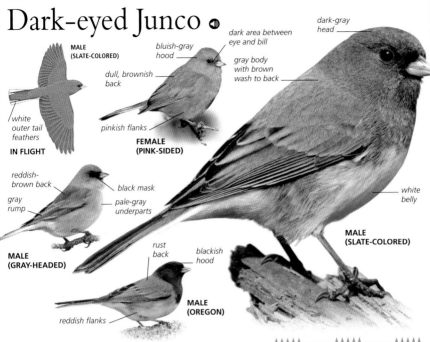

Dark-eyed Junco

MALE (SLATE-COLORED)
white outer tail feathers
IN FLIGHT

bluish-gray hood
dark area between eye and bill
dull, brownish back
pinkish flanks
FEMALE (PINK-SIDED)

dark-gray head
gray body with brown wash to back
white belly
MALE (SLATE-COLORED)

reddish-brown back
black mask
gray rump
pale-gray underparts
MALE (GRAY-HEADED)

rust back
blackish hood
reddish flanks
MALE (OREGON)

The Dark-eyed Junco's appearance at bird feeders during snowstorms has earned it the colloquial name of "snowbird." They generally prefer to feed on the ground, and can be found hopping about on the forest floor in search of seeds and insects, or on the ground underneath a bird feeder in backyards across North America. The name "Dark-eyed Junco" is actually used to describe a group of birds that vary geographically in an incredibly diverse way. Sixteen subspecies have been described. "Slate-colored" populations occur in central Alaska, Canada, and the northeastern US; the "White-winged" nests in the Black Hills of South Dakota; "Pink-sided" birds breed in Idaho, Montana, and Wyoming, and "Oregon" birds breed in the Pacific West, from coastal Alaska to British Columbia and the mountainous western US in the Sierras south to Mexico. "Red-backed" populations reside in the mountains of Arizona and New Mexico, while "Gray-headed" birds range between the "Red-backed" and "Pink-sided" populations. Dark-eyed Juncos can form large flocks in the winter; where ranges overlap, several subspecies may be found foraging together with sparrows and other birds.

VOICE Loud, smacking *tick* and soft *dyew* calls; flight call a rapid, twittering, and buzzy *zzeet*; song a simple, liquid, 1-pitch trill.

NESTING Cup placed on ground hidden under vegetation or next to rocks; 3–5 eggs; 1–2 broods; May–August.

FEEDING Eats insects and seeds; also berries.

FLIGHT: low and direct, staying within cover whenever possible.

PINK-SIDED MALE
Like most juncos, this male is brighter with greater contrasts, darker eye areas, and more vivid colors.

OCCURRENCE
Breeds in coniferous and mixed forests across Canada, south to the east Appalachians and Georgia. In the West, in mountains from Alaska and British Columbia to New Mexico and northern Baja California. Winters from southern Canada to northern Mexico.

Length **6–6 3/4in (15–17cm)**	Wingspan **8–10in (20–26cm)**	Weight **5/8–1 1/16oz (18–30g)**
Social **Flocks**	Lifespan **Up to 11 years**	Status **Secure**

DATE: ____________ TIME: ____________ LOCATION: ____________

Order **Passeriformes**	Family **Passerellidae**	Species ***Zonotrichia leucophrys***

White-crowned Sparrow

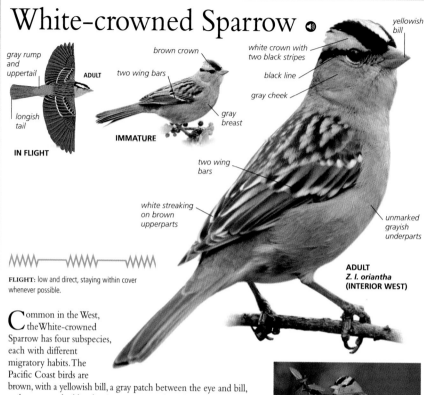

gray rump and uppertail

ADULT

longish tail

IN FLIGHT

brown crown

two wing bars

gray breast

IMMATURE

white crown with two black stripes

yellowish bill

black line

gray cheek

two wing bars

white streaking on brown upperparts

unmarked grayish underparts

ADULT
Z. l. oriantha
(INTERIOR WEST)

FLIGHT: low and direct, staying within cover whenever possible.

Common in the West, the White-crowned Sparrow has four subspecies, each with different migratory habits. The Pacific Coast birds are brown, with a yellowish bill, a gray patch between the eye and bill, and a gray-washed head stripe; western and northwestern birds are gray below, with a gray patch between the eye and bill, an orange bill, and a white head stripe. The eastern and Rocky Mountain birds have a pink bill, a black patch between the eye and bill, and a bright-white head stripe, while birds in southwest Canada are darker.

VOICE Call a sharp *tink*; flight call a thin *seep*; song a buzzy whistle followed by buzzes, trills, and whistles.

NESTING Bulky cup of grass placed on or near the ground in bushes; 4–6 eggs; 1–3 broods; March–August.

FEEDING Forages for seeds, insects, fruit, buds, and even grass.

BOLD MARKING
Perched on a shrub, this sparrow's black-and-white striped head is highly visible.

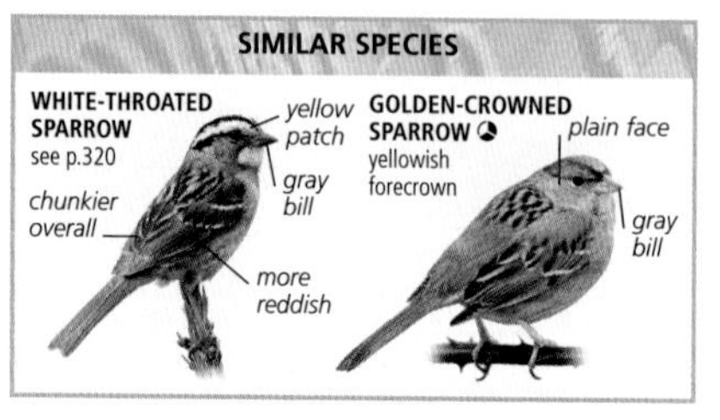
SIMILAR SPECIES
WHITE-THROATED SPARROW
see p.320
yellow patch
gray bill
chunkier overall
more reddish
GOLDEN-CROWNED SPARROW
yellowish forecrown
plain face
gray bill

OCCURRENCE
Widespread across the boreal forest and tundra limit, from Alaska eastward to Quebec and Labrador, and southward from British Columbia to coastal California and the interior mountainous West. Preferred nesting habitats include dense brush near open grasslands; in winter, open woods and gardens.

Length **6½–7in (16–18cm)**	Wingspan **9½–10in (24–26cm)**	Weight **$^{11}/_{16}$–1¼oz (20–35g)**
Social **Flocks**	Lifespan **Up to 13 years**	Status **Secure**

DATE: ____________ TIME: ____________ LOCATION: ____________

Order **Passeriformes**	Family **Passerellidae**	Species ***Zonotrichia querula***

Harris's Sparrow

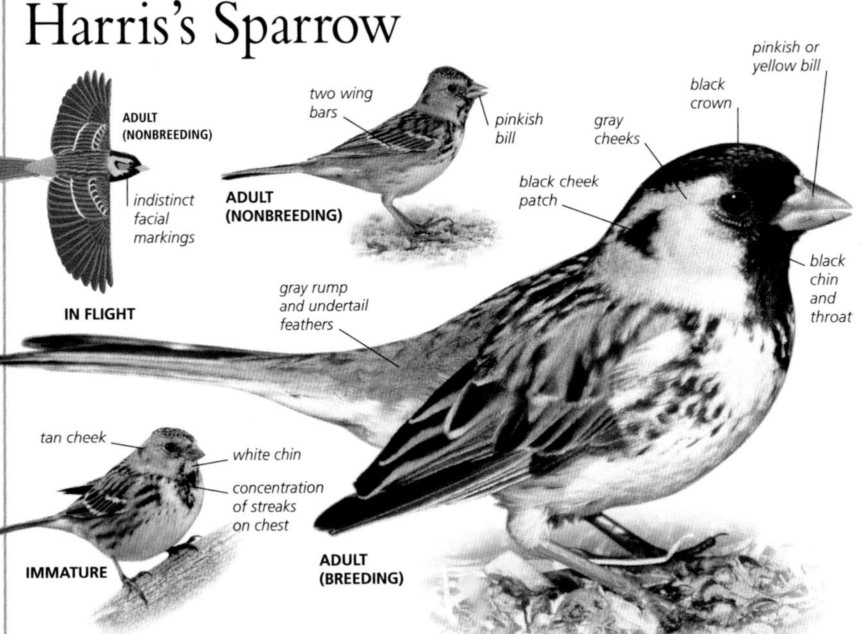
ADULT (NONBREEDING)
indistinct facial markings
IN FLIGHT
two wing bars
pinkish bill
ADULT (NONBREEDING)
pinkish or yellow bill
black crown
gray cheeks
black cheek patch
black chin and throat
gray rump and undertail feathers
tan cheek
white chin
concentration of streaks on chest
IMMATURE
ADULT (BREEDING)

An unmistakable black-faced, pink-billed bird, Harris's Sparrow is the only breeding bird endemic to Canada. It can be seen in the US during migration or in winter on the Great Plains. This species is occasionally found in large flocks of White-throated and White-crowned Sparrows. Harris's Sparrow is the largest sparrow in Canada, approaching the Northern Cardinal in size. Its scientific name, *querula*, comes from the plaintive quality of its whistled song. The first Harris's Sparrow nest was found in 1907 in the Northwest Territories.

VOICE Call a sharp *weeek*; song a melancholy series of 2–4 whistles on the same pitch.

NESTING Bulky cup placed on ground among vegetation or near ground in brush; 3–5 eggs; 1 brood; June–August.

FEEDING Eats seeds, insects, buds, and even young conifer needles in summer.

FLIGHT: low and direct, staying within cover whenever possible.

NORTHERN ACROBAT
This nonbreeding Harris's Sparrow grips two different weeds, one in each foot.

SIMILAR SPECIES

HOUSE SPARROW see p.294

WHITE-THROATED SPARROW see p.320

much smaller
lacks bright-pink bill
white throat
smaller and shorter-tailed

OCCURRENCE
Breeds in scrub-tundra along the Canadian taiga–tundra timberline from northern Northwest Territories to north Ontario. Winters in the US Great Plains from South Dakota and Iowa south to northern Texas. Nonbreeders found in thickets and hedges. Casual to rare in the East and West.

Length **6¾–7½in (17–19cm)**	Wingspan **10½–11in (27–28cm)**	Weight **1¹⁄₁₆–1⁷⁄₁₆oz (30–40g)**
Social **Flocks**	Lifespan **Up to 12 years**	Status **Secure**

DATE: ____________ TIME: ____________ LOCATION: ______________________

Order **Passeriformes**	Family **Passerellidae**	Species ***Zonotrichia albicollis***

White-throated Sparrow

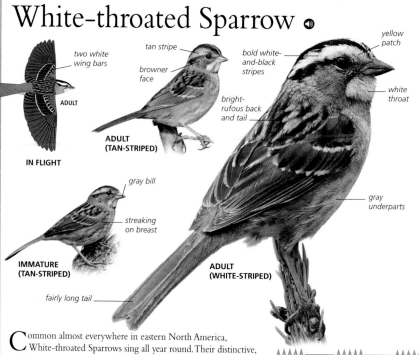

two white wing bars
ADULT
IN FLIGHT

tan stripe
browner face
ADULT (TAN-STRIPED)

yellow patch
bold white-and-black stripes
white throat
bright-rufous back and tail
gray underparts
ADULT (WHITE-STRIPED)

gray bill
streaking on breast
IMMATURE (TAN-STRIPED)

fairly long tail

Common almost everywhere in eastern North America, White-throated Sparrows sing all year round. Their distinctive, whistled, rhythmic song can be remembered with the popular mnemonic *Oh sweet Canada Canada Canada*, or the less accurate *Old Sam Peabody*. This species has two different color forms, one with a white stripe above its eye, and the other with a tan stripe. In the nonbreeding season, large flocks roam the leaf litter of woodlands in search of food. Often, the only indication of their presence is the occasional moving leaf or thin, lisping flight call.

VOICE Call loud, sharp *jink*; flight call lisping *tssssst!*; song clear whistle comprising 1–2 higher notes, then three triplets.

NESTING Cup placed on or near ground in dense shrubbery; 2–6 eggs; 1 brood; May–August.

FEEDING Mainly forages on the ground for seeds, fruit, insects, buds, and various grasses.

FLIGHT: low and direct, staying within cover whenever possible.

DIFFERENT COLOR FORMS
The presence of white or tan stripes on White-throated Sparrows is not related to their sex.

SIMILAR SPECIES

WHITE-CROWNED SPARROW slimmer overall; see p.318
no yellow patch
orange or pink bill

GOLDEN-CROWNED SPARROW
yellowish forecrown
plain grayish breast

OCCURRENCE
Breeds in forests from eastern Yukon to Newfoundland, south into the Great Lakes and northern Appalachians. Nonbreeders prefer wooded thickets and hedges. Winters across the eastern US and extreme south of the Southwest. Rare but regular along the Pacific Coast.

Length **6½–7½in (16–17.5cm)**	Wingspan **9–10in (23–26cm)**	Weight **11/16–1¼oz (20–35g)**
Social **Flocks**	Lifespan **Up to 10 years**	Status **Secure**

DATE: ____________ TIME: ____________ LOCATION: ____________

Order **Passeriformes**	Family **Passerellidae**	Species ***Pooecetes gramineus***

Vesper Sparrow

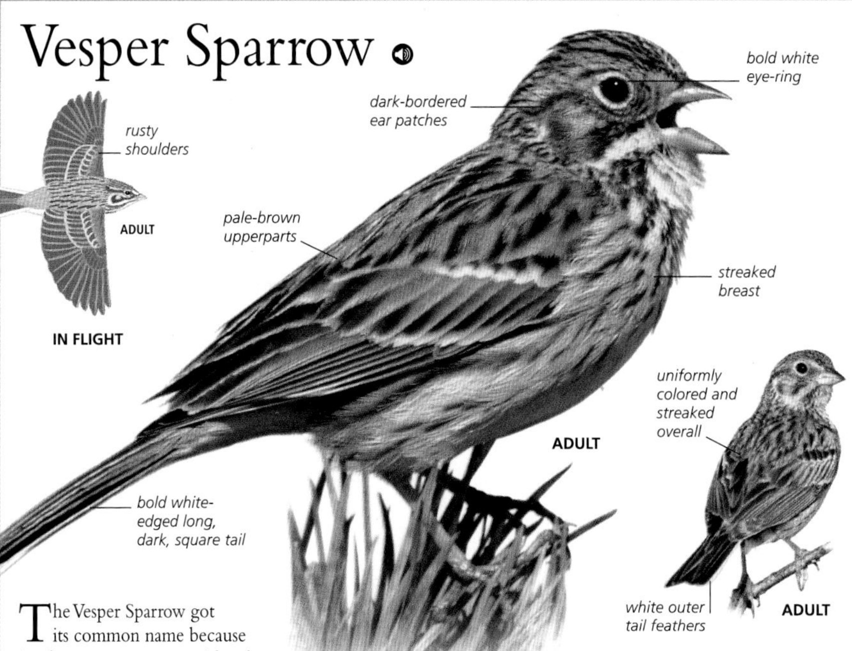

rusty shoulders
ADULT
IN FLIGHT
dark-bordered ear patches
bold white eye-ring
pale-brown upperparts
streaked breast
uniformly colored and streaked overall
ADULT
bold white-edged long, dark, square tail
white outer tail feathers
ADULT

The Vesper Sparrow got its common name because its pleasant song was considered to sound sweetest in the evening, when prayers known as "vespers" are sung in the Catholic and Eastern Orthodox churches. When Henry David Thoreau wrote of this species, he called it the "Bay-winged Bunting," because of its (sometimes concealed) rusty shoulder patches and its resemblance to the Old World Emberizidae buntings. The Vesper Sparrow needs areas with bare ground to breed, so it is one of the few species that can successfully nest in areas of intense agriculture; the bird's numbers seem to be declining in spite of this.

VOICE Full *tchup* call, flight call thin *tseent*; song consists of two whistles of same pitch, followed by two higher-pitched ones, then trills, ends lazily.

NESTING Cup placed on patch of bare ground, against grass, bush, or rock; 3–5 eggs; 1 brood; April–August.

FEEDING Eats insects and seeds.

FLIGHT: strong, often perches when flushed; often moves on ground.

GIFTED SONGSTER
The sweet song of the Vesper Sparrow is a characteristic sound of more northerly open areas.

OCCURRENCE
Breeds in sparse grassland, cultivated fields, recently burned areas, and mountain parks across south Canada and the northern US. Winters in sparsely vegetated, open habitats from the southern US to southwest Mexico. Found in patches of bare earth in all seasons.

SIMILAR SPECIES

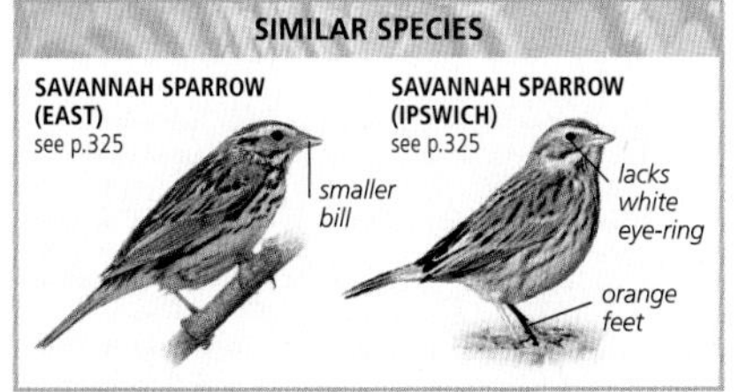

SAVANNAH SPARROW (EAST)
see p.325
smaller bill
SAVANNAH SPARROW (IPSWICH)
see p.325
lacks white eye-ring
orange feet

Length **6¼in (16cm)**	Wingspan **10in (25cm)**	Weight **11/16–1 1/16oz (20–30g)**
Social **Flocks**	Lifespan **Up to 7 years**	Status **Declining**

DATE: ______________ TIME: ______________ LOCATION: ______________________________

Order **Passeriformes**	Family **Passerellidae**	Species ***Ammospiza leconteii***

LeConte's Sparrow

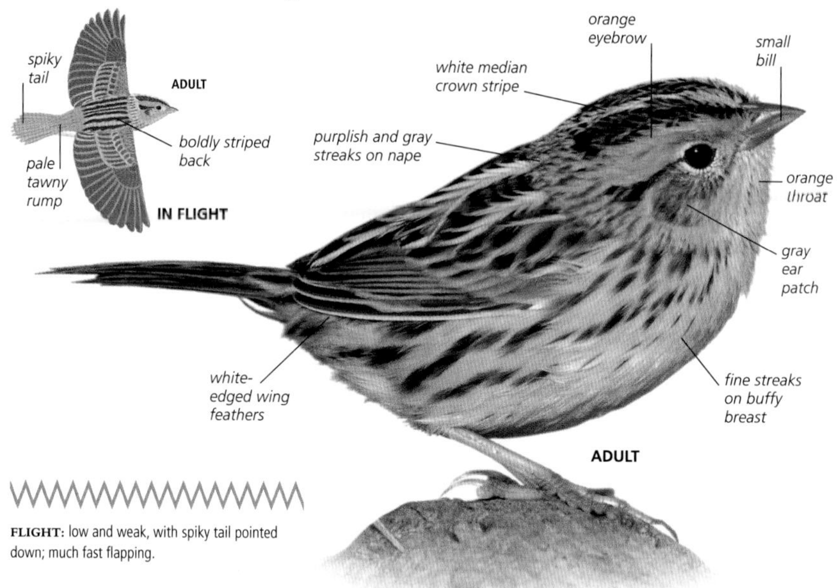
spiky tail
ADULT
boldly striped back
pale tawny rump
IN FLIGHT
orange eyebrow
small bill
white median crown stripe
purplish and gray streaks on nape
orange throat
gray ear patch
white-edged wing feathers
fine streaks on buffy breast
ADULT

FLIGHT: low and weak, with spiky tail pointed down; much fast flapping.

Although intricately patterned in glowing colors, LeConte's Sparrow is usually very difficult to see. Not only is it tiny—one of the smallest of all sparrows—but in the grasslands and marshes of interior North America where it lives, it prefers to dart for cover under grasses instead of flushing when disturbed. Meanwhile, the flight call and song of this elusive little bird are remarkably insect-like. Many people who hear it often pass off the unseen bird as a grasshopper. Its nest is even harder to find, making this bird a real challenge to study or observe.

VOICE Call long, downslurred *zheeep*; flight call similar to grasshopper; song insect-like, buzzy *tik'-uht-tizz-ZHEEEEEE-k*.

NESTING Concealed little cup placed on or near ground; 3–5 eggs; 1 brood; June–August.

FEEDING Forages on the ground and in grasses for insects and their larvae, spiders, and seeds.

HIDEAWAY BIRD
LeConte's Sparrow is usually found skulking in medium-to-tall grass in all seasons.

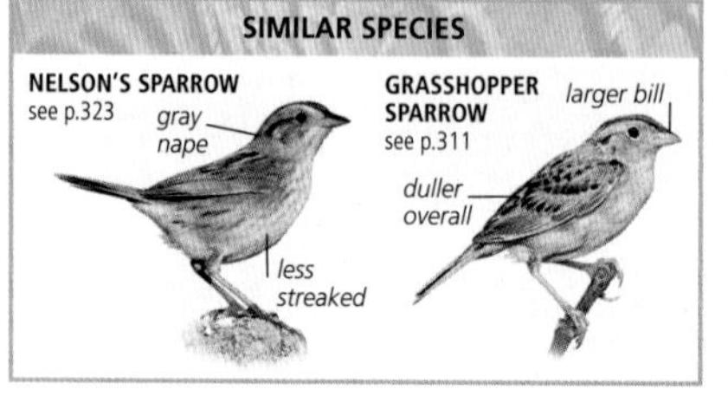
SIMILAR SPECIES
NELSON'S SPARROW
see p.323
gray nape
less streaked
GRASSHOPPER SPARROW
see p.311
larger bill
duller overall

OCCURRENCE
Breeds in marshes, wet meadows, and bogs from southwest Yukon to Lake Superior and west Quebec. Migrants or wintering birds found in tall grass and marshes from southwest Kansas to south Indiana, and central Texas to the coastal Carolinas.

Length **4½–5in (11.5–13cm)**	Wingspan **6½–7in (16–18cm)**	Weight **7/16–9/16oz (12–16g)**
Social **Solitary/Loose flocks**	Lifespan **At least 4 years**	Status **Secure**

 DATE: ____________ TIME: ____________ LOCATION: ____________

Order **Passeriformes**	Family **Passerellidae**	Species ***Ammospiza nelsoni***

Nelson's Sparrow

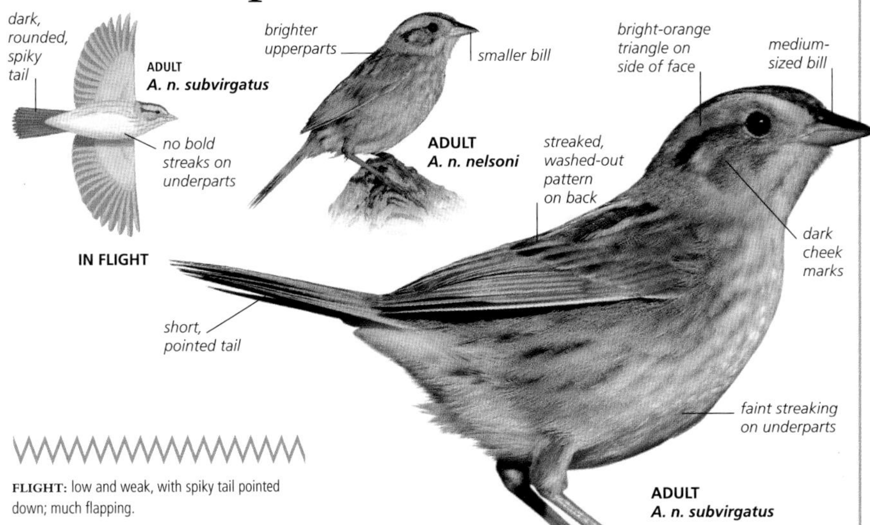

dark, rounded, spiky tail
ADULT
A. n. subvirgatus
no bold streaks on underparts
IN FLIGHT
brighter upperparts
smaller bill
ADULT
A. n. nelsoni
bright-orange triangle on side of face
medium-sized bill
streaked, washed-out pattern on back
dark cheek marks
short, pointed tail
faint streaking on underparts
ADULT
A. n. subvirgatus

FLIGHT: low and weak, with spiky tail pointed down; much flapping.

This rather shy species includes three subspecies that differ in plumage, as well as breeding habitat and location. *A. n. nelsoni* is the most brightly colored, and is found from the southern Northwest Territories south to northwest Wisconsin. *A. n. subvirgatus* breeds in coastal Maine and the Maritimes, and along the St. Lawrence River. It is visually duller than *A. n. nelsoni*, with a longer bill and flatter head. The intermediate-looking *A. n. alterus* breeds along the southern and western coasts of the Hudson Bay.

VOICE Sharp *tik* call; song a husky *t-SHHHHEE-uhrr.*

NESTING Cup of grass placed on or just above ground; 4–5 eggs; 1 brood; May–July.

FEEDING Forages on the ground mainly for insects, spiders, and seeds.

SIMILAR SPECIES

SALTMARSH SPARROW — longer bill; darker streaks

LeCONTE'S SPARROW see p.322 — white crown stripe; white stripes on back; darker streaking

IDENTIFYING MARKS
The orange-and-gray facial pattern and streaks on the breast are clearly visible.

OCCURRENCE
Breeds in a variety of marsh habitats across North America. Nonbreeders found in marshes and wet, weedy fields. *A. n. nelsoni* and *A. n. alterus* winter on coast from Texas northeast to New Jersey; *A. n. subvirgatus* from eastern Florida to New Jersey.

Length **4¾in (12cm)**	Wingspan **7in (17.5cm)**	Weight **7/16–11/16oz (13–20g)**
Social **Solitary/Flocks**	Lifespan **Unknown**	Status **Secure**

DATE: ____________ TIME: ____________ LOCATION: ____________________

Order **Passeriformes**	Family **Passerellidae**	Species ***Centronyx henslowii***

Henslow's Sparrow

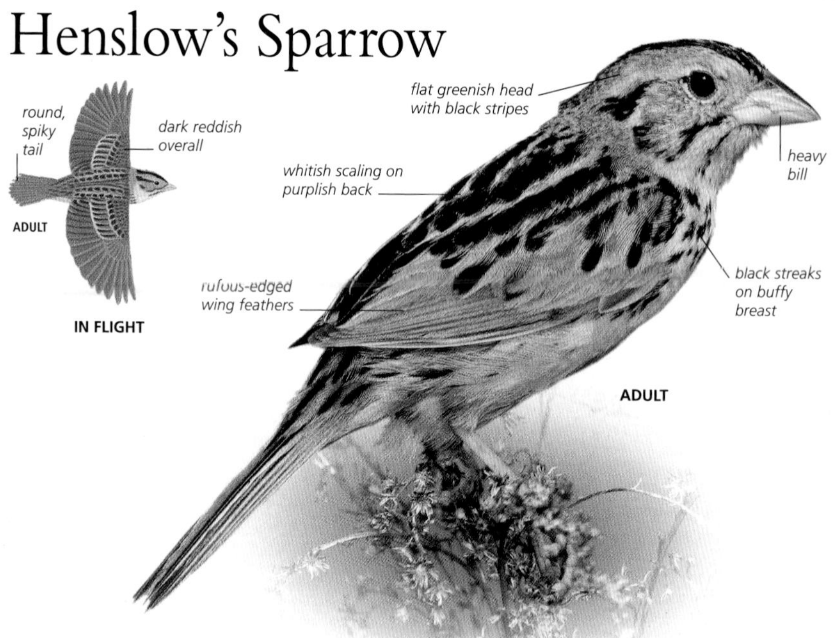
round, spiky tail
dark reddish overall
ADULT
IN FLIGHT
flat greenish head with black stripes
whitish scaling on purplish back
heavy bill
rufous-edged wing feathers
black streaks on buffy breast
ADULT

The combination of a large, flat greenish head, and purplish back are unique to Henslow's Sparrow. A bird of the tallgrass prairies and wet grasslands, the breeding range of this sparrow closely mirrors the extent of its habitat. While it has suffered greatly from the drainage, cultivation, and urbanization of much of its preferred breeding grounds, the Henslow's Sparrow has also recently started to use reclaimed strip mines in northwest Missouri and Iowa for breeding.

VOICE Call a sharp *tsik*; flight call a long, high, shrill *tseeeeee*; song a hiccupping sputter with second note higher *tsih-LIK!*

NESTING Cup of grass placed on or near ground; 2–5 eggs; 1–2 broods; May–August.

FEEDING Eats seeds; forages for insects and insect larvae, and spiders in the summer.

FLIGHT: low and weak, with spiky tail pointed down; much flapping.

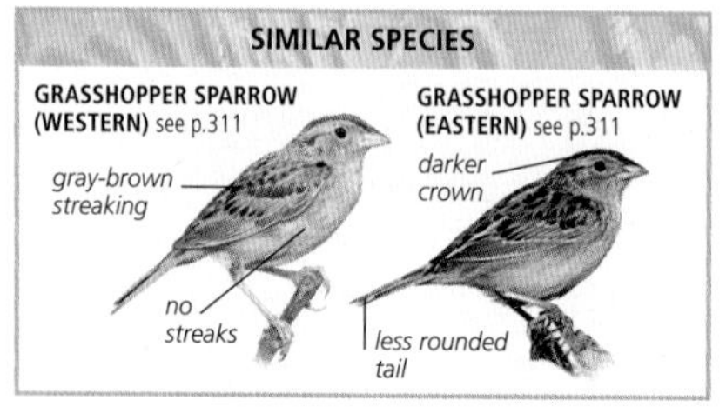
SIMILAR SPECIES
GRASSHOPPER SPARROW (WESTERN) see p.311
gray-brown streaking
no streaks
GRASSHOPPER SPARROW (EASTERN) see p.311
darker crown
less rounded tail

INTO THE AIR
The male puts considerable effort into his short, but surprisingly far-carrying song.

OCCURRENCE
Breeds predominantly in tallgrass prairie and wet grasslands from Oklahoma eastward to New York and up into southeastern Canada, and southward to North Carolina. Winters in weedy, brushy fields, grassy pine woods, and undergrowth along the Gulf Coastal Plain from Texas to North Carolina.

Length **4¾–5in (12–13cm)**	Wingspan **6½in (16cm)**	Weight **⅜–½oz (11–15g)**
Social **Solitary/Loose flocks**	Lifespan **At least 6 years**	Status **Endangered**

DATE: ____________ TIME: ____________ LOCATION: ____________

Order **Passeriformes**	Family **Passerellidae**	Species ***Passerculus sandwichensis***

Savannah Sparrow

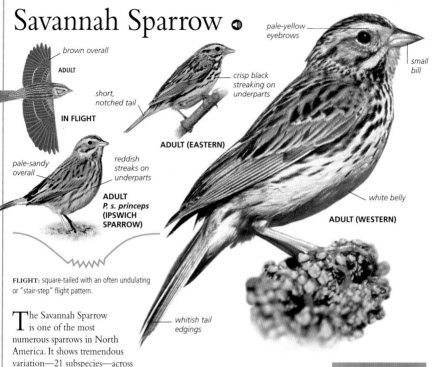

pale-yellow eyebrows

small bill

brown overall

ADULT

short, notched tail

IN FLIGHT

crisp black streaking on underparts

ADULT (EASTERN)

pale-sandy overall

reddish streaks on underparts

ADULT *P. s. princeps* (IPSWICH SPARROW)

white belly

ADULT (WESTERN)

FLIGHT: square-tailed with an often undulating or "stair-step" flight pattern.

whitish tail edgings

The Savannah Sparrow is one of the most numerous sparrows in North America. It shows tremendous variation—21 subspecies—across its vast range, but it is always brown, with dark streaks above and white with dark streaks below. The pale "Ipswich Sparrow" (*P. s. princeps*), originally described as a species, breeds on Sable Island, Nova Scotia, and winters along the East Coast. The "Large-billed Sparrow" (*P. s. rostratus* and *P. s. atratus*) breeds in Baja California and Sonora, Mexico. Their distinct song consists of three buzzy trills, and their flight calls are lower and more metallic than other populations.

VOICE Call a sharp but full *stip*; flight call a thin, weak, downslurred *tseew*; song a *sit sit sit sit suh-EEEEE say*, from perch or in display flight with legs dangling.

NESTING Concealed cup of grass placed in depression on ground, protected by overhanging grass or sedges; 2–6 eggs; 1–2 broods; June–August.

FEEDING Forages on the ground, mostly for insects; in summer also eats seeds in summer; in winter, berries and fruit when available; also small snails and crustaceans.

SWEET LOW DOWN
Savannah Sparrows like to vocalize from low vegetation and fenceposts near farms.

SIMILAR SPECIES

SONG SPARROW see p.326
larger overall
longer rounded tail

VESPER SPARROW see p.321
rusty shoulder
dark tail

OCCURRENCE
Breeds in meadows, grasslands, pastures, bushy tundra, and some cultivated land across northern North America. Also along the Pacific Coast and in Mexican interior. Nonbreeders use varied open habitats. Winters across the southern US to Honduras; also Cuba, the Bahamas, and the Cayman Islands.

Length **5½–6in (14–15cm)**	Wingspan **6¾in (17cm)**	Weight **½–1¹⁄₁₆oz (15–30g)**
Social **Solitary/Loose flocks**	Lifespan **Up to 8 years**	Status **Secure**

DATE: ______________ TIME: ______________ LOCATION: ______________________________

Order **Passeriformes**	Family **Passerellidae**	Species ***Melospiza melodia***

Song Sparrow

ADULT (WEST COAST)

streaked underparts

IN FLIGHT

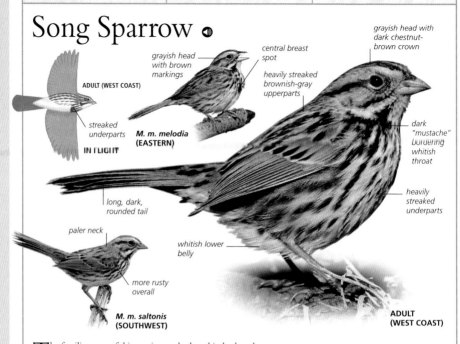

grayish head with brown markings

central breast spot

***M. m. melodia* (EASTERN)**

heavily streaked brownish-gray upperparts

grayish head with dark chestnut-brown crown

dark "mustache" bordering whitish throat

heavily streaked underparts

long, dark, rounded tail

paler neck

whitish lower belly

more rusty overall

***M. m. saltonis* (SOUTHWEST)**

ADULT (WEST COAST)

The familiar song of this species can be heard in backyards across the continent, including in winter, although it varies both individually and geographically. In the southeastern US, where it does not breed, migrant birds start singing in early spring before departing for northern areas. The Song Sparrow may be the North American champion of geographical variation—about 30 subspecies have been described. These vary from the large, dark birds of the Aleutian Islands (*M. m. maxima*) to the smaller, paler birds of southern Arizona (*M. m. saltonis*). Eastern birds, such as *M. m. melodia*, fall between the two in size.

VOICE A dry *tchip* call; flight call a clear *siiiti*; song a jumble of variable whistles and trills, *deeep deeep deep-deep chrrrr tiiiiiiiiiiii tyeeur* most common.

NESTING Bulky cup on or near ground, in brush or marsh vegetation; 3–5 eggs; 1–3 broods; March–August.

FEEDING In summer, feeds mainly on insects; in winter, eats mainly seeds, but also fruit.

FLIGHT: low and direct, staying within cover whenever possible.

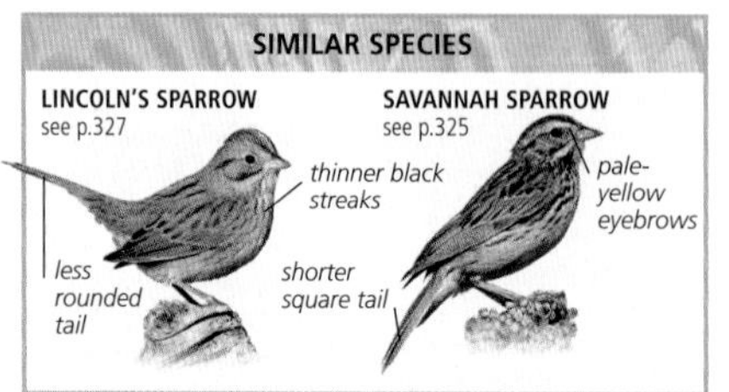
SIMILAR SPECIES
LINCOLN'S SPARROW
see p.327
thinner black streaks
less rounded tail
SAVANNAH SPARROW
see p.325
pale-yellow eyebrows
shorter square tail

BREAST SPOT
The Song Sparrow often sings from exposed perches, showing off its characteristic breast spot.

OCCURRENCE
Widespread in a range of habitats (although not in dense forests) across Canada and the US, from the Atlantic to the Pacific Coasts and north to Alaska. Some populations move south of their breeding range in winter.

Length **5–7½in (13–19cm)**	Wingspan **8½–12in (21–31cm)**	Weight **7/16–1¾oz (13–50g)**
Social **Solitary/Flocks**	Lifespan **Up to 9 years**	Status **Secure**

DATE: ____________ TIME: ____________ LOCATION: ____________

Order **Passeriformes**	Family **Passerellidae**	Species ***Melospiza lincolnii***

Lincoln's Sparrow

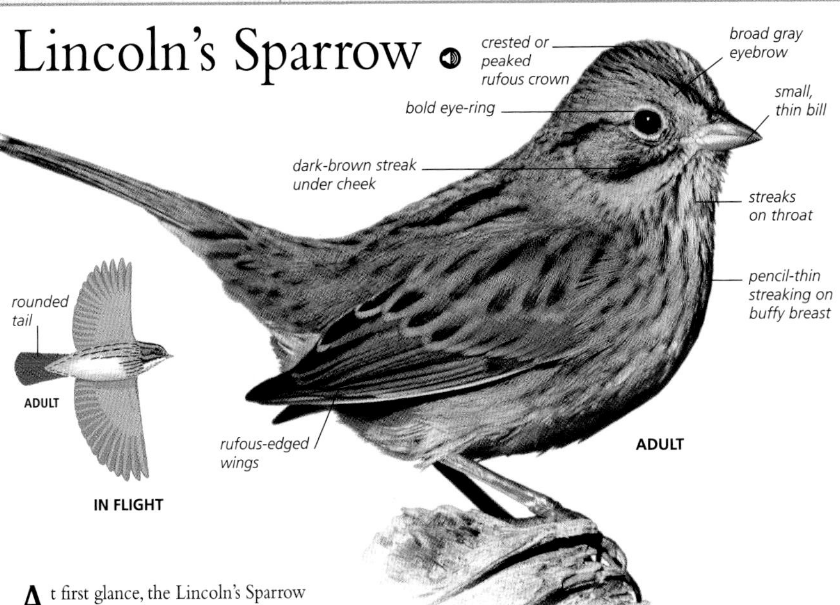
crested or peaked rufous crown
broad gray eyebrow
small, thin bill
bold eye-ring
dark-brown streak under cheek
streaks on throat
pencil-thin streaking on buffy breast
rounded tail
ADULT
rufous-edged wings
ADULT
IN FLIGHT

At first glance, the Lincoln's Sparrow appears plain, but on close inspection it reveals itself to be a bright-eyed little bird with subtly varying, but crisply outlined, markings. In the breeding season, it seeks out predominantly moist willow scrub at the tundra-taiga timberline; outside the breeding season, Lincoln's Sparrow can be found in scrubby habitats right across North America. It will occasionally visit backyard feeders in winter, but it is generally a secretive bird that stays within fairly dense cover wherever it can. However, Lincoln's Sparrow's rich, musical song is unmistakable, and it varies remarkably little from region to region.

VOICE Call a variable, loud *tchip*, flight call a rolling *ziiiit*; song series of rich, musical trills, *ju-ju-ju dodododo didididi whrrrrr.*

NESTING Grass cup, lined with fine grass, and hidden in depression in ground under overhanging sedges or grasses; 3–5 eggs;1 brood; June–August.

FEEDING Mainly seeds in winter; in summer, mostly insects, such as beetles, mosquitoes, and moths.

FLIGHT: low and direct, staying within cover whenever possible.

RAISE THE ALARM
When disturbed, the Lincoln's Sparrow often raises its central crown feathers, which form a crest.

SIMILAR SPECIES

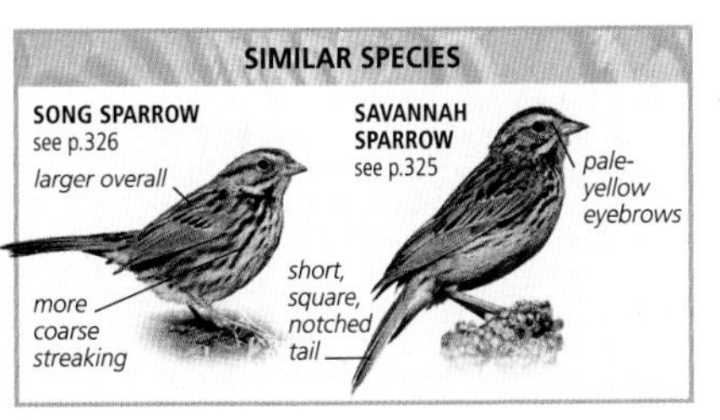
SONG SPARROW
see p.326
larger overall
more coarse streaking
SAVANNAH SPARROW
see p.325
pale-yellow eyebrows
short, square, notched tail

OCCURRENCE
Breeds in muskeg and wet thickets across northern North America, also south into the western ranges of California and Arizona. Migrants and wintering birds use a variety of scrubby habitats. Winters in the southern US (and farther south), and on the Pacific Coast north to British Columbia.

Length **5¼–6in (13.5–15cm)**	Wingspan **7½–8½in (19–22cm)**	Weight **½–⅞oz (15–25g)**
Social **Solitary/Small flocks**	Lifespan **Up to 7 years**	Status **Secure**

DATE: ______________ TIME: ______________ LOCATION: ______________________________

Order **Passeriformes**	Family **Passerellidae**	Species ***Melospiza georgiana***

Swamp Sparrow

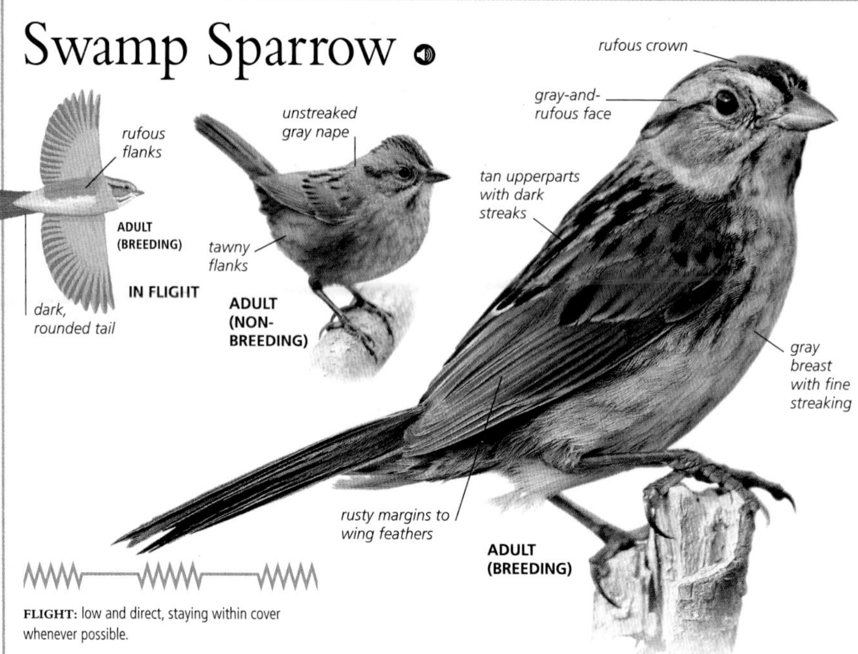
rufous crown
gray-and-rufous face
unstreaked gray nape
rufous flanks
ADULT (BREEDING)
tawny flanks
IN FLIGHT
dark, rounded tail
ADULT (NON-BREEDING)
tan upperparts with dark streaks
gray breast with fine streaking
rusty margins to wing feathers
ADULT (BREEDING)

FLIGHT: low and direct, staying within cover whenever possible.

The Swamp Sparrow is a common breeder in wet habitats across eastern North America and Canada west to the Yukon and British Columbia. It is especially abundant in its preferred habitat of tall reed marshes. A somewhat skittish bird, the Swamp Sparrow is often seen darting rapidly into cover, but usually repays the patient observer with a reappearance, giving its characteristic *chimp* call. Though often confused with both the Song Sparrow and the Lincoln's Sparrow, the Swamp Sparrow never shows more than a very faint, blurry streaking on its gray breast, and sports conspicuous rusty-edged wing feathers.

VOICE Call a slightly nasal, forceful *chimp*, flight call a high, buzzy *ziiiiii*; song a slow, monotonous, loose trill of chirps.

NESTING Bulky cup of dry plants placed 1–4ft (30–120cm) above water in marsh vegetation; 3–5 eggs; 1–2 broods; May–July.

FEEDING Mostly insects in the breeding season, especially grasshoppers; seeds in winter; occasionally fruit.

WATCH TOWER
This male Swamp Sparrow is perusing his territory from atop a seeding cattail flower.

SIMILAR SPECIES

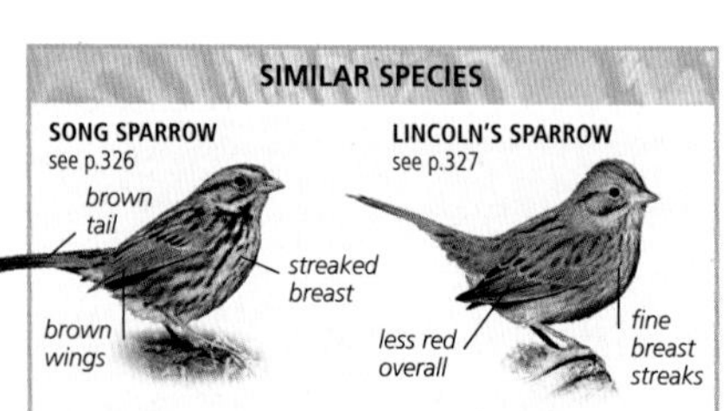
SONG SPARROW
see p.326
brown tail
streaked breast
brown wings
LINCOLN'S SPARROW
see p.327
less red overall
fine breast streaks

OCCURRENCE
Breeds in marshes, cedar bogs, damp meadows, and wet hayfields, from Yukon east to Newfoundland and south to Nebraska and the Delmarva Peninsula; winters in marshes in the eastern US and south through Mexico; rare but regular on the Pacific Coast.

Length **5–6in (12.5–15cm)**	Wingspan **7–7½in (18–19cm)**	Weight **½–⅞oz (15–25g)**
Social **Solitary/Small flocks**	Lifespan **Up to 6 years**	Status **Secure**

DATE: ______________ TIME: ______________ LOCATION: ______________

Order **Passeriformes**	Family **Passerellidae**	Species ***Pipilo erythrophthalmus***

Eastern Towhee

white corners to tail
single white patch in each wing
ADULT
IN FLIGHT
black hood and upperparts
reddish eye
MALE
white belly
white wing patches
long tail
brown hood and upperparts
small white markings on wings
rusty flanks
FEMALE

The Towhees get their name from the upslurred *chew-eee* (or *to-whee*) call they make. The Eastern Towhee is famous for its vocalizations and has one of the best-known mnemonics for its song: "drink your tea." The Eastern Towhee was once lumped with the Spotted Towhees under the name "Rufous-sided Towhee," because they interbreed in the Great Plains. In the southeastern US, Eastern Towhees have paler eyes the farther south they are located; individuals with nearly white eyes are found in Florida. Like all towhees, the Eastern Towhee feeds noisily by jumping backward with both feet at once to move leaves and reveal the insects and seeds that may be hidden underneath.

VOICE Call a nasal, upslurred *chew-eee*; flight call *zeeeooooweeet*; song sounds like *dweee, dyooo di-i-i-i-i-i-i-i-i-i-i-i*.

NESTING Large cup in depression on ground under cover, also low in thicket; 3–5 eggs; 1–2 broods; May–August.

FEEDING Eats seeds, fruits, insects, and buds.

FLIGHT: low and direct with much gliding, usually within cover.

TERRESTRIAL LIFE
The bird stays close to the ground and is usually found not more than a few yards off it.

SIMILAR SPECIES

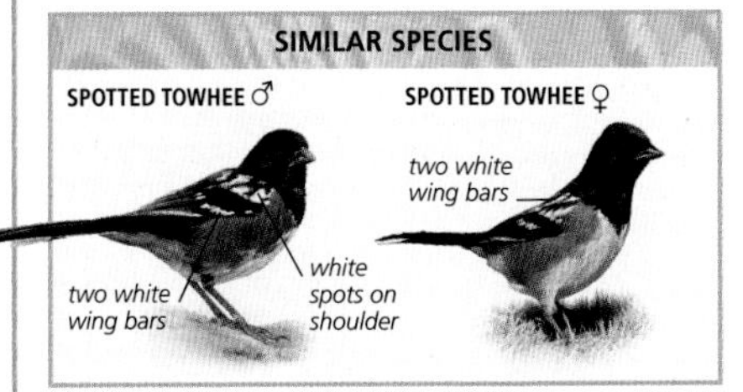
SPOTTED TOWHEE ♂
SPOTTED TOWHEE ♀
two white wing bars
white spots on shoulder
two white wing bars

OCCURRENCE
Found in dense thickets, woodland, dense shrubbery, forest edges and disturbed forests from southeast Saskatchewan, east Nebraska, west Louisiana, east to south Quebec, south Maine, and south Florida. Retreats from the northern parts of its range to winter in the southeastern US.

Length **7½–8in (19–20cm)**	Wingspan **10½in (27cm)**	Weight **1¹⁄₁₆–1¾oz (30–50g)**
Social **Solitary/Small flocks**	Lifespan **Up to 12 years**	Status **Secure**

DATE: ______________ TIME: ______________ LOCATION: ______________

Family **Icteridae**

ORIOLES AND BLACKBIRDS

THE ICTERIDS exemplify the wonderful diversity that exists among birds. Its members are common and widespread, occurring from coast to coast in nearly every habitat in North America. The species reveal extremes of color, nesting, and social behavior—from the vibrant, solitary orioles to the vast nesting colonies of comparatively drab blackbirds.

ORIOLES

Generally recognized by their contrasting black-and-orange plumage, although some species tend more toward yellow or chestnut shades, orioles are common tropical to subtropical seasonal migrants to North America. Their intricate hanging nests are an impressive combination of engineering and weaving. Most species boast a melodious song and tolerance for humans, a combination that makes them popular throughout their range.

COWBIRDS

These strictly parasitic birds have been known to lay eggs in the nests of close to 300 different species in North and South America. The species found in Canada is readily identified by its thick bill and dark, iridescent body contrasting with a brown head.

BLACKBIRDS

As their name suggests, this group of birds is largely covered in dark feathers, and their long, pointed bills and tails add to their streamlined appearance. Not as brilliantly colored as some other Icterids, these are among the most numerous birds on the continent after the breeding season, and form an impressive sight during migration.

SUBTLE BRILLIANCE
Although its plumage is dark, the Common Grackle displays a beautiful iridescence.

MEADOWLARKS

The Eastern and Western Meadowlarks are the only two species in this group in North America, but they are distinctive (although difficult to tell apart). Birds of open country, both species have a characteristic bright-yellow chest with a black bib but differing sweet songs.

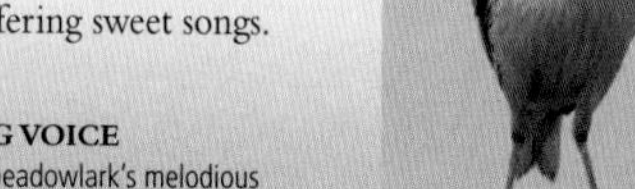

BIG VOICE
A meadowlark's melodious voice is a defining feature in many rural landscapes.

NECTAR LOVER
The magnificently colored Baltimore Oriole inserts its bill into the base of a flower, taking the nectar, but playing no part in pollination.

Order **Passeriformes**	Family **Icteridae**	Species ***Icteria virens***

Yellow-breasted Chat

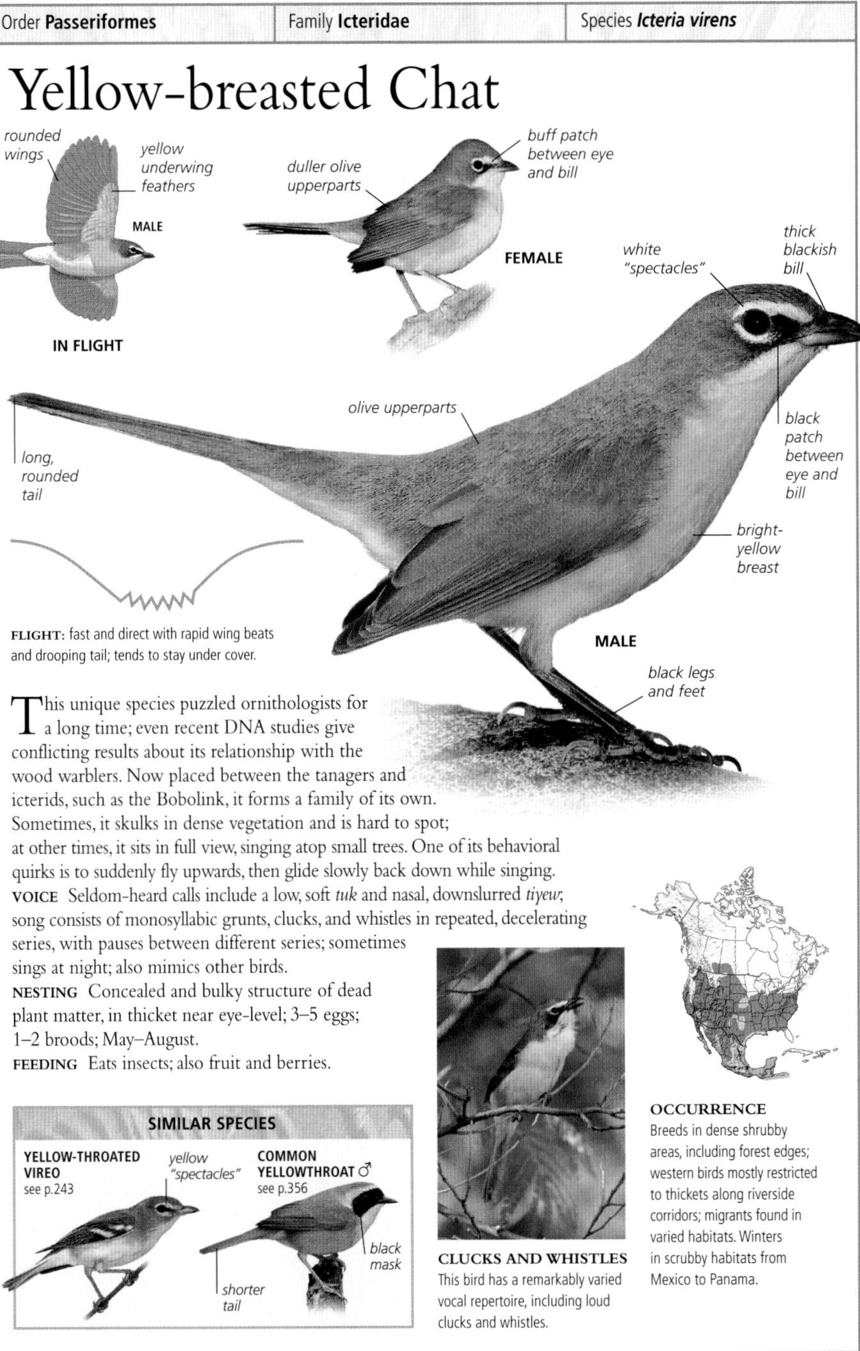

rounded wings
yellow underwing feathers
MALE
IN FLIGHT
duller olive upperparts
buff patch between eye and bill
FEMALE
white "spectacles"
thick blackish bill
olive upperparts
long, rounded tail
black patch between eye and bill
bright-yellow breast
MALE
black legs and feet

FLIGHT: fast and direct with rapid wing beats and drooping tail; tends to stay under cover.

This unique species puzzled ornithologists for a long time; even recent DNA studies give conflicting results about its relationship with the wood warblers. Now placed between the tanagers and icterids, such as the Bobolink, it forms a family of its own. Sometimes, it skulks in dense vegetation and is hard to spot; at other times, it sits in full view, singing atop small trees. One of its behavioral quirks is to suddenly fly upwards, then glide slowly back down while singing.

VOICE Seldom-heard calls include a low, soft *tuk* and nasal, downslurred *tiyew*; song consists of monosyllabic grunts, clucks, and whistles in repeated, decelerating series, with pauses between different series; sometimes sings at night; also mimics other birds.

NESTING Concealed and bulky structure of dead plant matter, in thicket near eye-level; 3–5 eggs; 1–2 broods; May–August.

FEEDING Eats insects; also fruit and berries.

CLUCKS AND WHISTLES
This bird has a remarkably varied vocal repertoire, including loud clucks and whistles.

OCCURRENCE
Breeds in dense shrubby areas, including forest edges; western birds mostly restricted to thickets along riverside corridors; migrants found in varied habitats. Winters in scrubby habitats from Mexico to Panama.

SIMILAR SPECIES

YELLOW-THROATED VIREO see p.243
yellow "spectacles"

COMMON YELLOWTHROAT ♂ see p.356
black mask
shorter tail

Length **7½in (19cm)**	Wingspan **9½in (24cm)**	Weight **¹¹⁄₁₆–1¹⁄₁₆oz (20–30g)**
Social **Solitary**	Lifespan **Up to 9 years**	Status **Declining**

DATE: ______________ TIME: ______________ LOCATION: ______________________________

Order **Passeriformes**	Family **Icteridae**	Species ***Xanthocephalus xanthocephalus***

Yellow-headed Blackbird

MALE

yellow head

conspicuous white wing patches

IN FLIGHT

black conical bill

black mask and crown on yellow head

IMMATURE MALE

bright-yellow head and chest

brownish overall

yellowish throat and facial patch

FEMALE

black overall

white wing patch

MALE

long tail

FLIGHT: direct with shallow rise and fall pattern; flaps and glides.

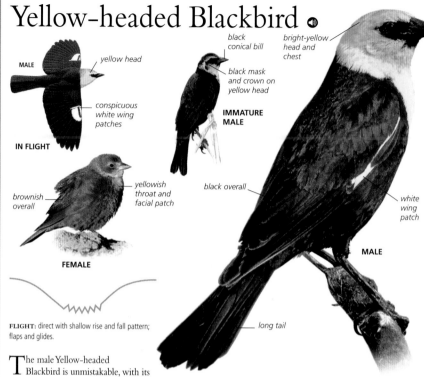

The male Yellow-headed Blackbird is unmistakable, with its conspicuous bright-yellow head contrasting with a dark body. Females, however, are more drab. Populations of this species fluctuate widely but locally according to available rainfall, which controls the availability and quality of its breeding marshland habitat. In some wetlands, the Yellow-headed Blackbird can be extremely abundant, and is easily noticed due to its amazing song.

VOICE Call a nasal *whaah*; song a series of harsh, cackling noises, followed by a brief pause, and a high, long, wailing trill.

NESTING Cup of plant strips woven into standing aquatic vegetation; 3–4 eggs; 1 brood; May–June.

FEEDING Eats insects while breeding; agricultural grains and grass seeds in winter.

SIMILAR SPECIES

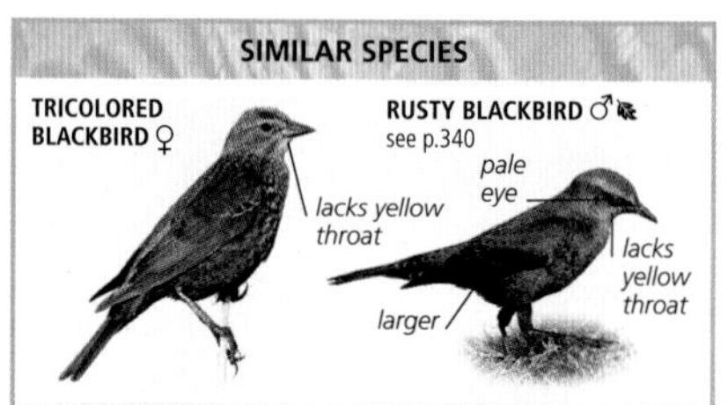
TRICOLORED BLACKBIRD ♀
lacks yellow throat
RUSTY BLACKBIRD ♂
see p.340
pale eye
lacks yellow throat
larger

YELLOW GARLAND
Five evenly spaced Yellow-headed males watch over their wetland habitat from a twig.

OCCURRENCE
Widely distributed in western Canada and the central and western US, this species breeds in marshes with cattail and bullrush vegetation, and also, locally, in wetlands within wooded areas. Winters in Mexico; resident in Baja California.

Length **8½–10½in (21–27cm)**	Wingspan **15in (38cm)**	Weight **2⅛–3½oz (60–100g)**
Social **Flocks/Colonies**	Lifespan **Up to 9 years**	Status **Localized**

DATE: ______________ TIME: ______________ LOCATION: ______________

Order **Passeriformes**	Family **Icteridae**	Species ***Dolichonyx oryzivorus***

Bobolink

black wings
buff-colored hindneck
MALE (BREEDING)
IN FLIGHT

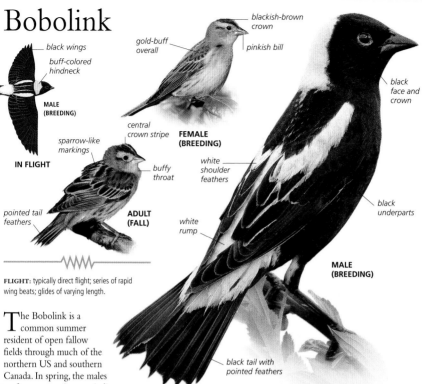

gold-buff overall
blackish-brown crown
pinkish bill
central crown stripe
FEMALE (BREEDING)

sparrow-like markings
buffy throat
pointed tail feathers
ADULT (FALL)

black face and crown
white shoulder feathers
black underparts
white rump
black tail with pointed feathers
MALE (BREEDING)

FLIGHT: typically direct flight; series of rapid wing beats; glides of varying length.

The Bobolink is a common summer resident of open fallow fields through much of the northern US and southern Canada. In spring, the males perform a conspicuous circling or "helicoptering" display, which includes singing, to establish a territory and to attract females. Bobolink populations have declined on their breeding grounds and in wintering areas because of habitat loss and changing agricultural practices.

VOICE Calls like the end of its name *link*; song a long, complex babbling series of musical notes varying in length and pitch.

NESTING Woven cup of grass close to or on the ground, well hidden in tall grass; 3–7 eggs; 1 brood; May–July.

FEEDING Feeds mostly on insects, spiders, grubs in breeding season, but seasonally variable; also cereal grains and grass seeds.

TAKING A BREAK
This male has fled the sun of the open fields to seek shelter in the shade of a tree.

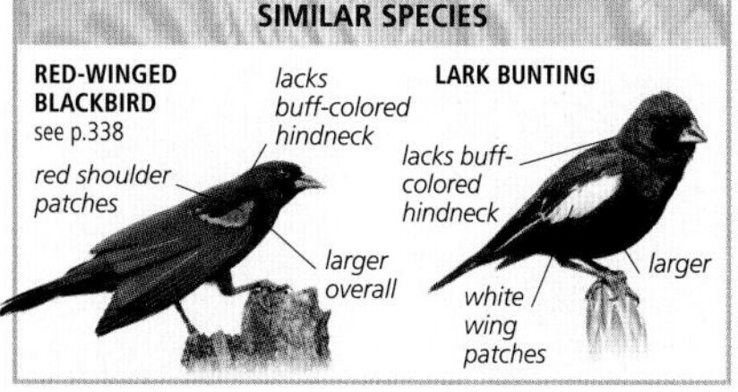
SIMILAR SPECIES
RED-WINGED BLACKBIRD
see p.338
lacks buff-colored hindneck
red shoulder patches
larger overall
LARK BUNTING
lacks buff-colored hindneck
larger
white wing patches

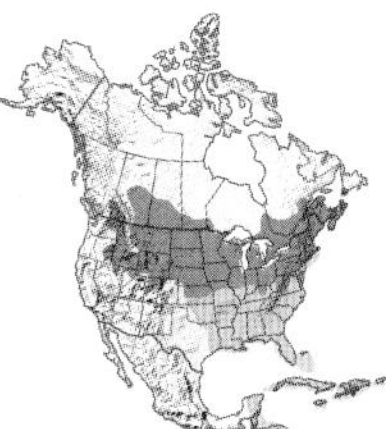

OCCURRENCE
Breeds in open fields with a mixture of tall grasses and other herbaceous vegetation, especially old hayfields. In Canada from British Columbia to the Atlantic Coast; in the US, from Idaho to New England. Migrates through the southern US and the Caribbean; winters in northern South America.

Length **6–8in (15–20cm)**	Wingspan **10–12in (25–30cm)**	Weight **1¹⁄₁₆–2oz (30–55g)**
Social **Winter flocks**	Lifespan **Up to 10 years**	Status **Threatened**

DATE: ____________ TIME: ____________ LOCATION: ____________________

Order **Passeriformes**	Family **Icteridae**	Species ***Sturnella magna***

Eastern Meadowlark

black-and-white striped crown
ADULT
rounded wings
IN FLIGHT
buffy wash on face
buffy mottling in black breastband
FALL
long, pointed bill
black stripe behind eye
brown upperparts streaked with buff and black
whitish face
yellow throat
yellow breast with black "V"
short tail with white outer tail feathers
yellow belly
BREEDING
long toes

FLIGHT: moderately fast; flushes with a series of rapid wing beats, then begins to flap and glide.

A bird of the eastern grassy fields, the colorful Eastern Meadowlark is well known for its plaintive sounding song. During courtship, the male sings enthusiastically from the highest available perch. This species overlaps with the very similar-looking Western Meadowlark in the western Great Plains, but is the only meadowlark farther east. Where they overlap, these birds are most easily distinguished by their different calls and songs. Throughout its range, numbers of the Eastern Meadowlark have fallen due to human encroachment on its habitat, although in the last decade or so, the species has made a slow (and local) comeback.

VOICE Call a sharp *dzzeer*; song a series of clear, descending whistles consisting of 3–8 notes, *tseeeooou tseeeeou*; higher pitched than the rattle of the Western Meadowlark.

NESTING Loosely woven, usually domed, cup of grasses and other plants, located on the ground in tall grass fields; 3–8 eggs; 1 brood; March–May.

FEEDING Forages on ground, mainly for insects, especially grasshoppers, but also caterpillars and grubs; seeds and grain in winter.

FAVORITE PERCH
Eastern Meadowlarks are partial to fenceposts as a favorite perch for singing.

SIMILAR SPECIES

AMERICAN PIPIT
see p.295
more slender, shorter bill
no yellow on chest

WESTERN MEADOWLARK
see p.335
slightly paler
more yellow at corner of bill

OCCURRENCE
Breeds in native tallgrass openings, pastures, and overgrown roadsides. Widespread in eastern North America, from Quebec to New Mexico and Arizona; also in Mexico and Cuba, and locally in South America. Partial migrant in the US, resident in Mexico and South America.

Length **7–10in (18–25cm)**	Wingspan **13–15in (33–38cm)**	Weight **2⅛–4oz (60–125g)**
Social **Pairs/Winter flocks**	Lifespan **Up to 9 years**	Status **Threatened**

DATE: ____________ TIME: ____________ LOCATION: ____________

Order **Passeriformes**	Family **Icteridae**	Species ***Sturnella neglecta***

Western Meadowlark

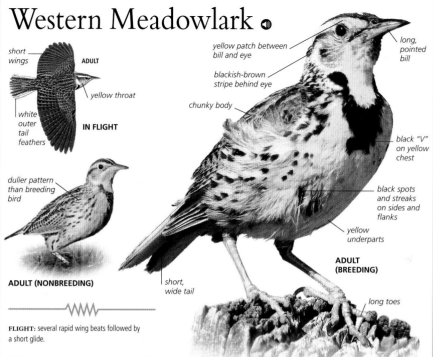

short wings
ADULT
yellow throat
white outer tail feathers
IN FLIGHT
dulier pattern than breeding bird
ADULT (NONBREEDING)
yellow patch between bill and eye
blackish-brown stripe behind eye
chunky body
long, pointed bill
black "V" on yellow chest
black spots and streaks on sides and flanks
yellow underparts
ADULT (BREEDING)
short, wide tail
long toes

FLIGHT: several rapid wing beats followed by a short glide.

The Western Meadowlark is one of the most abundant and widespread grassland birds in North America. It inhabits open country in the western Great Plains, the Great Basin, and the Central Valley of California. It is frequently encountered along roadsides, singing its melodious song from atop a fencepost or utility pole. Although the range of the Western Meadowlark overlaps widely with that of its eastern counterpart, hybrids between the two species are very rare and usually sterile.

VOICE Series of complex, bubbling whistled notes; lower frequency with no ascending whistles as heard in the Eastern Meadowlark.

NESTING Domed grass cup, well hidden in tall grasses; 3–7 eggs; 1 brood; March–August.

FEEDING Feeds mostly on insects, including beetles, grubs, and grasshoppers; also grains and grass seeds.

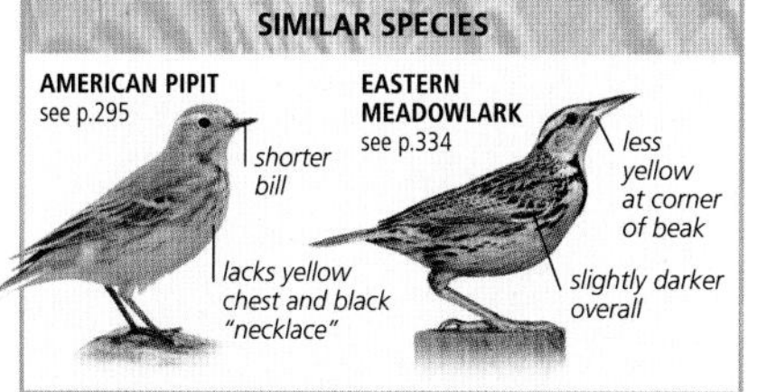

SIMILAR SPECIES
AMERICAN PIPIT
see p.295
shorter bill
lacks yellow chest and black "necklace"
EASTERN MEADOWLARK
see p.334
less yellow at corner of beak
slightly darker overall

A SHRUB WILL DO
In spring and summer, male Western Meadowlarks can be seen perching on shrubs to sing.

OCCURRENCE
Common in western North America, across much of southern Canada and the western US, south to Mexico. Breeds primarily in open grassy plains, but also uses agricultural fields with overgrown edges and hayfields. Partial migrant in the US, winters south to Mexico.

Length **7–10in (18–26cm)**	Wingspan **13–15in (33–38cm)**	Weight **2⅞–4oz (80–125g)**
Social **Pairs/Winter flocks**	Lifespan **Up to 10 years**	Status **Secure**

DATE: ____________ TIME: ____________ LOCATION: ____________

Order **Passeriformes**	Family **Icteridae**	Species ***Icterus spurius***

Orchard Oriole

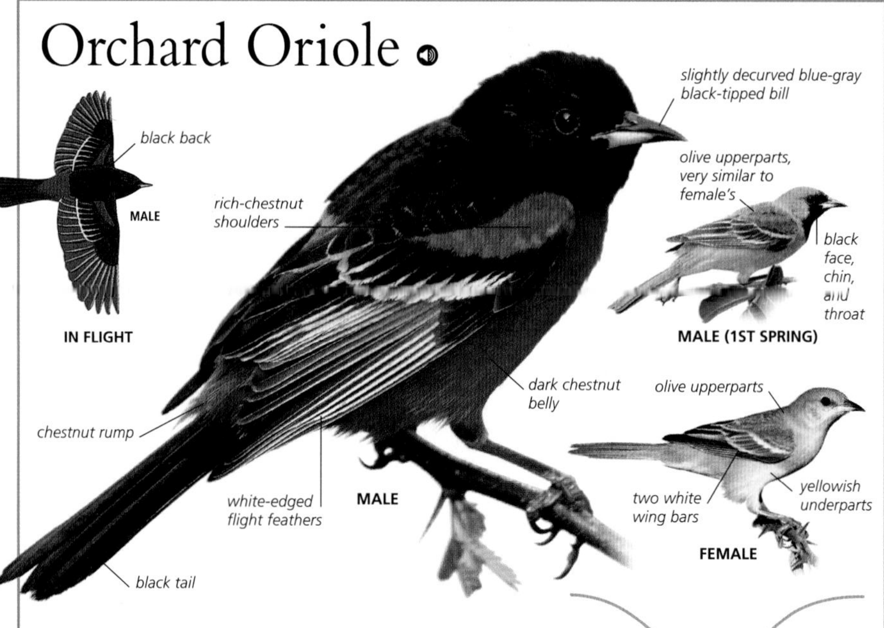
black back
MALE
IN FLIGHT
rich-chestnut shoulders
slightly decurved blue-gray black-tipped bill
olive upperparts, very similar to female's
black face, chin, and throat
MALE (1ST SPRING)
dark chestnut belly
olive upperparts
chestnut rump
white-edged flight feathers
MALE
two white wing bars
yellowish underparts
FEMALE
black tail

A small oriole, the Orchard Oriole resembles a large warbler in size, color, and the way it flits among leaves while foraging for insects. It bobs its tail, unlike other orioles. It spends less time on the breeding grounds than other migrant orioles, often arriving there as late as mid-May and leaving as early as late July. The Orchard Oriole tolerates humans and can be found breeding in suburban parks and gardens. In recent years, its numbers have increased in the eastern part of its range.

VOICE Fast, not very melodious, series of high warbling notes mixed with occasional shorter notes ending in slurred *shheere*.

NESTING Woven nest of grass suspended in fork between branches; 4–5 eggs; 1 brood; April–July.

FEEDING Mainly eats insects during breeding season, but will also feed on seeds, fruit, and occasionally, nectar; in winter, mostly fruit and nectar, and some insects.

FLIGHT: quite bouncy flight due to shallow, quick wing beats; interrupted by glides.

CHESTNUT SPLASH
The male Orchard Oriole has distinctive black upperparts and rich-chestnut underparts.

SIMILAR SPECIES

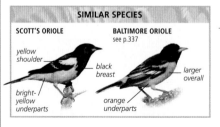

SCOTT'S ORIOLE
yellow shoulder
black breast
bright-yellow underparts

BALTIMORE ORIOLE
see p.337
larger overall
orange underparts

OCCURRENCE
Breeds in the eastern US and south-central Canada, in open forest and woodland edges with a mixture of evergreen and deciduous trees, especially along river bottoms and in shelter belts surrounding agricultural land. Winters in Mexico, Central America, and South America.

Length **7–8in (18–20cm)**	Wingspan **9in (23cm)**	Weight **11/16oz (20g)**
Social **Pairs**	Lifespan **Up to 9 years**	Status **Secure**

DATE: ______________ TIME: ______________ LOCATION: ______________________

Order **Passeriformes**	Family **Icteridae**	Species ***Icterus galbula***

Baltimore Oriole

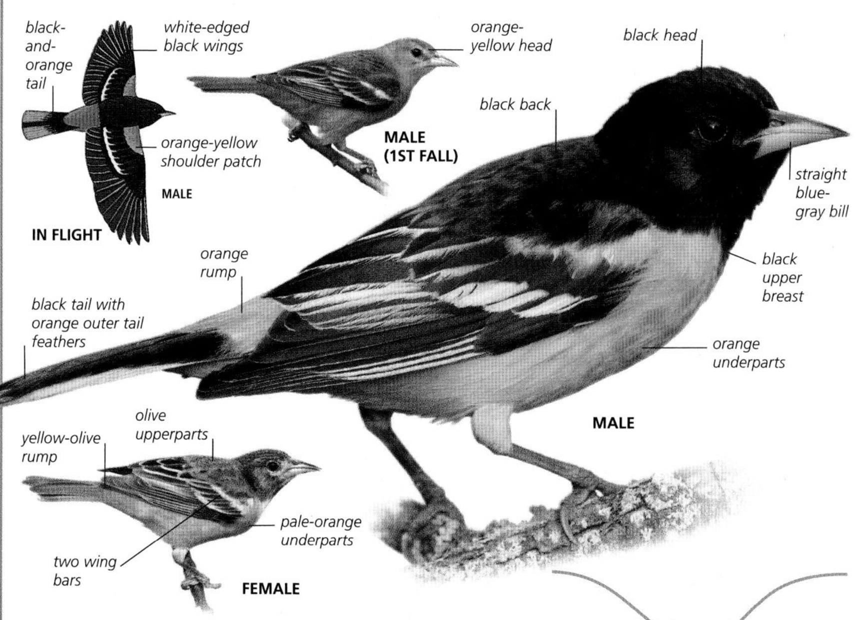
black-and-orange tail
white-edged black wings
orange-yellow shoulder patch
MALE
IN FLIGHT
orange-yellow head
MALE (1ST FALL)
black head
black back
straight blue-gray bill
black upper breast
orange rump
black tail with orange outer tail feathers
orange underparts
MALE
olive upperparts
yellow-olive rump
pale-orange underparts
two wing bars
FEMALE

The Baltimore Oriole's brilliant colors are familiar to many in eastern North America because this bird is so tolerant of humans. This species originally favored the American elm for nesting, but the Dutch elm disease decimated these trees. The oriole has since adapted to using sycamores, cottonwoods, and other tall trees as nesting sites. Its ability to use suburban gardens and parks has helped expand its range to incorporate areas densely occupied by humans.

VOICE Loud, clear, melodious song comprising several short notes in series, often of varying lengths.

NESTING Round-bottomed basket usually woven from grass, hung toward the end of branches; 4–5 eggs; 1 brood; May–July.

FEEDING Hops or flits among leaves and branches picking insects and spiders; fond of caterpillars; also eats fruit and sips nectar.

FLIGHT: strong with rapid wing beats; full downstrokes during flight provide great power.

PERFECT FOR FORAGING
The Baltimore Oriole forages alone in the dense foliage of trees and bushes, or on the ground.

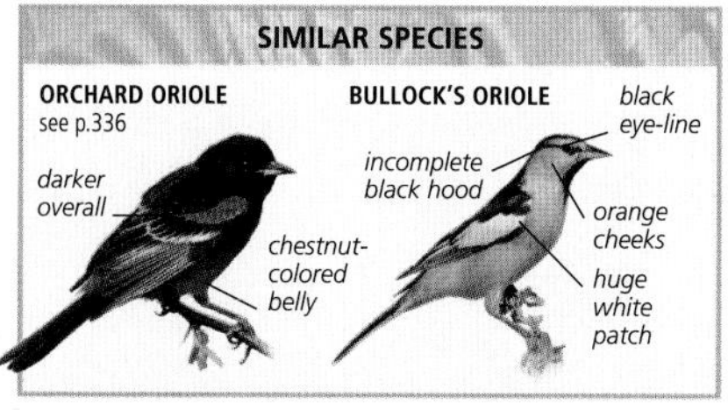
SIMILAR SPECIES
ORCHARD ORIOLE
see p.336
darker overall
chestnut-colored belly
BULLOCK'S ORIOLE
black eye-line
incomplete black hood
orange cheeks
huge white patch

OCCURRENCE
Forest edges and tall, open mixed hardwoods, especially close to rivers; regularly uses forested parks, suburban and urban areas with abundant tall trees. Small numbers winter in the southeastern US and Florida, but most birds move to Central and South America.

Length **8–10in (20–26cm)**	Wingspan **10–12in (26–30cm)**	Weight **1$\frac{1}{16}$–1$\frac{1}{4}$oz (30–35g)**
Social **Solitary/Pairs**	Lifespan **Up to 11 years**	Status **Secure**

DATE: ____________ TIME: ____________ LOCATION: ____________________

Order **Passeriformes**	Family **Icteridae**	Species ***Agelaius phoeniceus***

Red-winged Blackbird

MALE
red-and-yellow "flags"
black outer wings
IN FLIGHT

dark grayish-brown body
pale throat
IMMATURE (BICOLORED)

no clear yellow edging on red shoulder patches
MALE (BICOLORED)

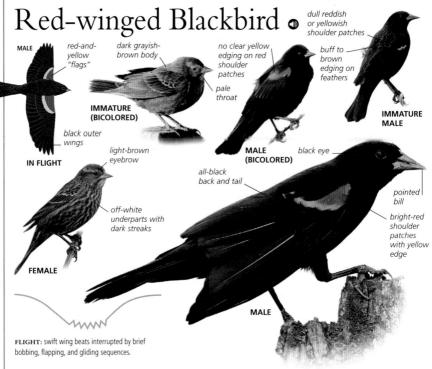

dull reddish or yellowish shoulder patches
buff to brown edging on feathers
IMMATURE MALE

light-brown eyebrow
off-white underparts with dark streaks
FEMALE

black eye
all-black back and tail
pointed bill
bright-red shoulder patches with yellow edge
MALE

FLIGHT: swift wing beats interrupted by brief bobbing, flapping, and gliding sequences.

One of the most abundant native bird species in North America, the Red-winged Blackbird is also one of the most conspicuous in wetland habitats. The sight and sound of males singing from the tops of cattails is a sure sign that spring is near. This adaptable species migrates and roosts in flocks that may number in the millions. There are numerous subspecies, one of the most distinctive being the "Bicolored" Blackbird (*A. p. gubernator.*)

VOICE Various brusk *chek*, *chit*, or *chet* calls; male song a *kronk-a-rhee* with a characteristic nasal, rolling and metallic "undulating" ending.

NESTING Cup of grasses and mud woven into dense standing reeds or cattails; 3–4 eggs; 1–2 broods; March–June.

FEEDING Forages for seeds and grains; largely insects when breeding.

DENSE FLOCKS
The huge flocks of Red-winged Blackbirds seen in migration are quite an amazing sight.

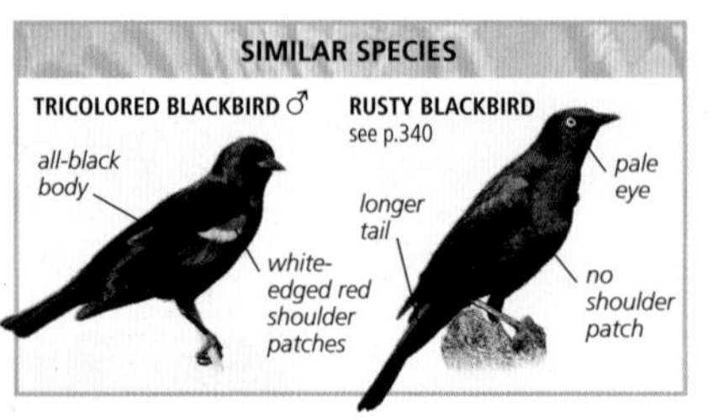
SIMILAR SPECIES
TRICOLORED BLACKBIRD ♂
all-black body
white-edged red shoulder patches
RUSTY BLACKBIRD
see p.340
longer tail
pale eye
no shoulder patch

OCCURRENCE
Widespread across Canada and the US from Alaska to the Maritimes, and south to Mexico, Central America, and the Bahamas. Lives in wetlands, especially freshwater marshes but also saltwater; wet meadows with tallgrass cover and open woodlands with reedy vegetation.

Length **7–10in (18–25cm)**	Wingspan **11–14in (28–35cm)**	Weight **1⁹⁄₁₆–2½oz (45–70g)**
Social **Flocks**	Lifespan **At least 14 years**	Status **Secure**

 DATE: ____________ TIME: ____________ LOCATION: ____________

Order **Passeriformes**	Family **Icteridae**	Species ***Molothrus ater***

Brown-headed Cowbird

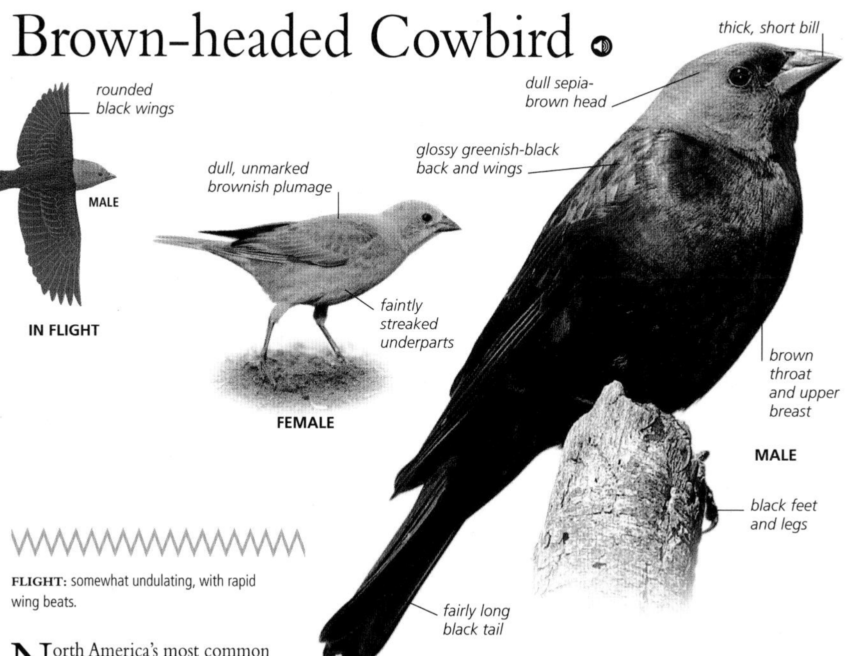

rounded black wings
MALE
IN FLIGHT
dull, unmarked brownish plumage
faintly streaked underparts
FEMALE
thick, short bill
dull sepia-brown head
glossy greenish-black back and wings
brown throat and upper breast
MALE
black feet and legs
fairly long black tail

FLIGHT: somewhat undulating, with rapid wing beats.

North America's most common and best known brood parasite, the Brown-headed Cowbird was once a bird of the Great Plains, following vast herds of bison to prey on insects kicked up by their hooves. Now, due to forest clearance and suburban development, it is found continent-wide. It has recently become a serious threat to North American songbirds, laying its eggs in the nests of more than 220 different species, and having its young raised to fledglings by more than 140 species, including the highly endangered Kirtland's Warbler.

VOICE High-pitched, squeaky whistles and bubbling notes, *dub-dub-come-tzeee*; also various clucks and *cheks*.

NESTING No nest, lays eggs in nests of other species; a single female may lay 25–55 (or more) eggs per season; April–August.

FEEDING Primarily eats grass seeds and cereal grains; also eats insects when available, especially grasshoppers and beetles.

AT A FEEDER
A female Brown-headed Cowbird enjoys a snack of seeds at a suburban feeder.

SIMILAR SPECIES

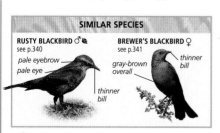

RUSTY BLACKBIRD ♂
see p.340
pale eyebrow; pale eye; thinner bill

BREWER'S BLACKBIRD ♀
see p.341
gray-brown overall; thinner bill

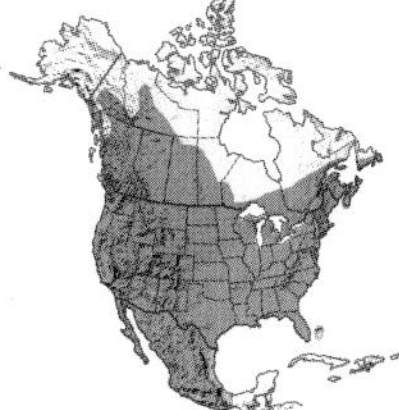

OCCURRENCE
Favors habitats modified by human activity, such as open wooded patches, low grass fields, fruit orchards, agricultural pastures with livestock, and gardens and residential areas. Widespread across North America except in Alaska and northern Canada.

Length **6–8in (15–20cm)**	Wingspan **11–13in (28–33cm)**	Weight **1⁷⁄₁₆–1³⁄₄oz (40–50g)**
Social **Large flocks**	Lifespan **Up to 16 years**	Status **Secure**

DATE: ____________ TIME: ____________ LOCATION: ______________________

Order **Passeriformes**	Family **Icteridae**	Species ***Euphagus carolinus***

Rusty Blackbird

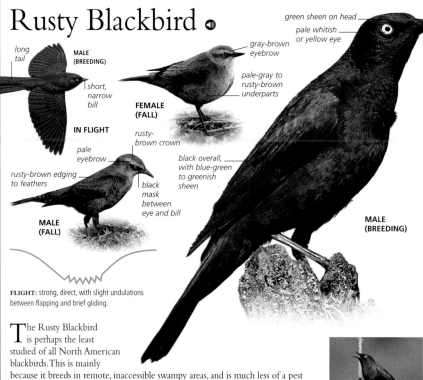

long tail
MALE (BREEDING)
short, narrow bill
IN FLIGHT
gray-brown eyebrow
pale-gray to rusty-brown underparts
FEMALE (FALL)
green sheen on head
pale whitish or yellow eye
rusty-brown crown
pale eyebrow
rusty-brown edging to feathers
black mask between eye and bill
black overall, with blue-green to greenish sheen
MALE (FALL)
MALE (BREEDING)

FLIGHT: strong, direct, with slight undulations between flapping and brief gliding.

The Rusty Blackbird is perhaps the least studied of all North American blackbirds. This is mainly because it breeds in remote, inaccessible swampy areas, and is much less of a pest to agricultural operations than some of the other members of its family. Unlike most other blackbirds, the plumage on the male Rusty Blackbird changes to a dull reddish-brown during the fall—giving the species its common name. It is also during the fall migrations that this species is most easily observed, moving south in long, wide flocks that often take several minutes to pass overhead. Its vocalizations are useful for distinguishing it from Brewer's Blackbird.

VOICE Both sexes use *chuk* call during migration flights; male song a musical *too-ta-lee*.

NESTING Small bowl of branches and sticks, lined with wet plants and dry grass, usually near water; 3–5 eggs; 1 brood; May–July.

FEEDING Eats seasonally available insects, spiders, grains, seeds of trees, and fleshy fruit or berries.

OPEN WIDE
Seldom seen, the male's courtship display includes gaping and tail-spreading.

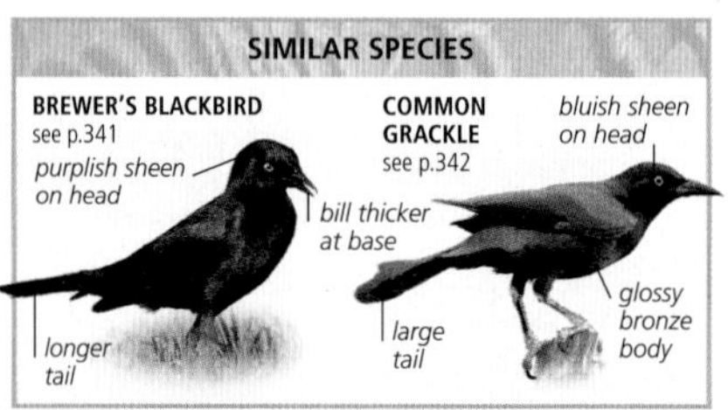
SIMILAR SPECIES
BREWER'S BLACKBIRD
see p.341
purplish sheen on head
bill thicker at base
longer tail
COMMON GRACKLE
see p.342
bluish sheen on head
glossy bronze body
large tail

OCCURRENCE
Breeds in moist to wet forests up to the timberline in the far north (farther north than any other species of North American blackbird); winters in eastern US, in various swampy forests.

Length **8–10in (20–25cm)**	Wingspan **12–15in (30–38cm)**	Weight **1⁹⁄₁₆–2⁷⁄₈oz (45–80g)**
Social **Pairs/Winter flocks**	Lifespan **At least 9 years**	Status **Declining**

DATE: ____________ TIME: ____________ LOCATION: ____________

Order **Passeriformes**	Family **Icteridae**	Species ***Euphagus cyanocephalus***

Brewer's Blackbird

stout bill

MALE

long, dark tail

IN FLIGHT

brown eyes

gray-brown overall

FEMALE

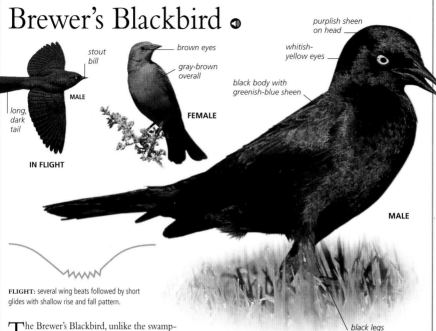

purplish sheen on head

whitish-yellow eyes

black body with greenish-blue sheen

MALE

black legs and feet

FLIGHT: several wing beats followed by short glides with shallow rise and fall pattern.

The Brewer's Blackbird, unlike the swamp-loving Rusty Blackbird, seems to prefer areas disturbed by humans to natural ones throughout much of its range. It is likely that the relatively recent eastward range expansion of the Brewer's Blackbird has been aided by changes in land practices. Interestingly, when its range overlaps with that of the Common Grackle, it wins out in rural areas, but loses out in urban areas. This species can be found feasting on waste grains left behind after the harvest or even in supermarket parking lots.

VOICE Buzzy *tshrrep* song ascending in tone.

NESTING Bulky cup of dry grass, stem and twig framework lined with soft grasses and animal hair; 3–6 eggs; 1–2 broods; April–July.

FEEDING Forages on the ground for many species of insects during breeding season, also snails; seeds, grain, and occasional fruit in fall and winter.

BROWN-EYED BIRD
Brown eyes distinguish the female Brewer's from the yellow-eyed female Rusty Blackbird.

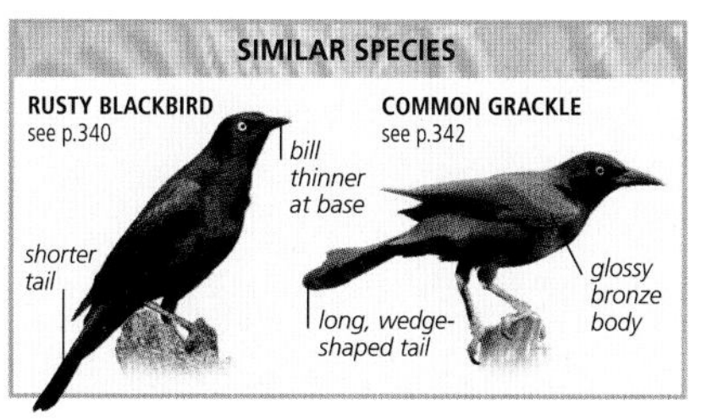
SIMILAR SPECIES
RUSTY BLACKBIRD
see p.340
bill thinner at base
shorter tail
COMMON GRACKLE
see p.342
glossy bronze body
long, wedge-shaped tail

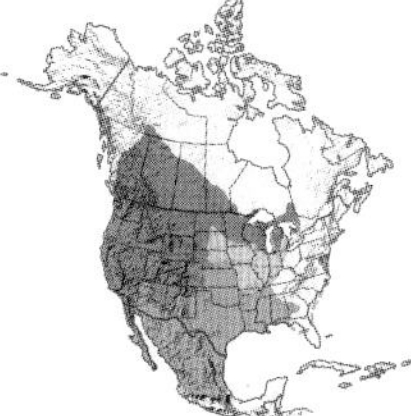

OCCURRENCE
Breeds and winters in open areas, readily adapting to, and preferring, disturbed areas and human developments, such as parks, gardens, supermarket parking lots, clear-felled forests, and fallow fields edged with dense trees or shrubs.

Length **10–12in (25–30cm)**	Wingspan **13–16in (33–41cm)**	Weight **1¾–2½oz (50–70g)**
Social **Flocks/Colonies**	Lifespan **Up to 13 years**	Status **Secure**

DATE: ________ TIME: ________ LOCATION: ________

Order **Passeriformes**	Family **Icteridae**	Species ***Quiscalus quiscula***

Common Grackle

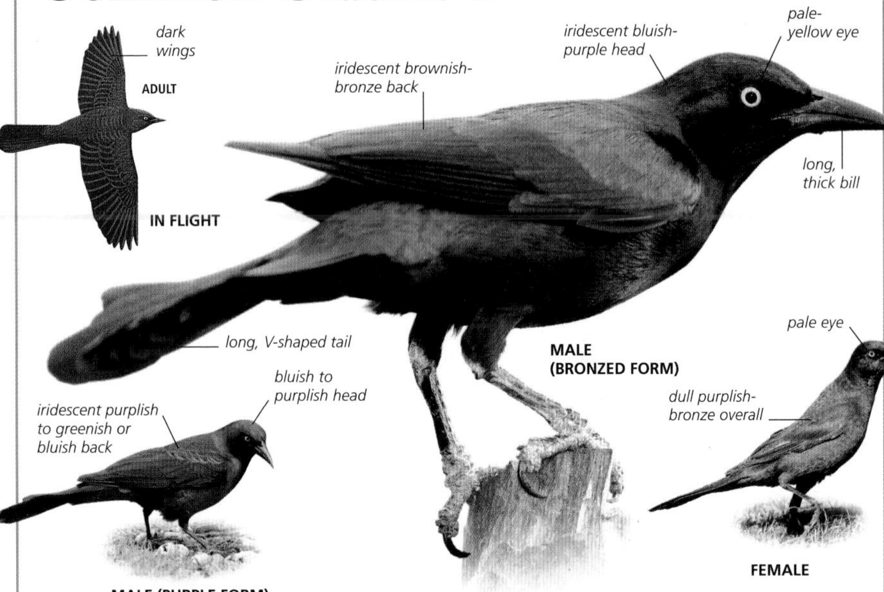
dark wings
ADULT
IN FLIGHT
iridescent brownish-bronze back
iridescent bluish-purple head
pale-yellow eye
long, thick bill
long, V-shaped tail
MALE (BRONZED FORM)
pale eye
dull purplish-bronze overall
FEMALE
bluish to purplish head
iridescent purplish to greenish or bluish back
MALE (PURPLE FORM)

This adaptable species has expanded its range rapidly in the recent past, thanks to human land-clearing practices. The Common Grackle is so well suited to urban and suburban habitats that it successfully excludes other species from them; it is often a nuisance at bird feeders. During migration and winter, Common Grackles form immense flocks, sometimes numbering over 1 million individuals. This tendency, combined with its preference for cultivated areas, has made this species an agricultural pest in some regions.

VOICE Call a low, harsh *chek*; loud song series of odd squeaks and whistles.

NESTING Small bowl in trees, with a frame of sticks filled with mud and grasses; 4–6 eggs; 1–2 broods; April–July.

FEEDING Eats beetles, flies, spiders, and worms, as well as small vertebrates; also seeds and grain, especially in nonbreeding season; an omnivore.

FLIGHT: straight, level, and direct without the up and down undulation of blackbird species.

HIGHLY ADAPTABLE
This grackle is comfortable near human developments, resulting in the expansion of its range.

OCCURRENCE
The Common Grackle lives in a wide variety of open woodlands, suburban woodlots, city parks, gardens, and hedgerows. It is absent west of the Great Plains. Wintering range extends south to the Gulf Coast.

SIMILAR SPECIES

GREAT-TAILED GRACKLE larger; purplish gloss to feathers; very long, deeply wedged tail

BOAT-TAILED GRACKLE longer tail; bluish gloss on black feathers

Length **11–13½in (28–34cm)**	Wingspan **15–18in (38–46cm)**	Weight **3⅛–4oz (90–125g)**
Social **Flocks**	Lifespan **Up to 20 years**	Status **Secure**

DATE: ______ TIME: ______ LOCATION: ______

WOOD WARBLERS

THE FAMILY PARULIDAE IS REMARKABLE for its diversity: in plumage, song, feeding, breeding biology, and sexual dimorphism. In general, though, wood warblers share similar shapes: all are smallish birds with longish, thin bills (unlike thick vireo bills) used mostly for snapping up invertebrates. Their varied colors and patterns make the lively, busy, mixed groups seen on migration especially appealing and fascinating to watch. Ground-dwelling warblers tend to be larger and clad in olives, browns, and yellows, while many arboreal species are small and sport bright oranges, cool blues, and even ruby-reds. The color, location, and presence or absence of paler wing bars and tail spots is often a good identification aid. Warblers recently underwent an explosion of speciation in the East, and over 30 species may be seen there in a morning of spring birding. The arrival of beautiful singing males in spring is the birding highlight of the year for many birdwatchers. Eastern-breeding species utilize three different migration strategies to deal with the obstacle of the Gulf of Mexico when coming from and going to their Neotropical wintering grounds. Circum-Gulf migrants fly through Mexico, along the western shore of the Gulf of Mexico. Caribbean migrants travel through Florida and island-hop through the Caribbean. And finally, trans-Gulf migrants fly directly across the Gulf of Mexico between the Yucatan Peninsula and the northern Gulf Coast. Birds flying this last and most deadly route are subject to abrupt weather changes over the Gulf, which sometimes yield spectacular fallout events at famed locations like High Island, Texas. The family is restricted to the Americas.

VARIABLE PLUMAGE
Many male *Setophaga* warblers (like this Blackburnian) are only brightly colored when breeding.

FEEDING STRATEGIES
Some warblers, such as this Black-and-white, probe the cracks in tree trunks for food.

STATIC PLUMAGE
In other warbler species, such as this Golden-winged, males keep their stunning plumage year-round.

Order **Passeriformes**	Family **Parulidae**	Species ***Seiurus aurocapilla***

Ovenbird

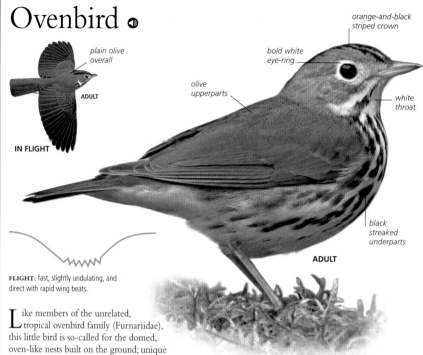

plain olive overall

ADULT

IN FLIGHT

orange-and-black striped crown

bold white eye-ring

olive upperparts

white throat

black streaked underparts

ADULT

FLIGHT: fast, slightly undulating, and direct with rapid wing beats.

Like members of the unrelated, tropical ovenbird family (Furnariidae), this little bird is so-called for the domed, oven-like nests built on the ground; unique structures for North American warblers. The Ovenbird is also noted for its singing. Males flit about boisterously, often at night, incorporating portions of their main song into a jumble of spluttering notes. In the forest, one male singing loudly to declare his territory can set off a whole chain of responses from his neighbors, until the whole forest rings.

VOICE Call variably pitched, sharp *chik* in series; flight call high, rising *siiii*; song loud, ringing crescendo of paired notes *chur-tee' chur-tee' chur-tee' chur-tee' chur-TEE chur-TEE chur-TEE.*

NESTING Domed structure of leaves and grass on ground with side entrance; 3–6 eggs; 1 brood; May–July.

FEEDING Forages mainly on the forest floor for insects and other invertebrates.

STRUTTING ITS STUFF
The Ovenbird is noted for the way it struts across the forest floor like a tiny chicken.

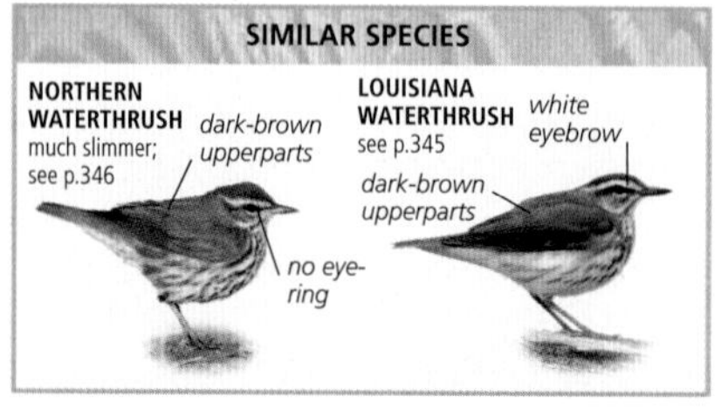
SIMILAR SPECIES
NORTHERN WATERTHRUSH
much slimmer; see p.346
dark-brown upperparts
no eye-ring
LOUISIANA WATERTHRUSH
see p.345
white eyebrow
dark-brown upperparts

OCCURRENCE
Ranges from parts of the Yukon and British Columbia to the eastern US; breeds in closed-canopy mixed and deciduous forests with suitable amount of fallen plant material for nest building and foraging; migrants and wintering birds use similar habitats.

Length **6in (15cm)**	Wingspan **9½in (24cm)**	Weight **9/16–7/8oz (16–25g)**
Social **Solitary/Flocks**	Lifespan **Up to 7 years**	Status **Declining**

 DATE: ____________ TIME: ____________ LOCATION: ____________

Order **Passeriformes**	Family **Parulidae**	Species ***Parkesia motacilla***

Louisiana Waterthrush

short tail
dull brown overall
ADULT
IN FLIGHT
white eyebrow flares behind eye
buffy area near bill and eye
large bill
unstreaked throat
thick, sparse breast streaking
white underparts contrasting with buffy flanks
ADULT
long bright-pink legs

FLIGHT: fast, slightly undulating, and direct with rapid wing beats.

The Louisiana Waterthrush is one of the earliest warblers to return north in the spring; as early as March, eastern ravines are filled with cascades of its song. Both the stream-loving Louisiana Waterthrush and its still-water cousin, the Northern Waterthrush, bob their tails as they walk, but the Louisiana Waterthrush arcs its entire body at the same time. In spring, this species shows brighter pink legs than the Northern Waterthrush.

VOICE Call a round *spink*; flight call a rising, buzzy *ziiiit*; song a loud, descending, ringing, whistled cascade, ending with sputtering *see'-oh see'-oh see'-uh see'-uh tip-uh-tik-uh-tip-whee'ur-tik*.

NESTING Bulky mass of leaves, moss, and twigs, under steep stream bank over water; 4–6 eggs; 1 brood; May–August.

FEEDING Forages in streams for insect larvae, snails, and small fish; also catches flying insects, such as dragonflies and stoneflies.

TAKING A LITTLE DIP
In many ways, this species is the "dipper of the East," picking invertebrates from shallow streams.

SIMILAR SPECIES

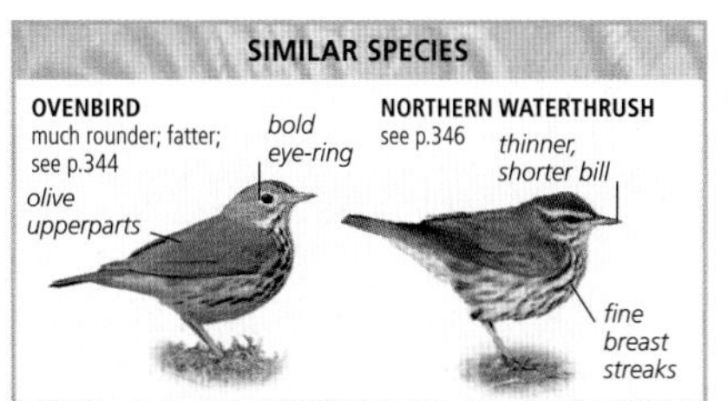
OVENBIRD
much rounder; fatter; see p.344
bold eye-ring
olive upperparts
NORTHERN WATERTHRUSH
see p.346
thinner, shorter bill
fine breast streaks

OCCURRENCE
Breeds along fast-moving streams in deciduous forests in the eastern US and southern Ontario; migrants stop over near running water, including gardens; winters along wooded streams and rivers in mountains and hills in the Caribbean, Mexico, Central America, and northern parts of South America.

Length **6in (15cm)**	Wingspan **10in (25cm)**	Weight **5/8–7/8oz (18–25g)**
Social **Solitary**	Lifespan **Up to 8 years**	Status **Threatened**

DATE: ____________ TIME: ____________ LOCATION: ____________________

Order **Passeriformes**	Family **Parulidae**	Species ***Parkesia noveboracensis***

Northern Waterthrush

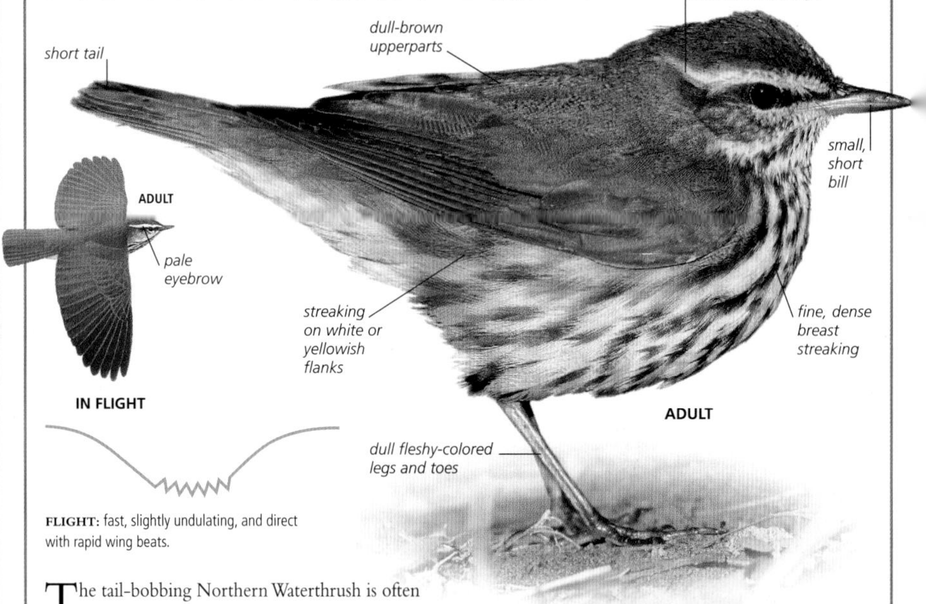

short tail

dull-brown upperparts

pale eyebrow narrows behind eye

small, short bill

ADULT

pale eyebrow

streaking on white or yellowish flanks

fine, dense breast streaking

IN FLIGHT

ADULT

dull fleshy-colored legs and toes

FLIGHT: fast, slightly undulating, and direct with rapid wing beats.

The tail-bobbing Northern Waterthrush is often heard giving a *spink!* call as it swiftly flees from observers. Although this species may be mistaken for the closely related Louisiana Waterthrush, there are clues that can help identify it. While the Northern Waterthrush prefers still water, its relative greatly prefers running water; in addition, its song is quite unlike that of the Louisiana Waterthrush.

VOICE Call a sharp, rising, ringing *spink!*; flight call a rising, buzzy *ziiiit*; song a loud series of rich, accelerating, staccato notes, usually decreasing in pitch *teet, teet, toh-toh toh-toh tyew-tyew!*

NESTING Hair-lined, mossy cup placed on or near ground, hidden in roots of fallen or standing tree or in riverbank; 4–5 eggs; 1 brood; May–August.

FEEDING Mostly eats insects, such as ants, mosquitoes, moths, and beetles, both larvae and adult, plus slugs and snails; when migrating, also eats small crustaceans, and even tiny fish.

YELLOW FORM
Many Northern Waterthrushes have yellow underparts, like this one, while others have white.

SIMILAR SPECIES

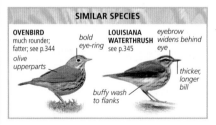

OVENBIRD
much rounder; fatter; see p.344

bold eye-ring

olive upperparts

LOUISIANA WATERTHRUSH
see p.345

eyebrow widens behind eye

thicker, longer bill

buffy wash to flanks

OCCURRENCE
Breeds right across northern North America in dark, still-water swamps and bogs; also in the still edges of rivers and lakes; migrant birds use wet habitats; winters in shrubby marshes, mangroves, and occasionally in crops, such as rice fields and citrus groves.

Length **6in (15cm)**	Wingspan **9½in (24cm)**	Weight **½–⅞oz (14–23g)**
Social **Solitary**	Lifespan **Up to 9 years**	Status **Secure**

DATE: ____________ TIME: ____________ LOCATION: ____________

Order **Passeriformes**	Family **Parulidae**	Species ***Vermivora chrysoptera***

Golden-winged Warbler

gray back
bright-yellow wing panel
MALE
white outer tail feathers
IN FLIGHT
black mask
bright-yellow crown
gray back suffused with yellow
unstreaked wings
black throat
yellow wing panel
white undertail
gray mask
greenish-yellow crown
FEMALE
MALE

One of the continent's most beautiful warblers, this species is unfortunately being genetically swamped by the more southerly Blue-winged Warbler. This situation is worsening as more habitat is cleared and climate changes intensify. The Golden-winged interbreeds with the Blue-winged, resulting in two more frequently seen hybrid forms: the Brewster's Warbler, which resembles the Blue-winged Warbler, and the Lawrence's Warbler, which looks like a Blue-winged Warbler with the mask and black throat of a Golden-winged.

VOICE Call a sharp *tsip*; flight call high, slightly buzzy *ziiih;* song buzzy *zee zuu zuu zuu*, first note higher; birds that deviate from this song pattern may be hybrids.

NESTING Shallow bulky cup, on or just above ground; 4–6 eggs; 1 brood; May–July.

FEEDING Hangs upside down at clusters of curled-up dead leaves; feeds on moth larvae, other winged insects, and spiders.

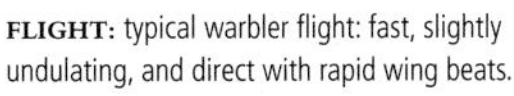

FLIGHT: typical warbler flight: fast, slightly undulating, and direct with rapid wing beats.

SMALL TREES REQUIRED
Golden-winged Warblers breed in shrubby habitats created by clearance and re-growth.

SIMILAR SPECIES

BLUE-WINGED WARBLER
see p.348

CHESTNUT-SIDED WARBLER
see p.366

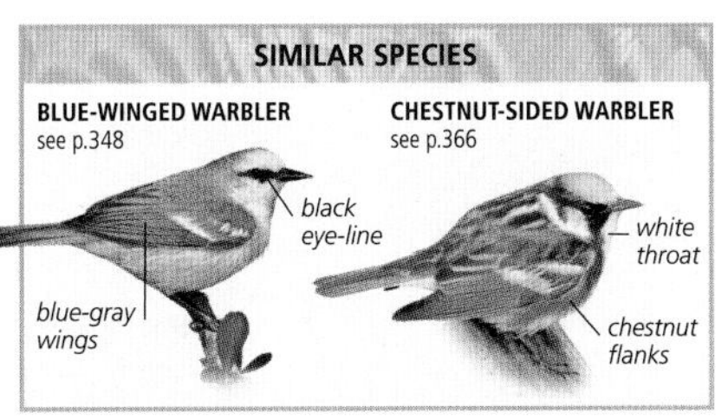
black eye-line
blue-gray wings
white throat
chestnut flanks

OCCURRENCE
Breeds in the northeastern US and southeastern Canada in short secondary growth habitat with dense patches of deciduous shrubs or tangles, or in marshes with a forest edge; uses any wooded habitat on migration; winters in Central America from Guatemala to north Colombia; mostly on the Caribbean side.

Length **$4^3/_4$in (12cm)**	Wingspan **$7^1/_2$in (19cm)**	Weight **$^9/_{32}$–$^3/_8$oz (8–11g)**
Social **Migrant/Winter flocks**	Lifespan **Unknown**	Status **Threatened**

DATE: ____________ TIME: ____________ LOCATION: ____________

Order **Passeriformes**	Family **Parulidae**	Species ***Vermivora cyanoptera***

Blue-winged Warbler

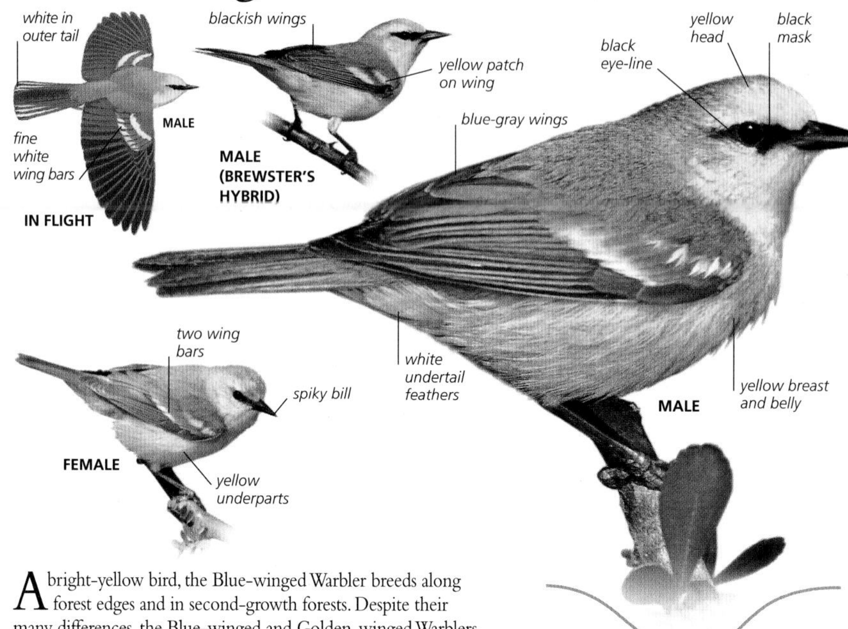
white in outer tail
fine white wing bars
MALE
IN FLIGHT
blackish wings
yellow patch on wing
MALE (BREWSTER'S HYBRID)
blue-gray wings
black eye-line
yellow head
black mask
two wing bars
spiky bill
white undertail feathers
yellow breast and belly
MALE
FEMALE
yellow underparts

A bright-yellow bird, the Blue-winged Warbler breeds along forest edges and in second-growth forests. Despite their many differences, the Blue-winged and Golden-winged Warblers are closely related and interbreed freely, producing a variety of fertile combinations. The most frequently produced hybrid, Brewster's Warbler, named in 1874, was once believed to be a different species. It is similar to the Golden-winged Warbler (yellowish breast, two yellow wing bars), but has the Blue-winged's facial pattern, without the black mask and throat.

FLIGHT: typical warbler flight: fast, slightly undulating, and direct with rapid wing beats.

VOICE Sharp *tsip* call, like *Spizella* sparrows; flight call: a high, slightly buzzy *ziiih;* song is a low, harsh, buzzy *beee-burrrrr,* second note very low in pitch and rattling; deviation from this song pattern may hint at hybrid origin.

NESTING Deep, bulky cup of vegetation, just off the ground in grasses; 4–5 eggs; 1 brood; May–June.

FEEDING Hangs upside down at clusters of dead leaves; probes for moth larvae and small insects.

DECEPTIVE HYBRID
The black border to this bird's ear patch indicates a Blue- and Golden-winged ancestry.

OCCURRENCE
Breeds in areas of second-growth forest, but is less picky than the Golden-winged Warbler and can use older and taller stands. Occurs in any wooded habitat on migration. Migrates across the Gulf of Mexico to winter in southeastern Mexico and central Panama.

SIMILAR SPECIES

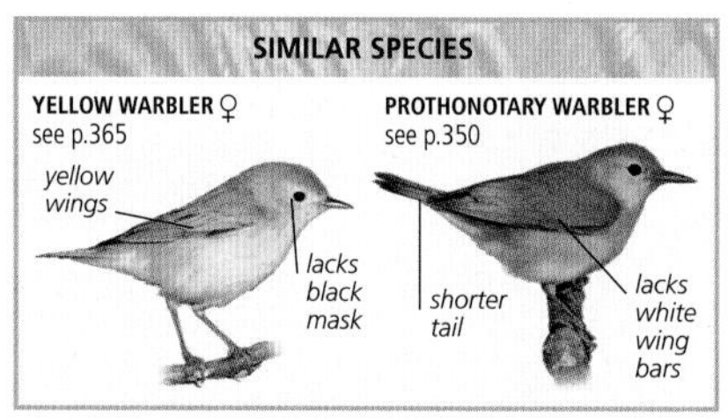
YELLOW WARBLER ♀
see p.365
yellow wings
lacks black mask
PROTHONOTARY WARBLER ♀
see p.350
shorter tail
lacks white wing bars

Length **4¾in (12cm)**	Wingspan **7½in (19cm)**	Weight **9/32–3/8oz (8–11g)**
Social **Loose flocks**	Lifespan **Up to 7 years**	Status **Secure**

DATE: ______________ TIME: ______________ LOCATION: ______________

Order **Passeriformes**	Family **Parulidae**	Species ***Mniotilta varia***

Black-and-white Warbler

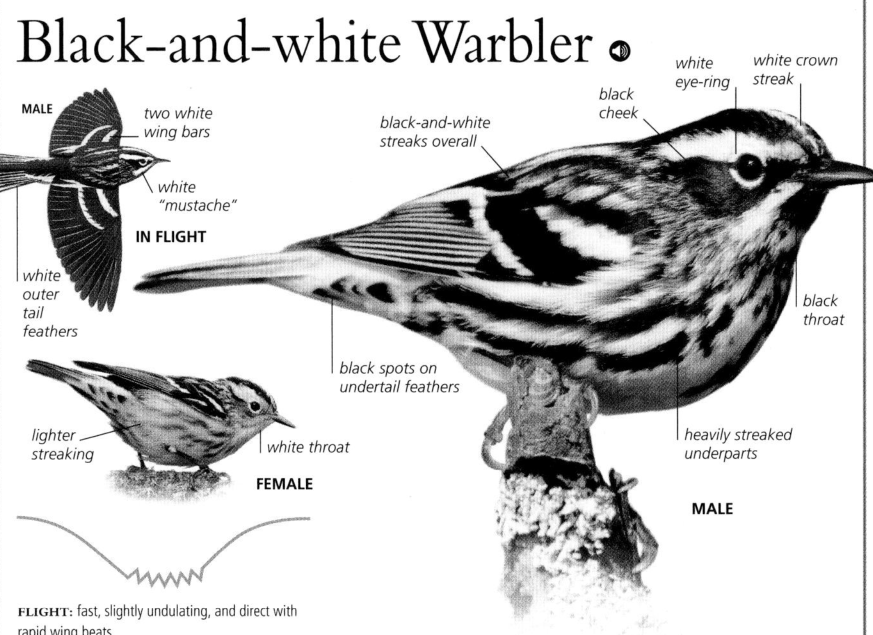
MALE
two white wing bars
white "mustache"
IN FLIGHT
white outer tail feathers
black-and-white streaks overall
black cheek
white eye-ring
white crown streak
black throat
black spots on undertail feathers
heavily streaked underparts
MALE
lighter streaking
white throat
FEMALE

FLIGHT: fast, slightly undulating, and direct with rapid wing beats.

The Black-and-white Warbler is best known for its creeper-like habit of feeding in vertical and upside-down positions as it pries into bark crevices, where its relatively long bill allows it to reach into tiny nooks and crannies. These habits, combined with a streaked plumage, make this bird one of the most distinctive warblers in North America. It is a long-distance migrant, with some birds wintering in parts of northern South America.

VOICE Sharp *stik* call; flight call a very high, thin *ssiit*, often doubled; song a thin, high-pitched, wheezy series *wheesy wheesy wheesy wheesy wheesy wheesy*.

NESTING Cup on ground against stump, fallen logs, or roots; 4–6 eggs; 1 brood; April–August.

FEEDING Creeps along branches and trunks, probing into bark for insects and insect larvae.

SQUEAKY WHEEL
The high-pitched, wheezy song of this warbler is said to be reminiscent of a squeaky wheel.

UPSIDE DOWN
Black-and-white Warblers often creep headfirst along trunks and branches of trees.

SIMILAR SPECIES

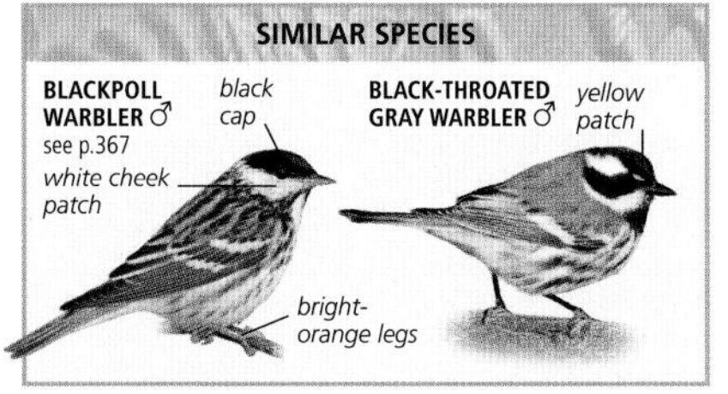
BLACKPOLL WARBLER ♂
see p.367
black cap
white cheek patch
BLACK-THROATED GRAY WARBLER ♂
yellow patch
bright-orange legs

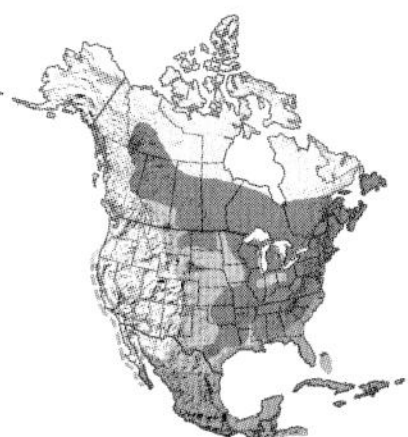

OCCURRENCE
Breeds in deciduous and mixed mature and second-growth woodlands; migrants occur on a greater variety of habitats; winters in a wide range of wooded habitats in the southern US, Mexico and into Central and South America.

Length **5in (13cm)**	Wingspan **8in (20cm)**	Weight **5/16–1/2oz (9–14g)**
Social **Migrant/Winter flocks**	Lifespan **Up to 11 years**	Status **Secure**

DATE: ____________ TIME: ____________ LOCATION: ____________

Order **Passeriformes**	Family **Parulidae**	Species ***Protonotaria citrea***

Prothonotary Warbler

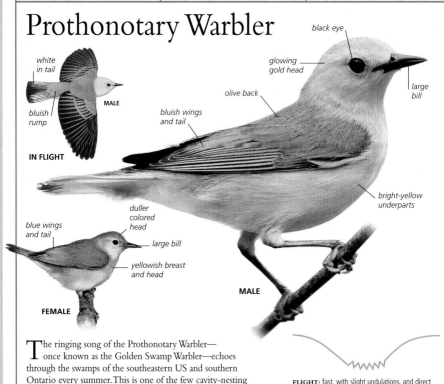

white in tail
bluish rump
MALE
IN FLIGHT
black eye
glowing gold head
olive back
bluish wings and tail
large bill
bright-yellow underparts
MALE
duller colored head
blue wings and tail
large bill
yellowish breast and head
FEMALE

The ringing song of the Prothonotary Warbler—once known as the Golden Swamp Warbler—echoes through the swamps of the southeastern US and southern Ontario every summer. This is one of the few cavity-nesting warbler species; it will use human-made birdhouses placed close to still water. Prothonotary Warblers also tend to stay fairly low over the water, making them easy to spot. This warbler's yellow head and breast reminded an early naturalist of the bright-yellow robes worn by Prothonotaries (high-ranking papal clerks), and he passed on the name to this colorful bird.

VOICE Flight call a loud, high *sviit*; call note a loud *chip*; song a loud series of penetrating and internally rising notes *tsveet tsveet tsveet tsveet tsveet tsveet tsveet.*

NESTING Over or near still water; woodpecker holes often used; 3–8 eggs; 1–2 broods; April–July.

FEEDING Mostly eats insects and small mollusks; also seeds, fruit, and nectar.

FLIGHT: fast, with slight undulations, and direct with rapid wing beats.

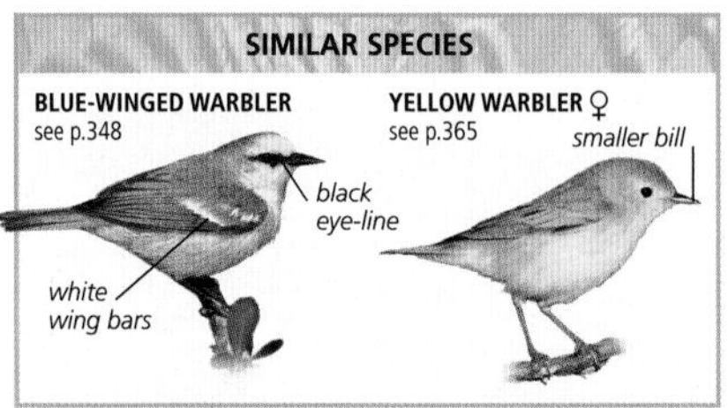
SIMILAR SPECIES
BLUE-WINGED WARBLER
see p.348
black eye-line
white wing bars
YELLOW WARBLER ♀
see p.365
smaller bill

GOLDEN SONGBIRD
Visible in the darkness of a southern swamp, a Prothonotary Warbler sings its ringing song.

OCCURRENCE
Breeds in wooded areas over or near still water, especially in cypress swamps and bottomlands across the southeastern US and up into southern Ontario. Winters in mangroves and dry forests in southern Mexico.

Length **5½in (14cm)**	Wingspan **9in (23cm)**	Weight **½–⅝oz (14–18g)**
Social **Winter flocks**	Lifespan **Up to 8 years**	Status **Endangered**

DATE: ____________ TIME: ____________ LOCATION: ____________

Order **Passeriformes**	Family **Parulidae**	Species ***Leiothlypis peregrina***

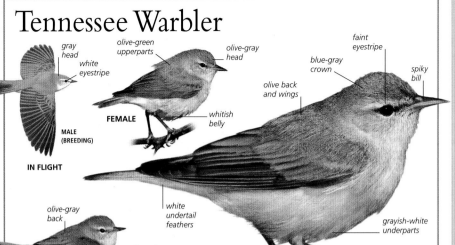

Tennessee Warbler

gray head
white eyestripe
MALE (BREEDING)
IN FLIGHT

olive-green upperparts
olive-gray head
whitish belly
FEMALE

faint eyestripe
blue-gray crown
spiky bill
olive back and wings
white undertail feathers
grayish-white underparts
MALE (BREEDING)

olive-gray back
yellowish throat and breast
MALE (FALL)

The Tennessee Warbler was named after its place of discovery, but this bird would have been on migration, as it breeds almost entirely in Canada and winters in Central America. These warblers inhabit fairly remote areas, and their nests are difficult to find. It is one of a number of species that takes advantage of outbreaks of spruce budworm; the population of Tennessee Warblers tends to increase in years when budworms are abundant.

VOICE Call a sharp *tzit*; flight call a thin slightly rolling *seet*; song usually three-part staccato series, *chip-chip-chip*, each series increasing in pitch and usually in tempo.

NESTING Nest woven of fine plant matter, in ground depression, concealed from above by shrubbery; 4–7 eggs; 1 brood; June.

FEEDING Searches outer branches of trees for caterpillars, bees, wasps, beetles, and spiders; also eats fruit in winter and drinks nectar by piercing the base of flowers.

FLIGHT: fast, slightly undulating, and direct with rapid wing beats.

UNIQUE UNDERPARTS
The breeding male is the only North American warbler with unmarked grayish-white underparts.

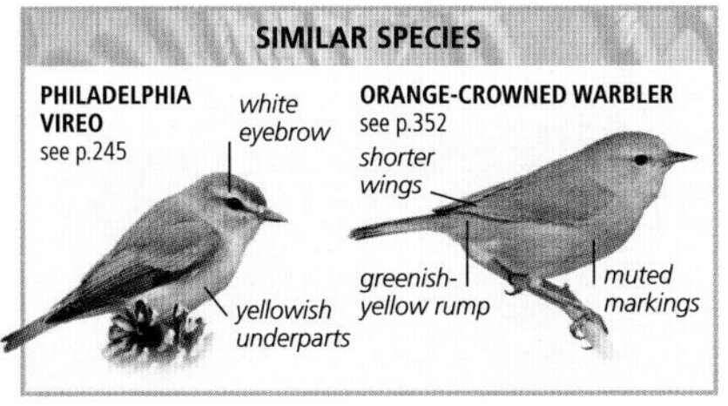
SIMILAR SPECIES
PHILADELPHIA VIREO
see p.245
white eyebrow
yellowish underparts
ORANGE-CROWNED WARBLER
see p.352
shorter wings
greenish-yellow rump
muted markings

OCCURRENCE
Breeds in a variety of habitats, especially woodlands with dense understory and thickets of willows and alders. Very common in suburban parks and gardens during migration, particularly in the Midwest. Winters from southern Mexico to northern Ecuador and northern Venezuela.

Length **4¾in (12cm)**	Wingspan **7¾in (19.5cm)**	Weight **9/32–5/8oz (8–17g)**
Social **Flocks**	Lifespan **Up to 6 years**	Status **Secure**

DATE: ______________ TIME: ______________ LOCATION: ______________________________

Order **Passeriformes**	Family **Parulidae**	Species ***Leiothlypis celata***

Orange-crowned Warbler

dull olive overall
MALE
IN FLIGHT
crown shows orange when bird is alarmed
pale-yellow eyebrow
olive-green upperparts
short wings
greenish-yellow rump
muted breast markings
ADULT (WEST)
gray head
drabber plumage overall
yellow undertail feathers
EAST; 1ST WINTER

FLIGHT: fast, slightly undulating, and direct with rapid wing beats.

Common and relatively brightly colored in the West but uncommon and duller in the East, the Orange-crowned Warbler has a large breeding range. The 19th-century American naturalist Thomas Say described this species on the basis of specimens collected in Nebraska. He was struck by the tiny orange cap, but because it was so concealed in the plumage of the crown, he named it *celata*, which is Latin for "hidden." The orange cap is not usually visible in the field.

VOICE Call a clean, sharp *tsik*; flight call a high, short *seet*; song a loose, lazy trill; eastern birds lazier, western birds more emphatic.

NESTING Cup of grasses, fibers, and down, usually on the ground under a bush; 4–5 eggs; 1 brood; March–July.

FEEDING Gleans mostly arthropods, such as beetles, ants, spiders, and their larvae; also eats fruit; collects nectar by piercing the base of a flower.

FACE MARKINGS
The eastern populations of this warbler have whitish facial markings during their first winter.

SIMILAR SPECIES

TENNESSEE WARBLER see p.351

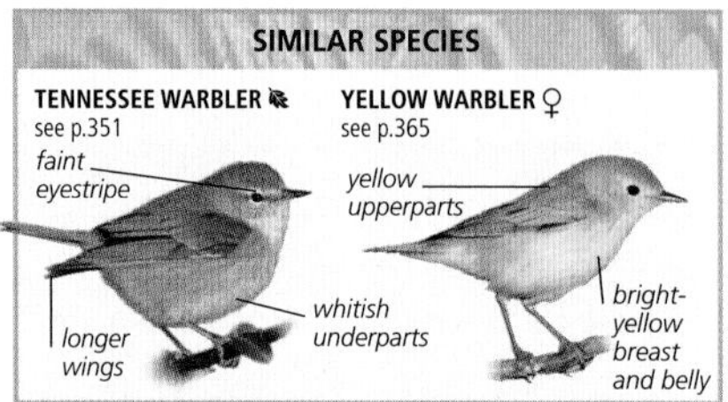
faint eyestripe
longer wings
whitish underparts

YELLOW WARBLER ♀ see p.365

yellow upperparts
bright-yellow breast and belly

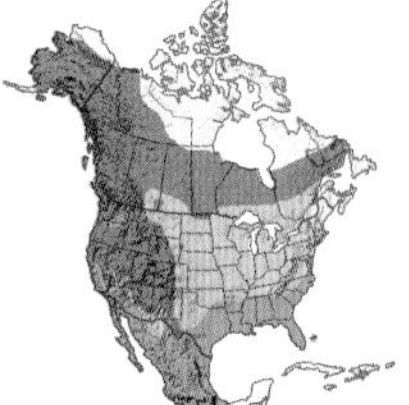

OCCURRENCE
Breeds in varied habitats across North America from Alaska eastward to Newfoundland, and in the West from British Columbia southward to California, New Mexico, and western Texas. Prefers streamside thickets. Some winter in the West, while others go to Mexico and Guatemala.

Length **5in (13cm)**	Wingspan **7¼in (18.5cm)**	Weight **¼–⅜oz (7–11g)**
Social **Winter flocks**	Lifespan **Up to 6 years**	Status **Secure**

DATE: ______ TIME: ______ LOCATION: ______

Order **Passeriformes**	Family **Parulidae**	Species ***Leiothlypis ruficapilla***

Nashville Warbler

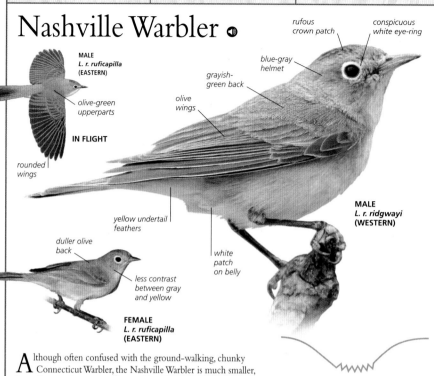

MALE
L. r. ruficapilla
(EASTERN)
olive-green upperparts
IN FLIGHT
rounded wings
rufous crown patch
conspicuous white eye-ring
blue-gray helmet
grayish-green back
olive wings
yellow undertail feathers
white patch on belly
MALE
L. r. ridgwayi
(WESTERN)
duller olive back
less contrast between gray and yellow
FEMALE
L. r. ruficapilla
(EASTERN)

Although often confused with the ground-walking, chunky Connecticut Warbler, the Nashville Warbler is much smaller, hops about up in trees, and has a yellow throat. Nashville has two subspecies: *L. r. ruficapilla* in the East and *L. r. ridgwayi* in the West. Differences in voice, habitat, behavior, and plumage hint that they may, in fact, be separate species. *L. r. ridgwayi* can be distinguished as it has more extensive white on its belly and a grayish-green back.

VOICE Call sharp *tik*, sharper in West; flight call high, thin *siit*; eastern song two parts: first part lazy, second faster trill *tee-tsee tee-tsee tee-tsee titititititi*; western song slightly lower and fuller with lazier second part, a seldom trilled *tee-tsee tee-tsee tee-tsee weesay weesay way*.

NESTING Cup hidden on ground in dense cover; 3–6 eggs; 1 brood; May–July.

FEEDING Gleans insects and spiders from trees.

FLIGHT: fast, slightly undulating, and direct, with rapid wing beats.

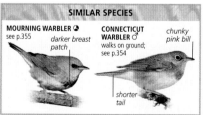

SIMILAR SPECIES

MOURNING WARBLER see p.355

darker breast patch

CONNECTICUT WARBLER ♂ walks on ground; see p.354

chunky pink bill

shorter tail

FIELD MARKS
The white eye-ring and belly are evident on this singing male.

OCCURRENCE
Ruficapilla breeds in wet habitats of Saskatchewan east to Newfoundland and south to West Virginia; migrates to winter mainly in Mexico. *Ridgwayi* breeds in brushy montane areas in the Sierras and northern Rockies and winters in coastal California and south Texas to Guatemala.

Length **4¾in (12cm)**	Wingspan **7½in (19cm)**	Weight **¼–7/16oz (7–13g)**
Social **Migrant/Winter flocks**	Lifespan **Up to 7 years**	Status **Secure**

DATE: ______________ TIME: ______________ LOCATION: ______________________

Order **Passeriformes**	Family **Parulidae**	Species ***Oporornis agilis***

Connecticut Warbler

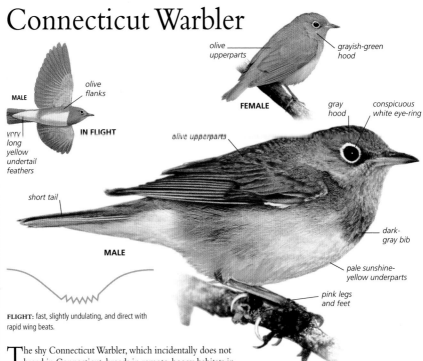

olive upperparts
grayish-green hood
FEMALE

MALE
olive flanks
IN FLIGHT
very long yellow undertail feathers

gray hood
conspicuous white eye-ring
olive upperparts
short tail
dark-gray bib
pale sunshine-yellow underparts
pink legs and feet
MALE

FLIGHT: fast, slightly undulating, and direct with rapid wing beats.

The shy Connecticut Warbler, which incidentally does not breed in Connecticut, breeds in remote, boggy habitats in Canada and is hard to spot during its spring and fall migrations. It arrives in the US in late May and leaves its breeding grounds in August. It is the only warbler that walks along the ground in a bouncy manner, with its tail bobbing up and down.

VOICE Seldom-heard call a nasal *champ*, flight call a buzzy *ziiiit*; song a loud "whippy," accelerating series, often ending with upward inflection *tweet, chuh WHIP-uh chee-uh-WHIP-uh chee-uh-WAY.*

NESTING Concealed cup of grass or leaves, lined with fine plant matter and hair; placed near or on the ground in damp moss or grass clump; 3–5 eggs; 1 brood; June–July.

FEEDING Gleans a variety of adult insects, insect larvae, and spiders from under leaves; also eats small fruit.

EXCEPTIONAL UNDERTAIL
The yellow undertail feathers nearly reach the tip of the Connecticut Warbler's tail.

SIMILAR SPECIES

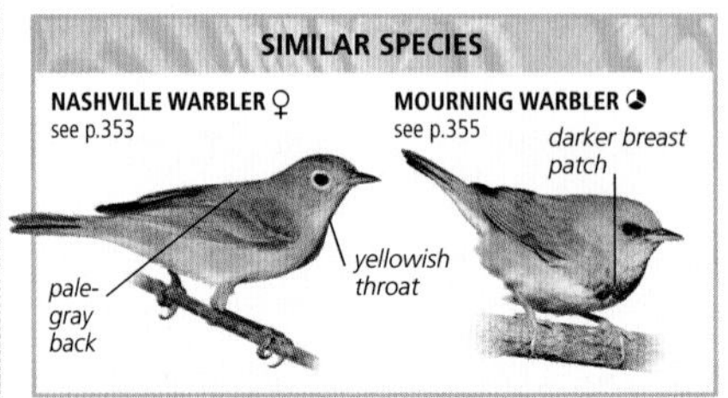
NASHVILLE WARBLER ♀
see p.353
pale-gray back
yellowish throat
MOURNING WARBLER
see p.355
darker breast patch

OCCURRENCE
Breeds across Canada from British Columbia to Quebec and in the US, in Minnesota and the Great Lakes region, in bogs and pine forests. Winters in forest habitats of Amazonian Peru and Brazil.

Length **6in (15cm)**	Wingspan **9in (23cm)**	Weight **7/16–11/16oz (13–20g)**
Social **Solitary**	Lifespan **Up to 4 years**	Status **Secure (p)**

 DATE: ____________ TIME: ____________ LOCATION: ____________

Order **Passeriformes**	Family **Parulidae**	Species ***Geothlypis philadelphia***

Mourning Warbler

MALE (BREEDING)

yellow undertail feathers

"hooded" look

IN FLIGHT

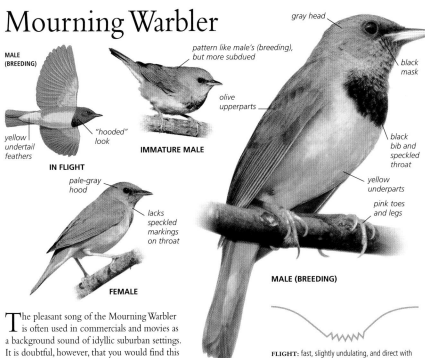

pattern like male's (breeding), but more subdued

olive upperparts

IMMATURE MALE

pale-gray hood

lacks speckled markings on throat

FEMALE

gray head

black mask

black bib and speckled throat

yellow underparts

pink toes and legs

MALE (BREEDING)

The pleasant song of the Mourning Warbler is often used in commercials and movies as a background sound of idyllic suburban settings. It is doubtful, however, that you would find this gray-headed, gray-throated warbler in a backyard, as it prefers dense, herbaceous tangles—both for breeding and during migration. These birds are late spring migrants and the leaves are fully out when they arrive in the eastern US, making it difficult to see them. The easiest way to see a Mourning Warbler is to track a male by its song.

VOICE Call a flat *tchik*; flight call a high, thin, clear *svit*; song a very burry series of paired notes with low-pitched ending: *churrr-ee churrr-ee churrr-ee churr-ee churrr-ee-oh.*

NESTING Well-concealed cup of leaves, lined with grass, on or near ground in dense tangle; 2–5 eggs; 1 brood; June–August.

FEEDING Mainly gleans insects and spiders in low foliage; eats some plant material in winter.

FLIGHT: fast, slightly undulating, and direct with rapid wing beats.

FOLLOW THAT BIRD
Tracking down a singing male is the easiest way to find this skulking species.

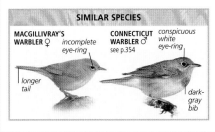

SIMILAR SPECIES

MACGILLIVRAY'S WARBLER ♀ *incomplete eye-ring*; *longer tail*

CONNECTICUT WARBLER ♂ see p.354 *conspicuous white eye-ring*; *dark-gray bib*

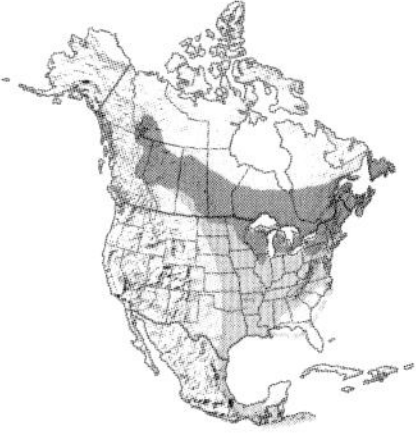

OCCURRENCE
Breeds in dense thickets of disturbed woodlands from the Yukon and British Columbia, east to Quebec and Newfoundland, south to the Great Lakes, New England, New York, and the Appalachians. Winters in dense thickets in Central and South America.

Length **5in (13cm)**	Wingspan **7½in (19cm)**	Weight **3/8–7/16oz (10–13g)**
Social **Solitary**	Lifespan **Up to 8 years**	Status **Secure**

DATE: ____________ TIME: ____________ LOCATION: ____________

Order **Passeriformes**	Family **Parulidae**	Species ***Geothlypis trichas***

Common Yellowthroat

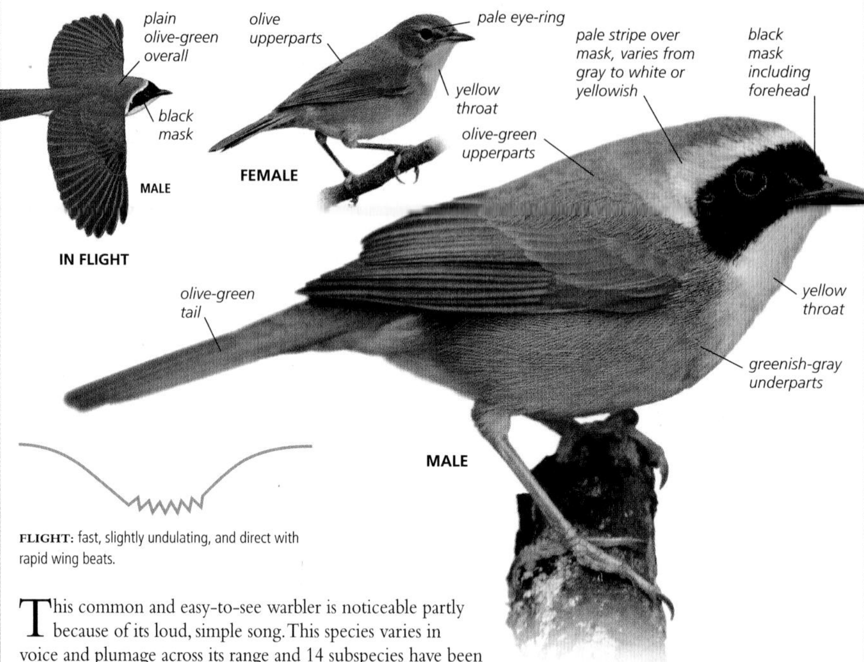
plain
olive-green
overall
black
mask
MALE
IN FLIGHT
olive
upperparts
pale eye-ring
yellow
throat
FEMALE
pale stripe over
mask, varies from
gray to white or
yellowish
black
mask
including
forehead
olive-green
upperparts
olive-green
tail
yellow
throat
greenish-gray
underparts
MALE

FLIGHT: fast, slightly undulating, and direct with rapid wing beats.

This common and easy-to-see warbler is noticeable partly because of its loud, simple song. This species varies in voice and plumage across its range and 14 subspecies have been described. In the western US, the birds have yellower underparts, brighter white head stripes, and louder, simpler songs than the eastern birds. The male often flies upward rapidly, delivering a more complex version of its song.

VOICE Call a harsh, buzzy *tchak*, repeated into chatter when agitated; flight call a low, flat, buzzy *dzzzit*; song a variable but distinctive series of rich (often three-note) phrases: *WITCH-uh-tee WITCH-uh-tee WITCH-uh-tee WHICH*; more complex flight song.

NESTING Concealed bulky cup of grasses just above ground or water; 3–5 eggs; 1 brood; May–August.

FEEDING Eats insects and spiders in low vegetation; also seeds.

UNFORGETTABLE CALL
The song of the male Common Yellowthroat is an extremely helpful aid in its identification.

SIMILAR SPECIES

KENTUCKY WARBLER ♂
much larger; see p.388

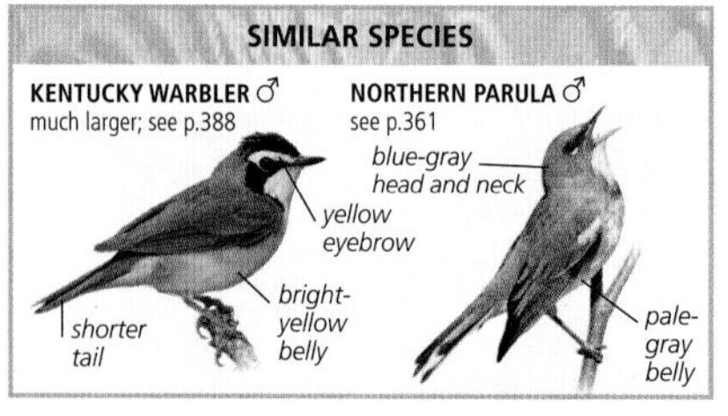
yellow
eyebrow
bright-
yellow
belly
shorter
tail

NORTHERN PARULA ♂
see p.361

blue-gray
head and neck
pale-
gray
belly

OCCURRENCE
Found south of the tundra, from Alaska and the Yukon to Quebec and Newfoundland, and south to California, Texas, and to the southeastern US. Inhabits dense herbaceous understory, from marshes and grasslands to pine forest and hedgerows. Winters from Mexico to Panama and the Antilles.

Length **5in (13cm)**	Wingspan **6¾in (17cm)**	Weight **5⁄16–3⁄8oz (9–10g)**
Social **Migrant/Winter flocks**	Lifespan **Up to 11 years**	Status **Secure**

DATE: ____________ TIME: ____________ LOCATION: ______________________

Order **Passeriformes**	Family **Parulidae**	Species ***Setophaga citrina***

Hooded Warbler

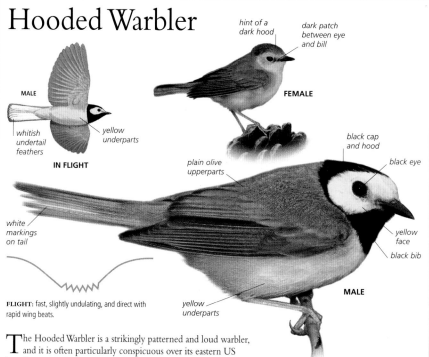

hint of a dark hood
dark patch between eye and bill
FEMALE
MALE
whitish undertail feathers
yellow underparts
IN FLIGHT
black cap and hood
black eye
plain olive upperparts
white markings on tail
yellow face
black bib
MALE
yellow underparts

FLIGHT: fast, slightly undulating, and direct with rapid wing beats.

The Hooded Warbler is a strikingly patterned and loud warbler, and it is often particularly conspicuous over its eastern US breeding range. Both male and females frequently flash the white markings hidden on the inner webs of their tails. The extent of the black hood varies in female Hooded Warblers; it ranges from none in first fall birds to almost as extensive as males in some adult females. Populations have been increasing recently, possibly due to their ability to live in disturbed forest habitat.

VOICE Call a metallic *tsink*; flight call a high, thin *sveep*; song a rich, whistled series, ending loudly and emphatically: *tu-wee' tu-wee' tu-wee-TEE-tee-yu.*

NESTING Bulky cup of leaves lined with hair, in shrub near eye level; 3–5 eggs; 1–2 broods; May–July.

FEEDING Eats many different kinds of insects found low in vegetation.

STRIKING MASK
The black-and-yellow face of the Hooded Warbler makes the male an unmistakable bird.

SIMILAR SPECIES

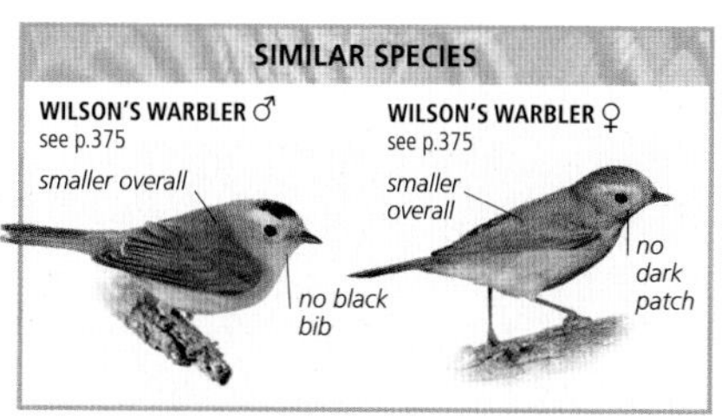
WILSON'S WARBLER ♂
see p.375
smaller overall
no black bib
WILSON'S WARBLER ♀
see p.375
smaller overall
no dark patch

OCCURRENCE
Breeds in moist deciduous forests with dense understory in eastern US and southern Ontario; has bred in some moist mountain canyons. Migrants like similar habitat. Winters in moist woodlands with good understory, especially lowland rainforest, from eastern Mexico to Panama and the West Indies.

Length **5¼in (13.5cm)**	Wingspan **7in (17.5cm)**	Weight **5/16oz–7/16oz (9–12g)**
Social **Migrant/Winter flocks**	Lifespan **Up to 8 years**	Status **Secure (p)**

DATE: ____________ TIME: ____________ LOCATION: ____________

Order **Passeriformes**	Family **Parulidae**	Species ***Setophaga ruticilla***

American Redstart

MALE

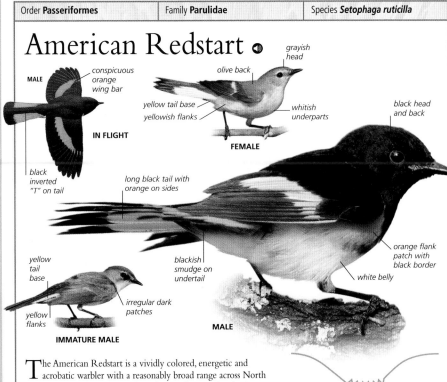

conspicuous orange wing bar

IN FLIGHT

black inverted "T" on tail

olive back

grayish head

yellow tail base

yellowish flanks

whitish underparts

FEMALE

black head and back

long black tail with orange on sides

orange flank patch with black border

white belly

blackish smudge on undertail

MALE

yellow tail base

yellow flanks

irregular dark patches

IMMATURE MALE

FLIGHT: fast, slightly undulating, and direct with rapid wing beats.

The American Redstart is a vividly colored, energetic and acrobatic warbler with a reasonably broad range across North America. One of its behavioral quirks is to fan its tail and wings while foraging, supposedly using the flashes of bold color to scare insects into moving, making them easy prey. It possesses well-developed rictal bristles, hair-like feathers extending from the corners of the mouth, which help it to detect insects.

VOICE Harsh *tsiip* call; flight call a high, thin *sweep*; song a confusingly variable, high, thin, yet penetrating series of notes; one version burry, emphatic, and downslurred *see-a see-a see-a see-a ZEE-urrrr.*

NESTING Cup of grasses and rootlets, lined with feathers and placed low in deciduous tree; 2–5 eggs; 1–2 broods; May–July.

FEEDING Gleans insects and spiders from leaves at mid-levels in trees; also catches moths, flies in flight; will also eat fruit.

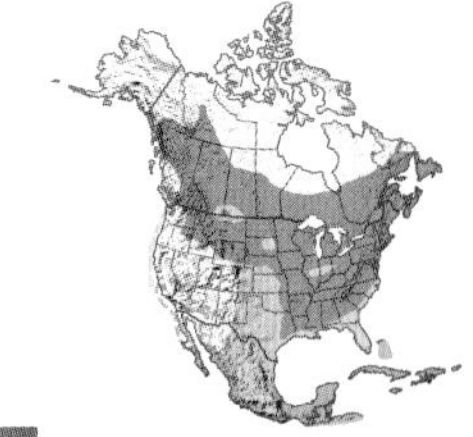

TRANSVESTITE BEHAVIOR
Immature males sneakily sport female plumage to gain access to mates and food.

MALE CAREGIVER
As with most warblers, male Redstarts help raise the young, though they may be polygamous.

OCCURRENCE
Breeds in moist deciduous and mixed woodlands across North America; migrants and wintering birds use a wide range of habitats. Winters from Baja California and south Florida through Middle America and the Caribbean to northern South America.

Length **5in (13cm)**	Wingspan **8in (20cm)**	Weight **7/32–3/8oz (6–11g)**
Social **Flocks**	Lifespan **Up to 10 years**	Status **Secure**

DATE: ____________ TIME: ____________ LOCATION: ____________

Order **Passeriformes**	Family **Parulidae**	Species ***Setophaga tigrina***

Cape May Warbler

MALE

white patches on wings

IN FLIGHT

gray back

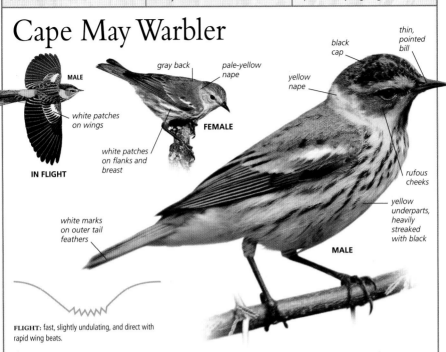

pale-yellow nape

FEMALE

white patches on flanks and breast

black cap

thin, pointed bill

yellow nape

rufous cheeks

yellow underparts, heavily streaked with black

white marks on outer tail feathers

MALE

FLIGHT: fast, slightly undulating, and direct with rapid wing beats.

The Cape May Warbler is a spruce budworm specialist, and so the populations of this bird increase during outbreaks of that insect. These birds often chase away other birds aggressively from flowering trees, where they use their especially thin and pointed bills and semitubular tongues to suck the nectar from blossoms. In its summer forest habitat, the Cape May Warbler uses its bill to feed on insects by plucking them from clumps of conifer needles.

VOICE Song a high, even-pitched series of whistles *see see see see.*

NESTING Cup placed near trunk, high in spruce or fir near top; 4–9 eggs; 1 brood; June–July.

FEEDING Gleans arthropods, especially spruce budworms, but also flies, moths, and beetles from mid-high levels in canopy; also takes fruit and nectar during the nonbreeding season.

SPRING FLASH
Magnificently colored, a male warbler displays its chestnut cheek, yellow "necklace," and yellow rump.

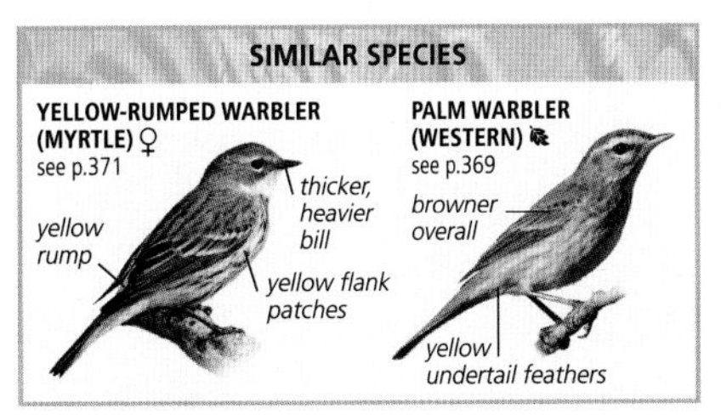
SIMILAR SPECIES
YELLOW-RUMPED WARBLER (MYRTLE) ♀
see p.371
yellow rump
thicker, heavier bill
yellow flank patches
PALM WARBLER (WESTERN)
see p.369
browner overall
yellow undertail feathers

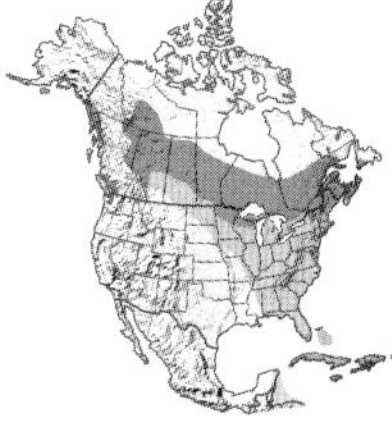

OCCURRENCE
Breeds from the Yukon and British Columbia to the Great Lakes, the Maritimes, and New England in mature spruce-fir forests. Migrants found in varied habitats. Winters in varied habitats in Central America, as far south as the Honduras.

Length **5in (13cm)**	Wingspan **8in (20cm)**	Weight **5/16–7/16oz (9–13g)**
Social **Migrant flocks**	Lifespan **Up to 4 years**	Status **Secure**

DATE: ____________ TIME: ____________ LOCATION: ____________________

Order **Passeriformes**	Family **Parulidae**	Species ***Setophaga cerulea***

Cerulean Warbler

whitish eyebrow
pale-blue crown
sea-green upperparts
yellowish underparts
FEMALE

bright-blue crown
black breastband
MALE

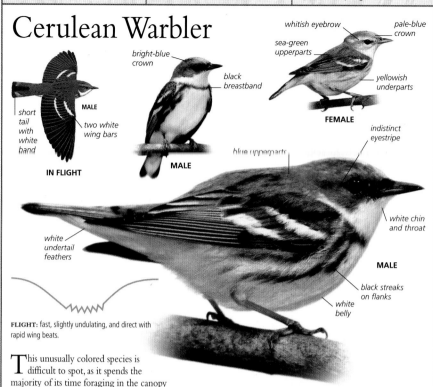

short tail with white band
MALE
two white wing bars
IN FLIGHT

blue upperparts
indistinct eyestripe
white chin and throat
white undertail feathers
MALE
black streaks on flanks
white belly

FLIGHT: fast, slightly undulating, and direct with rapid wing beats.

This unusually colored species is difficult to spot, as it spends the majority of its time foraging in the canopy of deciduous forests. It was once common across the Midwest and the Ohio River Valley, but its habitat is being cleared for agriculture and fragmented by development. In winter, this bird lives high in the canopy of the Andean foothills, but sadly this habitat is threatened by coffee cultivation.

VOICE Call a slurred *chip*; flight call a buzzy *zeet*; three-part, buzzy song consisting of a short series of low paired notes followed by a mid-range trill and upslurred high-pitched *zhree*.

NESTING Compact cup high on fork in deciduous tree, far from trunk; 2–5 eggs; 1 brood; May–July.

FEEDING Gleans insects high in canopy, especially from leaf bases.

UNIQUE COLOR
Female Cerulean Warblers have a unique blue color on their head and upperparts.

SIMILAR SPECIES

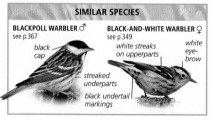

BLACKPOLL WARBLER ♂
see p.367
black cap
streaked underparts

BLACK-AND-WHITE WARBLER ♀
see p.349
white streaks on upperparts
white eye-brow
black undertail markings

OCCURRENCE
Mainly breeds in mature deciduous forests across the northeastern US and southeastern Canada; tends to prefer dense woodlands during migration. Winters in evergreen forests in the Andes, principally from Colombia to Peru.

Length **4¾in (12cm)**	Wingspan **7¾in (19.5cm)**	Weight **9/32–3/8oz (8–10g)**
Social **Migrant/Winter flocks**	Lifespan **Up to 6 years**	Status **Endangered**

DATE: ____________ TIME: ____________ LOCATION: ____________________

Order **Passeriformes**	Family **Parulidae**	Species ***Setophaga americana***

Northern Parula

MALE

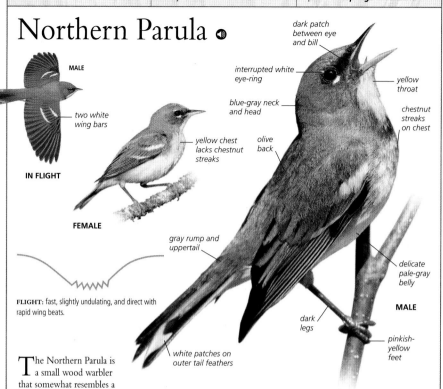

two white wing bars

IN FLIGHT

yellow chest lacks chestnut streaks

FEMALE

dark patch between eye and bill

interrupted white eye-ring

blue-gray neck and head

yellow throat

chestnut streaks on chest

olive back

gray rump and uppertail

delicate pale-gray belly

MALE

dark legs

pinkish-yellow feet

white patches on outer tail feathers

FLIGHT: fast, slightly undulating, and direct with rapid wing beats.

The Northern Parula is a small wood warbler that somewhat resembles a chickadee in its active foraging behavior. This bird depends on very specific nesting materials—*Usnea* lichens, or "Old Man's Beard," in the North, and *Tillandsia*, or Spanish moss, in the South. The presence of these parasitic plants on trees greatly limits the geographical range of this species. The Northern Parula interbreeds with the Tropical Parula in southern Texas where their ranges cross, producing hybrid birds.

VOICE Call a very sharp *tsip*; flight call a thin, weak, descending *tsiif*; song a variable, most common buzzy upslurred trill, variably continuous or in steps, ending very high, but then dropping off in an emphatic *zip*.

NESTING Hanging pouch in clump of lichens; 4–5 eggs; 1 brood; May–July (south) or April–August (north).

FEEDING Gleans for caterpillars, flies, moths, beetles, wasps, ants, and spiders; also eats berries, nectar, some seeds.

THE AMERICAN TIT

This small yellow- and chestnut-breasted bird was named by Carl Linnaeus in 1758.

SIMILAR SPECIES

COMMON YELLOWTHROAT ♀
see p.356

olive
upperparts

OCCURRENCE

Nests in almost any kind of wooded area with its preferred nesting material; migrants (some of which cross the Gulf of Mexico) occur in almost any habitat; winters in varied habitats from southern Texas and Florida across the Caribbean and Mexico south to Panama.

Length **4¼in (11cm)**	Wingspan **7in (18cm)**	Weight **¼–⅜oz (7–10g)**
Social **Winter flocks**	Lifespan **Up to 7 years**	Status **Secure**

DATE: ____________ TIME: ____________ LOCATION: ____________

Order **Passeriformes**	Family **Parulidae**	Species ***Setophaga magnolia***

Magnolia Warbler

yellow rump
gray crown
MALE (BREEDING)
broken white tail band
IN FLIGHT

greenish back
white undertail feathers
plain face with pale eye-ring
IMMATURE (FALL)

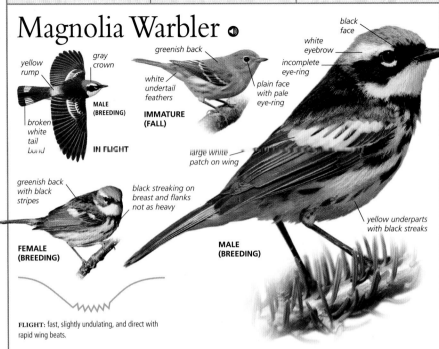

black face
white eyebrow
incomplete eye-ring
large white patch on wing
yellow underparts with black streaks
MALE (BREEDING)

greenish back with black stripes
black streaking on breast and flanks not as heavy
FEMALE (BREEDING)

FLIGHT: fast, slightly undulating, and direct with rapid wing beats.

The bold, flashy, and common Magnolia Warbler is hard to miss as it flits around at eye level, fanning its uniquely marked tail. This species nests in young forests and winters in almost any habitat, so its numbers have not suffered in recent decades, unlike some of its relatives. Although it really has no preference for its namesake plant, the 19th-century ornithologist Alexander Wilson discovered a Magnolia Warbler feeding in a magnolia tree during migration, which is how it got its name.

VOICE Call a tinny *jeinf*, not particularly warbler-like; also short, simple whistled series *wee'-sa wee'-sa WEET-a-chew*; short, distinctive flight call a high, trilled *zeep*.

NESTING Flimsy cup of black rootlets placed low in dense conifer against trunk; 3–5 eggs; 1 brood; June–August.

FEEDING Gleans mostly caterpillars, beetles, and spiders.

SPRUCE WARBLER
The conspicuous male Magnolia Warbler can be found singing its distinctive, loud song throughout the day, often in a spruce tree.

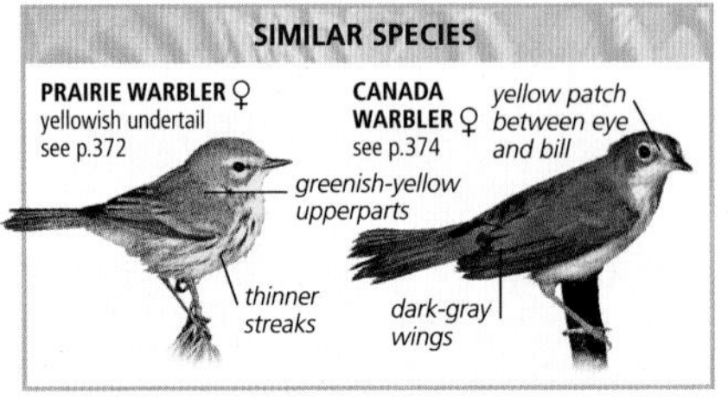
SIMILAR SPECIES
PRAIRIE WARBLER ♀
yellowish undertail
see p.372
CANADA WARBLER ♀
see p.374
yellow patch between eye and bill
greenish-yellow upperparts
thinner streaks
dark-gray wings

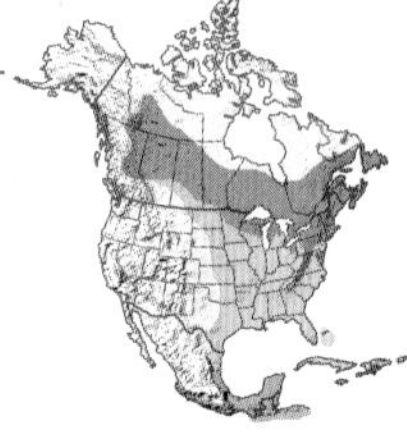

OCCURRENCE
Breeds in dense, young mixed and coniferous forests from Yukon east to Newfoundland and south into Appalachians of Tennessee; migrates across the Gulf and the Caribbean; winters in varied habitats in the Caribbean and from southeast Mexico to Panama; rare vagrant in the West.

Length **5in (13cm)**	Wingspan **7½in (19cm)**	Weight **7/32–7/16oz (6–12g)**
Social **Migrant/Winter flocks**	Lifespan **Up to 6 years**	Status **Secure**

DATE: ______________ TIME: ______________ LOCATION: ______________

Order **Passeriformes**	Family **Parulidae**	Species ***Setophaga castanea***

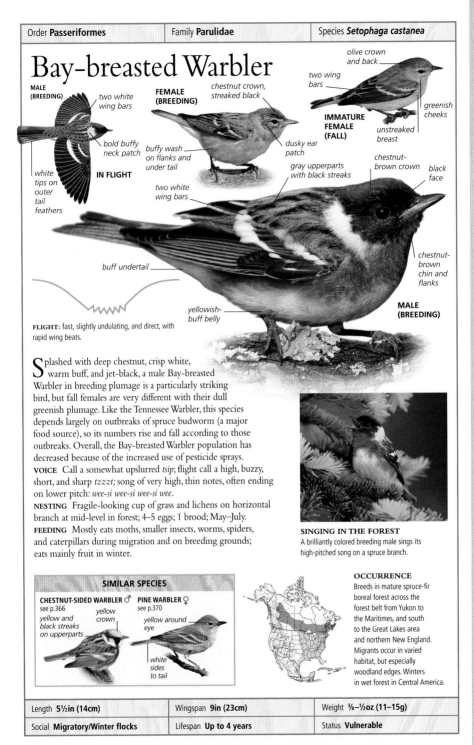

Bay-breasted Warbler

MALE (BREEDING)
two white wing bars
bold buffy neck patch
white tips on outer tail feathers
IN FLIGHT
FEMALE (BREEDING)
chestnut crown, streaked black
buffy wash on flanks and under tail
dusky ear patch
olive crown and back
two wing bars
greenish cheeks
IMMATURE FEMALE (FALL)
unstreaked breast
gray upperparts with black streaks
chestnut-brown crown
black face
two white wing bars
chestnut-brown chin and flanks
buff undertail
yellowish-buff belly
MALE (BREEDING)

FLIGHT: fast, slightly undulating, and direct, with rapid wing beats.

Splashed with deep chestnut, crisp white, warm buff, and jet-black, a male Bay-breasted Warbler in breeding plumage is a particularly striking bird, but fall females are very different with their dull greenish plumage. Like the Tennessee Warbler, this species depends largely on outbreaks of spruce budworm (a major food source), so its numbers rise and fall according to those outbreaks. Overall, the Bay-breasted Warbler population has decreased because of the increased use of pesticide sprays.

VOICE Call a somewhat upslurred *tsip*; flight call a high, buzzy, short, and sharp *tzzzt;* song of very high, thin notes, often ending on lower pitch: *wee-si wee-si wee-si wee.*

NESTING Fragile-looking cup of grass and lichens on horizontal branch at mid-level in forest; 4–5 eggs; 1 brood; May–July.

FEEDING Mostly eats moths, smaller insects, worms, spiders, and caterpillars during migration and on breeding grounds; eats mainly fruit in winter.

SINGING IN THE FOREST
A brilliantly colored breeding male sings its high-pitched song on a spruce branch.

SIMILAR SPECIES

CHESTNUT-SIDED WARBLER ♂ see p.366

PINE WARBLER ♀ see p.370

yellow and black streaks on upperparts
yellow crown
yellow around eye
white sides to tail

OCCURRENCE
Breeds in mature spruce-fir boreal forest across the forest belt from Yukon to the Maritimes, and south to the Great Lakes area and northern New England. Migrants occur in varied habitat, but especially woodland edges. Winters in wet forest in Central America.

Length **5½in (14cm)**	Wingspan **9in (23cm)**	Weight **⅜–½oz (11–15g)**
Social **Migratory/Winter flocks**	Lifespan **Up to 4 years**	Status **Vulnerable**

DATE: ____________ TIME: ____________ LOCATION: ____________

Order **Passeriformes**	Family **Parulidae**	Species ***Setophaga fusca***

Blackburnian Warbler

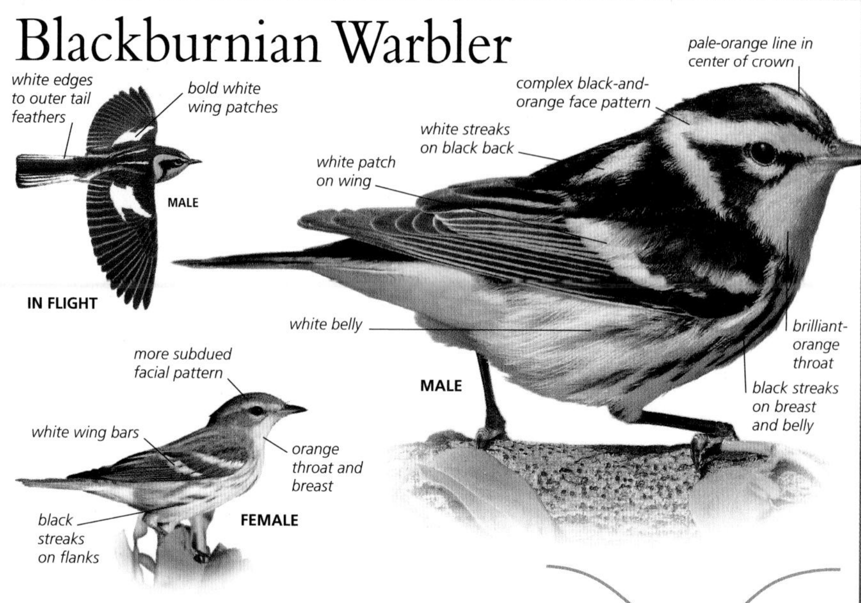
white edges
to outer tail
feathers
bold white
wing patches
MALE
IN FLIGHT
pale-orange line in
center of crown
complex black-and-
orange face pattern
white streaks
on black back
white patch
on wing
white belly
brilliant-
orange
throat
black streaks
on breast
and belly
MALE
more subdued
facial pattern
white wing bars
orange
throat and
breast
black
streaks
on flanks
FEMALE

FLIGHT: fast, slightly undulating, and direct with rapid wing beats.

This fiery beacon of the treetops is considered one of the most beautiful members of its family; its orange throat is unique among the North American warblers. The Blackburnian Warbler coexists with many other *Setophaga* warblers in the coniferous and mixed woods of the North and East, but is able to do so by exploiting a slightly different niche for foraging—in this case the treetops. It also seeks the highest trees for nesting.

VOICE Call a slightly husky *chik*; flight-call a high, thin *zzee;* song variable, but always high-pitched; swirling series of lisps, spiraling upward to end in an almost inaudible *trill.*

NESTING Fine cup in conifer on horizontal branch away from trunk, usually high in tree; 4–5 eggs; 1 brood; May–July.

FEEDING Gleans arthropods, such as spiders, worms, and beetles; also fruit.

DISTINGUISHING FEATURES
The female is like a dull adult male, but with two wing bars and no black on the face.

AVIAN FIREFLY
This male in breeding plumage glows when seen against a dark forest background.

SIMILAR SPECIES

BAY-BREASTED WARBLER (FALL) ♀ see p.363

BLACK-THROATED GREEN WARBLER ♂ see p.373

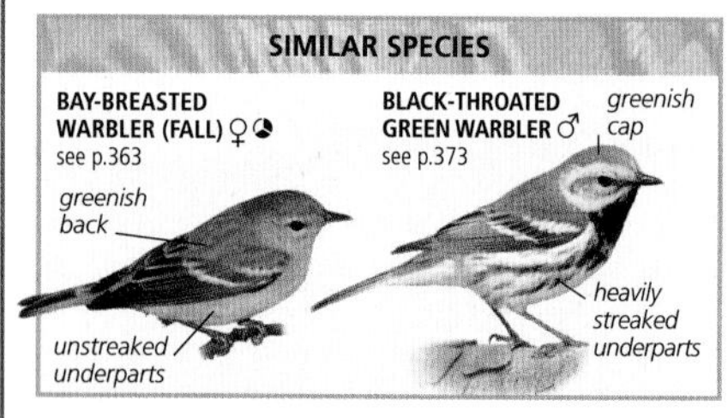
greenish
back
unstreaked
underparts
greenish
cap
heavily
streaked
underparts

OCCURRENCE
Breeds in coniferous and mixed forests from Alberta east through the North Great Lakes to Newfoundland and south into the Appalachians of Georgia; migrants found in wooded, shrubby, or forest edge habitats. Winters in wet forests in Costa Rica and Panama, and southward as far as Peru.

Length **5in (13cm)**	Wingspan **8½in (21cm)**	Weight **5/16–7/16oz (9–12g)**
Social **Winter flocks**	Lifespan **Up to 8 years**	Status **Vulnerable**

DATE: ____________ TIME: ____________ LOCATION: ____________

Order **Passeriformes**	Family **Parulidae**	Species ***Setophaga petechia***

Yellow Warbler

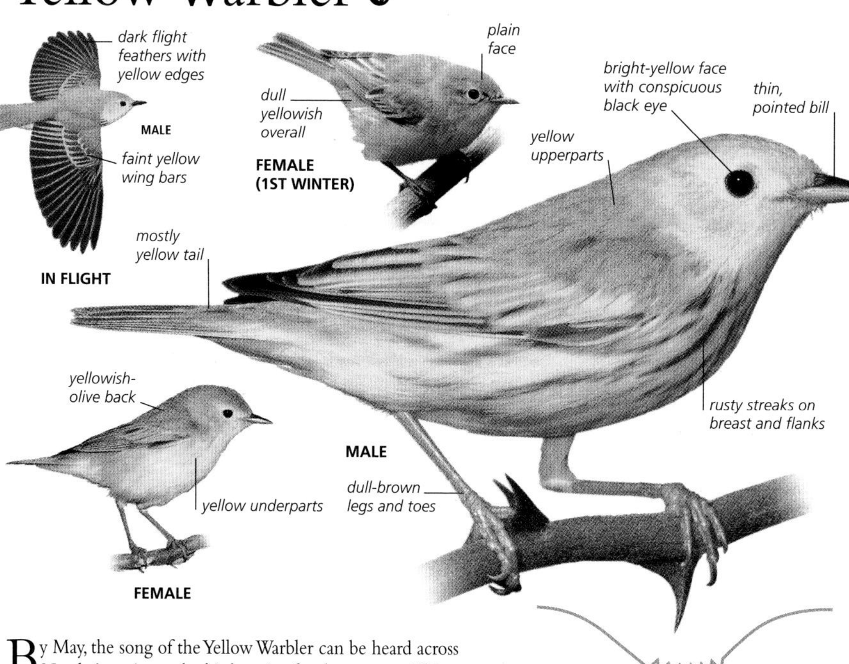
dark flight feathers with yellow edges
MALE
faint yellow wing bars
IN FLIGHT
mostly yellow tail
plain face
dull yellowish overall
FEMALE (1ST WINTER)
bright-yellow face with conspicuous black eye
thin, pointed bill
yellow upperparts
yellowish-olive back
yellow underparts
FEMALE
MALE
dull-brown legs and toes
rusty streaks on breast and flanks

By May, the song of the Yellow Warbler can be heard across North America as the birds arrive for the summer. This warbler is treated as a single species with about 35 subspecies, mostly in its tropical range (West Indies and South America). The Yellow Warbler is known to build a new nest on top of an old one when cowbird eggs appear in it, which can result in up to six different tiers. The Yellow Warbler does not walk, but rather hops from branch to branch.

VOICE Call a variable *chip*, sometimes given in series; flight call buzzy *zeep*; song variable series of fast, sweet notes; western birds often add an emphatic ending.

NESTING Deep cup of plant material, grasses in vertical fork of deciduous tree or shrub; 4–5 eggs; 1 brood; May–July.

FEEDING Eats mostly insects and insect larvae, plus some fruit.

FLIGHT: fast, slightly undulating, and direct, with rapid wing beats.

ONE OF A KIND

This species has more yellow in its plumage than any other North American wood warbler.

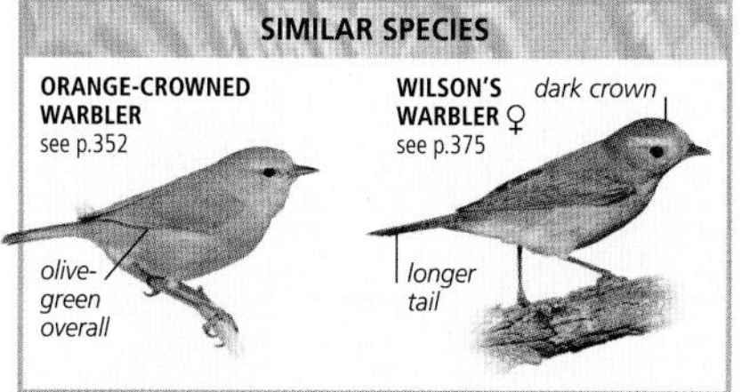
SIMILAR SPECIES
ORANGE-CROWNED WARBLER
see p.352
olive-green overall
WILSON'S WARBLER ♀
see p.375
dark crown
longer tail

OCCURRENCE

Widespread in most shrubby and second-growth habitats of North America. Migrates to the southern US and southward to Mexico, Central America, and South America. Resident populations live in Florida and the West Indies.

Length **5in (13cm)**	Wingspan **8in (20cm)**	Weight **$^9/_{32}$–½oz (8–14g)**
Social **Flocks**	Lifespan **Up to 9 years**	Status **Secure**

DATE: ____________ TIME: ____________ LOCATION: ____________

Order **Passeriformes**	Family **Parulidae**	Species ***Setophaga pensylvanica***

Chestnut-sided Warbler

MALE (BREEDING)
two yellow wing bars
IN FLIGHT
white outer tail feathers
yellow cap
black "mustache"
chestnut band along flanks
FEMALE (BREEDING)
white tail spots
yellow-and-black streaks on upperparts
conspicuous white cheeks
yellow crown
white throat
two wing bars
rich-chestnut flanks
MALE (BREEDING)
olive crown
bright lime-green above
plain face with white eye-ring
FEMALE (1ST FALL)
plain gray underside

The Chestnut-sided Warbler is one of the few wood warbler species that has benefited from deforestation, because it depends on deciduous second-growth trees and forest edges for breeding. Once a rare bird, it is more common now than it was in the early 19th century. These birds vary in appearance, immature females looking quite unlike adult males in breeding. In all plumages, yellowish wing bars and whitish belly are the most distinguishing characteristics. Its pleasant song has long been transcribed as *pleased pleased pleased to MEET'cha.*

VOICE Call a sweet *chip*; flight call a low, burry *brrrt;* song a series of fast, sweet notes, usually ending with emphatic *WEET-chew.*

NESTING Open, easy-to-find cup just off ground in small deciduous tree or shrub; 3–5 eggs; 1 brood; May–August.

FEEDING Eats insects, especially larvae; also berries and seeds.

FLIGHT: fast, slightly undulating, and direct with rapid wing beats.

MALE TERRITORY
This singing, territorial male prefers second-growth thickets as its habitat.

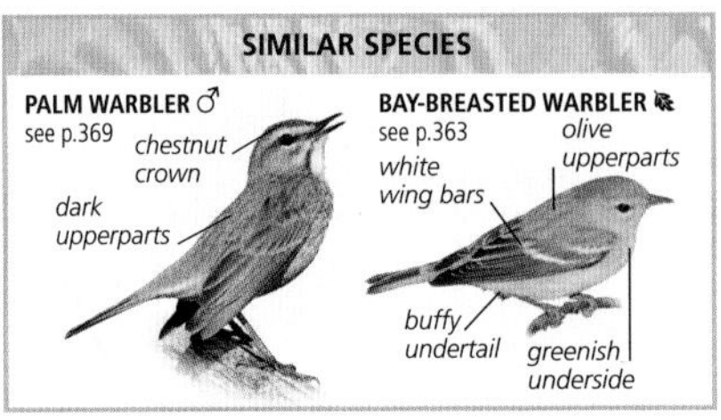
SIMILAR SPECIES
PALM WARBLER ♂
see p.369
chestnut crown
dark upperparts
BAY-BREASTED WARBLER
see p.363
white wing bars
olive upperparts
buffy undertail
greenish underside

OCCURRENCE
Breeds in successive stages of regrowth in deciduous forests, from Alberta to the Great Lakes, Nova Scotia, and the Appalachians; isolated populations in the Midwest. Winters in the Caribbean, Mexico, and Central America, south to Venezuela and northern Colombia.

Length **5in (13cm)**	Wingspan **8in (20cm)**	Weight **9/32–7/16oz (8–13g)**
Social **Winter flocks**	Lifespan **Up to 7 years**	Status **Secure**

DATE: ______________ TIME: ______________ LOCATION: ______________

Order **Passeriformes**	Family **Parulidae**	Species ***Setophaga striata***

Blackpoll Warbler

white tail spots
MALE
two white wing bars
IN FLIGHT
greenish upperparts with fine black streaks
faint, fine streaking on underparts
FEMALE (BREEDING)
black cap
white cheek
bold black streaks on gray back
greenish overall
streaking on breast
streaked underparts
MALE (FALL)
pale feet contrasting with darker legs
white undertail feathers
MALE (BREEDING)
orange legs

The Blackpoll Warbler is well known for undergoing a remarkable fall migration that takes it over the Atlantic Ocean from southern Canada and the northeastern US to northern Venezuela. Before departing, it almost doubles its body weight with fat to serve as fuel for the nonstop journey. In spring, most of these birds travel the shorter Caribbean route back north.

VOICE Call piercing *chip*; flight call high, buzzy yet sharp *tzzzt*; common song crescendo of fast, extremely high-pitched ticks, ending with a decrescendo *tsst tsst TSST TSST TSST tsst tsst;* less commonly, ticks run into even faster trill.

NESTING Well-hidden cup placed low against conifer trunk; 3–5 eggs; 1–2 broods; May–July.

FEEDING Gleans arthropods, such as worms and beetles, but will take small fruit in fall and winter.

FLIGHT: fast, slightly undulating, and direct, with rapid wing beats.

HITTING THE HIGH NOTES
The song of the male Blackpoll is so high-pitched that it is inaudible to many people.

SIMILAR SPECIES

CERULEAN WARBLER ♂ see p.360
blue upperparts
white belly

BLACK-AND-WHITE WARBLER ♂ see p.349
black cheek
distinct black-and-white stripes

OCCURRENCE
Breeds in spruce-fir forests across the northern boreal forest zone from Alaska eastward to Newfoundland, southward to coastal coniferous forests in the Maritimes and northern New England. Migrants fly over the Atlantic Ocean to landfall in the Caribbean and northern South America.

Length **5½in (14cm)**	Wingspan **9in (23cm)**	Weight **⅜–⅝oz (10–18g)**
Social **Flocks**	Lifespan **Up to 8 years**	Status **Secure**

DATE: ____________ TIME: ____________ LOCATION: ____________

Order **Passeriformes**	Family **Parulidae**	Species ***Setophaga caerulescens***

Black-throated Blue Warbler

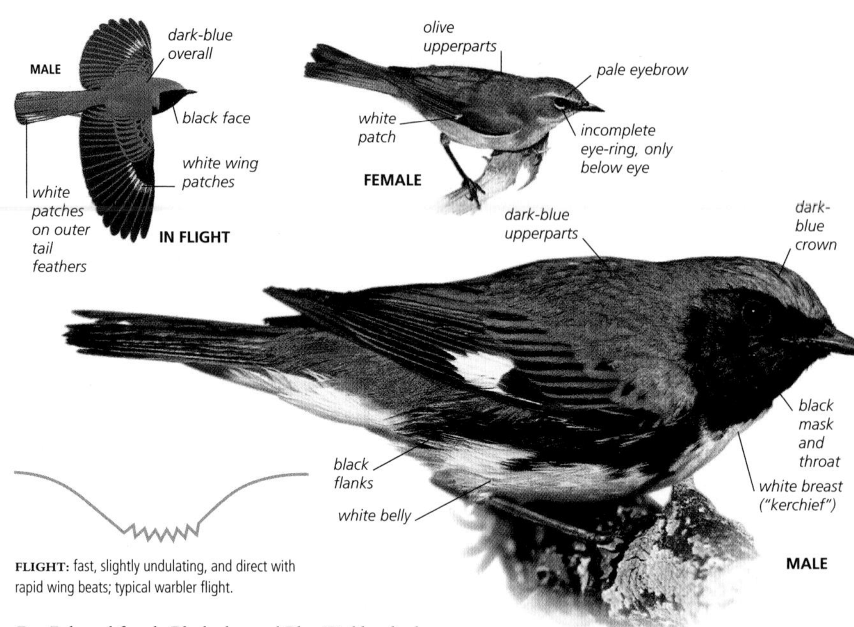
MALE
dark-blue overall
black face
white wing patches
white patches on outer tail feathers
IN FLIGHT
olive upperparts
pale eyebrow
white patch
incomplete eye-ring, only below eye
FEMALE
dark-blue upperparts
dark-blue crown
black mask and throat
white breast ("kerchief")
black flanks
white belly
MALE

FLIGHT: fast, slightly undulating, and direct with rapid wing beats; typical warbler flight.

Male and female Black-throated Blue Warblers look so dissimilar that early ornithologists thought they were different species. Many of the females have a blue wash to their wings and tail, and almost all have a subdued version of the male's white "kerchief," so identification is not difficult. This beautiful eastern North American species migrates northward in spring, along the eastern flank of the Appalachians, but a small number of birds fly, along an imaginary line, northwestward to the Great Lakes. This "line" is so clearly defined that this bird is common in Chicago but extremely rare in St. Louis.

VOICE Call a husky junco-like *tchunk*; flight call a distinctive, drawn-out, metallic *ssiiink,* reminiscent of some Northern Cardinal calls; song a relatively low-pitched series of upslurred buzzes *zu zu zo zhray zhree*, or slower *zhray zhray zhreee.*

NESTING Bulky cup of plant material a meter off ground in dense forest; 3–5 eggs; 1–2 broods; May–August.

FEEDING Gleans arthropods, mainly caterpillars, from mid-low level in forest; takes small fruit and nectar.

BLACK, WHITE, AND BLUE
Males are gorgeous year-round, especially when viewed against contrasting fall foliage.

SIMILAR SPECIES

CERULEAN WARBLER ♂
see p.360

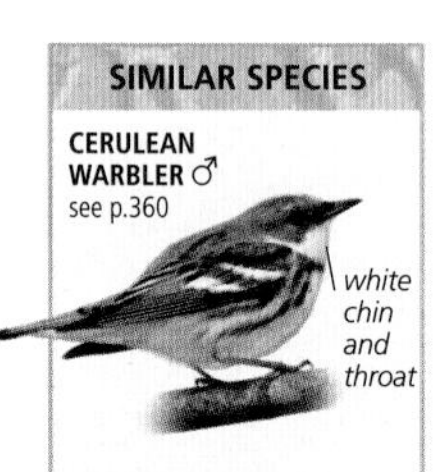
white chin and throat

OCCURRENCE
Breeds in relatively undisturbed deciduous and mixed hardwood forests from southern Ontario and northern Minnesota to Nova Scotia and into the Appalachians of Georgia. Fall migration through wooded habitats; a Caribbean migrant. Winters almost exclusively in the Antilles.

Length **5in (13cm)**	Wingspan **7½in (19cm)**	Weight **9/32–7/16oz (8–12g)**
Social **Migrant flocks**	Lifespan **Up to 10 years**	Status **Secure**

 DATE: ______________ TIME: ______________ LOCATION: ______________

Order **Passeriformes**	Family **Parulidae**	Species ***Setophaga palmarum***

Palm Warbler

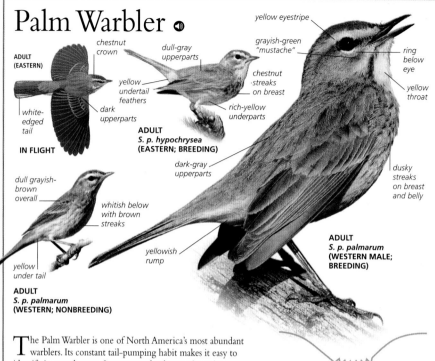

chestnut crown
white-edged tail
dark upperparts
ADULT (EASTERN)
IN FLIGHT

dull-gray upperparts
yellow undertail feathers
chestnut streaks on breast
rich-yellow underparts
ADULT *S. p. hypochrysea* (EASTERN; BREEDING)

yellow eyestripe
grayish-green "mustache"
ring below eye
yellow throat
dark-gray upperparts
dusky streaks on breast and belly
yellowish rump
ADULT *S. p. palmarum* (WESTERN MALE; BREEDING)

dull grayish-brown overall
whitish below with brown streaks
yellow under tail
ADULT *S. p. palmarum* (WESTERN; NONBREEDING)

The Palm Warbler is one of North America's most abundant warblers. Its constant tail-pumping habit makes it easy to identify in any plumage. It was named *palmarum* (meaning "palm") in 1789 because it was first recorded among palm thickets on the Caribbean island of Hispaniola. The western subspecies (*S. p. palmarum*) is found in Western and Central Canada. It is grayish-brown above and lacks the chestnut streaks of the eastern sub-species (*S. p. hypochrysea*), which has a yellower face, and breeds in southeastern Canada and northeastern US.

VOICE Call a husky *chik* or *tsip*; flight call a light *ziint*; slow, loose, buzzy trill: *zwi zwi zwi zwi zwi zwi zwi zwi*.

NESTING Cup of grasses on or near ground, often in peat moss, at base of small coniferous tree or shrub; 4–5 eggs; 1 brood; May–July.

FEEDING Eats insects, sometimes caught in flight; also takes seeds and berries.

FLIGHT: fast, slightly undulating, and direct with rapid wing beats.

SIMILAR SPECIES

BAY-BREASTED WARBLER ♀ see p.363

YELLOW-RUMPED WARBLER (MYRTLE) ♀ see p.371

dusky ear patch
streaking on back
white throat

FAR FROM THE PALMS This male Palm Warbler is far north of the coastal palms where its kin spend the winter.

OCCURRENCE
In North America, breeds in spruce bogs within the northerly forest zone, across Canada from Yukon to the Maritimes and Labrador, and in the US, from Minnesota to Maine. Often migrates through central portions of the eastern US; winters in the southeastern US, Florida, and Central America.

Length **5½in (14cm)**	Wingspan **8in (20cm)**	Weight **¼–⁷⁄₁₆oz (7–13g)**
Social **Flocks**	Lifespan **Up to 6 years**	Status **Secure**

DATE: ____________ TIME: ____________ LOCATION: ____________

Order **Passeriformes**	Family **Parulidae**	Species ***Setophaga pinus***

Pine Warbler

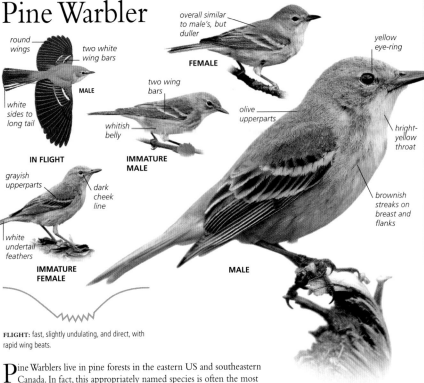

round wings
two white wing bars
white sides to long tail
MALE
IN FLIGHT

overall similar to male's, but duller
FEMALE

two wing bars
whitish belly
IMMATURE MALE

grayish upperparts
dark cheek line
white undertail feathers
IMMATURE FEMALE

yellow eye-ring
olive upperparts
bright-yellow throat
brownish streaks on breast and flanks
MALE

FLIGHT: fast, slightly undulating, and direct, with rapid wing beats.

Pine Warblers live in pine forests in the eastern US and southeastern Canada. In fact, this appropriately named species is often the most common bird in its namesake habitat, and its distinctive song can be heard from several birds at once. One of the few warblers that uses bird feeders, the Pine Warbler is a hardy bird, staying within the US throughout the winter.

VOICE Call a soft *tsip*, flight call a high, thin, slightly rolling, descending *ziit*; song a lazy, musical *trill*, variably of round or sharper notes.

NESTING Cup of grass high up, far out on horizontal branch, concealed by pine needles; 3–5 eggs; 1–2 broods; March–July.

FEEDING Gleans arthropods, especially caterpillars, from pine needles; will also eat seeds and fruit in nonbreeding season.

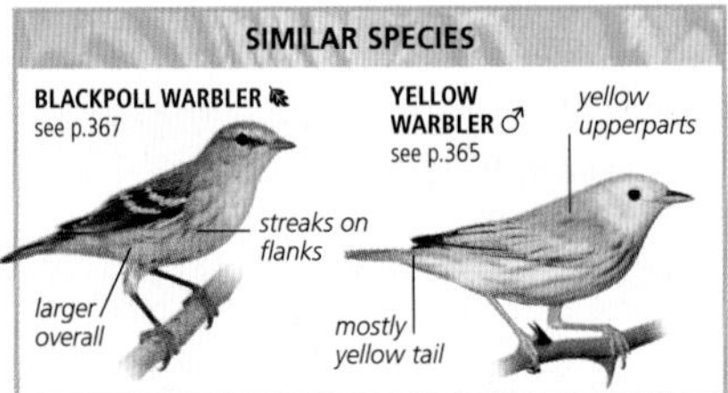
SIMILAR SPECIES
BLACKPOLL WARBLER
see p.367
streaks on flanks
larger overall
YELLOW WARBLER ♂
see p.365
yellow upperparts
mostly yellow tail

APTLY NAMED
In many areas, Pine Warblers are the most common breeding birds in mature pine woods.

OCCURRENCE
Pine and mixed forests from southern Canada and the eastern US, south to eastern Texas and Florida. Nests in deciduous forests if individual trees or small stands of pine are present. Resident in southern half of its US range. Breeds and winters in the Bahamas and in Hispaniola.

Length **5in (13cm)**	Wingspan **9in (23cm)**	Weight **5/16–1/2oz (9–15g)**
Social **Migrant/Winter flocks**	Lifespan **Up to 7 years**	Status **Secure**

DATE: ____________ TIME: ____________ LOCATION: ____________

Order **Passeriformes**	Family **Parulidae**	Species ***Setophaga coronata***

Yellow-rumped Warbler

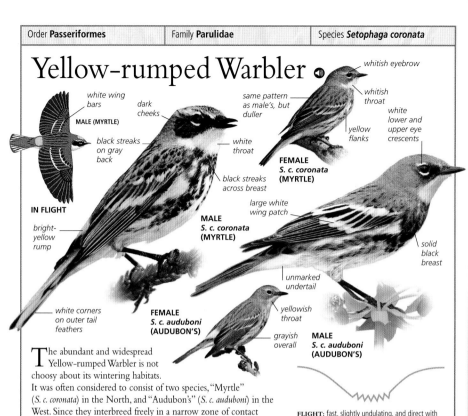

white wing bars
MALE (MYRTLE)
black streaks on gray back
IN FLIGHT
bright-yellow rump
dark cheeks
white throat
black streaks across breast
white corners on outer tail feathers
MALE
S. c. coronata
(MYRTLE)
same pattern as male's, but duller
whitish eyebrow
whitish throat
yellow flanks
FEMALE
S. c. coronata
(MYRTLE)
white lower and upper eye crescents
large white wing patch
solid black breast
unmarked undertail
MALE
S. c. auduboni
(AUDUBON'S)
yellowish throat
grayish overall
FEMALE
S. c. auduboni
(AUDUBON'S)

The abundant and widespread Yellow-rumped Warbler is not choosy about its wintering habitats. It was often considered to consist of two species, "Myrtle" (*S. c. coronata*) in the North, and "Audubon's" (*S. c. auduboni*) in the West. Since they interbreed freely in a narrow zone of contact in British Columbia and Alberta, the American Ornithological Society merged them. Recent evidence, however, suggests that they are indeed separate species so the designations may change again.

VOICE Myrtle's call a flat, husky *tchik*; Audubon's a higher-pitched, relatively musical, rising *jip*; flight call of both a clear, upslurred *sviiit*; song loose, warbled trill with an inflected ending; Myrtle's song higher and faster, Audubon's lower and slower.

NESTING Bulky cup of plant matter in conifer; 4–5 eggs; 1 brood; March–August.

FEEDING Feeds mostly on flies, beetles, wasps, and spiders during breeding; takes fruit and berries at other times of the year; often sallies to catch prey.

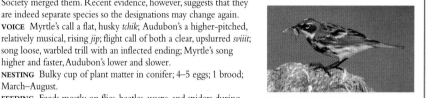

FLIGHT: fast, slightly undulating, and direct with rapid wing beats.

WIDESPREAD WARBLER
Yellow-rumped Warblers are widespread and are likely to be spotted often.

SIMILAR SPECIES

MAGNOLIA WARBLER ♂
see p.362

CAPE MAY WARBLER ♀
see p.359

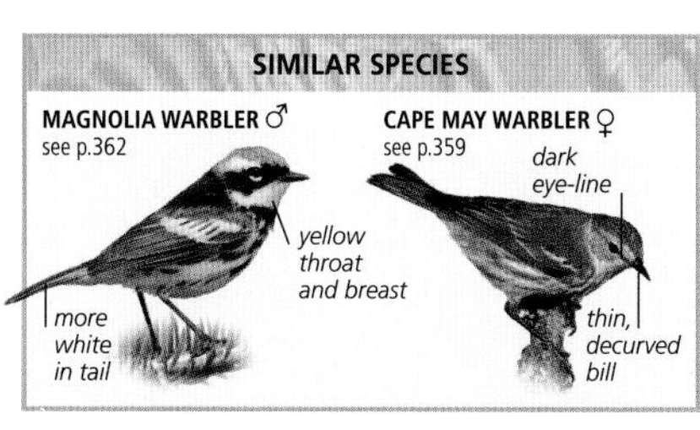
yellow throat and breast
more white in tail
dark eye-line
thin, decurved bill

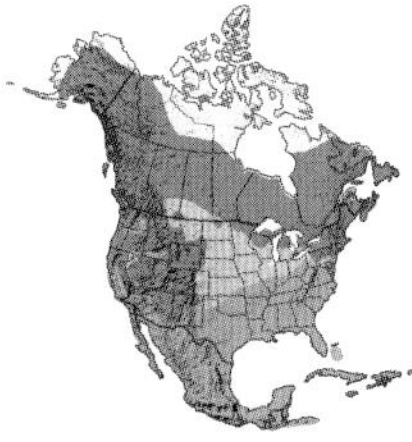

OCCURRENCE
Both northern and western populations are widespread across the continent from Alaska eastward to Quebec and Newfoundland, and westward in the mountains south to Arizona, New Mexico, and Northern Mexico. Prefers coniferous and mixed hardwood coniferous forests.

Length **5in (13cm)**	Wingspan **9in (23cm)**	Weight **3/8–5/8oz (10–17g)**
Social **Flocks**	Lifespan **Up to 7 years**	Status **Secure**

DATE: ____________ TIME: ____________ LOCATION: ____________

Order **Passeriformes**	Family **Parulidae**	Species ***Setophaga discolor***

Prairie Warbler

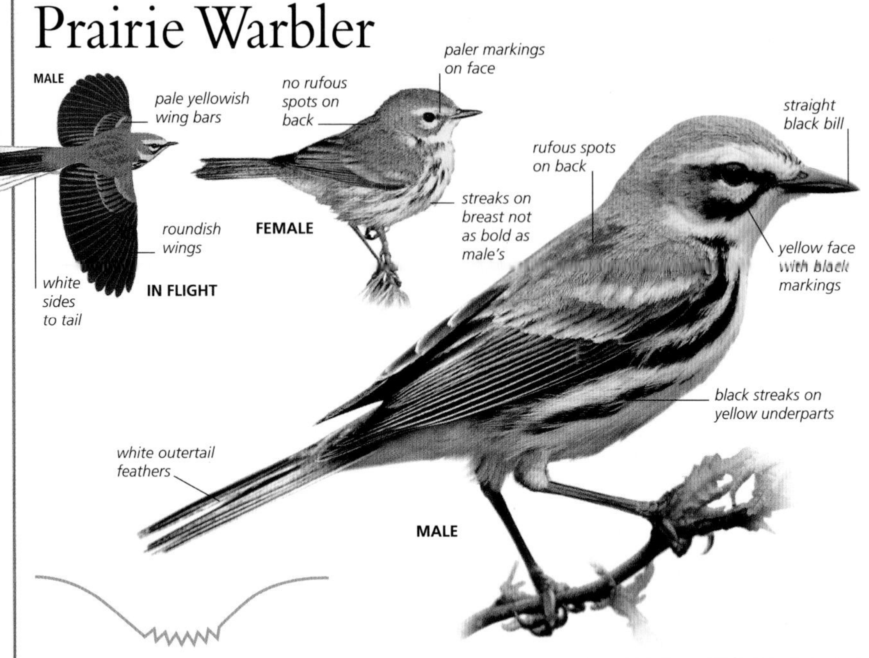
MALE
pale yellowish wing bars
roundish wings
white sides to tail
IN FLIGHT
no rufous spots on back
paler markings on face
FEMALE
streaks on breast not as bold as male's
rufous spots on back
straight black bill
yellow face with black markings
black streaks on yellow underparts
white outertail feathers
MALE

FLIGHT: fast, slightly undulating, and direct, with rapid wing beats.

Contrary to its common name, the Prairie Warbler does not live on the "prairie." Its distinctive song is a quintessential sound of scrubby areas across eastern North America. Although the population of this bird increased in the 19th century due to the widespread clearing of forests, the maturation of this habitat, along with human development, is having a negative impact on local populations.

VOICE Call a thick *tsik* or *tchip*, flight call a high, thin *sssip*; song variable in tempo, but always series of husky, buzzy notes that increase in pitch: *zzu zzu zzu zzo zzo zzo zzee zzee.*

NESTING Cup of plant material in fork of sapling or low trees, often within human reach; 3–5 eggs; 1 brood; May–July.

FEEDING Eats various insects, such as flies and crickets; also berries.

HIGH AND LOUD
Males sing from preferred elevated perches, producing their characteristic buzzy song that increases in pitch and tempo.

SIMILAR SPECIES

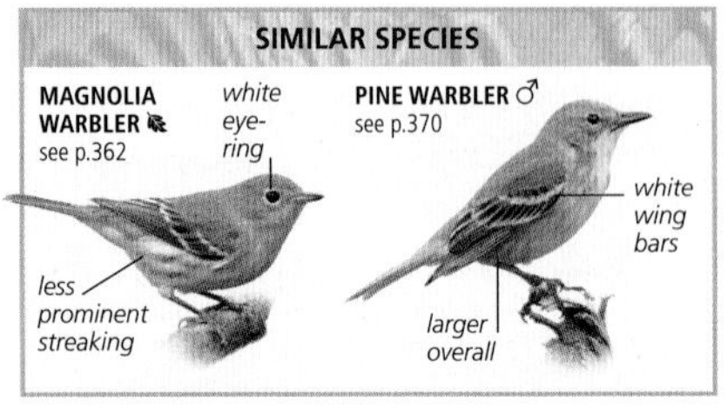
MAGNOLIA WARBLER
see p.362
white eye-ring
less prominent streaking
PINE WARBLER ♂
see p.370
white wing bars
larger overall

OCCURRENCE
Breeds in shrubby, open-canopied, second-growth habitats, and mangroves; migrant and wintering birds prefer similar brushy habitats. Breeds in parts of southern Ontario. Winters in the Bahamas, Greater and Lesser Antilles, and coasts of southern Mexico to El Salvador.

Length **4¾in (12cm)**	Wingspan **9in (23cm)**	Weight **7/32–5/16oz (6–9g)**
Social **Solitary/Winter flocks**	Lifespan **Up to 10 years**	Status **Declining**

 DATE: ______ TIME: ______ LOCATION: ______

Order **Passeriformes**	Family **Parulidae**	Species ***Setophaga virens***

Black-throated Green Warbler

olive-green back
MALE
two white wing bars
IN FLIGHT
same as male's, but duller
greenish flanks
FEMALE
greenish cap
yellow face
black bib and chin
heavily streaked underparts
white outer tail feathers
yellowish flanks
MALE

FLIGHT: fast, slightly undulating, and direct with rapid wing beats; typical warbler flight.

This species is easy to distinguish as its bright-yellow face is unique among birds inhabiting northeastern North America. It is a member of the *virens* "superspecies," a group of non-overlapping species that are similar in plumage and vocalizations—the Black-throated Green, Golden-cheeked, Townsend's, and Hermit Warblers. Sadly, this species is vulnerable to habitat loss in parts of its wintering range.

VOICE Flat *tchip* call; flight call a rising *siii*; two high-pitched, buzzy songs, fast *zee zee zee zee zoo zee*; and lower, slower *zu zee zu-zu zee*.

NESTING Cup of twigs and grasses at around 10–65ft (3–20m), on horizontal branch near trunk in the North, away from trunk in the South; 3–5 eggs; 1 brood; May–July.

FEEDING Gleans arthropods, especially caterpillars; also takes small fruit, including poison ivy berries, in nonbreeding season.

YELLOW-AND-BLACK GEM
From a high perch on a spruce tree, a male bird advertises his territory with a song.

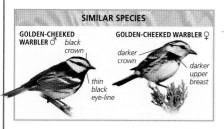

SIMILAR SPECIES

GOLDEN-CHEEKED WARBLER ♂ black crown; thin black eye-line

GOLDEN-CHEEKED WARBLER ♀ darker crown; darker upper breast

OCCURRENCE
Breeds in many forest types, especially a mix of conifers and hardwood, from British Columbia east to Newfoundland and into the southeast US along the Appalachians. Migrants and wintering birds use a variety of habitats. Winters from southern Texas to Venezuela; small numbers in Caribbean.

Length **5in (13cm)**	Wingspan **8in (20cm)**	Weight **9/32–3/8oz (8–11g)**
Social **Migrant/Winter flocks**	Lifespan **Up to 6 years**	Status **Secure**

DATE: ____________ TIME: ____________ LOCATION: ____________

Order **Passeriformes**	Family **Parulidae**	Species ***Cardellina canadensis***

Canada Warbler

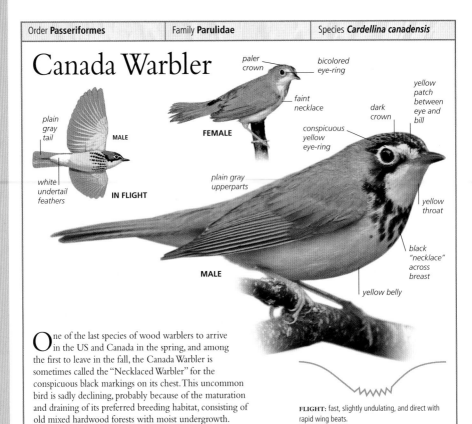

paler crown
bicolored eye-ring
faint necklace
FEMALE
plain gray tail
MALE
white undertail feathers
IN FLIGHT
yellow patch between eye and bill
dark crown
conspicuous yellow eye-ring
plain gray upperparts
yellow throat
black "necklace" across breast
yellow belly
MALE

One of the last species of wood warblers to arrive in the US and Canada in the spring, and among the first to leave in the fall, the Canada Warbler is sometimes called the "Necklaced Warbler" for the conspicuous black markings on its chest. This uncommon bird is sadly declining, probably because of the maturation and draining of its preferred breeding habitat, consisting of old mixed hardwood forests with moist undergrowth.

VOICE Call a thick *tchip;* flight call a variable, clear *plip;* song a haphazard jumble of sweet notes, often beginning with or interspersed with *tchip,* followed by a pause.

NESTING Concealed cup of leaves, in moss or grass, on or near ground; 4–5 eggs; 1 brood; May–June.

FEEDING Gleans at mid-levels for many species of insects; also catches flies and forages on ground.

FLIGHT: fast, slightly undulating, and direct with rapid wing beats.

TAKING FLIGHT
This species often waits for prey to fly by, before launching into flight to pursue it.

FAMILIAR MEAL
Flying insects, including crane flies, make up the bulk of the Canada Warbler's diet.

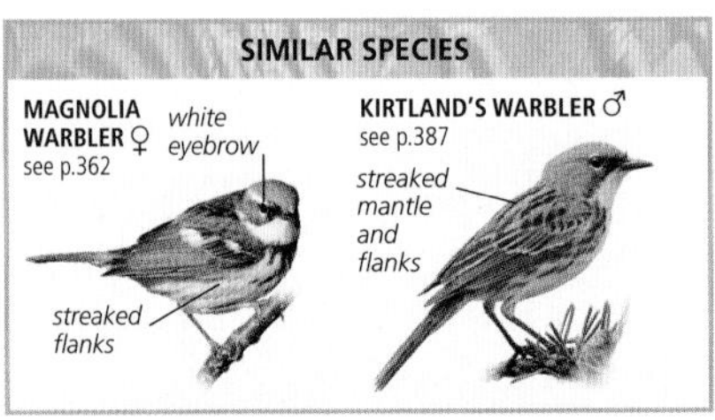
SIMILAR SPECIES
MAGNOLIA WARBLER ♀
see p.362
white eyebrow
streaked flanks
KIRTLAND'S WARBLER ♂
see p.387
streaked mantle and flanks

OCCURRENCE
Breeds in moist deciduous, mixed, and coniferous forests with well-developed understory, especially swampy woods; migrants use well-vegetated habitats; winters in dense, wet thickets and a variety of tropical woodlands in South America.

Length **5in (13cm)**	Wingspan **8in (20cm)**	Weight **$\frac{9}{32}$–$\frac{1}{2}$oz (8–15g)**
Social **Flocks**	Lifespan **Up to 8 years**	Status **Threatened**

DATE: ____________ TIME: ____________ LOCATION: ____________

Order **Passeriformes**	Family **Parulidae**	Species ***Cardellina pusilla***

Wilson's Warbler

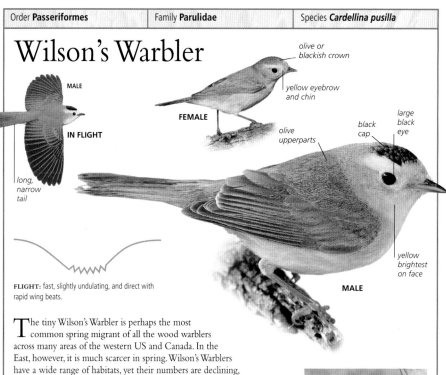

olive or blackish crown

MALE

IN FLIGHT

FEMALE

yellow eyebrow and chin

large black eye

black cap

olive upperparts

long, narrow tail

yellow brightest on face

MALE

FLIGHT: fast, slightly undulating, and direct with rapid wing beats.

The tiny Wilson's Warbler is perhaps the most common spring migrant of all the wood warblers across many areas of the western US and Canada. In the East, however, it is much scarcer in spring. Wilson's Warblers have a wide range of habitats, yet their numbers are declining, especially in the West, as its riverside breeding habitats are gradually being destroyed by development. This species is named after the renowned early 19th-century ornithologist, Alexander Wilson.

VOICE Call a rich *chimp* or *champ;* flight call a sharp, liquid *tsik;* song a variable, chattering trill, often increases in speed *che che che che chi-chi-chi-chit.*

NESTING Cup of leaves and grass placed on or near ground in mosses or grass, higher along the Pacific Coast; 4–6 eggs; 1 brood; April–June.

FEEDING Captures insects in foliage, leaf litter, or during flight; also takes berries and honeydew.

BRIGHT WESTERN BIRD
In its western range, male Wilson's Warblers have a glowing yellow-orange face; eastern birds are duller.

EASY IDENTIFICATION
The black cap and yellow face of the otherwise olive-colored Wilson's Warbler are good field markers.

SIMILAR SPECIES

YELLOW WARBLER ♀ see p.365
yellow edges to wing feathers
shorter tail
yellow overall

HOODED WARBLER ♀ see p.357
larger bill
larger body

OCCURRENCE
Breeds in wet shrubby thickets with no canopy, often along streams and lakes; Pacific slope birds use more varied habitats, including moist forests. Widespread in forests south of tundra, from Newfoundland to northern New England, west to Alaska and south through the western US to California and New Mexico down into Mexico.

Length **4¾in (12cm)**	Wingspan **7in (17.5cm)**	Weight **7/32–5/16oz (6–9g)**
Social **Flocks**	Lifespan **Up to 6 years**	Status **Declining**

DATE: ________ TIME: ________ LOCATION: ________

CARDINALS AND RELATIVES

BIRDS BELONGING to the Cardinalidae family are visually stunning, noisy birds. Some tanagers (those in the genus *Piranga*) and grosbeaks and buntings (those in the genus *Passerina*) are grouped together with the Northern Cardinal and Pyrrhuloxia in this family. Tanagers are slender-bodied, cone-billed, finch-like birds that feed on insects, such as wasps and bees, and fruits in high foliage. Males are brightly colored, while the females are duller and greener. They have similar songs but more distinctive calls.

CARDINALS

Cardinals are striking birds: the Northern Cardinal is almost entirely red, while the Pyrrhuloxia of the southwestern states is gray with vivid-red patches. Both species have pointed, upstanding crests. Females are grayer, but still have the crest. Their bills are stout but short, adapted to feed on tough fruits, berries, and seeds.

GROSBEAKS AND BUNTINGS

Grosbeaks in the genus *Pheucticus* are stocky, heavily built, sluggish species, with characteristically heavy, deeply triangular bills for splitting and peeling seeds. Again, males are bright and boldly colored, while females are duller but distinctively patterned. The colorful buntings in this family (with a preponderance of blues in their plumage) are similar to the grosbeaks, but more lightly built and with more delicate, triangular bills.

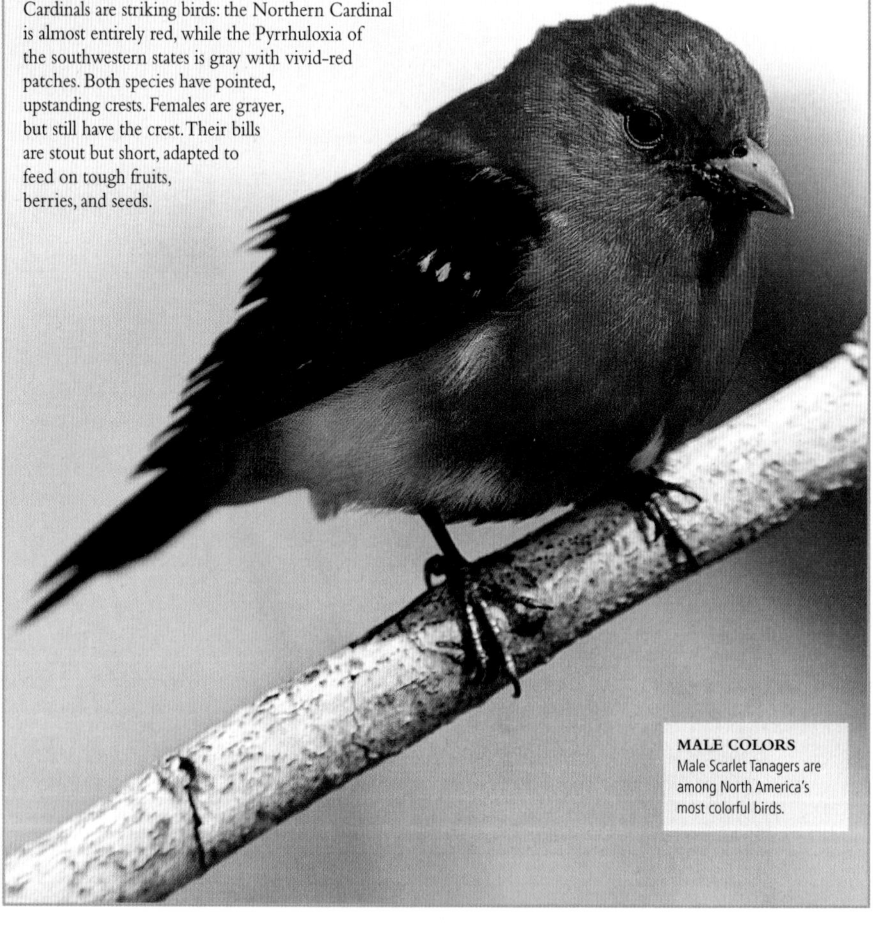

MALE COLORS
Male Scarlet Tanagers are among North America's most colorful birds.

Order **Passeriformes**	Family **Cardinalidae**	Species ***Piranga olivacea***

Scarlet Tanager

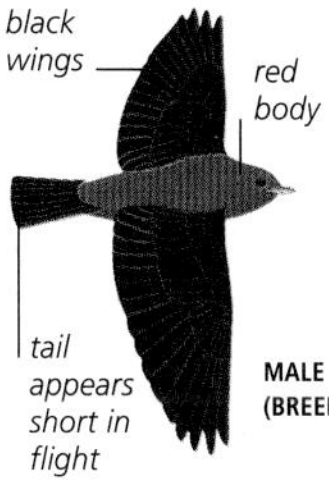

black wings
red body
tail appears short in flight
MALE (BREEDING)
IN FLIGHT

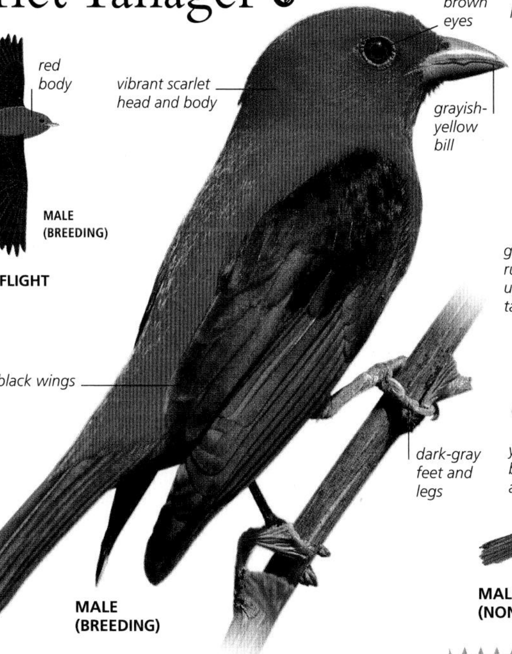

vibrant scarlet head and body
dark-brown eyes
grayish-yellow bill
black wings
black tail
dark-gray feet and legs
MALE (BREEDING)

yellow patches in red plumage
MALE (MOLTING)

greenish rump and upper tail
overall greenish upperparts
FEMALE

yellow-green body, head, and rump
MALE (NONBREEDING)

Although the male Scarlet Tanager in its breeding plumage is one of the brightest and most easily identified North American birds, its secretive nature and preference for the canopies of well-shaded oak woodlands make it difficult to spot. The male is most easily located by its distinctive and easily recognizable song. Male Scarlet Tanagers can vary in appearance—some are orange, not scarlet, and others have a faint reddish wing bar.

VOICE Call a hoarse, drawn out *CHIK-breeer*, often shortened to *CHIK*; flight call an upslurred, whistled *pwee*; song a burry, slurred *querit-queer-query-querit-queer*.

NESTING Loosely woven cup of grass, lined with fine material, high up in tree; 3–5 eggs; 1 brood; May–July.

FEEDING Gleans insects, larvae, fruit, buds, and berries.

FLIGHT: strong and direct; rapid wing beats.

STUNNING MALE
Taking a bath away from the treetops, a male Scarlet Tanager can be seen in all its glory.

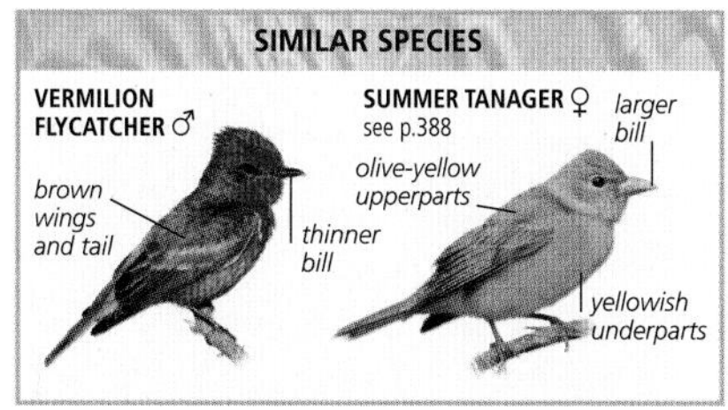
SIMILAR SPECIES
VERMILION FLYCATCHER ♂
brown wings and tail
thinner bill
SUMMER TANAGER ♀
see p.388
larger bill
olive-yellow upperparts
yellowish underparts

OCCURRENCE
Breeds in mature deciduous and mixed forests (especially with large oaks) from southern Manitoba and eastern Oklahoma east to the Maritime Provinces and the Carolinas. Trans-Gulf migrant. Winters in varied habitats along the eastern slope of the Andes from eastern Panama to Bolivia.

Length **7in (18cm)**	Wingspan **11½in (29cm)**	Weight **$^{11}/_{16}$–1¼oz (20–35g)**
Social **Solitary/Small flocks**	Lifespan **At least 10 years**	Status **Secure**

DATE: ____________ TIME: ____________ LOCATION: ____________

Order **Passeriformes**	Family **Cardinalidae**	Species ***Cardinalis cardinalis***

Northern Cardinal

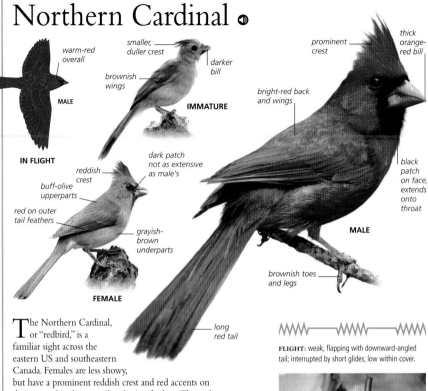

warm-red overall
MALE
IN FLIGHT
smaller, duller crest
darker bill
brownish wings
IMMATURE
prominent crest
thick orange-red bill
bright-red back and wings
dark patch not as extensive as male's
reddish crest
buff-olive upperparts
red on outer tail feathers
grayish-brown underparts
FEMALE
black patch on face, extends onto throat
MALE
brownish toes and legs
long red tail

The Northern Cardinal, or "redbird," is a familiar sight across the eastern US and southeastern Canada. Females are less showy, but have a prominent reddish crest and red accents on their tan-colored outer tail and wing feathers. The male aggressively repels intruders and will occasionally attack his own reflection in windows and various shiny surfaces.

VOICE Sharp, metallic *tik* call, also bubbly chatters; song a loud, variable, sweet, slurred whistle, *tsee-ew-tsee-ew-whoit-whoit-whoit-whoit-whoit.*

NESTING Loose, flimsy cup of grass, bark, and leaves, in deciduous thicket; 2–4 eggs; 1–3 broods; April–September.

FEEDING Eats seeds and insects, such as beetles and caterpillars; also buds and fruit.

FLIGHT: weak, flapping with downward-angled tail; interrupted by short glides; low within cover.

CONSPICUOUS COLOR
This Northern Cardinal's vivid plumage means that it is often easy to spot on snowy winter days.

SIMILAR SPECIES

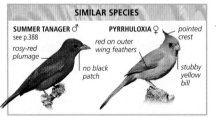

SUMMER TANAGER ♂
see p.388
rosy-red plumage
no black patch

PYRRHULOXIA ♀
pointed crest
red on outer wing feathers
stubby yellow bill

OCCURRENCE
Resident in thickets of various relatively moist habitats, such as deciduous woodland, scrub, desert washes, and backyards. Range spans across the eastern US, southernmost Canada, the extreme Southwest, and south into Mexico, northern Guatemala, and northern Belize.

Length **8½in (22cm)**	Wingspan **12in (30cm)**	Weight **1 7/16–1 3/4oz (40–50g)**
Social **Solitary**	Lifespan **Up to 16 years**	Status **Secure**

 DATE: ________ TIME: ________ LOCATION: ________

Order **Passeriformes**	Family **Cardinalidae**	Species ***Pheucticus ludovicianus***

Rose-breasted Grosbeak

black head and back
bold white wing patches
massive bill
rose-red breast
white belly
MALE (BREEDING)

white rump
MALE (BREEDING)
IN FLIGHT
short tail with white corners

rosy or orange breast
MALE (1ST FALL)

white marks on head
large pinkish bill
white wing bars
thick streaks on underparts
FEMALE

brown patches on back
streaked underparts
MALE (NONBREEDING)

For many birdwatchers in the East, the appearance of a flock of dazzling male Rose-breasted Grosbeaks in early May signals the peak of spring songbird migration. Adult males in their tuxedo attire, with rose-red ties, are unmistakable, but females and immature males are more somber. In the fall, immature male Rose-breasted Grosbeaks often have orange breasts, and are commonly mistaken for female Black-headed Grosbeaks. The difference is in the pink wing lining usually visible on perched birds, pink bill, and streaking across the center of the breast.

VOICE Call a high, sharp, explosive *sink or eeuk*, reminiscent of the squeak of sneakers on floor tiles, flight call an airy *vreee*; song a liquid, flute-like warble, rather slow in delivery, almost relaxed.

NESTING Loose, open cup or platform, usually in deciduous saplings, at mid to high level; 2–5 eggs; 1–2 broods; May–July.

FEEDING Eats arthropods, fruit, seeds, and buds.

FLIGHT: undulating but powerful flight with bursts of wing beats.

SIMILAR SPECIES
PURPLE FINCH ♀
see p.300
much smaller
smaller, dark bill
thick lateral throat stripe
BLACK-HEADED GROSBEAK ♀
tawny breast
pencil-thin streaks on underparts

STUNNING MALE
A striking male Rose-breasted Grosbeak in springtime is quite unmistakable on a tree.

OCCURRENCE
Breeds in deciduous and mixed woods, parks, and orchards across the northeastern quarter of the US, and across Canada westward from Newfoundland through Ontario to southeast Yukon. Winters from Mexico and the Caribbean, south to Guyana and Peru. Rare in the West.

Length **8in (20cm)**	Wingspan **12½in (32cm)**	Weight **1¼–2oz (35–55g)**
Social **Solitary/Small flocks**	Lifespan **Up to 13 years**	Status **Secure**

DATE: ____________ TIME: ____________ LOCATION: ____________________

Order **Passeriformes**	Family **Cardinalidae**	Species ***Passerina cyanea***

Indigo Bunting

blue overall; often appears black in flight
MALE (BREEDING)
IN FLIGHT
intermediate between male and female plumage
MALE (1ST SPRING)
darker head
indigo face
bright cyan-blue body
MALE (BREEDING)
dull brown overall
small bill
whitish throat
blurry streaks on breast
bluish cast to wings and tail
FEMALE

Few North American birds are more brilliantly colored than the Indigo Bunting. However, it is not particularly well named, because the bird is really not indigo but rather a vibrant, almost cyan-blue. The color only turns to indigo on the male's head before finally becoming a rich violet on the face. Indigo Buntings are specialists of disturbed habitats, originally depending on tree-falls within forests and the grassland-forest edge. Human activity, however, has radically increased suitable breeding habitats. As a result, Indigo Buntings are much more common and widespread than they were a hundred years ago. This adaptable species has even learned to nest in cornfields.

FLIGHT: slightly undulating, fast, and direct; gliding and fluttering in territorial encounters.

VOICE Call a sharp, dry, rattling *pik*!; flight call a long buzz; song a series of simple, high-pitched, paired whistles, often described as "*fire!-fire!*, *where?-where?*, *there!-there!*, *put-it-out!*, *put-it-out!*"

NESTING Open cup above ground in dense tangle or shrub; 3–4 eggs; 1–3 broods; May–September.

FEEDING Eats seeds, insects, fruit, and buds.

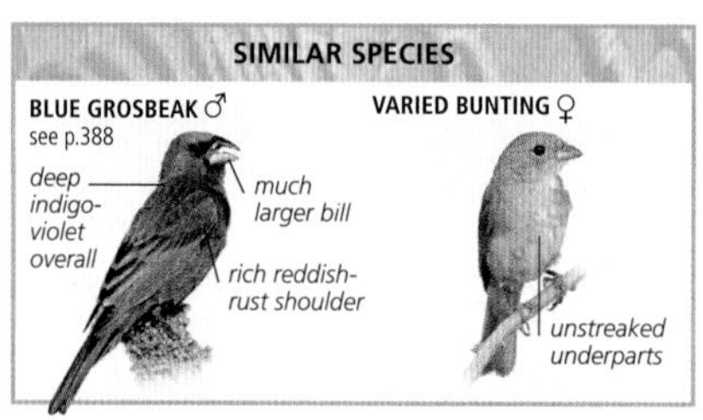
SIMILAR SPECIES
BLUE GROSBEAK ♂
see p.388
deep indigo-violet overall
much larger bill
rich reddish-rust shoulder
VARIED BUNTING ♀
unstreaked underparts

SOUND OF SUMMER
This is one of the most common and cheerful songbirds found in eastern North America.

OCCURRENCE
Breeds in moist disturbed habitats—weedy fields, forest edges, and areas of heavy cultivation across the eastern US, southeastern Canada, and also locally in the Southwest. Winters from Mexico and the Caribbean south to Panama, and in small numbers along the Gulf Coast and in Florida.

Length **5½in (14cm)**	Wingspan **8in (20cm)**	Weight **7/16–11/16oz (12–19g)**
Social **Large flocks**	Lifespan **Up to 11 years**	Status **Secure**

DATE: ____________ TIME: ____________ LOCATION: ____________________

Order **Passeriformes**	Family **Cardinalidae**	Species ***Spiza americana***

Dickcissel

streaked back

MALE (BREEDING)

IN FLIGHT

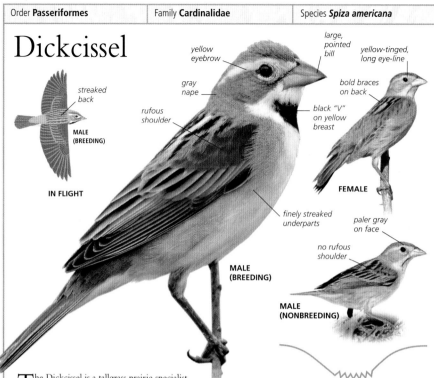

yellow eyebrow

gray nape

rufous shoulder

large, pointed bill

black "V" on yellow breast

finely streaked underparts

MALE (BREEDING)

yellow-tinged, long eye-line

bold braces on back

FEMALE

paler gray on face

no rufous shoulder

MALE (NONBREEDING)

The Dickcissel is a tallgrass prairie specialist and seldom breeds outside this core range. Known for its dramatic seasonal movements, the Dickcissel winters in Venezuela, with flocks in tens of thousands ravaging rice fields and damaging seed crops. Immature birds, without yellow-and-rusty plumage, are very similar to female House Sparrows—vagrant and wintering Dickcissels in North America are often mistaken for sparrows.

VOICE Call a flat *chik*; flight call a distinctive, low, electric buzz *frrrrrrt*; song a short series of sharp, insect-like stutters followed by few longer chirps or trill *dick-dick-dick-SISS-SISS-suhl*.

NESTING Bulky cup placed near ground in dense vegetation; 3–6 eggs; 1–2 broods; May–August.

FEEDING Forages on ground for insects, spiders, and seeds.

FLIGHT: strong, direct, and slightly undulating; flocks in tight balls.

UNIQUE SONG

The Dickcissel's onomatopoetic song is the classic sound of a healthy tallgrass prairie.

SIMILAR SPECIES

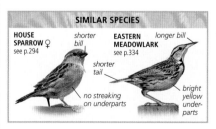

HOUSE SPARROW ♀ see p.294

shorter bill

no streaking on underparts

EASTERN MEADOWLARK see p.334

longer bill

shorter tail

bright yellow underparts

OCCURRENCE

Breeds in tallgrass prairie, grassland, hayfields, unmown roadsides, and untilled cropfields across the east-central US. Barely reaches southernmost Canada and northeast Mexico. Winters in huge flocks in Venezuela, in open areas with tallgrass-like vegetation, including rice fields.

Length **6½in (16cm)**	Wingspan **9½in (24cm)**	Weight **⅞–1¼oz (25–35g)**
Social **Large flocks**	Lifespan **Up to 5 years**	Status **Secure**

DATE: ____________ TIME: ____________ LOCATION: ____________

RARE SPECIES

Family **Anatidae**	Species ***Spatula querquedula***

Garganey

The Garganey is a small dabbling duck, the same size and shape as the Blue-winged Teal. A male in breeding plumage is unmistakable, its bold white eyebrow contrasting sharply with its dark brown head. In flight, it has a silver-gray forewing with a broad white trailing edge.

OCCURRENCE Native to Eurasia, records span North America; prefers wetland habitats with emergent vegetation.

VOICE Male a low, dry rattling *knerek* or *kerrek* call; female a high-pitched quack.

bold white eyebrow extends to nape
gray sides contrast with brown breast
MALE

Length **14½–16in (37–41cm)**	Wingspan **23½–25in (60–64cm)**

Family **Columbidae**	Species ***Zenaida asiatica***

White-winged Dove

This large gray-colored dove is best identified in flight by the conspicuous white bands on its wings. Perched birds display bright-blue skin around orange eyes and longish square tails with white tips. This species has been expanding its population northwards into Canada in recent decades.

OCCURRENCE Breeds and winters in dense, thorny woodlands, deserts, orchards, and residential areas. It is now expanding north into Canada.

VOICE Distinctive, drawn-out cooing: *who-cooks-for-you*; also makes five-note variation from the nest: *la-coo-kla-coo-kla.*

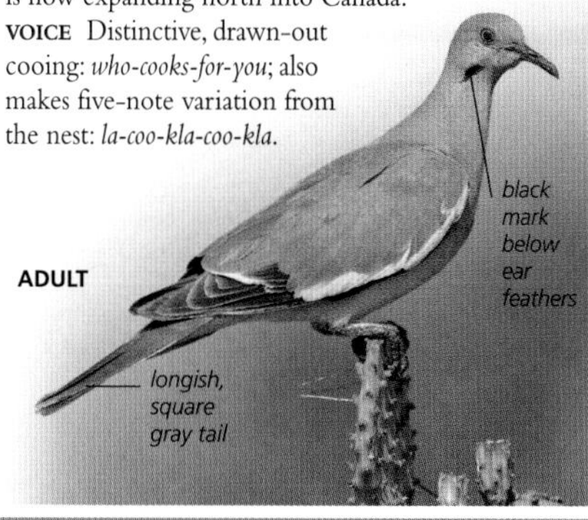
ADULT
black mark below ear feathers
longish, square gray tail

Length **11½in (29cm)**	Wingspan **19in (48cm)**

Family **Caprimulgidae**	Species ***Antrostomus carolinensis***

Chuck-will's-widow

The largest North American nightjar, the Chuck-will's-widow is also one of the least known. This species is very tolerant of human development and nests in suburban and urban areas. It often feeds by flying continuously and catching its prey in the air. It hunts mostly at dawn and dusk but also during a full moon.

OCCURRENCE Breeds in mixed forests and in open fields. Found mainly in the eastern US; sometimes seen in Ontario and the Maritimes. Winters in Florida, Mexico, and in northern Central America.

VOICE Whistled *chuck-will's-wid-ow*; begins softly, then increases in volume with emphasis on the two middle syllables.

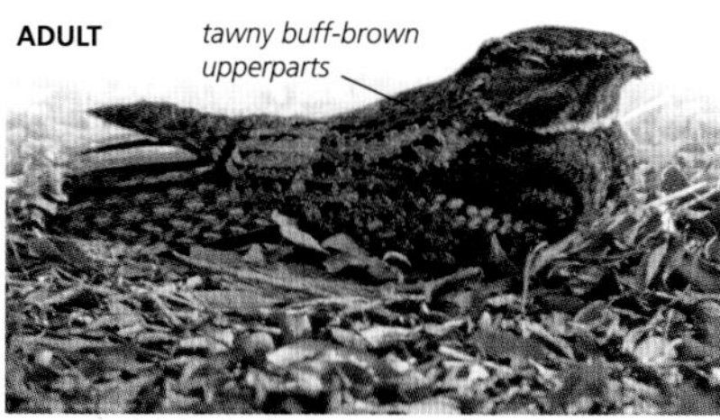
ADULT
tawny buff-brown upperparts

Length **11–12½in (28–32cm)**	Wingspan **25–28in (63–70cm)**

Family **Rallidae**	Species ***Porphyrio martinicus***

Purple Gallinule

The Purple Gallinule is conspicuous due to its vibrant coloring. Well known for long-distance vagrancy, far outside its normal breeding range, it has been found in Labrador, Switzerland, and South Africa.

OCCURRENCE Breeds and winters in freshwater marshes in the southeastern US; occasionally shows up in southern Ontario east to the Maritimes.

VOICE Call a chicken-like clucking; also grunts and higher-pitched single notes.

ADULT (BREEDING)
dark-blue breast and belly

Length **13in (33cm)**	Wingspan **22in (56cm)**

Family **Charadriidae** | Species ***Charadrius wilsonia***

Wilson's Plover

Wilson's Plover is the largest of the North American *Charadrius* species. Its distinctive habit of running horizontally, low to the ground, is a familiar sight on beaches. Wilson's Plover was listed as a species of "high concern" in 2000.

OCCURRENCE Found primarily in coastal habitats (beaches and sand dunes), mostly in the southeast, but sometimes up into Nova Scotia.

VOICE Flight call a short *pip*, or *pi dlit*; alarm calls include slurred whistle *tweet*, and short whistled *peet*.

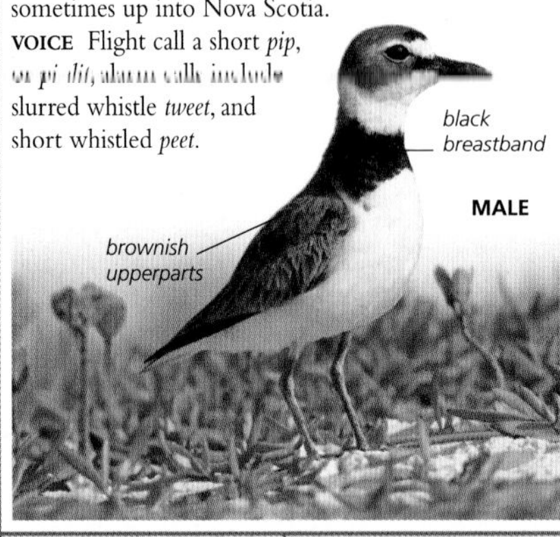
black breastband
MALE
brownish upperparts

Length **6½–8in (16–20cm)** | Wingspan **15½–19½in (39–49cm)**

Family **Scolopacidae** | Species ***Calidris pugnax***

Ruff

The Ruff is well known for the elaborately colored head ruffs and tufts of breeding male birds. Males are 20 percent larger than the females (known as Reeves), which are more muted in appearance.

OCCURRENCE Rare migrant along the Pacific Coast, occasional in St. Lawrence River and the Great Lakes.

VOICE Mostly silent; occasionally gives a soft *krruk*.

short, slightly drooped bill

JUVENILE (FALL)

Length **8–12in (20–30cm)** | Wingspan **19–23in (48–58cm)**

Family **Stercorariidae** | Species ***Stercorarius skua***

Great Skua

Similar to the South Polar Skua, this large and aggressive predator and scavenger can be differentiated by its heavier streaking and more reddish tones to its brown body. The Great Skua is closely related to several species of Southern Hemisphere skuas including the South Polar Skua.

OCCURRENCE Rare visitor, mostly in fall through spring, to pelagic waters off the Atlantic Coast of North America.

VOICE Rough, cackling *rah-rah-rah*.

dark nape
hooked dark bill
mottled-gray to warm brown plumage
ADULT

Length **19½–23in (50–58cm)** | Wingspan **4–4½ft (1.2–1.4m)**

Family **Stercorariidae** | Species ***Stercorarius maccormicki***

South Polar Skua

The South Polar Skua is a large, aggressive relative of the jaegers. Away from its breeding areas in the South Shetland Islands and along the coast and islands of the Antarctic, it is a daunting presence on the ocean. It lurks menacingly on the water when not badgering other seabirds for food, or battling for scraps behind fishing boats.

OCCURRENCE A scarce visitor to seas on the East and West Coasts; most numerous in spring and fall in the Pacific, and in spring in the Atlantic far offshore.

VOICE Deep gull-like burbling; generally silent at sea in North America.

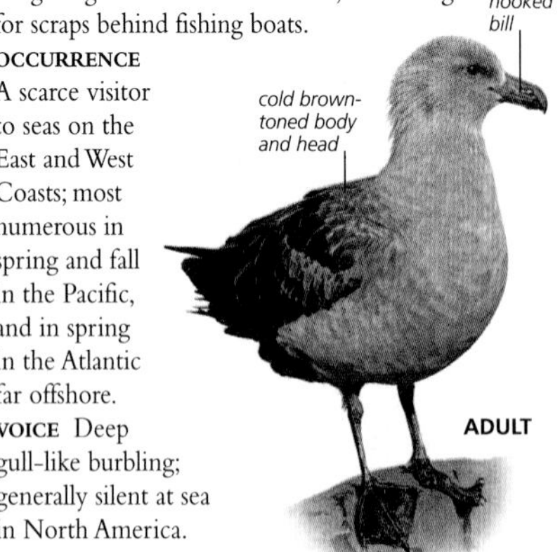
hooked bill
cold brown-toned body and head
ADULT

Length **21in (53cm)** | Wingspan **4¼ft (1.3m)**

Family **Laridae**	Species ***Pagophila eburnea***

Ivory Gull

The Ivory Gull, all-white with black legs, is unlikely to be confused with any other gull. Adults are pure white in summer and winter. Juveniles are patterned to varying degrees, with black spots on the tips of their flight feathers, including the tail and wing outer feathers; they also have a smudgy black face.

OCCURRENCE High-Arctic breeder; rarely strays far south of the pack ice, even in winter; casual in winter to British Columbia and the Maritime Provinces; accidental elsewhere.

VOICE Tern-like, harsh *keeuur*; rarely heard away from breeding grounds.

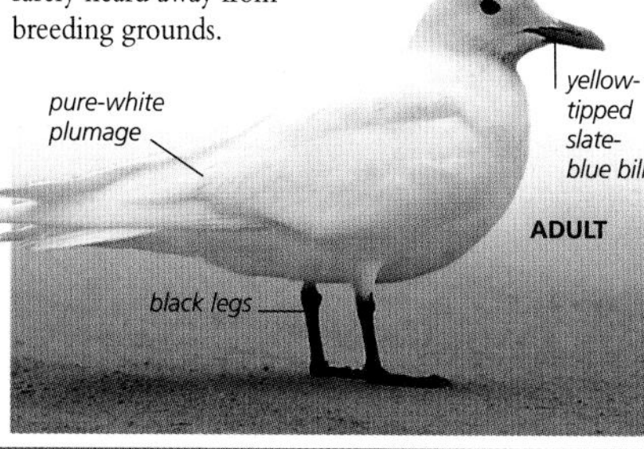
pure-white plumage
yellow-tipped slate-blue bill
ADULT
black legs

Length **15½–17in (40–43cm)**	Wingspan **3½–4ft (1.1–1.2m)**

Family **Laridae**	Species ***Rhodostethia rosea***

Ross's Gull

In adult breeding plumage, this small, delicate gull is unmistakable. Dove-gray upperparts, pale-pink underparts, red legs, and a black collar make it an elegant and beautiful-looking bird.

OCCURRENCE Siberian breeder found only along the Alaskan north coast in fall; expanded as a breeding bird into Arctic Canada; winter strays found across Canada and to the northeast and northwest US.

VOICE Rarely heard in winter; tern-like *kik-kik-kik*.

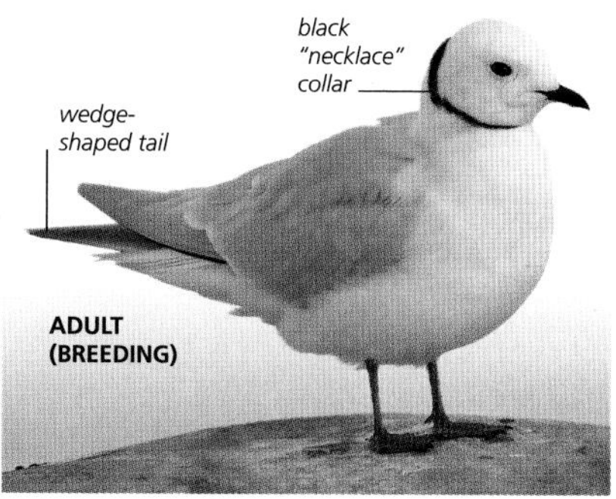
black "necklace" collar
wedge-shaped tail
ADULT (BREEDING)

Length **11½–12in (29–31cm)**	Wingspan **35–39in (90–100cm)**

Family **Laridae**	Species ***Larus schistisagus***

Slaty-backed Gull

This rare visitor from eastern Russia and Japan is most likely to be confused with the Western Gull. Adults have a series of white spots on the outer wing feather tips, referred to as "a string of pearls." Winter adults have heavily streaked heads with white linings to their underwings that contrast with the gray outer and inner wing feathers.

OCCURRENCE Occurs occasionally in northern and southwestern British Columbia; accidental in winter across Canada and the US.

VOICE Slow *aah-aah-aah*.

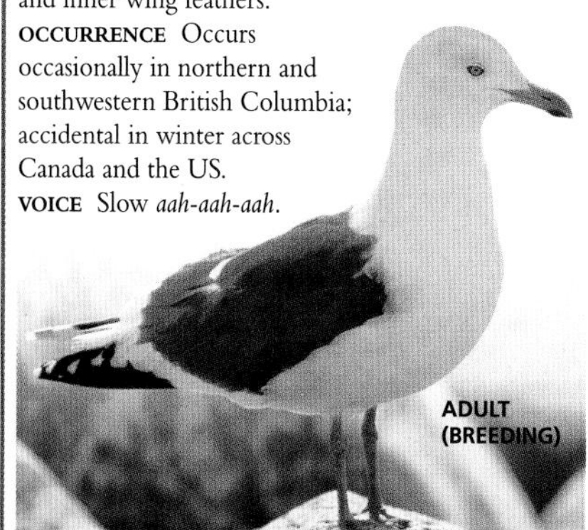
ADULT (BREEDING)

Length **24–26in (61–66cm)**	Wingspan **4½–5ft (1.4–1.5m)**

Family **Laridae**	Species ***Sternula antillarum***

Least Tern

The Least Tern is the smallest of the North American terns. In summer, its distinctive black cap and white forehead distinguish it from other members of its family. In the 19th century their numbers declined. They have rebounded but are now threatened by ongoing habitat loss.

OCCURRENCE Breeds along both coasts, major rivers, lakes, and reservoirs; favors sandy areas, such as beaches and sandbars. Scattered sightings across Canada.

VOICE Extremely vocal during breeding; a high-pitched *ki-deek, ki-deek*; also a rapid, almost non-stop chatter.

two dark outer wing feathers
ADULT (BREEDING)
yellow bill

Length **8½–9in (21–23cm)**	Wingspan **19–21in (48–53cm)**

Family **Ardeidae** | Species ***Egretta caerulea***

Little Blue Heron

The shy and retreating Little Blue Heron is often overlooked because of its blue-gray color and secretive eating habits. First-year birds, which may be mistaken for Snowy Egrets, are white. They gradually acquire blue-gray, mottled feathers before eventually molting into their all-dark adult plumage.

OCCURRENCE Breeds in various wetlands, such as swamps, marshes, lakes, streams, rivers, and flooded fields. Range has expanded north, particularly into eastern Canada.

VOICE Vocal during courtship; generally silent.

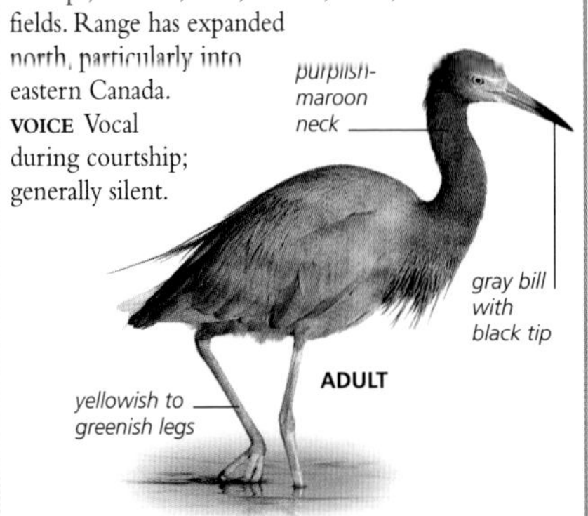
purplish-maroon neck
gray bill with black tip
ADULT
yellowish to greenish legs

Length **24in (61cm)** | Wingspan **3ft 3in (1m)**

Family **Ardeidae** | Species ***Nyctanassa violacea***

Yellow-crowned Night-Heron

The Yellow-crowned Night-Heron was unaffected by the 19th century plume hunting trade. It then expanded northward in the 20th century, but has since retreated slightly from the northern edge of its range. It can be seen in wooded areas.

OCCURRENCE Breeds near wetlands in the southeastern US and along the coast up to the Canadian Maritimes; also likes being near houses in wooded habitat.

VOICE Call an abrupt *quark* or *wok*, higher pitched than Black-crowned Night Heron; most vocal in the mornings, and after dusk.

ADULT
thick black bill

Length **19½–28in (50–70cm)** | Wingspan **3¼–3½ft (1–1.1m)**

Family **Cathartidae** | Species ***Coragyps atratus***

Black Vulture

Common in the southern and eastern states, the Black Vulture is often seen in large communal roosts in the evening. When not feeding on roadkills along highways and other carrion, Black Vultures sometimes kill the odd prey.

OCCURRENCE Range expanding in the northeastern US. Also widespread in Central and South America. Breeds in dense woodlands, caves, old buildings.

VOICE Usually silent; hisses and barks occasionally.

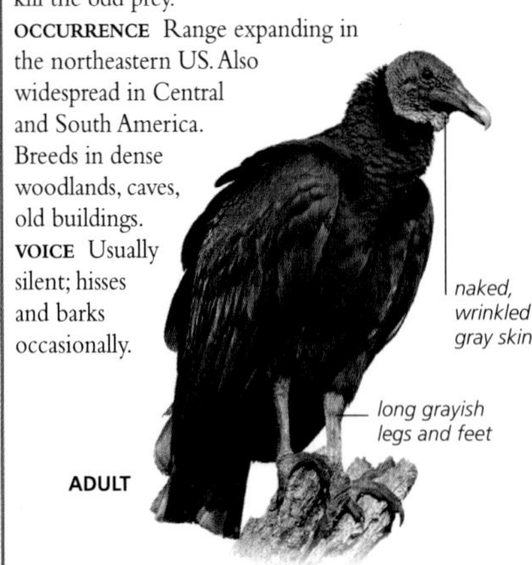
naked, wrinkled gray skin
long grayish legs and feet
ADULT

Length **24–27in (61–68cm)** | Wingspan **4½–5ft (1.4–1.5m)**

Family **Tyrannidae** | Species ***Tyrannus forficatus***

Scissor-tailed Flycatcher

Often perched on a wire or fence, the Scissor-tailed Flycatcher also has a spectacular aerial courtship display, with its long tail streaming behind it. Its nest incorporates many human products, such as string, cloth, and paper. Pre-migratory roosting flocks during late summer consist of 100 to 1,000 birds.

OCCURRENCE Breeds in the southern states and in Mexico; prairie, open grasslands, pastures, and golf courses. Sporadically appears from coast to coast in Canada.

VOICE Male song variable number of *pups* followed by *perleep* or *peroo* in breeding territories and communal roots.

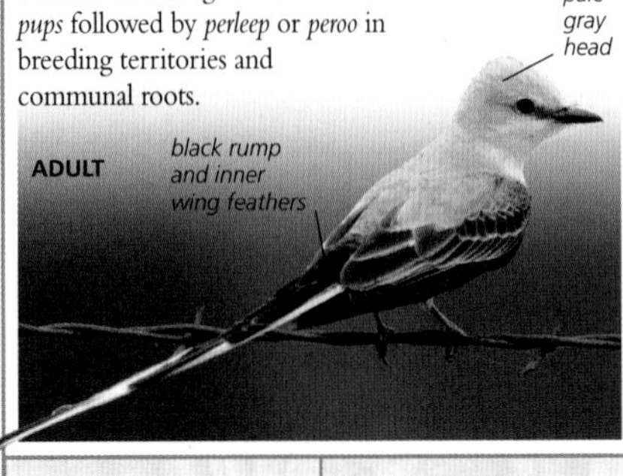
pale-gray head
ADULT
black rump and inner wing feathers

Length **9–15in (23–38cm)** | Wingspan **15in (38cm)**

Family **Corvidae**	Species ***Corvus ossifragus***

Fish Crow

The Fish Crow is common along the Eastern Seaboard of the US but is occasionally in Canada, where it occurs alongside the nearly identical, but slightly larger, American Crow. The Fish Crow is also distinguishable as it has a higher-pitched and more nasal call. This is a highly social species, which forages in flocks and breeds in small colonies.

OCCURRENCE Found in lowland coastal and riverbank habitats; also found inland and near human stuctures, such as parking lots in suburban malls.

VOICE Call a paired *ehn uhn*; with the second note lower.

slender neck and head
black overall
ADULT
strong black legs and feet

Length **14 –16in (36–41cm)**	Wingspan **36in (91cm)**

Family **Fringillidae**	Species ***Fringilla montifringilla***

Brambling

Widespread in northern Eurasia, from Scandinavia to the far east of Russia, the Brambling is unlike any native North American finch. In all seasons, males and females have a conspicuous white rump and orange outer wing feathers.

OCCURRENCE Regular migrant to the Aleutian and Pribilof Islands, and mainland western Alaska. Occasionally seen elsewhere in Canada and the US.

VOICE Call a characteristic, mewing *jee-eek*; song a trilled *zhreeeee*.

blackish head, with white spots
MALE
yellow bill with black tip
white rump and uppertail feathers
orange chin and breast

Length **5¾in (14.5cm)**	Wingspan **10–11in (25–28cm)**

Family **Parulidae**	Species ***Helmitheros vermivorum***

Worm-eating Warbler

The Worm-eating Warbler often hangs upside down, searching suspended dead leaves for inchworms and other caterpillars. Although this bird nests on the ground and tends to forage fairly low, singing males may perch quite high in trees.

OCCURRENCE Breeds in mature deciduous forests with abundant leaf litter and dense undergrowth; mostly in the eastern US but occasionally up into Ontario.

VOICE Thick *chip* call; flight call an upslurred, thin, rolling *ziiit*; song a thin, dry trill.

ADULT
blurry pattern on undertail feathers
tawny wash on breast

Length **5in (13cm)**	Wingspan **8½in (21cm)**

Family **Parulidae**	Species ***Setophaga kirtlandii***

Kirtland's Warbler

One of the rarest songbirds in North America, Kirtland's Warbler is threatened by habitat loss and brood parasitism from the Brown-headed Cowbird. Its pale lemon-yellow underparts can be seen as it sings from the top of young Jack pines.

OCCURRENCE Breeds in Jack pine stands regrowing after forest fires; rare in Ontario and Quebec.

VOICE Song a loud series of staccato *chips*, ending with bubbly, whistled *tup-CHUP-chup tup-CHEEP-cheep chew-EEP.*

interrupted white eye-ring
MALE
pale lemon-yellow underparts with marked streaks on flanks
streaked blue-gray upperparts

Length **6in (15cm)**	Wingspan **9in (23cm)**

Family **Parulidae** | Species ***Setophaga dominica***

Yellow-throated Warbler

The Yellow-throated Warbler is perhaps best known for its habit of creeping along branches, much like the Black-and-white Warbler. The species occasionally interbreeds with the Northern Parula, creating the so-called "Sutton's Warbler."

OCCURRENCE Breeds in the eastern half of North America, in woods with cypress, sycamore, or live oak trees. Its range has extended northwards with sightings in the southern parts of most provinces.

VOICE Flight call high, thin *siit*; song long, descending cascade of clear whistles, sometimes jumbled.

ADULT
unmarked white undertail feathers
white line from bill to nape

Length **5in (13cm)** | Wingspan **8in (20cm)**

Family **Parulidae** | Species ***Geothlypis formosa***

Kentucky Warbler

The loud and cheery song of the Kentucky Warbler is one of the characteristic sounds of forests in the southeastern US, but it is being heard more often in similar habitats along the southern border of eastern Canada. This is a rather secretive species. It forages close to or on the forest floor.

OCCURRENCE Breeds in moist deciduous forests with dense understory. Migrants prefer woodlands and thickets.

VOICE Call a low, hollow *chup*, flight call a buzzy *dziiip*; song a loud rolling series of paired notes *chur-ee' chur-ee' chur-ee' chur-ee' chur-ee'*.

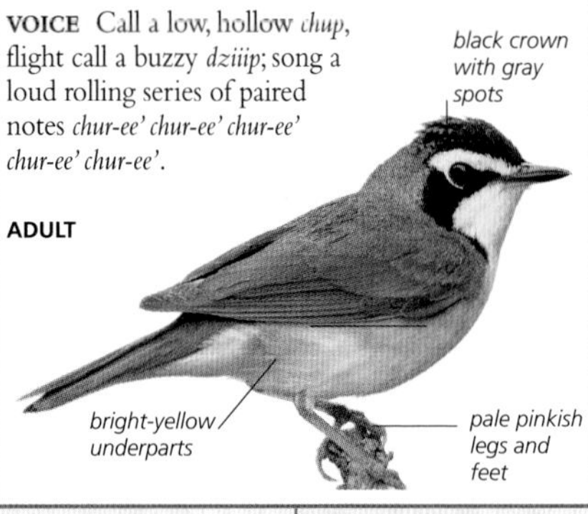
black crown with gray spots
ADULT
bright-yellow underparts
pale pinkish legs and feet

Length **5in (13cm)** | Wingspan **8½ in (21cm)**

Family **Cardinalidae** | Species ***Piranga rubra***

Summer Tanager

The stunning male Summer Tanager is the only North American bird that is entirely bright red. Immature males in their first spring plumage wear a patchwork of bright yellow-and-red plumage. Of the two subspecies, *P. r. rubra* breeds in the East while *P. r. cooperi* breeds in the West.

OCCURRENCE *P. r. rubra* breeds in deciduous and mixed woodlands in the East up into Canada; *P. r. cooperi* in cottonwood-willow habitats near streams in the West.

VOICE Call an explosive *PIT-tuck!* or *PIT-a TUK*; flight call a muffled, airy *vreee*.

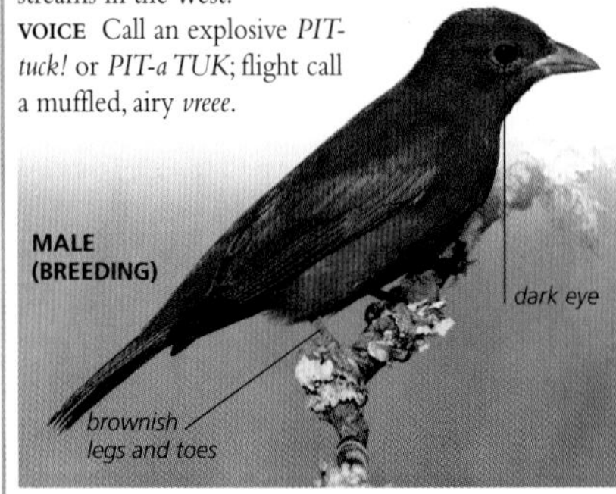
MALE (BREEDING)
dark eye
brownish legs and toes

Length **8in (20cm)** | Wingspan **12in (31cm)**

Family **Cardinalidae** | Species ***Passerina caerulea***

Blue Grosbeak

Blue Grosbeaks have expanded their range northward in recent years, especially in the Great Plains. However, they are still a rare find. Features that can help with identification are the Grosbeak's huge bill, uniformly dark plumage, black face, and reddish shoulder.

OCCURRENCE Breeds in dense undergrowth of disturbed habitats: old fields, hedgerows, and desert scrub across all of the southern US and expanding north into eastern Canada.

VOICE Call a loud, sharp, metallic *tchink*; similar to Indigo Bunting; song rambling, husky.

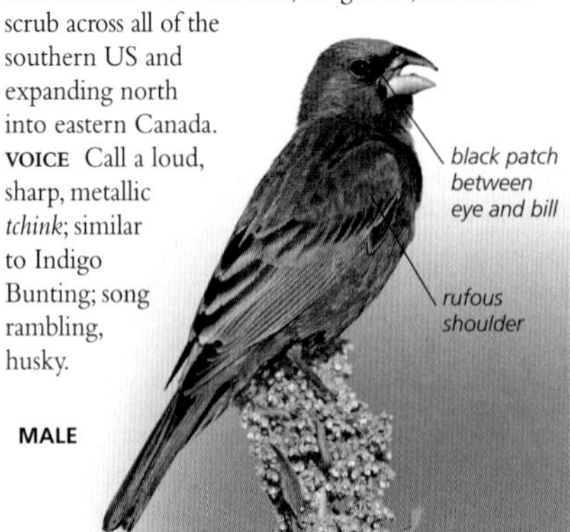
black patch between eye and bill
rufous shoulder
MALE

Length **6¾in (17cm)** | Wingspan **11in (28cm)**

GLOSSARY

Many terms defined here are illustrated in the general introduction (pp.10–21).

adult A fully developed, sexually mature bird. It is in its final plumage, which no longer changes pattern with age and remains the same after yearly molt, although it may change with season. *See also* **immature**, **juvenile**.
aerie The nest of birds of prey, like eagles or peregrine falcons, usually on a cliff, and often used by the same pair of adult birds in successive years.
alarm call A call made by a bird to signal danger. Alarm calls are often short and urgent in tone, and a few species use different calls to signify the precise nature of the threat. *See also* **call**.
allopreening Mutual preening between two birds, the main purpose of which is to reduce the instinctive aggression when birds come into close contact. In the breeding season, allopreening helps to strengthen the pair bond between the male and female. *See also* **preening**.
altitudinal migrant *see* **vertical migrant**
alula A small group of two to six feathers projecting from a bird's "thumb," at the bend of its wing that reduces turbulence when raised.
Audubon, John James (1785–1851) American naturalist and wildlife illustrator, whose best known work was his remarkable collection of prints, *Birds of North America*.
axillary A term describing feathers at the base of the underwing. Axillary feathers often form small patches, with coloration differing from the rest of the underwing.

barred With marks crossing the body, wing, or tail; the opposite of streaked. *See also* **streaks**.
bastard wing *see* **alula**
beak *see* **bill**
bill A bird's jaws. A bill is made of bone, with a hornlike outer covering of keratin.
bird of prey Any of the predatory birds in the orders Accipitriformes (eagles, hawks, kites, and osprey), Falconiformes (falcons), and Strigiformes (owls). They are characterised by their acute eyesight, powerful legs, strongly hooked bill, and sharp talons. These birds are also known as raptors. *See also* **talon, raptor**.
body feather *see* **contour feather**
booming A sound produced by bitterns and some species of grouse. The booming of male bitterns is a deep, resonant, hollow sound that can carry for several miles. The booming of male grouse is produced by wind from air pouches in the sides of the bird's neck.
brackish Containing a mixture of saltwater and freshwater.
breeding plumage A general term for the plumage worn by adult birds when they display and form breeding pairs. It is usually (but not always) worn in the spring and summer. *See also* **nonbreeding plumage**.
brood (noun) The young birds produced from a single clutch of eggs and incubated together. *See also* **clutch**. **(verb)** In birds, to sit on nestlings to keep them warm. Brooding is usually carried out by the adult female. *See also* **incubate**.
brood parasite A bird that lays its eggs in the nest of other birds. Some brood parasites always breed this way, while others do so only occasionally.
brood patch An area of bare skin on the belly of a parent bird, usually the female, that is richly supplied with blood vessels and thus helps keep the eggs warm during incubation. This area loses its feathers in readiness for the breeding season and is fully feathered at other times.

cagebird A species of bird commonly kept in captivity.
call A sound produced by the vocal apparatus of a bird to communicate a variety of messages to other birds. Calls are often highly characteristic of individual species and can help to locate and identify birds in the field. Most bird calls are shorter and simpler than songs. *See also* **alarm call**, **booming**, **contact call**, **song**.
casque A bony extension on a bird's head—seen in hornbills, for example.
cere A leathery patch of skin that covers the base of a bird's bill. It is found only in a few groups, including birds of prey, pigeons, and parrots.
claw In birds, the nail that prolongs their toes. *See also* **talon**.
cloaca An anal-like opening on the rear of a bird under its tail. It is present in both sexes and is used in reproduction—for example, to release sperm and eggs—and excretion.
clutch The group of eggs in a single nest, usually laid by one female and incubated together.
cock A term sometimes used to describe the adult male in Galliformes and songbirds. *See also* **hen**.
collar The area around a bird's neck, which in some species is a prominent feature of its plumage pattern and can be used for identification.
color form One of two or more clearly defined plumage variations found in the same species. Also known as a color morph or phase, a color form may be restricted to part of a species's range or occur side by side with other color forms over the entire range. Adults of different color forms are able to interbreed, and these mixed pairings can produce young of either form.
comb A fleshy growth of bare skin usually above the eyes.
contact call A call made by a bird to give its location as a means of staying in touch with others of the same species. Contact calls are used by birds in flocks and by breeding pairs. Contact calls are crucial for nocturnal migrants. *See also* **call**.
contour feather A general term for any feather that covers the outer surface of a bird, including its wings and tail. Also known as body feathers, contour feathers help streamline the bird in flight, and provide warmth and waterproofing.
cooperative breeding A breeding system in which a pair of parent birds are helped in raising their young by several other birds, which are often related to them and may be young birds from previous broods.
courtship display Ritualized, showy behavior used in courtship by the male, and sometimes by the female, involving plumage, sound (vocal and non-vocal), and movements.
covert A small feather covering the base of a bird's flight feather. Together, coverts form a well-defined feather tract on the wing or at the base of the tail. *See also* **feather tract**.
creche A group of young birds of about the same age, produced by different parents but tightly herded together. One or more adults guards the entire creche.

crepuscular Relating to the period just before dusk, when many birds are active, especially during courtship. In reference to birds, the term is sometimes used to mean both twilight and dawn.
crest A group of elongated feathers on top of a bird's head, which may be raised during courtship or to indicate alarm.
crissum *see* **vent**
crown The area on top of a bird's head. It is often a prominent plumage feature, with a different color from the feathers on the rest of the head.

dabble To feed in shallow water by sieving water and obtain food through comblike filters in the bill; used mostly for ducks (dabbling ducks or dabblers).
decurved A term describing a bird's bill that curves downward from the forehead toward the tip.
dimorphism *see* **sexual dimorphism**
display *see* **courtship display**, **distraction display**, **threat display**
distraction display A display in which a bird deliberately attempts to attract a predator's attention in order to lure it away from its nest or nestlings.
diurnal Active during the day.
down feather A soft, fluffy feather, lacking the system of barbs of contour or flight feathers, that provides good insulation. Young birds are covered by down feathers until they molt into their first juvenile plumage. Adult birds have a layer of down feathers under their contour feathers. *See also* **contour feather**, **juvenile**.
drake An adult male duck. The adult female is known as the duck.
drift The diversion of migrating birds from their normal migration route by strong winds.
dynamic soaring *see* **soaring**

ear tuft A distinct tuft of feathers on each side of a bird's forehead, with no connection to the true ears, which can be raised as a visual signal. Many owls have ear tufts.
echolocation A method of sensing nearby objects using pulses of high-frequency sound. Echoes bounce back from obstacles, enabling the sender to build up a "picture" of its surroundings.
eclipse plumage A female-like plumage worn in some birds, especially waterfowl, by adult males for a short period after the breeding season is over. The eclipse plumage helps camouflage them during their molt, when they are flightless.
elevational migrant *see* **vertical migrant**
endemic A species (or subspecies) native to a particular geographic area—such as an island, a forest patch, a mountain, or province, or country—and found nowhere else.
escape An individual bird that has escaped from a zoo or other collection to live in the wild. *See also* **exotic**
eye-ring A ring of color, usually narrow and well defined, around the eye of a bird.
eyestripe A stripe of color running as a line through the eye of a bird.
eyrie *see* **aerie**
exotic A bird found in a region from which it is not native. Some of these are escapes, or were originally, but now live as wild birds.

feather tract A well-defined area on a bird's skin where feathers grow, leaving patches of bare skin in between. *See also* **pterylae**.
fledge In young birds, to leave the nest or acquire the first complete set of flight feathers. Known as fledglings, these birds may still remain dependent on their parents for some time. *See also* **flight feather**.
fledging period The average time taken by the young of a species to fledge, timed from the moment they hatch. Fledging periods in birds range from 11 days in some small songbirds to as long as 280 days in the Wandering Albatross.
fledgling *see* **fledge**
flight feather A collective term for a bird's wing and tail feathers, used in flight. More specifically, it refers to the largest feathers on the outer part of the wing, the primaries and secondaries.
forewing The front section of a bird's wing, including the primary coverts and secondary coverts. *See also* **hindwing**.

gamebird Generally, any bird that is legally hunted, including some doves and waterfowl. This name is generally used for members of the order Galliformes.
gular sac Also known as a gular pouch, it is a large, fleshy, extendable sac just below the bill of some birds, especially fish-eaters such as pelicans. It forms part of the throat.

habitat The geographical and ecological area where a particular organism usually lives.
hen A term sometimes used to describe the adult female in Galliformes, especially grouse and songbirds. *See also* **cock**.
hindwing The rear section of a bird's spread wing, including the secondary feathers, especially when it has a distinctive color or pattern. *See also* **forewing**.
hybrid The offspring produced when two species, sometimes from different genera, interbreed. Hybrids are usually rare in the wild. Among birds, they are most frequent in Galliformes and waterfowl, especially ducks. Hybrid progeny may or may not be fertile.

immature In birds, an individual that is not yet sexually mature or able to breed. Some birds pass through a series of immature plumages over several years before adopting their first adult plumage and sexual maturity. *See also* **adult**, **juvenile**.
incubate In birds, to sit on eggs to keep them warm, allowing the embryo inside to grow. Incubation is often carried out by the female. *See also* **brood**.
incubation period In birds, the period when a parent incubates its eggs. It may not start until the clutch is completed.
injury feigning *see* **distraction display**.
inner wing The inner part of the wing, comprising the secondaries and rows of coverts (typically marginal, lesser, median, and greater coverts).
introduced species A species that humans have accidentally or deliberately brought into an area where it does not normally occur.
iridescent plumage Plumage that shows brilliant, luminous colors, which seem to sparkle and change color when seen from different angles.
irruption A sporadic mass movement of animals outside their normal range. Irruptions are usually short-lived and occur in response to food shortage. Also called irruptive migration.

juvenile A term referring to the plumage worn by a young bird at the time it makes its first flight and until it begins its first molt. *See also* **adult**, **immature**.

keratin A tough but lightweight protein. In birds, keratin is found in the claws, feathers, and outer part of the bill.
kleptoparasite A bird that gets much of its food by stealing it from other birds, usually by following them in flight and forcing them to disgorge their food.

lamellae Delicate, comblike structures on the sides of the bill of some birds used for filtering tiny food particles out of water.
leap-frog migration A pattern of migration in which some populations of a species travel much further than the other populations, by "leap-frogging" over the area where these sedentary (nonmigratory) birds are found. *See also* **migration**.
lek An area, often small, used by males as a communal display arena, where they show off special plumage features accompanied by vocal and non-vocal sounds, to attract females. Females wait along the lek and select the male or males that they will mate with.
lobed feet Feet with loose, fleshy lobes on the toes, adapted for swimming.
lore A small area between a bird's eye and the base of its upper bill.

mandible The upper or lower part of a bird's bill, known as the upper or lower mandible, respectively.
mantle The loose term used to define the back of a bird between its neck and rump.
migrant A species that regularly moves between geographical areas. Most migrants move on an annual basis between a breeding area and a wintering area. *See also* **partial migrant, sedentary**.
migration A journey to a different region, following a well-defined route. *See also* **leap-frog migration, partial migrant, reverse migration, sedentary, vertical migrant**.
mobbing A type of defensive behavior in which a group of birds flock together to harass a predator, such as a bird of prey or an owl, swooping repeatedly to drive it away.
molt In birds, to shed old feathers so that they can be replaced. Molting enables birds to keep their plumage in good condition, change their level of insulation, and change their coloration or markings so that they are ready to breed or display.
monogamous Mating with a single partner, either in a single breeding season or for life. *See also* **polygamous**.
morph *see* **color form**

nape The back of the neck.
nares Paired nasal openings located in different places on the bill, depending on the species.
nestling A young bird still in the nest.
New World The Americas, from Alaska to Cape Horn, including the Caribbean and offshore islands in the Pacific and Atlantic oceans. *See also* **Old World**.
nictitating membrane A transparent or semitransparent "third eyelid," which moves sideways across the eye for protection and moistening. Diving waterbirds often use them to aid in their vision underwater.
nocturnal Active at night.
nomadic Being almost constantly on the move. Birds of deserts, grasslands, and the coniferous forests of the far north are commonly nomadic.
nonbreeding plumage The plumage worn by adult birds outside the breeding season. In many species, particularly in temperate regions, it is also known as winter plumage. *See also* **breeding plumage**.
nonmigrant *see* **sedentary**
nonpasserine Any bird that is not a member of the order Passeriformes (or passerines). *See also* **passerine**.

oil gland Also called the preen gland or the uropygial gland, a gland at the base of a bird's tail that secretes oils that are spread over the feathers for waterproofing them during preening.
Old World Europe, Asia, Africa, and Australasia. *See also* **New World**.
orbital ring A thin, bare, fleshy ring around the eye, sometimes with a distinctive color. *See also* **eye-ring**.
outer wing The outer half of the wing, comprising the primaries, their coverts, and the alula (the "thumb").

partial migrant A species in which some populations migrate while others are sedentary. This situation is common in broadly distributed species that experience a wide range of climatic conditions. *See also* **migration, sedentary**.
passerine A bird belonging to the vast order Passeriformes (the passerines). This group contains more species than all other orders of birds combined. Passerines are also called songbirds or perching birds. *See also* **nonpasserine**.
pelagic Relating to the open ocean. Pelagic birds spend most of their life at sea and only come to land to nest.
phase *see* **color form**
polygamous Mating with two or more partners during the course of a single breeding season. *See also* **monogamous**.
population A group of individual birds of the same species living in a geographically and ecologically circumscribed area.
preening Routine behavior by which birds keep their feathers in good condition. Each individual feather is pulled through the bill, sometimes with oil added from the preen gland, to help smooth and clean the plumage. *See also* **allopreening**.
primary feather One of the large outer wing feathers, growing from the digits of a bird's "hand." *See also* **secondary feather**.
pterylae Bare patches of skin lying between the feather tracts. *See also* **feather tracts**.

race *see* **subspecies**
range A term to indicate the geographical distribution of a species or population.
raptor A general name for birds belonging to the orders Accipitriformes, Falconiformes, and Strigiformes. Often used interchangeablely with bird of prey. *See also* **bird of prey**.
ratite A member of an ancient group of flightless birds that includes the ostrich, cassowaries, emus, rheas, and kiwis. In the past, the group was larger and more diverse.
resident *see* **sedentary**
reverse migration A phenomenon that occurs when birds from a migratory species mistakenly travel in the opposite direction from normal, causing birds to turn up in places far outside their normal range. *See also* **migration**.
roost A place where birds sleep, either at night or by day.
rump The area between a bird's back and the base of its upper tail coverts. In many species, the rump is a different color from the rest of the plumage and can be a useful diagnostic character for identification.

sally A feeding technique (sallying), used especially by tyrant flycatchers, in which a bird makes a short flight from a perch to catch an insect, often in midair, followed by a return to a perch, often the same one.
salt gland A gland located in a depression of the skull, just above the eye of some birds, particularly seabirds. This enables them to extract the fluids they need from saltwater and then expel the excess salts through the nostrils.
scapular Any one of a group of feathers on the "shoulder," forming a more or less oval patch on each side of the back, at the base of the wing.
scrape A simple nest that consists of a shallow depression in the ground,

which may be unlined or lined with material such as feathers, bits of grass, or pebbles.
secondary feather One of the row of long, stiff feathers along the rear edge of a bird's wing, between the body and the primary feathers at the wingtip. *See also* **primary feather**.
sedentary Having a settled lifestyle that involves little or no geographic movement. Sedentary birds are also said to be resident or nonmigratory. *See also* **migration**.
semipalmated The condition in which two or more of the toes are partially joined by an incomplete membrane at their base.
sexual dimorphism The occurrence of physical differences between males and females. In birds, the most common differences are in size and plumage.
shield In birds, a hard structure on the forehead that joins the bill and often appears to be an extension of it.
shorebird Also known as a wader, any member of several families in the order Charadriiformes, including plovers, sandpipers, godwits, snipe, avocets, stilts, oystercatchers, and curlews. Not all species actually wade in water and some live in dry habitats.
soaring In birds, flight without flapping of the wings to preserve or gain altitude and save energy. Updraft soaring usually results from rising air hitting cliffs and mountain ridges or rising thermals of warm air. Some seabirds, flying for days at a time, use dynamic soaring by repeatedly catching rising air deflected off the waves.
song A vocal performance by a bird, usually the adult male, to attract and impress a potential mate, advertise ownership of a territory, or drive away rival birds. Songs are often highly characteristic of individual species and can be a major aid in locating and identifying birds in the field. *See also* **call**.
songbird A general term used to describe a member of the suborder Passeri (or oscines), a subdivision of the largest order of birds, the Passeriformes (passerines).
species A group of similar organisms that are capable of breeding among themselves in the wild and producing fertile offspring that resemble themselves, but that do not interbreed in the wild with individuals of another similar group, are called a species. *See also* **subspecies**.
speculum A colorful patch on the wing of a duck, formed by the secondary feathers. *See also* **secondary feather**.
spur A sharply pointed, clawlike structure at the back of the leg of some birds, like the Wild Turkey.
staging ground A stopover area where migrant birds regularly pause while on migration, to rest and feed.
stoop A near-vertical and often very fast dive made by falcons and some other birds of prey when chasing prey in the air or on the ground.
streaks Marks that run lengthwise on feathers; opposite of bars.
subspecies When species show geographical variation in color, voice, or other characters, these differentiated populations are recognized by ornithologists as subspecies (formerly also called races). *See also* **species.**
supercillium Also called supercillial stripe, a stripe running from the base of a bird's beak above its eye.
syrinx A modified section of a bird's trachea (windpipe), equivalent to the voicebox in humans, that enables birds to call and sing.

talon One of the sharp, hooked claws of a bird of prey.
territory An area that is defended by an animal, or a group of animals, against other members of the same species. Territories often include useful resources, such as good breeding sites or feeding areas, which help a male attract a mate.
tertial Any one of a small group of feathers, sometimes long and obvious, at the base of the wing adjacent to the inner secondaries.
thermal A rising bubble or column of warm air over land that soaring birds can use to gain height with little effort. *See also* **soaring**.
threat display A form of defense in which a bird adopts certain postures, sometimes accompanied by loud calls, to drive away a rival or a potential predator.
tiercel A term referring to a male falcon.
trachea The breathing tube in animals, also known as the windpipe.
tubenose A general term used to describe members of the order Procellariiformes, including albatrosses, petrels, and shearwaters; their nostrils form two tubes on the upper mandible and are used to expel salt.

underwing The underside of a bird's wing, usually visible only in flight or when a bird is preening, displaying, or swimming.
upperwing The upper surface of a bird's wing clearly exposed in flight but often mostly hidden when the bird is perched with its wings closed.

vagrant A bird that has strayed far from its normal range. Usually, vagrants are long-distance migrants that have been blown off course by storms, have overshot their intended destination due to strong winds, or have become disoriented.
vent Also called the crissum, the undertail feathers between the lower belly feathers and tail feathers, which in some species are differently colored from either belly or tail feathers. Can be helpful in identification.
vertical migrant Also called altitudinal migrant, a species that migrates up and down mountains, usually in response to changes in the weather or food supply. *See also* **migration**.

wader *see* **shorebird**.
waterfowl A collective term for members of the family Anatidae, including ducks, geese, and swans.
wattle A bare, fleshy growth that hangs loosely below the bill in some birds. It is often brightly colored, and may play a part in courtship.
wildfowl *see* **waterfowl**
Wilson, Alexander (1766–1813) A contemporary of J.J. Audubon, Wilson's seminal *American Ornithology* marks the start of scientific ornithology in the US.
wing bar A line or bar of color, sometimes more than one, across the upper surface of the wing, often used in identification. Most obvious when a bird is on the ground or perched with its wings closed. Sometimes obvious in flight in some birds.
wingbar A line or bar of color across the upper surface of a bird's wing. Wingbars can often be seen when a bird is on the ground or perched and its wings are in the closed position, but they are normally much more obvious in flight. Wingbars may be single or in groups of two or more.
wingspan The distance across a bird's outstretched wings and back, from one wingtip to the other.

zygodactyl Having two toes pointed forward and two backward, often seen in tree climbers like woodpeckers.

INDEX

A

B

C

D

E

F

G

UV

W

XY

Z